Marketing
Management
Casebook

The Irwin Series in Marketing

Consulting Editor
Gilbert A. Churchill, Jr.
University of Wisconsin,
Madison

EDITED BY:

ROBERT T. DAVIS, D.C.S.
Sebastian S. Kresge Professor of Marketing
Graduate School of Business
Stanford University

HARPER W. BOYD, JR., Ph.D.
Donaghey Distinguished Professor of Marketing
College of Business Administration
University of Arkansas at Little Rock

FREDERICK E. WEBSTER, JR., Ph.D.
E. B. Osborn Professor of Marketing
The Amos Tuck School of Business Administration
Dartmouth College

Marketing Management Casebook

FOURTH EDITION

RICHARD D. IRWIN, INC.
Homewood, Illinois 60430

1984

ISBN 0-256-03017-0

Library of Congress Catalog Card No. 84–80442

Printed in the United States of America

1 2 3 4 5 6 7 8 9 0 MP 1 0 9 8 7 6 5 4

Preface

This edition represents a considerable update from the 1980 version—an update that involves new material, revised material, and a better balance of market types. To be specific, there are 44 cases included in the collection, of which 20 are new, 6 are revisions, and 18 have been retained from the earlier edition.

More importantly, the cases are spread quite uniformly among industrial, service, and consumer markets. The split is 13 industrial, 16 consumer, and 15 service (assuming that retailers and distributors are classified as service organizations). As was true in the earlier edition, there are a number of international cases, as well as a sprinkling from the newer electronic industries.

The focus of the cases is reasonably broad. Most of them encompass a range of issues far beyond their specific labeling. As in the 1980 edition, we have divided the cases into eight subject areas—the role of the marketplace, development of marketing strategy, product and product line, price, channels of distribution, personal selling and advertising, organization, and development of marketing plans.

It is generally true that the eight subject areas represent the major decision categories within which marketing managers must operate. We would argue further that the sequencing of the eight is reflective of how marketing managers think about their tasks.

As with all books, there were many individuals who collectively made the final result possible. In particular, we are most grateful to the executives who made their company materials available and who typically devoted many hours of their time to the development of the case studies. Our colleagues were of inestimable value, particularly in their willingness to teach many of these cases and provide us with feedback which could be used to improve the presentation. Special thanks for particular cases go to David Montgomery, Gerald J. Erskin, and David

Weinstein—and also to INSEAD. Elaine Hubbard at Stanford went to unusual lengths to chaperone the new cases through "the system," and Mrs. Roberta Moore at Arkansas, as well as Marlene Dawson at Stanford, did yeoman secretarial jobs.

Robert T. Davis
Harper W. Boyd, Jr.
Frederick E. Webster, Jr.

Contents

SECTION FOUR

Price

SECTION FIVE

Channels of Distribution

SECTION SIX

Personal Selling and Advertising

SECTION SEVEN

Organization

SECTION EIGHT

Development of Marketing Plans

Index of Cases, 609

Role
of the
Marketplace

C A S E 1–1

Freeman Roller Rink

In late August 1982, Dr. Garman P. Freeman and his brother, Al E. Freeman, Jr., formed a partnership for the possible purchase of a building for the operation of a combination roller rink and video game arcade in Little Rock, Arkansas. The building, located on the corner of 24th and High Streets (see Exhibit 1), was originally a Safeway supermarket. Both men felt that sufficient financing would be available if a feasibility study revealed that a skating rink and arcade could generate reasonable profits.

Dr. Garman Freeman, a dentist who had been in practice since 1949, had built a reputable clientele over the years. Although not retired, he had participated actively in SCORE (Senior Corps of Retired Executives) in past years, but stated that "I think they needed a black to serve, so they asked me even though I didn't quite fit in." He had been active in business, civic, and church affairs for many years. In addition to his dental practice, he had been engaged in real estate work including the construction and ownership of two one-story office buildings. Al Freeman, vice president and sales manager for Bond All Laboratories, Inc., located in Madison, Arkansas, received his college degree in 1948 and had served as a dental technician in the U.S. Army during the Korean War. Later he helped establish Bond All Laboratories for the purpose of manufacturing chemically related products of which embalming fluid was the leading seller. The brothers did not intend to manage the new venture themselves; rather, they planned to hire a full-time, experienced rink/arcade manager.

In an effort to determine the feasibility of their rink/arcade project, the Freeman brothers turned for help to the Small Business Assistance Program housed in the College of Business, University of Arkansas at

© 1983 by the College of Business, University of Arkansas, Little Rock. This case is based on a feasibility study prepared by Mr. John Fornier under the supervision of Professor Ray B. Robbins, Department of Management, College of Business Administration, University of Arkansas, Little Rock.

Exhibit 1
Map Showing Freeman's Marketing Area

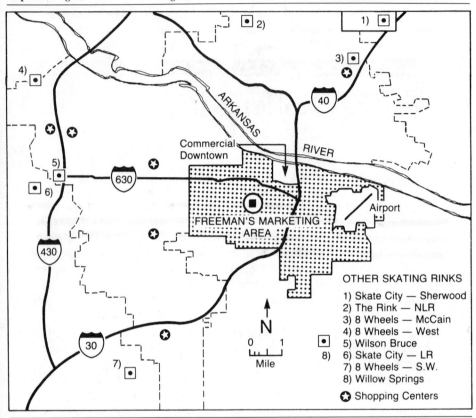

Little Rock. The analysts assigned to conduct the study focused first on the market potential for the proposed services and second on the construction of a simulated profit and loss statement.

The geographical market which could be served was determined primarily on the basis of other skating rinks. A list of these is as follows (see Exhibit 1).

1. The Rink, North Little Rock.
2. Skate City, Sherwood.
3. 8 Wheels (McCain Mall), North Little Rock.
4. Willow Springs, Little Rock.
5. 8 Wheels (S.W.), Little Rock.
6. 8 Wheels, Little Rock.
7. Wilson Bruce, Little Rock.
8. Skate City, Little Rock.

The three 8 Wheel franchised rinks were substantially larger than the proposed Freeman operation. All had modern facilities, hardwood floors, and were certified for national competition. The Sherwood Skate City rink was larger than any of the 8 Wheel operations, had modern facilities including a hardwood floor, and was also certified for national competition. It also featured an attached ice skating rink. The other Skate City was similar in size and facilities to the 8 Wheel rinks. The remaining three rinks were "independents" and had approximately the same size operation as was planned by the Freemans. These rinks had artificial flooring and were not certified for national competition.

All of the competitors served food and had pinball and video games. Each of the three 8 Wheel rinks had two game machines, the large Skate City rink had six, and the small Skate City had four. The independents had three to four machines. The extent of the food service operation varied with the size of the rink; i.e., the larger the rink, the more extensive the food service. Two of the three independents provided only food and beverage vending machines.

The skating rink nearest to the proposed enterprise would be four miles away since no skating rinks existed in central Little Rock. The market boundaries were set on the basis of proximity to the nearest rink, natural boundaries, and major streets and highways. It included census tracts 1–14, 25, 26, 28, and 29, which had a combined population of 41,738 individuals and 15,800 households. About 80 percent of the population was black. (For further demographic data see Exhibit 2.) It was estimated that the Freeman rink would attract 90 percent of the prospective skaters in the area; i.e., 10 percent would go to other rinks. Further, it was estimated that the Freeman rink would attract 1 percent of the skating admissions of the remaining area.

According to a survey conducted by the National Family Opinion, Inc., a marketing research organization located in Dayton, Ohio, some 39.2 million Americans enjoy roller skating. Nationwide this represented one skater in 23 percent of all households. Another study revealed that 62 percent of all skaters were between the ages of 15 and 18. Only 27 percent were over 18. The study from National Family Opinion, Inc., showed that the head of skater households was younger than the average family head and that 66 percent of skater households had a total annual income above $20,000. In general, skaters came from larger households (4 or more members) and lived in smaller metropolitan areas. Nationally, the average skater visited a rink 26 times a year. Winter months represented the peak skating period while summer was the off-season, although this varied by geography.

Exhibit 2
Freeman Market Area, 1980 Census Demographic Data

1. Age Distribution

Little Rock

62% skaters all skaters

Age	Total	Male	Female
5–9	12,559	6,300	6,295
10–14	11,441	5,714	5,727
→ 15–19	12,569	6,120	6,449
20–24	15,766	7,153	8,613
25–34	30,711	14,650	16,061
35 & over	75,415	33,374	42,005
Total	158,461	73,311	85,150

North Little Rock

Age	Total	Male	Female
5–9	4,814	2,439	2,375
10–14	4,593	2,332	2,261
→ 15–19	5,243	2,540	2,703
20–24	5,814	2,700	3,114
25–34	10,623	5,154	5,469
35 & over	33,201	15,307	17,894
Total	64,288	30,472	33,816

Freeman market area

Age	Total	Male	Female
5–9	3,483	1,680	1,803
10–14	3,053	1,537	1,516
lowest 15–19	3,739	1,796	1,943
20–24	4,627	2,158	2,469
25–34	6,962	3,397	3,565
35 & over	19,874	8,373	11,645
Total	41,738	18,941	22,941

2. Racial Breakdown—Freeman Market Area

80% of pop.

White...............	10,392
Male.............	4,618
Female...........	5,774
Black.............	31,136
Male.............	14,226
Female...........	16,910
Other.............	210
Male.............	97
Female...........	113

3. Family Data

	Little Rock	North Little Rock	Freeman market area
Total families	40,804	17,603	9,118
Families with children	20,938	8,649	4,893

4. Housing Value and Income Data—Freeman Market Area

a. Median housing unit value = $25,236 versus $39,950 for Little Rock and North Little Rock
b. Average median household income = $9,308 versus $14,375 for Little Rock and $15,190 for North Little Rock
c. Households with income over $20,000 = 2,358
d. Households with income under $20,000 = 13,442

Using the data in Exhibit 2, it was possible to estimate the number of skaters who would patronize the Freeman rink during a two-week period. The calculations are as follows:

Little Rock population	158,461
North Little Rock population	62,288
Freeman market area population	41,738
Average persons per household, Little Rock	2.55
Average persons per household, North Little Rock	2.57
Average persons per household, Freeman market area	2.62
Number of households, Little Rock	62,142
Number of households, North Little Rock	25,015
Number of households, Freeman market area	15,800

Skaters per 2-week period $= .90(15,800) + .01(87,157 - 15,800) \times 23\% =$ 3,435

The Freeman brothers planned to modernize the building and to use bright colors and eye-catching designs to provide an atmosphere for fun and enjoyment. They also recognized the importance of properly maintaining the building and its parking lot, including the use of adequate lighting and security. A new polyurethane rink floor would be installed at a cost substantially below (50 percent) that of a wooden floor. This type of floor also required less maintenance, but did not last as long.

Special programs would be used to attract customers. These would include lessons, clinics, dance sessions, contests, shows, and exhibitions. Prices would vary by the time and day of the week. Competitors typically divided the week into daily sessions from 4 to 7 P.M. and 7 to 10 P.M. The peak periods were Friday and Saturday nights for which the large competitors charged either $3.50 or $4.00. The Saturday afternoon price was $3.00, and all other sessions were $2.00. The Freemans planned to charge $2.50 for the two peak periods and $2.00 for all other sessions. The average admission was expected to be $2.00, which would take into account price promotions. They hoped to be able to rent the rink at least one weekday night each week at a price of $250 for such special events as birthdays, company parties, and charity-sponsored activities. They planned to investigate the use of special price deals, such as an unlimited-use monthly ticket for $20, group discounts, two back-to-back sessions for the price of one, and the use of dollar-off coupons. A 50-cent fee would be charged for rental skates per session.

In an effort to learn more about the arcade game portion of the business, several distributors were contacted. On the basis of what was learned, it was concluded that 12 electronic games could be placed in operation on a commission basis; i.e., the machines would be owned by a local distributor who would not only purchase the machines but maintain them. Distributors typically required a 60 percent take on all

receipts. The alternative was to buy such games at a cost of $2,600 to
$3,100 each. Based on national data from grocery stores, it was esti-
mated that each game would, on average, provide revenues of $150 per
week.

It was not clear whether to install food and beverage machines or to
open a snack bar similar to those operating in movie theaters. The
latter involved an additional investment and higher fixed costs, but
had a higher revenue potential if the rink attracted large numbers of
skaters. The average skater was expected to spend $1.25 per month on
food and beverages.

Considerable time was spent in preparing an estimate of the costs of
setting up the rink/arcade venture. These costs were broken down as
follows:

Land and building	$ 69,000
Remodeling/decorating:	
Furniture/fixtures	28,500
Polyurethane floor ($2 × 8,250 sq. ft.)	16,500
Walls/partitions	2,500
Carpeting ($3 × 916 sq. ft.)	2,750
Lighting, air conditioning, heating, electrical, and plumbing	30,000
Enlarged office area	1,500
Snack bar equipment	7,000
Outside lighting	150
Music P.A. system	4,000
Signs	1,800
Inventory:	
Skates, 300 pair @ $31.95	9,585
Extra wheels and parts	650
Snack bar supplies/inventory	1,000
Office and cleaning supplies	1,000
Other costs:	
Working capital	15,000
Legal and professional fees, licenses/permits, utility deposits, and initial advertising	5,000
Total investment	$199,435

It was likely that, of the nearly $200,000 investment required,
$150,000 could be borrowed from several sources. The expected aver-
age interest rate which would have to be paid at that time was 11.5
percent. The land was estimated to be worth $30,000 and the building
$36,000. It was anticipated that a 20-year mortgage of $35,000 could be
obtained on a variable interest basis; i.e., the actual interest charged
would vary depending on prevailing rates.

From a variety of sources it was possible to put together an estimate
of monthly expenditures in the form of percentage of sales ratios for a

rink similar in size to the one being considered. These estimates are given below.

	Percent of sales
Salaries	8%
Wages	12
Advertising	3
Interest/mortgage	22
Supplies/food	12
Telephone/utilities	5
Insurance	2
Maintenance	2
Taxes/licenses	5
Security	7
Repairs	3
All other	5
Total	86%

Source: Roller Skating Business Fact Book and Roller Skating Operator Trade Association.

Total sales per 4-week period were estimated as follows:

1. Admissions:
   6,870 skaters[a]   Price = $2.00 with own skates;
   4,000 with own skates[b] $2.50 with rental skates
   2,870 with rental skates[b]

   4,000 × $2.00 = $8,000 own skates
   2,870 × $2.50 = $7,175 rental skates $15,175.00 total

2. Arcade games:
   12 games × $150/week[c] × .40[d] × 4 weeks   2,880.00

3. Snack bar:
   Average skater spends $1.25 per 4-week period × 6,870[e]   8,587.50

   Total sales $26,642.50

[a] From earlier data.
[b] National survey shows 66 percent of skaters are from households with incomes of $20,000 or more. It is assumed that such skaters own their own skates.
[c] Based on national average of machines in grocery stores.
[d] Commission rate charged by suppliers in Little Rock and North Little Rock.
[e] Estimated from data provided by local theater operators.

Based on a profit before tax margin of 14 percent, the venture was estimated to yield profits of $3,729.95 per average four-week period or an annual profit before taxes of $48,489.35 without taking into account depreciation which was estimated to be about $20,000 annually. At this level, state and federal income taxes were expected to total about 20 percent. The Freemans recognized that their rink/arcade would not be profitable from the outset, although they did think that it would be possible to break even the first year of operation.

C A S E 1–2

Grantree Furniture Rental (A)

In February 1972, Mr. Donald Bjorklund, founder and president of Grantree[1] Furniture Rental Corporation, was reviewing his company's progress. Sales and profits had grown nicely during the company's history, but current economic prospects were shaky, and Mr. Bjorklund wanted to be certain that his firm's position was sound.

Company History

The idea of renting home furnishings to householders occurred to Mr. Bjorklund while he was running a retail furniture store in Seaside, Oregon. He noted that many young adults, high mobiles (e.g., stewardesses), and certain senior citizens whose children had left home shared a need for inexpensive but appropriate furnishings for their new and often temporary households. Although there had long been the option of renting furnished apartments, direct rental of furniture was not readily available.

There were two apparent alternative approaches—direct to tenants and through apartment house owners and managers. For both targets there seemed to be legitimate potential need for rental. The challenge was to switch the tenant from "purchase on time" to rental and to switch the owner-manager from investing funds in a depreciating asset to rental. The challenge appealed to Mr. Bjorklund.

This case was written by Professor Robert T. Davis and is partially based on a case written by Phillip D. Fuchs in 1972. © 1979 by the Board of Trustees of the Leland Stanford Junior University.

[1] From 1963 to 1974, the company was called Custom Furniture Rental Corporation; it became Grantree in 1974. For reasons of simplicity, however, the company will be referred to as "Grantree" throughout this case.

Thus, in May 1963, he launched his new business, operating from an existing store in Portland. There were few employees, and deliveries were made in one old truck. By 1965, the firm had been incorporated and operated branches in the San Francisco Bay Area, including Sunnyvale, San Mateo, Burlingame, San Francisco, and the East Bay—all areas with high apartment growth rates. Early sales were modest but encouraging, as indicated in Exhibit 1.

Exhibit 1
Summary of Growth and Profit

	Original		Restated	
	Revenues	**Net income**	**Revenues**	**Net income**
June 30, 1975–				
February 28, 1966.........	$ 178,507	$ 18,824		
FYE February 28, 1967.......	597,514	46,304		
FYE February 29, 1968.......	1,046,045	71,236	$1,054,102*	$75,293*
FYE February 28, 1969.......	1,922,171	80,591	2,883,059†	65,978†
FYE February 28, 1970.......	4,239,987	216,352		
FYE February 28, 1971.......	5,358,286	275,212		
FYE February 29, 1972.......	6,090,562	397,993		

* During FYE 2/28/69, rental income was recognized on a full accrual basis with appropriate provision for uncollectible accounts.
† In December 1969, Home Furnishers Acceptance Corporation was acquired by merger and for financial accounting purposes was treated as a pooling of interests.

In subsequent years, Grantree acquired two local rental firms with strong managers (a rarity in this business) and, by the end of 1971, had 24 domestic showrooms, one Canadian showroom, 12 warehouses, and 6 used furniture outlets. Expansion had been limited to the West Coast and included Vancouver, Seattle, Edmonds, Bellevue, Portland, Beaverton, Corvallis, Eugene, Oakland, San Leandro, Walnut Creek, San Francisco, Burlingame, San Carlos, Sunnyvale, San Jose, Hollywood, Mira Loma, La Habra, Anaheim, Costa Mesa, and San Diego. Sales had climbed to over $5 million.

Although Exhibit 1 reveals a healthy growth in volume and profits, Mr. Bjorklund wondered if success were not due, in part at least, to a countercyclical aspect of the business—Did furniture leasing thrive in hard times? Regardless of the explanation, faster growth was limited by capital requirements. The investment in furniture, both in stock and on lease, was substantial.

To relieve the financial strain, the firm merged in July 1971 with a Portland financial institution, Granning and Treece. (Granning and Treece was a family-owned business which specialized in loans.) Mr. Bjorklund remained president of the furniture rental operation; two other executives ran smaller but profitable consumer finance and equipment leasing divisions. Walker Treece continued as chairman of the surviving company.

The Industry

The furniture industry consisted of 5,300 companies making wood, metal, or upholstered furniture for home and contract (industrial) markets. Most manufacturers were small and specialized by raw material or type of furniture. After 1960, however, there had been a trend toward large manufacturers diversifying into the furniture business by acquisition. Examples of these "newcomers" included Mohasco Industries, Armstrong Cork, Litton Industries, U.S. Plywood, Sperry Rand, and Beatrice Foods. Some of these companies had experience in closely allied businesses (Simmons, Magnavox), while others were novices.

By far the majority of the furniture manufacturers were family-owned, tradition-bound outfits, concentrated in North Carolina, Virginia, New York, Illinois, Indiana, and California, all close to sources of raw material and low labor costs. They have been described by *Fortune* as ". . . insignificant in size, inbred in management, inefficient in production, and inherently opposed to technological change."

In recent years, however, automation and new technologies have altered the labor cost situation in case goods (i.e., wood furniture) operations. Upholstered furniture, on the other hand, was not as adaptable to these innovations and had remained largely a custom, hand-crafted business. When synthetics and more efficient machinery gained acceptability, productivity was expected to improve considerably. This would presumably attract more large-scale manufacturers and impact significantly on marketing and manufacturing.

Distribution

Furniture distribution was as inefficient as its production. A number of distribution channels existed:

		Manufacturers (5,300)		
Furniture Markets (10s)	Furniture Rental (60)	Wholesalers (3,400)	Manufacturers Agents (100s)	Decorators (1,000s)
		Retailers (35,000)		

Despite the profusion of intermediaries, 80 percent of the volume went direct from manufacturer to retailer. The retailers, both chain and independent, could be classified by type and by function:

A. By Type
   1. Specialty furniture stores.
   2. Department stores.
   3. Mail-order houses.
   4. Premium houses.
   5. Catalog offices.
   6. Dealers in office furniture.
   7. "Wholesale showrooms"—(a misnomer since these were actually retailers selling to the ultimate user).
   8. Warehouse/showrooms—e.g., Levitz Furniture Company.
   9. Interior designers.
  10. Discounters.
B. By Function
   1. Deluxers—uncrate, assemble, check for damage and repair; usually more expensive than prepackers.
   2. Prepackers—reship to buyer in original crate.

The remaining major intermediaries were wholesalers, interior designers, and rental firms. The furniture rental firms were few in number, perhaps 60 in 1972. Most were offshoots of retail stores and concentrated on the East and West Coasts. Grantree was the leader; the second largest was two-thirds its size. Competition was generally local and restricted to a single outlet. Most competitors were tiny, inefficient mom-and-pop operators. Service was limited. The major competitive tactic was price cutting, and advertising was confined to the classified ads, the yellow pages, and occasional display ads in local newspapers. There were no data on share of market, although the recent establishment of the Furniture Rental Association of America augured well for the infant industry.

Purchase of used furniture was an important alternative to furniture rental. Competition in used furniture was keen. In addition to used furniture outlets, there were garage sales, householder sales, and institutional outlets like Goodwill and the Salvation Army.

Leasing in general seemed to be "in." The socioeconomic and cultural changes that had taken place since World War II had altered the value systems and lifestyles of many people. Gone was the Puritan ethic of "pay-as-you-go"; it was no longer a sin to buy on credit. Particularly for young adults, a lease provided the convenience of product use without the obligation of ownership.

The advantages of furniture rental, described in a brochure distributed by Grantree's salespeople, were these:

Have the furniture you want and need now—low in cost.
Select the furniture yourself.
Immediate delivery.
No large investment.

No personal property taxes.

No moving expenses.

No maintenance costs.

Saves time and expense of shopping for furniture.

Flexibility of style and need through easy exchange privileges—an ideal arrangement for persons who require frequent moves or are in an area on a temporary basis.

Robert C. Hampton, executive director of the Furniture Rental Association, stated that ". . . in 1969, for the fifth consecutive year, furniture rental volume in America grew more than 30 percent. Several companies, Grantree for one, have seen rental volume nearly doubling annually during this period." He predicted that in the 1970s at least 10 percent of the apartments in the United States would be furnished with some item acquired on lease.

Industry Problems

Whereas the rental segment of the furniture business seemed to offer potential promise, the traditional furniture industry had many problems. Retailers dominated the channels, a phenomenon which had diminished the effectiveness of distribution. These retailers had not been capable "channel captains," due to a lack of marketing or distribution skill and their preoccupation with other tasks. In most other industries, manufacturers were channel captains.

The major problem of the industry was product damage incurred either in materials handling or during shipment. Case goods were the most vulnerable and required great care by shippers and packers. The high incidence of damage meant the maintenance of repair and refinishing facilities along the channels. In some instances, damaged goods had to be disposed of at markdown prices.

Slow delivery was another vexing problem, particularly for retailers and their customers. Orders received by manufacturers were usually limited to a single consumer order, frequently for individual units. Typically, the manufacturers held these small orders until a sufficient number in one geographical destination had been accumulated, thereby avoiding the higher LCL and LTL shipping rates. Inevitably, the delay often inhibited purchase.

In merchandising, the major problems revolved around inadequate brand promotion and cooperative advertising. Except for a few national labels, most advertising was store oriented. Little assistance was provided by manufacturers to dealers in regard to promotion, display, sales training, or general management practices.

The retail furniture markets were highly competitive. Price competition was rife, as illustrated by many markdowns, special sales, cash-

and-carry sales, and discounts to certain "club members." Nonprice competition was primarily advertising, done only by the largest firms.

The most exciting competitive development of the early 1970s was warehouse-showroom marketing, best illustrated by Levitz Furniture Company. Practically unheard of a few years earlier, the warehouse-showroom format cornered nearly $400 million in annual sales volume, about 4 percent of the total furniture sales volume in the United States. It was expected to capture a 15 percent share by 1975. The full import of this new competition was uncertain, but the prime targets for warehouse-showrooms were young householders and bargain hunters, all important potential subscribers to furniture leasing.

The Markets for Rental Furniture

Data on rental furniture penetration among households were scarce. One broad estimate was that 5 percent of total consumer expenditures in 1972 were for furniture and appliances, either purchased or rented. Executives at Grantree reasoned that rentals were primarily found among apartment renters. It was their considered judgment that for every 100 apartment units in 1972 in the West Coast markets.[2]

75 were furnished by the tenants with their own furniture.

25 were furnished with rented furniture.

1 or 2 of the 25 would be furniture rented from firms like Grantree—the rest provided by the owner-builder.

The ultimate rental consumers, whether dealing direct with Grantree or through an owner/manager, were described by one Grantree executive as:

> Young marrieds, the transferred executives, ballplayers, stewardesses. Many of our customers are young persons who formerly rented furnished apartments and homes. High interest rates make young people unwilling to take on long-term financial obligations unless they are definitely ready to commit themselves to a particular style of furniture.
>
> Another major segment of our market is the mobile element of our society. These are people of all ages; people who want "instant living," who don't want to buy furniture until they finally select their permanent home.
>
> Income brackets of people who rent furniture are mixed—high income families rent for convenience, while the "economy class" rents to spread a limited budget.

---

[2] The percentage of "furnished" apartments on the East Coast seemed to be much lower. The West Coast had the highest percentage regionally in the United States. Seventy percent of the apartments in Phoenix, for example, were furnished.

Mr. Bjorklund felt that there were two separate segments of consumers, the buyers and the renters. He saw little evidence that consumers switched readily from one group to the other.

An important factor in the demand for home furnishings (either purchase or rental) was the degree of population mobility. U.S. population studies indicated that each year about 20 percent of the people changed residence. Of these relocations, about two thirds moved within the same county and one third moved to other counties. The most mobile segment of the population was the 18–34 age group. The mobiles were young and well educated, held higher status occupations, had above-average incomes, tended to be socially active, and generally needed to revise their household inventories to suit new living quarters. Mobiles represented a unique opportunity for furniture marketers.

The reasons for migration, as discussed recently among psychologists, had potential marketing relevance. Human dignity was frequently an important factor in the change of surroundings. A new environment was perceived as giving one a new and better chance for success. Voluntary relocations might be perceived as a way of destroying the past or of moving up. Many people relocated to achieve social and personal growth. Others looked for economic gain.

Mr. Bjorklund, in describing the prime markets, reasoned that there were several bases for segmentation:

1. Demography—geography, family composition and size, educational attainments of the family head, occupation, income, ethnic origin, race, home ownership, marital status, and number of wage earners in the household.
2. Physical characteristics—age, health, sex, height, weight.
3. Psychological traits—personality, intelligence level, avocational interests, political bias, psychological needs, and preferences.
4. Behavioral patterns (with respect to the product)—product use, product loyalty, brand use, brand preference, buying habits, buying behavior.
5. The commercial market—which accounted for 40 percent of Grantree's revenues, mainly apartment owners, and institutional customers.

Grantree considered its major competitors to be the owners of furnished apartments, not other rental outfits. Apartment house owners needed furnished apartments primarily to help rent their units. Prospective tenants without furniture, unless they knew about direct renting, would shy away from unfurnished quarters; or, if they favored a particular apartment, might not return if they had to leave to rent furniture, and thus be potentially exposed to other apartment alternatives.

Why so many owners continued to supply their own furniture in rental units was presumably caused by inadequate knowledge of their own furniture costs, strong sales arguments by contract furniture salespeople, and inadequate knowledge about the existence of rental firms. In many ways, the apartment owners were not strong competitors for furniture: They rarely gave much service to the tenants. Furniture ownership was a traditional necessity, and an expensive one at that. The typical owner invested between $600 and $1,000 per one-bedroom apartment and had to assume the costs of storage, maintenance, theft, damage, replacement, tied-up capital, diversionary use of the apartment manager's time, and an asset that dwindled to zero value (due to selling costs) after five years.

Grantree's Marketing Strategy

Grantree leased home furnishings for one month or longer, the typical commercial contract being of longer initial duration than the direct-to-tenant. During 1971, the company rented furniture to 13,000 customers in the United States and 700 in Canada. Sixty percent of the rentals were to individual tenants and could be canceled by the customer on 30 days prior written notice. The average term of rental agreement was nine months.

On direct-to-tenant business, the firm realized a 9-month payback (i.e., 11 percent per month), but 20 months (5 percent) on commercial. The commercial rentals had the offsetting benefits of less physical handling, larger unit transactions, and hopefully a more responsible lessee. The latter assumption, however, was tenuous.

The owner included the tenant's furniture rental in a single figure for the "furnished apartment." He then paid Grantree, but often after a five- or six-month delay. The firm picked up the rental on its books as income as soon as the tenant signed the apartment lease. If a builder went broke, Grantree would find itself with five or six months of income write-off; in fact, in one case, the bankrupt builder sold the Grantree furniture as if it were his own. Although commercial failures were not all that frequent, it was difficult for Mr. Bjorklund to know which business was the more profitable. It was his opinion that both markets were equally attractive.

Grantree let the tenant or lessee select any one item or coordinated group of items from a wide assortment of styles. Delivery and installation of the selection was made within 24 hours after the lease was signed. Rental rates, which required a monthly advance, depended upon the selections. The average charge was $30 per month, which covered furnishings for a living room, dinette, and bedroom. The company's rental fees were competitive with the time payments on purchased furniture; in some cases Grantree's prices were lower than either monthly payments due on purchased furniture or on rental rates charged by competing firms. In the San Jose area, for example, Grantree's rate for a minimum group was $22.50 per month—local competitors charged $25 to $30. The company also offered a much wider selection and generally higher quality furniture than its rental competitors.

A deposit of $35 was required for each account but was returned if the lease was in effect at least 12 months. This fee covered the cost of delivery and installation. Customers could make additions, deletions, or changes of items, but there was a $15 charge for each such order. The rate was, in effect, a delivery charge and applied to any or all pieces of furniture involved in the service call.

If the lessee moved, there was a $20 charge to shift the furniture. If a customer transferred to another geographical area serviced by Grantree, the lessee could return the furniture and ask for delivery at the new location. The company required 30 days' written notice of this change of address.

Grantree's customers had the option of buying part or all of the rented furniture. The purchase price amounted to 25 times the monthly rental fee. A selection of furniture carrying a monthly rental of $30 would bear, therefore, a total purchase price of $750. The purchase option offer provided that credit toward the total purchase price be given as follows:

100 percent of the first year's rent.

75 percent of the second year's rent.

50 percent of the third year's rent.

80 percent of this credit could be applied to the purchase of a similar piece of new furniture.

Using the example of a $30 per month rental and $750 purchase price, the customer having paid the first year's rental fees would be given a credit of $360 and pay the balance of $390 to complete the purchase. The customer who had completed making rental payments for two years would be given credit of $630 (100 percent of $360 plus 75 percent of $360) toward the $750 purchase price, leaving a balance of $120.

Persons opting to buy their rented furniture generally did so after the first year and certainly not beyond the second year. In 1971, there were 1,400 customers who decided to purchase one or more pieces of rented furniture. Gross receipts from those sales were $330,000. However, less than 8 percent of the total customer base exercised their buying option.

Used furniture was sent out for rental "like new," but the company openly invited all of its customers to return any piece that failed to meet the "like new" test. In the words of Mr. Bjorklund, "We sell service and there's no sense trying to pass off shabby merchandise on the renter. It is in this quality control that we have a big advantage over most of our competition."

Used Furniture Sales. Reporting to the local rental managers were six used furniture stores in the major Grantree markets. Furniture that was considered unusable for rental was disposed of on an "as is" basis at bargain cash prices. Sales volume in these stores by 1972 approximated $1.5 million per year, but the profit or loss was not clear. It was estimated that losses were about $250,000 each year. Although a significant portion of the original buying price was recovered in the used sale, there was no clear-cut policy about where to set the used furniture selling price in terms of depreciated value and selling costs of disposal. At these six used stores, some new furniture was sold (less than 10 percent in 1971) in order to highlight the "good values" on the used. Mr. Bjorklund thought that the new furniture sales were profitable. Used furniture employees were typically ex-warehouseworkers and drivers who wanted to sell. Being in the used furniture business was considered a necessary evil to being in the rental business.

The Product Mix. An important aspect of the company's marketing mix was the product line, which had been carefully selected by company personnel highly knowledgeable about furniture buying. The line was under constant review for style and compatibility with consumer preferences and demand.

Grantree's product line included the following:

Davenports	Dining chairs
Chairs (living room)	Beds
Table lamps	Mattresses
Stereo systems	Pictures
Bars	Love seats
Dinette sets	Cocktail tables
Headboards	Television sets
Box springs	Bookcases
Rugs	Dining tables
Sofas and sofa beds	Buffets
End tables	Bed frames
Floor lamps	Night stands and lamps
Room dividers	Refrigerators
Bar stools	

In terms of decor, the firm offered 12 living room and 3 bedroom choices in 1972, a significant increase over the past three years. The quality of the furniture had likewise been upgraded as evidenced by the steadily increasing "average monthly rental charge."

Grantree acquired 90 percent of its furniture from about 25 major suppliers, mostly located in the West in order to minimize inventory requirements. It was considered prudent to have duplicated suppliers (there were three, for example, for upholstered furniture) in order to guarantee merchandise in the case of emergencies. Another 75 companies supplied Grantree with the remaining 10 percent of its needs, mostly in knickknacks, lamps, and small specialty items. Because of its size and importance, Grantree had considerable leverage with its suppliers.

The Promotion Mix.   The major components of the Grantree promotion mix were: (1) personal selling, (2) advertising, (3) sales promotion, (4) publicity and public relations, and (5) miscellaneous promotions. The total marketing budget came to between 10 percent and 12 percent of net sales, and most of that was reflected in costs attributed to personal selling. Advertising was concentrated in telephone directories (Yellow Pages) and occasionally placed newspaper display advertisements for special events. Media advertising accounted for about 2.5 percent of new sales.

It was estimated that 50 percent of the direct-to-tenant sales came from recommendations by owners/managers. The other half came from the yellow pages, friends, and customers.

The Sales Forces.   There were three distinct kinds of salespeople in Grantree, reflecting three sales approaches. First, there were the showroom salespeople, who waited on customers who came into the showroom. These salespeople did not customarily make any sales off the premises. Second, there were the sales and service representatives who worked in the field, calling on apartment managers and owners. They did not make actual sales but paved the way for future sales by making known Grantree's service for apartment tenants. (Given apartment vacancy rates of 10 to 15 percent, the owners and managers were anxious to gain a competitive edge and thus represented a fairly responsive market segment.) The third kind of salesperson attempted to make contracts with large commercial accounts. Typically, these were the veteran salespeople or sales managers.

Sales Management Duties.   In addition to selling commercial accounts, sales managers were responsible for recruiting, selecting, and training new personnel. They were also expected to assist top management in the development of sales plans and strategies. They were judged on their ability to supervise, stimulate, evaluate, and control the salespeople in their respective jurisdictions.

Grantree recruited most of its salespeople from employment agencies but occasionally used referrals from customers and other employees. Immediately after being hired, the new salesperson was given an orientation to the firm's policies and practices by the sales manager. Following the indoctrination, a new employee received on-the-job training for about one week and was then assigned as a showroom salesperson. Field selling assignments were earned only after a salesperson was considered well informed on company policy, product line, lease agreements, and selling techniques.

Sales compensation was straight salary. Reimbursement was made for travel expense at the rate of 12 percent per mile. Employees also received a number of fringe benefits such as discounts on furniture, nine paid holidays and vacation pay (one week's pay for one year's service), sick pay, health insurance, and life insurance (the company's share of the premium was two thirds, while employees paid one third). The firm had a profit sharing plan. Furthermore, salespeople participated in prize contests and could earn P.M.s for good performance.[3] The compensation plan applied to each type of salesperson.

Advertising. Grantree made limited use of mass media advertising, and relied primarily on the yellow pages. Classified ads in local newspapers were made occasionally. Mr. Bjorklund recalled that the company had tried a radio campaign, but it was unproductive and had been discontinued. Advertising was handled by Grantree personnel, and there were plans to establish an in-house agency to handle this function in the future.

The company favored use of four-color brochures displaying the product lines available to potential renters. It also believed that adver-

Exhibit 2
Sources Perceived by Residents as Most Helpful in Selection of Furniture and Bedding

Source	Furniture (percent)	Bedding (percent)
Discussion with family, friends, neighbors	47	49
Discussion with professional designers and/or interior decorators	8	3
Seen in other homes	27	9
Visiting model homes	12	1
Window-shopping	43	21
Newspaper ads	28	46
Home shows	2	1
Magazine articles	21	20
Magazine ads	30	17
Manufacturers' booklets/mailing pieces	8	8
TV programs and/or commercials	3	11
"Know what I want"	3	7
Catalogs	2	3

---

[3] Premium money, sometimes called "push money."

tising specialties such as ballpoint pens, bumper stickers, book matches, four-foot rulers, and so on were good promotional tools. Mr. Bjorklund expressed the opinion that word-of-mouth advertising was very effective, as was the development and maintenance of a good corporate and product image.

In-Store Display.   In-store (showroom) display appeared to be important in the marketing of furniture, either rented or purchased. A study made in May 1968 by the research department of Fairchild Publications threw some light on the effectiveness of various promotional devices (see Exhibit 2).

Organization

When Grantree was first established, and during its formative years, the organization was highly centralized. Like many entrepreneurs, Mr. Bjorklund was largely a one-man show. As the firm expanded, Mr. Bjorklund recognized the need to formalize and decentralize his organization. It was his intention to shove the operating decisions down to the district managers, while reserving the strategic and policy matters to himself.

The company maintained showrooms and warehouses in Washington, Oregon, California, and Vancouver, B.C. Each branch was manned by sales and warehouse personnel. Personal selling, the major element in the Grantree promotional mix, was handled both in the showroom and by field operations. Each branch maintained facilities for repairing, cleaning, fumigating, assembling, servicing, and installing. The delivery-drivers played a key role in the development and maintenance of a favorable company image.

Growth Alternatives

Mr. Bjorklund's main line of attack had been to first blanket the western apartment market before turning to geographic expansion, the penetration of new markets such as commercial offices, or vertical integration back into manufacturing. Coverage of the West was attained by internal growth (i.e., establishing company units in new locations) and by acquisition. It was not easy, however, to decide when a particular market had been satisfactorily penetrated.

When asked how he measured penetration, Mr. Bjorklund stated that a reasonable penetration rate for a single company seemed to be 5 percent of the total apartment units.[4] The total obviously included a large number of low-income apartments for which the rental of furni-

---

[4] The count of apartment units was purchased from the federal government which maintained a Post Office Mail Carrier Survey.

ture was practically out of the question. Thus, Mr. Bjorklund was pleased with his firm's 5 percent penetration in Portland and Eugene, but not with the 1 percent in San Francisco. Confirmation of the reasonableness of the 5 percent target figure came from a study of market penetration elsewhere. In Washington, D.C., for example, the penetration rate was 25 percent, but the business was shared by three strong competitors and several smaller concerns. Similarly in Houston, there was a high penetration rate (20 percent), but no single firm had more than 6 percent.

The company's long-range plans called for expansion by entering additional market areas. The normal procedure for breaking a new market was to open a warehouse with attached showroom and trucks. Later, additional showrooms were added closer to prime apartment areas. Finally, after a critical mass of furniture was on rental (probably two to three years), a used furniture store was opened.[5]

Before making a decision to enter any given market, the company made a series of market studies. The investigations produced a "census" of existing multiple housing units, housing under construction, and plans for future construction. Market profiles were prepared with emphasis on classes of people and their lifestyles. Demographic data were included. These surveys and analyses were made by Grantree district managers and reviewed by Mr. Bjorklund and the executive vice president. In addition, the proposed market was traversed by automobile and airplane for observation of its physical characteristics.

The typical requirements for an attractive market were a high mobility rate (such as a political center) and active apartment construc-

Exhibit 3
U.S. Census Bureau Projection

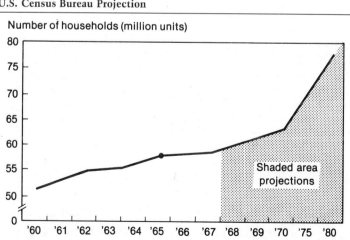

_____

[5] Exhibit 3 includes some generally useful information about market potentials.

Exhibit 3 *(concluded)*

Number of Household and Family Units (000)

| | Projections | |
	Total household	Family units
1980:		
Highest	76,494	62,967
Lowest	73,601	61,977
1975:		
Highest	70,036	57,670
Lowest	67,730	56,865

Households

Year	Total	Urban and rural nonfarm	Rural farm	Primary family units
1970	62,874	60,150	2,724	51,110
1969	61,805	58,935	2,870	50,416
1968	60,444	57,501	2,944	49,734
1967	58,845	55,910	2,934	48,791
1966	58,092	54,875	3,214	48,169
1965	57,251	53,899	3,350	47,720
1964	55,996	52,651	3,345	47,278
1963	55,189	51,725	3,464	46,813
1962	54,652	50,890	3,762	46,185
1961	53,464	49,115	3,749	45,299

Note: All years as of March; projections are as of July. A household includes all of the persons who occupy a house, an apartment or other group of rooms, or a room that constitutes a dwelling or housing unit. The term "family" as used here refers to a group of two or more persons related by blood, marriage, or adoption and residing together, all such persons considered as members of one family.

Source: U.S. Department of Commerce.

tion. Sacramento and Phoenix, for example, were prime targets, whereas Bakersfield and Fresno were less attractive in the short run.

The company's marketing effectiveness in the past two years had been improved significantly by several strategies. One of these was the relocation of showrooms/salesrooms from back streets to high traffic streets. Another was the establishment of used furniture outlets in six major areas.

The Issue

Mr. Bjorklund, as stated earlier, was not displeased with his firm's progress, but he had the uneasy feeling that he wasn't sure about the best strategy. His company was still small, and there was little real evidence that there was a realizable market potential.

C A S E 1–3

Cummins Engine Company

At 10:25 on the morning of Monday, August 23, 1976, Mr. John Tilling[1] of the Cummins Engine Company called Ray Peterson in service: "I need your help on a problem. Mr. Thompson J. Throckmorton has been complaining to McPhail that he couldn't take his yacht out on Saturday because something was wrong with the engine. Can you get with your service manager in the area and the distributor to find out what's wrong and get back to me? We need to get back to Throckmorton as soon as possible."

As director of marine sales for Cummins, Mr. Tilling was responsible for the marketing of diesel engines destined for use in all types of boats. Over two thirds of Cummins' sales of marine engines were to the pleasure craft market, less than one third to the commercial market, although the latter was estimated to be twice as large as the former. Diesels for pleasure craft (see Exhibit 1) has been one of Cummins original product lines when the company was started in 1919, but the marketing effort was discontinued after the stock market crash of 1929. Cummins had reentered the field in the early 1960s, with somewhat disappointing results. The profit margins were among the lowest of all Cummins products. The warranty expense was among the highest. And the line commanded an inordinate amount of executive concern because of calls like Mr. Throckmorton's. Two weeks before, Mr. Tilling's supervisor, Mr. Andrew McPhail, executive vice president of the Industrial Products Group, asked Mr. Tilling to reevaluate Cummins' participation in the pleasure craft market. Some executives thought that complete withdrawal from the marine market should be seriously considered, whereas others advocated a significant change in Cummins' positioning in and approach to the marine market.

---

[1] All personal names are fictitious. Copyright © 1976 by the Trustees of Dartmouth College. All rights reserved.

Exhibit 1
A Page from Cummins' Promotional Literature

Cummins V8 pleasure boat engines

Powerful, reliable, compact diesels

Cummins V8 marine diesels provide high horsepower and reliable performance in pleasure craft. The oversquare cylinder concept, in which the bore diameter is greater than the stroke, provides more power in a compact, light configuration—ideal for pleasure boat installations. Because of this concept, Cummins was able to achieve high power in a small, light weight package and to retain heavy-duty, commercial component design for exceptional reliability.

Proven performance

To prove the performance and reliability of the new over-square cylinder design concept, Cummins entered V8 engines in the grueling Miami to Nassau Power Boat Race in 1962. As a result of their performance, Cummins diesels were the first engines to be awarded the Ocean Tested Seal of Approval by the racing organization.

Since then thousands of Cummins V8 engines have been installed in pleasure craft built by leading boat builders and have been specified by naval architects in custom designed boats. And Cummins has refined the V8

engines to provide improved performance and reliability from today's engines.

Style leadership

Cummins was the first engine manufacturer to use professional industrial designers to control the outside appearance of the engine. They developed the low profile designs which contribute to neater engine installation. The inherent compact size of the V8 design permits reduction of engine room size and Cummins internal fuel and oil line design eliminates leaks to retain a clean appearance during operation and to reduce engine room fire hazard.

Warranty protection

Cummins warranty provides for the repair or replacement of defective parts in pleasure boat engines for 3,600 hours or 2 years, whichever occurs first. For half of this period, Cummins pays reasonable labor expense in addition to replacing or repairing the defective part. For

the remainder of the warranty, Cummins replaces or repairs defective parts and pays a portion of the labor.

200 to 450 horsepower

Five compact V8 models cover a range of 202 horsepower (151 kW) to 450 horsepower (336 kW). They are built in 504 cubic inch (8.3 l), 555 cubic inch (9.1 l), and 903 cubic inch (14.8 l) configurations. The 504 cubic inch (8.3 l) and 555 cubic inch (9.1 l) models are naturally aspirated while the 903 cubic inch (14.8 l) configuration is available as naturally aspirated, turbocharged, and turbocharged aftercooled models.

More power available for large boats

In addition to the V8 engines listed in this brochure, Cummins in line six and V12 work boat diesels are available for ocean yachts requiring up to 1045 hp (780 kW) for single engine installations and 2090 hp (1560 kW) for twin engine vessels.

The Product

Because of their weight (over 2,000 pounds each) and their relative expense ($8,000–$20,000 cost to OEM boatbuilders) Cummins engines were limited to the high horsepower relatively small segment of the total pleasure craft market. (Cummins diesels were used in twin-engine pleasure craft exclusively.) These boats, mostly with fiberglass hulls, exceeded 35 feet in length and ranged in cost to the end-user from $150,000 to $300,000 and more. About one third were purchased from dealer and manufacturer stock, and two thirds were special-ordered with either standard or custom designs. All were available with a wide variety of fittings and accessories. The boats were most commonly used for fishing, cruising, and business and personal entertainment. On the average, they were operated about 200 hours per year. Their home ports typically were near coastal population centers in the United States and abroad. The boats often ranged over large areas especially on the East Coast of the United States where northern customers would winter the boats in Florida.

In 1976 Cummins was anticipating completing its first $1 billion calendar sales year. It was the largest producer of diesel engines over 200 horsepower, and its products were used in all applications, automotive and industrial. The company had its headquarters and extensive research facilities in Columbus, Indiana, and foreign subsidiaries located in Mexico, Brazil, England, India, and Japan. Over the years, Cummins had developed a reputation for the quality, reliability, and economy of its engines.

Cummins' involvement in the pleasure craft market dated almost all the way back to the company's inception in 1919. However, when demand dwindled after the stock market crash of 1929, Cummins dropped out and did not reenter the field until 1961. During the intervening 30 years, Cummins continued to sell engines for use in commercial boats. But the mainstay of its line, an in-line six-cylinder unit, was too large and heavy for use in most pleasure boats.

In 1961 Cummins introduced as part of its regular line a new short-stroke vee configuration eight-cylinder diesel, considerably smaller and lighter than the in-line six. In formulating the marketing plans for this new engine, Cummins executives decided to use it for the pleasure marine market, among other uses. They hired a prominent industrial designer to restyle the engine and make it more compact and aesthetically appealing to pleasure craft owners, who, unlike fishermen and tugboat operators, would take pride in opening an engine hatch to the sight of a sleek, chromed engine. With the addition of marine gearing, wet manifolds, a longer camshaft, heat exchanger, gear oil cooler, sea water pump, and other changes, this engine became the marine version of a diesel already in use in trucks and industrial equipment.

The new vee engine was a success technically and commercially. It powered the winning entry in the Miami-Nassau offshore ocean race of 1962, the first year it was entered. And in sales, it quickly grabbed a significant market share. Competitors soon developed similar engines, and from 1964 on, Cummins found itself in a marine diesel horsepower race, with the most sales going to the engine with the most power in

Exhibit 2

Cummins
pleasure boat engines

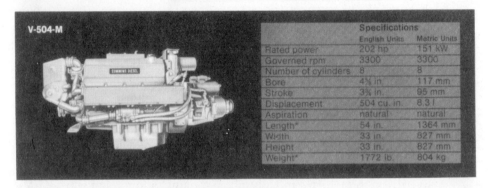

V-504-M

	Specifications	
	English Units	Metric Units
Rated power	202 hp	151 kW
Governed rpm	3300	3300
Number of cylinders	8	8
Bore	4¾ in.	117 mm
Stroke	3¾ in.	95 mm
Displacement	504 cu. in.	8.3 l
Aspiration	natural	natural
Length*	54 in.	1364 mm
Width	33 in.	827 mm
Height	33 in.	827 mm
Weight*	1772 lb.	804 kg

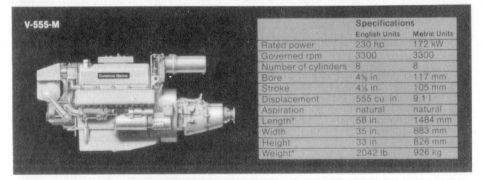

V-555-M

	Specifications	
	English Units	Metric Units
Rated power	230 hp	172 kW
Governed rpm	3300	3300
Number of cylinders	8	8
Bore	4¾ in.	117 mm
Stroke	4⅛ in.	105 mm
Displacement	555 cu. in.	9.1 l
Aspiration	natural	natural
Length*	58 in.	1484 mm
Width	35 in.	883 mm
Height	33 in.	826 mm
Weight*	2042 lb.	926 kg

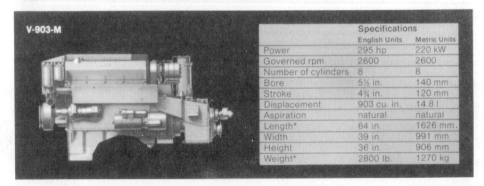

V-903-M

	Specifications	
	English Units	Metric Units
Power	295 hp	220 kW
Governed rpm	2600	2600
Number of cylinders	8	8
Bore	5½ in.	140 mm
Stroke	4¾ in.	120 mm
Displacement	903 cu. in.	14.8 l
Aspiration	natural	natural
Length*	64 in.	1626 mm.
Width	39 in.	991 mm
Height	36 in.	906 mm
Weight*	2800 lb.	1270 kg

its class. When a new engine was developed, it would immediately be marinized and entered in the race. In the more recent stages of the race, first turbocharging and then aftercooling had been employed. In 1976, Cummins and its principal competitor. Detroit Diesel (a division of General Motors), offered engines rated at 450 horsepower. Cummins' full line for the pleasure marine market is illustrated in Exhibit 2. Exhibit 3 offers a comparison with the lines offered by the two major competitors.

Exhibit 2 *(concluded)*

VT-903-M

	Specifications	
	English Units	Metric Units
Rated power	400 hp	298 kW
Governed rpm	2600	2600
Number of cylinders	8	8
Bore	5½ in.	140 mm
Stroke	4¾ in.	120 mm
Displacement	903 cu. in.	14.8 l
Aspiration	turbocharged	
Length*	65 in.	1662 mm
Width	41 in.	1041 mm
Height	38 in.	970 mm
Weight*	3200 lb.	1453 kg

VT-903-M1

	Specifications	
	English Units	Metric Units
Rated power	340 hp	254 kW
Governed rpm	2800	2800
Number of cylinders	8	8
Bore	5½ in.	140 mm
Stroke	4¾ in.	120 mm
Displacement	903 cu. in.	14.8 l
Aspiration	turbocharged	
Length*	64 in.	1626 mm
Width	41 in.	1041 mm
Height	38 in.	970 mm
Weight*	2950 lb.	1340 kg

VTA-903-M

	Specifications	
	English Units	Metric Units
Rated power	450 hp	336 kW
Governed rpm	2600	2600
Number of cylinders	8	8
Bore	5½ in.	140 mm
Stroke	4¾ in.	120 mm
Displacement	903 cu. in.	14.8 l
Aspiration	turbocharged and aftercooled	
Length*	70 in.	1778 mm
Width	38 in.	975 mm
Height	41 in.	1044 mm
Weight*	3650 lb.	1660 kg

* With typical reverse and reduction gear.

Exhibit 3
U.S. Marine Competitive Comparison: Pleasure Boat Application (marine gear, heat exchanger, electrics)

Cummins (1/1/76)				Detroit Diesel (9/1/75)				Caterpillar (9/1/75)			
Model	HP at rpm	Price	$/HP	Model	HP at rpm	Price	$/HP	Model	HP at rpm	Price	$/HP
V-504M (Warner 73 2:1)	189 at 3,300	$ 5,800	$30.69	6V-53 (Warner 73 2:1)	197 at 2,800	$ 5,575	$28.30	3208 (MG-502 2:1)	204 at 2,800	$5,520	$27.06
V-555-M (Warner 73 2:1)	216 at 3,300	6,482	30.01	6-71N (Allison M 2:1)	257 at 2,300	8,070	31.40				
V-903-M (Capital 4 HE-10200 2:1)	276 at 2,600	9,649	34.96	6-71TI (Allison M 2:1)	325 at 2,300	10,636	32.73				
VT-903-MI (Capital 4 HE-10200 2:1)	318 at 2,800	10,639	33.46	8V-71N (Allison M 2:1)	325 at 2,300	10,423	32.07				
VT-903-M2 (MG-509 2:1)	374 at 2,600	11,821	31.61	8V-71TI (Allison M 2:1)	425 at 2,300	12,629	29.72				
VTA-903-M (Capital HYC 22000 2:1)	421 at 2,600	12,686	30.13								

Note: All prices to boatbuilder, assuming similar distributor margins.

One unexpected offshoot of the horsepower race was the discovery of a new market segment containing the U.S. Navy and Coast Guard and foreign navies. These customers sought for their patrol boats light engines with maximum power and reliability. Mr. Tilling estimated that currently one half of the total sales of the 903 marine series were made to the U.S. Coast Guard.

In the process of his involvement in the horsepower race, Mr. Tilling learned some of the desires of pleasure boat customers. They obviously liked the idea of having power in excess of what was needed to do the job. The second most important buying criterion related to the "noticeability" of the engine. The typical boat owner wished it to be as quiet as possible, and he reacted very unfavorably to the white smoke associated with starting a diesel engine, preferring to leave the yacht harbor with as little smoke and noise as possible. Mr. Tilling found that the owners were suitably impressed at boat shows by Cummins' uniquely aesthetic design, and some volunteered that they would be proud to lift the hatch and show off this engine, but this turned out to be not as important a buying criterion as power and noticeability.

One advantage which Cummins enjoyed in all areas of its business was that while its prime competitor GM produced two-cycle engines, Cummins produced four-cycle engines, which were significantly more efficient and thus offered superior fuel economy. In 1976 one boat manufacturer compared Cummins' 450 HP unit with a Detroit Diesel unit and found that the Cummins model used over 20 percent less fuel at cruise speed. However, Mr. Tilling had found that pleasure boat owners care little about marginal fuel savings in relation to performance. He reasoned that "if a guy spends $250,000 on a boat and only uses it about 200 hours a year, he really isn't going to care much if he saves a penny here or there on fuel costs."

Cummins' highly regarded research and engineering staff responded to the market demands by concentrating on the power, noise, and smoke problems. Chief engineer Charles Lampon explained, "We can get more power from any given engine for the marine market because it won't be subject to the same government emission standards as engines for the truck market, and it won't need the torque necessary for, say, a dump truck. Moreover, these engines will only have 200 hours per year running time, so we don't have to build them to last 150,000 miles or so, as we do truck engines."

Distribution and Market Characteristics

Cummins and its competitors all sold to exclusive regional distributors, who inventoried engines, had service responsibility, and occasionally did minor customizing to the specifications of their cus-

ORIGINAL ENGINE MANUFACTURERS

tomers, the OEM boatbuilders. These were full-line distributors, who sold and serviced engines destined for all automotive and industrial markets. They had sales responsibility for all OEMs within their territories, so that those most active in the marine market were the ones located near the coastal concentrations of OEM boatbuilders. (See Exhibit 4.)

Exhibit 4
U.S. Distributor Marine History

Distributor	10-year total	Highest year Year	Volume	Cumulative share of total
1	871	1972	171	21%
2	835	1972	218	41
3	374	1972	94	51
4	326	1966	51	59
5	321	1970	54	67
6	293	1970	51	74
7	155	1969	31	78
8	130	1970	31	81
9	104	1968	19	83
10	88	1967	27	86
11	79	1970	14	88
12	75	1965	26	89
13	62	1970	12	91
14	52	1970	12	92
15	48	1968	8	93
16	33	1972	11	94
17	30	1964	13	95
18	26	1968	6	96
19	22	1972	13	96
20	20	1971	12	97
17 others	119		49	
Total	4,063		683	

Cummins employed the same basic marketing strategy in the pleasure boat market as it did in the truck market. Half of the ultimate purchasing decision was attributed to the OEMs and half to the end-users. One third of all pleasure craft were bought straight from OEM and dealer stock on hand. The remainder were ordered specially and drew on either a standard OEM design package or a custom-design package. Occasionally the engine choice was restricted by the hull configuration of a particular model, but usually the OEM had to decide which engine best completed the package. As in the truck market, the OEMs offered each model with a particular engine designated as standard equipment, but with others available as options. With this in mind, Cummins directed half its marketing efforts toward the end-user through boat shows and promotional activity at the dealership level, and half toward the OEMs. The two leading OEMs accounted for almost 50 percent of the total market, while the top six controlled about 80 percent. Again, as in the truck market, some OEMs had their own exclusive dealership networks and some sold through independents.

Exhibit 5 describes the 1976 pleasure craft market through the month of July. Cummins was restricted to the 36 ft.–40 ft. and 41 ft.

Exhibit 5
July 1976 Industry Pleasure Boat Sales

Fiberglass Inboard Boats Only:

	Units	Factory value
This month.	892	$ 21,317,895
Same month last year	828	16,781,544
Percent gain or loss	+7.7%	+27.0%
Model year-to-date	7,174	154,562,344
Same period last year.	6,369	124,733,565
Percent gain or loss	+12.6%	+23.9%

Units:

Boat lengths	This month		Model year-to-date		Percent of total
	Runabouts	Cruisers	Runabouts	Cruisers	
25 ft. and under.	403	92	3,231	725	55.1
26 ft.–30 ft.	3	183	21	1,616	22.8
31 ft.–35 ft.	5	107	7	818	11.5
36 ft.–40 ft.		40	2	371	5.2
41 ft. and over.		59		383	5.3
Total	411	481	3,261	3,913	
Grand Total	892		7,174		

Factory Value:

Boat lengths	This month		Model year-to-date	
	Runabouts	Cruisers	Runabouts	Cruisers
25 ft. and under.	$2,404,084	$ 966,037	$18,335,161	$ 7,237,546
26 ft.–30 ft.	75,916	3,454,310	414,219	29,941,415
31 ft.–35 ft.	304,966	3,463,678	361,966	27,053,632
36 ft.–40 ft.		2,063,574	24,750	20,446,497
41 ft. and over.		8,585,330		50,747,158
Total	$2,784,966	$18,532,929	$19,136,096	$135,426,248
Grand Total	$21,317,895		$154,562,344	

and over categories because smaller boat hulls could not support the weight of the large diesel engines. Of course, some of the boats in these categories were fitted with gasoline engines. Exhibit 6 shows Cummins' share of the market of U.S. shipments of pleasure boat diesel engines. Exhibit 7 breaks down the 1975 diesel sales by horsepower range, with Cummins' engines starting at 200 horsepower. Mr. Tilling estimated that Cummins' total available market for 1976 would be

Exhibit 6
Marine—Pleasure—Cummins Range (201 + HP Diesels)

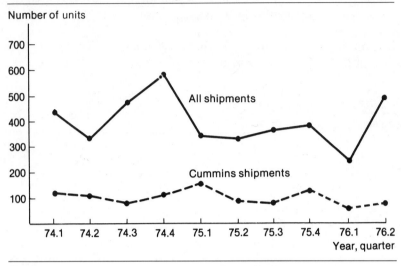

Number of units

Exhibit 7
1975 Industry Sales, Domestic Manufacturers Diesel
Engines for Pleasure Craft (by horsepower)

101–150.	620
151–200.	620
201–250.	359
251–300.	284
301–350.	284
351–400.	86
401–500.	172
501–600.	53
601–800.	53
801–1,200.	1
1,201–1,600	1
Total.	2,533

Total 1974 Marine Engine Sales (domestic, commercial
and pleasure)

Gasoline	90,000
Diesel	8,940

about 1,200 engines, representing 600 pleasure craft. He thought that
Cummins' share would be about 30 percent, or about 360 engines, for
an estimated sales revenue of roughly $3.6 million.

The pleasure craft diesel market was mostly domestic, with only
about 25 percent of the business coming from foreign OEMs. There
were several OEMs in Europe, with a concentration on the western

coast of Italy, but most of the diesel business there went to European firms producing smaller and less powerful diesels. Mr. Tilling thought that Cummins' split between domestic and foreign pretty much reflected the market. He and his assistant both spent some time traveling to the foreign markets, and he pointed to a tentative order from the Taiwan navy for 40 903s. The travel was not only for the pleasure craft business, since about 85 percent of the commercial boat market was international. Indeed, Mr. Tilling spent much of his time dealing with the commercial market, since even domestically it was twice as large as the pleasure craft market. Cummins' share of this market was only 5 percent, so it was here that he perceived the greatest potential growth opportunities.

Order Administration

Mr. Tilling was of the opinion that there were two main facets to the marketing of engines for pleasure craft: (1) selling the product to the end-user with a push approach through the boat dealers and a pull approach through advertising and boat show participation; and (2) making the product available to the OEMs at the distributor level. Over the years, Cummins had enjoyed a reputation with its distributors for product availability. This was crucial in the marine market, for OEMs would often give no more than two days' notice on an order.

In 1973 and 1974, Mr. Tilling had experienced a real problem in making his diesels available to the market. During that period, total demand for Cummins engines in all markets had exceeded the company's production capacity, and production lines were constantly behind schedule. Preferential treatment had been given to other departments, since marine engines were ordered in small quantities and yet produced on the same lines as the truck engines. The situation was compounded by the fact that marine engine orders took twice as long to expedite anyway, because of the several unique parts which had to be ordered from outside suppliers. Consequently, Cummins had lost much of its reputation for delivery reliability in the marine OEM community.

In 1975, Cummins' overall business was down slightly, and there was again sufficient capacity to supply all markets. The company expressed regret over what it had lost in the marine markets and committed itself to improving its tarnished reputation. However, in 1976, when business again picked up and production again lagged behind schedule, it was only natural that preference on the lines by given to the larger orders. In July some adjustments were made in the lead times necessary for marine orders. Engines ordered without marine gears could be ordered with lead times comparable to other Cummins

products, but engines with gears had the longest lead-time requirement.

Mr. Tilling felt that he had to respond somehow to the lead-time
problems or face the demise of the pleasure craft business. One alternative discussed was to sell standard engines to those distributors who
were equipped to do the marinizing themselves. Detroit Diesel had
this kind of arrangement with one of its largest distributors. However,
Cummins preferred to retain full responsibility for the engineering of
its products to avoid the risk of having distributors release products
which did not meet Cummins standards.

The problem was not as crucial to the commercial marine market,
which was much more flexible on lead times and which did not get the
special marinized package. But facing the possibility of losing much of
his department's business, Mr. Tilling approached Mr. McPhail, the
executive vice president of the Industrial Division, and asked him for
some relaxing of the production line policy. Mr. McPhail was sympathetic to the problem and said that he did not want to lose the business, but that in a crunch situation the dollars and cents alternative
had to prevail. However, Mr. Tilling had an alternate proposal. He
suggested that he be allowed to order from the production department
on the basis of periodic forecasts. Mr. McPhail approved the request on
a trial basis. Unfortunately, the plan didn't work as hoped. One month
later, Mr. Tilling discovered that he had marine engines sitting along-
side the production line in various stages of completion. He investi-
gated and found that this was due to the fact that production line
quotas were based on units shipped, not units completed, and so he
found himself back where he had started.

Service

The one activity which contributed the most to Cummins' overall
profit picture was its parts supply business. Any given engine in a
crawler tractor, for example, would normally be overhauled about
every 15 months. The same engine in a push boat or commercial fishing vessel would normally be overhauled every two or three years. The
pleasure craft engines, because of such limited use, would function
during the expected life span of a fiberglass hull (10–12 years) with
only minor maintenance. So the pleasure craft business did not generate the future income from parts which Cummins anticipated when
selling into any other market.

Although the pleasure boat market generated little parts business
for Cummins Engine Company, in certain high concentration areas,
the labor and parts business was quite profitable for the distributors.

The business available to the distributors was enough to justify purchasing service trucks and assigning full-time mechanics. These same trucks and service personnel also were used to service the commercial marine business. The commercial marine business did generate high parts demand and was an emphasis market for Cummins.

In spite of the lack of income-generating service, Gene Fowler, Cummins' Industrial Division service manager, estimated that the pleasure craft business occupied 15 percent of the regional service representatives' time, while only accounting for 3 percent of the division's total unit sales. He pointed to the boat owner complaints which were communicated directly to upper management, about 1 per week, with about 10 or 12 per year going directly to the chairperson of the board of directors. He described the situation, "The same man who owns a boat with a Cummins engine and a hundred or more industrial or automotive units with Cummins engines will always go through normal channels with the service problems of his business, but he might very well complain directly if he has a problem with his boat's engine. While downtime in commercial applications has a financial impact, downtine in a pleasure boat reduces a man's recreation time. Most people who can afford these pleasure craft work hard and expect to have the full use of their boats when they do have time off. Witness the case of Mr. Thompson Throckmorton; just one day of downtime and he's irate. And every time a complaint is passed down from upper management, we have to assume that it's a supersensitive issue. One boat can take up to three weeks of a service rep's time, and I sometimes have to write daily progress memos. Some rep's enjoy the work, but it can be demoralizing in the light of the lack of business generated by the extra time spent. We often give as much attention to the guy with two engines as to the guy with a thousand. This is one business we just don't need."

Warranty expenses were also relatively high (see Exhibit 8). And

Exhibit 8
Industrial Markets—Warranty Policy Expense versus Engine
Volumes, First Half of 1974 (all engines)

Market segment	Units	Policy (percent)
Construction, mining, logging	54	62
Marine:		
Pleasure	4	10
Commercial	2	2
Agriculture	10	5
Bus	2	3
Generator set, fire pump, power unit	13	12
Other	15	6
	100	100

they were of a different nature in the pleasure craft business. Because of damage done by a sudden puff of smoke or an oil leak, the repair could entail repainting and cleaning or replacing drapes and carpets. Cummins' industrial customers were not generally as sensitive to these problems.

Mr. Tilling saw no immediate solution to this problem. He pointed out that service was a necessary component of the business. And he suggested that one way Cummins might be able to segment its market and grab a bigger market share would be on the strength of offering a truly extensive consumer protection plan, freeing the customer from all service concerns and making Cummins service available to him at almost every port of call.

Sales Coverage

Mr. Tilling was also concerned with his sales coverage. With his assistant, he was responsible for making the engines available to the domestic and international markets through the regular Cummins distributor network. The contacting of the OEMs and the retailers was the responsibility of the distributor salespeople. They could count on Mr. Tilling for sales aids, handbooks, and promotions such as trade shows and boat shows. Occasionally one of the two Cummins people could assist in a presentation to a customer.

As examples of his problem, Mr. Tilling cited the situations in Florida and Los Angeles. In Florida, where there were several OEMs, the two salespeople for the Cummins distributor earned over $50,000 each from salaries and indirect sales bonuses of between $60 and $75 per engine. They were responsible for all Cummins products, industrial and automotive, and so did not spend much time calling on boat dealers. The OEMs were covered and the engines were made available, but there was no encouragement at the dealer level.

In Los Angeles there were no major OEMs but several dealers and a considerable refitting business often involving a change in engines. The Cummins distributor here had one salesman whose only responsibility was pursuing marine business. He spent much time with the local dealers and was very effective at chasing down the refitting jobs.

Mr. Tilling was considering two possible ways of dealing with this problem. Looking at the efforts of the Los Angeles salesman, he thought that Cummins might subsidize distributor marine-specialist salespeople in key areas to follow that example. His second thought was building up his own staff, for, as he said, "Five years ago there were nine people in this department, and now there are just two of us. So we split the globe in two and each takes half. We are not getting to where we should, the dealers."

Pricing

Mr. George Ferguson, in charge of all pricing for Cummins, felt that there was little room for pricing actions in the pleasure boat market. He did not want to lower prices because the engine families used in the pleasure boats already had lower margins than most Cummins engines. And he did not think he could raise prices. As he said, "I know our product is superior, but what can I do? Our superiorities just don't mean as much in this particular market." Within the management group at Cummins there was a wide range of opinion on the best product and pricing strategy in this market. Some managers believed that Cummins had no choice but to focus on the premium power, premium price segment of the pleasure boat market. Others disagreed, arguing for a major change in strategy to focus on the commercial market.

The Commercial Market

The commercial market consisted of fish boats, tugboats, tow boats, ferries, other work boats, and offshore crew boats and supply boats (for transportation between shore and offshore facilities or ships). Fish boats were the most important application in Cummins horsepower range accounting for over 50 percent of the total commercial market. The market was worldwide with concentrations wherever there were ports, navigable waterways, or concentrations of seafood. Engines for the commercial market ranged from the light 5-horsepower units to 50,000-horsepower engines found in large ships. Cummins engines competed for the market in the 200- to 1,000-horsepower segment.

Because of the wide diversity of the market, it was difficult to develop an accurate estimate of the size of the world market. In North America, the annual market was in excess of 2,500 engines (see Exhibit 9). The worldwide market in the 200- to 1,000-horsepower range was estimated at 20,000 units annually. Nearly all the engines in this market were diesels.

Commercial owners had very definite opinions on the engines installed in their boats. Because the boat was the key to their livelihood and lives, they could not afford to be indifferent to the engine. Of primary importance was the need for reliable and durable power. A reliable fish boat engine was one which would bring the fisherman safely home when caught in a storm. Average annual usage was over

Exhibit 9
Marine—Commercial—Cummins Range (201 + HP Diesels)

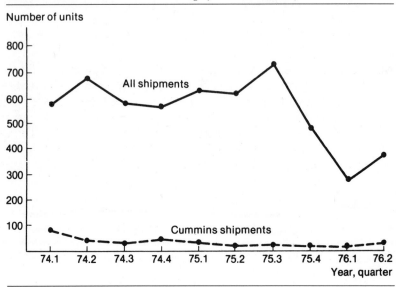

Number of units

3,000 hours with an engine trade cycle of about 10 years. Engines would be serviced and overhauled during this time, but major service work was expected to be infrequent and planned in advance.

After the owner was satisfied about an engine's reliability and durability, other factors such as service support and price became important. When a commercial owner needed service, he needed it quickly in order to meet his contractual obligation or to participate in peak fishing seasons. In recent years, with the substantial increase in petroleum prices, fuel economy was becoming a factor in engine selection. (As a general rule, every horsepower used required .05 gallons of fuel per hour).

Boat owners were tradition oriented and very slow to move away from proven products. Commercial owners normally had a great deal of experience prior to being in a position to make their first purchase. In a recent survey, approximately 75 percent indicated their choice of engine was based on past experience. Only 7 percent said they relied on the builder's recommendation with the rest relying on general reputation or friends' recommendations. In some instances a boat owner physically carried the engine of his choice from the engine distributor to the boatbuilder for installation.

Boat ownership was highly fragmented with average fleet size under 10 units. Although over half of the boats were owned by corporations, a large proportion were owned by individual corporators who might purchase two or three vessels in their lifetime. The boatbuilders similarly were quite numerous with only a few volume production (over 50 per year) yards.

Cummins' Participation in the Commercial Market

The world market was supplied from many American, European, and Japanese engine producers who had developed certain market areas or groups of loyal customers. No single company dominated the market. (Prior to the introduction of Cummins K6 engine, Caterpillar "owned" the 300- to 400-horsepower trawler market.) Within North America, Caterpillar and Detroit Diesel led with Cummins' share consistently under 10 percent. This poor showing was based primarily on past product line limitations and lack of emphasis at both the factory and distributor levels.

Throughout the 1960s and early 1970s, Cummins primary engines for use in commercial applications were in the NH and V1710 families. The NH was an in-line 6-cylinder engine and the V1710 was the 12-cylinder version with double the cubic inch displacement. Both the NH and V1710 were available in naturally aspirated and turbocharged versions. The turbocharged NH was the highest volume Cummins' product and North America's number one heavy truck engine.

While the product features of the NH and V1710 generally met the needs of the commercial boat market, Cummins was limited to competing in the 200- to 300- and 400- to 600-horsepower markets. Both Caterpillar and Detroit Diesel offered more extensive product lines with Caterpillar having an additional 1,200 RPM product line which appealed to many of the tradition-minded owners. In 1975, Cummins released the new K6 and K12 engines. The K6 engine, in its marine configuration, provided an entry into the 300- to 500-horsepower segment. The K12 extended Cummins range up to 1,000 horsepower. The K engine family was designed to surpass the NH and V1710 engines in durability, reliability, and fuel economy.

Throughout the early 1970s, truck demand for the NH exceeded Cummins ability to supply. In order to help protect this important market, engine supply to the marine market was restricted. At times the V1710, which was important in construction and mining equipment, also suffered from restricted availability. Because the commercial marine market potential for Cummins was small compared to other markets and engine availability was limited, Cummins placed little emphasis on improving its position in the commercial marine market.

Most distributors followed Cummins lead in ignoring the commercial marine market. The growth in the truck market, with its attendant parts and service demand, occupied most of the resources of the distributors. Also, limited engine availability and uncertain factory emphasis helped to curtail any efforts at developing waterfront service and sales. The effort which was developed was usually directed at the pleasure boat market where Cummins had an established position and where relatively higher volume boat manufacturers could be found.

Profitability

The commercial market offered higher potential profits than the pleasure boat business both on the initial sale and in the parts market. Exhibit 10 compares approximate dollars per horsepower pricing for

Exhibit 10
Approximate Marine Engine Pricing (including engine, gear, cooling, and electrics)

Horsepower	Pleasure boats ($/HP)	Commercial marine ($/HP)
200.	$30	$55
400.	$30	$50
600.	$35	$55
800.	n.a.	$60
1,000.	n.a.	$65

n.a. = Not applicable.
Note: Pleasure boat engines normally are rated at the top of their capability while commercial engines are derated 20 to 30 percent to improve engine life.

pleasure and commercial engines. Because the commercial boat engines were produced on the same lines as the high-volume truck and construction engines, overhead costs could be spread over more units and the operating margin per unit was higher. More importantly, annual parts sales were much higher. In 10 years, a pleasure boat engine would have operated 2,000 to 4,000 hours. In the same time period, a commercial engine would have run 25,000 to 65,000 hours and had three to five complete rebuilds.

As Mr. Tilling reflected on the difficulties he faced in the pleasure craft market, he was not at all sure that the commercial market represented a better opportunity given Cummins' product line and distribution. He had been instructed by Mr. McPhail to develop a recommendation "to either fish or cut bait in the pleasure craft market."

C A S E 1–4

Yankee International Medical Research, Limited

Late in November 1983, John Hinsley, president of Yankee International Medical Research and Manufacturing, Ltd., turned his attention to the marketing plans for his new company. In the rush to put together a proposal to attract capital for his new venture from private investors, Mr. Hinsley had been able to do no more than put together a brief statement of proposed marketing activities (Exhibit 1). Now he realized a much more detailed marketing plan was called for, but he was uncertain where or how to begin. His own background in financial administration for a large hospital and in his own small business, a collection agency, had given him little exposure to marketing, which he knew would be a key to the success of this new venture.

Yankee International was incorporated in July 1983 to manufacture and sell a new and improved version of hemodialysis equipment for the treatment of kidney disease. The new concept in hemodialysis equipment was designed by a group of research scientists and engineers, the same group who formed the company to market the equipment and hired John Hinsley to develop the business from the ground floor. Initial financing was provided by the group, but $230,000 start-up capital was being solicited from individual investors and venture capitalists to cover the costs of further research and development, prototypes, lab tests, clinical trials, patent filings, and initial overhead and sales expenses. The first working prototype was due in John Hinsley's hands in mid-February 1984. Up until this time, venture capitalists had been enthusiastic but wary of the project. Hinsley hoped to gain venture

This case was prepared by Mr. John Wong, Research Assistant, under the supervision of Frederick E. Webster, Jr., E. B. Osborn Professor of Marketing, Amos Tuck School of Business Administration, Dartmouth College. © 1984 by the Trustees of Dartmouth College.

Exhibit 1
Marketing Plan, Venture Capital Proposal

MARKETING

Distribution channels:
We intend to use a combination of:

a. Direct sales.
b. Manufacturers' representatives (agents).
c. Distributors.

We intend to commence with direct sales, selling only our products. This gives us good control of prices, control over the level of service, good feedback from our market, and the possibility of giving discounts.

We intend to use manufacturers' representatives in some areas to lower our sales cost, decrease time spent recruiting and training salesmen, and maintain good price control. This channel can be used with representatives already well established in his territory.

Distributors may be used in foreign sales and possibly in the continental United States. The final distribution channels have not yet been set. We will seek intensive distribution based upon our production capacity, seeking to maximize profits, not sales volume.

We intend to continually analyze and evaluate our competition through a competitive marketing audit. An honest appraisal should lead us to focus on marketing functions which need management attention.

Source: Venture capital proposal, company files.

support with the presentation of the working prototype, but he also was considering other options for raising capital.

Hinsley hoped to achieve a 2 percent market share in the first full year of operation through the use of two company sales representatives, namely himself and one other person. He planned to focus on the New England and Mid-Atlantic states initially, rolling out nationally as resources permitted. He also saw potential in international markets and made some preliminary contacts with international business and market research firms such as the World Trade Group, a subsidiary of the Bank of Boston. He also was considering employing manufacturer's agents for the rest of the country on a region by region basis.

"Once we begin production, we're all going to sell!" Hinsley exclaimed, "I can cover a lot of New England and the Mid-Atlantic states myself by traveling in a motor home. We're both going to know how to strip the machines down if we have to, to demonstrate how these things work. I plan to spend the first year on the road at least, but first I need to know where to start and how to build a good sales force and sales follow-up program. I've only got three months to get the company's house in order before I hit the road."

Hemodialysis

End-stage renal disease (ESRD) (irreversible uremia) is the fourth most common major health problem in the United States. Dialytic therapy began in the late 1960s for a small, select group of patients in Seattle and in the past two and a half decades had become the preferred method of sustaining life for ESRD patients.

The basic principles of hemodialysis have remained unchanged over the past two decades. The patient's blood is passed through a dialyzer, a disposable blood filter, and through the use of differential pressure, urea and other waste matter are extracted from the blood to a saline solution. The patient's blood is then returned to his/her body. Dialysis is continued until the patient's blood is cleaned, a process normally taking four to six hours. Patients normally take dialysis treatment three times a week.

The hemodialysis unit, which houses the dialyzer and the cleaning solutions, has essentially remained unchanged for the past 20 years. The way in which solutions are prepared for use is the essential difference among hemodialysis units. The two schematics in Exhibit 2 show the manual mixing unit and the automatic proportioning system.

Exhibit 2
Two Dialysis Processes

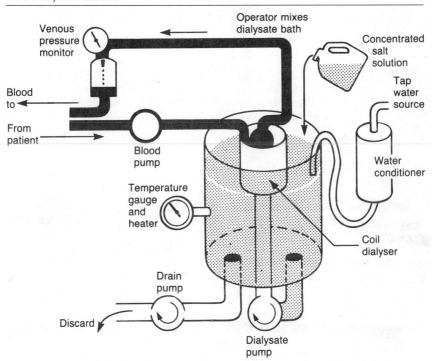

Schematic Representation of the Kolft Travenol
Tank Batch Dialysis Machine

Twenty years after its introduction, it remains a safe, low-maintenance system dependent on recirculation of dialysate prepared in a batch.

Exhibit 2 *(concluded)*

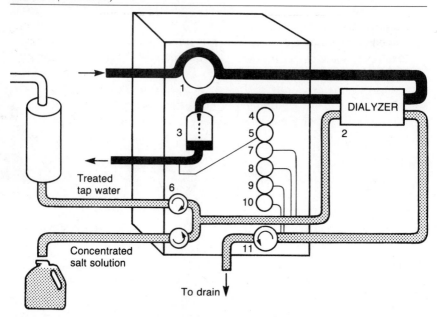

Schematic Representation of a Proportioning
System

The numeral 1 denotes the blood pump, 2 hemodialyzer, 3 drip chamber, 4 venous-pressure monitor, 5 air-bubble detector, 6 water and salt-solution proportioning pumps, 7 conductivity monitor, 8 temperature monitor, 9 negative-pressure monitor, 10 blood-leak detector, and 11 negative-pressure pump. Ps denote pumps, arrows monitors, and Xs detectors.

Yankee International Product Line

Yankee International planned to market five products and a line of dialytic supplies including cleaning solutions, surgical tubing, etc. The product line included the following:

1. Single-patient dialysis machine—this machine will be modular in design and will weigh significantly less than current systems on the market. Add-ons include a dialyzer cleaning module and a water purifier.
2. Multi-patient dialysis machine—this machine will be sold to hospitals and dialysis clinics. Like the single-patient unit, it is modular in design and the production personnel simply need to vary the size of the pumps and heaters to vary the capacity of the machine from 5 patients to 20 patients.
3. Single dialyzer cleaning unit (reuse machine)—this module is designed to clean the single-patient dialysis machine, which has been

in the past a disposable product. Patients may now get many more uses out of the dialyzer. It also will be sold as a standalone unit for hospitals.

4. Multi-unit dialyzer cleaning unit—same as above, only for multi-patient systems. The machine has the capacity to clean up to 20 dialyzers simultaneously.

5. Water purifier—patients, clinics, and hospitals located in areas with less than pure water may purchase this module to plug into either the single-patient or multi-patient dialysis machines.

The Yankee International dialysis machines were designed to increase patient comfort and provide more flexibility to treatment providers. The Yankee International machines offered new safety and convenience features designed to give patients unprecedented mobility and comfort. The single-patient system was the first truly portable dialysis machine designed to give patients the option of in-home use with a bare minimum of technical knowledge.

The Competition

In the venture capital proposal, Donald Brous, the chief engineer and founder of Yankee International, had described three major competitors in the single-patient hemodialysis market—Drake-Willock, Cobe, and Organnon. A comparison of features of each of the systems is provided in Exhibit 3.

Drawbacks for each of the three competitors were numerous according to Brous. The Drake-Willock system was the heaviest of all single-patient machines, weighing 120 pounds. According to the Yankee International users panel, a collection of leading specialists, it employed a hydraulic system which required frequent overhaul and replacement of parts. The system also was "overwhelmingly complex." The Cobe system also employed highly complex electronics. It was the second heaviest machine and required casters or wheels for mobility. One of the important pumps required frequent replacement. The Organnon system used an absorbent system which required replacement often before completing a single dialysis treatment, adding unnecessary costs to the cost of care. There was also said by Brous to be some question as to the relative safety of the unit. Brous did not know the selling prices of any of the competitive units, and he was not sure how they were distributed.

Brous reported two major competitors in the multi-patient systems market—Drake-Willock and Bio-Systems. The Drake-Willock machine was large and had a maximum capacity of 10 patients. The Bio-Systems model also was large and very slow. It provided capacity for 10

Exhibit 3
Comparisons with Competitive Single-Patient Systems

	Yankee International	Drake-Willock	Cobe	Organnon
Height	15"	40"	43"	14"
Width	15"	26"	19"	24"
Depth	12"	18"	12"	15"
Weight	35 lbs.	120 lbs.	87 lbs.	50 lbs.
Bicarb	Yes	Option	Option	Optio. ,
Ultrafilter	Yes	Calculated	Yes	Yes
Instrumentation	Digital redundant	Analog single	Analog single	Analog single
Conductivity cal	In situ	External	External	None
Temperature cal	In situ	External	External	None
Flow	Digital	Analog	None	Analog-limited
Service	Plug-in—no tools	More difficult	More difficult	More difficult
Requires absorbent cartridge	No	No	No	Yes
Blood system	Yes	Yes	Yes	None

Source: Venture capital proposal, company files.

to 20 patients or more. He believed that the Yankee International multi-patient system had advantages over both in terms of weight and size, the fact that it was serviceable without tools, and its simple design.

No reuse systems, the units designed to clean dialyzers, were available for home use. The only single reuse system available was too expensive to use in the home. The two multiple reuse systems were complex and expensive and relied on an outdated method of cleaning using Clorox and formaldehyde. Both Yankee International versions employed milder cleaning agents in the cleaning solutions and were not as harsh on patient and dialyzer. These cleaning solutions were thought to represent a very large potential market for Yankee International.

Brous later believed that the market share for dialysis equipment was broken down as follows:

Cobe	40%
Drake-Willock	25
Extracorporeal	25
Gambro	10

The Market

Public Law 92–603 of 1972 made 90 percent of the United States patients with end-stage renal disease eligible for treatment funding through medicare. As a consequence, the number of maintenance hemodialysis treatment patients grew from a select handful of patients two decades ago to 35,000 in 1978 and an estimated 70,000 in 1982. The number was expected to increase approximately 10 percent per year. Also, the number of patients receiving hemodialysis treatment outside of the United States was estimated to be 100,000 in 1982. The medicare mandate greatly accelerated the availability of maintenance hemodialysis in the United States relative to the rest of the world because the annual treatment cost, estimated at $30,000 per patient per year in 1979, was prohibitive for most Asian, African, and South American countries.

The U.S. federal government was greatly interested in reducing the costs of hemodialysis treatment, which was estimated to cost the government $242 million in 1979 and over $2 billion in 1982. The federal government was encouraging home dialysis treatment, as it cost 30 percent less than treatment in hospitals or clinics.

Yankee International hoped to capitalize on the medicare program's cost-reduction emphasis through the marketing of its reuse machines, which would lower the average cost of dialysis and in-home systems.

Sales of reuse equipment in the United States were forecast to be
approximately $20 million per year for the next three years (1983–85).

Yankee International also hoped to capitalize on its line of dialysis
supplies, especially the unique cleaning solutions required by Yankee
International systems.

The Company

John Hinsley was appointed president of Yankee International in the
summer of 1983. The company's organization consisted of a board of
directors, the president, and an administrative assistant. The board of
directors included a microbiologist, four engineers, including Donald
Brous who founded the company, and an attorney. Brous also retained
a staff position within the company as the chief production engineer.
Plans to hire additional staff were in the discussion stage.

Yankee International initially was based in a small office in Man-
chester, New Hampshire. Several sites for a production facility were
being considered, but one site in Northern New Hampshire seemed to
be gaining favor. The location of the potential production facility was
in Littleton, New Hampshire, and was owned and managed by Northern Community Investment Corporation, a nonprofit investment corporation set up to stimulate business in northern New Hampshire and
Vermont. Hinsley believed there was an opportunity to get initial capital from the firm as well as low-cost production space, as there was an
interest in attracting new business to provide jobs in a relatively high
unemployment area.

Production Plans

The first prototypes of the Yankee International hemodialysis systems were scheduled for March 1, 1984. Hinsley hoped to begin manufacturing the equipment by April 1. A brief description of production
plans is found in the venture capital proposal (Exhibit 4). The Yankee
International systems were to be built primarily using purchased, standard parts. Thus, the production process was an assembly operation
and only semiskilled labor was necessary.

Marketing/Distribution Plans

Hinsley had targeted several groups for sales and other promotional
effort including nephrologists, other specialists, dialysis centers, professional organizations, and health cooperatives. There were currently

Exhibit 4
Production Plans

The principal manufacturing operations consist of purchase, testing, and assembly of components offered by suppliers to the bioengineering industry; therefore, requirements for space, production tooling, and test instrumentation are modest. However, since the design, manufacture, quality assurance, distribution, and performance of hemodialysis equipment is regulated by the Bureau of Medical Devices and Diagnostic Products of the FDA, the company's manufacturing facility must be registered with this government agency as a Medical Device Manufacturing Establishment, and all operations must be conducted in accordance with FDA Good Manufacturing Practices for Medical Devices.

Discussions are underway to obtain facilities under an attractive lease-tax agreement for manufacturing on a commercial scale.

After completion of prototypes, of manufacturing drawings and specifications, orders will be issued to selected vendors and subcontractors for sheet metal, plastics, assemblies and subassemblies. All incoming materials will be subjected to rigid inspection and testing and traceability recorded per GMP requirements of the FDA.

The testing of components, subassemblies, and the final product is of the utmost importance. Detailed test procedures and requirements and recording results will be adhered to.

The present facility is adequate for the prototype and R&D work.

The time frame is (approximately):

Breadboards	3 months.
Mock-ups	5 months
Prototypes for clinicals	7 months
First production	10 months

Assembly time for a single-patient dialysis system (in production run) is estimated to be approximately 60 hrs.

For a multi-patient dialysis system	120 hours
For a single-patient reuse	40 hours
For a multi-patient reuse	100 hours

Production lead-time is relatively short, and an assembly group of 15 should turn out 40 single-patient dialysis systems per month or 60 single-patient reuse.

It may be determined during years two or three that all or part of the subcontract work should be performed in-house. This would substantially increase the labor content, of course.

Source: Venture capital proposal, company files.

2,632 nephrologists in the United States, a figure which represented approximately 1 percent of the total number of physicians. Hinsley estimated there were approximately 5,000 subspecialists. Many of the 3,000 dialysis clinics in the United States, which were private, profit-based kidney treatment centers, were run by nephrologists. Brous believed that many of these centers were quite profitable and represented a strong economic force in the health care industry.

Hinsley planned to advertise in the *American Journal of Kidney Disease* and to list the company with the *American Hospital Association Purchasing Directory* and the *Medical and Health Care Marketplace Guide*. He also planned to display the Yankee International product line at the national nephrologists conference, the American

Exhibit 5
Materials and Subcontracting Cost Estimates, Single-Patient Artificial Kidney

| | | Production | | |
	Quantity	Estimated lots of 100	Estimated lots of 1,000	Each prototype
Heater	1	$ 35.	$ 30.	$ 50.
Blood leak	1	80.	60.	500.
Water purity	1	20.	10.	150.
By-pass flow	1	30.	20.	200.
Line volt meter	1	20.	15.	30.
Flowmeter, digital	1	400.	300.	3,000.
Solenoid valves	4	100.	80.	400.
Conductivity systems	2	300.	200.	1,500.
Temperature control	1	100.	50.	200.
Temperature digital	1	70.	50.	300.
Temperature backup system	1	70.	50.	100.
Blower	1	20.	15.	50.
Dialysis pump	1	250.	100.	550.
Effluent pump	1	200.	100.	350.
Heater manifold	1	30.	20.	100.
De-Aeration tank	1	70.	50.	350.
Proportioning tank	1	70.	50.	350.
Conc. meter pump	1	50.	40.	500.
Conductivity digital	2	150.	100.	400.
Pressure digital	2	150.	100.	400.
Transducers	5	250.	150.	900.
Pressure switch	1	40.	30.	200.
Flow switches	2	60.	50.	200.
Battery and charger	1	30.	15.	100.
Current leakage meter	1	50.	25.	250.
Blood pump with monitor	1	400.	200.	1,000.
Sonic detectors	2	300.	200.	900.
Solenoid clamps	2	50.	40.	600.
Digital pressure	2	400.	200.	1,000.
Blood flow digital	1	100.	50.	500.
Heparin pump	1	200.	100.	500.
Cabinet	1	100.	50.	500.
Front panel	2	60.	30.	500.
Back panel	2	60.	30.	300.
Chassis	2	100.	75.	600.
Hydraulics, misc.		150.	100.	600.
Electrics, misc.		100.	50.	500.
		$4,665.	$2,835.	$18,630.

Source: Venture capital proposal, company records.

Society for Internal Organs national meeting, and other regional health
care shows. There were 10 such professional meetings and trade show
opportunities available in 1984.

Sales were projected by Brous to be:

First full year	$	800,000
Second full year		4,000,000

Third full year	8,000,000
Fourth full year	14,000,000
Fifth full year	19,000,000

✶The first-year sales estimate was figured on sales of 100 units at an average of $8,000 per unit, a level Brous thought to be easily attainable given his contacts. The sales figures also were based on sales of dialysis and reuse systems.

Pretax manufacturing profits were estimated to be:

Year 1	$ (135,000)
Year 2	1,062,000
Year 3	3,363,000
Year 4	6,246,000
Year 5	7,507,000

Cost estimates for the single-patient hemodialysis system are listed in Exhibit 5. The company's projected P&L statement is Exhibit 6.

Exhibit 6

YANKEE INTERNATIONAL MEDICAL RESEARCH
Manufacturing Profit and Profit and Loss Projections
Years 1–5
(in thousands)

	Year 1	Year 2	Year 3	Year 4	Year 5
Sales	$ 800	$4,000	$8,000	$14,000	$19,000
Costs:					
Materials	470	1,900	2,835	4,903	7,500
Labor	40	200	360	450	600
Manufacturing Overhead	83	150	244	345	478
Cost to manufacture	593	2,250	3,439	5,698	8,578
Gross profit	207	1,750	4,561	8,302	10,422
General and Administrative					
and sales expense	242	368	498	656	915
Net profit (Loss)	(35)	1,362	4,063	7,646	9,507
Royalties, R&D, consultants	100	300	700	1,400	2,000
Pretax profit	(135)	1,062	3,363	6,346	7,507

Source: Venture capital proposal, company records.

John Hinsley had collected a large number of articles and books on marketing but had barely had time to scan these. He had only a small amount of money available to spend for market research and other forms of assistance in developing his marketing program. He felt there was extreme urgency to getting the firm's marketing activities under-way, but he was uncertain as to which decisions and information-gathering activities should have highest priority.

Discussion Questions

1. Define the market for Yankee International's new hemodialysis equipment and supplies. What does Mr. Hinsley need to know about this market? How can he obtain the needed information?

2. What marketing decisions does Mr. Hinsley need to make?

3. Outline an introductory marketing program for this company.

Development of Marketing Strategy

C A S E 2–1

The Texas Canning Company

Bradford Williams, president of the Texas Canning Company (TCC), had just received the financial statements for the latest quarter. It showed that profits were down to $371,000, compared to $984,000 the previous year. Sales had remained flat, but what truly alarmed Brad were the revised projections that Mark Womack, vice president of finance, had given him along with the results of the quarter. It showed that the company would run a loss of $782,000 in the last three quarters and finish the year in the red. As Williams looked at the financial trend, (see Exhibit 1) he saw a flattening of sales and declining profitability. He wondered what he could do to solve the immediate problems and to encourage significant growth in the company in the next few years.

History of the Company

The company traced its origins back to 1893 when Thadeus Thornberry formed a company to sell vegetables to ranchers and local residents in Texas. Since the population was scattered, it was important to buy and store merchandise for long periods of time. Thornberry started by canning corn and peas, and his company flourished until the Depression years. The company, at that time, was sold to Fred Atkins who remained CEO until 1965 when Bradford Williams, a son-in-law,

Financial support for the production of this case was provided in part by the Marketing Management Program of the Graduate School of Business, Stanford University. This case was written by George Varughese, under the supervision of Robert T. Davis, Professor of Marketing. © 1982 by the Board of Trustees of the Leland Stanford Junior University.

Exhibit 1

TEXAS CANNING COMPANY
Income Statement
(in thousands)

	1981	1980	1979	1978
Net sales	$40,466	$38,273	$35,973	$33,740
Cost of sales	29,945	27,174	25,181	21,931
Gross margin	10,521	11,099	10,791	11,809
Selling, general administrative	7,688	8,802	8,473	9,696
Interest expense	2,013	1,259	1,200	508
Earnings before taxes	820	1,038	1,118	1,605
Taxes	340	465	510	760
Net earnings	480	573	608	845

TEXAS CANNING COMPANY
Balance Sheet
(in thousands)

	1981	1980
Assets		
Cash	$ 574	$ 786
Accounts receivable	3,101	1,958
Inventory	8,163	7,800
Prepaid expenses	1,425	657
Total current assets	13,263	11,201
Land	515	486
Buildings	4,575	4,520
Machinery	13,265	12,823
Less accumulated depreciation	(8,148)	(6,550)
Total assets	$23,470	$22,480
Liabilities		
Notes payable	$ 4,101	$ 3,200
Accounts payable	4,484	4,320
Accrued liabilities	2,392	2,892
Current portion of long-term debt	786	11,412
Total current liabilities	11,763	10,412
Deferred credits	982	1,220
Long term debt	2,182	3,055
Equity	380	380
Retained earnings	8,163	7,683
Total liabilities	$23,470	$22,480

took over and expanded the company by buying several plants in various parts of the state. By 1982, Texas Canning owned four plants in southwestern Texas (El Paso, Peco, Midland, and Odessa) where it processed a variety of vegetables. The company continued as a private concern with most of the shares held by the Atkins family.

The Business

TCC sold a line of canned and frozen products under private and franchise (company) labels. The business was split approximately into the following segments:

Canned products—asparagus, spinach, carrots, beans, peas, corn, squash.

Frozen products—beans, carrots, corn, peas.

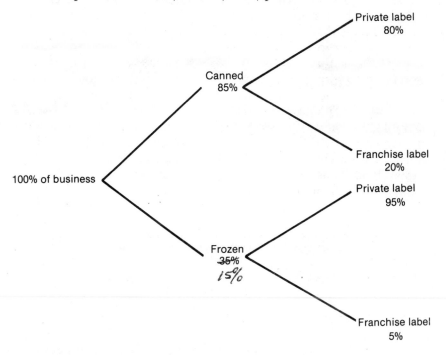

In the canned food segment, private labels were supplied to several large chains which covered the southwestern part of the country. The franchise label was distributed under the "Tastee" name to stores primarily in Texas. The frozen products had a similar distribution pattern except that most of the business was done in Texas. Private label was essentially a commodity business where the canner served as a contract food processor. The vegetables were harvested under contract, processed and canned under the customer label, and then shipped for eventual resale. In this regard, the retailer assumed most of the marketing risks and, of course, captured any excess margins. In the franchise business, on the other hand, the processor assumed the processing and marketing risks. The labeled products were distributed to the stores though a network of brokers.

This duality of label meant that TCC needed marketing as well as processing skills. Moreover, the marketing requirements for the franchised line were not simple and called for advertising, promotion, positioning, and pricing knowhow as well as a good broker organization. The offset was, hopefully, better margins. The trade-off in terms of profits was not fully evident however because competition in the business was severe. Significant label preferences were difficult to establish, and the strongest national labels were a constant threat. There was a real question that a regional canner could have the clout to consistently hold a differential position. In recent years, for example, TCC had seen the share in its markets erode (on the Nielsen index) from 45 percent to 30 percent (see Exhibit 2). What was equally worrisome was that the competitors, led by several other regionals, were increasing their expenditures for promotion while reducing advertising. The trade did not typically pass these savings along to the consumers. Mr. Williams guessed that promotion outlays now exceeded advertising in the ratio of 70 to 30. Several of the smallest canners were experimenting with generic labels to complement their traditional strategy of marginal costing and deep discounts. Hence, one of Williams' choices was between the straight commodity, i.e., private label, approach and the more risky franchise label.

Exhibit 2

Market Share for Franchise-Label Business in Texas					
	1977	1978	1979	1980	1981
Texas Canning Company	45%	38%	36%	32%	30%
Regional firm #1	15	18	19	21	25
Regional firm #2	10	12	15	16	18
National brands	20	21	20	21	22
Other	10	11	10	10	5
Total	100%	100%	100%	100%	100%

Flow of the Business

Williams' choice was, to some extent, a guessing game because he had to contract with growers several months in advance of delivery and then predict what the prices and costs would be at the time of actual delivery to his retailers. The cycle started each August when Williams met with his staff to decide on the production requirements for the following year. These requirements were then contracted out to farmers by the middle of February, with guaranteed prices and quantities. The planting schedule was controlled by TCC, which also supervised the quality of the crop through its field representatives. TCC owned most of the harvesting equipment and leased it to the farmers.

The crops were harvested in the summer months and brought directly to the plants where they were weighed, checked for quality, cleaned, and blanched. If selected for canning, the products received a second check for quality and were sent directly to the line. Produce to be frozen was processed and put into large containers and stored. Upon receipt of an order, the items were sent to the labeling operation and then shipped to the customers. The cost data in a representative month during 1981 for this flow is shown below:

Cost per Case of Private Label Canned Corn (24 cans)

Variable costs:

Raw corn	$1.90
Container cost	2.60
Shipping	.16
Labels and supplies	.42
Labor	.45
Overhead	.31
Field expenses	.03
Broker commission	.43
Warehousing	.22
Total variable costs	6.52
Fixed costs (financing, plant OHD)	2.00
Total cost	$8.52
Revenue per case	8.60
Profit per case	.08

Breakeven Revenue

Total revenue = 100%
Variable revenue = 75.8
Contribution margin = 24.2
Fixed cost = 23.5
Profit margin = .7
Total absolute fixed cost in 1981 = $9,388,000

$$\text{Breakeven revenue} = \frac{\text{Fixed cost}}{\text{Contribution margin}}$$

$$= \frac{9,388,000}{.242}$$

$$= \$38,793,000$$

Calculation of Key Ratios

		1981	1980
Return on sales (ROS)	$= \dfrac{\text{Income}}{\text{Sales}}$	1.2%	1.5%
Asset turnover (asset turn)	$= \dfrac{\text{Sales}}{\text{Assets}}$	1.72%	1.70%
Return on assets (ROA)	$= \dfrac{\text{Income}}{\text{Assets}}$	2.0%	2.5%
Leverage (LEV)	$= \dfrac{\text{Assets}}{\text{Equity}}$	2.74×	2.78×

Return on equity (ROE)	$= \dfrac{\text{Income}}{\text{Equity}}$	5.6%	7.1%
Sustainable growth*		5.6%	7.1%
Current ratio	$= \dfrac{\text{Current assets}}{\text{Current liabilities}}$	1.12×	1.08×

* ROS × Asset turn = ROA
ROA × LEV = ROE
ROE × Retention ratio = Sustainable growth

Organization and Operations

TCC was run on a functional basis with Williams firmly in control (see Exhibit 3 for organizational chart). John Atkins, son of Fred

Exhibit 3
Organization Chart

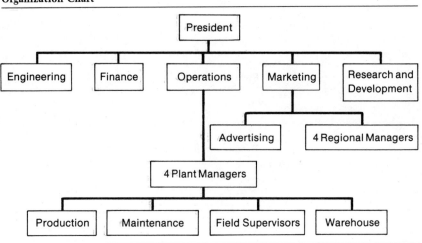

Atkins, was chairman of the board but did not participate in daily operations. Thomas Sowell, operations vice president, Mark Womack, and John Hellman, marketing vice president, formed the decision-making group but there was no doubt that Williams called the shots. Over the years the firm had adapted to the centralized style in which most of the decisions were made in the president's office. The functional heads operated primarily as staff advisors to the president. Communication was typically one-dimensional from the top down. There was hardly a decision of any type that didn't pass across Williams' desk. To be fair to Williams, it must be said that he seldom procrastinated in deciding what to do.

Production. Thomas Sowell administered the production department through plant managers, each of whom was given specific expense and production targets against which s/he was measured. Bonuses were determined by these standards, as well as Williams' appraisal, and made up 40 percent of total compensation. Each plant manager had subordinates in charge of maintenance, warehouse, supervisors, and field service. Sowell wondered whether a profit-center management was a better model because, in his opinion, the plant managers had little incentive to maximize company profits under the current setup.

Marketing. TCC used brokers to reach their retail and food service outlets, and the marketing program was administered by John Hellman. The firm had split the market into four regions whose managers reported to Hellman. These regional managers were responsible for sales, which meant they had to maintain personal relationships with the brokers and accounts. Even though the brokers carried other items, Hellman was satisfied that he could exercise enough control since the TCC line was important to most of the brokers. Occasionally, the company had run promotional campaigns to unload inventory or to attract attention to new products. Typically, the brokers had cooperated on these occasions. Besides these special programs, TCC ran a modest advertising program (in regional issues of selected consumer magazines and newspapers), though its promotional outlays exceeded the advertising expenditures.

Engineering, Research and Development, and Finance. Engineering was primarily a maintenance function—making sure that the equipment was kept up to date. There was very little basic or application research since management was content to let the large competitors pioneer any major innovations. Management prided itself on being able to copy rapidly. Finance served both the internal accounting and external reporting requirements, and the company supported a small data processing and work processing department.

Competition. Competition came from several national and about four regional firms. In private label, the competition was intense and varied from very small opportunistic canners to large processing companies. Since the farmers were contracted early (before prices were certain) and since there was little planning or market research, this business was characterized by oversupply. It was a dog-eat-dog world with little product differentiation. Hence the private label business was marginally profitable at best.

The franchise label business was a somewhat different story. Here, the company competed with such national brands as Heinz and Del Monte and two other companies in Texas. However, Williams knew that he had advantages in transportation costs and timely service since his plants and warehouses were located within 100 miles of his major accounts. The company also had built an image of quality for the Tastee brand. In blind consumer tests, TCC's products normally came out as "preferred." Although advertising was modest, it had been sustained for many years and had always been unique in its presentation. Hence, the consumer awareness level was measured in a recent study at 55 percent, trial at 35 percent, and repeat at 30 percent. Repeat had been 50 percent in an earlier (five years) study.

TCC tried hard to copy immediately product and package innovations and was generally regarded as a competent house by the trade. But Williams knew that trade loyalty was a tenuous asset at best. He had recently seen a research study made by a Stanford University professor (David Montgomery) on why chain store buyers accepted or rejected new product offerings. The study could be summarized as follows:

Factors Affecting Buying Decision

	Product Unique	Product "Me-too"
Seller Well-known	Buy	Buy IF: Presentation good; promotion package good
Seller Not well-known	Buy IF: Presentation good; promotion package good	Don't buy

Williams wondered if this model was relevant to his markets and, if so, how could he make use of it.

The value of a premium image was obvious. TCC had margins of up to 10 percent for its franchised specialty items, but only ±1 percent for the commodity lines. Del Monte and other large competitors tended to spend much more in absolute dollars on advertising and promotion, while the regional operators were more modest. In terms of positioning, one representation of TCC's position would be:

Full line

(X) National brands

(Y) TCC franchise label

**Commodity
emphasis**

**Quality
emphasis**

(Z) TCC private label

(Q) Local competitors

Limited lines

Current Trends

As Williams looked over the financial projections, he decided to make a list of the major trends that he foresaw:

1. Packaging costs had been increasing at a rapid pace and had become so expensive that a can was more expensive than its contents.
2. Transportation costs were also rising very fast due to the increases in energy costs.
3. The industry had too much capacity. As processors decided on production requirements, they were trying to outguess the market. Usually, this resulted in oversupply and depressed prices and margins.
4. The trend toward fresh and healthy foods had reduced the market for some products and had resulted in lower growth in others. This squeeze had culminated in severe price cutting by a number of processors.
5. The industry continued to be seasonal, which demanded high financing costs.
6. Government regulations had forced expensive changes in certain manufacturing operations.
7. Inflation and high interest rates had been costly, and there would be increasing pressure to raise productivity—to get more mileage out of the present assets.
8. Machinery cost increases were especially evident and averaged 500 percent over the past 10 years. Since the machinery was only used for about four months each year, it had become extremely difficult to justify purchasing. The company had been stuck with a lot of old machinery.
9. Frozen items were growing faster than canned.
10. Brand switching, at least in the Texas markets, was on the increase, and there was no letup in sight.
11. Retailers were increasing their pressures for trade deals, which

they normally pocketed instead of passing along to the consumers.

Some Options

There was a limited number of options that Williams could pursue. In commonly used marketing shorthand (the so-called Ansoff matrix) he could try to grow his firm in either of four ways.

		Markets*	
		Present	**New**
Products	**Present**	Market penetration strategy *option 1*	Market development strategy *option 2*
	New	Product development strategy *option 3*	Diversification *option 4*

* See Exhibit 4 for further elaborations.

Was it wiser, he pondered, to go for market share (penetration), new markets, new products, or complete diversification? Or maybe a no-growth posture was preferable—maximize cash flow from his present operations. From this approach it would be a short step to liquidation, gradual or immediate. Liquidation had never really occurred to Williams before, but the discouraging trends made him at least consider such a distasteful alternative.

Exhibit 4
Some Product Portfolio Matrices

1. Segments of Business

		Product: Frozen	Product: Canned	
Market	Private label	33%	52%	85%
Market	Franchise label	2%	13%	15%
		35%	65%	100%

2. Product Portfolio

		Margins: High	Margins: Low
Growth	High	Franchise label frozen	Private label frozen
Growth	Low	Franchise label canned	Private label canned

3. Product Market Matrix

		Market: Old	Market: New
Product	Old	Existing business	International other states
Product	New	New mixtures of vegetables	Frozen juices, etc.

C A S E 2–2

Victoria Station

In June 1976, management at Victoria Station, a San Francisco-based restaurant chain, was contemplating action to maintain the position the company had established after only six and a half years in business. The company's principal business came from operating 46 Victoria Station restaurants made up of disused railroad boxcars decorated with imported British Railways memorabilia.[1] The restaurants served a limited menu of seven items, featuring prime rib (51 percent of sales), and were a popular rendezvous not only for dinner but also cocktails and lunch, where sandwiches and chuckburgers were also offered. Three other restaurants with diversified themes in the San Francisco Bay Area had been early additions to the company's business/product portfolio: Thomas Lord's on San Francisco's fashionable Union Street was designed after an English sporting tavern, with a bar and restaurant serving a variety of sandwiches and hot entrees. The Royal Exchange in the San Francisco financial district had an English stock exchange atmosphere and was open primarily for lunch and afterwork cocktails. These two units served a higher proportion of alcoholic beverages than the Victoria Station's norm of 26 percent. Across the Bay, next to the Oakland Victoria Station, Quinn's Lighthouse was located in a renovated Coast Guard lighthouse and featured seafood as well as beef entrees.

The company also operated the Plantation Gardens at Poipu Beach on the Island of Kauai, Hawaii. This restaurant, in the former home of the plantation manager of the first sugar plantation on the island, was at the entrance to a 200-unit condominium development, itself sur-

---

This case was written by Charles Cross. © 1977 by the Board of Trustees of the Leland Stanford Junior University.

[1] The history of Victoria Station from conception in 1967 through the fall of 1973 is outlined in a case written by D. Daryl Wycoff, Associate Professor in Business Administration, Harvard Business School, and a Victoria Station director, ICCH 9–674–012.

rounded by tropical gardens. Native specialties, as well as beef and seafood, were served.

Atlanta, Georgia (site of the second Victoria Station), was also the location of the most radical major diversification to date, Quinn's Mill, which had just been opened in the spring of 1976. Designed in-house by Victoria Station's architectural team, the restaurant resembled an old grist mill and featured an expanded menu including appetizers, which no other Victoria Station served. The restaurant was spectacularly located on a lakeshore close by a major shopping center.

The company's achievements had been recognized nationally: CBS, in a TV production entitled "Mr. Rooney Goes to Dinner" (a survey of eating houses across America), had selected Victoria Station, of all so-called theme restaurants, as a "model" of effective execution of the concept. *Business Week* had interviewed President Richard Bradley and was to feature the company in a double-page article in August 1976. Bradley had been nominated against stiff competition for the prestigious "Man of the Year" award by the Multi-Unit Food Service Operators Association of America,[2] sponsored by *Nation's Restaurant News*, probably the most important trade publication in the food service industry.

Now faced with increasing competition concentrated in fewer and fewer hands, management was determining strategy for its long-term domination of the industry.

The Marketing Function

In December 1973, with 21 restaurants open and another 15 due to be opened within the next year, the company established a marketing department under Harlow White with the charter of generating sales growth in existing restaurants. Mr. White, an original investor in the company, had been national personnel manager for Pfizer, Inc. until March 1972, when he joined Victoria Station as director of human resources. Marketing was to be in addition to his personnel tasks. Mr. White explained that, at the time of his taking the job, the company's management information system was producing information which was not being used to best advantage. Management felt that the present restaurants were losing market opportunities because they had lacked a formal function to utilize the information to generate additional business. "I view the marketing function as first and foremost a development of information and later on taking that information, going to school on it, and using it to develop things to further enhance the competitive position," Mr. White commented.

---

[2] Bradley subsequently won the award.

First, marketing attempted to determine why the company had been so successful. To quote Mr. White again:

> It was product definition that made us do so well. We concluded we were selling a product that was more than a piece of meat on a plate, more than an ounce-and-a-quarter shot in a 13-ounce glass. It was a total experience. The general ambience of the restaurant, the quality of the product, the size of the portions, and the architecture of the place all contributed.

The success had been achieved without paid advertising except for direct mail announcements at the time of each restaurant's opening. Indeed, industry sources viewed restaurant advertising as generally indicative that the establishment was "in trouble." Instead, some free publicity had been sought. While the restaurants were under construction, management encouraged TV and press coverage, which was generally forthcoming because of the unusual nature of the project. Then, in the weeks prior to opening, the manager assigned to the restaurant would compile lists of prospective customers from country club memberships, banking contacts, etc. These would be supplemented by purchase of the area's American Express mailing list to facilitate, where possible, a mailing of 20,000 prospective customers, done from San Francisco, within five days of the opening of the restaurant. Management felt that the food, atmosphere, and service product offered in operating the restaurant, resulting in word-of-mouth advertising, was the best form of promotion.

In 1973, however, the company's two restaurants in Houston, Texas, were suffering increased competition, largely as a result of the abolition of the restrictive Texas liquor laws, which itself had resulted in restaurants opening at the rate of about one a week. Management wondered whether sales could be improved by advertising, and engaged a local advertising agency for the "Texas test," a series of local radio commercials.

The results were so encouraging that the company felt they would extend advertising into other markets. However, working with an agency in Texas posed communication problems with the home office and, equally important, the Texas agency had difficulty in assimilating the Victoria Station corporate thought process. Consequently, in late 1974, Pritikin and Gibbons, a San Francisco advertising agency (itself as recently formed as Victoria Station) was selected as the company's advertising agency.

Agency head Jerry Gibbons proposed to management that his organization would operate best with a profile of Victoria Station's customers, and therefore the company should engage in some primary research to determine the market segments attracted to the restaurants.

Drossler, a market research and counsel organization located in San Francisco, was selected to conduct the suggested research. The two-part report gathered information from the Los Angeles, Indianapolis, and Atlanta markets. The first report, submitted to management in January 1975, used interviews in the restaurants to establish a Victoria Station consumer profile and market target areas. In March 1975, the second report gave quantitative awareness and trial levels and consumers' perceptions of Victoria Station, based on telephone interviews.

Customers, it was found, tended to:

Be under 35.

Have annual incomes of $20,000 or more.

Be college educated.

Be married.

Fall into one of three main occupational groups: professional/technical, managers/officials/proprietors, or sales workers.

The second report showed that people most often mentioned liking the food and atmosphere at Victoria Station:

	Percentage of patrons interviewed		
Likes	**Atlanta**	**Indianapolis**	**Los Angeles**
Net food mentions	66	78	71
Net atmosphere mentions	57	61	70
Net service mentions	25	24	23

Approximately two thirds of those aware of Victoria Station saw it as specializing in red meat, one in three mentioning prime rib as the specialty. Awareness and trial statistics are shown in Exhibit 10.

Management expressed some surprise that atmosphere was mentioned so often by consumers, because they had spend a great deal of time and effort to ensure that the food product was first class. They envisaged that a restaurant's success should not be based on atmosphere, because this advantage was subject to erosion as other restauranteurs produced newer, and perhaps more fashionable, theme stores. Future advertising, it was decided, would stress the food part of the product mix. Accordingly, the marketing department in San Francisco and the agency developed a billboard campaign, "Perhaps the Finest Prime Rib Ever," and small brochures were printed with prominent pictures of the food, and similar headlining. Radio advertising was also developed, featuring Paul Frees, one of the most famous "voices" in America, and then Johnny Cash, the country singer whose various past recordings reflected his railroading interest. Their advertisements, broadcast by radio stations whose consumer profile matched Victoria Station's, attempted to draw out first the food quality, then the atmosphere.

Advertising expense (including selling expense) rose from $64,090 in fiscal 1974 (year ended March 31, 1974) to $295,850 in fiscal 1975 and $984,788 in fiscal 1976. This represented expense of the San Francisco operation; local managers were not involved in advertising policy decisions. During that time, sales rose from $24,759,691 (26 restaurants open—fiscal 1974) to $46,968,788 (44 restaurants open—fiscal 1975), then to $68,891,487 (51 restaurants open—fiscal 1976). In that time net earnings grew from $1,553,448 to $2,408,195, then to $3,979,785.

Development of Theme Restaurants

Industry sources acknowledged that the development of restaurants "on a theme" had been preceded by development of limited menu restaurants, themselves the creation of a Hawaiian, Chuck Rolles. Rolles graduated from the Cornell Hotel School in the early 1960s and returned to Oahu, Hawaii, where he opened a restaurant in the cellar of his father-in-law's hotel. He featured cocktails and served a limited selection of meat dishes. The restaurant was very popular, particularly among single people on the Island. Chuck's Cellar spread to the Mainland with the establishment of a limited menu restaurant in Los Altos, California, which again proved especially popular with the "singles crowd." As Rolles developed his restaurants in California, other limited menu restaurants appeared, including the Ancient Mariner and the Winery, which appealed to the same market segments.

Victoria Station was to early incorporate a "theme" with the limited menu. President Richard Bradley pointed out, however, that "themes" were not new: for example, Trader Vic's, an old established chain of restaurants located in prominent hotels worldwide, complemented their eastern food with Polynesian decor.

By 1976, the limited menu theme restaurant business had blossomed. Victoria Station, however, concentrated on building the dinner business rather than attracting the singles crowd. They had many imitators; small chains of as many as six restaurants had been opened featuring "dining in a boxcar." Additionally, in various parts of the country, it was possible to eat in an old bank vault, an old church, a converted Douglas DC3 and, in Dick's Fender and Body Shop in Detroit, a converted Ford Edsel and 1936 Chevrolet truck. Benihana of Tokyo, which had popularized Japanese cuisine with hibachi exhibition cooking, announced plans to develop a restaurant chain to be called the "Orient Express," noted by a spokesman to have "vibrating sensations of a moving train, and a station atmosphere very similar to

Victoria Station." Benihana's partner in this venture was Hardwicke Companies Inc., a public holding company which had invested in New York's Maxwell's Plum and Tavern on the Green, and a chain of Lord Hardwicke Pubs along the eastern seaboard.

Other major companies, principally food manufacturers, had acquired some of Victoria Station's principal competitors. Pillsbury had recently acquired Steak & Ale, a Dallas-based chain of 98 limited menu old English pub themers which had commenced operations four years before Victoria Station. General Mills reported that 10 percent of corporate profits were being contributed by its chain of 174 Red Lobster seafood restaurants. They were also planning to develop beef and seafood restaurants under the Hannahan's name. W. R. Grace had acquired the Irvine, California-based Far West services, operators of Reuben's, The Plankhouse, Moonraker, and the Reuben E. Lee chains. Saga Corporation, the Menlo Park, California, contract food service company, had diversified by acquiring the Velvet Turtle, Stuart Anderson's Black Angus, and The Refectory, a total of 63 restaurants different within themselves but all broadly in the Victoria Station market segment. Victoria Station's units and volumes were believed to exceed most if not all of the competition. The extent of manufacturer or conglomerate commitment to the food service industry beyond dinner houses is shown in Exhibit 7.

Hotels were also redefining their food service operations: *Restaurant Business* in October 1975 quoted a New York hotel executive as saying:

> Hotel dining rooms—that said it all. That was what hotels had for quite a long time, just a dining room. Why? Because all these people bringing money into a hotel and staying overnight had to be fed. A dining room was like a telephone—you had to have one.

A spokesman for the Hyatt Corporation based in Burlingame, California, declared that Hyatt Hotels' restaurants were not competing with the limited menu theme restaurants, and were developing Hugo's Rotisserie (continental, fine service), Mrs. O'Leary's (Chicago-style delicatessen), and Jonah's Oyster Kitchen (seafood, earth-tone decor). To date, approximately 40 of Hyatt's 150 hotel restaurants had been converted. The spokesman cited the captive audience already staying at the hotel together with the hotel's highly trained kitchen staff, who were capable of preparing food items a limited menu restaurant could not produce, as being strong factors favoring success.

Holiday Inns also felt that they were not attracting sufficient off-the-street patronage, and decided that their restaurants should compete with others in the local area. Theme restaurants installed in Holiday Inns to date included:

The Transatlantic Steamship Company—furnished in polished brass, mahogany, oak, and artifacts of transoceanic travels of 80 years ago.

The Spice Rack—fashioned after an old-fashioned spice store, with waitresses in floor-length colonial outfits and a needlepoint design menu.

The Club Pompeii—with a 26-foot-high Mount Vesuvius replica that erupted every half hour, 28 carved statues from Italy, and 300 feet of hand-painted murals.

Holiday Inns hoped to improve the quality of food offered by stressing regional specialties and fresh and seasonal items in different areas to avoid "plasticizing the food business." To improve the image of Holiday Inn food, the company successfully entered an 18-chef culinary team in various competitions.

Action at Victoria Station

In considering locations for the early restaurants, Victoria Station had followed a policy of building only in areas with a population of 1 million or more (see Exhibit 6). It was felt that such a population was required to maintain a consistently high volume all during the week. Management had, however, revised this view and, aware that its prime trading area lay within a distance of six miles of the restaurant, was building in lower populated areas. Eight openings were scheduled before the end of fiscal 1977—in Toronto, Ontario; Montreal, Quebec; Virginia Beach, Virginia; Wauwatosa, Wisconsin; Alexandria, Virginia; Rockville, Maryland; West Covina, California; and a third restaurant in Atlanta, Georgia.

The company had avoided the New York/New Jersey areas, and Wayne White, vice president of development, cited this as illustrative of difficulties lying in the way of developing the traditional boxcar format. Along the Atlantic seaboard, it was difficult to get approval for many requisites, including liquor licenses—an extreme example being Paramus, New Jersey, where a liquor license cost $175,000. Sewage, water, heat, and light hookups were also becoming harder to obtain. Besides these difficulties, it was estimated that construction costs had risen 40 to 50 percent in the past three years.

There were attractions to developing the business using the free-standing boxcar format. Four so-called prototypes existed which were standard designs and could be taken "off the shelf" and put down in various locations according to site and seating capacity requirements. These prototypes had been refined to give maximum operating efficiencies. Developments in New York and New Jersey might have to involve establishing a restaurant within an existing building, which would involve designing efficient interiors from scratch.

Management thought of their market areas as containing a certain volume of "Restaurant $," and that consumers would, on any given night, be "in the mood" for prime rib and, on another night, perhaps prefer other foods. A second expansion choice, then, was to have a second restaurant in selected market areas. To quote Wayne White:

> We have two other concepts now close by existing Victoria Station restaurants.[3] This demonstrates the great potential to pull more dollars out of some areas. Why can't we be the people who pull the dollars out of the base audience by building a different theme so a customer can say, "I want to go to the Station tonight for the prime rib" or, "I want to go to Quinn's for the pork and apples." This is as attractive as going to the smaller markets like Boise, Albuquerque, and Tucson and putting in one of the prototype Victoria Stations.

Quinn's Mill was the first large-scale example of the execution of this idea. Thomas Lord's and Quinn's Lighthouse had smaller seating capacities. The Royal Exchange did not compete with the restaurants as it did not have full food service and was not open on weekends. Quinn's Mill, however, seated 300 and had a much more extensive menu (see Exhibit 2). The seating capacity of Thomas Lord's and Quinn's Lighthouse were, however, to be extended. A second Royal Exchange, seating 280, was to be opened on the ground floor of a condominium complex in Honolulu and would serve full dinners.

Management had decided not to actively pursue acquisitions, but had made two. The first was Plantation Gardens, which the Moana property group had offered the company in December 1974. Second, having been offered each of the imitator chains of railroad theme restaurants except one, management had found the Train Station in Fort Lauderdale, Florida, up to its standards and had purchased the business in September 1975. Wayne White explained the history of the deal:

> I was in Fort Lauderdale in July 1975, and Dick Bradley had suggested I go look at the Train Station. First of all, I looked at some property up the street, brought to my attention by a broker I had known for some time. I liked the property, thought there was a good possibility to build there, but knew there wasn't room for two train restaurants in one town. I walked into the Train Station looking for the owner, who wasn't there. I left my card, saying 'when he comes in, tell him I was in town looking at sites.' About a month later he called me. By chance he said he was thinking of selling.

The Train Station was closed on acquisition, remodeled as a Victoria Station, and then reopened.

The biggest project to date was due to break ground in August—a 600-seat, $3 million restaurant on a hilltop beside the entrance to the

---

[3] Quinn's Lighthouse, Oakland, California; Quinn's Mill, Atlanta, Georgia.

Universal movie lot in Hollywood, California, where some 3 million people a year paid $5 each to tour the studios. Plans called for the customers to be moved from the studio's parking lot to the restaurant by funicular elevator. Instead of boxcars, old British Railway passenger cars were to be used, connected by a spacious central rotunda itself containing the huge clock that once was in London's own Victoria Station. Music Corporation of America (MCA), owners of Universal, which had sought out Victoria Station for this project, had agreed to an innovative ground-lease arrangement whereby their percentage of the restaurant's gross would increase at higher volumes. Victoria Station hoped this would encourage MCA to use their promotional capabilities. The location would also contain a Thomas Lord's type bar.

Day-to-Day Action in the Marketing Department

Management felt that the costs of doing business, together with the need for ever-increasing volumes, would lead multiunit operators to build bigger units, capable of sustaining $2 million a year sales. Accordingly, the newer Victoria Stations were being built where possible with 295 seats instead of 220 seats (the size to date). Harlow White explained that the maintenance of high volume was sometimes problematical in that, after a certain "honeymoon period" for the first few months of the restaurant, sales might tend to slacken. Advertising, it was hoped, would counteract this trend.

Marketing was also taking other action: to date, the policy of not accepting reservations had been changed so that groups of eight or more could, Monday through Thursday, be assured of not having to wait for a table. The appeal to groups was strengthened by mailings announcing this convenience to offices and local community groups.

On a local level, the company was sponsoring events to publicize the restaurants: these had included, during summer 1976, a sailboat race in the Oakland Bay outside Quinn's Lighthouse, a birthday party for a radio station in Seattle, and catering for the Indianapolis Clay Courts Tennis Championships.

Originally, one price had been charged throughout the country, but latterly a two-tier regional pricing system had been introduced, based on perceived value of the product in the local markets. Price rises per se were felt unacceptable, as this contravened the company's ongoing philosophy of offering value for money. However, price and portion size were closely related, and experiments were in hand to cut both portion size and price in a couple of test markets. For example, the lunchtime hamburger was thought possibly to be a more attractive product if made smaller than its current eight ounces and cut in price. The possibility of changing the lunchtime menu to make it "lighter" and so more appealing to nonbusiness people (for example, shoppers) was being considered.

Quinn's Mill offered the greatest chance to date to experiment with menu changes. Besides the greater diversity, the meat was made with top sirloin strip, roasted as if it were prime rib. There was reportedly less shrinkage and a lower food cost than if the meat were made along the lines of the traditional rib. Slightly smaller portions than those served at Victoria Station were reflected in the price, there being a 50 cent difference between a Quinn's Mill roast at $5.95 and the Victoria Station lowest price prime rib at $6.45. The difference was less marked in the sirloin steak, sold at Quinn's for $6.25 and in the Victoria Stations for $6.45. The five appetizers and one soup offered at Quinn's resulted in a slightly higher priced average check, with the only drawback being the extra time taken to serve the appetizer.

Discussing future strategies for the company in the British Railway's observation car, now a headquarters conference room in San Francisco, management generally agreed that at least 150 Victoria Stations could be developed in North America. President Bradley explained that the minimum number of people required to support a Victoria Station had not been determined. He felt that spiraling costs of construction would, industrywide, move emphasis away from decor and back to the food element of the mix. The entry of Pillsbury, Grace, and General Mills was, he thought a reflection of their hedging bets to ensure that, if the number of meals eaten away from home—and so away from their grocery store foods—materially increased, they would get their share of the business. Harlow White commented, "The business is moving into the hands of more sophisticated operators—multiunits and consumer-product manufacturers/marketers. We would like to be assured of maintaining our volumes in the face of such competition."

Exhibit 1

VICTORIA STATION INCORPORATED AND SUBSIDIARIES
Consolidated Balance Sheet

	March 31	
	1976	**1975**
Assets		
Current assets:		
Cash.	$ 7,626,699	$ 2,415,059
Accounts receivable	695,614	457,767
Inventories (Note A).	2,233,266	1,507,703
Prepaid expenses	687,788	377,423
Total current assets	11,243,367	4,757,952
Other assets:		
Liquor licenses	333,868	322,163
Deposits.	97,431	65,206
	431,299	387,369

Exhibit 1 *(continued)*

	March 31	
	1976	**1975**
Assets		
Property equipment and improvements:		
Land..	$ 1,965,935	$ 1,404,128
Buildings	2,805,424	1,564,339
Household improvements	19,256,994	17,570,235
Restaurant equipment	4,631,222	3,686,904
Furniture, fixtures and equipment......................	2,031,894	1,845,672
Construction in progress.............................	1,000,694	1,939,024
	31,692,163	28,010,302
Less: Accumulated depreciation and amortization	2,940,332	1,731,748
Deferred costs and intangibles:		
Deferred costs.......................................	877,663	660,017
Goodwill..	67,774	71,728
	945,437	731,745
	$41,371,934	$32,155,620

	March 31	
	1976	**1975**
Liabilities and Stockholders' Equity		
Current liabilities:		
Accounts payable	$ 3,547,068	$ 2,424,161
Accrued expenses....................................	1,791,616	1,784,456
Income taxes payable................................	1,583,538	531,975
Current installments on long-term debt	63,609	110,316
Total current liabilities	6,985,831	4,850,908
Long-term debt, less current installments:		
Senior...	3,717,611	11,432,945
Subordinated	3,784,328	3,663,899
	7,501,939	15,096,844
Deferred income taxes	1,171,224	755,090
Commitments		
Stockholders' equity:		
Preferred stock, par value $1:		
Authorized 500,000 shares, none issued		
Common stock, without par value:		
Authorized 10,000,000 shares in 1976 and 2,500,000 shares in 1975		
Issued and outstanding 2,642,790 and 2,000,325 shares...	115,640	83,516
Additional paid-in-capital	16,656,884	6,408,631
Retained earnings	8,940,416	4,960,631
	25,712,940	11,452,778
	$41,371,934	$32,155,620

Exhibit 1 *(concluded)*

VICTORIA STATION INCORPORATED AND SUBSIDIARIES
Consolidated Statement of Earnings

	Year Ended March 31	
	1976	**1975**
Sales:		
Food	$51,407,604	$34,511,284
Beverage	17,483,883	12,457,504
	68,891,487	46,968,788
Costs and expenses:		
Cost of sales:		
Food	23,840,335	16,270,095
Beverage	5,527,918	4,023,804
	29,368,253	20,293,899
Restaurant operating expenses:	21,116,805	13,946,989
Occupancy expenses:		
Rent.	2,926,605	2,087,929
Interest	966,006	1,434,408
Depreciation and amortization	2,166,295	1,895,707
Property taxes and insurance	702,656	478,096
	6,761,562	5,896,140
Advertising and selling expenses	984,768	295,850
General and administrative expenses	2,990,014	2,299,115
	61,221,402	42,731,993
Earnings before taxes on income.	7,670,085	4,236,795
Taxes on income.	3,690,300	1,828,600
Net earnings	$ 3,979,785	$ 2,408,195
Earnings per common and common equivalent share	$ 1.56	$ 1.18

$$\frac{68,891,487}{29,368,253} = 42.6\%$$

Exhibit 2
Quinn's Mill Menu

QUINN'S MILL

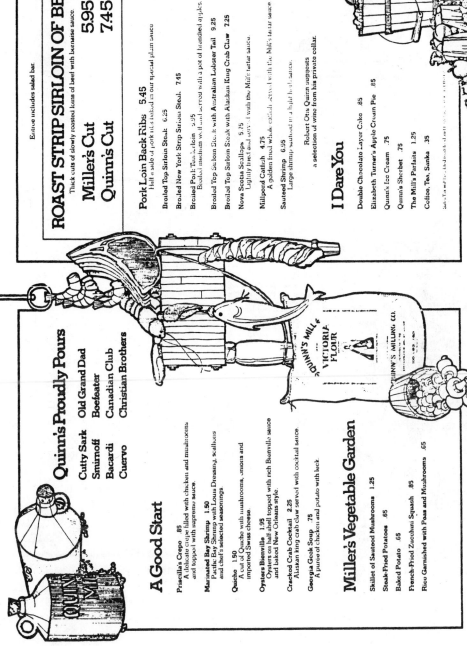

Entree includes salad bar.

ROAST STRIP SIRLOIN OF BEEF

Thick cuts of slowly roasted loins of beef with bernaise sauce.

Miller's Cut	5.95
Quinn's Cut	7.45

Pork Loin Back Ribs 5.45
Half a slab of pork ribs baked in our special plum sauce

Broiled Top Sirloin Steak 6.25

Broiled New York Strip Sirloin Steak 7.45

Broiled Pork Tenderloin 5.95
Broiled medium well and served with a pot of brandied apples.

Broiled Top Sirloin Steak with Australian Lobster Tail 9.25

Broiled Top Sirloin Steak with Alaskan King Crab Claw 7.25

Nova Scotia Scallops 5.75
Lightly fried and served with the Mill's tartar sauce.

Millpond Catfish 4.75
A golden fried whole catfish served with the Mill's tartar sauce

Sauteed Shrimp 6.95
Large shrimp sauteed in a light herb sauce.

Robert Otis Quinn suggests
a selection of wine from his private cellar.

I Dare You

Double Chocolate Layer Cake .85

Elizabeth Turner's Apple Cream Pie .85

Quinn's Ice Cream .75

Quinn's Sherbet .75

The Mill's Parfaits 1.25

Coffee, Tea, Sanka .35

Quinn's Proudly Pours

Cutty Sark	Old Grand Dad
Smirnoff	Beefeater
Bacardi	Canadian Club
Cuervo	Christian Brothers

A Good Start

Priscilla's Crepe .85
A delicate crepe filled with chicken and mushrooms
and topped with supreme sauce.

Marinated Bay Shrimp 1.50
Pacific Bay Shrimp with Louis Dressing, scallions
and chef's selected seasonings.

Quiche 1.50
A cut of Quiche with mushrooms, onions and
imported Swiss cheese.

Oysters Bienville 1.95
Oysters on half shell topped with rich Bienville sauce
and baked New Orleans style.

Cracked Crab Cocktail 2.25
Alaskan king crab claw served with cocktail sauce.

Georgia Geok Soup .75
A puree of chicken and potato with leek.

Miller's Vegetable Garden

Skillet of Sauteed Mushrooms 1.25

Steak-Fried Potatoes .65

Baked Potato .65

French-Fried Zucchini Squash .85

Rice Garnished with Peas and Mushrooms .65

Exhibit 2 *(concluded)*

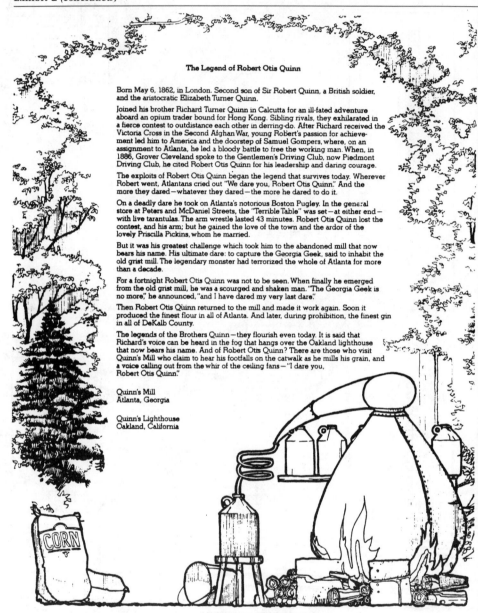

The Legend of Robert Otis Quinn

Born May 6, 1862, in London. Second son of Sir Robert Quinn, a British soldier, and the aristocratic Elizabeth Turner Quinn.

Joined his brother Richard Turner Quinn in Calcutta for an ill-fated adventure aboard an opium trader bound for Hong Kong. Sibling rivals, they exhilarated in a fierce contest to outdistance each other in derring-do. After Richard received the Victoria Cross in the Second Afghan War, young Robert's passion for achievement led him to America and the doorstep of Samuel Gompers, where, on an assignment to Atlanta, he led a bloody battle to free the working man. When, in 1886, Grover Cleveland spoke to the Gentlemen's Driving Club, now Piedmont Driving Club, he cited Robert Otis Quinn for his leadership and daring courage.

The exploits of Robert Otis Quinn began the legend that survives today. Wherever Robert went, Atlantans cried out "We dare you, Robert Otis Quinn." And the more they dared—whatever they dared—the more he dared to do it.

On a deadly dare he took on Atlanta's notorious Boston Pugley. In the general store at Peters and McDaniel Streets, the "Terrible Table" was set—at either end—with live tarantulas. The arm wrestle lasted 43 minutes. Robert Otis Quinn lost the contest, and his arm; but he gained the love of the town and the ardor of the lovely Priscilla Pickins, whom he married.

But it was his greatest challenge which took him to the abandoned mill that now bears his name. His ultimate dare: to capture the Georgia Geek, said to inhabit the old grist mill. The legendary monster had terrorized the whole of Atlanta for more than a decade.

For a fortnight Robert Otis Quinn was not to be seen. When finally he emerged from the old grist mill, he was a scourged and shaken man. "The Georgia Geek is no more," he announced, "and I have dared my very last dare."

Then Robert Otis Quinn returned to the mill and made it work again. Soon it produced the finest flour in all of Atlanta. And later, during prohibition, the finest gin in all of DeKalb County.

The legends of the Brothers Quinn—they flourish even today. It is said that Richard's voice can be heard in the fog that hangs over the Oakland lighthouse that now bears his name. And of Robert Otis Quinn? There are those who visit Quinn's Mill who claim to hear his footfalls on the catwalk as he mills his grain, and a voice calling out from the whir of the ceiling fans—"I dare you, Robert Otis Quinn."

Quinn's Mill
Atlanta, Georgia

Quinn's Lighthouse
Oakland, California

A VICTORIA STATION RESTAURANT
Quinn's Mill Restaurant, 3300 Northlake Parkway, Atlanta, Georgia

Exhibit 3

NOTICE

Platform #1

£ $

Baggage cart salad bar . . . . . .   Included with dinner

Platform #2

Roast Prime Rib of Beef
  Track #1—Julia C. Bulette Cut **53/6**   **6.45**
  Track #2—Enginemen's Cut **66/3**   **7.95**
  Side Track—Owners' and Friends' Cut **87/1**   **10.45**
Bar-B-Que Beef Ribs—Limited **45/6**   **5.45**
Filet **70/6**   **8.45**
Top Sirloin **53/6**   **6.45**
Teriyaki Beef Kebob **49/6**   **5.95**
Shrimp Victoria—Giant shrimp sautéed
                in wine and garlic sauce **53/6**   **6.45**
Steak and Shrimp **63/6**   **7.65**

Platform #3

Sautéed Mushrooms served in a skillet . . . **10/6**   **1.25**
Baked Idaho potato . . . . **5/6**   **.65**

Platform #4

Station Master's Desserts . . . . **7/1**   **.85**
Coffee, Tea, Sanka . . . . **3/—**   **.35**

Dinners include salad, bread and butter

FRANK A. DICKENS
CHIEF GENERAL SUPERINTENDENT

Sales Tax will be added on all food and beverages

San Francisco	Miami	Newport Beach	Marin
Atlanta	Cincinnati	Northbrook	Tampa
Oakland	Kansas City	Sacramento	Honolulu
New Orleans	Houston II	Tahoe City	Villa Park
Denver	Columbus	Torrance	Southfield
Sunnyvale	Seattle	Arlington	Toledo
Los Angeles	Darien	Vancouver	Pittsburgh
Phoenix	Louisville	Memphis	St. Louis
Dallas	King of Prussia	Rocky River	Charlotte
Houston I	Boston	Schaumburg	Toronto
Portland	Woodland Hills	Birmingham	Montreal
Indianapolis	San Diego	Jacksonville	Fort Lauderdale

Exhibit 4

Properties (the following table sets forth information as of May 31, 1976, concerning the company restaurants which have been opened and restaurants for which sites have been acquired)

Location	Name	Dining capacity	Date opened or to be opened	Lease expiration*
San Francisco				
50 Broadway	Victoria Station	210	December 1969	11/1/94
San Francisco				
2000 Union	Thomas Lord's	70	November 1970	9/30/90
Atlanta				
631 Lindbergh N.E.	Victoria Station	218	December 1970	4/28/90
Oakland				
55 Embarcadero Cove	Victoria Station	140	April 1971	11/29/92
New Orleans				
111 Rue Iberville	Victoria Station	180	September 1971	5/18/96
Denver (Glendale)				
4330 E. Alameda	Victoria Station	170	September 1971	12/7/90
Oakland				
51 Embarcadero Cove	Quinn's Lighthouse	100	April 1972	11/29/92
Sunnyvale (Calif.)				
855 E. Homestead	Victoria Station	205	July 1972	9/13/2016
San Francisco				
301 Sacramento	The Royal Exchange	150	August 1972	1/31/91
Los Angeles				
2001 S. Sepulveda	Victoria Station	205	August 1972	3/24/97
Phoenix				
1720 E. Camelback	Victoria Station	205	September 1972	11/30/2021
Dallas				
2910 Routh	Victoria Station	205	September 1972	11/30/96
Houston I				
3015 S. Post Oak	Victoria Station	205	January 1973	1/31/93
Portland (Oreg.)				
6500 S.W. Macadam	Victoria Station	220	March 1973	3/30/98
Indianapolis				
7279 N. Keystone	Victoria Station	220	May 1973	5/30/98

Location	Chain	No.	Opened	Closed
Miami 6301 N.W. 36th St.	Victoria Station	220	May 1973	2/28/98
Cincinnati 939 W. Eighth	Victoria Station	220	June 1973	5/31/2023
Kansas City 100 W. 3rd St.	Victoria Station	288	July 1973	Purchase
Houston II 7807 Kirby	Victoria Station	220	September 1973	6/30/2003
Columbus 1691 Dublin-Granville	Victoria Station	220	October 1973	5/31/2008
Seattle 1880 Fairview Ave. East	Victoria Station	220	November 1973	7/31/2008
Darien (Conn.) 54 Boston Post Road	Victoria Station	254	December 1973	11/30/92
Louisville 920 Dupont	Victoria Station	220	December 1973	8/31/98
Philadelphia (King of Prussia) 151 North Henderson Road	Victoria Station	220	December 1973	3/14/98
Boston 64 Sleeper St.	Victoria Station	292	January 1974	2/28/97
Los Angeles (Woodland Hills) 20621 Ventura Blvd.	Victoria Station	220	March 1974	9/30/98
San Diego 7919 Mission Center Court	Victoria Station	220	May 1974	9/30/2003
Newport Beach 990 Dove St.	Victoria Station	220	June 1974	6/30/99
Chicago (Northbrook) 200 Skokie Blvd.	Victoria Station	220	June 1974	11/30/98
Sacramento 1792 Tribute Rd.	Victoria Station	220	June 1974	3/31/97
Tahoe City (Calif.) 425 North Lake Blvd.	Victoria Station	250	June 1974	6/30/2004
Los Angeles (Torrance) 23805 Hawthorne Blvd.	Victoria Station	220	July 1974	1/31/99
Arlington (Texas) 804 N. Watson	Victoria Station	220	August 1974	6/30/2009

Exhibit 4 (*concluded*)

Location	Name	Dining capacity	Date opened or to be opened	Lease expiration*
Vancouver (B.C.)				
1414 Hornby...............	Victoria Station	220	September 1974	9/30/97
Memphis				
2734 S. Mendenhall......	Victoria Station	220	September 1974	6/29/2018
Cleveland (Rocky River)				
1340 Depot St...........	Victoria Station	220	September 1974	6/30/2009
Chicago (Schaumburg)				
675 Mall Dr.............	Victoria Station	220	December 1974	3/31/99
Birmingham (Ala.)				
2023 Morris Ave.	Victoria Station	250	December 1974	2/28/99
Jacksonville				
7579 Arlington Expy......	Victoria Station	220	December 1974	12/31/2010†
Kauai (Hawaii)				
Poipu Beach............	Plantation Gardens	150	December 1974	12/31/99
Tampa				
2903 N. Dale Mabry Hwy. ..	Victoria Station	220	January 1975	10/31/99
Honolulu				
1599 Kapiolani Blvd.	Victoria Station	164	January 1975	3/31/94
Marin County (Greenbrae) (Calif.)				
17 E. Francis Drake Blvd. ..	Victoria Station	292	January 1975	12/31/2010†
Chicago (Villa Park)				
298 W. Roosevelt Rd......	Victoria Station	220	March 1975	7/31/99
Detroit (Southfield)				
28565 Northwestern Hwy. ..	Victoria Station	295	May 1975	1/31/2011†
Toledo (Maumee)				
1418 Reynolds Rd........	Victoria Station	220	May 1975	12/31/2010†
Ft. Lauderdale				
1390 Northeast 62nd St.....	Victoria Station	280	December 1975	Purchase
St. Louis				
11550 Page Service Drive	Victoria Station	220	January 1976	Purchase

Location / Address	Restaurant	Seats	Opened	Lease Expiration*
Charlotte				
3061 N. Sharon Amity Road	Victoria Station	220	March 1976	Purchase
Pittsburgh (Monroeville)				
2725 Stroschein Blvd.	Victoria Station	295	March 1975	Purchase
Atlanta				
3300 Northlake Parkway	Quinn's Mill	300	March 1976	9/30/2009

Restaurant Sites Acquired (10)

Location / Address	Restaurant	Seats	Opened	Lease Expiration*
Toronto				
Queen's Quay	Victoria Station	280	Fall 1976 (est.)	8/31/2003
Atlanta (Cumberland)				
Cumberland Parkway	Victoria Station	295	Fall 1976	Purchase
Virginia Beach				
Columbus St.	Victoria Station	205	Fall 1976	7/14/2021
Honolulu				
Ala Moana Blvd.	Royal Exchange	200	Fall 1976 (est.)	12/31/95
Montreal				
De La Savane	Victoria Station	295	Winter 1976	8/31/2020
Milwaukee (Wauwatosa)				
Mayfair Road	Victoria Station	295	Winter 1976	Purchase
Alexandria				
Van Dorn St.	Victoria Station	295	Early 1977	Purchase
Cleveland (Orange)				
Orange Place	Victoria Station	295	Early 1977	Purchase
Rockville, Maryland				
Shady Grove Lane	Victoria Station	295	Early 1977	Purchase
Los Angeles				
Universal City	Victoria Station	600	Early 1977	3/31/2006

* Including renewals at the option of the company.
† Restaurants which were sold and leased back by the company.

Exhibit 5
Leading Manufacturers with Food Service Chains

Manufacturer or conglomerate	Name of food service chain and headquarters	Total number food service units	Estimated annual food service chain volume (millions)
Pillsbury	Burger King (Miami) Steak & Ale (Dallas) Poppin' Fresh Pies (Minneapolis)	1,730	$920
Ralston Purina	Jack-in-the-Box Judge Tibbs Chicken Continental Restaurants (San Diego)	800	300
United Brands	A & W (Santa Monica, Calif.)	2,000	300
General Foods	Burger Chef (Tarrytown, N.Y.)	950	275
General Mills	Red Lobster, Hannahan's (Orlando)	175	150
International Multifoods	Mr. Donut, Sveden House, T. Butcherblock, Boston Sea Party (Minneapolis)	580	127
Greyhound	Greyhound Food (Phoenix)	385	125
Orange-Company	Arthur Treacher's (Columbus)	450	120
W. R. Grace	Far West Services (Irvine, Calif.)	136	110
Del Monte	Service Systems (Buffalo) (contract feeder)	1,175	100
Consolidated Foods	Lyons (Burlingame, Calif.) L-K Enterprises (Marion, Ohio)	210	73
Campbell Soup	Hanover Trail (Camden, N.J.) Herfy's, Pietro's (Seattle)	85	45
Borden	Borden Burger, Homer Filby's (Columbus)	40	15

Source: *Nation's Restaurant News.*

Exhibit 6
Rank of Standard Metropolitan Statistical Areas in the United States by Population: 1970

Rank	SMSAs	1970 population
1	New York, N.Y.	11,571,899
2	Los Angeles–Long Beach, Calif.	7,032,075
3	Chicago, Ill.	6,978,947
4	Philadelphia, Pa.–N.J.	4,817,914
5	Detroit, Mich.	4,199,931
6	San Francisco–Oakland, Calif.	3,109,519
7	Washington, D.C.–Md.–Va.	2,862,123
8	Boston, Mass.	2,753,700
9	Pittsburgh, Pa.	2,401,245
10	St. Louis, M.–Ill.	2,363,017
11	Baltimore, Md.	2,070,670
12	Cleveland, Ohio	2,064,194
13	Houston, Tex.	1,985,031
14	Newark, N.J.	1,856,556
15	Minneapolis–St. Paul, Minn.	1,813,647
16	Dallas, Tex.	1,555,950
17	Seattle–Everett, Wash.	1,421,869
18	Anaheim–Santa Ana–Garden Grove, Calif.	1,420,386
19	Milwaukee, Wis.	1,403,688
20	Atlanta, Ga.	1,390,164
21	Cincinnati, Ohio–Ky.–Ind.	1,384,851
22	Paterson–Clifton–Passaic, N.J.	1,358,794
23	San Diego, Calif.	1,357,854
24	Buffalo, N.Y.	1,349,211
25	Miami, Fla.	1,267,792
26	Kansas City, Mo.–Kans.	1,253,916
27	Denver, Colo.	1,227,529
28	San Bernardino–Riverside–Ontario, Calif.	1,143,146
29	Indianapolis, Ind.	1,109,882
30	San Jose, Calif.	1,064,714
31	New Orleans, La.	1,045,809
32	Tampa–St. Petersburg, Fla.	1,012,594
33	Portland, Ore.–Wash.	1,009,129
34	Phoenix, Ariz.	967,522
35	Columbus, Ohio	916,228
36	Providence–Pawtucket–Warwick, R.I.–Mass.	910,781
37	Rochester, N.Y.	882,667
38	San Antonio, Tex.	864,014
39	Dayton, Ohio	850,266
40	Louisville, Ky.–Ind.	826,553
41	Sacramento, Calif.	800,592
42	Memphis, Tenn.–Ark.	770,120
43	Fort Worth, Tex.	762,086
44	Birmingham, Ala.	739,274
45	Albany–Schenectady–Troy, N.Y.	721,910
46	Toledo, Ohio–Mich.	692,571
47	Norfolk–Portsmouth, Va.	680,600
48	Akron, Ohio	679,239
49	Hartford, Conn.	663,891
50	Oklahoma City, Okla.	640,889
51	Syracuse, N.Y.	636,507
52	Gary–Hammond–East Chicago, Ind.	633,367
53	Honolulu, Hawaii	629,176

Exhibit 6 *(continued)*

Rank	SMSAs	1970 population
54	Fort Lauderdale–Hollywood, Fla.	620,100
55	Jersey City, N.J.	609,266
56	Greensboro–Winston–Salem–High Point, N.C.	603,895
57	Salt Lake City, Utah.	557,635
58	Allentown–Bethlehem–Easton, Pa.–N.J.	543,551
59	Nashville–Davidson, Tenn.	541,108
60	Omaha, Nebr.–Iowa.	540,142
61	Grand Rapids, Mich.	539,225
62	Youngstown–Warren, Ohio	536,003
63	Springfield–Chicopee–Holyoke, Mass.–Conn.	529,922
64	Jacksonville, Fla.	528,865
65	Richmond, Va.	518,319
66	Wilmington, Del.–N.J.–Md.	499,493
67	Flint, Mich.	496,658
68	Tulsa, Okla.	476,945
69	Orlando, Fla.	428,003
70	Fresno, Calif.	413,053
71	Tacoma, Wash.	411,027
72	Harrisburg, Pa.	410,626
73	Charlotte, N.C.	409,370
74	Knoxville, Tenn.	400,337
75	Wichita, Kans.	389,352
76	Bridgeport, Conn.	389,153
77	Lansing, Mich.	378,423
78	Mobile, Ala.	376,690
79	Oxnard–Ventura, Calif.	376,430
80	Canton, Ohio	372,210
81	Davenport–Rock Island–Moline, Iowa–Ill.	362,638
82	El Paso, Tex.	359,291
83	New Haven, Conn.	355,538
84	Tucson, Ariz.	351,667
85	West Palm Beach, Fla.	348,753
86	Worchester, Mass.	344,320
87	Wilkes–Burro–Hazelton, Pa.	342,301
88	Peoria, Ill.	341,979
89	Utica–Rome, N.Y.	340,670
90	York, Pa.	329,540
91	Bakersfield, Calif.	329,162
92	Little Rock–North Little Rock, Ark.	323,296
93	Columbia, S.C.	322,880
94	Lancaster, Pa.	319,693
95	Beaumont–Port Arthur, Tex.	315,943
96	Albuquerque, N. Mex.	315,774
97	Chattanooga, Tenn.–Ga.	304,927
98	Trenton, N.J.	303,968
99	Charleston, S.C.	303,849
100	Binghamton, N.Y.–Pa.	302,672
101	Greenville, S.C.	299,502
102	Reading, Pa.	296,382
103	Austin, Tex.	295,516
104	Shreveport, La.	294,703
105	Newport News–Hampton, Va.	292,159
106	Madison, Wis.	290,272
107	Stockton, Calif.	290,208
108	Spokane, Wash.	287,487

Exhibit 6 *(concluded)*

Rank	SMSAs	1970 population
109	Des Moines, Iowa	286,101
110	Baton Rouge, La.	285,167
111	Corpus Christi, Tex.	284,832
112	Fort Wayne, Ind.	280,455
113	South Bend, Ind.	280,031
114	Appleton–Oshkosh, Wis.	276,891
115	Las Vegas, Nev.	273,288
116	Rockford, Ill.	272,063
117	Duluth–Superior, Minn.–Wis.	265,350
118	Santa Barbara, Calif.	264,324
119	Eric, Pa.	263,654
120	Johnston, Pa.	262,822
121	Jackson, Miss.	258,906
122	Lorain–Elyria, Ohio	256,843
123	Huntington–Ashland, W. Va.–Ky.–Ohio	253,743
124	Augusta, Ga.–S.C	253,460
125	Salinas–Monterey, Calif.	250,071
126	Vallejo–Napa, Calif.	249,081
127	Pensacola, Fla.	243,075
128	Columbus, Ga.–Ala.	238,584
129	Colorado Springs, Colo.	235,972
130	Scranton, Pa.	234,107
131	Ann Arbor, Mich.	234,103
132	Evansville, Ind.–Ky.	232,775
133	Lawrence–Haverhill, Mass.–N.H.	232,415
134	Charleston, W.Va.	229,515
135	Raleigh, N.C.	228,453
136	Huntsville, Ala.	228,239
137	Hamilton–Middletown, Ohio	226,207
138	Saginaw, Mich.	219,743

Exhibit 7
Universal City Project

Exhibit 8
Universal City Project

Exhibit 9
Universal City Project

Exhibit 10
Excerpts from the Drossier Report

2. Conclusions and Recommendations

Los Angeles.   Unaided awareness of Victoria Station is lower in Los Angeles than in the other two markets. Unaided awareness of the Los Angeles unit is also low relative to competitors. This suggests a need for building "Top-of-Mind" awareness. Such an augmentation is dependent on the development of a memorable positioning and on repeat exposure, ideally through a variety of media. Development of a memorable positioning for Victoria Station is especially important in Los Angeles as a means of differentiation from the profuse selection of restaurants available to respondents in this market. With customer conversion for the Los Angeles unit topping that of the other two cities and equaling that of competitors, it appears that the Victoria Station unit is in a good position to convert trial customers to repeat or loyal customers. However, efforts to maintain and increase repeat patronage and customer loyalty should be made.

Indianapolis.   Findings suggest that the Indianapolis market shows a potential for growth of total awareness of Victoria Station. Increasing total awareness means reaching as many people as possible to bring to their attention the existence and nature of the restaurant. The shopping center location of this unit, while being central, also tends to limit awareness to those who shop in the center or happen to live near by. While unaided (Top-of-Mind) awareness of this unit is equal to or greater than *selected* competitors, wider Top-

Exhibit 10 *(continued)*

of-Mind awareness of other restaurants in the market makes the building of unaided awareness also desirable.

Atlanta.   While total and unaided awareness of the Atlanta unit are high compared to
the other two cities, findings indicate that awareness of Victoria Station could be improved,
relative to its competitors. In addition, a comparison of customer conversion ratios of the
Atlanta unit to the two other units as well as to its competitors, indicates that an important
element of this unit's strategy for nurturing market growth should be to increase repeat
patronage and customer loyalty. Both repeat patronage and customer loyalty generally are
built through greater emphasis on the individual customer. The usual elements of customer
satisfaction such as food quality and service are of course essential. In addition, programs
to induce customer conversion and loyalty, such as customer discount coupons, should be
explored.

III. Awareness and Patronage

The following measures of awareness and patronage, and the relationships between
them, provide valuable insights into the types of strengths and weaknesses an eating
establishment has. Later chapters which discuss image and attitudes provide some explanation of the reasons *why* these strengths and weaknesses exist.

In order to provide a frame of reference against which to evaluate the levels of awareness and patronage achieved by Victoria Station, comparable measures have been obtained for three selected competitors in each of the three cities surveyed.

1. Awareness

Total Awareness.   Total awareness is important in determining whether respondents
have to be educated as to the existence of a particular eating establishment. Total awareness has two components—unaided and aided awareness. In this study, unaided awareness was elicited by asking the respondent to name all the restaurants he or she could
think of which specialize in steak or prime rib. If the respondent did not name a specific
preselected restaurant, aided awareness was elicited by asking the respondent if he/she
had ever heard of it. Total awareness is the sum of aided and unaided awareness.

Previous experience has shown that total awareness appears to discriminate only in a
negative direction. That is, if awareness is high (85 percent or more) it does not mean it's a
good restaurant, but if awareness is *low*, it is likely to be a restaurant which has potential for
improvement.

The markets in Indianapolis and Los Angeles show a greater potential for growth in
awareness of Victoria Station, with present total awareness levels being somewhat lower
than Atlanta's.

Total Awareness of Victoria Station
Restaurants (total sample $N = 250$)

	Total awareness
Atlanta	84%
Los Angeles	75
Indianapolis	71

In Atlanta, two competitors display even higher levels of total awareness than Victoria
Station. This suggests that there is potential for growth of total awareness of Victoria Station
in the Atlanta market, even though the present level of awareness is high.

Exhibit 10 *(continued)*

Total Awareness Compared to Atlanta
Competitors (total sample *N* = 250)

	Total awareness
Red Lobster...............	99%
Steak and Ale	91
Victoria Station	84
Sandpiper	84

In Indianapolis, total awareness of Victoria Station (71 percent) is greater than that of two of the selected competitors—Cork'n Cleaver (64 percent) and Friday's (56 percent). The Jolly Ox has a substantially higher awareness level (92 percent) than Victoria Station.

Total Awareness Compared to
Indianapolis Competitors (total sample
N = 250)

	Total awareness
Jolly Ox....................	92%
Victoria Station	71
Cork'n Cleaver..............	64
Friday's	56

The total awareness level of Victoria Station in Los Angeles (75 percent) is greater than that of Chuck's (64 percent), on par with that of the Warehouse (77 percent), and slightly less than that of the Velvet Turtle (83 percent).

Total Awareness Compared to Los
Angeles Competitors (total sample
N = 250)

	Total awareness
Velvet Turtle................	83%
Warehouse.................	77
Victoria Station	75
Chuck's	64

Unaided Awareness.   While total awareness is important in determining whether respondents have to be educated as to the existence of a particular restaurant, another awareness measure is *unaided recall*. As mentioned earlier, this is the percentage of persons who volunteer the name of a particular restaurant when asked to name eating places with which they are familiar. In this case, people were asked to name restaurants specializing in *steak* or *prime rib*.

Unaided recall approximates a measure of the different restaurants which "run through" a person's mind when he/she is actually making a selection. As such, it tends to correspond closely to patronage patterns in the recent past and/or plans for the immediate

Exhibit 10 *(continued)*

future.* This selectivity concept is important since awareness is built in a competitive atmosphere.

A comparison of the three markets shows unaided awareness of Victoria Station to be higher in Atlanta and Indianapolis (16 percent, respectively) than in Los Angeles (5 percent). The significantly lower level of unaided awareness of Victoria Station in Los Angeles is crucial in understanding the relatively unsatisfactory sales trend of the Los Angeles unit. However, all three markets show potential for improvement of unaided awareness.

Unaided Awareness of Victoria Station
(total sample N = 250)

	Unaided awareness
Atlanta	16%
Indianapolis	16
Los Angeles	5

In Atlanta, one competitor. Steak and Ale, has a higher level of unaided awareness than Victoria Station. Two restaurants which were not preselected competitors were also mentioned on an unaided basis—Sizzler and Bonanza.

Unaided Awareness Compared to Atlanta
Competitors (total sample N = 250)

	Unaided awareness
Steak and Ale	24%
Victoria Station	16
Sizzler	14
Bonanza	11
Red Lobster	6
Sandpiper	3

In Indianapolis, three restaurants which were not preselected competitors were mentioned on an unaided basis. Two of these, Ponderosa and Bonanza, have higher levels of unaided awareness than Victoria Station. Victoria Station has a higher level of unaided awareness than the three preselected competitors.

Unaided Awareness Compared to
Indianapolis Competitors (total sample
N = 250)

	Unaided awareness
Ponderosa	23%
Bonanza	18
Victoria Station	16
Jolly Ox	16
Sizzler	14
Cork'n Cleaver	9
Fridays	1

---

* Because of the profusion of eating places to choose from, consumers tend to be selective in the number of restaurants which they will recall on an unaided basis.

Exhibit 10 *(continued)*

Unaided awareness of Victoria Station in Los Angeles (5 percent), while lower than that of the other two units, is on par with two competitors, Chuck's (6 percent) and the Velvet Turtle (6 percent), and is higher than that of another competitor, the Warehouse (1 percent). Besides these restaurants, two others had high levels of unaided recall—Lawry's (40 percent) and Sizzler (10 percent). It should be noted that Lawry's bills itself as "the prime rib restaurant."

Unaided Awareness Compared to Los Angeles Competitors (total sample N = 250)

	Unaided awareness
Lawry's.	40%
Sizzler	10
Chuck's	6
Velvet Turtle.	6
Victoria Station	5
Warehouse.	1

2. Patronage

Patronage Measures.   Three patronage measures were obtained for Victoria Station and selected competitors.

1. Ever Patronized. The percentage of respondents saying that they have ever been to Victoria Station/competitor.
2. Current Customers. The percentage of people saying that they would consider Victoria Station/competitor when choosing a place to eat. (These people are also included in the "Ever Patronized" percentage.)
3. Patronize Most. The percentage of people saying that Victoria Station/competitor is the restaurant they go to most often. (These people are also included in the "Current Customer" percentage.)

These figures for the three units are as follows:

Patronage of Victoria Station (total sample N = 250)

	Atlanta	Indianapolis	Los Angeles
Ever patronized.	51%	42%	38%
Current customers.	41	34	32
Patronize most.	5	8	8

A larger percentage of people in Atlanta have ever patronized Victoria Station than have people in either Indianapolis or Los Angeles. This probably reflects the Atlanta unit's greater length of time in the market.

While the Victoria Station patronage figures in Atlanta are high relative to the other two Victoria Stations, they are lower than the three selected competitors—Red Lobster, Steak and Ale, and Sandpiper. Patronage figures for Red Lobster are particularly high, with 84 percent of the people having ever eaten there.

Exhibit 10 *(continued)*

Patronage of Victoria Station and Competitors—Atlanta (total sample
$N = 250$)

	Ever patronized	Current customers	Most often
Red Lobster.	84%	65%	20%
Steak and Ale	57	50	14
Sandpiper	53	48	14
Victoria Station	51	41	5

In Indianapolis, patronage figures for Victoria Station are second only to Jolly Ox.

Patronage of Victoria Station and Competitors—Indianapolis (total
sample $N = 250$)

	Ever patronized	Current customers	Most often
Jolly Ox	51%	42%	14%
Victoria Station	42	34	8
Cork'n Cleaver.	34	26	6
Friday's	32	24	5

Patronage figures for Victoria Station and three competitors in Los Angeles do not differ significantly one to another.

Patronage of Victoria Station and Competitors—Los Angeles (total
sample $N = 250$)

	Ever patronized	Current customers	Most often
Warehouse.	40%	35%	8%
Chuck's	40	34	10
Victoria Station	38	32	8
Velvet Turtle	38	31	8

3. Trial Ratio and Customer Conversion Ratios

Trial Ratio.   Trial ratio is used as a tool in analyzing patronage relative to total aware-ness. It shows what percentage of those *aware* of a restaurant have ever *tried* it. Trial is important in overall strategy, because once awareness has been built, the restaurant positioning must be sufficiently appealing to stimulate consumers to try it.

$$\frac{\text{Ever patronized}}{\text{Total awareness}} = \text{Trial ratio}$$

Customer Conversion Ratios.   By looking at the percentage of respondents who are "current customers" of a restaurant relative to the percentage who have "ever patronized it," we see what proportion of those that have tried a restaurant, are converted to repeat customers. This also offers a reading of general satisfaction.

$$\frac{\text{Current customer}}{\text{Ever patronized}} = \text{Repeat customer conversion ratio}$$

Exhibit 10 *(continued)*

And, by comparing the percentage of respondents who patronize a restaurant "most often" to the percentage who have "ever patronized" the restaurant, we see what proportion of those that have tried a restaurant become extremely loyal customers, patronizing this particular restaurant more than any other restaurant.

$$\frac{\text{Patronize most often}}{\text{Ever patronize}} = \text{Loyal customer conversion ratio}$$

These three ratios for the three Victoria Station units are as follows:

	Trial ratio	Customer conversion ratio	
Victoria Station	**Ever patronized total awareness**	**Current customer ever patronized**	**Most often ever patronized**
Atlanta	.61	.80	.10
Indianapolis	.59	.81	.19
Los Angeles	.51	.84	.21

Several important points which can be drawn from this data help in understanding the three distinct markets:

a. Trial ratio for Los Angeles is lower than for the other two cities. Yet both customer conversion ratios are relatively high. This suggests that marketing strategy for Los Angeles should concentrate on building trial by increasing awareness and by inducing patronage.

b. While Atlanta's trial ratio is relatively high, the loyal customer conversion ratio is lower than those of the other two cities. This probably reflects the heavy competition in the Atlanta market. The difference between trial and customer conversion suggests that a marketing strategy, besides maintaining and improving the high level of awareness and trial, should concentrate on increasing repeat patronage and loyalty.

c. Trial and conversion ratios are both relatively high for the Indianapolis unit. However, awareness of Victoria Station in Indianapolis is lower than awareness in the other two cities. These findings show the need for building awareness which leads to trial visits.

A comparison of trial and customer conversion ratios of Victoria Station and selected competitors gives further insight into the specific positioning of Victoria Station in the three separate markets.

In Atlanta, trial ratio for Victoria Station is on par with two of the three selected competitors. However, trial ratio for Red Lobster (.86) is much higher than Victoria Station (.61). Victoria Station's customer conversion ratios are relatively low. This again indicates that the main marketing objective in Atlanta should be to increase repeat patronage and customer loyalty.

Trial and Customer Conversion Ratios of Victoria Station and Competitors—Atlanta

	Victoria Station	Steak and Ale	Sandpiper	Red Lobster
Trial ratio				
$\frac{\text{Ever patronized}}{\text{Total awareness}}$	.61	.63	.63	.86
Customer conversion ratios				
$\frac{\text{Patronize currently}}{\text{Ever patronized}}$	.80	.88	.91	.77
$\frac{\text{Patronize most often}}{\text{Ever patronized}}$	.10	.25	.26	.24

Exhibit 10 *(concluded)*

In Indianapolis, trial and customer conversion ratios are high, relative to competitors. However, Jolly Ox has a higher conversion ratio for "patronize most often." Given the even sales trend of this unit, the strategy offering the best leverage would be to increase total awareness and maintain or improve the existing favorable levels of repeat patronage.

Trial and Customer Conversion Ratios of Victoria Station and Competitors—Indianapolis

	Victoria Station	Jolly Ox	Friday's	Cork'n Cleaver
Trial ratio				
Ever patronized / Total awareness	.59	.55	.57	.53
Customer conversion ratios				
Patronize currently / Ever patronized	.81	.82	.75	.76
Patronize most often / Ever patronized	.19	.27	.16	.18

The Alhambra State Bank

The Alhambra State Bank, located in a medium-sized metropolitan area in the Northwest, was founded in 1923. The bank was situated downtown in modernized facilities with ample parking space nearby. Alhambra had prospered throughout most of its history and, over the years, had developed a conservative image. The bank served primarily individuals and commercial accounts, rather than industrial accounts. This distribution of accounts had occurred largely because of the area's history. Originally an agricultural community, the area became somewhat industrialized during the immediately following World War II. There were, however, only a few large industrial firms in the area, and these were concerned mainly with the processing of forest products. Further, the headquarters of such activities were located elsewhere, and their financial needs were not serviced locally.

In the late 1960s, the bank came under new management. An evaluation of profitability at that time revealed that on relative basis the bank was not performing satisfactorily. Consequently, a five-year plan of action was instituted to improve earnings. Major elements in the plan consisted of modernizing the bank interior, adding more parking space, increasing advertising expenditures, training personnel to be better "salespeople," and increasing small loans by adopting less stringent standards.

A statement of corporate purpose was part of this plan and read as follows:

> We want our bank to be the quality leader in our area. We will raise our banking standards and support and participate in the area's growth. As a result, our bank should be exceptionally profitable.
>
> Quality is a result of talent, and we want our bank to attract top-caliber people. We want a working environment where performance is the main criterion for advancement. To be successful, we must build on

This case was written by Eric E. Abell and Charles M. Johnson. © 1978 by the Board of Trustees of the Leland Stanford Junior University.

the talent we now have and attract top-caliber people to all levels of our organization. To all our people, we must offer an unusual opportunity for growth in career and growth in income.

We must recognize that we cannot be all things to all people. We must be selective in choosing the customers and customer groups we serve. We cannot serve an uneconomic customer professionally, and our best work will be done with our best customers. Thus, we should not spread ourselves too thinly but rather concentrate our resources—human and capital—on those customers and customer groups that we particularly want to serve. This will take time, but given time, we can develop customers that truly establish our position of leadership.

In short, we don't want to be the biggest bank in the state, just the best.

During the early to mid-1970s, the bank's total deposits grew more rapidly than those of its major competitors. The compounded annual growth rate in total deposits was 20.9 percent for this period, but earnings failed to keep pace—primarily because of a disappointing growth in demand deposits, which grew only 6.7 percent annually. Overall profits were extremely sensitive to demand deposit growth due primarily to the fact that a bank had to pay interest on time deposits, but not on demand deposits. On the other hand, reserve requirements were higher for demand deposits (13 percent) than for time deposits (6 percent).

During the same period, savings deposit growth totaled only $2.2 million, while the increase in certificates of deposit amounted to $14.2 million. Alhambra paid the same rate of interest as did the other banks in the area on its savings passbook accounts. Its recent average rate for certificates of deposit (a highly competitive market) was nearly 9 percent. The average return on assets amounted to only 0.77 percent. Return on capital was considered "good" (15.5 percent), but only because of the bank's relatively low capitalization. Returns on loans and investments had, however, been quite exceptional. The performance of Alhambra and major competitors on these items is shown in Exhibit 1.

Exhibit 1
Return on Assets, Loans, and Investments of Alhambra Bank and Major Competitors.

	Return (percent)			
	Assets*	Capital†	Loans‡	Investments§
Alhambra	0.77	15.5	10.1	5.5
First National	1.03	19.6	9.7	4.3
Northwest National	0.98	13.6	9.4	3.8
Pacific State	0.79	13.1	8.7	4.6

* Profit after tax divided by total assets.
† Profit after tax divided by end of year capital, excluding loan reserves.
‡ Interest income before tax on loans, divided by total loans.
§ Income before tax on investments (securities) divided by total investments.

Alhambra's loan-deposit ratio was 56 percent, which was less than their competitors. (See table.) Alhambra was also leveraged at 21 : 1 (the maximum permitted by regulatory authorities was 26 : 1).

	Loan-deposit ratio*	Leverage†
Alhambra	56%	21 : 1
First National	69	18 : 1
Northwest National	60	16 : 1
Pacific State	62	19 : 1

* Total loans divided by total deposits.
† Liabilities divided by capital accounts.

High personnel and "other" expenses had overshadowed this performance. Alhambra's head count (employees per $1 million of deposits) was the highest of any of the four leading banks; further, its loan losses as a percent of operating income were the largest. The expense profile of Alhambra and its leading competitors is shown in Exhibit 2.

Exhibit 2
Expense Profile

	Alhambra	First National	Northwest National	Pacific State
Operating expense	9.4%	14.6%	14.8%	12.2%
Taxes	2.2	7.8	1.0	5.0
Interest	27.4	27.2	29.2	25.4
Personnel	32.4	29.2	31.5	33.9
Loan losses	4.0	3.8	1.5	3.3
Net occupancy costs	7.0	2.7	4.7	7.3
Other expenses*	17.6	14.7	17.3	12.9
Total	100.0%	100.0%	100.0%	100.0%

* Includes depreciation and rent.

A factor of concern to the officers of Alhambra was the bank's dependence on time deposits which, if continued, would result in higher interest rates in the future. Data for the past year covering Alhambra and its competitors are shown in Exhibit 3.

Exhibit 3
Demand and Time Deposits as a Percent of Total Deposits

	Demand	Time	Demand deposit growth*
Alhambra	37%	65%	6.7%
First National	41	59	10.8
Northwest National	41	59	12.5
Pacific State	43	57	20.6

* Compound annual growth rate past 3 years.

No major bank in the area had shown a significant deposit market share increase in the past several years. Alhambra's share had increased only slightly, and its overall share was low when compared to First National and Northwest National. Share data are shown in Exhibit 4.

Exhibit 4
Share of Market for Alhambra and Leading Competitors by Total and Demand Deposits

	Share	
	Total deposits	**Demand deposits**
Alhambra	8.5%	8.5%
First National	24.7	25.9
Northwest National	30.7	33.1
Pacific State	7.5	9.2
All other	28.6	23.3

In its efforts to find ways to develop and maintain a strong customer group orientation, the bank commissioned a study of the impact of various customer groups on overall bank profitability. Exhibit 5 shows the funds used and supplied by some 11 customer segments as of June 30 of the present year. The data were obtained from a sampling of the bank's deposit and loan accounts, and the results were projected to the June 30 balance sheet. Customer segments were identified by bank officials.

The analysis of funds used and supplied was relatively straightforward. Total loans outstanding represented simply the amount the bank had lent to individuals comprising the segment. The total deposits of this group were obtained by tracing the individuals' checking, savings, and other accounts to determine the amount on deposit by type of deposit. The amount the bank was required to hold "on reserve" was then deducted from the total of each type of deposit. At that time, the bank's net demand reserve requirement was 13 percent, for savings 3 percent, and for other time deposits 6 percent.

The data contained in the column headed "net funds supplied" represented the difference between a segment's outstanding loans and the amount on deposit less the amount required for reserves. Individuals, dealers, and home builders were the largest "cash consumers," in the sense that they required the largest net funds. High-asset individuals, public organizations, and nonprofit groups were the largest cash contributors in that their total deposits (less reserves) far exceeded their outstanding loans.

Next, a profitability analysis was made of each segment. First, the total income for the segment was estimated. Interest received from the

Exhibit 5
Funds Used as of June 30 (annualized)*

Customer segment	Total loans outstanding ($000)	Total deposits (less reserves) ($000)				Net funds supplied ($000)
		Demand	Savings	Time deposits	Total	
1. Individuals	$ 6,445	$ 2,505	$1,579	$ 131	$ 4,215	$ (2,230)
2. High-asset individuals	855	794	1,515	984	3,293	2,438
3. Retail/wholesale	1,982	1,623	79	299	2,001	19
4. Dealers†	2,923	131	20	30	181	(2,742)
5. General contractors	1,789	857	40	96	993	(596)
6. Home builders‡	3,366	179	27	11	117	(3,149)
7. Public organizations	—	1,918	53	14,953	16,924	16,924
8. Professional firms	219	606	58	29	693	474
9. Nonprofit groups	722	1,397	421	398	2,216	1,494
10. Petroleum companies	131	153	—	236	389	258
11. Financial institutions	638	715	68	91	874	236
12. Other	2,152	1,299	391	642	2,372	220
Total	$21,222	$12,177	$4,251	$17,900	$34,268	$13,346

* Based on sample of deposit and loan accounts, and expanded to June 30 balance sheet.
† Includes all mobile homes and auto dealers, and accounts of individuals carrying indirect loans.
‡ Includes FHA loans and savings, as well as accounts of individuals carrying FHA loans.

Exhibit 6
Profitability of Customer Segments of Alhambra State Bank—June 30 (annualized)*

Customer segment	Net funds supplied ($000)	Total income ($000)		Interest paid	Charge for funds	Salary and other expenses	Net contributions ($000)
		Interest and service charges	Credit for funds				
1. Individuals	$(2,230)×9% $789	$ 789	—	$ 78	$201	$ 948	$(438)
2. High-asset individuals	2,438	97	$ 220	136	—	45	136
3. Retail/wholesale companies	19	219	13	25	11	103	93
4. Dealers†	(2,742)	281	—	2	247	51	(19)
5. General contractors	(596)	168	—	8	54	64	42
6. Home builders‡	(3,149)	451	1	2	285	65	100
7. Public organizations	16,924	20	1,523	1,335	—	30	178
8. Professional firms	474	29	43	5	—	39	28
9. Nonprofit groups	1,494	97	134	47	—	35	149
10. Petroleum companies	258	16	23	17	—	63	(41)
11. Financial institutions	236	72	35	9	13	35	48
12. Other	220	233	29	66	9	60	127
Total	$13,346	$2,472	$2,021	$1,730	$820	$1,538	$ 403

*Based on sample of deposit and loan accounts, and projected to June 30 balance sheet.
†Includes all mobile homes and automobile dealers, and accounts of individuals carrying indirect loans.
‡Includes FHA loans and earnings, as well as accounts of individuals carrying FHA loans.

[handwritten annotations: "negative contributors costing bank" near Net contributions column; arrow pointing to $201 in Charge for funds column; "$(2,230)×9%" next to Individuals Net funds supplied] service charges paid by segment members were determined from bank records. The "credit" for funds necessitated assigning a monetary value to a segment's "net funds supplied." The same was true in reverse in determining the expenses of a segment; i.e., if a segment was a net borrower, then a value had to be assigned to the "deficit."

Thus, it was necessary to assign a transfer price to either the "surplus" or the "deficit" of each segment. The analyst responsible for the profitability study had the option of using a cost- or market-oriented transfer price. He computed his cost of funds at five percent, by dividing his interest paid on deposits by net deposits available after reserve requirements. He chose the market price, however, because he reasoned that since the bank was trying to attract deposits, the market price was more appropriate. As his "rate," he selected the Federal Funds rate. This figure was the amount charged by one bank lending another bank money on a one-day basis. This was a common practice for banks, and for the time period involved the rate ranged from 6 percent to 10 percent; the analyst used the current price, which approximated 9 percent. The profitability analyses by customer segment is shown in Exhibit 6.

Salary and related expenses for each segment were determined on both a direct and indirect basis. First, the analyst allocated all those expenses directly involved with the applicable segment. Thus, certain personnel worked exclusively with selected groups. This was especially true with the real estate and car dealer segments. The remaining expenses were allocated by a variety of methods that were considered satisfactory by all concerned.

The analyst also studied a number of factors relating to various customer groups. The purpose of these studies was to add additional insights into the profitability of each group. The results of these studies are summarized below:

1. **Speed of Customer Service.** A survey taken revealed that Alhambra's services (judged on the basis of the number of people waiting per teller window) were superior to their competitors.
2. **Average Size Checking Account.** From a recent FDIC *Biennial Call Report*, it was determined that Alhambra's average size checking account under $1,000 was $255, versus a combined average of $279 for the two larger banks in the area.
3. **Area Economic Forecast.** The population of the area was expected to grow from a present size of 315,000 to 378,000 over the next five years. Total personal income for this same period was forecast to grow from $1.13 billion to $2.7 billion and average personal income from $4,035 to $6,556.
4. **Impact of FHA Loans on Deposits.** From a sample of 50 Federal Housing Administration loans made during the past six months, it

appeared that such loans to noncustomers did not result in new deposit accounts.

5. **Impact of Installment Loans on Deposits.** From a sample of 95 currently outstanding installment loans made during the past six months, it appeared that such loans to noncustomers did not result in new deposit accounts.

6. **Comparison of Alhambra's Ratios to Those of Two Largest Competitors.** From the most recent FDIC *Biennial Call Report* and the *ASB Summary of Deposits Report*, the following was determined:

	Two largest competitors combined	Alhambra	Ratio
Total number of deposit accounts............	116,307	19,804	5.87
Total deposits ($000,000)	244.4	37.5	6.52
Total number of savings accounts $1,000–$100,000	9,410	717	13.12
Total dollars ($000,000) in savings accounts $1,000–$100,000	45.0	3.01	15.0
Average account size	$4,780	$4,198	

If Alhambra could maintain the same ratio of savings deposits between $1,000 and $100,000 to total deposits as the other two banks, then its aftertax profits would increase by $82,500—or 28 percent.

7. **Analysis of High-Asset Individuals.** From an analysis of 217 high-asset individuals with either a checking or savings account, only 25 percent had both types of accounts. Such individuals were "arbitrarily" defined as ones having $1,000 in checking and/or an average savings account balance of $2,500.

8. **Distribution of Gross Receipts by Type of Activity.** The most recent report showing the distribution of gross receipts by industry type for the entire state was as follows:

Industry	Percent of total gross receipts
a. Retail/wholesale..................................	39.9%
b. Construction.....................................	15.2
c. Finance and real estate...........................	10.8
d. Transportation, communications and utilities............	9.8
e. Manufacturing....................................	9.4
f. Service	3.8
g. Petroleum	3.4
h. Agriculture and forestry...........................	2.4
i. Other...	5.3
Total	100.0%

9. **Impact of Automobile Loans.** A sample of automobile loans revealed that out of 49 "customers," some 25 had deposit accounts, with the average-size account totaling about $300.

The organization of the Alhambra State Bank was relatively traditional and was essentially organized around functional activities. At one time or another, bank officials had discussed a variety of organizational changes. The president felt that the present organization was too functionally oriented and that not enough attention was being paid to different customer groups. As an example of his thinking on this subject, he pointed out that organizing around the credit function (e.g., loan officers) led to a neglect of the bank's more profitable groups—i.e., those large depositors with minimal credit needs, such as high-asset individuals and public organizations. He felt that by organizing responsibilities for similar accounts to some one person or group within the bank, it would be possible to develop a better understanding of a customer group's unique financial needs.

Other bank officials were not so certain that such an organizational change would be productive, especially if it were not recognized that a whole new way of "running the business" was involved. As one manager said, "It's one thing to talk about organizing around customer groups, but quite another to talk about how we proceed to develop target accounts, set up marketing plans, coordinate and control our overall marketing efforts, and reward our lower-level managers on the basis of some profitability measure. I see a whole new management philosophy unfolding, and it's hard for me to see at this time what kind of an organizational structure we should have in order to articulate and implement this philosophy."

At a meeting of the executive group (composed of the chairman, president, manager of administration, and manager of operations), the data on overall bank profitability, customer segments, profitability of individual segments, and various related data were reviewed in depth with the analyst. In addition, the subject of organization change was discussed briefly. At the conclusion of the meeting, it was decided that the bank should attempt to state what it hoped to accomplish over the next five years. It was argued by the president that the basic issue was one of setting market share targets. He believed that the bank should seek to increase its market share of demand and time deposits to 11.5 over the next five years. He admitted that this target might not be realistic, but that the group had to "start somewhere." At this point, the meeting was adjourned with the request from the chairman that they reassemble a week hence and be prepared to talk specifically about *how* they would attempt to obtain this market share objective, what its attainment might mean from a profit point of view, and what the organizational implications would be.

The Weisman Bottling Company

The Weisman Bottling Company, located in a large midwestern metropolitan area of nearly 2 million people, produced and marketed a line of carbonated beverages consisting mainly of flavored soft drinks, soda water, and tonics. These were sold in a number of different container types and sizes to a wide variety of retail and commercial outlets. In 1974, total company sales were about $3 million.

The company was founded in 1924 by Solomon Weisman and had remained in the family ever since. In 1975 Eli Weisman, the grandson of the founder, succeeded to the presidency upon the death of his father. He had recently completed an evening MBA program at one of the local universities and was anxious to apply what he termed "the newer and more sophisticated management concepts and techniques" to a tradition-oriented firm operating in an increasingly complex and dynamic industry. In particular, he wanted to develop a strategic plan for his company. He planned to accomplish this by working with his sales manager, Gerry Stires, and his controller, Irving Tass. Both had served under his father for many years in similar capacities.

The company's marketing area consisted essentially of the metropolitan area which in 1972 numbered 1.8 million. Since 1960 the area had experienced a 20 percent population increase, and while the growth rate was slowing, the area was expected to increase to 2.1 million by 1980. As one of the leading areas in the Midwest, it generated over $6 billion in personal income and had retail sales of $3.8 billion in 1970. Its citizens were, on the average, better educated than for the United States as a whole. Median household income was also higher. Within the area there were 2 major universities, 3 four-year colleges, 7 junior colleges, 80 high schools, and over 300 elementary schools.

The company faced strong competition within its marketing area. Both the Coca-Cola and Pepsi Cola franchises were large and aggressive units. Mr. Weisman pointed out, however, that while they dominated the cola market—both for the regular and diet products—they by no means dominated the flavor market. Part of the reason for this, he said, was because of their understandable preoccupation with cola which trade sources estimated accounted for some two thirds of the market expressed in cases. On a dollar basis the cola share was even higher because of the predominance of national brands. The flavor market, on the other hand, tended to be dominated by local bottlers who competed mainly on a price basis. Private labels were considerably more important in flavors than in cola.

Thus, the company faced strong competition which took a variety of forms including local bottlers who also held a national franchise such as 7 Up, Squirt, and a nationally advertised brand of ginger ale. At one time or another, the Weisman Company had been offered a franchise for a nationally advertised noncola soft drink. These had been rejected because the company felt acceptance would constrain the way the business was run. Eli Weisman felt that in retrospect such a policy had been a mistake but noted that there were at present no opportunities to pick up a "good" franchise.

Industry competition centered around an ever-increasing array of container types and sizes, merchandising "deals" (mostly in "cents-off"), media advertising, and "in-store" activities. Distribution was becoming of major importance because of the growing policy of most outlets to carry only one brand of flavored soft drinks. Often the "one line" was the store's private label. Some large outlets carried two flavor lines—a nationally advertised brand (e.g., those offered by Coke and Pepsi) and a local or private label brand. Eli Weisman stated that while his product was equal in quality to any other brand in the market he was forced to price some 20 percent lower than the national brands "simply because we don't have the name." In general the company maintained a price parity policy with respect to its local competition.

The company produced a line of 10 flavors which was bottled in the same type and size containers used by competitors. Thus, the company packaged its product in glass and disposable bottles and cans. It sold its 12-ounce product in both glass and cans, its 16-ounce in glass, and its 32-ounce in a nonreturnable bottle with a screw cap.

The company had traditionally set aside seven cents per case for advertising, merchandising, and driver-salesmen incentives. Most of this amount was spent on in-store, cents-off promotions. Some had gone for incentives to the sales force for opening new accounts and building in-store displays. Rarely did the company spend any monies in media advertising nor did the company allocate funds for the purchase of vending machines or fountain equipment. These two market segments tended to be dominated by the large national brand franchises.

About 90 percent of the company's sales derived from take-home sales through retailers and on-site cold bottle consumption. Of these sales, private labels accounted for 18 percent. Syrup sales to a number of route vending companies accounted for the remaining 10 percent. An average of 10 truck routes serviced approximately 3,500 accounts of which some 15 percent accounted for about 50 percent of total cases sold. The number of routes and accounts varied according to the season of the year. During the summer, extra routes were added to service a substantial number of small accounts which were open only during the summer months or which added a line of soft drinks for the "season."

In thinking through the procedures to follow in preparing a strategic plan, Mr. Weisman decided that the first step should consist of obtaining trend data on the company's share of the market. Company total case sales had remained relatively static for quite some time, but there had been a change in the mix; e.g., sales of the 12-ounce cases were declining while sales of the 32-ounce cases were increasing. Even so, given the population growth of the area over recent years, it seemed clear that the company had lost share.

In order to determine market share trends, Mr. Weisman had the company's case sales by package size and type tabulated for 1969 and 1974 (the last complete year on which such data were available). He had wanted to go back to 1960, but the type and size packages had shifted to such an extent that he felt they would obscure the trend analysis. Since 1969 the company's product line had remained stable. In his case sale tabulations, he excluded soda water and tonics but included syrups (on a case equivalent basis) and his private label "business." Although costs varied slightly by flavor type, he decided not to break them out separately since he reasoned that he could do little to change the sale of any specific one.

The next step was to convert his raw case sales for the two years into case equivalents of 24 units of 8 ounces each, which was the way the trade reported its sales data. Following this, he determined what were his dollar marginal contributions per case equivalents.[1] (The results of this analysis are in Exhibit 1.) In 1969, his per case marginal contribution was 45.3, and in 1974 it was 46.9 cents. While this change represented an increase, Mr. Weisman noted that his expenses had increased at a higher rate because of the rapid inflation which had

---

[1] Marginal contribution was defined as factory price less direct (variable) costs which included plant labor, ingredients, breakage, and container costs.

Exhibit 1

Case Sales, Revenues, and Marginal Contributions by Product Item, 1969 and 1974 (includes private label and syrup but not soda and tonic)

Package	Marginal contributions (MC)*	Sales price*	Case sales	Total MC	Total sales	Case equivalents*
1969:						
12-ounce (returnable)	$0.89	$1.75	130,450	$116,100	$ 228,287	195,675
12-ounce (can)	0.85	2.50	182,910	155,473	457,275	274,365
16-ounce (returnable)	0.88	2.00	69,680	61,318	139,360	139,360
32-ounce (not returnable)	0.79	2.50	487,760	385,330	1,219,400	975,250
Total			870,800	$718,221	$2,044,322	1,584,920
1974:						
12-ounce (returnable)	$0.95	$2.30	110,500	$104,975	$ 254,150	165,750
12-ounce (can)	0.90	3.00	206,600	185,940	619,800	309,900
16-ounce (returnable)	0.93	2.65	48,800	45,384	129,320	97,600
32-ounce (not returnable)	0.83	3.05	531,700	441,311	1,621,690	1,063,400
Total			897,600	$777,610	$2,624,960	1,636,650

Note: Syrup sales converted into 12-ounce units and included in 12-ounce (returnable) data for 1969 and 1974.

* Per case. All package sizes come in cases of 24 units except the 32-ounce which comes in cases of 12 (case equivalents are 24 units of 8 ounces each). The price per case is that of Weisman to the trade at year's end as is the per case marginal contribution. Marginal contribution is sales price less direct costs such as labor, ingredients, breakage, and container.

taken place during this period. In any event his profits before taxes over this period had declined despite higher turnover.

Following this analysis, he calculated the area's population growth for the period 1969 to 74. In the future, population growth was expected to slow substantially. Some demographic changes had occurred favoring the younger age groups which were the heaviest consumers of soft drinks.

The area's per capita consumption of all soft drinks was estimated by a reliable trade source as being 275 8-ounce equivalents in 1969 and 331 in 1974. Of these amounts, cola and diet drinks (which were dominated by the cola flavor) were estimated to account for some 68 percent. Vending sales were estimated at between 10 and 12 percent of total sales, while fountain sales were estimated at 16 percent. Mr. Weisman thought these percentages had remained relatively constant between 1969 and 1974. In attempting to get an estimate of his relevant market, he figured the annual per capita consumption of his product to be 74 8-ounce units in 1969 and 89 in 1974.[2] He next calculated total industry sales of his company's product line in 8-ounce equivalent cases of 24 units each and obtained the following:

Year	Population	Per capita (flavors) 8-ounce units	Total market equivalent case sales
1969	1,680,000	74	5,180,000
1974	1,921,000	89	7,458,000

Since company equivalent cases were 1,584,920 in 1969 and 1,636,650 in 1974, market share had dropped from 30.5 percent to 21.8 percent. In discussing these data with his controller and sales manager, the latter pointed out that the loss should also be interpreted in light of a change in industry structure. Two small bottling companies selling about 10 percent of the flavor market had gone out of business during the past two years thereby reducing the number of competitors to a total of six. Mr. Weisman estimated that Coke and Pepsi together

---

[2] These figures were obtained by reducing the total per caps by the amount represented by cola and diet drinks (68 percent) and by fountain drinks (16 percent). The latter, however, had to be adjusted for the amount of cola and diet product sold by fountains; thus, the fountain per caps were reduced from 16 percent to 5.1 percent (68% × 16% = 10.88% and 16% − 10.88% = 5.12%). Thus, the "relevant" market was estimated at 26.9 percent of the total per caps for 1969 and 1974. No adjustment was made for vend sales since the company sold syrup into that market. Although colas were an important seller here, it was not known what share they represented. Mr. Weisman knew that by not adjusting for such sales his relevant market figure was somewhat inflated—perhaps by as much as 6 to 7 percent.

accounted for about 20 percent of the total flavor market, that two other competitors each held about 10 to 12 share points, and the largest seller accounted for about a third of the market. In the opinion of the sales manager, it was this latter company which had benefited most from Weisman's loss in share.

In the near term, Mr. Weisman was pessimistic about prices and costs. He felt that competition would continue to force price adjustments to lag increased costs. In particular he was concerned about the rapid increase which was occurring in connection with delivery costs. His plant was relatively new and could handle up to 25 percent more sales. He knew, however, that the largest competitor had recently installed a high-speed packaging line which probably reduced marginal per case costs by about two cents.

It seemed clear to Mr. Weisman that he must attempt to strategize in ways which would impact on volume. He expected some "help" from the area's increased population growth, coupled with an increase in per capita consumption of perhaps as much as 3 percent a year. But he felt that he must seek ways to grow shares. He thought that the private label business—now estimated at 25 percent of the take-home flavor market—would increase only slightly. He noted that his major competitor was actively seeking such business at prices below those Weisman was quoting.

The three men next turned their attention to the area's store population and the company's accounts. The sales manager had recently put together some information which showed that there were just under 11,000 retail outlets handling soft drinks in the company's marketing area. Of these, some 312 were supermarkets, 588 were convenience stores, 712 were small food outlets, and 9,245 were "all other" units. The latter included such outlet types as bars, restaurants, filling stations, discount stores, and liquor stores. Based on an analyses of Weisman accounts, it was thought that the company had the following distribution by type of outlet:

Supermarkets*	18%
Convenience	16
All other food	23
All other	24

* Includes private label. Six supermarket chains accounted for more than half of all supermarket units in the area and about two thirds of the dollar sales of such outlets.

The sales manager had located a recent study made by a local newspaper which indicated that supermarkets accounted for about 35 percent of all bottled soft drinks being sold, that convenience and all other food stores sold 20 percent of the total, and that all other units sold the remainder.

Given the above data, Mr. Weisman instructed his two associates to prepare for a meeting in the near future at which time they would further discuss and, hopefully, come to an agreement on what should be the company's future strategy. Mr. Weisman noted that he hoped each would be as specific as possible in recommending what strategies to adopt and that he expected them to be able to support their recommendation with as much documentation as possible.

The Needlework Company (A)

The Needlework Company was founded in early 1971 as a publisher of instructional leaflets for the needlework trade. Soon afterwards, the company also began to distribute books of other publishers in addition to certain supplies (e.g., yarn and fabrics) as well as tools and accessories (e.g., scissors, hoops, and needles). After a modest beginning, company sales and profits experienced rapid growth—particularly for the period 1979–81 (see Exhibit 1 for the company's income statement for this period). In late 1981, the company hired a new marketing manager, Robert Fisher, who, in addition to his other duties, was assigned the responsibility for preparing the company's first strategic plan.

The needlework skills which the company targeted with respect to its line of instruction leaflets were quite varied. The more popular ones included counted cross stitch, crewel, crocheting, cross stitch, embroidery, knitting, needlepoint, preworked needlepoint, and stamped cross stitch. Exhibit 2 provides a glossary of these terms.

The company's goal or mission was "to become the dominant supplier of noncommodity products to the U.S. needlework industry."[1] To accomplish this, the company felt it must provide the retail trade with a full line of products including both proprietary (own label) or jobbed items. The former could be manufactured by the company or produced to specifications by an outside source. In the case of jobbed items, the company simply served as a distributor.

To date, the company had produced over 300 leaflets (instructional manuals). The production process starts with a design prototype (the end-use product) usually submitted by a freelance designer. If accepted by the company's product management staff, it is then placed in production, which involves reworking the instructions that accompany

---

[1] The biggest commodity type product (in sales) was acrylic yarn, which was purchased by fiber specification and color—rarely by brand name.

Exhibit 1
Company Sales and Profits, 1972–1981 ($000)

Year	Net sales	Cost goods sold	Gross profit	Expenses	Profit Before tax	After tax
1972	$ 166	$ 113	$ 53	$ 97	$ (44)	—
1973	648	431	217	240	(33)	—
1974	1,352	814	538	495	43	$ 41
1975	3,087	1,627	1,460	1,117	343	202
1976	3,981	1,913	2,068	1,638	430	239
1977	4,430	2,088	2,342	1,823	519	281
1978	6,097	2,814	3,283	2,360	923	481
1979	8,406	4,110	4,296	2,992	1,304	702
1980	14,250	7,330	6,920	4,753	2,167	1,187
1981*	28,393	14,605	13,788	9,048	4,740	2,494

* Estimated

Exhibit 2
Glossary of Needlework Terms

Counted cross stitch: A form of cross stitch embroidery worked on an unmarked even-weave fabric base using a coded design chart to determine color changes. The size of the finished embroidery is defined by the number of threads per square inch of the fabric and the "stitch count" of the charted design. Commonly used materials are embroidery floss and Aida cloth.

Crewel: Surface embroidery worked with wool or wool-like yarn.

Crocheting: The creation of an interlocking fabric by using yarn and a single hooked tool.

Cross stitch: Simple embroidery form whereby two stitches of the same length are used creating an x when complete.

Embroidery: Fabric decoration created with a needle and thread. Distinctive from sewing in that the primary purpose is embellishment rather than joining.

Knitting: The creation of an interlocking fabric by using yarn and two needles.

Needlepoint: An embroidery form utilizing yarn on an openweave mesh canvas base to create a very durable fabric.

Plastic canvas: A needlepoint canvas, usually seven mesh (threads per inch) molded from a plastic material rather than woven on a loom. The canvas is stable yet flexible making it easy to create three-dimensional projects.

Preworked needlepoint: A partially completed canvas on which the design has been embroidered, but the background has not. Most commonly used for furniture pieces such as chair seats. Also known as prefinished or preembroidered needlepoint.

Stamped cross stitch: A form of cross stitch embroidery in which the design is pre-printed on the fabric surface.

Surface stitchery: Any of a variety of embroidery techniques used to embellish a fabric and/or canvas base by drawing a needle threaded with yarn through the base.

the prototype, testing them, and designing the leaflet cover and interior in terms of graphics and color. The last step is the actual printing which is done by a large local printer.

Shortly after its founding, the company began to job floss, fabrics, and a variety of tools and accessories. By the end of fiscal year 1981, the company had in excess of 5,000 stockkeeping units, all of which were warehoused in a single location. Recently, the company began to produce and market kits. The basic difference between an instructional leaflet and a kit, according to Mr. Fisher, "is that the customer buys all the material needed to accomplish the pattern while, with kits, all the materials are already assembled." The kits contained plastic needlepoint canvas as opposed to the more traditional cotton canvas. Different lines of kits were made for chains and the specialty store trade. Kit lines were produced for the fall and spring seasons as well as for Christmas. The distribution of company sales by product line for the year 1980–81 is shown in Exhibit 3. As might be expected, margins varied

Exhibit 3
Sales of Major Lines Carried, 1980 versus 1981 ($000)

	1980	1981
Proprietary: ~ own label		
1. Leaflets/books..................	$ 5,962	$ 8,989
2. Plastic canvas kits	657	4,653
Subtotal	6,619	13,642
Jobbed/distributed:		
1. Leaflets/books..................	$ 3,080	$ 5,681
2. Thread/floss	2,595	5,206
3. Fabric	805	1,882
4. Needles......................	445	843
5. Tools/accessories.............	706	1,139
Subtotal	7,631	14,751
Net Sales........................	$14,250	$28,393

substantially with proprietary products (leaflets and kits) averaging substantially above 50 percent versus 30 percent for jobbed items.

The company sold its product line to about 14,500 needlework specialty shops (called the regular trade) and about 75 chain organizations—all located in the United States.[2] The company sold only its proprietary lines (leaflets and kits) to the chains.

The Market

The company's end-user market consisted of women and a relatively small number of men who knit/crochet and/or do surface stitchery. In 1981, the company commissioned a telephone survey of some 2,300 households distributed randomly throughout the United States. Its purpose was to provide quantitative data at the consumer/house-

---

[2] The company also sold a relatively small amount to large Canadian distributors.

hold level which could be used as a check on industry sales estimates provided by the trade. In addition, it provided company management with certain demographic information about those individuals who were interested in the various needlework skill areas. Exhibit 4 contains a summary of the findings obtained from this research.

Exhibit 4
Market Research Survey

In 1981, the company commissioned a telephone survey of 2,300 households distributed randomly throughout the United States. Its purpose was to provide quantitative data at the consumer level which could be used as a further check on the industry estimates provided by the trade. The major findings from this study are as follows:

1. Some 36 percent of all U.S. households (77 million) had one or more individuals who had knitted, crocheted, done needlepoint, or cross stitch during the past 12 months. This totaled 28 million households; of the individuals involved, 92 percent were female and 8 percent were male.
2. About half of the adult females who practiced some sort of needlework during the past 12 months also practiced other needlework-related skills such as crewel and embroidery.
3. Of the 28 million practicing households, 28.2 percent had someone who had knitted/crocheted, 16.1 percent had someone who had done needlepoint, and 9 percent had someone who did counted cross stitching.
4. The demographics of those who have practiced some kind of needlework skill during the past 12 months are summarized as follows:
    a. 92 percent were female, and 12 percent were under 18 years of age.
    b. 8 percent were males, and nearly half (48 percent) were under 18 years.
    c. The median age of females practicing knit/crochet was 45 years versus 38 years for needlepoint and 36 for counted cross stitch.
    d. There was considerable variation of needlework skill by region of the country with knit/crochet highest in the West North Central region, needlepoint in the South Atlantic, and counted cross stitch in both of these regions.
    e. 42 percent had some college or were college graduates versus 34 percent for the total population.
    f. The median income was $17,280 versus $15,150 for the total population.
5. The sources used most often for instructions/designs were:

| | Those practicing: | | |
Source	Knit/crochet	Needlepoint	Counted cross stitch
Leaflets/booklets	32.2%	10.6%	31.0%
Magazines	18.6	6.9	8.8
Hard/soft-cover books	9.5	8.5	7.1
Complete kits	7.7	42.4	36.6
Did own design	2.8	11.2	3.1
Other person	11.8	0.6	4.1
Other	2.8	—	3.6

Exhibit 4 (*continued*)

6. The usual supply source for instructions/designs was:

	Those practicing:		
Source	Knit/crochet	Needlepoint	Counted cross stitch
Specialty stores .... (regular trade including department stores)	52.7%	77.8%	84.1%
Chains......................	47.3	22.1	15.9

7. The usual supply source for yarn/thread was:

	Those practicing:		
Source	Knit/crochet	Needlepoint	Counted cross stitch
Specialty stores .... (regular trade)	40.1%	72.6%	63.2%
Chains......................	59.9	27.4	36.8

8. The usual supply source for needles/hooks was:

	Those practicing:		
Source	Knit/crochet	Needlepoint	Counted cross stitch
Specialty stores .... (regular trade)	39.1%	67.2%	N/A
Chains......................	60.9	32.8	N/A

9. The usual supply source for complete kits was:

	Those practicing:		
Source	Knit/crochet	Needlepoint	Counted cross stitch
Specialty stores .... (regular trade)	69.0%	78.4%	81.9%
Chains......................	31.0	21.6	18.1

10. Twice as many females crochet than knit.
11. Knitters and crocheters made the following items during the past 12 months:

	Knitters			Crocheters		
Item made	Percent	Number of items*	Cost*	Percent	Number of items*	Cost*
Sweaters	63	2	$21.00	9.3	2	$15.00
Afghans/quilts/ blankets	33	2	23.00	65.0	2	25.00
Baby items	18	5	16.00	16.0	4	14.00
Hats/caps/scarves...	17	4	8.00	9.8	3	4.00
Mittens............	8	4	4.00	.5	1	2.00
Pillows/pillow covers	6	4	6.00	12.0	3	8.00
Slippers...........	10	5	9.00	6.0	5	10.00
Toys..............	3	6	6.00	6.0	5	7.00
Vests	3	1	6.00	2.0	3	7.00

* Average number of items made and average cost of materials used.

Exhibit 4 (*continued*)

12. The major sources of design/instructions for knitters and crocheters were as follows:

Source	Ever used	Used most often	Most enjoy
Subscription or newsstand needlework magazine	44.7%	17.3%	18.1%
Instructional leaflet	62.4	31.3	27.9
Hard/soft-cover books	26.5	9.3	8.8
Complete kits	33.2	7.5	7.1
Other magazines	2.7	0.9	1.8
Other person	15.5	11.5	10.2
Made myself	4.9	2.7	3.1
Other	3.1	2.7	1.8
Don't know	14.6	16.0	21.0

13. The best known knit/crochet leaflets were those published by the yarn companies. The awareness of the company's name among knitters/crocheters was as follows:

Leaflets published by*	Leaflets on hand	Leaflet companies that come to mind (unaided)	Total awareness (unaided and aided)
Needlework Company	3.1%	1.8%	27.0%
Coats/Clark	8.8	12.8	83.6
Columbia-Minerva	7.5	4.4	48.2
Bernat	6.2	7.1	43.4
Brunswick	1.3	2.2	53.5

* All but the Needlework Company are basically yarn companies which prepare and sell leaflets as a way of promoting their brand of acrylic yarn. The company does not sell such yarn because it is basically a commodity product sold by the yarn companies either direct or through distributors.

14. Over the next year, the level of knitting/crocheting activities was expected to increase. The figures below do not take into account those who will enter the market.

Expected activity in next year:	
Will do more	27.2%
Will do less	15.6
Will do same	54.7

15. Pictures and wall hangings are the most popular needlepoint projects at an average cost of $15.

Item made	Percent making	Number of items*	Material costs per item*
Pictures/wall hangings	52.7%	2	$15.00
Pillows/pillow coverings	32.3	2	19.00
Chair covers	11.4	2	24.00
Christmas items	8.0	5	11.00
Household items	5.0	7	9.00
Purse/tote bags	4.5	3	13.00
Samplers	2.5	1	16.00
Animals/toys/trains	3.5	—	—
Bell pulls	1.0	1	14.00
Miniatures	.5	10	3.00

* Average number of items made and average cost of materials used.

Exhibit 4 (*concluded*)

16. Of those who had done needlepoint during the past 12 months, 15 percent were familiar with the company's kit brand. Some 2.5 percent had purchased such a kit, and all indicated satisfaction with their purchase(s).
17. Counted cross stitch was done by 9 percent of all U.S. households. Of those practicing this skill, 40 percent had done so for less than a year.
18. Current counted cross stitchers do not expect to increase the level of their activity over the next 12 months.
19. Projects done in counted cross stitch are similar to items done in needlepoint; that is, pictures/wall hangings, pillows, and Christmas items.
20. While only 5.4 percent of counted cross stitchers recall (on an unaided basis) the Needlework Company as a publisher of instructional leaflets, nearly 50 percent do so on an aided/unaided basis.

The Industry

The company sold its products to both chain and the regular trade. The former consisted of such well-known retail organizations as K mart, Wal Mart, Target, Woolworth, Ben Franklin, and TG&Y. The company estimated that several thousand chain store units carried their leaflets and kits. Sales to chains represented about 15 percent of total company sales. Chains sold these products at about the same price as the regular trade. In the past, chains had purchased mostly knit and crochet leaflets but, in recent months, had evidenced strong interest in the company's surface stitchery leaflets.[3] The sale of kits depended for the most part on the buyer's reaction to a kit line. The company produced several new lines each year since a given line was popular for only a few months.

The regular trade consisted of small independent specialty stores which sold instructional leaflets/books, yarn, fabric, thread/floss, needles, kits, and tools/accessories. Most were small with sales of less than $100,000 a year. They existed, to a considerable extent, because of the owner's interest in needlework. Some were even located in the owner's home. About 10 to 15 percent turned over annually. A recent analysis revealed that some 20 percent of the company's regular trade accounts bought in excess of $2,000 of company merchandise annually and accounted for over 70 percent of sales to the regular trade. At the other extreme lay those stores (some 50 percent) buying $500 or less annually which represented less than 10 percent of sales. Company sales and share data are presented in Exhibit 5.

---

[3] This is an umbrella term which includes a variety of embroidery skills used to embellish a fabric and/or canvas base by drawing a needle threaded with yarn through the base. See Exhibit 2 for more specifics relating to the skills involved.

Exhibit 5
Market Potential by Product Line: Chain versus Regular Trade

	1981			
	Market size ($000)	Company sales ($000)	Share	Average annual growth rate*
Regular trade:				
Leaflets/books	$ 24,790	$10,856	43.8%	20%
Plastic canvas kits	9,006	4,653	52.0	25
Thread/floss	33,810	5,206	15.4	15
Fabric	19,600	1,882	9.6	15
Needles	17,560	843	4.8	10
Tools/accessories	27,780	1,139	4.1	20
Total†.	132,546	24,571	19.0	—
Chains:				
Leaflets/books	$ 8,150	$ 3,814	46.8%	15%
Plastic canvas kits	3,440	0.0	0.0	25
Thread/floss	13,760	0.0	0.0	15
Fabric	1,750	0.0	0.0	20
Needles	18,920	0.0	0.0	10
Tools/accessories	‡	0.0	0.0	—
Total†.	$ 46,020	$ 3,814	8.0%	—

* Next five years. Includes annual inflation of 10 percent.
† Does not include yarn and specialty/miscellaneous products.
‡ Less than $1 million in sales.

Regular trade outlets tended to keep minimum inventories and to maintain little stock control. They relied heavily on suppliers—including local distributors—to maintain backup stocks. Retailer studies consistently showed a high out-of-stock condition on many items. For the most part, such stores did not engage in price promotions and followed the retail prices suggested by their suppliers which, on an average, provided margins of between 40 and 50 percent.

The regular trade was mostly serviced by a large number of small suppliers. In the leaflet/book area, there were over 100 companies selling to the regular trade. Some 16 companies dominated the fabric market, while 6 did much the same with thread and floss. The latter was dominated by a French company (DMC), which accounted for over 60 percent of total category sales. Needles were supplied primarily by only two companies—both American (Boye and Bates). As might be expected, there were a large number of companies selling tools and accessories—several hundred, of which a number were European. There were also a large number of kit companies. While there were but a few acrylic yarn producers, there were several hundred small specialty yarn sellers.

Manufacturers typically used distributors and/or sales reps to sell the regular trade. Only a very few used direct selling, and most of these used a dual system in which company salesmen handled only the very large accounts. Small manufacturers often had a difficult time gaining access to the market since sales reps typically did not carry competing lines. Thus, they were forced to rely on small local jobbers of which there were several hundred. The latter operated on margins in excess of 30 percent but found it difficult to inventory a full line of products. The Needlework Company, with jobbed sales in excess of $14 million and an inventory in excess of 5,000 stockkeeping units, was the nation's largest distributor of needlework products.

The Marketing Department

The company had a traditional organizational structure consisting of five departments—marketing, finance, accounting, personnel, and operations. Marketing contained sales (both regular trade and chain), product management, leaflet preparation (including art), marketing research (including sales analysis), merchandising, and order receipt/customer service. Operations included receiving and shipping (referred to as warehouse operations), kit manufacturing, building maintenance, and the computer. Purchasing reported to finance. All departments reported directly to the president.

The company had two sales forces—one each for chains and the regular trade. Both were headed by vice presidents. The former consisted of six men, five of whom had in excess of 15 years' industry experience each. As indicated earlier, all chain sales were made direct. All chain salesmen were paid a salary plus bonus (as well as expenses) with salary representing about 70 percent of total compensation. The bonus was based on actual sales versus target and was tailored for each man depending on his contribution to meeting the target. Thus, in effect, each man had a quota to meet and his bonus depended in large measure on the extent to which he exceeded this target. The bonus of the vice president in charge of chain sales (who also handled several large accounts) was based on the target set for his accounts and total chain sales. In 1981, he was expected to receive about $135,000 in salary and bonus, while the average of the other chain salesmen would be around $85,000.

Sales to the regular trade were handled by 37 sales reps (32 men and 5 women) who also handled other noncompeting lines. It was estimated that company sales accounted for better than 80 percent of their total sales. Each rep had an exclusive territory and was expected to call on all key accounts (defined as purchasing annually in excess of $1,000 from the company the prior year) at least every three months. Because of the independent nature of these middlemen, the company did not receive any call reports on their activities. The vice president in charge of regular trade sales estimated, however, that his sales force concentrated on the upper 30 percent of stores and called on them three to four times a year. The balance of the accounts were handled via regional and national trade shows; periodic general mailings (three to four times a year) mostly pertaining to price changes, new items, and discontinued items; telephone calls to and from customers; and leaflet automatics (new leaflet shipments five times yearly). The latter was on a subscription basis. About 27 percent of the regular trade (mostly larger stores) had signed up for this service.

Sales reps received a commission on their sales the size of which depended on the product line's gross margin. Thus, proprietary products (leaflets and kits) provided higher commissions than did jobbed items. In 1980, commissions averaged about 7 percent. The reps received commissions on all sales to their territory (except for chains) regardless of whether they solicited or serviced the business. Sales from leaflet automatics, trade shows, unsolicited accounts, and phone/mail orders received directly from retailers were credited to their account. Sales reps paid their own travel expenses and were primarily concerned with product placement and, therefore, tended to focus on new products. Even so, informal field studies showed that product placement was weak, especially with respect to jobbed items. The sales manager thought that this would always be a problem given that the company carried some 5,000 such items. "After all," he said, "we can't expect them to average more than two to three calls a day, given the geographical dispersion of their accounts. They probably can't spend more than two hours with a customer, and a lot of this is waiting time since the store manager has to handle customers while he's there." He also noted that, because of the long industry experience of most of his reps, a considerable amount of time was spent in answering questions about industry trends and the trade's acceptance of new products.

The company did not hold national sales meetings. These were not thought necessary in view of the fact that each rep was visited twice a year by either the sales manager or his assistant, met with company officials at one or more trade shows each year, and talked to the home office frequently by phone. A newsletter was sent out monthly summarizing industry trends and reporting on average company sales to date by product line. In addition, each sales rep received an individualized monthly statement showing sales and commissions for the month as well as year to date. A computerized sales by account report was sent to each rep quarterly. Information concerning special promotions, new products, product deletions, and price changes were sent out as they occurred. In 1980, there had been over 100 such announcements. Sales reps were expected to keep their own product files which, for the most part, contained four-color product information sheets ($8\frac{1}{2} \times 11$). The company had some 14 order forms (one for each major line), which also served as price listings. The cost of a complete set of order forms was 58 cents. A set was inserted with each customer shipment.

The sales organization had experienced little turnover over the years. Of the six who had left during the past four years, only one departure had been initiated by the company. Most had dropped other lines to concentrate more on the sales of company products.

The company received an average of over 1,600 orders daily of which 83 percent were by phone and mostly customer originated. In terms of the regular trade, the sales force submitted 7 percent of all orders which represented 18 percent of sales. Better than 95 percent of all orders received were shipped within 72 hours. To minimize backorders, the company maintained high inventories (the average inventory for 1981 was $3.8 million).

The Marketing Department's product management group consisted of three product units—one each for knit and crochet leaflets, surface stitchery, and kits. Each unit was comprised of a manager and several assistants, including instruction writers. In 1981, the company published 16 knit and crochet leaflets, 28 surface stitchery leaflets, and 4 different kit lines which contained a total of 63 individual items.

The merchandising group consisted of a manager and two assistants. They studied sales trends by products and made recommendations to the product managers and the purchasing unit regarding the addition and deletion of items, what leaflets to consider producing, and what inventories to carry on major items. In addition, the unit was charged with the development of special in-store displays although, to date, only a few had been prepared. The merchandising manager was also the chairperson of the new product's committee which met weekly to discuss product additions and deletions.

The art unit took the instructional material and turned it into the finished product. Thus, the manager and her 10 artists and production people were responsible for all design, layout, and photography work, plus managing the printing operation which was contracted to a local supplier. A considerable amount of time was spent in proofing and checking quality at each stage in the process. In addition, this unit prepared all the packaging and instructional materials for the kit line.

What little marketing research was done was initiated by the marketing manager. He typically determined what information was needed and how it was to be obtained before turning it over to an outside contractor. All sales analysis was done by the assistant sales manager who was assisted by one clerical employee. They did both chain and regular trade analyses, although the latter dominated the time spent on this activity.

Opportunities and Threats

One of the major reasons for the company's increase in sales had been the strong market demand for its surface stitchery products. There was, however, substantial disagreement among company managers as to the total market growth rates for such products over the next three years. For example, the president forecast a market growth rate over the next three years of 50 percent–25 percent–0 percent versus 25 percent–0 percent–0 percent by the marketing manager.

To confound and aggravate the problem, the surface stitchery forecasts impacted not only on leaflets, but also on those for yarn, fabrics, and many accessories. Thus, overall differences of many millions of sales dollars were involved depending on what growth rates were assumed. Since the company produced its own surface stitchery leaflets and also jobbed substantial quantities, there was the question of how much should be invested in company leaflets versus simply selling leaflets produced by other companies.

It was also difficult to forecast the sales of kits since much depended upon the consumer's response to both the product concept and the design. Some kits appeared to have faddish overtones and, thus, could impact strongly on primary demand. The company was considering selling the same kit line to both chains and regular trade. Such a move would save considerable monies and add about 10 percentage points to the line's gross margin. In the past, the company had produced separate and distinctly different lines for chains versus regular trade in an effort to minimize any discontent on the part of the latter.

The president was concerned about the company's future mix of proprietary and jobbed items and its impact on margins and costs. In recent years, the sale of distributed products had increased faster than that of the company's own products, thereby impacting gross margins. Further, such a shift increased the company's vulnerability versus local jobbers who, for the most part, sold the same products and brands as the company. The president wondered if the company should move towards private labels.

Yet another problem was the effect of growth and inflation on the company's cash flows, capital requirements, and costs. The company's account receivables were $4,800,000, and the 1981 average collection time was 63 days. Notes payable were $2,101,000. The company paid no dividends, and its stock was closely held.

In looking to the future, the marketing manager suggested that the company's economic objective should be to achieve a five-year compounded annual growth rate (real dollars) of 20 percent in sales and 22 percent in earnings. The president argued for a 30 to 35 percent compounded increase in sales and 33 to 38 percent in earnings. Both men felt that at least 70 percent of total revenue should come from the regular trade and that the company should become an increasingly important supplier of proprietary needlework products.

Moore Printing, Office Products, and Furniture Company

In early 1982, Mr. Robert Moore, president and chief executive officer of the company bearing his name, received a preliminary report
from the public accounting firm preparing the company's 1981 tax
returns. It revealed that an operating loss of about $180,000 was ex-
pected. This was substantially more than had been forecast and meant
that over the past five years (1977–81) the company had experienced
operating losses totaling $508,000. While "other income" had substan-
tially dampened the impact of these losses, the situation as Mr. Moore
noted was becoming increasingly serious—even dangerous—with respect to the family's investment (see Exhibit 1 for company income
statements 1976–80).

The company, located in a medium-size city in the southeastern
part of the United States, was founded in 1916 by Joseph Moore primarily as a distributor of office products/supplies including paper and stationery. During his tenure as owner-manager, he added office furniture
and opened a retail store which sold both office products and office
furniture. Upon his death in 1946, he was succeeded by his only child,
Joseph Moore, Jr., who at that time was only 25 years old. In the mid-
1950s the company entered yet a third business—printing. At the outset, the company operated letterpresses which were used for relatively
small black and white runs of stationery, mailing inserts, announcements, business cards, and circulars. By the late 60s, the printing business had been enlarged to include both two- and four-color work, com-

---

This case was written by Professor Harper Boyd, College of Business Administration,
University of Arkansas. Included in *Stanford Business Cases 1983* with permission. ©
1983 by the Board of Trustees of the Leland Stanford Junior University.

Exhibit 1

MOORE COMPANY
Income Statements
1976–1980

inflation - 10% (handwritten)

	1980	1979	1978	1977	1976
Sales...................	$11,647	$11,221	$8,303	$6,854	$8,010
Cost goods sold............	7,582	7,371	5,274	4,434	5,068
Gross profit................	4,065	3,850	3,029	2,420	2,942
Expenses	4,238	3,742	3,044	2,740	2,894
Operating income	(173)	108	(15)	(320)	48
Other income*	127	133	109	92	95
Income before taxes.........	(46)	241	94	(228)	143

* Includes discounts earned, interest earned, and miscellaneous.

12,500,000 (handwritten)
Sales should be (handwritten)

posing, and binding. The company operated three color presses along with seven small letterpresses in 1982.

Robert Moore, the grandson of the founder, entered the business in 1968 shortly after graduating from college. He served first as an office products salesman and later as a print salesman handling mostly house accounts; i.e., large accounts on which no sales commissions were paid. In 1975, Joseph Moore, Jr., retired from all participation in the business because of ill health. His only son, Robert, took over command. In addition to his other duties as president, Robert continued to service a number of large printing accounts because of their strong historical ties to the company and, more especially, to the Moore family. Under Joseph Jr.'s management, sales had increased fourfold, and the company had never experienced a loss. Joseph Jr. had prided himself on his financial management and accomplishment, and even though he was no longer active in the business, he considered the company to be in sound financial shape despite recent losses.

At the end of 1981, current assets were in excess of $4 million (including an investment account of nearly $1 million which was earmarked for the purchase of new color presses) versus current liabilities of only about $900,000—mostly in accounts payable. The company had no short- or long-term debt. The company owned a recently renovated building which Joseph Moore, Jr., considered to be "excellent for our purpose." The building's location, which housed all the company's businesses, was near the downtown area and included ample parking facilities. The Moore family owned all the company's stock.

Economic Environment

In commenting on the company's economic environment over the past several years, Mr. Moore noted that,

In general, both the state and our metropolitan area have experienced a steady growth in economic activity as measured in terms of population, retail sales, employment, per capita income, and the like. While it's difficult to relate the impact of these increases on our business units in any measurable way, they obviously should have been quite favorable. More specifically, these increases were and are strongly associated with services industries such as ours. For example, increases in employment are highly correlated with use of office supplies and office furniture—and, to some extent, with printing.

Our state, not unlike other southern states, has had an economic growth rate better than the national average. Our trade association reports that office supplies and office furniture at the national level have been growing in recent years at an annual rate of 6 to 8 percent and are expected to average 11 percent in the decade of the 80s—all in constant dollars. Of course, we've all been bothered by inflation which has been troublesome for the past several years. I don't know what the state rate of inflation has been, but the national rate ran between 6 and 8 percent for 1976–80, about 11 percent for 1979, and 14 percent for 1980. I hope the current lower rate holds up.

Company Organization

The company's organizational structure and most of its management personnel had remained much the same over the past 10 years. In addition to the three operating departments (office products, furniture, and printing), there were three other departments—accounting, receiving and delivery, and sales. The office products and furniture departments each had their own retailing, warehousing, and buying operations. All except receiving and delivery were headed by vice presidents who reported directly to Mr. Moore. The office products department had a purchasing unit comprised of two individuals, while the managers of both printing and furniture assumed direct responsibility for this activity. Accounting handled the purchasing of all consumable supplies and services including all occupancy items. Since accounting was responsible for personnel, it also handled health and life insurance.

Mr. Moore was concerned with the performance of his accounting department, particularly so in terms of the company's cost accounting system. He stated that,

> We have a very real problem when it comes to knowing what's going on at the departmental level. We are never really sure what a department's operating income is from month to month. We computerized two years ago and have never been the same since. I suspect that our prior manual system wasn't all that good and we simply compounded the problem when we went to computers. Another problem is that there are too many record systems in the company, none of which agree with the others. Sales is particularly bad in this respect. Their records never agree

with accounting on commissions due the salesmen. There's a constant battle over who's right, which not only eats up time but is demoralizing to the sales force. A similar problem exists with sales forecasting. Our sales department has yet to come up with a reasonable forecast. As a consequence, we've found it nearly impossible to set up useful budgets for each operating division and for the company as a whole.

Printing Department

Over the years, the company had found it difficult to determine the size and growth of any market segments for its printing products because of a lack of secondary source data as well as a lack of internal historical records. The sales management activity, according to Robert Moore, had never functioned well with respect "to market outreach potentials by product and customer type, sales call frequencies, pricing, customer satisfaction, and product profitability." He went on to say that "while this department is losing 'less,' part of the 1980 improvement versus 1979 was due to a change in the way rent and energy costs were allocated." He estimated that this change favored 1980 over 1979 by $63,000. (See Exhibit 2 for sales and profits for each department—1977–1980.)

Exhibit 2
Sales and Operating Income by Departments, 1977–1980 (in thousands)

	Printing		Office products		Furniture	
	Sales	Income	Sales	Income	Sales	Income
1977	$3,969	$(369)	$1,869	$ 8	$1,016	$41
1978	3,943	(197)	3,426	171	934	41
1979	5,052	(100)	5,117	153	1,052	55
1980	6,484	(18)	4,087	(198)	1,068	43

The company had three different printing systems. One was a high-speed Webb color operation which specialized in the printing of inserts, small brochures, and coupons. These were sold to large consumer-goods firms (e.g., petroleum companies), almost all of which were located out of state. In 1980, sales were $1,774,512 with an estimated profit of $72,000. Over the years, sales had remained reasonably stable. Mr. Moore said that his company was at a disadvantage in this highly competitive market because "not only is our equipment not modern, but we don't provide our customers with an integrated system. By that I mean we don't have several high-speed Webbs and collaters plus an automated envelope-stuffing machine. Thus, we get only the single-insert business. The trouble is, it would cost us at least $4 million to set up a modern system—and we'd have to build or lease a

new building to house it. Besides, there is currently an overcapacity in
the industry."

The company sold its Webb products via brokers who resided primarily in Atlanta, New York, and Chicago. Most had represented the
company for a number of years and received 5 percent of sales for their
service. They tended to place their smaller jobs with Moore because of
system constraints. With but a few exceptions, they also represented
larger, more integrated printers. Mr. Moore thought that because his
equipment was largely written off and because of the use of nonunion
labor, his prices were highly competitive. However, he felt it was just a
question of time before he'd have to decide whether to modernize or
accept a declining sales situation.

Letterpress products still represented a substantial part of the remaining print business. The company operated seven such presses of
various sizes and speeds. All of these presses had been written off,
although many had been rebuilt; and all were considered to be in excellent condition. These presses turned out a variety of products including form letters, envelopes, price lists, tickets, registration forms,
counter cards, business cards, flyers, invoices, labels, ledger sheets,
brochures, catalog sheets, and even scratch pads. A recent study
showed that, in one month, 121 different products (such as those indicated above) were printed—mostly in small quantities. This same
study revealed the following with respect to the distribution of letter
press sales by order size.

	Orders	Dollars
Less than $50	11%	2%
50–99	25	6
100–199	26	15
200–499	27	32
500–999	7	20
1,000 and over	4	25
Total	100%	100%

Despite the number of small orders, Mr. Moore thought the letterpress operation to be profitable—"perhaps in the amount of $75,000
per year. But our sales here have been declining steadily because of the
greater use of more sophisticated office copy machines and the opening
of small quick-printing franchises like Jiffy. As more of the bigger jobs
go out for bid, we'll have more trouble. I'm not sure that even buying
new equipment will help because the mom-and-pop printers are increasing in number, and their costs make them hard to compete with."

Color represented the third type of printing and included both four-
color and two-color work. The main products printed were 8½ × 11

brochures, catalogs, and annual reports. The company operated three large color presses. In 1980, color sales totaled over $3 million. In commenting on color sales, Mr. Moore noted, "we have done well here in recent years—at least sales-wise. In the last two years, we picked up several very large orders which helped considerably. We've always had an overcapacity problem with color. To make money with such equipment, you've got to run two shifts—at least part of the time. Last year we lost over $160,000 on color printing."

Mr. Moore estimated that color equipment utilization was about 60 percent versus some 80 percent for the letterpress. Color efficiency was still only about 70 percent (number of worker hours available divided by the number of hours worked). There was also the fact that when the color work force was not fully loaded—see idle time ahead—there was the inevitable tendency to not work all out. Because of the shortage of skilled color pressmen, the company was reluctant to lay off such workers. Over the years the company had, however, lost a number of its skilled color pressmen who were attracted elsewhere because of job security and overtime pay.

In recent years, competition had increased—and particularly from large out-of-state printers. This was particularly the case with large local bid jobs. "These printers," said Mr. Moore, "are simply buying business to keep their presses running. They charge considerably higher prices elsewhere. We find it difficult to compete; and besides, we're never certain who is bidding what on a given job. I suppose we could go out of state and play the same game, but we'd have to hire some really talented salespeople to do so at an individual cost of at least $75,000 per year. We tried to work through brokers a while back but never had any success."

The company also faced increased competition from its largest local competitor who had recently installed a new computer-controlled five-color press at a cost of over $2 million. This equipment, on average, ran at twice the speed of Moore's and turned out higher quality end products. Since the installation of this new press, Moore had found it more difficult to get the longer run high-quality local jobs. Moore targeted medium- to short-run jobs and stressed their ability to provide fast delivery, since having three presses provided more flexibility. In looking to the future, Mr. Moore thought that the company would have to purchase new color presses, but he didn't want to do so until he had found a market niche in which he could compete successfully.

Office Products

Sales of this department increased substantially from 1977 to 1979 due mainly to increased state and local contracts (see Exhibit 2). The

office products line consisted of some 10,000 stock-keeping items including paper, pens and pencils, ink pads, glue, envelopes, adhesives,
tapes, staplers, pencil sharpeners, binders, calendars, briefcases, desk
lamps, and even hand-held calculators. In addition, the department
sold a full line of data-processing supplies. In 1980 the business was
comprised of several different parts as follows:

State/local government contracts.	56%
Commercial sales.	26
Retail, cash, and charge	4
Phone orders.	9
Data processing supplies	5
	100%

Note: No sales commissions were paid on government
contracts or retail sales. Commissions were paid on all other
sales except those phone orders from unassigned accounts. It
was estimated that only about 30 percent of the department's
total sales were commissionable.

   In 1978 and 1979, the department's profitability was largely a function of government contracts which were let on a bid basis. In 1980,
the company was less successful in its bidding; and as a consequence,
sales declined substantially. In addition to the year-to-year risks inherent in any government contract situation, Mr. Moore thought that
they had a negative effect on the commercial business. His reasoning
was that because of the irregular flow of orders involving different
quantities of basic stock items, it was difficult to avoid a large number
of stock-outs. Further, since the state evoked a penalty for late delivery, the tendency was to take care of the government first. Mr. Moore
went on to say that "we do get better prices from our suppliers because
of our volume, but I know for a fact that we have lost commercial sales
because of our poor service—particularly stock-outs. Over the years
we've played into the hands of several of our competitors who specialize in selling office products to just the commercial market. Even our
own sales force is negative about our failure to perform here. They
always had a problem anyhow because of the thousands of items they
have to sell—you'd be surprised how many pens we keep in stock, in
all the different colors and tip sizes. It takes a lot of time to write up a
decent-size office-products' order."
   The department's inventory was not computerized—rather a manual cardex system was used. A card was maintained for each stock-
keeping unit showing orders, current inventory, and purchases. In
1980, it was estimated that over 50,000 orders were processed—an
average of better than 200 per day. At the end of the year, there was
always a negative variance between the value of the physical inventory

and that shown on the books—often as high as $50,000. Mr. Moore felt that while some was due to theft most of it was simply paper mistakes.

Small orders represented a particularly difficult problem. Some 30 percent of the total number of tickets written were, in 1980, for less than $10 and represented about 3 percent of sales (see table). At the other extreme, orders of $100 and over accounted for 14 percent of total orders and 66 percent of sales. At one time, the company had considered putting in place a service charge for any order under $10, but the sales force opposed it so strongly that the idea was dropped.

Distribution of Office Product Order Tickets by Size

	Percent of orders	Percent of sales
Less than $10.00	29%	3%
10–19.99	18	4
20–29.99	12	4
30–39.99	6	3
40–49.99	6	4
50–99.99	15	16
100 and over	14	66
Total	100%	100%

Office products typically carried high margins (over 50 percent on retail) and hence were frequently discounted. Moore's gross margin was, in 1980, about 30 percent mainly due to the low government bids and some discounting to its commercial customers. Because of the commoditylike nature of the products involved, coupled with high initial markups, the market for office products was extremely competitive. More and more of the large buyers were putting their business up for bid for either six months or one year. These contracts were bid on an off-list basis, not by item, but on the total dollar amount of each order. Typically, the buyer promised to place weekly orders except for "emergencies." The source of the list prices was a monthly release published by a reputable trade organization. Mr. Moore said that he had declined to bid aggressively on commercial business so far because he didn't feel he could adequately service these accounts. He reported that he knew of bids which were as high as 28 percent off list.

Furniture

Sales of the office furniture department had remained relatively stable over the past several years (see Exhibit 2). The department carried both metal and wooden lines of furniture as well as accessories (e.g., lamps, clocks, ash trays, and porcelain figurines). In metal, it carried both a price and a quality line of desks, chairs, tables, and files. In wood, it carried only relatively expensive products from a variety of suppliers including executive desks and chairs, tables, sofas, coffee tables, cupboards, and occasional chairs. A part-time decorator was available for free consultation with any prospective customer.

Moore emphasized its wooden furniture and, over the years, had furnished the executive offices of a large number of local firms—some at a cost of $20,000 to $25,000. The department manager noted, however, that the high-quality segment was declining in importance at the expense of steel furniture. Part of this was because of the growth in sales of office plan systems which used colored partitions and a combination of furniture which included a desk, file drawers, and space for a desk-top computer or CRT. There were many different system configurations which posed a display and stocking problem. This new segment was expected to have sales in excess of conventional furniture by 1990. Even so, the latter was expected to grow at an average annual rate of 10 percent (in constant dollars) over the next several years.

One of the main difficulties with the system's segment was its lower margins owing to greater involvement by manufacturers in the sale. Since this was primarily bid business of some magnitude, many manufacturers were giving higher than normal discounts. Despite this, many of the jobs yielded the dealer a margin of less than 10 percent. Since the manufacturer paid the freight and typically shipped direct to the account, the dealer was primarily concerned with the on-site assembly of this furniture. Obviously the dealer and the manufacturer had to work closely together in soliciting and bidding such accounts.

Regular metal furniture had become increasingly a commodity, and Moore sold almost none at full list. Competition was described as fierce and was expected to become even more so in the future. One of the many furniture department problems faced by Moore was the size of its inventory which averaged over $200,000. Even so, the company was forced to fill many of its orders via distributors, which resulted in lower margins.

In the future, Mr. Moore felt the department should continue to emphasize its high-quality wooden office furniture but add new lower priced wood and metal lines. He hoped that these additions would enable him to bid more aggressively on medium-size jobs. He planned to set up a market information system which would identify all new construction, thereby alerting the sales force to future furniture business. He also planned to have the manager of the furniture department make regular calls on the leading architectural firms in the state (about 70 percent of furniture sales were commissionable). He felt that by becoming more aggressive it would be possible to increase the department's sales by 10 percent per year, thereby improving profits considerably.

Sales Department

The sales department was comprised of a sales manager, an assistant sales manager, a sales statistician, two secretaries, two inside salesmen, six county salesmen, a data processing supplies sales specialist, and 11 city salesmen. All outside salesmen were commissioned, but the company paid fringe benefits and all traveling expenses. In addition to the above, the company had a number of salaried retail salespersons who sold both office products and furniture.

As noted earlier, there were a number of house printing accounts, all of which were large and involved mostly color work. Most had been associated with Moore for a number of years—some had been opened by Joseph Moore, Jr. In addition to Mr. Moore, the sales manager and the printing vice president had house accounts which, for the three men in 1980, totaled $1,141,834.

Three of the 11 city salesmen specialized in color printing and ranged statewide in their search for business for which they received a 10 percent commission. Inevitably they sold some letterpress work, although they did not aggressively sell such printing. Without exception, these men sold no other Moore products, although they had frequently been helpful in "opening doors" for other salesmen. Of Moore's top 50 printing accounts (exclusive of house accounts), these three men handled 23. Mr. Moore felt that none of these men was a "star"—that each was much too content to earn about the same each year. "While we get good repeat business out of them, they don't really show much initiative in going after new accounts, unless pushed. Of course, getting a new account is difficult these days and especially if it's on a bid basis. Still they could be more aggressive than they are."

The six county salesmen covered the entire state except for the metro area in which Moore was located. Most had been with the company for a long period of time—three in excess of 20 years. They had fixed geographical territories which they tried to cover every two months. Most of their sales were made to county and local governments, commercial accounts, and industrial firms. Over the years, they had tended to specialize in certain kinds of letterpress printing, stationery, expensive binders, and furniture. They sold very little office products. Commissions were 12 percent on printing and 10 percent on everything else. In recent years, their sales had decreased to a total of $1,715,000 of which 15 percent represented furniture sales, 18 percent office products (mostly binders), and 67 percent printing (mostly letterpress). Mr. Moore felt that county sales would continue to decline because of more local competition, the computerization of certain county and local records, and the trend toward omnibus state contracts which enabled other political entities within the state to use them. Mr. Moore doubted whether the county business was very profitable, but he planned no changes because of the age and length of service of the sales force.

The city sales force of seven men (one of whom specialized in data processing supplies) and two women sold all company products. Their commissions were the same as those paid to the county sales force. They too received lower commissions when sales were made at below list. One of the women and one of the men were new and on a salary draw; i.e., they received a guaranteed monthly income until their commissions equaled their draw. All salesmen worked on the basis of assigned accounts, regardless of location. In recent years, the city sales force had experienced substantial turnover with the result that the large accounts had gravitated to those who remained. Thus, three salesmen accounted for over 50 percent of sales. The sales manager, in commenting on this situation, said, "One of these days we're going to have to redistribute some of our big accounts—otherwise there's little chance for our younger salesmen to ever make it. Our top men spend most of their time servicing a limited number of accounts. They've forgotten what it is to sell. But right now they know their accounts, and I'd hate to think of their leaving and taking some of them with them."

C A S E 2–7

Consolidated Airlines

Paul Adams, president of Consolidated Airlines, was concerned that his firm's marketing strategy needed a major overhaul despite having the largest share of its regional market. Consolidated's position had eroded 15 share points in the past five years, and there was increasing talk that a major carrier was about to expand into the geography. In an effort to generate as many new ideas as possible, Adams asked his marketing manager to gather diverse examples of actual strategies, military as well as business. (These examples are included in Exhibit 1.)

Consolidated offered passenger air service within northern California and served a territory of 100,000 square miles with an expanding population of 3 million. Except for local industry in five reasonably sized cities, the major business of the area was scattered and included forestry, agriculture, and recreation as well as a number of plants and other facilities owned by national firms. The geography was extensive and rugged enough that air travel was growing at a rate above the national average and had succeeded in attracting a growing clientele of business people as well as individuals on nonbusiness trips. As a result, passenger miles for Consolidated had been expanding nicely since the firm's start-up in 1965, and revenues topped $35 million in 1982. However, the rate of growth had begun to taper off late in the 1970s.

The firm's early success was due to its pioneering a hitherto unserved territory by means of 25-seater turbo props. The firm's start happened to coincide with a boom in the territory's economy resulting from the heavy population flow into California, a decentralization of many businesses, and an expanding tourist business. Consolidated offered a full-service package including convenient schedules, curbside

This case was written by Professor Robert Davis, Graduate School of Business, Stanford University. Financial Support for preparing this case provided in part by the Marketing Management Program of Stanford Graduate School of Business, Stanford University.
© 1983 by the Board of Trustees of the Leland Stanford Junior University.

check-in, extra roomy seats as well as deluxe cabin interiors, free drinks, a quality deli service, and small gifts for family members. In return, the airline charged a premium price. As Mr. Adams said, "We are the Cadillac of the industry. We sell entirely on the basis of a quality experience."

During its first five years, the company was without airline competition, and its growth was limited primarily by the speed with which Consolidated could convert passengers from other forms of transportation. The major selling problems in those early days were: (1) a premium selling price, (2) the need to convince customers that air service was more efficient than the alternatives, (3) the difficulty of identifying potential customers from within the large base that made up the original geographic segment, and (4) developing believability in Consolidated's ability to deliver what it promised.

Sales were handled through a limited sales force as well as a few independent representatives. The salespeople sold mostly to wholesalers and dealers, i.e., travel agents, though they did make direct sales to large accounts. The cost of maintaining each company salesperson in 1982 was about $60,000—which included salary, incentives, and direct expenses. The reps earned a commission of 7 percent of sales. Advertising, promotions, and direct mail were modest, with combined costs about equal to the cost of the sales force.

By 1972, Consolidated was confronted with its first competition, and by 1982, there were four viable competitors who split 60 percent of the business, leaving the other 40 percent to Consolidated. The competitors' marketing strategies varied. One, for example, was a heavy price cutter who offered "no frills economy." Another split its business between travelers and cargo and served only the major population areas at peak hours for a price about 10 to 15 percent below Consolidated's. A third advertised its "tie in" to a national carrier operating out of San Francisco and adjusted its schedules to dovetail with the national affiliate's schedules. A fourth used smaller planes designed to go in and out of rural areas—in a sense, the equivalent of a "door-to-door" operation. The customer also could save his ticket stubs for a substantial future discount.

One informal poll taken by Mr. Adams at a recent travel convention indicated that Consolidated was considered a quality house which was getting a little too stodgy and tough to deal with. The cabin crews, for example, were rated as "OK, but not outstanding." Schedule cutbacks were cited as evidence that the airline was less customer oriented. The sales force was criticized for being overly concerned with large customers and didn't do as much prospecting as the competition. These criticisms were by no means an avalanche, but they disturbed Mr. Adams nonetheless.

Questions

1. In reexamining his strategic approach, what changes should Mr. Adams consider?
2. How do you account for this firm's loss in market position?

Exhibit 1
Strategy Examples

U.S. Time Company (Timex)

The post-World War II strategy of Timex was to create and maintain a leading market position in one clearly defined user segment—people who wanted stylish watches at very low cost. Such buyers were tired of having a Swiss watch that had to be cleaned and adjusted every three or so years for $15.

At the same time, Timex identified an underutilized retailing outlet—retail drug stores—resulted in a coordinated product/market niche. This niche was left untouched by other watch companies. The beauty of the strategy lay in its consumable nature. For the low price, people apparently were willing to forego longevity, which ensured substantial replacement sales. This fast replacement tendency was encouraged through an emphasis upon style and design. As new markets emerge, such as electronic timepieces, Timex was able to garner its share, still in the low price range, thus increasing its market depth while maintaining its position within its segment.

Sears, Roebuck & Company

During the postwar period, Sears developed a highly successful strategy based on the primary consideration that its customers did not belong to any clearly definable group. Its segmentation approach was *not* to segment the market; the average American, wherever he lived, was a Sears target. The success of the Sears retailing operation derived mainly from its ability to provide easy access to its stores. Sears moved with the suburban trend—away from downtown locations—thus anticipating the onrush of shopping centers. Sales were effectively supplemented by catalog retailing, thus extending the Sears arm into virtually every home in America.

Marks & Spencer

In Britain, during a period characterized by "stagflation," Marks & Spencer experienced booming sales and profits. The company began as a conventional variety store chain, but its success was obtained through a careful redefinition of its goals and consequently its marketing strategy.

First, it decided to concentrate on wearing apparel for the working and lower middle classes, at prices they could afford, but with upper-class quality—made possible by mass production procedure and recently developed new textile fibers. Second, M&S deliberately restricted its new store openings, electing instead to increase throughout in existing stores. By continually upgrading its merchandising, display, and sales per customer, M&S was able to maintain a perstore sales level of about $4 million a year on only 20,000 square feet of selling space.

Seven-Up Company

7up was a lemon-flavored brand of soft drink that, until 1969, was an "also ran" in an industry dominated by Coca-Cola and Pepsi-Cola. By 1977, 7up had battled its way to an overall number three in the industry, this despite the emergence of several closely competitive brands introduced in the 1960s, including Coca-Cola's Sprite, Pepsi-Cola's Teem, and Royal Crown's Upper 10.

The turnaround came in 1968, when a market research study revealed that consumers had little top-of-the-mind awareness of 7up. Soft drinks were typically equated with colas, a drink category that accounted for over 50 percent of the market. 7up was further constrained by a number of factors: a traditional seven-ounce bottle (in a market of rapid

Exhibit 1 *(continued)*

package innovation by the colas); a high price image; an adult drink identification; a reputation as a mixer for alcoholic drinks; and possessing somewhat of a therapeutic property (i.e., "good for indigestion and hangovers").

J. Walter Thompson came up, in 1968, with "7up, the Uncola" theme and pushed the idea that 7up was the only leading soft drink type with distinctively different qualities. The theme was introduced nationally and supported with a massive advertising effort. A concurrent program aimed at reinforcing the efforts of the local bottlers, including an extensive sampling campaign, was also launched. The results of the campaign were dramatic. Sales rocketed, and the product image was converted to one appealing to the younger segments.

Raychem

A Fabian strategy is an indirect approach consisting primarily of evasion. In ancient times, Thebes avoided contact with Spartan armies while developing a powerful spearhead composed of picked professionals. This model force, though inferior to the Spartan army in actual number, soundly defeated its enemy.

A modern business example of this type of strategy is Raychem, a West Coast firm. The company developed a process of irradiating a proprietary plastic with "memory"—that is, under a broad range of temperature and pressure extremes, the plastic returns to its original shape. It is used in numerous applications, such as airtight wrapping, solderless wire connections, etc.

During its first three years, Raychem selected out-of-the-way markets and applications with limited potential—deliberately choosing small, secondary segments. When the company had acquired the skills and wherewithal to prove its basic discipline, it then rapidly expanded into its major markets.

IBM—Copiers

Xerox is to the copier industry what IBM is to computers. In an effort to gain a foothold in what is foreseen as a huge growth market, IBM decided to introduce its own copiers. In order to save time, only a single model was launched initially. The machine was slower than Xerox's for copies exceeding 10 (though faster under 10) and priced higher than the comparable Xerox models. It used roll paper, rather than single sheets, and had less flexibility than Xerox.

Since IBM was already well entrenched in the office equipment business with its typewriters (electric and programmed) and a well-respected line of dictating equipment, the copier was positioned as part of a system—"word processing." It was advertised as "the answer to your unduly high duplicating costs;" i.e., speed encourages proliferation of copies and therefore costs.

Versatec

Between 1964 and 1970, Varian and Gould, both high-technology firms, tried to build significant sales in electrostatic printers. These machines were nonimpact printers that could print electronically—about 10,000 characters per second—speed that was in keeping with the speed of large computers. The firms had limited success, though they managed to push the technology towards its maximum.

In 1969, Versatec was formed and, by 1974, was the leader in a now rapidly growing industry. Instead of concentration on maximum speed (which is costly), Versatec designed a machine that did 1,000 characters per second (still far ahead of alternative output devices); made all parts modular and interchangeable so that printers and plotters were assembled from the same standard parts; selected specifically the small computer, end-user, and OEM research markets; set the price at one half the competitive level (with a gross margin of 50 percent); sold through exclusive representatives (rather than company salespeople); and restricted its communication to trade shows, technical literature, and customer-slanted brochures.

Pillsbury—Funny Face

Until Funny Face (a drink mix for kids), Pillsbury was mostly involved in flour and baking. The introduction of Funny Face entailed an entirely new approach, both to the market and to top management.

Exhibit 1 *(continued)*

As to the market, Pillsbury began with the discovery that its Sweet 10, an artificial sweetener, was being used by some mothers instead of sugar to sweeten Kool-Aid, a competitor's product. Pillsbury's thinking progressed through various stages until it decided to market its own drink mix with the premeasured sweetener already included. The early strategy sessions, however, were nearsightedly focused on the same issue as that of the competition—selling a drink mix to mothers for their children.

Finally, Pillsbury broke through the well-entrenched position of Kool-Aid by deciding to merchandise not a drink mix, but fun. All marketing efforts were then brought into line with this concept; in particular, the strategy would be aimed at selling to kids, not their mothers. Instead of practical pictures of pitchers on the envelope, Pillsbury struck on the plan (using their own kids as idea sources) of putting funny-faced oranges, apples, etc. on the packages. In line with the basic concept, the Pillsbury name was de-emphasized, and Sweet 10 as an ingredient was also played down. Both of these decisions involved risks and moved substantially away from the original plan, which was to build business for the sweetener—in other words, a manufacturing, produce-oriented approach. But Funny Face came through and provided a new base for launching other nonflour products.

As a result of its experience with Funny Face, Pillsbury freed its new-products people from individual division relationships, forming an entirely new group directly responsible to the president. Thus their vision is not limited to the particular process of products of any one division but is free to move in any direction.

Weight-Watchers

Market strategy zeroes in on the extremely widespread concern for weight control. The firm has focused on the nonfad segment of the market, beginning with a carefully controlled program for balanced nutrition and weight control provided for a modest fee. "Product positioning" eliminated extremes—fast weight loss, single-focus dieting. Appeal is thus to people who are serious about losing weight. After developing an established base through national "distribution" centers, the company has increased its depth through introduction of food products and whole meals derived from the elements of its weight-control program.

In a sense, the weight-loss programs have provided a secure test base from which to launch clearly related products. Weight-Watchers presumably has a comparatively low advertising budget, since primary (and effective) communications are accomplished by word of mouth.

Burroughs

A 1978 article in the *Harvard Business Review* singled out three companies which had launched and maintained effective marketing strategies despite holding small market shares. Burroughs was one of the three companies.

In an industry dominated by IBM, Burroughs had emerged as a strong number two by 1978. The company's marketing strategy was the following:

1. Hold the annual growth to a rate that the company could manage successfully—no wild, tough-to-handle, accelerated growth.
2. Segment in every portion of the business, including markets, products, production processes, and research. In short, concentrate totally on the game of "nichemanship."
3. Devote ample capital to research and development to ensure the high quality of products.

Sweda

In the mid-1970s, Sweda's market share had dropped from second largest to fifth largest in the cash register market. Sweda's slide was due to its delay in switching from the traditional impact cash register to the electronic cash register. In the late-1970s, under the direction of George Saterson, Sweda started to reverse its slide and, by 1981, again was regarded as one of the three most successful companies in the cash register market. Sweda's renewed success was due largely to Saterson's aggressive marketing program which reflected the following attitudes:

Exhibit 1 *(continued)*

1. Research and development should keep the company at the forefront of the industry. In the years 1976 to 1980, Sweda's research and development expenses more than doubled.
2. All segments of the cash register market should be identified and penetrated. Sweda was the only company exclusive of NCR with products in every major segment of the cash register market.
3. Products should be low-priced. Sweda's prices were consistently among the lowest in the industry.
4. The field force (salespeople and customer support personnel) should be sufficiently large to provide proper customer service. From 1978 to 1980, Sweda more than tripled its U.S. field force to 200 salespeople and 300 customer support personnel.
5. Independent dealers should be utilized to supplement the field force's sales efforts. In high-technology industries, independent dealers were not widely used because customers often questioned their sophistication, reliability and responsiveness. Sweda executives insisted, however, that they precluded this problem through intensive dealer training.

Dupont—Nylon

Nylon hosiery was one of Dupont's first, and most successful, nylon products. When sales for nylon hosiery began to level off, the company sought to enlarge the nylon hosiery market and to develop new nylon products.

Nylon products developed to penetrate new markets included tires, rugs, and bearings. The company's strategy to enlarge the nylon hosiery market took the following three steps: First, through advertising, it reinforced the social necessity of wearing hose; second, a full range of colors and textures were introduced (for the first time) to encourage more varied usage; and third, the company expanded its market by appealing to teenagers.

Texas Instruments

Transistors were once prohibitively expensive to make and thus enjoyed only a very limited market. A development in mass production techniques effectively lowered the unit price, but wider markets were still to be identified. In marketing the transistor, Texas Instruments chose to approach the portable radio market. This entailed finding a way to get through, or around, the vacuum tube producers, who enjoyed a close relationship with radio manufacturers. Texas Instruments elected to sneak around by way of the independent radio manufacturers. These manufacturers, however, lacked the capital and expertise to produce such small radios. Consequently, Texas Instruments took on the burden of circuit design and basic support of the independents. Texas Instruments' effort led to the building of a profitable mass market from which it benefited greatly.

Wang Laboratories

Wang's marketing strategy was a classic case of market segmentation. In 1979, Wang further segmented the information processing market by introducing an automated office system which combined both data processing and word processing. Wang's integrated system was ideal for small- to medium-sized businesses. Realizing that the new market it had helped to create would soon attract the industry giants, Wang's strategy was to move first—and fast. To establish itself as the market leader, Wang permeated the market with a "nonstop" flow of products users desired and backed its lead with support for end-users. In responding to the needs of users, Wang went so far as to establish a joint research and design program with its customers. Commenting on their commitment to users, Carl Masi, VP-marketing at Wang, was quoted as saying, "Our primary competitors, IBM and Xerox, design products, bring them to the customers, and say: 'Take it or leave it.' We are more influenced by what customers want."

Wang's marketing ability helped establish the company as a leader in small business computers. In the years 1978, 1979, and 1980, Wang's sales increased $345,136,000—from $198,134,000 to $543,270,000.

Video Disks

In 1981, many companies around the world were waiting to see what technology would become the standard of the video disk industry before entering into that market. However,

Exhibit 1 *(continued)*

some companies, like Sanyo, became impatient. Early in 1981, Sanyo announced that within one year it would enter the video disk market with both an optical video disk player and a capacitance video disk player. Industry experts in 1981 agreed that the lack of a product standard would temporarily impede the growth of the video disk industry but would not dampen its tremendous growth potential.

RCA, MCA, and Matsushita: The Video Disk War

The video disk player was a visual version of the phonograph. Using prerecorded disks, video disk players could play back movies, sporting events, etc. The impact of video disk, however, went far beyond the consumer market. For instance, uses of the video disk in industry were infinite; business uses ranged from training sessions to sales presentations. The video disk player was in direct competition with the video tape recorder (VTR). In 1981, there were three companies in the lucrative video disk market: RCA, MCA, and Matsushita. Each of the three companies had different marketing strategies and product technologies. However, despite their different approaches, all three firms had the same goals. Each was competing not only for market share, but also for acknowledgment of its technology as the industry standard. Brief descriptions of the marketing strategy and product technology of the three companies are as follows.

RCA.   RCA's marketing strategy was to distinguish its video disk player from its competitors by price. The RCA player, often referred to as a "capacitance" player, used a microscopic diamond stylus that traveled through 12 miles of grooves to play one side of the disk (an hour's worth of programs). The disk used by RCA was stamped out much like a phonograph record, except that 38 of its grooves were squeezed into the space occupied by a single audio groove.

MCA.   While RCA's strategy was to develop a low-priced video player, MCA's marketing strategy was to procure new technologies to develop features that competitors could not match. In contrast to RCA's player, MCA's machine utilized laser technology. Somewhat more versatile than a "capacitance" player, the MCA player could search for and display any single frame on the disk—an option that the RCA player did not have. Although MCA's technology, unlike RCA's, precluded the wearing out of a disk, MCA's disks were much more expensive to produce than RCA's.

Matsushita.   Matsushita's marketing strategy was to price its players between RCA's and MCA's and equip them with as many features as was technologically possible. The Matsushita player was similar to RCA's in that it too was a "capacitance" player. Matsushita's disk, however, did not have any grooves. Instead, a flat metal shoe rode the disk surface, guided by tracking signals from the disk.

The Military

Although the goals may differ, military successes depend on strategy somewhat similar to business strategy.

> Effective results in war have rarely been attained unless the approach had such indirectness as to ensure the opponent's unreadiness to meet it. The indirectness has usually been physical and always psychological. In strategy, the longest way 'round is often the shortest way home. . . . While the strength of an opposing force or country lies outwardly in its numbers and resources, these are fundamentally dependent upon stability of control, morale, and supply.*

Summarizing the concept of indirect approach, the strategy is to suddenly dislocate the enemy physically by taking the line of least resistance, and psychologically by taking the line of least expectation. Further, the aim is to distract the enemy, thus depriving him of his freedom of action. Finally, a concentration of forces may be brought to bear on the now weakened and demoralized enemy forces. "True concentration is the fruit of calculated dispersion."

1. Adjust your end to your means.
2. Keep your object always in mind.

* From *Strategy*, B. H. Liddell Hart (New York: F. A. Praeger, 1967), p. 25.

Exhibit 1 *(concluded)*

3. Choose the line of least expectation.
4. Exploit the line of least resistance.
5. Take a line of operation which offers alternative objectives.
6. Keep plan and disposition flexible.
7. Don't hit where your opponent is strong.
8. Don't renew an attack on the same line after it once has failed.

Hitler's Success.   Early in 1940, Hitler's strategy was specifically to avoid any direct assault on the heavily fortfied French Maginot Line. Instead, he chose to bait the Allies into a vulnerable position away from their defenses on the Belgian frontier. When they had been lured deep into Belgium (having been allowed to advance without opposition), the Germans struck a deadly thrust in behind them. The Germans made effective use of their armored divisions, relying on mechanics rather than mass. The success of this approach was largely due to the inability of the French to depart from convention, in that they concentrated almost their entire fighting power in the advance into Belgium, and left only a few second-rate divisions to guard their rear. Their thought apparently was that the naturally rough terrain at their back offered enough resistance to the mechanized divisions of the Germans. On the contrary, the Germans had learned that natural obstacles are not nearly so formidable as human resistance in strong defenses.

Nimitz.   During World War II, when the Japanese were thoroughly dug in throughout the Pacific, the Navy strategy was to leapfrog from one key island to another, cutting off Japanese supply lines and starving out everything behind. The Navy was therefore able to bypass the big fixed Japanese base at Truk, as well as many other well-defended positions.

General Alexander.   Alexander of the Allied Forces, successfully outmaneuvered the Germans on a line between Tunis and Bizerta by stretching the enemy's front in order to produce a weak joint. His flexible plan called for drawing the enemy's attention to their left flank, then pressing hard on their right, following with his main punch at their left center. When this was effectively checked, Alexander swung to the right, where the Germans believed themselves to be strong enough. This process of distraction allowed Alexander to succeed with a final blow, using his forces to simultaneously attack Tunis and Bizerta, which collapsed German resistance along the northern half of the front. The battle was concluded with a successful attack on the enemy's rear, where the Germans had not been able to recover quickly enough.

Napoleon.   In attacking the enemy, logic may dictate that attacking the enemy's strongest point directly will yield victory. This theory, however, may not take cost into account nor a recognition that the leverage point could be elsewhere. It was Napoleon's strategy to attack, not the strong point, but the vulnerable critical joint of the enemy's alliance. Thus, instead of battering away at Austria directly, his plan was to first knock out the frontier of Piedmont in northern Italy—Austria's junior partner—from whence he could gain an open road into Austria.

Schriever's Puzzle.   For General Bernard Schriever, the objective was to develop an intercontinental ballistic missle system. Schriever had to develop a complex system, which reasonably could be expected to take 10 years. Even five years, however, was longer than the experts considered safe, so Schriever devised a method in which all facets of the system would be designed, tested, and built at the same time—the technique of concurrency, very like independently fashioning the pieces of a jigsaw puzzle—in the hopes that the pieces would all fit when brought together. Through the use of independent contractors, thousands of scientists and engineers—each assigned to a specific aspect of the project—the latest in computer control systems, and a massive "war room" command post to monitor all phases, the Atlas was successfully launched just four years after the start of the program.

C A S E 2–8

The Kingston-Warren Company

In August 1983, John Grant, sales manager for the controls systems group of the Kingston-Warren Company, was reviewing several customer proposals for the CAPS system. CAPS, a computerized order-picking system for warehouses, had been introduced by Kingston-Warren a year ago and had generated significant interest in the order selection trade. The interest had not translated into firm orders, however. John was more than a little puzzled and concerned about the slow flow of actual orders for CAPS. Many proposals had been submitted, often at considerable expense, to prospective customers, and there were still many under active consideration in those customers' organizations. It was proving extremely difficult to actually close the sale. The customer buying process had proven to be very complex and time-consuming. John thought that the level and quality of promotional effort on CAPS had been more than adequate, as had been the level of financial and other forms of support from top management. He was concerned about pricing, the ability of the dealer organization to sell CAPS, and the emergence of several new competitors. Clearly, the economic recession was having an impact on all capital goods markets, but John wasn't sure that an improving economy would help CAPS very much.

The stack of proposals revealed few clues as to why only three systems, out of 25 proposals, had been sold and installed over the past 12 months. As he reviewed the proposals and the sales representatives' correspondence, he felt that each system had been justified economi-

This case was written by Kim Borden, Research Assistant, under the direction of Frederick E. Webster, Jr., E. B. Osborn Professor of Marketing, Amos Tuck School of Business Administration, Dartmouth College. Not to be reproduced without permission. Copyright © by Trustees of Dartmouth College.

149

cally, solved a customer problem more than adequately, and had been priced competitively. He remembered outlining his strategy to Kingston-Warren's president, Herb Grant, Jr., last year and the initial excitement from the sales representatives.

Herb Grant, Jr., and John Grant had met at the end of June to review the results of the marketing strategy for CAPS over the past year. John and the company's sales representatives had become discouraged after having put so much effort into pushing the CAPS system. John was concerned that the Kingston-Warren dealer network did not have the high-level management contacts in customer companies to effectively sell CAPS, and he was thinking about revising the CAPS dealer policy. In their meeting, the president had also mentioned CAPS pricing. Kingston-Warren had always sold very high-quality materials-handling equipment and had also always commanded the highest price. Herb Grant, Jr., was worried that the recent discounts the control systems group had quoted in order to close a few sales would establish a low price level in the marketplace. He felt Kingston-Warren had put out "confusing" signals in regard to CAPS pricing. During most of the meeting, however, Herb Grant, Jr., had urged John Grant to maintain the current strategy. Despite the sales representatives' frustration and the growing number of competitors, Herb Grant, Jr., honestly believed that the original strategy was sound and well focused.

The Company

The Kingston-Warren Corporation was founded in 1946 to manufacture weatherseals for automobile windows. Located in Newfields, New Hampshire, the company was owned by Herb Grant, and his son, Herb Grant, Jr., managed its day-to-day operations. In 1982, total sales were $40 million, employees numbered 850 people, and the factory and office space occupied a handsome, modern 256,000-square-foot building. Kingston-Warren's proprietary metal roll-forming process, initially developed in 1946, was the basis for many new products developed since that time. The company was organized into three divisions in 1983: automotive; metal products; and materials handling.

The automotive division manufactured rubber and metal/rubber composite channels to weather seal automobile windows. The size of the market for this product was determined by automobile industry sales and usually accounted for about 55 percent of annual company sales. General Motors was the auto division's largest customer, and GM valued Kingston-Warren as a supplier. GM would keep their order quantities constant or increasing at the expense of other weatherseal suppliers during economic downturns. The metal products division produced custom steel components for the television, construction, computer, and electronics industries. The division's customers included IBM, General Electric, RCA, and Armstrong World Industries.

The Materials Handling Division

The materials handling division was created 20 years ago when the Chairman of Grand Union grocery stores thought it would be a good idea to make an automatic stocking retail shelf. The chairman intended for grocery stores to have inclined shelves so the products would slide to the front of the shelves automatically. In theory, when a customer selected a product, another would slide into place; the goal was to have a store that always looked fully stocked and neat. Kingston-Warren was contracted to manufacture these shelves because of their highly precise roll-forming process. Unfortunately, the application of a gravity-fed shelf did not work well in retail stores. Customers could not replace items they had selected but did not want to buy, and soon the store aisles were littered with grocery items.

Gravity-flow shelving did have another very useful application however—warehouse order selection systems. Order selection systems involve shelving, a conveyor with totes (bins for collecting items), and a picker. A useful example for explaining order selection systems is a gift item mail-order house. In their catalog, the mail-order house may have 700 different items, each of which is held in inventory at their warehouse. When a customer sends in an order, the order is translated to a "pick list." The pick list will have information about which items are to be picked, the quantity needed for each item, and (usually) information about where the items are located in the warehouse.

The picker will take the pick list and locate the goods on shelves, filling the tote with the necessary items. (See Exhibit 1 for a typical order-picking setup.) Usually, a conveyor runs through the picking aisle, and totes, with the pick list attached, move along a conveyor. A picker will only be responsible for a certain number of items (his or her zone), and several people may be responsible for filling the same order. As items are picked, the corresponding line on the pick list is checked or marked in some way to indicate that item on the order has been filled.

Gravity-flow shelving enhanced this basic system by providing a method to keep inventory (stock) easily available. Each inclined shelf was equipped with roll track, so open cases of goods slid to the front of the shelf. Handling of goods was far more efficient because restocking of gravity-flow shelves could be handled from the back of the unit, while picking was taking place simultaneously at the front of the shelf. Warehouse space was saved because the available stock was kept in a single row on the shelf, rather than having several cases stacked across

Exhibit 1
A Typical Warehouse Order-Picking Situation

the front of the shelf as required in static shelving. As a result of the improved utilization of warehouse space, picker productivity was also greatly increased. Pickers did not have to walk as far, nor did they have to search for products on static shelving. (See Exhibit 2 for typical static and gravity-flow layouts.)

Exhibit 2
Gravity-Flow and Static Shelving

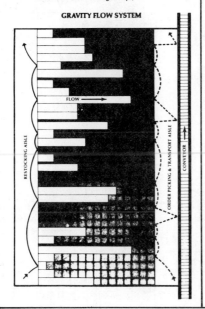

GRAVITY FLOW:
Pickers spend 85% of their time doing productive work.

A gravity flow system may cost a little more than conventional shelving, but it dramatically cuts labor costs. How? By decreasing the distance a picker has to walk between the items being picked, and the time spent looking for them (see illustration). Frontage per item is usually reduced to a single case except for a few of the fastest movers.

In a typical gravity flow system, about 85% of the picker's time is spent actively picking and marking order forms—and only 15% walking. Thus, a picker can save as much as three quarters of each hour, often making it possible to eliminate three out of four workers.

Similar savings can be made in restocking goods.

Finally, a gravity flow system makes the most efficient use of floor space. Fewer aisles are required. And 50% or more goods can be stocked in the same area.

- - - - ORDER PICKER (Shown making ten stops.)
———— RESTOCKER (Shown making six stops.)

GRAVITY FLOW SYSTEM

STATIC SHELVING:
Pickers spend 15% of their time doing productive work.

Static shelving systems are relatively inexpensive. The big hidden cost factor is labor—the amount of time and energy spent by people restocking and picking.

In the drawing below, notice how many wasted steps are taken between the items being picked.

In the typical static system, pickers actually waste about 85% of their time walking. That means only about 15% of their time is left for productive work—picking and marking order forms.

Compare the two systems . . .

	GRAVITY FLOW	STATIC SHELVING	GAIN WITH GRAVITY FLOW
Total floor space	equal	equal	none
Items stored (each case, 1 cubic foot)	155	120	29%
Shelves high	5	3	2
Cases per opening	15	12	3
Total cases	2325	1440	61%

STATIC SHELVING SYSTEM

King-Way Sales and Distribution

Kingston-Warren marketed its gravity-flow shelving and other order selection hardware under the brand name King-Way. The internal sales structure consisted of the president, who supervised the sales activities

Exhibit 3: Organization Chart

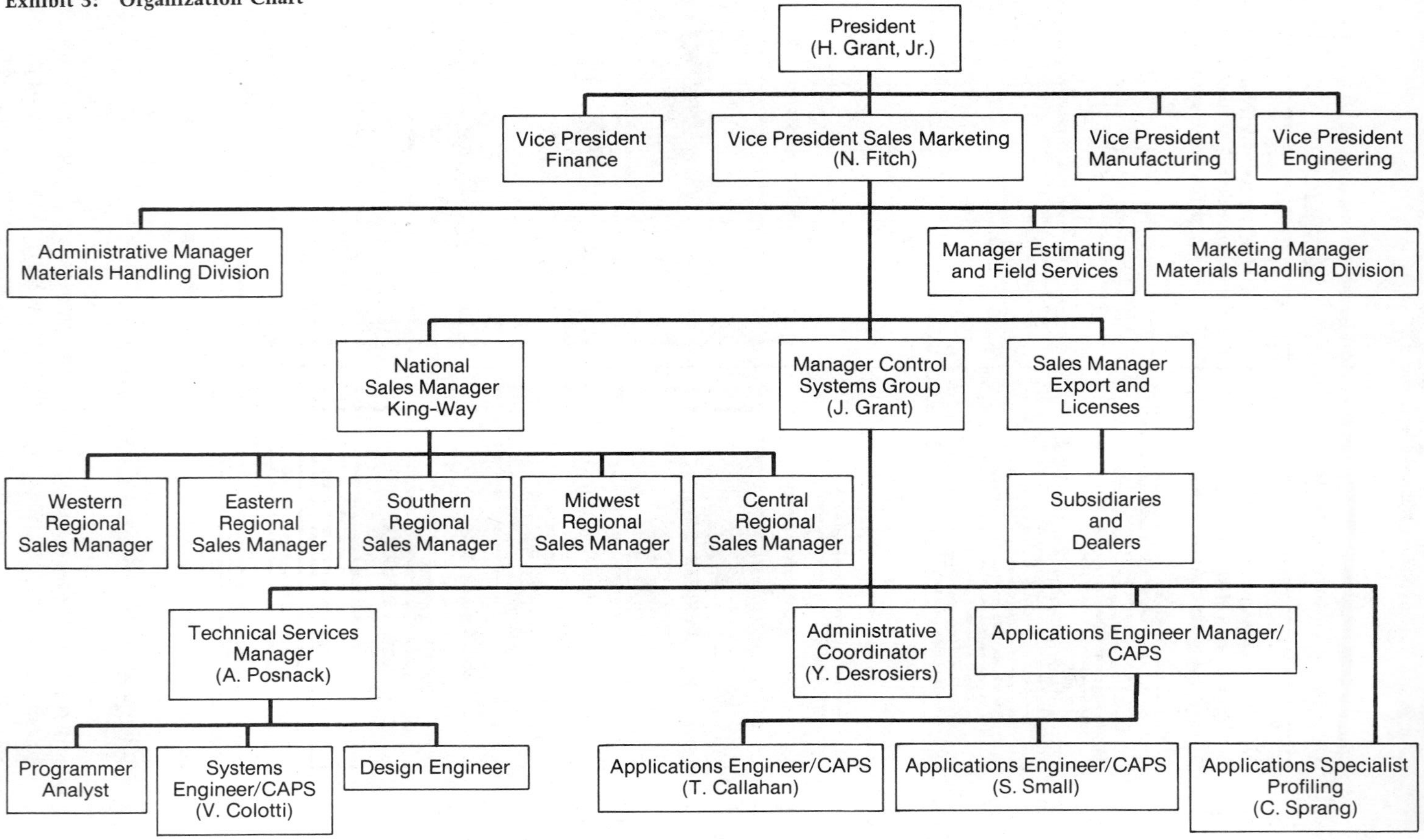

- President (H. Grant, Jr.)
  - Vice President Finance
  - Vice President Sales Marketing (N. Fitch)
    - Administrative Manager Materials Handling Division
    - Marketing Manager Materials Handling Division
    - Manager Estimating and Field Services
      - Sales Manager Export and Licenses
        - Subsidiaries and Dealers
    - National Sales Manager King-Way
      - Western Regional Sales Manager
      - Eastern Regional Sales Manager
      - Southern Regional Sales Manager
      - Midwest Regional Sales Manager
      - Central Regional Sales Manager
    - Manager Control Systems Group (J. Grant)
      - Technical Services Manager (A. Posnack)
        - Programmer Analyst
        - Systems Engineer/CAPS (V. Colotti)
        - Design Engineer
      - Administrative Coordinator (Y. Desrosiers)
      - Applications Engineer Manager/CAPS
        - Applications Engineer/CAPS (T. Callahan)
        - Applications Engineer/CAPS (S. Small)
        - Applications Specialist Profiling (C. Sprang)
  - Vice President Manufacturing
  - Vice President Engineering

of all divisions, a vice president of sales for the materials handling division, a sales manager for the control systems group, and four regional sales managers. The regional sales managers were responsible for developing their territories, each of which was roughly one quarter of the United States. These regional sales managers were salaried and reported to the vice president of sales. (See Exhibit 3 for an organization chart for Kingston-Warren.)

Exhibit 4
An Explanation of the "Profiling" Service

An Exclusive Service

PROFILING is a service which provides the King-Way flow rack user with an essential tool to assist in the planning and installation of King-Way order selection systems. Available only to King-Way users, **PROFILING** can yield significant dollar savings in such areas as floor space, hardware costs, installation labor, stocking and picking.

Using carton data provided by the user, King-Way's computer will "stock" the Flow Rack System—before anyone ever touches a carton! The user can measure the effect of various stocking strategies long before the flow rack is installed, and choose the arrangement that satisfies his requirements best. The finished **PROFILE** tells the installers exactly where to mount each shelf and lane guide; it tells the stockers what cartons to put where; and it provides input to the user's data processing system for recording slot locations.

KING-WAY ®
ORDER SELECTION SYSTEMS

Kingston-Warren sold King-Way products through approximately 120 dealers located across the United States. They were independent companies and usually represented a wide range of materials handling equipment and machinery, including fork lifts, dollies, pallets, pallet racks, conveyors, and automated picking systems.

In 1982, sales for King-Way products were $12 million. Customers included firms in a wide variety of industries including health and beauty aids, food and tobacco, hardware, toys, printed matter and stationery, and shoes, for example. Although there was a price list available to dealers for standard King-Way items, approximately 75 percent of the dollar volume of sales was quoted in Newfields by estimators. The quotations were usually part of proposals prepared by the regional sales managers for customer-designed facilities.

Kingston-Warren, considered by many to be the leader in order-picking systems, had installed thousands of systems throughout the world and had an excellent reputation for quality, durability, and functional equipment. Competition had increased over the years, and King-Way, as the highest priced system, had seen some erosion in its share of the market. In recent years, several new manufacturers had entered the market, mostly steel fabricators who sold flow rack and pallet rack at a low price. Kingston-Warren prided itself on selling "total systems" and actively promoted this advantage in its advertising and product focus. Their "Profiling" service was a computer-generated efficient layout for customer order selection systems. (See Exhibit 4.)

CAPS: Computer Assisted Picking System

In July 1982, Kingston-Warren introduced CAPS; an abbreviation for "computer assisted picking system". CAPS was a microprocessor-based system designed to increase picker productivity and reduce picking errors by doing away with the pick list. Instead of a paper pick list, LED (light emitting diodes) displays on the front of gravity-flow racks indicated how many of an item should be picked to fill a particular order. The complete CAPS system consisted of a control console, zone controllers, bay lamps, and pick modules. (See Exhibit 5.)

The *CAPS Control Console* consisted of a keyboard and CRT screen. Customer order information was passed to this microprocessor from a company's main computer via direct communications line or formatted diskette. The console tracked orders, inventory status, bottlenecks, and backlogs and could be used for entering rush orders, canceling orders, or calling up specific orders. The main function of the controller, however, was to direct the pickers in their activities with LED signals on the face of gravity-flow racks.

A zone is an area where one picker works, and there may be up to 40 zones in a warehouse. The *zone controller* was located in the first bay

Exhibit 5
The CAPS System

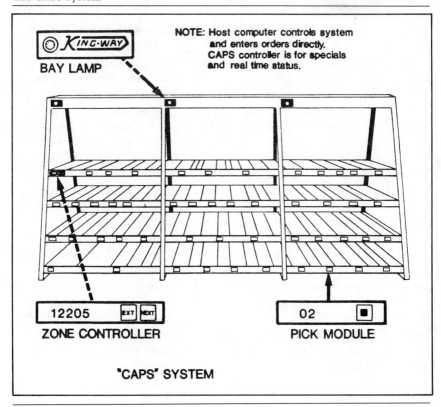

(shelving unit) of a picking zone and indicated the order number of the order currently being picked in that zone. When the picker had finished with the active order, he or she pushed the "next" button on the zone controller to receive a new order.

The *bay lamp* was located at the top of each bay and, when illuminated, served as a highly visible indicator that there were picks to be made from that bay on the active order. When all the picks had been made in a particular bay, the bay lamp would automatically extinguish. The bay lamps made it easier for pickers to locate bays that had pick activity and ignore those bays without activity.

The *pick module* was positioned at the front of each item in the system—usually a single runway or lane in a gravity-flow shelf. When lit, the pick module indicated to a picker the item to be picked and in what quantity. As the pick was completed, the picker pushed the button on the module to extinguish the quantity number and to signal to the computer that the pick was complete. The pick module could also be used to report shorts and stock-outs.

The advantage of CAPS was that it simplified the picker's job, reducing picking errors and increasing productivity, while also reducing order processing time. CAPS provided a wealth of instantaneous information on inventory and active orders in the order selection system. The system was very flexible and could work in a variety of zone configurations. CAPS easily retrofitted to existing King-Way gravity-flow racks and could be adapted to fit other manufacturers' equipment.

The CAPS system was originally introduced by Dimension, Inc., in 1979. Kingston-Warren was licensed for exclusive worldwide distribution rights (except for Europe other than the United Kingdom and Australia) from Dimension, Inc., in September 1981. CAPS systems were shipped from the Dimension plant in Reston, Virginia. The first "paperless picking" system had been installed in Rubbermaid's Party Plan warehouse in Chillicothe, Ohio, which supplied products to housewives who acted as dealers by setting up neighborhood parties and taking orders. Several thousand orders were shipped each week, and the average order had 50 items in it. Customer and dealer satisfaction was extremely important in this business, and Rubbermaid had many checking procedures to ensure that orders were shipped correctly. The productivity increases and error reduction results of the Dimension installation were impressive: An initial study showed that picking output rose from 400 items picked per hour to 600 picks per hour, and errors decreased from .5 percent to $1/10$ of 1 percent. These improvements were possible because pickers no longer had to refer to written documents listing the product and quantity ordered. Also, location of items in the warehouse did not need to be memorized. System and installation cost payback was achieved in one year.

CAPS Marketing Strategy

John Grant and his colleagues based the preliminary marketing strategy plan for CAPS on a situational analysis covering the company, the supplier, and the external environment. CAPS was to be an integral part of the product line, expanding the King-Way equipment range and furthering the company's goal to continue to be the foremost supplier of order selection systems. Although not a "high-tech" company, Kingston-Warren had the customers and sales network from King-Way to effectively market CAPS. The supplier of CAPS, Dimension, Inc., had already produced and installed computer-aided picking systems, and the technology had been tested and proven. Future research and development expenses would be jointly shared by Dimension and Kingston-Warren, and software improvements that would add different management report options to the basic system were under way.

Materials handling personnel seemed ready for a product that offered greater productivity and less errors but was less costly than fully automated storage and retrieval units. Fully automated order-picking systems had been developed that required no human pickers, but these were prohibitively expensive and prone to breakdowns. A computerized system like CAPS that aided pickers was regarded as an ideal compromise in cost and efficiency. The market for computer-aided picking systems was estimated to reach $23 million by 1988 and to level off after that point. Kingston-Warren, because of their excellent reputation for quality products, expected to achieve a 60 percent market share.

Distribution/Sales Network

Originally, John Grant and his colleagues decided to use the existing sales network of regional sales managers and dealers to sell CAPS. Most of the dealers had been with King-Way for over 10 years and had established relationships with the local companies using order selection systems, their warehouse managers, and often the company engineers who helped design and set up each facility. In addition, Kingston-Warren hired two applications engineers to be specialists in CAPS, to help regional sales managers and dealers lay out system proposals, and to assist in sales calls on request from the dealer and regional sales manager.

Over the past year, it had become obvious that CAPS must be sold to a different organizational level than King-Way products. The investment for a CAPS system was large and usually considered a capital budgeting decision by the customer. The economic return on a CAPS system and approval by the customer's financial officer were at least as important in closing a sale as the recommendation of the warehouse manager. Only 10 or so Kingston-Warren dealers were judged to have well-developed contacts at these levels of customers' organizations. The regional sales managers and applications engineers had had to forcefully step into several situations and do the actual selling of a project. For the dealers, learning about CAPS and assigning or hiring personnel to promote it could be expensive. CAPS was extraordinarily different from most materials handling equipment, and many dealers could not make the transition from a basic industrial product to a high-tech product.

Some dealers had expressed grievances about the commission structure on the CAPS systems. King-Way products were quoted to the dealers at list price minus a standard discount. The dealer's actual commission was determined by the selling price to the customer, which was ultimately determined by the dealer with many transactions below list price. The materials handling equipment market had a "notorious" discount structure, with many commodity items selling at 50 to 60 percent off list. Kingston-Warren offered CAPS to dealers at list minus a discount that was less than half the percentage offered on

King-Way but which was consistent with dealer discounts in the computer field. Dealer earnings on a CAPS sale could still be significantly higher than on an average King-Way sale because of the dollar value of the transaction. Dealers reported encountering significant problems with warehouse managers who were expecting a materials handling type discount on the computer-assisted picking system.

The control systems staff was considering setting up a structure involving A and B dealers. A dealers would have to meet several objective requirements before they would be qualified to receive commissions on CAPS sales in their territories. These requirements, yet to be determined, would relate to product training and knowledge, general management and financial capabilities, and size of the dealership. B dealers would receive a finder's fee for sales leads that led to CAPS sales in their territory. These B dealers would not be expected to learn about CAPS, however, nor would they be expected to participate in the sales process after they had passed on the sales lead.

In order to execute the CAPS high-level management sell, Kingston-Warren had put together a senior strike force to help close sales. Depending on the sales situation, the strike force would include the president, the vice president of sales, the vice president of finance, and other senior management officials and technical personnel. In a "textbook" sale, the dealer in the area would make the first contact with the customer, then an applications engineer would arrange a visit to the customer's plant. Proposals and a quotation would be prepared, and then the strike force would be used either during a potential customer's visit to the Kingston-Warren plant or at an on-site call. This approach worked very well because the senior management at Kingston-Warren knew the CAPS product very well and could effectively communicate to the higher management levels in the customer's company.

Pricing

Prices for a CAPS system including hardware, software, spare parts, training, and a one-year warranty were estimated as follows for the purpose of developing a proposal:

SKUs*	List price
500	$185,000
1,000	290,000
2,000	525,000
4,000	975,000

* An SKU is a stock-keeping unit, a single item in inventory. Each item—product, color, size, etc.—would be counted as a separate SKU.

When a customer was quoted a CAPS system, he was supplied an extensive cost justification based on raw data the customer supplied on his order selection system. From Kingston-Warren studies and data from installations, picker productivity improvement and error reduction would be 50 to 100 percent. For analysis, Kingston-Warren used 75 percent productivity improvement and 75 percent error reduction. See Exhibit 6 for an example of a CAPS cost justification.

Exhibit 6
CAPS System Cost Analysis for Wesley Pharmaceuticals, Inc.

	Year 1	Year 2	Year 3	Year 4	Year 5
Pickers	10	10	10	10	10
Average salary	33,680	33,680	33,680	33,680	33,680
Labor costs	336,800	336,800	336,800	336,800	336,800
Productivity increase	.75	.75	.75	.75	.75
Labor savings	144,343	144,343	144,343	144,343	144,343
Picks	1,137,500	1,137,500	1,137,500	1,137,500	1,137,500
Error rate	.0040	.0040	.0040	.0040	.0040
Cost/error	25.00	25.00	25.00	25.00	25.00
Error costs	113,750	113,750	113,750	113,750	113,750
Error reduction	.75	.75	.75	.75	.75
Error savings	85,313	85,313	85,313	85,313	85,313
Maintenance	(5,869)	(7,826)	(7,826)	(7,826)	(7,826)
Total savings	223,786	221,830	221,830	221,830	221,830
Pretax analysis:					
Items	800	0	0	0	0
Caps investment	(225,000)	0	0	0	0
Caps savings	223,786	221,830	221,830	221,830	221,830
Cash flow	(1,214)	221,830	221,830	221,830	221,830
Cum cash flow	(1,214)	220,616	442,445	664,275	886,105
ROI	0	0	0	0	0
Aftertax analysis:					
Caps investment	(225,000)	0	0	0	0
Investment tax credit	22,500	0	0	0	0
Net cost	(202,500)	0	0	0	0
Depreciation	33,750	49,500	47,250	47,250	47,250
Caps savings	223,786	221,830	221,830	221,830	221,830
Total net savings	126,837	133,630	132,522	132,522	132,522
Net cash flow	(75,663)	133,630	132,522	132,522	132,522
Cum net cash flow	(75,663)	57,966	190,488	323,010	455,532
ROI	0	76.61	147.40	166.84	172.92

Most prospective customers for a computer-assisted picking system would solicit bids from several different companies. Few companies had actually awarded purchase orders over the past few years, however, and Kingston-Warren had dropped the price on several bids in the hopes of closing a sale. Competitive companies were also offering low prices, trial periods, extended warranties, and other incentives in the hopes of being able to develop initial "showcase" installations as a way of developing the market. Potential customers seemed hesitant to invest in a computer-aided picking system which they regarded as an unproven technology.

Kingston-Warren initially had planned to follow the high-quality/high-price/market leader strategy on CAPS that had been successful with King-Way. When it became clear that orders were developing much more slowly than expected, Kingston-Warren lowered prices almost to the level of their cost on several proposals, hoping to develop a few "showcase' installations, and to close these orders quickly. Unfortunately, few orders were actually closed, the bid periods had dragged on, and now Herb Grant, Jr., worried that Kingston-Warren had established a low price precedent in the market. Price competition had increased as the number of competitors had increased over the past year. In one recent bid, one competitor had bid at one half the price of a CAPS system. John Grant wondered how he could compete with this alarming price competition and differentiate CAPS so that it could command a higher price.

Marketing Communications

Advertisements for CAPS had been placed in the major trade journals. During the introductory six months, a full-page, four-color advertisement had been run in each of the two major trade publications. (See Exhibit 7.) After six months, the frequency had been reduced to every other month. The advertising stressed the general concept of computer-assisted picking rather than the CAPS system. Kingston-Warren had received about 100 requests for literature from each ad placed. Two magazine articles, one in *The Howard Way Letter—A Guide for Improving Productivity in Warehousing and Distribution* (August 1982) and one in *Modern Materials Handling* (November 5, 1982), gave glowing reports about the CAPS system and features. Glossy brochures were printed and distributed to the dealers, and CAPS was included in general King-Way advertisements and guidebooks.

CAPS had been featured at two materials-handling trade shows, where it was displayed in operation on two King-Way gravity-flow racks. Each trade show had generated 400 to 500 good leads. These people received a follow-up letter giving the name of the local dealer, and the lead was then turned over to the dealer.

Another promotional effort was dealer-sponsored regional sales presentations. Dealers were encouraged to hold one-day miniconferences inviting potential CAPS customers. The regional sales manager, an applications engineer, and several of the corporate officers gave informal talks with visual aids throughout the day. (See Exhibit 8 for daily schedule.) A CAPS system was available for hands-on use and a picking demonstration using the attendees as pickers. These presentations had two objectives—to inform prospective customers of CAPS advantages

Exhibit 7
An Introductory Advertisement

and to give the dealer a better understanding of the system and its applications. Attendees ranged from vice presidents of distribution to consultants to warehouse managers and foremen, and generally numbered 30 to 50. Six such sessions had been held around the country, and more were planned.

The control systems group and the regional sales managers believed these presentations to be a very effective form of selling. Audience interest and attention had been consistently high, and the prospects

Exhibit 8
CAPS Seminar Agenda

FRANK BOUFFORD CO., INC.

MATERIALS HANDLING EQUIPMENT & STORAGE SYSTEMS

HUNTING RIDGE MALL • BEDFORD, NEW YORK 10506 • 914-234-7286 • 914-234-9253

FRANK BOUFFORD CO., INC. - "CAPS" SEMINAR AGENDA
TARRYTOWN HILTON - JUNE 21-24, 1983

9:00 - 9:15 AM	Welcome & Orientation with KW Tape
9:15 - 9:45 AM	Kingston-Warren Corporation History
9:45 - 10:15 AM	CAPS Picking Demo
10:15 - 10:30 AM	Break
10:30 - 12:00 Noon	Introduction to CAPS
12:00 - 1:00 PM	Lunch
1:00 - 2:30 PM	Introduction to CAPS continued including profiling
2:30 - 2:45 PM	Break
2:45 - 3:30 PM	Cost Justification
3:30 - 4:30 PM	Cocktails with Discussion

SPEAKERS

	Tuesday	Wednesday	Thursday	Friday
Welcome	Frank Boufford	Frank Boufford	Frank Boufford	Frank Boufford
KW History	Herb Grant, Jr.	Neil Fitch	John Grant	John Grant
Picking Demo	Terry Mackin	Tim Callahan	Terry Mackin	Terry Mackin
Intro to CAPS	Tim Callahan	Al Posnack	Tim Callahan	Tim Callahan
Cost Justification	Al Posnack	Terry Mackin	Terry Mackin	Terry Mackin

were available for an entire day. The cost was not considered expensive at approximately $2,000 per day, split 50-50 with the dealer in the area to give him incentive to bring in good prospective customers and to actively participate in the seminar. About one month after the seminar, one of the applications engineers would do follow-up calls with the dealer. John Grant felt that it would be possible to hold seminars in New York and Los Angeles three times a year and still not reach every good potential customer in those markets.

Competition

At the time of its introduction, CAPS had only one serious competitor. In August 1983, there were five computer-aided picking systems on the market, and John Grant expected that others would appear over the next year. Many were small companies and had been attracted to the field by the promotion efforts of Kingston-Warren. Acme, the leading manufacturer of warehouse conveyors, was the original competitor and had promoted the picking system that was tied to its own conveyor system. Acme's Pick Pack system was not as flexible as CAPS, but Acme was well respected among materials-handling equipment suppliers. Although Acme had not promoted their product recently, several people at Kingston-Warren thought they were reevaluating the market and would come out soon with a system comparable to CAPS. Others at Kingston-Warren felt that Acme would leave the market and drop the product altogether. This was in part due to the recent takeover of Acme by Consolidated Engineering, Inc., a large, diversified company.

Of the other competitive products, only one, the Bosworth Rackamatic system, had actually been installed. Al Posnack, the technical services manager for control systems, felt that the Rackamatic system was the only system that could rival CAPS for features; he was unsure of its quality, however. Bosworth was a small regional manufacturer of conveyors, flow rack, and other materials-handling equipment, and John Grant believed the Rackamatic might be the product to bring Bosworth up to the level of national supplier. Bosworth had a good understanding of the productivity increases possible with computer-aided picking and was the only manufacturer that could compete with Kingston-Warren in supplying total systems.

The two other competitors, Saturn Automated Industries and Multinational Materials Handlers, were believed to have sold one system, and none of the companies had actually installed a system. Al Posnack believed all of them could deliver a working product, although none could offer the experience that Kingston-Warren had in materials handling. All were small companies buying the equipment and software from outside suppliers.

Difficulties Closing Orders

John Grant pulled five file folders from the stack he was going through. They were in Terry Macklin's territory, and Tim Callahan, one of the CAPS applications engineers, had also worked on these jobs. Both were in the office that day, and John decided to call them in to discuss the five proposals, as well as to discuss his thoughts on the dealers and pricing. Terry had been on the phone all morning, chasing leads and updating the status reports on several jobs. The meeting would have to be brief because several more proposals were due out that week and a potential customer was coming in on Friday for a CAPS demonstration. Tim was busy preparing a training session for one of the first CAPS' customers.

That afternoon, John, Terry, and Tim sat down in the conference room over coffee. The first job they looked at was Wesley Pharmaceuticals, Inc. Wesley was a large, international manufacturer of pharmaceuticals, and one of their industrial engineers had first expressed interest in response to a CAPS ad in *Modern Materials Handling*. She had called Kingston-Warren and had been put in touch with Terry, who immediately sent her the CAPS questionnaire. Wesley had numerous picking lines scattered across the United States and Europe and was looking to buy a trial system. Terry started the conversation.

Terry: Good news on this one. It became an order this morning! Not bad for a year's worth of work. Once this one is up and running, I'm sure we'll get other orders from them—both domestically and in Europe. The dealer will be pleased, even though he hasn't done much on this order.

John Grant reviewed the Wesley file that was started a year ago March. All the correspondence was directly from Kingston-Warren to the customer, without so much as a brief note of communication to or from the dealer, which John thought was perhaps for the best, given the dealer in that area. He was fine for flow-rack sales but did not have the contacts in the upper management of his client companies. Terry was obviously annoyed because he had had to do all the work on this order with Tim; but at least it was an order.

John: What do you think of the idea of A and B dealers for CAPS?

Terry: In some ways I'd like to do the whole sell myself—but there are a few excellent dealers. Besides, those who can't sell CAPS do a good job in general with King-Way. We can't afford to lose them—so the finder's fee is a good way of keeping the Bs happy. You asked me earlier about criteria for A dealers. Well the Pyramid job is a great example. EDS (a King-Way dealer) has got to be one of the classiest outfits in materials handling.

Tim: They've been truly professional with that job. Jay, the dealer's sales representative, is dedicated solely to CAPS and has really taken the time to understand it. He has the features down cold—it has really been a pleasure working with him.

Terry: But we still don't have an order.

John: Have all the right people in every functional area been contacted?

Terry: Yes and then some. Everybody, from the warehouse foreman on up, is excited, and I'm sure we'll see an order by the fourth quarter. Pyramid is one of the largest home care catalog operations we've looked at. CAPS systems in all their pick lines could save them hundreds of thousands of dollars.

John: But you've been working on this one for more than a year!

Tim: Bad timing again. Once we got all their questions answered—and they had plenty, but none we couldn't solve—the economy turned down.

Terry: Dave, the senior engineer, told me that they had to lay off people for the first time *ever* this summer. The times are just not right to bring in a productivity improvement. They were ready to close in March, after they visited here, but then their market began to decline. But I'm sure we'll see this one yet. EDS is keeping on top of things.

John looked at the Pyramid file that was thick with correspondence from the dealer to Kingston-Warren and from the dealer to the customer. Everything has proceeded smoothly, but still Kingston-Warren would have to wait for the order.

The next job they looked at was Emerson Distributors. Emerson was a distributor of general merchandise and had over 2,000 SKUs in their warehouse. They were updating their static shelving system to flow rack, and the control systems group had put together an add-on CAPS proposal to the King-Way bid. Emerson was building a new warehouse, and the flow-rack order was worth approximately $400,000. Although Kingston-Warren received the flow-rack order, the Emerson's president had decided that the company could not justify an additional investment for CAPS at this time. He purchased King-Way, however, with the expressed intention of purchasing CAPS at a later date. The control systems group had used the senior strike force to push this sale, and John Grant felt it had been extremely successful.

Terry next mentioned Manlius Wholesale, a distributor serving a large grocery store chain.

Terry: Pounds, the president, is sold on CAPS, but he must win approval from *his* boss. Manlius is a subsidiary of Eastern Provision, and Pounds perceives CAPS as a radical step for the company—and it *is* very different from their current picking methods. Currently, we're trying to arrange for several people at Eastern Provision to visit our factory, but until we get to this higher level, the job is only barely active. It's strange that Pounds, who does have the authority to commit to this project, is hesitant to do so without corporate approval.

Tim: We even offered him a three-month free trial—and surprisingly he won't take us up on that either.

John: Do you think it will become an order?

Terry: Eventually, but there is still a lot of selling to do. These certainly aren't like King-Way orders where you can usually get a commitment in 100 days.

John: What about Wellington Imports? They sell giftware, don't they?

Terry: Yes and that job is still pending. The project has been delayed because they've decided to build a warehouse rather than lease one. The prospect still looks good, but it won't be until the first quarter next year that they'll be ready to move on CAPS.

The meeting ended with a discussion of various proposals that were being prepared. Tim and Terry were excited about the upcoming customer demonstration planned for that day. The company that was visiting was a large mail-order house, and the senior management

would be attending the presentation. The warehouse manager had become interested in CAPS after attending a trade where CAPS had been
displayed.

John was very concerned about the closure record for CAPS. The
Wesley Pharmaceuticals job could be added to the list of sales, but four
closed sales in over a year did not seem like a good record. He thought
that maybe the lead time for CAPS systems was longer than he had
anticipated. There were certainly many good proposals out for CAPS.
The A-B dealer system would need approval by the president, and John
Grant had to come up with some quantitative criteria for selecting A
dealers. Pricing was another issue to be considered. He knew that
CAPS would have to be differentiated from its competitors, but had
not decided how this should be done. He called Herb Grant, Jr., to
arrange a meeting the next day. Although John Grant did not think
major changes were needed, he felt he should go over some of the
issues with Herb, who had shown signs of also becoming concerned
about the lack of firm orders in the face of continuing significant increase in marketing expenses.

SECTION THREE

Product and
Product Line

C A S E 3–1

Gillcable, Inc.

The Immediate Issue

On September 1, 1982, Robert Hosfeldt, executive vice president of
Gillcable, Inc., presided over the annual planning meeting of his management team. The topic to be discussed concerned a new product
package called Superbasic that Hosfeldt and his marketing vice president, Ben Reichmuth, had devised and for which an implementation
plan was needed. But there were important complications.

An early entrant into an industry just emerging from its infancy, the
company had become the largest independent cable system in the
United States. It was known throughout the cable industry as a model
of modern technology and innovation in marketing and programming.
Because of this, Hosfeldt saw tremendous opportunities in Superbasic
for increasing penetration and generating additional profits. But paral-
leling this apparent opportunity were many worrisome operating problems, the two most serious of which were the continued loss of cable
equipment through subscriber theft and the increase in bad debts—
both related to rapid growth. Additionally, there was considerable uncertainty about the likely changes in the cable industry and how these
changes would affect the future.

Cable Business

Cable technology is almost as old as broadcast television technology, though it became an important force only after the mid-1970s.
The first cable systems were established in the early 1950s to provide

This case was written by David J. Katz under the supervision of Professor Robert T.
Davis, Stanford Graduate School of Business. Financial support for this project was
provided in part by the Marketing Management Program. © 1983 by the Board of Trustees of the Leland Stanford Junior University.

reception in areas that did not receive clear signals because of distance or terrain. The widespread introduction of satellite-delivered pay television in the late 1970s revolutionized the industry and provided an enormous increase in revenues without significant additional investment. The number of cable-subscribing households virtually doubled between 1978 and 1982 and was expected to double again before the end of the decade (see Exhibit 1). In 1982, cable reached nearly one

Exhibit 1
U.S. Cable Television Penetration, 1976–1990

Year	Basic subscribers (in thousands)	Percent of television households	Pay TV subscribers (in thousands)	Percent of television households
1976	12,094	17	565	1
1977	13,194	18	1,466	2
1978	14,155	19	2,980	4
1979	16,023	21	5,341	7
1980	18,672	24	7,780	10
1981	22,596	28	11,804	14
1982	27,500	32	15,000	20
1983*	30,636	37	18,216	22
1984*	35,448	42	21,944	26
1985*	40,467	47	25,830	30
1986*	45,656	52	29,852	34
1987*	49,280	55	33,152	37
1988*	52,098	57	36,560	40
1989*	54,988	59	40,076	43
1990*	58,900	62	43,700	46

* Projected

Source: *CableVision Magazine*, November 8, 1982.

third of all television households. Optimistic industry estimates projected that this figure could reach as high as 70 percent by 1990. The number of subscribers to "pay services" increased five times during the 1978–82 period and was expected to triple by 1990. Geographically, it was estimated that the greatest growth would occur in major metropolitan areas, many of which were just being wired in 1982. (See Exhibit 2 which describes how a cable television system works.)

There were three types of cable television programming: basic, pay or premium, and pay-per-view. Most franchise agreements (granted by municipalities) required that multiple service operators (MSOs) such as Gillcable provide at least 12 channels for a basic monthly charge. These channels included local broadcast stations, which were designated "must carries" by the FCC, as well as some national basic services. These national services were provided only to cable operators and were supported through advertising income or a per-subscriber charge. Often these services gave some advertising time to MSOs in

Exhibit 2
How a Cable Television System Works

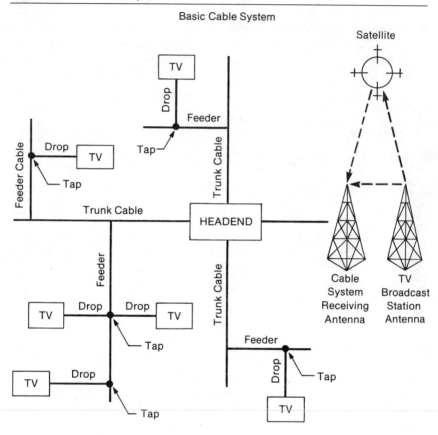

A television camera takes pictures and sounds and encodes them in the form of an electric current. A television receiver decodes the current and converts it into the original pictures and sounds. Transmission has traditionally been the radiating of an electromagnetic wave from a transmitting antenna. This "broadcast" wave loses energy (an effect known as attenuation) as it travels, but for a distance of about 50 miles it can be intercepted by any receiver that lies in its path and is turned to its wavelength. The wave can be intercepted at greater distances with more elaborate equipment, but after about a hundred miles, the curvature of the earth begins to block the receiver from the transmitter, and the signal is lost.

An alternative to the method is cable transmission. The components of a cable system are antennas to receive broadcast television signals, a "headend" to process them and add other signals, and the cable distribution network that carries the signals to subscribers' receivers. Distribution is on a "party-line" basis from the headend, with each subscriber having access to exactly the same programming.

A separate antenna is used for each station received, so that it can be turned to the broadcast frequency and aligned to pick up the strongest signal. If the cable operator wants to bring in distant signals which originate too far away to be received directly by an antenna, he must relay the signal to the system's headend. This is usually done by microwave transmission, often by satellite, at frequencies specially licensed by the FCC.

Exhibit 2 *(concluded)*

As shown in the diagram, broadcast signal is connected by cable to the headend facility, which contains the electronic equipment necessary to process signals for distribution on the cable network. The headend performs several functions, including filtering out undesired signals, translating UHF signals to VHF, separating or "demodulating" information from distant signals from the microwave transmission carrier, combining or "modulating" signals that originate within the cable system to match a channel in standard VHF band, and mixing all signals into a composite signal and amplifying them before distributing them on cable.

The main cables that carry signals from the headend are called trunk cables, which can be strung on utility poles or through underground ducts. Television signals are attenuated throughout the cable system so that amplifiers must be placed throughout the cable route to build the strength up to usable levels. Each amplifier degrades signal quality slightly, and the effect is cumulative. For this reason, trunk cable systems must be minimized. To minimize trunk runs, many current systems use a "hub" concept, with the headend at the center of a group of trunk cables strung radially. Large systems often require multiple headends.

When a trunk cable passes an area of subscriber density, a smaller feeder cable is used to distribute signals from the trunk to that area. A small drop cable brings the signal to the home from the closest feeder line. A coupler, or tap, connects the drop to the feeder cable.

Each cable carries a practical limit of 12 channels, which matches the 12 channels of the standard VHF tuner on television receivers (channels 2–13). UHF frequencies are too high for the cable system to carry directly. Channel capacity can be expanded by running multiple cable systems and using a switch at the receiver to regulate the signal, and/or by using a converter to change a nonstandard frequency channel to one that can be tuned directly on the subscriber's television. Use of both expansion devices simultaneously can expand system capacity to over 100 channels.

---

return. Most franchise agreements also included a stipulation that some channels be reserved for public access, a requirement that was expected to grow. A final category of basic services consisted of broadcast channels from outside the immediate geographic area, which were not "must carries." The most popular of these were the so-called superstations, located in various major cities, which broadcast sports, movies, news, and other programming of national interest. Federal regulation practically restricted the number of distant broadcast stations to three. In 1982, there were 35 national basic services (including superstations), most of which provided 24-hour programming of specialized nature such as sports, news, music, arts, or religion. The largest services reached over half of all cable homes.

Pay or premium services covered special programming, usually broadcast on a 24-hour basis, for a fee in excess of the basic charge. The most popular were the late-run movies, but adult programming, sports, and foreign language programming were available also. The pay service operators purchased the rights to movies and special events and usually sold their entire programming packages to MSOs on a per-subscriber basis. About 75 percent of revenues were retained by MSOs, with 25 percent going to the pay services.

Pay services were usually received outside the basic (VHF) band through a converter. A device called a "trap" was placed on the roof of the subscriber's residence, and depending on how the trap was set, the subscriber received a clear or scrambled signal. When the subscriber wanted to add or change a pay service, an installer had to go to the home to reset the trap. A recent major technological breakthrough, the addressable descrambler, allowed the MSO to provide or change pay services to each subscriber simply by sending a signal; but few systems used these addressable descramblers in 1982.

The addressable descrambler further allowed the MSO to provide programming on an individual screening, or pay-per-view basis. This option was not fully developed by the industry. Through 1982, pay-per-view events had been confined largely to boxing matches and late-run movies. Agreements typically allowed MSOs to keep 50 percent of the revenues from these events. As the use of addressable descramblers grows, however, cable should be able to compete with network television for major events like the Super Bowl and World Series. In addition, Gill expected that major movies would be released to cable for pay-per-view on the same day as they were released to movie theaters. Hosfeldt commented:

> We expect same-day release by 1983 or 1984. Even more desirable may be a system in which we get a movie for the entire first month after its release with an option to show it as many times as we choose.
>
> This would be better for a movie like *E.T.*, which had good advance publicity but went crazy at the box office in its first week.

Gill's president, Allen Gilliland, added:

> We expect that cable will have the major events like the Super Bowl by the late 1980s because the numbers are incredible. Cable could generate up to $50 million for a single pay-per-view event. Because of the potential buying power, we will be able to create our own events in music and sports, for example. The main obstacle is the availability of addressable boxes. If MSOs move quickly to develop addressability, you could see national pay-per-view events occurring by 1984 or 1985.

Gillcable, Inc.

Gillcable was a multiple-service operator serving San Jose, Campbell, and part of Cupertino, California. With 1,600 miles of dual cable, it served 93,000 subscribers of a possible 191,000 homes. As Exhibit 3 illustrates, growth to 1982 had been highly satisfactory. All subscribers received Gill's 24-channel dual cable basic package which included 15 "must carry" local channels. Of the remaining nine, one was reserved for community access programming, and the others were filled by a

Exhibit 3
Gillcable Growth, 1971–1982

Date	Number of basic subscribers	Number of premium subscribers*
1971	16,963	—
1972	18,589	—
1973	32,839	—
1974	42,016	—
1975	57,432	—
1976	65,208	—
1977	68,704	—
1978	70,178	—
1979	71,922	—
1980	80,372	3,000
1981	89,175	28,000
1982	93,616	33,375

* Introduced December 1980. Figures are approximate; premium subscribers are basic subscribers who have descrambler boxes.

combination of distant broadcast signals, either within California or from a "superstation" like WTBS in Atlanta, along with some channels reserved specially for cable.

In addition to the basic package, subscribers had the option to purchase one or more of five premium services, all of which required a descrambler to receive. Three of the five services were "foundation" channels which provided 24-hour service that appealed to a broad spectrum of viewers. These consisted of The Movie Channel, which showed 40 late-run movies per month; Home Box Office, which offered 24 movies per month as well as sporting events; and Showtime, which had movies, special shows, and other events. There was considerable duplication among the movies, although the separate services, particularly HBO, were increasingly differentiating themselves. The other two services were "wraparounds" which appealed to particular market segments. These two were Rendezvous, a Gill channel which showed three adult movies each evening, and Galavision, a national Spanish-language station. Gill planned to add at least three additional wraparounds in 1982: Cinemax, which showed slightly older movies than the foundations; The Disney Channel, which offered children's programming and family entertainment; and The Entertainment Channel, which had exclusive rights to BBC programming and was positioned as an arts/cultural channel. Subscribers with descrambler boxes could also purchase pay-per-view events, such as championship fights and movies not yet released to the pay channels. Exhibit 4 depicts Gill's program offerings.

Gillcable had an unusual start. It sprang from a San Jose bakery which Allen T. Gilliland, Sr., bought in 1933 for $3,000. By 1955, the

Exhibit 4
Gillcable Channel Offerings

| | A switch | | | | B switch | |
Channel	Affiliation	Broadcast signal	Basic service	Channel	Affiliation	Broadcast signal
KTVU	Independent*	2	2	Community Service		—
KNTV	ABC*	11	3	KDTV	SIN*	14
KRON	NBC*	4	4	KQEC	Independent*	32
KPIX	CBS*	5	5	Bay Area Religious Network		—
KICU	Independent*	36	6	KTZO	Independent*	20
KGO	ABC*	7	7	WTBS Atlanta	Independent*	17
Cable News Network†		—	8	KCSM	PBS*	60
KTEH	PBS*	54	9	KQED	PBS*	9
Cable Health Network†		—	10	KSTS		48
MTV: Music Channel†		—	11	KVOF	Independent*	38
G Channel		—	12	KBHK	Independent*	44
ESPN: Sports Channel†		—	13	USA Cable Network*		—
Premium channel:‡						
Pay-per-view		—	A			
Rendezvous		—	C			
The Movie Channel		—	D			
			E	KTXL	Independent	40
Galavision		—	G	KMST	CBS	46
Home Box Office		—	H			
Showtime		—	I			

* Must carry channel.
† National Cable network.
‡ Premium channels can be received only with a descrambler.

Sunlite bakery operated 75 delivery routes and dominated the San Jose area market. Gilliland became interested in television broadcasting in the late 1940s and early 1950s and organized a group of local investors to apply for a television license in San Jose. In 1955, Sunlite Bakery became the owner of Standard Radio and Television Company.

At the time, San Jose was a small city, and conventional wisdom held that a broadcast station in such a small market so close to San Francisco was suicidal. But Gilliland did not share this view. He brought his son Allen Jr. the current president, into the business after his graduation from Stanford in 1946. Although Allen Jr. had been brought up in the bakery business and had assumed a number of production and management positions at Sunlite from 1946 to 1960, his heart was in television. He became a founding partner of Standard, and when his father died in 1960, Allen, a self-described risk taker and entrepreneur, assumed the presidency of Standard—which became Gill Industries in 1964.

Standard used its FCC license to build KNTV (Channel 11), which operated as an independent from 1955 until 1960 when it became an ABC affiliate. Shortly thereafter, Allen, became one of the first generation of broadcasters who took an interest in cable.

By 1965, Gill had built and was operating two cable systems in California and had a half interest in a third. The company, which had previously been a food processing company with investments in communications, now became a communications company with food processing interests. Consequently, the bakery interests were sold in 1966. In 1968, Gilliland began building a cable system in San Jose in partnership with Ridder Newspapers. Gill Cable began construction in 1970, and in 1972, when about one third of the cable had been laid, Gill Industries acquired full ownership of the system.

Because of the tremendous up-front fixed costs required to build a cable system, the new company experienced cash flow problems in its early years. A solution to this problem was provided in 1978 when Gill Industries was required by the FCC to divest either the cable company or its KNTV broadcast station. Gilliland chose to sell KNTV because of his belief in the future of the cable industry. The sale brought $25 million. In 1982, the company produced revenues of about the same amount. Being privately owned, Gillcable did not disclose earnings, but industry sources believed that the company had increased the net worth of Gill Industries from $50 million to $150 million. Margins were estimated at 40 percent.

Gillcable had become known throughout the industry as one of the best run and most innovative companies. Two of these innovations warrant particular mention, addressability and the Bay Area Interconnect Network.

Beginning in late 1980, Gill was the first system west of the Mississippi with addressable control of services. About one third of its subscribers had descramblers, which allowed them to receive pay channels as well as pay-per-view events. The integration with the on-line data base management system allowed a customer with a descrambler to call the telephone sales office to order a pay service or special event, receive an unscrambled picture on their set in minutes, and be automatically billed on their next statement. The dual cable/descrambler system gave the company a capacity of 58 channels.

In 1979, Gillcable innaugurated the Bay Area Interconnect Network by linking through a central headend (by means of cable and microwave relay) 30 cable systems from Napa to Salinas. The major benefit to such a network had to do with economic clout. The larger viewing audience permitted more and larger advertising income and higher bids for pay-per-view events. The interconnect, needless to say, encouraged the separate franchisees to buy programming from Interconnect. The system included four cable networks (Cable News Network, The Sports Channel, Music Television, and Cable Health Network) and planned to expand. Total subscribers were 500,000 (35 percent of the area's viewing audience), and advertising revenues of $3 million in 1982 were expected to grow 50 percent a year over the next five years.

Gill Management Services

In keeping with his history of innovation, Gilliland diversified the company vertically. Complex offerings and equipment inventory requirements generated by the use of addressable descramblers made complex tracking of subscriber use critical. To this end, Gilliland founded Gill Management Services, a computerized record-keeping service that enabled cable firms to have immediate access to subscriber data. GMS served 20 cable systems nationwide and produced about $5 million in annual revenue. It was expected to become the star in Gill's portfolio, particularly as addressability became more common and problems of software development and reliability—the burdens of early entry into the field—were corrected.

Being first was not without its problems. The Gill descramblers had been among the first on the market and were relatively easy to "defeat." This was done by opening the box and rewiring it to bypass the addressable mechanism so that all pay services could be received even if only one was ordered. Such manipulation was a significant problem, particularly in a high-technology area like San Jose. Reichmuth saw this as a serious drag on premium sales. While he had no way to measure accurately how many boxes were altered, he suspected that it ranged between 10 percent and 25 percent of all installations. Gill planned to solve this problem over the next one to three years by switching to a new descrambler, which could be defeated but only with the replacement of a costly and complicated microprocessor.

A second problem was descrambler loss which averaged 10 percent of the boxes, which cost $100 each. With a more aggressive recovery program, Hosfeldt thought he could cut the losses in half, but even so this expense was expected to remain high since the new descrambler was estimated to cost $150. The dilemma was evident: To maximize revenues, Hosfeldt hoped to have boxes in all subscriber homes by the end of 1984. But given the high loss level (20 percent in some parts of the service area), Hosfeldt wondered how much greater penetration was warranted.

Bad debts were another aggravating issue which threatened growth plans. As the economy went into a recession in the early 1980s, payment of cable bills seemed to take a back seat to essential utilities such as gas, electricity, and telephone. Bad debt expense had skyrocketed recently and threatened to exceed 5 percent of revenues. Collection was problematic. Unlike tangibles, cable service was consumed immediately Further, court costs were excessive in relation to the amounts usually owed. Hosfeldt was unsure about how to handle this issue. To clamp down and disconnect earlier on slow payers would restrict growth. Hosfeldt estimated that by moving the date for disconnect up from the 110th day past due to the 90th day would hold growth to zero for four or five months.

The Marketing and Sales Strategy

The Gillcable organization was designed by Gilliland and Hosfeldt to balance the mesh the wide variety of management tasks. Gilliland stayed away from daily operations, devoting himself instead to the financial management of Gill Industries. Hosfeldt thus operated Gillcable. He brought to bear 20 years of experience and had served in a similar capacity at KNTV.

In the early days, the organization had been quite informal. Each manager had a direct reporting relationship to Hosfeldt, and his office was accessible to all. Hosfeldt's rich experience allowed him to keep track of everything from the highly technical equipment system to the sales operation. With growth, however, this system became cumbersome, and Hosfeldt responded by dividing the company into six divisions, each headed by a vice president: engineering, finance, operations, broadcast, marketing, and community relations. (A Gillcable organization chart is shown in Exhibit 5.) Each division was unique

Exhibit 5
Gillcable Organization Chart

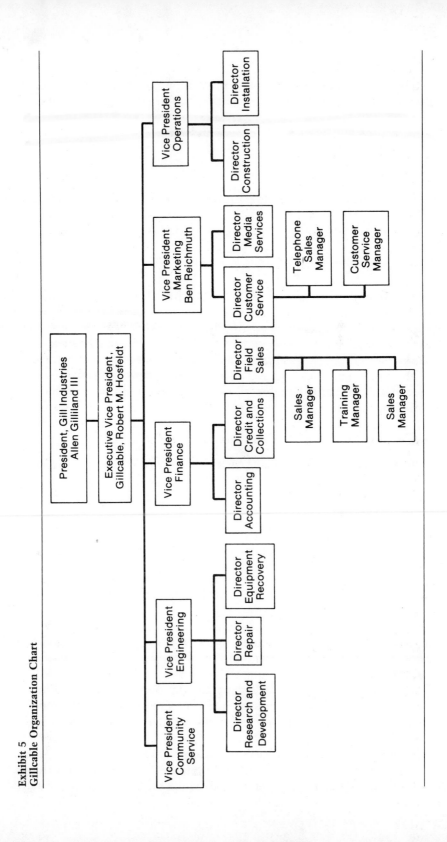

and hence operated with a considerable degree of autonomy. Nonetheless, Hosfeldt applied a strong hand in coordinating their activities.

Marketing consisted of three departments: field sales, customer services, and media services—each of which was supervised by a director.

Field Sales

Field sales consisted of 20 selling and 3 support personnel working under Rick Muhlbach who had been director of sales for four years. Three of the sales people also had management duties, two as sales managers and one as recruiter and trainer.

There were three selling tasks.

1. Remarket. Thirteen members of the sales force worked on periodic sweeps throughout the service area. The area was divided into 39 regions, and the sales crew spent an average of two to three nights in each region. Leads were generated by computer-generated call cards of the serviceable addresses in the area that were cold; i.e., not connected at the tap. Each salesman got about 30 lead cards each night. Cards listed the important available information about each address that was stored in the computer system. An example of a call card is shown in Exhibit 6A. Reichmuth felt that the size of the remarket sales force was dictated by the size of the service area:

> We want to avoid scorching the earth. If we move through the region faster than once every four months, we're at the door too frequently, and we're going to upset people. If we aren't there just about that often, people are going to forget about our service. We used to divide the service area into territories and give each salesman a territory, but we found that we got the worst of both worlds. Salesmen tended to get preconceived ideas about their territories—they knew which streets they thought were good and hit them too often, and they had ideas about which street and houses were bad, and they avoided them altogether. With the periodic sweep, we've found a happy medium.

2. Hot Moves. Salespeople who were successful for a year in remarket were normally promoted to the hot move program. A hot address was one which was connected at the tap but had no active subscriber. A new resident could thus hook up the cable and receive service. Gill had a policy of leaving an address hot for about 30 days after a voluntary disconnect. The hot move salesperson would receive a computer printout of all hot addresses with the last active subscriber date and the scheduled tap disconnect date. A computer printout for the hot move program is shown in Exhibit 6B.

The hot move sales force had individual territories. Reichmuth felt that "scorched earth" was not an issue since the salesman was usually

Exhibit 6

A. Sales Call Card

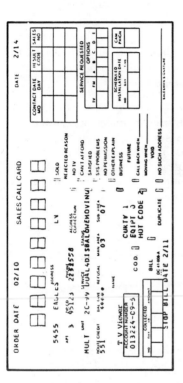

B. Hot Move Sheet

MA SA CHL	ADDRESS	RESIDENTIAL	APT#	NAME	PHONE	ACCOUNT#	BAL OWED	CAMPN	START DATE	STOP DATE	OLD SM
CB	21 A1 271 SHELLEY	CURREI1 IV-0- FM-0- EQ-0- HB-0-	AV ST-0- MV-0-	D TATMAN RZ-0- GV-0-	371-1397	421656-012		199	9/00/82	1/10/83	255
CB	A1 2254 SHELLEY	CURREI1 IV-0- FM-0- EQ-0- HB-0-	AV ST-0- MV-0-	JM TONKEL RZ-0- GV-0-	371-9171	445201-017		137	10/20/79	2/11/83	16
CB	A1 2332 SHELLEY	CURREI1 IV-0- FM-0- EQ-0- HB-0-	AV ST-0- MV-0-	Z CHOU RZ-0- GV-0-	371-0516	445221-015	.51	231	9/00/82	2/09/83	520
CA	13 C1 195 UNION	CURREI1 IV-B- FM-J- EQ-0- HB-0-	AV ST-0- MV-0- 56	J DUGAN RZ-0- GV-0-	559-4021	435971-026	125.66	099	11/00/82	2/07/83	202
CB	00 01 330 UNION	CURREI1 IV-0- FM-0- EQ-0- HB-0-	AV ST-0- MV-0-	M OCOYNELL RZ-0- GV-0-	999-9999	486654-019	14.85-	099	2/00/82	1/31/83	205
CB	21 A1 1710 WHITE JAKS	CURREI2 IV-0- FM-J- EQ-J- HB-0-	AV ST-0- MV-0-	T WELLS RZ-0- GV-0-	371-4491	808543-020		179	10/20/81	10/07/82	506
CB	21 A1 1956 WHITE OAKS	CURREI1 IV-0- FM-J- EQ-J- HB-0-	AV A ST-0- MV-0-	M BUYETTE RZ-0- GV-0-	371-8068	808671-039		171	3/10/81	1/31/83	205
OA	20 A1 1541 MUDDARD	CURREI2 IV-J- FM-J- EQ-J- HB-0-	RU ST-0- MV-0-	J WALSER RZ-0- GV-0-	377-4515	063159-010		124	12/20/77	1/09/83	20

meeting new residents who had not seen a Gill representative before. Further, a salesperson who knew the territory was aware when houses became vacant or had new residents. There were, in 1982, five hot move salesmen. Each had a territory of about eight management areas. Hot moves were critical to growth because they minimized the negative impact of churn (disconnects and reconnects at the same address) on the subscriber base. The faster an address could be resold, the smaller the financial loss caused by a cancelled subscriber. Churn was a substantial problem in the cable industry—Reichmuth estimated that about 3 percent of the subscriber base turned over each month for voluntary reasons or because of nonpayment.

3.   Special Territories.   Two sales individuals had special territories. One worked only apartments, and the other handled newly wired areas. Reichmuth tried to de-emphasize apartment sales because of the problem of turnover:

> Sometimes half of our subscribers in an apartment complex disappear on the first of June because that's when leases expire. The problem has diminished because of economic conditions, but it's still an issue. When one salesman concentrates on apartments, he gets to know the managers and so knows when a unit is vacant or about to become vacant, and he knows which units have high turnover rates.

Telephone Sales and Customer Service

Telephone sales had become important during the last year primarily because of increased mention of the firm's telephone number in advertisements. Telephone sales accounted for 35 to 40 percent of sales in 1981 but had grown to almost 50 percent by 1982, reaching as high as 56 percent in one month. Reichmuth felt, however, that 50 percent was about the limit of telephone sales.

Gill maintained a central telephone room with 19 operators, each working at a computer terminal. Nine of the operators took sales calls, seven took customer service calls (billing questions, programming complaints or suggestions, and other questions), and three took repair calls. When lines for one group were filled, calls automatically transferred to the other group. Each had access to all subscriber information and could input orders directly.

Media Services

The media services department was responsible for all advertising and promotional activities. It was Reichmuth's opinion that advertising posed an interesting problem for cable television:

> Television advertising is very effective for our premium services, but only for our current subscribers. We can advertise on our Interconnect

channels, but nonsubscribers don't see it. The most effective medium for nonsubscribers is print, and we make good use of that, particularly newspapers. For current subscribers who we want to upgrade to premium, we use television.

Media services also published a monthly programming guide, which was sent to all subscribers, and coordinated direct mail activities. Direct mailings preceded each sweep of a sales area, pay-per-view events, and special promotions.

Hiring and Training

Turnover of sales personnel at Gill was high, particularly in the first few weeks of employment. Selling was hard, and the six-day workweek as well as long daily working hours caused burnout. Job expectancy for all but a few was two to three years. The training manager, who also sold, commented:

> It's important for these people to learn the ABCs of cable TV and what Gill has to offer, but you just can't prepare people for the realities of door-to-door selling. A good door-to-door salesperson is born, not made. You've got to be able to take the personal rejection of having 10 doors in a row slammed in your face and still be the friendly cable representative at the 11th. You can tell after three or four days if somebody's going to make it. If they start straggling in with a hangdog expression, you can write them off.

Salespeople were recruited through newspaper ads and by word-of-mouth. Because of the difficulty of the sales task, there was an extensive two-week training period. The training manager conducted classes in which he explained the technology, the service, and sales techniques.

The selling objective clearly was to maximize sales, which sometimes created problems—particularly because there was little new construction. Most addresses had been sold at one time or another. Reichmuth felt he constantly had to be vigilant for "kinks"—deals on which salespeople changed the name or phone number to get a previously poor-paying subscriber back on service. Those who did this were disciplined, however, and Reichmuth felt the problem was under control. This problem raised the bad debt issue since some addresses consistently produced nonpay disconnects. He wondered if these areas should be designated off limits to the sales force.

Compensation

Telephone and field sales personnel received vastly different levels of compensation. Field sales were paid at the highest level of any cable sales force in the country. Reichmuth felt that this was justified because sales were much more difficult in an area that was almost entirely remarket. Field sales personnel were paid $18 for each basic sale plus $6 for each level of premium service. In addition, they were paid a bonus of $50 for making 15 sales in a week, $100 for reaching 20 sales, and an additional $100 for each 5 sales over 20. Telephone sales personnel received a base salary plus $1 for each basic sale and $.50 for each premium upgrade. Customer service operators were paid an additional retention bonus based on a percentage of growth each month. This tended to make their salaries equivalent to telephone sales personnel, who received more sales calls.

Muhlbach remembered his first look at the compensation package:

> When Hosfeldt first showed me the package, I said, "There's no way these guys can make any money." Then he showed me their salaries, and I saw how the bonus mounts up. If people stay with us for a year, they should make $30,000 to $50,000 a year. A hot move salesperson should make $50,000 to $75,000. The key is consistency. If they go out and hit three every night, they'll do all right, but the money really comes when they hit four and five. They all know the number I hate most—its 19. When someone hits 20, he/she has it made.

While there was no commission increase for length of stay with the company, salespeople tended to move from remarket to managerial positions or hot moves the longer they stayed with the company. Exhibit 7 lists salaries and other pertinent data for field sales personnel.

Exhibit 7
Data of Field Salesmen*

Salesman	Length of time at Gill	Age	Type of sales	Approximate salary last 12 months
A	8 years	34	Hot move	$100,000
B	2 years	31	Hot move	50,000
C	9 months	37	Hot move	—
D	2½ years	36	Hot move	65,000
E	1 year	26	Hot move	34,000
F	1½ years	27	Apartments	75,000
G	2 years	29	New construction	55,000
H	1½ years	26	Remarket	40,000
I	1½ years	26	Remarket	35,000
J	1 year	32	Remarket	40,000
K	2 months	42	Remarket	—
L	1 year	33	Remarket	45,000
M	1 month	40	Remarket	—
N	3 months	28	Remarket	—
O	2 months	24	Remarket	—
P	1½ years	27	Remarket	26,500
Q	5 months	26	Remarket	—
R	1 month	45	Remarket	—

* Data intended to be illustrated and to reflect actual data.

Monthly commissions for telephone sales operators amounted to $250 to $350. With base salary, annual salaries amounted to $15,000 to $18,000. There was little compensation advantage to job longevity, although operators tended to move into supervisory positions if they stayed with the company. These positions carried higher base salaries.

Reichmuth defended the disparity in salaries:

> Our field sales force is very expensive—we spent about a million dollars on commissions last year. But direct sales is the backbone of our growth. Our sales force is often the only direct contact between the company and the subscriber, and we want quality people out there. The subscriber who calls in on the phone has already pretty much decided to buy, but the real selling job occurs in the field. The direct salesperson can turn around a potential customer who has heard about us but hasn't really made a commitment to buy the service.

Cost of Service

The table below lists prices for selected basic packages in the San Francisco Bay Area.

MSO	Monthly basic price
Gillcable	$14.85
Westinghouse Group W	10.95
Viacom of San Francisco	10.00
Concord TV Cable	8.10
Cablevision Corporation	6.65

Gill's $14.85 was by far the highest price in the area, which Hosfeldt justified on the basis of system reliability and product quality (Gill offered the only independent movie channel on basic service in the United States):

> Our 24-hour channel basic service is among the best in the industry, but we sell more than just a product package. We take good care of the subscriber from the moment we sell to the moment we disconnect. We install hookups or correct system problems in a fraction of the time it takes for other companies.

Gill's higher prices had not had much effect on penetration which, at 48.7 percent, was well above the industry average and one of the highest in the Bay Area. Gill research did show a significant price point at $40 per month. Many subscribers would not pay above this level no matter what the service quality.

Reichmuth explained his philosophy of pricing:

> Discounting is very big in the industry, but we don't do it. Companies
> are finding that if they give a discount on every level of pay, by the time
> they get to the third or fourth level, they've given it away. Furthermore,
> discounting gives cable a "cheap" image, which we want to avoid. We're
> proud of the quality of our system, and we think the price we charge is
> reasonable. Pay-per-view particularly is not price sensitive. For a big
> fight, you get 10 or 12 people in a front room, and $20 doesn't seem like
> much, particularly when you compare it to closed-circuit prices.

The Opportunities—and the Constraints

Industry analysts felt that cable TV stood poised to take over from
the broadcast network. Moreover, there were two other largely un-
tapped sources of future cable TV revenues, two-way television and
advertising.

Two-way services were the topic of much speculation, and it was
not clear to what extent they would be profitable. Potential services
included telebanking, videotext, teleshopping, and home security.
Only home security was generally regarded as a sure success, with
industry sources estimating a market share of 20 percent by 1990.
AT&T and the other phone companies were considered best positioned
for this business because of their financial strength and technical and
marketing abilities. Further, two-way required different wiring from
single-direction cable, and older systems like Gill's did not have two-
way capability as did most of the new systems.

Potential advertising revenues had barely been tapped by cable companies because cable systems tended to have viewing audiences that
were too small to attract significant advertising dollars. One way to get
around this problem was to join cable systems together through interconnect systems, so that each system in the interconnect would show
the same programs and advertisements at the same time. Gill, as previously noted, had developed the first and largest interconnect system in
the United States.

The industry was faced, at the same time, with important constraints. To start, cable was subject to regulation from federal, state,
and local governments. Although the FCC had decreased its influence
over the last several years, municipalities had continued to exert considerable control, primarily through franchising terms. Cable companies had to apply to municipalities for franchises, and local governments had become quite sophisticated in exacting heavy concessions
in return for potentially lucrative rights to build cable systems. Major
issues included franchise fees, rate regulation, municipal ownership,
content regulation, and mandated access. Of these, franchise fees im-

posed the greatest financial drain on MSOs. Municipalities received up to 5 percent of revenues for giving franchise rights. Gill, which had an older franchise, paid only a 2 percent franchise fee. Rates had to be approved by the municipality, and rate restrictions could conceivably be used to restrict profitability. Municipalities thus far had not denied reasonable rate increases.

Municipal ownership was a particularly volatile issue, with proponents advocating public ownership as a means of avoiding commercialism, retaining control over programming, and reducing cost. Municipalities had for the most part lacked the expertise and had been unable to develop the consensus necessary to own and operate their own systems.

Content regulation had not been a major concern. MSOs usually regulated themselves, and the argument that cable was a medium of choice—no subscriber *had* to watch anything—had thus far been persuasive. Mandated public access had been demanded—and received—by many recent franchises. As the number of channels available in new systems rose, cable companies were willing to designate more of them for public access, even though these channels generated no revenue.

Since MSOs received franchises, they did not encounter direct competition from other cable companies. As an entertainment medium, cable competed directly with movie theaters, live sports events, and other forms of entertainment. Of most significant concern to cable operators were other purveyors of pay television, including private cable systems (SMATV), single-channel subscription TV services (STV), and direct broadcast satellites (DBS), which were expected to beam about 36 channels nationwide by the late 1980s. All will make some dent in cable market penetration, but none is expected to compete successfully in urban markets. SMATV will be responsible for some "cream skimming" in large housing developments and multiunit dwellings. STV had been able to cover a larger area than most cable systems and could therefore make heavier use of advertising media to promote its product, but it could never offer the breadth of programming that cable systems could. DBS offered the most serious challenge, but cable systems should be well established by the time DBS comes into existence and will offer more channels and the benefits of addressability.

High costs were a particular problem for cable companies applying for new franchises. Cable systems were remarkable for their high fixed cost of construction and cable laying and the low variable costs associated with operation. Industry estimates were that a new two-way system with 54-channel capacity could cost as much as $800 per subscriber. This challenged cable marketing operations to sell a large proportion of pay services relative to basic in order to ensure a reasonable payback. Where high costs were coupled with high interest rates and the increasing demands exacted by municipalities in franchise agreements, cable companies were finding it increasingly difficult to weather the financial storms imposed by huge up-front costs in order to survive to the balmy atmosphere promised by high pay revenues.

The September Staff Meeting

Against this background, Gill management was taking a fresh look at its growth plans and selling strategies. A number of issues had been raised:

1. How fast to expand pay-per-view?
2. What payback to require?
3. How much penetration to seek?
4. Was product quality satisfactory?
5. How to use the 26 unfilled channels?
6. How many pay services to support?
7. How to handle bad debts and scrambler losses?

These issues had come to a head because management was considering a new product, "Superbasic."

Superbasic was a transitional product package designed to upgrade subscribers from basic to premium subscriptions and, in the process, make them eligible to purchase pay-per-view events. The product was a package of eight basic channels similar to those already included except that Superbasic could be received only on a descrambler because of the dual cable system's 24-channel capacity. (See Exhibit 8 for the proposed Superbasic package.)

Exhibit 8
Proposed Superbasic Package

Broadcast channels:
    Channel 3 (Sacramento, NBC affiliate)—particularly valuable as a backup for sports events blacked out in the Bay Area.
    Channel 40 (Sacramento, independent)—specializes in classic movies and syndicated programming.
    Channel 46 (Monterey, CBS affiliate)—backup for San Francisco CBS affiliate.

Cable channels:
    Satellite News Channel—24-hour news format similar to the Cable News Network.
    Nashville Country—24-hour country music and variety programming.
    Weather Channel—24-hour national weather service.
    Daytime/Arts—Programming for women during the day and cultural programming in the evening.
    Dow Jones Cable News—24-hour news format with emphasis on financial news.

Hosfeldt saw Superbasic as an excellent opportunity to increase descrambler penetration. He particularly favored a pricing strategy in which subscribers to premium services would receive Superbasic at no increase in price. He reasoned that, since there would be little increase in Gill's cost in bringing the eight channels, Superbasic could actually be a revenue producer without increasing total price for premium subscribers. This could be accomplished by designating a price for Superbasic and subtracting this price from the price of the first pay service. In this way, Gill's payment to the pay service, based on a percentage of price, would be reduced. This idea is illustrated below:

Package 1		Package 2	
Basic only	$14.85	Basic	$14.85
		Superbasic	x
Total price	$14.85	Total price	$14.85 + x
Package 3		**Package 4**	
Basic	$14.85	Basic	$14.85
Superbasic	x	Superbasic	x
Foundation pay service	12.55 − x	Foundation A	12.55 − x
		Foundation B	12.55
Total price	$27.40	Total price	$39.95

This pricing strategy would have the added advantage of keeping the price of a service package with a second foundation service under the $40 price point. Hosfeldt thought that it would also make the transition from basic to premium service easier for the subscriber.

One of the most frequently voiced concerns about immediate introduction of Superbasic was that Gill might be moving too quickly. If sufficient pay-per-view opportunities did not come about for three or four years, the investment in additional descramblers could be crippling financially. A further problem was that Superbasic would initially be available in only one of the two system hubs because wiring was not sufficient in one to carry Superbasic. This meant that about 20 percent of the system's subscribers would not be able to receive Superbasic until mid-1984. This argued for either a delay in introduction or at least a change in Hosfeldt's pricing plan, since it would be difficult to convince some subscribers to pay the same price for eight fewer channels. There was also some concern in the industry about program quality. One cable executive commented, "I would be surprised if a 30-channel system operator won't be scratching to find things to put on a couple of years from now. The current 35 national basic services are going to boil down to a handful." Some members of the Gill management team felt in would be counterproductive to risk offering an inferior product package or having to withdraw the package for lack of product at some future date.

Two issues that everyone agreed should be settled before Superbasic was introduced were the problems of box recovery and collection of past due accounts. One school of thought was that these issues were integrally related with sales and marketing. A staff member commented:

> I believe that marketing should be responsible for the whole customer loop, from the salesperson who signs up the customer; to the installer who connects the cable; to customer service while he is an active account; to collections, disconnects, and box recovery if that becomes necessary. There is a basic tension between finance and marketing. Finance feels a need to be tough—if subscribers are late with payments, finance wants to disconnect them. Marketing wants to keep them on service if possible. I think that collections and box recovery should be integrated with field sales, and salespeople should be paid a percentage of past-due amounts they collect and a bounty on each box they recover. This gives the company a chance to make one more contact with "a good guy" before we send "a bad guy" out to disconnect. The beauty of the idea is that you reduce churn, and with it the cost of sales commissions for resale, disconnect and reconnect costs, and lost revenue while an address is disconnected.

A member of the Gill management team disagreed:

> Having marketing handle collections and box recovery is like letting the fox in the henhouse. A company must have checks and balances if it is going to be successful. Marketing its just going to be too eager to see growth to do a responsible job of collecting. I think we should definitely step up collection and box recovery efforts, but it should be handled within the current organization structure.

There was a third point of view that argued that collections and recovery were not such critical issues:

> Our new descrambler will be almost impossible to defeat. This means that in two years, when we have switched our entire system to the new boxes, there will be no incentive to keep the old ones. Addressable boxes are going to generate so much revenue that it just isn't worth the high cost of going after them—we can just purchase new ones. Sure we have to tighten up on collections, but that's economy related. When the economy improves, so will our bad debt problem.

A final issue was brought up by marketing vice president Reichmuth who felt that Superbasic and increased penetration might require some new marketing ideas, particularly with regard to sales and promotion. He opened this to the group for some brainstorming.

C A S E 3–2

![bar]

Henkel-Trifft

In late January 1969, Herr Krabbe, product planner at Henkel Cie GmbH, was preparing for the next "weekly conceptual talks" with his colleagues and supervisors. In that meeting, ideas, developments, and problems within the product line would be discussed. One of the products which had been Herr Krabbe's responsibility for the last month was the new liquid spray cleaner Trifft, launched in August 1968 nationally on the German market. Trifft had not gained as wide consumer acceptance as expected. Facing a disappointing sales performance, product management was wondering how or whether Trifft's market performance could be improved. Herr Krabbe had a report from the advertising agency, Euro Ad, on his desk, suggesting that Trifft should be repositioned closer to other liquid household cleaners to share their success.

In 1876, Fritz Henkel founded a company in Dusseldorf, Germany, for bleaching powder, employing three workers. By 1900, Henkel & Cie employed 80 persons and was the first to apply a brand name to a product normally sold in bulk. Henkel's bleaching powder was produced in uniform quality, packaged in standard sizes, and supported by newspapers advertising. At that time, laundry still had to be scrubbed with laundry soap. Henkel's was the world's first self-acting washing preparation; i.e., the laundry had only to be boiled. On June 6, 1907, a Dusseldorf newspaper contained the first advertisement for this product called Persil, and a year later the company could claim "millions of housewives" used it. The original package has been retained over Persil's 62-year life. This brand was still the biggest selling brand on the market in 1969.

Copyright © by INSEAD—The European Institute of Business Administration, Fontainebleau, France. This case was prepared by Peter Mayer under the direction of Dr. David Weinstein, Associate Professor of Marketing, INSEAD. Reproduced by permission.

In 1969, Henkel was competing successfully with Procter and Gamble, Colgate, and Unilever—and was the world's fourth largest producer of detergents and cleaning agents. It employed some 32,000 people, one third of whom worked outside Germany. In Dusseldorf, its plants and offices spread over 275 acres. Henkel's sales in 1968 were close to DM 4,000 million, and its line was comprised of 8,000 products ranging from industrial chemicals, adhesives, detergents, to cosmetics, with detergents representing about half the total turnover.[1]

Some Henkel brands had been sold successfully for a long time—for example, Persil. Others were modified or dropped as market conditions changed. Thus, new products were constantly being developed by the firm. Henkel's established policy in "cleaners" was to obtain at least a 13 percent share for any new product in a particular market one year after its introduction. Otherwise, the product was deemed unsuccessful and phased out. Although the procedure for the development and introduction of a new product could vary substantially from one single product to the next, the company followed the policy of thoroughly testing the product concept and the physical product itself under a variety of conditions including "test" markets. Labels, containers, pricing, and advertising were similarly tested.

All-purpose household cleaners (APHCs) were defined as "cleaning agents for all household washable surfaces." APHCs had somewhat different chemical features which permitted them to perform in a different mix of applications (see Exhibit 1 for current market products). A number of studies performed for Henkel in 1965–67 showed, however, that they were used basically for the "big cleaning jobs." Other applications of APHCs included intermediate cleaning and stain removal, bathroom, kitchen, and door cleaning. Most of this cleaning occurred in the kitchen during and after cooking; therefore, besides cleaners and soap, housewives generally used dishwater. For manual dishwashing (automatic dishwashers at that time in Germany had a negligible share), housewives prepared a solution comprised of a special detergent and warm water. Dishwater was, thus, considered to be the strongest competitor of APHCs as far as intermediate cleaning was concerned.

In 1967, all-purpose household cleaners in Germany could be divided into powders and concentrated liquid cleaners. Both had to be diluted with water before application. Total industry sales for 1962–1967 are given in Table 1.

Henkel had already innovated twice in this field by introducing Dor, a powdered cleaner, which was the first mild, modern household cleaner for delicate surfaces (launched nationally in 1961) in Germany,

---

[1] Compiled from company sources, *Internal Management*, February 1972, and *Fortune*, August 1972. In 1969 $1 U.S. = DM 4.20.

Exhibit 1
Products on the Market in 1967 and 1968

Company	Product	Form	Cleaning power*	Color	Perfume	Use	On the market since	MS† 1967 (percent)	MS† last quarter 1968 (percent)
Henkel	Dor	Powder	Low	Light green	Lavender	Not for big dirt-"shine"	1961	25.8%	23%
	Clin	Liquid	Low	—	Pine/ammonia†	All purposes	1963	2.5	—
	WR Kraftreiniger	Liquid viscous	Medium	Milky	Soap/ammonia‡	All purposes, big dirt	1967 test marketed	0.5	—
	Imi Pulver	Powder	High	—	None	Not for delicate surfaces, esp. for grease	1929	9.9	Not known
Sunlicht	Imi Flüssig	Liquid viscous	Medium	Milky	Pine/ammonia‡	All purposes	1966	3.2	Not known
	Trifft	Liquid spray	Medium	Green	Pine/ammonia‡	All purposes	1968	—	8.9
	Andy	Powder	High	—	—	Not for delicate surfaces	1963	—	—
Unilever	Andy Flüssig	Liquid	Medium	Green	Pine/ammonia‡	All purposes	1965	—	—
	Vigor	Liquid spray	High	Blue	Pine/ammonia‡	Not for delicate surfaces	1968 test marketed	—	None
Procter & Gamble	Fairy	Powder	High	None	None	Not for delicate surfaces	1961	8.3	Not known
Colgate	Mr. Proper	Liquid	Medium	Green	Pine/ammonia‡	All purposes	1967	12.0	18
	Ajax Floor	Powder	High	None	None	Not for delicate surfaces	—	—	—
Palmolive	Ajax	Liquid	Medium	Milky	Pine/ammonia‡	All purposes	1974	28.1	28
	Schnip	Liquid spray	Low	None	Fruit	All purposes	1968 test marketed	—	1–7 in test market
Others	—	—	—	—	—	—	—	7.2	Not known

Notes: Very strong cleaners are aggressive on lacquers. Strength can be felt by the skin during use, especially in case of small scratches.
* This column expresses the alkalinity of the various cleaners corresponding, in general, to the perceived power in cleaning.
† MS = Market shares. These could vary between ≠ 20 percent geographically. This effect is especially true in test market areas where two products come into the most direct competition.
‡ Ammonia was perceived (due to extensive Ajax advertising) as a very good cleaning ingredient by users.

Table 1
Market Data for APHCs in Germany

	1962	1963	1964	1965	1966	1967
Market size (million DM)	39	62	80	97	100	100
Market shares (percent):						
Henkel.....................	79.5	63.5	49.5	43.0	43.9	42.0
Colgate (Ajax)..............	0	0	20.4	33.6	37.8	32.5
P&G (Fairy, Mr. Proper)	20.4	31.4	19.7	14.5	11.5	20.5
Unilever...................	0	4.0	9.5	7.9	5.0	2.5
Others	0.1	1.1	0.9	1.0	1.8	2.5
	100.0	100.0	100.0	100.0	100.0	100.0
Shares by texture (percent):						
Powder	96.8	82.5	64.2	61.4	59.2	52.0
Concentrated liquid	3.2	17.5	35.8	38.6	40.8	48.0
	100.0	100.0	100.0	100.0	100.0	100.0
Henkel's APHC						
product line (percent):						
Dor powder	65.0	36.6	25.8	22.3	23.3	26.0
Other powders.............	11.3	10.2	8.6	11.0	10.9	10.0
Concentrated liquid	3.2	16.7	15.1	9.7	9.7	6.0
Total	79.5	63.5	49.5	43.0	43.9	42.0

and Clin, a concentrated liquid cleaner (national in 1963). The latter
was the first concentrated liquid APHC to gain a significant market
share. In 1967, APHCs represented about 5 percent of Henkel's washing and cleaning agent sales in Germany. In spite of this small relative
share, management was increasingly concerned about its declining
share in the APHC market and about the success of competitive concentrated liquid APHCs.

The U.S. market was used by Henkel as one source of new product
ideas. In 1967, liquid cleaners held 70 percent of the American APHC
market. In addition to concentrated liquid and powder cleaners, there
were (since 1966) so-called spray cleaners (included in the 70 percent
market share for liquid cleaners). They were applied directly to the
surface by squirting a pump which served also as a container cap and
were promoted as "heavy duty cleaners" for spots and special purposes.
The pump was used in Germany only in connection with a liquid
window cleaner ("Sidolin").

Spray cleaner prices were well above those of liquid cleaners—on
the average they were 30 percent higher per ounce of liquid. However,
they came in larger bottles (22-ounce average versus 15-ounce) which
made price comparisons difficult for shoppers. Two brands dominated
the spray-cleaner segment (Fantastik and Formula 409).

In autumn 1967, Mr. Bertold, who observed the U.S. market for
Henkel in New York City, reported that spray APHCs were estimated
to have obtained a 23 percent market share of the APHC market. This

figure was used subsequently by product management in comparing the U.S. and the German market and its trends.

In the spring of 1967, Henkel received three U.S. spray cleaners, (Fantastik, Formula 409, and Cinch) for laboratory testing. The laboratory director, in reporting the results to product management, noted that, while he was impressed with the spray principle, these formulas were, in his opinion, chemically too aggressive for the German market. At the same time, product management was becoming increasingly concerned with Henkel's position in the growing market for liquid APHCs in Germany. While P&G (Meister Proper) and Colgate (Ajax) were successful in this field, Henkel's effort had not been very successful. The popular Dor powder had been developed in liquid form but had not yet been marketed. "The idea was not to jeopardize sales of Dor powder, when it still has a large market share and to save the liquid for a later date when powder sales had become too small," said Herr Krabbe.

Product management saw in the spray cleaner an opportunity to market a new liquid cleaner. It was felt that such a cleaner could improve Henkel's position in the liquid APHC segment and also anticipate competitive developments, since it was suspected that U.S.-based German competitors were preparing to launch similar products. It was planned to sell the Henkel spray cleaner for large surface cleaning as well as for spots and intermediate cleaning.

In September 1967, following several meetings, the desired features of the new spray cleaner were agreed upon. At this stage, two names were being considered, Hit or Swing. Eventually, neither Hit nor Swing would be used, since they had already been registered by other companies. The name finally selected was Trifft, a common expression in German for "hit the spot."

A study was carried out in September 1967 among 750 housewives who tested a strong formula and another 750 who tested the milder formula. This was done even though product management knew that the products being tested were not yet "perfect." The spray pump leaked, and the fluid contained in the transparent bottles was sensitive to light, i.e., it changed color when exposed to light over a long period of time. Despite these technical problems, product management felt that work on the project should proceed rapidly. A month after the initiation of the field study, it was decided to brief the Euro Ad agency to develop bottle and label ideas. The urgent need for fast development was stressed by a pencil note put on the product conception document by a leading marketing manager, "Es soll in dieser Richtung schnell weitergearbeitet werden" (We should work fast in this direction).

The final product conception document, which was completed in November 1967 (detailed in Exhibit 2), summarized the market opportunity; confirmed the positioning of Trifft as a convenient cleaner that

Exhibit 2
Summary of the Product Conception Report

Liquid household cleaners have achieved more than 50 percent share in Germany and more than 75 percent in the United States.
Henkel has no significant product in the liquid market.
In the United States, spray cleaners have already obtained 25 percent of the market. We believe that the German market will also be receptive to this new cleaner.
The main ideas of such a spray cleaner from Henkel are:

Easy and convenient application of a liquid household cleaner by means of a spray pump.
Without diluting with water.
Without rinsing and polishing.

A product test is being carried out to investigate which type will be the most likely to succeed in Germany:

A mild cleaner.
A stronger, better cleaning type.
A universal type between the two, with emphasis on the easy application.

Other data:

Contents: 300–400 g, eventually larger refill bottle.
Price (retail): DM 2.10–2.30 for 350 g.
Price level due to calculated necessities and to high-quality positioning.

Calculations:

	1969	1970	1971
Market share.......	8%	14%	18%
Market size*.......	105 DM	109	112
Revenue Trifft*....	12 DM†	15.3	20
Tons sold	2,500	3,600	4,700
Contributions*.....	5 DM	6.3	13

* In millions of DM.
† 8 percent market share + inventory.

could be sprayed undiluted on surfaces; gave details on the formulas, bottle capacity, and pricing policies; and forecast market shares of 8 percent in 1968, 14 percent in 1969, and 18 percent in 1970. Introduction was scheduled for autumn 1968.

The results of the formula test among housewives became available in January 1968. The report stated that:

Trifft has the potential to be well accepted by consumers in comparison to other cleaners, if well introduced with advertising support. During the introduction phase, Trifft should be differentiated from window cleaners in order to avoid confusion. The strong version Trifft had better results in most areas and results equal to the mild version in other areas. We therefore recommend production of the stronger type.

The results provide some insights concerning:

Housewives' opinion about household work (only 10 percent dislike household work).

Surfaces cleaned with Trifft (75 percent used it on both surfaces and spots).

Little use of Trifft on furniture (60 percent did not use it on kitchen furniture).

Complaints about spots and stains on lacquers (about 5 percent) after application (both types).

Trifft's cleaning power (90 percent saying either "good" or "very good").

There was no indication of differences by region, social class, or any other criteria. (For more details, see Exhibit 3.)

In January 1968, a spray cleaner (Nifti by Cyanamid) was introduced in Denmark, and product management had evidence that Colgate and Unilever were working on similar developments. Herr Krabbe (product management) put it this way: "When we knew that competition intended to do the same as we did, we agreed on not going regional first, as usual, but to go national with Trifft as soon as possible."

A conference with Euro Ad held in January 1968 produced the following agreement regarding the introductory advertising campaign:

1.   Use the name "Trifft" in the advertising copy.
2.   Show the easy handling ("It's like playing").
3.   Emphasize partial cleaning but also show large surface cleaning.
4.   Devise a good slogan which contains the new cleaning method.
5.   Avoid using the name "Henkel."
6.   The target group should be all housewives, with emphasis on the 25 to 35-year-olds.
7.   Avoid confusion with existing window cleaners by clear advertising and usage instructions.

The next step included setting up operational plans, designing the introductory campaign, and final selection of the label and the bottle.

A marketing research study showed that the most popular label was very similar to that of a competitor's laundry detergent (OMO). "Therefore," said Herr Krabbe, "we chose the second best rated label and changed the color from blue to green, because many housewives said they didn't like the blue with the red; it was too aggressive."

In May 1968, the results of another research study became available. This one tested the concept of spray cleaning through the use of depth-interviews with 40 housewives who discussed their cleaning needs, how they classified cleaners, and how they reacted to the spray concept. During the interview, they were shown a spray cleaner and al-

Exhibit 3
Excerpts of a Field Study for Henkel on a Liquid Spray Cleaner

Samples of Trifft were given free to two groups of 750 housewives. One group received the strong version (SP) and the other the milder one (MP). Interviews took place two weeks later.

Results	SP (trialists)	MP (trialists)
Cleaning power "good" or "very good"	90%	
Cleaning power "very good"	44%	36%
Good all-around cleaning	80	
Good stain cleaning.............................	52	37
"Practical when used"	75	72
Economical......................................	71	73
"Practical bottle"	64	66
Color and smell	positively judged	
Normally used cleaner smells better...............	3	9
Normally used cleaner cleans stains better	0	17
Normally used cleaner is less practical as to its bottle..	7	
Spray cleaner is a new thing.....................	50	
Spray is known from window cleaner (Sidolin)........	25	
I recommend Trifft for spot and large surface cleaning..	62	57
I recommend Trifft for larger surfaces..............	17	29
I recommend Trifft for spot cleaning...............	19	21
Trifft was sprayed directly on the surface to clean......	75	
Trifft was sprayed on the cleaning rag	10	
Pump is functioning perfectly	71	66
Product needs improvement	24	31
Especially the pump........................	12	
Especially the bottle......................	6	
I would pay more than DM 2 for the product	60	52
(average price)	DM 2.22	DM 2.13
Advantages of the spray mechanism:		
Economical	50	38
Good dosing	15	25
Practical.................................	17	16
Direct application	8	8
Clean working	5	4
Timesaving	4	4
I like household work............................	68	
I am indifferent to household work	22	

    Other cleaners normally used were: Dor (35 percent) and Ajax All-Purpose Cleaner (17 percent).
    Most housewives think that Trift is most closely related to Sidolin (25 percent) than to Dor (9 percent versus 16 percent).

lowed to use it. The results revealed considerable skepticism and insecurity about the new concept, the most important of which was that they perceived no real need for a spray cleaner. While it was recognized that these reactions presented obstacles to the success of Trifft, it was felt that they could be overcome by advertising and consumer education (see Exhibit 4).

In April 1968, Colgate introduced, on a regional basis, its liquid spray cleaner Schnip. It was milder than Trifft and advertised for inter-

Exhibit 4
Excerpts from a Research Study among 40 Housewives Using
Depth-Interviewing—May 1968

In a laboratory test with 40 housewives, the results of the depth interviews were:

A. General Findings
Major classifying dimensions relating to APHCs offered by interviewees were:

Application area.

Cleaning power.

Texture.

Liquid cleaners are said to be modern, practical. Having a broad range of uses, they are convenient, timesaving, and easy to mix—but expensive. There is a need for precise instructions as to the appropriate mixture for the surface type.

B. Spray Cleaners
1. Reactions to new concepts
   The new principle raised immediately a negative reaction due to inability to identify the concept. The spray principle is associated with aerosol spray cosmetics (hair spray) and slightly with window cleaning. It is rejected for household cleaning because:

   Difficult to control the amount used.

   Risk of spraying on a wider area than needed.

   Doesn't seem superior to conventional liquid cleaners.

   Spray APHC's can only be imagined in a form like window cleaners; i.e., in plastic bottle with a squirt top. But skepticism should, on the other hand, not be overestimated. If such a product is introduced, however, a long learning process will be necessary along with a very attractive presentation of the product.
2. Expectations of a spray APHC
   Basic areas of application were thought to be larger pieces of furniture (like tables and cupboards), but the product is perceived as being uneconomical. Doors, tiles, and windows were mentioned. These attitudes again stress the need for consumer education.
3. Reactions to a Trifft concept
   a. Spot cleaning endangers the whole product conception. Emphasis on spot cleaning power and use for delicate surfaces are important. The price, substantially higher than for comparable products, represents an economic barrier.
   b. Brand name Trifft: very original and appealing but lacks product specificity.
   c. Package: positively judged; close to window cleaners and dishwashing liquids. The label does not give precise areas of application. The bottle is easy to handle.
   d. Trifft on today's market: Trifft's image is close to Henkel's Dor and Mr. Proper but can be a good competitor given the following recommended changes:

      Dynamic, colorful package (against Mr. Proper!).

      Clear product profile, clear instruction of use.

      Emphasis on use for large surfaces to avoid "specialization".

      Stress on easy, timesaving applications.

mediate spot cleaning (see Exhibit 5). Unilever/Sunlicht introduced Vigor, a heavy duty spray cleaner for dirt and stains, regionally in the Saarland in May 1968.

The following cost calculations for Trifft and corresponding estimates for Schnip and Vigor were prepared in May 1968.

Exhibit 5
Profile and Prices of Some APHCs in Germany in 1968

		Price (in DM per kg)
Trifft*...............	All purpose cleaner, convenient because of the spray principle, concentration on a new application principle that needs no water, and is good for the hands.	4.87 (introduction) 5.87
Vigor*..............	Fights against the tough dirt and grayness, destroys the dirt from the inside without water, and restores shine without rinsing.	2.44 (introduction) 5.00
Schnip*	Gives a guaranteed shine and is always there to deal with a "disaster spot."	3.90 (introduction) 5.30
Mr. Proper	Concentrated liquid cleaner that leaves no marks and shades, restores every surface to a "mirror-like" condition, and also emphasizes fast and efficient cleaning.	3.97
Ajax liquid..........	Concentrated liquid cleaner (the "White Tornado") with tough cleaning power, especially for cleaning thoroughly and quickly in difficult situations.	3.26
Dor powder	Shine for tiles, doors, and furniture in kitchen and bathroom without attacking the surface in any way, mild for the hands, efficient when used.	5.70
Imi (powder and liquid)	Universal for kitchen, bathroom, cellar, stairs and floors, "cuts the grease" in these places and can also be used for dirty work clothes.	2.00 (powder) 3.30 (liquid)

* These cleaners were the only ones to be applied directly on a surface to be cleaned. Other cleaners were concentrated and had to be diluted with water before application with a sponge or a cleaning rag. Therefore, spray APHC's already consisted of a nonconcentrated liquid.

On the other hand, due to the spray principle, only a very small quantity of liquid was sprayed onto a given surface to be cleaned, whereas much more water/cleaner mixture was used with the other types of cleaners.

		Trifft (400 g)*		Schnip (500 g)		Vigor (450 g)
Introductory period:						
Retail price/unit (DM)		1.95		1.95		1.10
Factory list price to the wholesaler		1.27		1.30		.73
10 percent discounts for introduction and quantity discounts	.27		.27		.15	
Freight.........................	.06		.07		.07	
Manufacturing costs	.70		.75		.73	
Total variable costs...............		(1.03)		(1.09)		(.95)
Contribution per unit for marketing budget, overheads, and profits......		.24		.21		(.22)
After introduction period:						
Retail price/unit (DM)		2.35		2.65		2.25
Factory list price to the wholesaler		1.53		1.75		1.50
Quantity discounts	.15		.17		.15	
Freight†	.06		.07		.07	
Manufacturing costs‡	.70		.75		.73	
Total variable costs...............		(.91)		(.99)		(.95)
Contribution per unit for marketing budget, overheads, and profits......		.62		.76		.55

* g = grams.
† Freight for Trifft was less because of the use of 15-bottle cartons versus 10-bottle carton.
‡ The largest "manufacturing" cost items were the pump (Trifft: .28) and the bottle (.22)—not the liquid itself (.06).

Trifft was to be introduced with 3 million bottles at the lower price and then the regular price. Schnip and Vigor were planned to start with 100,000 bottles each on regional markets, one third of which were to be sold at the introductory price. The production for Trifft started in June with 4 million bottles which were to be in retail markets in August, and advertising was planned to start in September.

Introduction and Initial Results

Trifft was launched nationally in early August 1968 with a special introductory retail price of DM 1.95, compared to a "normal" price of DM 2.35. Within one month, about 15 consumers made complaints concerning stripes and stains on lacquers and two about insufficient cleaning power. Tests, however, in the laboratory showed that Trifft did not cause more damage than did other spray cleaners and less than strong cleaners. The damage resulted from the chemical features of old lacquers and could be avoided by careful application (spraying the cleaner on a cleaning towel first and then applying). The complaints were taken seriously enough by product management to change the use instructions on the label.

The point-of-sale promotion budget of DM 1 million was considerably larger than that which was normally used to introduce a new product. The advertising budget (DM 2 million) was spent mainly on television. It was beyond the usual advertising/sales ratio for other APHCs (see Exhibit 6).

Another research study with 80 housewives ranked Trifft TV spots higher than those of the competition both in recall and empathy. Housewives like the down-to-earth, educational approach towards the new cleaning principle. Based on this study, the following recommendations were made:

> Confusion with window cleaners should be avoided at all costs (not even showing windows in TV spots!). Emphasis should be placed on consumer education because there is still a need for information. TV spots should be dominated by a "static line," not by turbulent, fast-moving pictures. Application to delicate surfaces should be stressed, in order to keep well away from Ajax and Mr. Proper. Trifft ranges below them in cleaning power and slightly above Dor. To avoid criticism of high pricing, economy in use should be strongly emphasized.

A further conclusion from this study was that consumer acceptance for Trifft was still low. This conclusion was supported by the slowing sales of Trifft whose market share in December 1968 fell to 5.4 percent. Actual monthly sales until the end of 1968 are shown in the following table.

Exhibit 6
Advertising Expenditures for All-Purpose Household Cleaners in Germany 1967–1968
(in thousands DM)

Product	1967 Total (000) DM	1967 Total Precent	Jan.	Feb.	Mar.	Apr.	May	June
Dor.........	3,882.7	24.3	2.0	69.9	639.2	897.4	642.2	23.0
Trifft.........								
Imi Flussig....	1,601.5	10.0				313.2	292.5	144.0
W. R. Krafter ..	473.7	3.0	50.4	33.9	57.1	40.4	25.4	32.3
Saugermacht..								35.9
Vigor								30.9
Fairy.........	1,172.4	7.4	50.2	50.5	54.2	169.3	166.3	150.1
Meister RR†...	4,568.3	28.6	389.0	319.8	320.6	466.1	432.6	588.5
Ajax A lizw ...	4,258.3	27.6	441.4	662.2	581.9	533.4	224.7	235.9
Schnip.......							146.0	136.7
Pinarom......			18.5	12.4	98.7	59.2	11.7	10.0
Total.........	15,956.9	100%	951.5	1,148.7	1,751.7	2,479.0	1,941.4	1,357.3
Quarters......			I—3,851.9			I and II—9,629.6		

* Exceed 100 percent due to rounding.
† The 1967 media expenditure for Mr. Proper does not include seven million trial bottles distributed free in 1967.

In January 1969, Trifft was sold in 10,000 retail stores. Consumer awareness was at 30 percent with some 10 percent having tried Trifft and 5 percent still using it. Another research study again revealed favorable reaction to the TV spots but also reservations towards the product. Some 40 percent felt that they did not need Trifft, and 22 percent thought it would be too expensive to use.

Actual Monthly Sales ex Works

Month	Bottles (000)	Market share in the German APHC market percent
August 1968	500	—
September 1968	1,200	10.21
October 1968.	990	9.91
November 1968...............	590	8.0
December 1968...............	390	5.4

The report recommended the following:

Awareness is too high to explain the slowdown of Trifft sales so far. It is rather that existing cleaning habits regarding intermediate cleaning

for 1968						1968 Total	
July	Aug.	Sept.	Oct.	Nov.	Dec.	(000) DM	Percent*
447.4	498.0	418.7	301.1	136.1		4,075.0	22.2
	42.8	651.6	633.0	547.5	511.8	3,387.5	18.4
18.1	3.9					261.5	1.4
29.0		24.6	16.4	16.4	16.4	145.8	0.8
59.0	30.1	54.7	35.6	25.0		235.3	1.3
38.2	16.5		117.2	26.1	38.5	677.1	3.7
320.2	275.3	194.7	187.6	233.1	191.9	3,889.4	21.2
274.8	326.8	474.8	377.7	304.6	278.5	4,716.5	25
140.1	77.6	81.0	70.9	57.4	67.5	777.2	4.2
7.9	7.2	4.5	7.3	10.8	12.0	260.1	1.4
1,534.7	1,273.2	1,904.6	1,755.8	1,357.0	1,116.4	18,376.1	100%
	I–III—14,147.1						

are too fixed and there is a lack of emotional involvement with Trifft. The task-oriented spots, therefore, have advantages on the one hand but should be much more lively and emotionally engaging to compete innovatively against the "competition" of cleaning habits and dishwater.

Trifft's direct competitors, Schnip and Vigor, also had experienced a disappointing sales performance in their regional test markets; Schnip, which had achieved at one time a 7 percent market share of the regional APHC market, was faced with declining sales, and Vigor never got beyond 1 percent in its test market.

By January 1969, more precise information concerning the U.S. market was obtained, which revised previous estimates about the market share of sprays as follows:

U.S. Market Data on APHCs

	1966	1967	1968	1969 (est.)
Market size ($ million)	138	152	170	175
Shares by texture (percent):				
Powder	30.0	26.0	23.0	14.0
Liquid (without spray)	66.8	68.4	62.0	63.0
Spray	3.0	5.6	15.0	23.0
Total	100.0	100.0	100.0	100.0

U.S. Market Shares of Spray Cleaners (percent)

	1966	1967	1968	1969 (est.)
Fantastik.......................................	1.2	2.7	6.2	9.2
Formula 409....................................	1.8	2.7	5.0	6.9 .
Others (Cinch, Ajax, Power-On,				
Whistle, Clean and Kill)...................	0.0	0.2	3.8	6.9
Total..............................	3.0	5.6	15.0	23.0

Advertising/Sales Ratios of U.S. APHCs

	1967	1968	1969
Average advertising to sales ratio of spray APHC	1.00	.50	.14
Average/sales ratio of all APHCs (total average)	.20	.19	.15

The latest critical market review which had been prepared by Euro Ad now lay on Herr Krabbe's desk, and he was reviewing it in preparation for the weekly concept talks. It concluded as follows:

> Trifft was introduced in August 1968 in a market dominated by Ajax, Mr. Proper, and Dor. Trifft's disappointing sales performance reflects very fixed consumer cleaning habits towards which the three main products are oriented.
>
> The agency recommendation for immediate action is to change the present Trifft concept (retaining the spray) to get closer to existing household cleaners; i.e., to accept existing consumer habits. Therefore, the formula should be changed for heavy dirt.

C A S E **3–3**

Roots in Europe

On an overcast day in February 1978, Mr. Alan Jackson sat in his office overlooking the Lake of Geneva, in Geneva, Switzerland, and commented to his visitor, "Our business has reached a critical stage but I'll have to take a somewhat roundabout route to bring you to the point where you can understand my problem. Let me tell you the story of the Roots Shoe and how I came to be where I am today." What follows is Jackson's narrative:

Anna Kelso and the Earth Shoe

The 1978 story of Roots really begins almost 20 years ago in Copenhagen, Denmark, with a woman named Anna Kelso. She was a health enthusiast, a yoga practitioner, into health foods, and very much given to developing her body and doing the things which she thought made for a natural type of living. She noticed in her deep breathing exercises that it was important to tilt her pelvis and to hold her body in a certain way in order to get maximum breath. She also noticed that if she stood on the floor and put a book or other item underneath the front of her feet so that the balls of her feet were slightly elevated, it changed her pelvic position and she felt that this improved her deep breathing. Then on long walks in the country on soft ground and particularly on the hard-packed beach, she noticed as she walked along that her heels came down first and took the impact and then she rolled off the side of her feet and across the ball of her foot and off her toes, and she looked back on the imprint and saw that the heel left the deepest impression.

Working these ideas through in her mind, Anna Kelso came up with a wooden sandal in which the foot was placed to that the heel was lower. Now this made it rather awkward to walk since the wooden sandal didn't bend, so she developed a little rocker front end so that the whole wooden sandal could pivot forward. Slowly the concept of a sandal developed into a shoe which she felt allowed the wearer to walk in a natural way. It had a sole with a deeply recessed heel (which she called a "negative" heel) and a high arch support. It also had the rocker front end so that without bending the sole itself you could have a natural swing forward. She went to a few small craftsmen who made shoes in rather primitive ways and had them make up shoes along these designs.

Anna Kelso called her shoe design the Earth Shoe. She began to sell them in a little shop in the central part of Copenhagen. In order to keep the "natural" feeling, she decorated with lots of plants and rather rough-hewn natural wood. She put pebbles and sand in the window to emphasize the naturalness of walking on the beach. She talked about it being the best way to stand and walk and how it changed your stance. And for almost 20 years, nobody every heard of Anna Kelso and her Earth Shoe except a few fanatics in and around Copenhagen. These were people who were into deep breathing exercises, yoga, meditation, vegetarian eating, health foods, etc. But for the population at large, even in Copenhagen, not very many people had heard of Anna Kelso.

The Earth Shoe Introduced in the United States

Sometime about 1969, an American photographer, Ray Jacobs, and his wife were in Copenhagen and, as the story goes, Mrs. Jacobs suffered from some kind of back ailment and wasn't feeling very well. Apparently, they met in Copenhagen someone who told them about the Anna Kelso Earth Shoe and decided at least to try a pair. After purchasing them, they continued along their way in their trip throughout Europe. Two weeks later, Mrs. Jacobs' backache was gone. They rushed back to Copenhagen, according to the story, and ended up negotiating North American rights to import and distribute the Anna Kelso Earth Shoe. Just like Anna Kelso, Ray Jacobs was not a retail sales oriented person. He simply duplicated in New York City what Anna Kelso had in Copenhagen. He picked a site in a low-rent district, not a very commercial area, and duplicated her kind of store—a store in a location that didn't have a lot of walk-by traffic. He furnished the store with rather rough-hewn furniture and put pebbles and sand in the window. He had these rather crudely made shoes with the negative heel. He had the health charts showing the spine straightening out and gave the Anna Kelso story. He opened that store in 1970. There was no effort to do much advertising; no effort to do much in the way of public or press relations. Nevertheless, in 1970, a few of the North American health fanatics (we might even say "health nuts") slowly began to find their way to his New York store. Three years later, it's our understanding, there were three stores then opened by Ray Jacobs; the original one in New York City, another in Cambridge, Massachusetts, and the third in Ann Arbor, Michigan.

Any American who wore a tie in 1972 would most probably not have heard of Anna Kelso and the Earth Shoe. The only people who had by this time become familiar and adopted the shoe were truly the counterculture—those who had turned their backs on the so-called American materialism and had been looking for nature. They found in Anna Kelso and the background of the Earth Shoe a new meaning, a return to nature, the natural way to walk, the simple way to dress. Soon they were standing in line waiting for the next shipment to come in from Copenhagen.

In addition to the real counterculture and nature nuts, there were those university students and faculty that somewhat envied the counterculture but weren't prepared to make the entire change. They became familiar with this Earth Shoe phenomenon though it still had received no notice in the mainstream press. There still was practically no advertising. The Earth Shoe was, after three years in North America, a practically unknown item except for the counterculture group and the university campuses.

Don Green and Michael Budman in Toronto

In Toronto, at that same time, were living two young men from the Detroit area, Don Green and Michael Budman. Don was 23 years old and Michael 27. Michael had graduated from Michigan State University in Lansing and had gone to live in Toronto; Don had attended the university but not graduated. They had lived at the same place in Lansing. The two boys had known each other since childhood, had attended the same camp in Ontario, Canada, had lived in the same area, gone to the same high school, and, despite the four years difference in age, knew each other well. They had not done anything of a commercial nature and were really just hanging out in Toronto. Michael was working at a few odd jobs to earn some money. They occasionally visited family and friends in Detroit, and on one of those trips back home in 1972, they visited friends in Ann Arbor and were introduced to the Anna Kelso Earth Shoe.

At that time, it took some effort to become accustomed to the shoe. The negative heel was at a very severe angle, the arch support was very high, and for most people accustomed to wearing normal heeled shoes or even flat-soled shoes, there was quite a period of adjustment. The stretching of heel cord tendons and muscles and the adaptation of the arch all required some time, and it was only upon the encouragement of those who had already gone through the process that many people continued to persevere and wear the shoes until their bodies adapted. It took Don and Michael several weeks before they could wear the Earth Shoes for long periods of time, but after that period of adjustment, they really were converts. They felt the shoe was something not commercial; it was something worthwhile, it was back to nature. Since they liked the whole scene, they thought it would be nice if they could have a small store in Toronto similar to the one in Ann Arbor, where they could busy themselves with something meaningful—they could sell the Earth Shoe in Canada.

With this in mind, they contacted Ray Jacobs, and thus began a whole series of "lucky" circumstances that resulted in today's Roots Shoe and the company, Natural Footwear Limited. The first result of the contact was Ray Jacobs' refusal to grant them exclusive distribution rights in Canada. It was really rather presumptuous of these two young men to approach Ray Jacobs and ask for the total Canadian rights to the Earth Shoe. Of course he wasn't going to grant that. They then tried to negotiate rights for Toronto with an option on the rest of Canada if this proved successful. Then began a long series of negotiations into which Don's father, a very successful businessman, was called to help. After considerable time, Don and Michael came to the conclusion that it would be impossible to develop a meaningful relationship with Ray Jacobs and his Earth Shoe.

By this time, late 1972, the Earth Shoe had been on the North American market for a full three years. Don and Michael came to the conclusion that they could just as easily have a similar shoe manufactured locally in Toronto and equip the store themselves and sell it under a different name. The rejection by Ray Jacobs was their first bit of luck. The second bit of luck was when they went through the Yellow Pages of the Toronto telephone book looking for someone or some company to manufacture the shoes. Obviously, they could not go to a very large manufacturer because the quantities involved for one little store wouldn't justify it. Looking through the Yellow Pages of the telephone directory, they located the Boa Shoe Company and the Kowalewski family. The Boa Shoe Company consisted of John Kowalewski, a Polish immigrant whose father had made boots for the officers of Czar Nicholas II, and his four sons who were, essentially, handmaking snakeskin shoes primarily for the Florida tourist trade. When Don and Michael showed John Kowalewski and his sons the recessed heel (or negative heel-type shoe), the first reaction of the Kowalewskis was that it was a very cheaply made, low-quality shoe. Construction details had been ignored, and materials weren't of the best quality. The manufacturing details were primitive; in fact, they were designed to be primitive by Mrs. Kelso and had not been improved over the years that she had been manufacturing.

John Kowalewski indicated that if he was going to be involved, he would want to make a quality shoe. He would like to look for the best quality leathers. He wanted double stitching where it was required. He felt they had to have counters in the heal to support the shoe over a long period of time. When Don and Michael talked with him about the long period of adaptation because of the severe angle, he reached the conclusion that the arch support was too high and was placed too far back. Thus began a period of examining the Anna Kelso Earth Shoe to modify its construction both from a quality standpoint as well as from a functional standpoint in order to make it a more readily usable, more beneficial shoe. (See Exhibit 1.)

Exhibit 1
The Roots Shoe

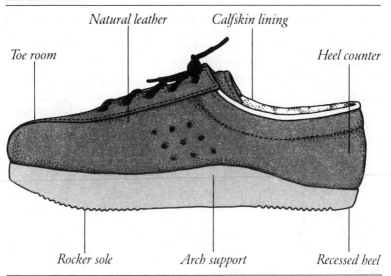

Natural leather   *Calfskin lining*

Toe room   *Heel counter*

Rocker sole   *Arch support*   *Recessed heel*

The next bit of luck was the discovery of Robert Burns. Robert Burns was an Englishman who had come to Canada and set up his own design and graphics shop. Working with Robert, the group came up with company logos, company brochures, and descriptive material that was definitely of an international standard in quality and design and gave a corporate image considerably more sophisticated than that of the Earth Shoe Company. Looking for a trade name, they wanted something close to nature. Knocking around ideas with friends one evening, a girlfriend came up with the name Roots, meaning roots in the sense of the foundation of life. So with the name Roots and with Robert Burns' graphics, they began to develop a corporate image that could appeal to a wide cross-section of the population.

Graphics and a name, of course, aren't enough, so a fourth piece of luck came along when Robert Burns introduced them to a Welshman who had also immigrated to Canada and had a flair for writing. He was a copywriter and editorialist, and his name was David Perry. David Perry's subtly sophisticated, deceptively simple language fit very nicely with the image that they were trying to create. It blended nicely with the natural feeling of the product and with Robert Burns' graphics.

Their luck in finding people at this critical time continued when they met Fred Kondo, a Japanese Canadian who was a master wood-worker. He made fine furniture and agreed to equip the stores with a style of fixtures manufactured out of polished oak and in keeping with the Earth Shoe concept. At the same time, they met Renny Delessing, an interior architect with a good grasp for space. And so in a very short time in this dynamic city of Toronto, they stumbled across, built up, and put together a creative team. There were Don Green and Michael Budman, who by the refusal of Ray Jacobs were thrown into the neces-sity of creating their own company. By chance they stumbled across these Polish immigrants John Kowalewski and his four sons, who just happened to be master shoemakers in the Old World tradition and were able to create from the original Earth concept a better quality product.

The first Roots store in North America opened in Toronto on Au-gust 15, 1973. It followed the tradition established by Anna Kelso and Ray Jacobs in New York City almost four years earlier, but it was definitely a higher quality presentation because of the contributions of these talented people in the areas of shoe making, graphic arts, writing, and design.

Growth beyond Toronto

The results were more than anyone expected. A couple of weeks after opening the store, with a little bit of advertising display in the city buses, the blue jean-wearing, semi-counterculture crowd of To-ronto went for the Roots recessed heel shoes in a big way. Sales were more than either Don or Michael had ever dreamed of, and of course, this was quickly transmitted to their families. Don's father had a neigh-bor who was in the shoe business and operated several retail shoe stores in the Detroit area. Upon hearing the boasting of Don's father, the neighbor agreed to visit Toronto and look at the operation. That look was enough to persuade him to open a new Roots store in the

Detroit area. Shortly thereafter, in early 1974, a Roots franchise outlet was opened in Birmingham, Michigan, by another neighbor of Green's father. Green also had a brother in San Francisco who decided that because Don was having so much success, he would also open a store; thus, San Francisco was activated. Michael Budman's brother, who resided in Los Angeles, hopped onto the bandwagon. Therefore, in early 1974, the Roots operations had spread from Toronto, to Detroit, San Francisco, and Los Angeles.

Simultaneously, the Earth group began to grant franchises to outsiders. As a result, by the spring of 1974, the countercultural devotees, the nature enthusiasts, the vegetarians, and the yoga people were beginning to hear about the recessed heel, or the negative heel shoe, with the Earth Shoe best known but Roots coming along fast.

Don's father, Irwin Green, had, 10 years earlier, entered a joint venture in Western Europe with another young man from Detroit, Alan Jackson. I had been living in Geneva, Switzerland, since 1957 and had been involved as a consultant primarily in international operations between Europe and the United States, with an emphasis on market development. I had, in fact, developed a European market for the products of a factory owned by Irwin Green, and the development of that market led to a three-way venture in which those products were manufactured in Italy. The manufacturing facility was owned jointly by Irwin Green, myself, and an Italian businessman. Irwin Green sold out of the venture about 1970 but remained in close contact with me. Thus, I was kept informed of Don's development of the shoe business. In 1973, when production was first started, I was asked to provide some assistance in expediting the delivery from Europe of molds for soles.

The Situation in Europe

In the spring of 1974, Irwin Green suggested that perhaps I might be interested in helping Don actually get established in Western Europe. After studying the possibilities, Don and Michael and I agreed on a joint venture for the development of the European market for Roots. That development was to take the form of setting up test stores in some of the leading European cities—the first in Munich and the second in Amsterdam.

By mid-1974, the Earth Shoe and the Roots shoe were in full international development, and the basic product concept was gaining favor with the public. In the United States, Earth Shoe and Roots franchises increased rapidly. By the spring of 1975, there were experimental Roots stores in Munich and Amsterdam, about 14 Roots stores across Canada and the United States, and roughly 30 to 40 Earth Shoe stores across the United States. And that was just the beginning.

The activity developed differently in North America than in Europe for a number of reasons. The first is that neither Ray Jacobs, for Earth, nor Don Green and Michael Budman, for Roots, had had any previous marketing experience, whereas in Western Europe, we had been consulting for many large international companies in many kinds of business activities. Therefore, I had somewhat more working experience and training in both general business practices and the very special field of new market development. Another reason for the difference was that Earth became a generic term in North America—it was *the* negative heel shoe, it was *the* recessed heel shoe, it was first in the marketplace, and it expanded most rapidly. Earth was the leader. In this way it was able to sell, at a relatively high price, a product that was not of the highest quality but had the magic of its introductory name. Roots, on the other hand, sold its products at the same price as Earth but had a product that was superior, presented in an atmosphere that was of a higher quality, and with advertising and promotional material that showed outstanding design and creativity. The competitive race was on. The product concept caught on in the United States as a fad, and neither Earth nor Roots could obtain enough shoes to satisfy their market. Earth bought manufacturing facilities in New England and began manufacturing facilities in New England and began manufacturing on its own, while Roots bought out the Kowalewskis, took over the Boa Shoe Company, and expanded its manufacturing facilities.

The Growth Stage

It was an exciting time as stores opened and the market seemed endless. Inventory turnovers were exceptionally high, and profits were therefore also high. Drawn into the business as franchisees were people who were university graduates but who had no experience in the retail business; people who were quite intelligent, but who had no business training. Franchises were granted to people who were undercapitalized. They could make money during this period of huge demand, but had yet to face a difficult time.

By 1975, the national press began to take notice of Earth, and major magazines carried editorial comments. Earth began to spend money on national advertising and on public relations. It was an exciting period with booming sales. Looking back, a store located anywhere could sell whatever it could get. By mid-1975, there were about 40 Roots stores in North America and perhaps 60 or 80 Earth stores. Most significantly, middle-class America was taking notice. The negative heel Earth shoe was definitely a roaring success.

At the first meeting of all the Roots franchisees and management, the Roots versus Earth situation was discussed. It was June 1975. Roots was not quite two years old in North America and only a few months into Europe.

Although they had virtually no consumer data or market analysis, Roots management believed that there were two different kinds of customers in this rush for the negative heel shoe. First, there were the Earth Shoe customers. These, according to Roots management, were the young blue jean-wearing kids, the real counterculture who were going into these rather seedy looking, rather neglected, rather rough Earth Shoe stores and buying the inflated priced, crudely made Earth Shoes. The second part of the market was the more affluent suburban middle-class consisting of somewhat older people looking for higher quality. This segment was more selective and willing to pay a higher price. They were the Roots customers.

With this in mind, Roots felt that they should direct their marketing approach towards the somewhat more affluent group. They selected a Madison Avenue advertising agency that had good experience in selective, upscale marketing—Lord, Geller, and Frederico—who had accounts like Tiffany's and the *New Yorker* magazine. At the June 1975 meeting of the franchisees, Lord, Geller, and Frederico were presented as the latest word in promotion for Roots. It was announced that there would be a major fall 1975 advertising program in national media for the brand, including advertisements in major magazines, large newspaper display ads, television, and heavy promotion. And Lord, Geller, and Frederico were going to give Roots the image which Roots felt it had— that of the quality product, the well-designed recessed heel shoe which was head and shoulders above Earth in quality and function.

The program proved to be a fiasco. The ads were not effective; the media were wrong; too much money was spent. It was a failure. Some $250,000 to $300,000 was spent across the United States, but the spending was poorly planned and poorly managed. The expected increase of sales did not result, and the entire effort proved very distasteful to management. From that time on, there was no major national advertising in North America for Roots; there was no consistent program of introducing and maintaining the company's name and product to the public.

The year 1975 did, however, draw the attention of U.S. shoemakers to the roaring success of both Earth and Roots across the country. By the end of 1975, there were 40 or 50 Roots stores across North America and more than double that in Earth Shoes. The U.S. shoemaking industry couldn't ignore this trend, and so 40 to 50 U.S. manufacturers introduced copies. Some of them actually did have recessed or negative heels, while others only looked like they had. Fortunately for both Earth and Roots, these manufacturers felt that the product was overpriced. So all of the copies, whether Florsheim at the higher end of the range or Thom McAn at the lower, entered with shoes (called Terra

Firma, Nature Shoe, the Natural Shoe, and so on) priced one third to one half that of the Earth or the Roots shoe. The copies were introduced as fashion items, put into conventional shoe stores, and sold as conventional shoes. They were displayed right along with the other casual and dressy shoes. There was nothing dramatically different about the way they were sold. It was just "this year's shoe." They did, in fact, become "this year's shoe;" there were an estimated 20 million pairs of recessed or negative heel-type shoe sold in North America in 1976. Of that 20 million, probably less than 5 percent (less than 1 million) were sold by Earth and Roots combined. Earth and Roots were the only ones selling the shoes in a distinctive atmosphere. They were the only ones that had specialized shoe stores selling only their products. All of the competing brands were sold as conventional shoes under conventional methods, but they were successful. Mr. and Mrs. Middle-class America and Middle-class America's children swept into the recessed heel shoe. It was in all the fashion magazines; it was in all the newspapers. Promotion was heavy. It was a roaring success.

At the same time, Roots had a very active public and press relations campaign. Unfortunately, practically all of it was devoted to the success story of the company, to the great growth the company was having, to the exciting personalities of Don Green and Michael Budman. Emphasis was not on the product. In 1976, both Earth and Roots began to feel the problems created by not having adequate local management and not being familiar with all of the tiny details necessary to manage retail stores and national distribution. Store site selection was one of the critical details that Roots management lacked familiarity with and which was to become a problem for them. Personnel supervision was another.

The European Situation

At the same time in Europe, things were developing differently. In 1975, three stores had been opened, Amsterdam, Munich, and Paris; early 1976 saw the opening of a second store in Holland in the Hague and a store in London. Sales in each of the five stores reached 80 to 100 pairs per week during the first year. Those stores all began to sell modestly and correctly, following the basic Roots concept. They all had advertising and promotion programs from day one, with heavy emphasis on press and public relations since the single stores couldn't afford much ordinary paid-for advertising. Contacts were made with physiotherapists, orthopedists, and nurses. We contacted people in the health area who are on their feet during much of the day and who take care of their feet. We also contacted other professionals like models, photographers, and fashion people, who also spend long days standing.

We wanted to establish Roots as a healthy, fashionable shoe. We called these people on the telephone, wrote letters to them, demonstrated Roots, and let them test the shoe with no obligation. We wanted them talking about us. We also went to the press, especially journalists who write about fashion, sports, business, and outdoor life. We stressed that Roots was an exciting, new, healthy, fashionable concept. We told them about Roots and let them wear them. We didn't have money to spend, but we had the time to spend. There was an organized press relations activity and an organized direct-mail activity. Store site selections had been made with a great deal of care. Standard store operating procedures had been established. It was a relatively well-organized business. Furthermore, Roots was alone in the European marketplace; Earth was not active.

Market Maturity and Management Problems in North America

In North America, by the end of 1976, the craze for the Earth-type shoe was over. Earth and Roots were both in difficulty, and some of the things which they had been ignoring were beginning to show up. In the fall of 1975, there had been no national product advertising emphasizing the functional features of the product by Roots. Promotional material provided to the dealers did not emphasize the product's functions or its characteristics. There had been absolutely no contact by the factory with the field salespeople. There had been only the most minimal contact between the factory and the franchisees and the store managers. Roots owned and operated more than 20 of its own stores in the United States. There was no proper organization for that activity; none of the generally accepted techniques for management, motivation, or control were used. The people at Roots in Toronto were concerned with producing the product but not with contact in the field— not with organizing and managing their own stores or with the kinds of guidance and help that the franchisees required. It was a catastrophic situation producing shoes of better and better quality but not with the necessary marketing follow-through. At the same time they lost control of their account receivables, they also lost control of some of their production statistics, and sales began to fall.

Similar problems were developing with Earth. As a matter of fact, the Earth home office in New York was building up very sizable overhead, and by the end of 1976, they had more than 120 people in their central offices. There were about 120 stores, almost all of which were franchise Earth stores that never seemed to have on hand, ready for sale, the product styles that were selling. Back at the factory, however, and in the warehouse, there was a reported 250,000-pair inventory—

always in the wrong style, the styles that weren't selling—whereas the stores were screaming for the shoes they could sell. It was a catastrophic situation for Earth.

In Europe, the success of the Roots stores continued; every store was profitable. Expansion was planned. The success was most prevalent in Holland where, at a very early date, the press had shown particular interest in the shoes and the Roots people were able to generate a favorable rapport with the press. Stories about the shoe constantly appeared in the Dutch press. This resulted in some interesting statistics. For example, the Amsterdam store averaged 104 pairs of shoes sold per week in its first year, 1975. It needed only about 60 pairs a week to break even. The 1976 sales were 194 pairs per week, so it was an exceptionally profitable store which encouraged some aggressive developments in Europe in 1977. These positive signs in Europe were to be compared with the devastation coming to North America.

By spring of 1977, both Earth and Roots were in disaster situations in the United States. The total mismanagement of the Earth Shoe Company resulted in the company's forced bankruptcy on March 4, 1977. Roots was somewhat different. The failure to pick proper sites and the failure to perform the functions necessary for the successful marketing of name brand products began to have disastrous results. However, back in the factory in Toronto, although acknowledging some of the management faults as well as the failure to promote and manage, the real reason for the North American failure was said to be the fickle public's attitude. The fad was over, management believed. The recessed heel shoe was dead as a fashion item in management's opinion, and a decision was made to go into other products. In spring of 1977, Toronto made the decision to produce other types of shoes with a normal raised heel and to change its image from that of a manufacturer of the quality recessed heel shoe to one of a manufacturer of quality comfortable casual shoes. A fall 1977 line was designed based on a wedge sole.

Market Growth Continues in Europe

In Western Europe, however, the emphasis was still along the conventional product line, and considerable expansion took place. First of all, the company opened a number of additional stores. Secondly, the company went into leased departments in major department stores where it recreated within the department store the same kind of selling environment it had in its own stores including natural wood furniture, green plants, and very little product in a small but well-defined physical space. Well, success was immediate. In 1977, previous sales records were exceeded in all of the European stores and particularly in Holland.

The Amsterdam sales figures were almost unbelievable. On Thursday nights when the stores were open for late shopping and on Saturdays, they had to close the door and let customers in only when customers came out.

What had happened was that, in 1975 and 1976, the European public was buying Roots primarily for its natural comfort feature. All the promotion emphasized the natural comfort. The company was careful to make no medical claim in its promotion but observed that most normal people seemed to feel less tired after a long day of standing or walking in Roots recessed heel shoes. That message, repeated over and over again, was accompanied by the secondary message of high-quality materials and high-quality Canadian craftsmanship. The European market in 1975 and 1976 was a cross-section of the European public in terms of age and economic status. What they all seemed to have in common was interest in foot comfort. Little old ladies were driven there by their chauffeurs; young athletes came in; fashion models came in—all kinds of people came in. Somewhere in that group of people must have been some young, fashion trendsetters, perhaps from the Amsterdam and the Hague high schools, because by the spring of 1977, the Roots shoe became a *must* in the minds of young teenagers in Holland. Sales in the Amsterdam store, for example, that had been 104 pairs per week the first year and 194 the second year, shot up to 400, 500, and 600 pairs a week until they reached 700 pairs Easter week 1977. And they maintained astronomical levels—500 and 600 pairs per week well into the summer. It was at this point that we began opening leased departments in department stores.

By fall 1977, there were 10 retail outlets in Holland, 5 company stores and 5 leased stores, and sales were booming. During the second year, however, sales in London, Paris, and Munich had remained more or less constant with problems developing in sales in those stores when inventories were not properly managed and orders were either not placed or not filled properly. This experience in England, France, and Germany emphasized the importance of attention to the details of inventory and store management. These conclusions combined with the tremendous success in the Netherlands convinces me that our marketing strategy and the Roots concept were basically sound.

There were also rumors of competition coming as in North America, bringing in some of the cheap shoes that had been sold in the United States. Roots European management came to the decision that it was important to get additional outlets quickly, at least in Holland where the success was phenomenal. A Roots authorized dealer program was created. Rather than just let the product loose, as Florsheim and Thom McAn had done in the United States, the Roots authorized dealer program was established on the basis that there would be one or at least a limited number of authorized dealers in each major city, that the dealer who was selected would be furnished with a lot of marketing and merchandising assistance, and that he would be obligated to use it. For example, the shoes had to be displayed in a Roots corner or a Roots wall area. The basic display fixtures would be furnished at cost to the dealer, and he would be required to use them. The dealer was provided with a detailed program of training and other material. The program was announced to the Dutch retail industry in November 1977. Meetings were held in December to which potential dealers came and heard about the program in detail. In January 1977, 40 Dutch dealers were selected; the program actually opened, with tremendous success, on March 1, 1978.

The Turnaround in North America

In the meantime back in North America, Earth had gone bankrupt, the Roots organization in the United States had had to close about 20 dealers and about 25 of its own retail stores, had to write off as an unrecoupable loss perhaps a half a million dollars in accounts receivable, and had completely changed its marketing goal. In addition to developing its range of wedged shoes, it came out with a line of classic shoes with rubber soles and rubber heels and with styles somewhat reminiscent of the 1950s, along with some very new styles.

In March 1978, Natural Footwear Limited (the manufacturing arm of Roots) was able to offer the remaining Roots Company stores and franchises in Canada and the United States a truly outstanding line of casual footwear of high quality and high price beginning with the original concept of the Roots recessed heal shoe, going on to a wedge, and continuing to a classic sole. However, the company was not able to offer its retail outlets any of the supporting material and assistance commonly required of successful name brand products. In fact, the owner-management of Natural Footwear had decided that it did not want to be directly involved in retail activities. They had successfully obtained as outlets Saks Fifth Avenue in the United States and the Eaton chain in Canada, and they were negotiating with Bloomingdale's in New York. Each of these retailers was expected to produce a significant portion of Roots total sales. The feeling of the Toronto management of Natural Footwear was that they would be able to market directly to these major department store chains without the necessity and cost of providing a log of backup material and backup assistance.

In March of 1978, none of the established Roots dealers were obtaining from the factory the full quantity of shoes they were ordering. All of them were enthused about the new styles and were prepared to slowly change the outlook of their retail stores. It's difficult to know exactly what North American sales were, but it seems that about 4,000 pairs a week were being sold in Canada and the United States.

Continued Success in Europe

At the same time, the boom in Europe was continuing. Including the Dutch authorized dealer program, there were now almost 60 retail outlets in Europe. Sales were about 4,500 pairs a week, slightly above the North American rate, and there was a major program to develop franchisees and leased departments in France and Germany. Consumer demand for the recessed heel was continuing, and this is the crux of today's problem. The Toronto management is frightened that this so-called fad for the recessed heel will die in Europe as it did in the United States and that the European operation is in for a very difficult time. On the other hand, I feel strongly that when the fad dies, when the teenagers walk away, if the store site locations have been properly selected and if the sales people have been properly dealt with, if the store managers received the same kind of continuing contact and the buildup required, and if the dealers are serviced properly, then the residual market is still a very substantial and successful market and need not die as it did in the United States.

Backing this up is the fact that, despite the introduction of the wedge and the classic heel and despite the fact that the recessed heel had not been promoted since the fall of 1975, the sale of the few remaining recessed heel shoes offered in the franchise stores represented 40 to 60 percent of the volume, it was learned in the March dealer meetings. I am against the introduction, even on the test basis, of anything that would reduce the impact of the Roots advertising and promotional message in Europe. Our emphasis on the "natural" look and way of walking in Roots shoes, carried over into our store design, is almost anti-fashion, and I don't think we can switch to a fashion orientation. In Europe, I want to stick with the basic Roots concept of a comfortable, high-quality casual shoe whose comfort is based not only on the high quality of its materials and construction, but also on the unique recessed heel design. Whereas my colleagues in Toronto think we should prepare for the end of the recessed heel fad in Europe by the introduction of new products during the height of the fad, I believe that a better approach is to rely upon adequate promotion of the product and strong relationships with all the retail outlets, so that when abnormal fad sales fall off, the remaining sales will still be very, very profitable.

In a typical Roots store in Europe, selling only the recessed heel, some 20 styles are sold, and the average inventory is between 1,000 and 2,000 pairs, with inventory turnover between 7 and 20 times a year. In the Roots stores in North America, where the expanded line includes wedges and classic soles, the number of styles is perhaps 40 to 60, with larger inventories and lower turnovers. As you go into a conventional shoe store, the numbers of models increase dramatically, and inventory turnovers fall equally dramatically. It's a different kind of business. It seems that with the unique recessed heel approach, the business can be managed profitably in much simpler terms and with a more direct method. Anyway that's the problem today to decide: whether the company can successfully continue in Europe along the lines originally established by the company in Toronto in 1973 and 1974, but abandoned by the company when the sales fell dramatically in North America.

The plan for Holland is to have approximately 50 Roots authorized dealers. So far, the typical outlet is selling about 30 pairs per week from an inventory of 120 to 150 pairs. The normal shoe retailer expects to turn his inventory only three times per year, so this is very good. If there is a fad component in our current sales, there is also a comfort component that should at least guarantee sales of 15 to 20 pairs per week per outlet or continuing sales of 750 to 1,000 pairs per week through the authorized dealers network in Holland alone. Our five company-owned stores can also be expected to generate sales of 500 pairs per store per week when the fad dies and the five leased departments another 375 to 500 each. Furthermore, the situation in the test store in Munich has finally improved in terms of both personnel and inventory management, and sales are now running at more than 150 pairs per week. A new franchise store in Berlin is selling over 200 pairs per week. This positive evidence of the growing German acceptance of the Roots concept opens the way for creating a national distribution pattern in Germany similar to the one so successfully established in the Netherlands. A reasonable objective would be between 10 and 20 German franchise stores selling at 150 to 200 pairs per week, while the fad lasts, and at half that rate thereafter. This could be followed in 1979 by a program to start about 100 leased departments. Similar efforts are also possible in France and England. Then I see a potential for 3,000 pairs per week in Europe *after* the fad has passed.

Discussion Issues:

1. Do you agree that "luck" played an important role in what Budman and Green accomplished in Toronto? Why *was* Roots successful in Toronto?

2. Is the basic Roots shoe concept fad or fashion?

3. If it's a fad, will there be a residual of loyal customers?

4.   What skills must be developed if the American company expects to compete successfully in the fashion shoe business?

5.   If you were in Alan Jackson's shoes, would you broaden your product line in Europe to include the new fashion shoes?

6.   Why was the original Roots shoe concept successful?

7.   How did the American market differ from the national markets in Europe?

C A S E 3–4

Johnston, Inc.

Bob Johnston, president of a children's high-quality apparel firm, was concerned about his company's future strategy. Although his company was doing well, there were a number of unsettling industry trends.[1] It wasn't as if there were one or two major problem areas; rather, discernible developments in the children's wear industry were unfocused and contradictory. Bob found it difficult, therefore, to assess his best future course of action in respect to such marketing issues as exclusive versus nonexclusive retail arrangements; the use, or combination, of such diverse retail outlets as specialty shops, department stores, mass merchandisers, catalog houses, and discounters; product line definition and price policies; the appropriate mix among selling, advertising, and promotional alternatives; and the very issue of growth—Was growth desirable and in what form?

It was not that doing business through the company's traditional outlets, specialty retailers, had ever been simple. Volatility in those channels was traditional; doing business with specialty merchants had been a constant challenge given the ever changing requirements of consumers, retail store buyers, merchandise managers, and store presidents. In a real sense, the country's general environmental changes in lifestyles, attitudes, and population priorities were magnified at the retail level. The desire of most successful retail managers was to be "relevant—exciting—in the lead."

Channel changes, needless to say, made it difficult for a smallish firm like Johnston's (less than $6 million in sales) to adapt easily to new requirements. And they increased greatly the risks of growth. Johnston's size called for larger commitments to style, the spreading of

---

This case was written by Isabelle Schmid. © 1979 by the Trustees of the Leland Stanford Junior University.

[1] See Appendix A: Notes on the Clothing Industry.

224

an already thin management base, and even greater anticipation of future needs of the trade and consumers. Needless to say, it had always been a gamble in clothing to guess correctly the designs, fabrics, styles, and colors for presentation to the buyers. There was also the ever present concern that the styles and fabrics shown in the women's wear industry might not translate into consumer acceptance in children's clothing; or the reverse, that the women's industry would corner the supply of a specific, widely demanded fabric (such as corduroy).[2]

Thus, it was natural for Bob to ask, "How should my company expand? Should we seek more volume from present customers, from wider geographic penetration, from new distribution, from product line extension (such as the recent additions of christening and layette garments), or from vertical integration into the channels? In fact, can there be much aggressive growth given the financial implications (heavier debt), the three-year breaking-in period for personnel and equipment in new plants, and the danger that size might tarnish the company's image of exclusivity?"

Company History

Forty-eight seasons, or 16 years ago, Johnston began to produce an infant designer collection exclusively for Lord & Taylor, a well-known Fifth Avenue prestige retailer. The brand name Betti Terrell (Johnston's designer at the time) was adopted for this collection. As the line gianed in popularity, Johnston began to look toward expanded distribution. Other retailers coveted the Betti Terrell designer collection due to Lord & Taylor's reputation in the fashion industry.

Under the franchise agreement, Johnston could not sell his Betti Terrell line to another store based in the same city. However, he could market an "open line," Little One. Because Betti Terrell was also limited to the infant line, Johnston introduced a third label, Fischèl (Priscilla Fischèl was vice president for sales, headquartered in New York), aimed at toddlers and four- to seven-year-olds. These separate brand decisions reflected the historical importance and strength of Lord & Taylor to Johnston.

By 1977, Johnston had 800 active accounts, some franchised and some not. A third of the firm's sales came from 15 customers. There were five labels covering the following age categories: newborn, infant, toddler, girls 4 to 6 and girls 7 to 12. Each year, the company designed and manufactured about 1,200 styles, not including different sizes and

---

[2] Women's and men's clothing was traditionally designed and manufactured ahead of children's; hence those cutters purchased fabrics first. These fabric purchases normally indicated the trend in clothing.

colors. A summary of their current production revealed eight major lines as follows:

Types of Apparel Produced

One-piece.	*Long*—B'alls, jiffies, j'alls, skipsuits, pants, etc.
One-piece.	*Short*—Sunsuits, shortalls, bubbles, shorts, etc.
Two-piece.	*Long*—Overall sets, pant-suits, etc.
Two- and Three piece.	*Short*—Shortall and shirt, skip and jacket, etc.
Coats, coat sets, jackets.	
Shirts, blouses, toys.	
Dresses, jumpers, dress sets, etc.	
Miscellaneous—Beachwear, bonnets, pram bags, bear suits, etc.	

A small sample of some 1977 baby items is included in Exhibit 1. The following table summarizes the label and age matrix:

Size Range

	Newborn (0–6 mo.)	Infant (6, 9, 12, 18 mo.)	Toddler (2–4)	Girls (4–6)	Girls (7–12)
Franchise labels	—	Betti Terrell	Fischèl	Fischèl	—
Open labels	Johnston	Little One	Little One	Little One	Johnston
Low		**Style and price sensitivity**		**High**	

Reproductions of the five major labels as well as some lesser ones are continued in Exhibit 2.

Competition for Johnston was difficult to assess. There were, of course, a number of well-regarded small firms—Florence Eiseman, Grace Company, Sylvia Whyte, Ruth of Carolina and Dorissa—but it was also true that the market was so diffuse that a small manufacturer like Johnston tended to ignore competition and just "go for a share." In reality, it was difficult to pinpoint specific competition. Very few firms, for instance, offered designer collections, although there were plenty of specialists (i.e., pants, skirts, swimsuits) for any particular type of clothing. Some operators were imitators or knockoff artists, who copied and sold at a discount. In a way, it was easy to break into the industry because start-up costs were relatively low. But it was difficult to gain credibility with store buyers as a new supplier. They valued economy, perhaps, but even more, they had to be sure of delivery, quality, and follow-through. And buyers had long memories in these matters.

Exhibit 1

BETTI TERRELL DESIGNER COLLECTION
FOR BABIES

Designed by

Carolyn Hogue

Spring–Summer, 1977

In Our 48th Season

Johnston, Inc.
P.O. Box 15125
Dallas, Texas 75201

For delivery—Spring—as ready—complete March 1
For delivery—Summer—as ready—complete March 31

Terms: 8/10 EOM

"Stripe It Fun"

Estimated shipping December 15 on early orders,
complete March 1

Style no.	Garment	Price	Size
9188	Girl Popover dress and panties—sun popover in white precured b/c (65% Kodel/35% Cot) with elastic neckline—angel wing sleeves—accents of green binding & orange tulip applique. Panties of bold stripe (50% Avril/50% Cot) in green/orange/gold/white. Suggested retail—19.00 (50.0) White stripe	9.50	6–9–12–18
9619	Girl sun hat—ruffle brim completely lined hat in bold stripe (50% Avril/50% Cot) in green/orange/gold/white—white pique binding & bow. Suggested retail—8.00 (50.0) Stripe	4.00	9–12–18
9158	Shortall—zip front shortall with half the back & half the front in white twill (65% Kodel/35% Cot) and the other half in bold stripe (50% Avril/50% Cot) in green/orange/gold/white—stripe patch pockets on white front. Suggested retail—12.50 (50.0) White/Stripe	6.25	6–9–12–18
9624	Sun hat—white twill sun hat with bright orange and green button trim. Could be worn by boy or girl. All fabrics 65% Kodel/35% Cot. Suggested retail—8.00 (50.0) White	4.00	9–12–18
9189	Girl sun bubble—in white precured b/c (65% Kodel/35% Cot)—with orange tulip applique on bib—bold green/orange/gold stripe ruffling accents (50% Avril/50% Cot). Suggested retail—12.50 (50.0) White	6.25	6–9–12–18

Exhibit 2

Johnston, Inc., had done reasonable well financially by comparison with its competition. For example, a reporting service (Robert Morris Associates) published in 1974 a composite index of 26 children's clothing manufacturers with sales under $10 million, which can be compared with Johnston's record (see Exhibit 3).

Exhibit 3

	Robert Morris Associates	Johnston
Assets		
Cash	2.3	2
Receivables net	33.1	46
Inventory net	45.8	46
Other current	3.6	—
Total current	84.9	94
Fixed assets net	11.0	5
Other noncurrent	4.1	1
Total	100.0	100
Liabilities		
Due banks (short-term)	19.6	6
Due trade	23.6	10
Income taxes	2.3	—
Current maturities long-term debt	.7	—
All other current	8.1	12
Total current debt	54.3	28
Long-term debt	5.6	—
Net worth	40.1	72
Total	100.0	100

	Robert Morris Group
Income statement	
Net sales	100.0
Cost of sales	75.1
Gross profit	24.9
All other expenses—net	22.7
Profit B/T	2.2

Johnston stated that although his company's gross was significantly greater than industry average, profits were only slightly better due to high sales and design costs attributable to a designer's collection. Sales costs, including offices, showrooms, sales compensation, and samples, were 10 percent of sales.

Organization and Production

Bob Johnston summarized his firm's key functions as design, production, marketing, and sales. Because of the nature of the business, all were interconnected around the concept of seasons.

From an overall point of view, Johnston had organized his operations as shown in Exhibit 4.

The key marketing/sales locations were in two major buying centers, New York and Dallas. Because of the firm's size, relationships

Exhibit 4

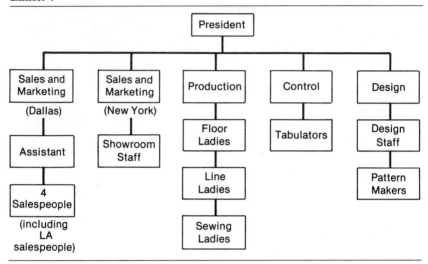

among the various groups were much more informal than formal and circumscribed.

Design

The design function was directed by Carolyn Hogue, with a small staff of designers and pattern makers. Typical of her schedule and duties was the timetable for the 1978 spring line for the labels Betti Terrell, Fischèl, and Little One:

> *July–September 1977.* Carolyn winnowed information from buyers, the company's showroom staff, other designers, and the fabric industry, as well as her own intuitions. She also previewed domestic and international fabric shows. Then, from five-yard sample swatches, she created five lines, styles within each line reflecting her feelings about what the line "needed" to present a well-balanced collection. These results were previewed by the top five Johnston executives. At this time, certain items were eliminated as not being "right" for the line in terms of price, design, and classification (classification meant grouping by type of garment, such as pant, dress, coverall). The surviving items were priced by the controller. During this same period, the company forecasted the required yardage necessary to produce the number of garments it estimated would be sold. Samples for showrooms and salespeople were made.
>
> *October.* The lines went into production.
>
> *October–November.* Key retail buyers made garment selections at the plant and typically left specific orders. These key customers nor-

mally selected a few items as exclusives, for which they had to guarantee a minimum cut. On the basis of these early orders and buyer comments, the line was "put to bed." Delivery terms and prices were finalized and fabric purchases completed. Production of the remaining lines was finished.

December–March 1978. Repeat of the July–September schedule, for the fall 1978 line.

Perhaps the best summary of the sales pattern can be shown as in Exhibit 5.

Exhibit 5
Sales Pattern, Fall 1976

Report no.	Report date	Sales to date—all lines total season sales (ratio)
1	4/5/76	0.30
2	4/13/76	0.51
3	4/21/76	0.64
4	4/29/76	0.82
5	5/6/76	0.91
6	5/13/76	0.94
7	5/20/76	0.97
8	5/27/76	0.99
9	6/10/76	1.00
10	6/18/76	1.00
Final	8/5/76	1.00

These data refer to orders received; i.e., purchase orders from retail buyers, on a weekly basis. Notice the time periods required for the gradual accumulation of total sales. It is also evident that information on selling trends is difficult to read early in the selling season, when accumulated sales are limited.

Production

The basic rule was "first come, first served." That is, the buyer who first ordered received the first shipment. Moreover, second cuttings were seldom made. Consequently, if a buyer ordered too little, there was scant opportunity to ask for a subsequent factory run. This rule created an interesting buyer trade-off: sufficient orders versus ordering flexibility.

The first production steps consisted of making patterns and coordinating the cutting and sewing schedule with market demand. Separate bolts of fabric were distinguished from each other with care to guarantee matched coloring and shading. All pieces of a style were grouped and assigned to a production line.

These lines consisted of 8 to 11 women, working sequentially on each garment as it passed through to the head of the line, where it emerged completed. This production technique contrasted to the "bundle" system, where each worker always performed the same operation and pieces were joined at the very end. Johnston's technique sacrificed some efficiency for accuracy and flexibility, which was in keeping with the firm's need for small runs of many items, where schedules were tight and small margins called for minimum errors. Each line had a supervisor, who served as leader and adviser on the intricacy of the next garment coming through. The last production step included finishing details, inspection, pressing, hanging, and bagging.

Generally speaking, the Johnston manufacturing operation was a critical factor to success. Some of the sewing techniques were complex and unusual; yet the quality of the finished product was expected to be noticeably superior to that of competition—no loose threads, garments equally well finished inside and out, finished seams, and collars cut on the bias.

One of the key influences upon profit was inventory turnover; it was essential to hold inventories to a minimum and yet be responsive to the requirements of a seasonal market.

Production Constraints

Three requirements affected production constraints: the need to fully sell out all runs, a policy of no reorders, and quality standards. Profits depended upon sold-out production runs which, in turn, were a function of plant capacity (both in-house and outside-contract) and fabric and trim availability. However, these constraints were relatively flexible at the beginning of each season. Once the rough sales forecast of the styles was determined, supplies purchased, and production schedules set, however, flexibility was greatly diminished. Notwithstanding, certain production adjustments were possible as sales information improved. Still, poor early information could lead to expensive wrong cuts.

Full production requirements were a function of small margins. Unused fabrics usually had to be sold off at a loss. Laying off employees was undesirable because of the company's dependence on the local work force and the general difficulty of finding skilled workers. Expanding production greatly beyond average plant capacity was only possible (short run) by contracting out various garments. In these cases, the question of quality was problematical. Within the greater Dallas area, nobody was able or willing to match Johnston's quality standards. Moreover, the time factor was critical. Usually about four to five extra weeks had to be allowed for outside production schedules. Given very tight production schedules, such flexibility was often unavailable.

In the long run, increased capacity was possible with the purchase of an existing plant, the construction of a new plant, or the development of additional contractors. In the case of a new plant, the learning curve was about three years.[3] Regardless of the choice, Johnston had two other considerations to keep in mind: the costs of servicing any additional financial debt and the ability to stimulate demand while maintaining the quality, reputation for uniqueness, and exclusively presently attached to Johnston products.

Reorders were not in the plan. A request could be serviced if unsold stock was on hand, but Johnston would not cannibalize signed orders to the benefit of a more important customer. Although some production adjustment was possible, reorders were usually unavailable due to fabric limitations and tight schedules. Furthermore, reorders generally arrived after the production line had been shifted to producing for the next season. (Reorders came in after the merchandise had had a one-month selling time on the retail floor, or about two to four months after production was finished.)

The third production constraint was a function of quality standards. For three reasons, quality limited production:

1. Uniqueness of design, which caused an intricate production requirement.
2. Quality of workmanship and the shortage of properly skilled workers.
3. The logistical problem of on-time delivery of individual items and groups of items (an important dimension of supplier quality).

Marketing and Sales

As mentioned earlier, Johnston carried five labels: Betti Terrell, Fischèl, Little One, Johnston, and Toymaker Designs. The target audience consisted of those consumers described as "middle-upper class, with understated tastes, preferring pastel towards bright colors, a city-type, and department or specialty store patron."

As we have noted, there was a wide variety of retail operations in the garment industry. But for a firm like Johnston's, with its high-priced, exclusive lines, the only pertinent categories were specialty stores and department stores. In fact, Bob Johnston found it easier to

---

[3] Johnston could figure a contractor premium of 15 to 20 percent above factory labor; a $1,500 premium per operator above asset cost in the case of buying an existing plant; and $125,000 (or $2,500 per operator, assuming 50) if a plant were built.

talk about specialty stores (such as I. Magnin) and department stores (such as Macy's). When pressured to generalize how he saw the differences between these two types, he summarized as follows:

Area of contrast	Specialty stores	Department stores
Margins..............	Higher	Tight
Sales orientation.......	Higher gross	Volume
Merchandise..........	Insists on original label	Sometimes buys for $10 less from a knockoff artist, such as a copy of Pierre Cardin produced in the Orient.
Depth of line..........	Breadth in selective lines	Buys deep in one resource (like one half of Johnston's output) and hence makes the product into a commodity ("you can buy it at the Emporium")

The consumer was a different matter. In Johnston's opinion, the buying decision was normally made by either the mother or grandmother. Not until the teen years did one find strong user input into the buying decision. The decision makers often had very different ideas about how they wanted to dress the offspring. The mother emphasized practicality: "Is it wash 'n wear, permanent press?" Grandmothers tended to overlook these features. Further value differences encompassed such dimensions as quality workmanship, colors, relevance to lifestyle, and the image the garment should convey. In addition to these contrasts, geographical differences were significant in the American market. Chicago and New York favored classical, traditional styles, somber or pastel colors, and wool, corduroy, and lightweight cotton fabrics. The West and South were attracted to bright, "sun and sport" styles and colors, and materials which were adaptable to year-round wearing.

The characteristics of the consumer were difficult, therefore, to generalize. In this respect, it is interesting to note remarks made during an interview with some Macy's children's wear buyers in June 1977:

Young marrieds get quite practical when buying. They wouldn't buy a "way out" gift because it would reflect on the giver.

The high end market is not shrinking; rather there is increasing concern with quality, durability, practicality, and style.

The mother, after all, can't dress the little girl fancier than she is dressed.

The grandmother is interested in the brand name. The mother is more interested in copying what "she" is like—a bit trendy, somewhat unique, but wash 'n wear.

There are two kinds of customers—those who want their kids to look like miniature adults and those who want them to look like children.

An important part of the firm's strategy had to do with its overall image in the trade. The trade was, of course, Johnston's first level of customer. When asked to comment on "What does a retailer buy when he deals with Johnston?" the president replied: "Exclusive designs that stand out on the rack; prompt, reliable deliveries; quality; a New York office that can facilitate the purchasing process enormously; longevity—a proven name; prestige customers; ethical behavior."

The interface between manufacturer and retailer was an important constraint, as well as opportunity, in the Johnston strategy. For example, one buyer made the following observation: "The real problem in the store is the fixtures and racks. They limit what you can do in presentation—what, in fact, can be displayed."

Not all department stores were interested in having a children's apparel department. Although a good department hopefully could generate store traffic and create long-term customers, the margins and ROI were average; the space could be better put to fast-moving merchandise; and total sales volume was relatively small (about 4½ percent of total store sales).

Because of the fundamental changes taking place in the channels (see "Notes on the Clothing Industry"), it was unclear to Johnston in 1977 whether major retailers would continue to carry and support major designer labels or try to revert to their earlier role of being fashion dictators—the "Fifth Avenue" tradition; whether they would be more insistent upon exclusive arrangements or willing to accept selected local competition. It is significant to note that in the Johnston Company, Carolyn was designer, merchandiser, and market researcher in that she maintained close contact with the key store accounts.

Pricing was another important ingredient of marketing strategy. Price levels were arrived at among the controller, the designer, and the New York showroom (in the person of Priscilla Fischèl) and reflected history, competition, market trends, degree of risk inherent in a style, and season. For example, spring-summer items generally contributed more to the overall margins than labor-intensive winter clothing.

Typically, Johnston catered to the high end of the price segment. The normal procedure was to multiply a garment's cost by a factor to arrive at a selling price. This formula, of course, was not rigid, since it was necessary that after the retailer had added his mark-on, the eventual retail selling price still be in an appropriate "price line." The company had done little price experimentation. Bob explained that management instinctively believed that if the price were set too high, obviously all sales would disappear.

Selling strategy was premised upon the existence of three key purchase "points": the factory, the showrooms, and the traveling sales force. A select few retailers came to the factory to purchase, indicating that these buyers were sure of their consumers and the appropriateness

of the Johnston merchandise fit in terms of the preferred store "look."
In short, these buyers purchased on the basis of their feelings and the
historical record of the manufacturer, regardless of what the retail
market shows offered as to design, price, fabric, or color.

The major apparel cities (New York, Chicago, Dallas, Los Angeles)
offered "market weeks" in which buyers visited a number of manufacturer's showrooms and placed orders. These "markets" were seasonal,
including fall/holiday, spring/summer. Department store buyers were
of two types. "Key buyers" normally purchased about the same number of pieces. The others "shopped the market" seeking particular
items with which to enhance their department. This second approach
was not so much a "fill in the gap" approach as it was an attempt to
give their departments a broader "look." The strategy, of course, was
intended to increase the selection for the customer in order to foster
store loyalty as well as to create a feeling of "theater." It was important, needless to say, to be competitive in these regards. It was not
surprising that this second type of buyer was not very brand loyal. She
or he would only buy in terms of specific look, price, color, and design.

The third sales point was the traveling sales force, the traditional
channel for smaller store buyers. Due to increased travel costs and the
great popularity of market shows, traveling salespeople were steadily
diminishing in importance.

Store buyers had a number of criteria for buying, common among
which were the following:

1. Does the line reflect "the look" I want?
2. Does the merchandise "jump off the rack?"
3. Does the line fit in with other merchandise I have purchased?
    Does it enhance my total department image?
4. Are the price points right for my department? (Is it too expensive?
    Not expensive enough?)
5. Will it be delivered when I want it?
6. Does the supplier have delivery credibility?
7. Does it fit into my departmental budget?
8. How much should I buy, for which stores, and which pieces of the
    collection?
9. Is the line confined?
10. Can I wait until the last minute to order so as to read the market
    better, to maximize my "open-to-buy," and to be flexible in case a
    new item, new designers, new look or color takes off in the mar-
    ket?
11. Is the merchandise convenient to handle? Does it have to be
    steamed first? Preticketed? Supplied with hangers?

The manufacturer's showroom personnel, as well as salespeople,
played a critical role, despite the implied dominance of the garments

themselves. Many supplier intangibles, including integrity, dependability, workmanship, appropriateness of line, were inferred from the salespersons' behavior. Moreover, the field people recognized the inherent conflict between the tightness of the production schedule and the buyers' preferences to commit at the last minute. The trick was to balance the two so as to satisfy the customer while protecting the company. This was a selling role demanding understanding and interpersonal skills. It was a selling role that required sound communications between buyers, the New York office, other field personnel, and the plant. Feelings were as important as facts.

Advertising was a final key ingredient to Johnston's marketing strategy. It was not easy, in this regard, to decide the correct relative emphasis to place upon the consumer and the trade. Was pull or push more appropriate? Traditionally, Johnston had spent little on consumer advertising (about $20,000).[4] Management's assumption was that brand awareness among consumers was high, particularly among long-time Betti Terrell and Fischèl customers. Therefore, the firm relied on the quality and design of the merchandise to move garments off the rack. Even among buyers, Johnston advertised infrequently, depending upon name reputation, to induce a visit to the showroom during market week. Co-op advertising with particular retail outlets was not considered feasible due to high cost and limited exposure. Each year, one or two half-page ads (at $2,000) were run in *The New Yorker*, a reflection of the era when that magazine was read by Johnston's primary market.[5]

But management had important advertising concerns, particularly given brand proliferation in the markets. Should the advertising budget be redirected? Was it possible to increase brand awareness? Could a small company compete with the well-known women's clothing designers who were entering the children's market? Or should the emphasis be placed upon retail buyer promotions, with price-off deals and co-op newspaper ads?

A brand campaign was not easy. If the attempt were made, it was not clear whether the emphasis should be placed upon "best sellers" (a standard, simple item) or "fashion" items. Should the message be directed at the mother or grandmother? Which aspect of the products should be mentioned—line, color, design, practicality, quality?

Finally, store contacts might be enhanced by spending money educating the selling personnel about merchandising techniques, including how to display the groups, how to coordinate the Johnston gar-

---

[4] This amount of advertising is deceptively low. Frequently, leading specialty and department stores will advertise in catalogs and newsprint the brand label in order to enhance their prestige among consumers.

[5] See Exhibit 6.

Exhibit 6

My Friend Charlie on my clothes,
in my arms, and in my book.
Charlie Goes Fishin' sundress and
panties in white polyester/cotton
with blue edging and applique,
about $22. 9, 12 and 18 mo. sizes.
Stuffed bear, about $9. 32-pg.
"My Friend Charlie" book about $4.

*Godchaux's / Joseph Horne / Lord & Taylor
and other fine stores*

Box 15125, Dallas, Texas 75201

1 col. × 71 lines, space & production cost
$1,453, *The New Yorker*, March 28,1977.

ments with those from other resources, and how to order appropriately.

Bob Johnston also considered the greater use of selected promotional techniques which would substitute value attributes for quality attributes. For example, spring sunsuits could be "offered at a special price due to surplus fabric and labor." In this offering, there would be no markdown money, advertising money, or rebates. But if the company made such offerings, even late in a selling season, would the result cannibalize the regular line? Would the firm lower the reputation of its name?

In recapping Johnston's marketing strategy, it is revealing to note Bob's answer to two questions:

1. What is your firm's uniqueness—your essential strength?
   "Complete designer collections with matching wardrobes, quality in design, product flexibility, and our inherent belief in good taste."
2. What are your company's goals and objectives?
   "To survive; to grow within limits so as to maintain our niche; to do better by expanding present accounts and adding new ones; to increase in a timely manner our productive capacity; to optimize the impact of our sales force by teaching them how to relate even better to customers."

Growth Possibilities

Bob Johnston liked to describe the prospects for growth as dependent upon four variables: design; production/organization; contact with the "rest of the world" (ROW); and image with store buyers. It was his philosophy that these four were interrelated and that growth was premised upon the proper balance among them.

Take, for example, a new design concept created by Carolyn and requiring increased production capability. For the design to succeed, it had to be accepted by the retail buyers, an acceptance based upon their reading of the "ROW" (i.e., the consumer market). Similarly, if the buyers "wanted" a particular design from a manufacturer in order to broaden their look, the "ROW" must be induced to want this design, and the plant must be made capable of producing it. The interdependence between manufacturer, buyer, and consumer was critical and delicate.

Growth, in Johnston's opinion, could be viewed a number of ways. In the first place, growth could be defined as increased revenue sufficient to cover inflated costs. Unfortunately, raising prices for this purpose was not always possible. In many markets, for example, there seemed to be some psychological price barriers. A $25 gift might be acceptable, but not one for $26. Hence, growth to cover costs might have to be obtained through volume and, therefore, lower unit costs.

Or growth might be more strategically oriented, such as "present products, expanded distribution." Such a move would probably entail maintenance of the multilabel format (namely, exclusive franchise lines and open lines) but selling to more outlets. The question would be how to accomplish this goal. If exclusiveness were the selling proposition, then expansion would only be possible by finding markets not already covered by stores presently carrying the line. This would basically require selling to smaller stores in areas outside the mainstream of department store operations, because most major cities already had at least one store carrying the Johnston franchise line. Moreover, selling to smaller stores involved greater risk and uncertainty. These markets represented a credit-sensitive area of the market in which total quantities purchased were smaller. The mortality rate of small specialty stores was excessive. Thus, it would probably require that new sales rely heavily on the "open lines."

Unfortunately, certain key buyers who presently had the franchise felt very strongly about exclusives. They argued that their department's reputation was based primarily on image and uniqueness. They resented new franchises. Whether they would cease ordering Johnston garments if the firm expanded was unknown. (Of the top 15 buyers, at least 3 were adamant about retaining exclusivity.)

Or growth could come from produce redefinition with the same or expanded distribution. Product redefinition might consist of shrinking to one label, reducing or expanding size availability, and reducing or expanding collection designs. Let's consider these separately.

One Label or Many.   The issues introduced by this alternative were several. Would the firm's focus be on present customers or new ones? Would the concept be applied to present or to new ones? What did "exclusivity" mean as department stores expanded from coast to coast? Did "exclusivity" matter to a customer? What effect would one label have on small shops which had positioned themselves on the concept of "uniqueness, originality, and exclusivity?" Would sales drop because fewer items were offered (consolidation of line with Betti Terrell for infants, toddlers, and kindergarten)? Would those customers who now bought from both the franchise and open lines buy less because all garments carried the same label? Was a buyer concerned with how many labels a department carried? If the lines were consolidated and therefore the number of styles reduced, would the buyer purchase collection groups in greater depth or as sparingly as at present?[6] Would departments who presently carried the Fischèl line and the Betti Terrell label experience a reduction in sales because of customer unfamiliarity with the name? Did customers buy labels? Store image? Store names?

Size Availability

As mentioned earlier, Johnston manufactured layette, infant, toddler, girls 4 to 6 and girls 7 to 12-year-old lines. Was it possible to further expand into the 7 to 12 size bracket in order to fill a need,

---

[6] Carolyn designed several groups, each around a unique theme, integrating fabric, color, and style. Each group normally consisted of interchangeable dresses, skirts, pants, jackets, overalls, and boy's shortalls or overalls.

expressed by various buyers, for elegant but "young looking" clothes (in contrast to most 7 to 12 sizes, which were miniature versions of the junior market)? The size of the market was hard to estimate. And there were important differences among retailers and users. For instance, the buying staff was generally different; the department was located in a different area on the children's floor; the child himself had more involvement in the buying decision (she/he wants the grown-up look); and the Johnston name was unfamiliar to consumer and retailer.

Collection Design

Johnston could eliminate certain designs from the line, by concentrating on dresses or sportswear, for example. However, the Johnston brand was essentially strong because the company manufactured a "total concept." If this concept were eliminated, then the company might lose buyers who purchased for this reason. And Johnston would find itself in direct competition with established children's clothing manufacturers who had always specialized. Usually these specialists' strong selling point was the "total look" composed of interchangeable dresses, pants, skirts, jackets, blouses, and matching brother-sister outfits. Thus, any change from the present "total" format would probably shift the buying patterns, both in stores and quantity purchased.

Appendix A: Notes on the Clothing Industry (with Particular Reference to Children's Clothing)*

In the classic sense of perfect competition, the industry is characterized by thousands of highly competitive manufacturers and retailers. Mortality rates are high. Some 1972 data, summarized in Exhibit 1A, outline the structure of the supply side of the industry.

Notice that the concentration of business by size of establishment is less significant than its dispersal among hundreds of competitors. The textile trade has long had a reputation for fragmentation, entrepreneurship, and volatility. And yet, in recent years, there has been a dramatic shift away from this tradition. Large corporations have started to take an interest in high fashion; witness the acquisitions by Norton Simon (Halston), Consolidated Foods (Gamut, Russell Taylor), Takihyo (Anne Klein), and Warnaco (Jerry Silverman). As the magazine *MBA* reported in a December 1976 story:

> New York's garment business, once a bastion of small, immigrant entrepreneurs, is no longer a father and son, nickel and dime, cottage

---

* These notes were prepared by Nitsa Lallas and Candy Neville. © 1979 by the Board of Trustees of the Leland Stanford Junior University.

Exhibit 1A
Percent of Value of Shipments Accounted for by the Largest Companies in Selected Apparel and Textile Industries, 1972

SIC code	Industry description	Number of companies	Total ($000,000)	Value of shipments Percent accounted for by			
				4 Largest companies	8 Largest companies	20 Largest companies	50 Largest companies
2311	M&B suits and coats	721	$2,397	19%	31%	48%	65%
2321	M&B shirts and nightwear	518	2,104	22	31	50	69
2322	M&B underwear	67	239	49	71	91	99
2323	M&B neckwear	291	295	26	36	53	74
2327	M&B separate trousers	463	1,745	29	41	60	76
2328	M&B work clothing	297	1,738	38	53	70	84
2329	M&B other clothing N.E.C.	481	783	20	27	41	63
2331	W&J blouses	886	1,255	18	26	38	55
2335	W&J dresses	5,294	3,580	9	13	18	28
2337	W&J suits & coats	1,547	1,805	13	18	26	40
2339	W&J other outerwear N.E.C.	1,247	1,638	18	25	37	52
2341	W&C underwear	608	1,332	15	23	41	63
2342	Corsets and allied garments	220	647	31	45	67	86
2351	Millinery	215	58	17	26	42	63
2352	Hats and caps	253	171	26	39	57	77
2361	Children's dresses and blouses	440	655	17	26	42	63
2363	Children's suits and coats	155	189	18	31	55	83
2369	Children's outerwear N.E.C.	372	578	22	32	48	69
2371	Fur goods	797	220	7	12	23	39

Note: M = Men's; W = Women's; B = Boy's; C = Children's; J = Juniors'.

Source: Focus: Profile of the Apparel Industry, American Apparel Manufacturers Association, Inc., 1976.

industry. Bottom-line money managers and advertising whiz kids have replaced the brother-in-law in the shipping department. Modern marketing techniques have arrived along with automated, computerized marking for style and size changes and laser cutting systems.

   . . . The sudden interest of larger corporations in the merchandising of high fashion is, more than anything else, a function of demographics. That postwar baby boom is now moving into the highest spending bracket in the population: the 25- to 45-year-old group. With the spread of singles' lifestyles, childless marriages, and higher educational levels, this generation has much more income than ever before to expand on good taste and fine design.

Accompanying this vertical integration tendency has been a parallel move among several important women's clothing manufacturers to move away from purely exclusive lines to mass distribution, ready-to-wear garments. Examples here include Anne Klein, Calvin Klein, Halston, Bill Blass, Yves St. Laurent, Givenchy, Gucci, and Pierre Cardin. Additionally, a number of these well-known names have been buying up even smaller firms and expanding into accessories and children's clothing. As a result, by 1977, there was a distinct tug-of-war between foreign and domestic design and between manufacturer label and store label. The balance of "values important to the consumer" attributed to retailer and supplier was beginning to shift. In fact, a significant change in the development of fashion had recently developed.

For many years, it was assumed that American fashion was determined by the major designers, both at home and more particularly in Paris. But they came the total failure of the anticipated midilength in 1970, and the garment industry was brought up short. No longer were Americans passive as to what styles they would wear; the risks for manufacturers suddenly escalated. Style and fashion became difficult to plan.[1]

Children's apparel represents a distinct subdivision of the general market, adapting some of the trends witnessed in men's and women's styles while rejecting others. The manufacturer here is faced with deciding which designs to miniature, restrained by the risk that the lag in his production cycle might be delayed beyond the popularity of the style in adult garments.

In the long term, an intriguing but unanswered query about children's apparel has been whether general trends in women's fashion would take hold in the children's market. Consider, for example, the noticeable shift away from pants to dresses and skirts or the increased awareness of European tendencies toward high styling. Would the American consumer shift toward greater concern with appearance? Would this trend bring back coats and dresses for little girls and suits for little boys?

---

[1] Style is a particular mode of presentation. Fashion is the style currently in vogue.

Retailers

Most clothing moves directly from cutter (i.e., garment maker) to direct account. The intermediaries in this flow are company salespeople, sales agents (independents), company show rooms, and local trade shows. Wholesalers are not a significant factor.

The general types of pertinent retailers can be broken out usefully into five major categories:

1. Mom/Pop Stores
   a. Single (or few) unit operation.
   b. Specialize in one category; e.g., children's, women's, sports, men's.
   c. Small-volume buyer.
   d. Small selection.
   e. Small city or resort locations.
   f. Rely on supplier salespeople.
   g. Buy for specific store.
   h. Few ads.
   i. Steady clientele.
2. Specialty Stores
   a. Multiunit.
   b. Wide geographical distribution of outlets.
   c. Mid-size volume buyers.
   d. Selective customers.
   e. Offer limited selection.
   f. Only clothing.
   g. Slightly higher prices.
   h. Medium ads.
   i. Fairly steady clientele.
   j. Exclusive couturier and ready-to-wear clothing.
3. Department Stores
   a. Multiunit.
   b. Limited geographic distribution of outlets.
   c. Large-volume buyers.
   d. Wide range of customers.
   e. Wide selection of goods.
   f. Competing departments within store.
   g. Clothing, household goods, etc.
   h. Price very competitive.
   i. Heavy advertising.
   j. Erratic client.
   k. Ready-to-wear.
4. Mass Merchandisers or Chains
   a. Frequently multiunit.
   b. Self-service primarily.

    c. Wide coverage of merchandise.
    d. Retail and catalog (i.e., Sears, Ward).
    e. Shopping center oriented.
    f. Low prices.
    g. Heavy merchandising.
    h. Lots of store brands.
    i. Staple oriented.
    j. Bargain image.

5. Discounters
    a. Often single outlets.
    b. Prefer national labels at deep discounts.
    c. Usually hardware, not soft goods oriented.
    d. More often associated with large city–peripheral area location.
    e. In and out on hot items.
    f. Price oriented.

No description of distribution channels would be meaningful without recognizing a fundamental area of conflict between manufacturer and retailer, for it turns out that the best strategy for either manufacturer or retailer is not the best for the other, as summarized next:

Strategy	Manufacturer	Retailer
Product line	Broad	Selective
Exclusivity (at retail)	Yes	No
Emphasis given at retail	Specialty selling/management	Part of regular inventory
Payment	In advance	Long terms
Advertising	Large retailer effort	Large manufacturer effort
Price	No price cutting	Price to sell
Brand	Manufacturer franchise	Store franchise
Return privilege	No	Yes

There are several reasons for this inherent conflict. Consider the role of the retailer: Is he the manufacturer's "salesperson" or the customer's "buyer?" The latter is presumably the more desired position; however, given the heterogeneity of the various markets, the retailer is faced with a formidable task. How does he/she cater in an intimate, personalized manner to one set of customer values without losing another customer group? Which type of merchandise should be selected to please the greatest number of clients (steady and browsers), without selecting such diverse merchandise as to please no one? Retailers, in other words, may select merchandise for a variety of reasons that are foreign to the supplier.

The manufacturer faces a similar problem on a larger scale. Producing for a national market, how does he balance out regional differences as well as contradictory store outlet demands? This balancing act is complicated by the fact that the manufacturer's point of inflexibility is

his factory. He is committed to a certain range of output by his investment in bricks and mortar. On the other hand, his point of flexibility is
the sales/marketing function. He can send his salespeople "anywhere." The retailer, on the other hand, is most flexible in his "manufacturing" (i.e., purchasing function) and least flexible in selling (i.e.,
the customer must come to his store[s]).

Hence, there is a tugging and pulling between manufacturer and
retailer. If the merchandise involved is a commodity (i.e., the consumer has choice; there are multiple brands; and price is the critical
variable), then the retailer controls. Not only can he select from numerous sellers, but the consumer patronizes particular retailers less
because of brands carried than because of retailer attractions (i.e., shopping values, such as location, decor, selection, credit, convenience, and
fun). On the other hand, the manufacturer with a strong brand franchise can influence the channels. With a limited choice of supply, the
trade and consumer are dependent upon a particular supplier. The
manufacturer's values, in other words, outweigh retailer values.

Thus, we have the two worlds of national labels and private (or
store) labels. The manufacturer tries to build consumer loyalty; the
retailer, store loyalty. This competition is reflected, of course, in the
balance of expenditure between advertising and promotion. Advertising is normally the manufacturer's chief weapon for building a consumer brand franchise. "Promotion," on the other hand, is aimed at
gaining retailer support, and "a point of sale" inducement to buy.

Against this general background, one can identify two major trends
in the clothing industry over the last 15 years. One has been the growing importance of the retailer, and the other, accelerating competition,
both among manufacturers and retailers.

The retailer's growing influence can be attributed in part to the fact
that many items of clothing have become commodities. Hence, marketing control shifts to the side of shopping values. This commodity
trend has been due primarily to advanced mass-production techniques.
Today, large quantities of skirts, pants, shirts, and dresses of almost
identical style, material, and quality can be made by competing manufacturers. Stanley Marcus, former chairman of Neiman-Marcus and
presently executive vice president of parent Carter Hawley Hale, made
the following comments about the sameness of department stores in
the January 21, 1977, issue of *Women's Wear Daily:*

> Any objective observer visiting a modern shopping center . . . must get
> a sense of fatigue from seeing virtually the same goods and colors and
> textures in store after store. Exclusivity in a mass-production market,
> even when legally possible, is hard to come by.

Because of this growth in the mass production of clothing, consumer
buying behavior has changed. Instead of seeking a "designer" dress or a

handmade blouse, many shoppers will opt for a mass-produced item that looks of equal quality "but is half the price."

Since many buyers will select the mass-produced item, exclusive franchise agreements between manufacturers and retailers have suffered. No longer is it so obvious that the manufacturer and retailers have suffered. No longer is it so obvious that the manufacturers can grant exclusives to retailers to guarantee the retailer a competitive edge. No longer are retailers dependent upon prestige labels to succeed. It used to be that the Fifth Avenue retailers were the "elitest of the elite." B. Altman's, Lord & Taylor, Saks Fifth Avenue, Bonwit Teller, and Bergdorf Goodman were symbols of high fashion and prestige. But their lock on the high fashion market has weakened. As an article from *Clothes*, December 1, 1976, said, "It's been years since the Fifth Avenue stores' private labels which said 'made expressly' for Saks or Lord & Taylor had any clout."

The retailing scene is thus in a state of flux. Retailers, in general, have become more influential—and yet they may have lost their opportunity to differentiate on the basis of prestige labels.

Cost pressures have also been important, particularly as fashion influences have shifted. In a *Fortune* article (December 1976), the writer summarized the problems of department stores:

1. Margins have dropped.
2. Suburban growth has slowed.
3. Shopping center development has slowed.
4. There has been heated competition in fashion goods from such mass-merchandisers as Sears, Penney, and Montgomery Ward, who had themselves been squeezed by the discounters.

Fortune concluded:

> Two powerful forces now emerging will dominate the retailing business in the United States for many years to come. One is heightened competition among all sellers of general merchandise as an era of easy growth comes to an end. The other is the pervasive influence of fashion in determining what consumers buy and stores sell. Together these forces are challenging the strategies of the big retailers and reshaping their prospects.

Buying merchandise for retail department stores is unquestionably one of the most critical jobs in the organization. Although conceptually straightforward, the multitude of alternatives available to the buyer (in terms of manufacturers, merchandise, and consumers to target) make the job difficult to implement. Even when fundamental style decisions have been made, buyers are plagued with color, size range, and quantity details. One can easily imagine the problems involved with tracking the sales of several styles each available in three colors and eight sizes.

Buyers earn a relatively low salary, work long hours, and are the targets for a multiplicity of salespeople. Entertainment, gifts, theater tickets—these are all favors/temptation thrust at most buyers by a great range of selling organizations. Ethical standards, needless to say, vary. Most major firms, both supplying and buying, are scrupulously honest; a few are quite the reverse.

Company benefits for the buyer might include three or four buying trips to New York (or elsewhere) each year, the normal 20 percent employee buying discount, a low-interest revolving credit arrangement with the retailer, and a real opportunity for advancement. Typical progression might be from salesperson to sales manager (perhaps several departmental assignments here) to assistant buyer to merchandise supervisor to floor manager to buyer, a criss-cross path. Pressures to beat "same day last year" are high, and "open to buy" is standard buyer vocabulary.[2]

The buyers and their assistants operate from central headquarters and buy for all retail outlets. In an organization with less than five retail outlets, the buyer can tailor merchandise to the various stores. For example, a buyer may want different merchandise or different proportions of the same merchandise in stores located in downtown San Francisco and suburban Palo Alto. As the organization grows and adds more retail outlets, the buyer is much less able to cater to regional differences. There are simply too many products in too many sizes and colors to effectively alter the merchandise regionally.

Typically, assistant buyers spend the bulk of their time keeping track of the details; i.e., tracking sales, budgets, shipments, etc. More and more department stores utilize point-of-sale, computerized "cash registers," which generate very useful and up-to-date computer reports for buyers and their assistants. The reports include sales volume information by vendor, style, size, color, and retail outlet. If, for example, one item is selling particularly well, the buyers may go back to the vendor and attempt to get more merchandise shipped out to the stores quickly. If, on the other hand, one store is selling much more than another, they may transfer merchandise internally. These decisions must be made and implemented quickly before sales patterns change. For example, in the boys' and girls' departments, "Star Wars" T-shirts may sell for the first four weeks after opening night, but not before or after.

---

[2] Every six months, the buyer projects opening inventory, sales, and closing inventory for each month. "Open to buy" is the amount of purchases available each month to balance these estimates.

Buyers' Relationships with Manufacturers

Buyers commit millions of dollars to manufacturers throughout the year. Each year, a buyer develops a pro forma balance sheet and income statement which guide the year's buying. Prior years sales and styles are extrapolated to the future to develop the pro formas. The pro formas are then broken down by month, and each month the buyer has "open to buy" a certain dollar volume of merchandise. This is allocated among the buyer's various product lines each month but varies over the year with inventory levels and sales. For example, if sales of a particular product have been lower than expected and the inventory level is therefore higher than desired, the buyer will allocate dollars to other products in a given month.

Buyers want to remain as flexible as possible in their commitments to manufacturers so that they can respond to changes in demand. Historically, clothing buyers have ordered merchandise six months in advance of shipment, with few changes in the orders possible. Although initial orders are often placed about a half year in advance, modifications of the orders (styles, colors, sizes) are accepted by manufacturers up to two months before shipment without penalty to the buyer. Additionally, orders can be canceled up to one month before shipment without penalty. Since buyers are evaluated almost exclusively on their bottom line performance and merchandise selection, the pro formas and flexibility in placing orders are particularly important to them.

Reliable and well-packaged shipments are also important to buyers. Typically, buyers develop relationships with vendors over time and know what to expect from them. It is much easier and less risky for buyers to order merchandise from well-known, established vendors. Also, as the retail outlets allow more and more customer returns of merchandise, the merchandise is collected and returned to the vendor, who credits the buyer's account for the next purchase. Continuing relationships with vendors ensure that returned merchandise can be redeemed for credit. Yet thousands of very small, backyard manufacturers continually present their merchandise to buyers. Many fad items come out of this group, and although they present a much higher risk to the buyer, this group of vendors cannot be ignored. If they are, a buyer's competition may pick them up and gain the advantage of being first.

Buyers use a wide variety of criteria to select their merchandise, the most important being "Will the merchandise suit the target customer?" Other criteria include, "Does it fit well in the department; does it add value to the department; how well can it be displayed; can it be displayed with current merchandise, how reliable is the manufacturer, when can it be delivered; and does it meet the buyer's quality standards?"

Buying for the Infant's Department

Children's clothes are broken down into two groups: infants sizes and children's sizes. Infant sizes include birth to 3 months, 6 months, 9 months, 12 months, 18 months, and 24 months. Then come toddler sizes which are two years, three years, and four years. Beyond that are the children's sizes which include 4 to 6x and 7 to 14 sizes. Some stores include an infant's high-fashion boutique, which is a subset of the infant's department. Generally, children's clothes are a very low net item for a retailer.

Selling seasons are most pronounced in the Midwest and East, where weather changes are more dramatic. The rule of thumb for stocking stores for seasons is:

Inventory, markdowns	Late January
Spring merchandise.	January and February
Easter frills	February and March, sell out by Easter
Summer clothes	Heaviest sales in May and beginning of June
Back to school	July, heavy sales in August
Christmas	Merchandise arrives in October, heavy sales in November (Thanksgiving weekend especially), last-minute shoppers in December

The Consumers of Children's Wear

There has been a fair amount of consumer research in the clothing industry. In April 1978, *Ernshaw's*, a trade publication, reported some interesting observations about children's wear:

Department store share of children's wear has dropped from 50 percent to 25 percent in the past 15 years (the gainers are chains and discounters).

Store loyalty among housewives has been displaced by desire for shopping variety.

Casual living has meant an increased demand for play clothes that are durable and easy to maintain.

Mothers view the purchase of children's clothing as "nothing but problems," particularly with regard to size and price.

As children get older, there is a "conflict of interest" problem in the purchase between mother and child.

Shoppers tend to resist imports, particularly from the Far East.

Brand names are considered guarantees of security, consistency, reliability, and quality—up to a point where price becomes a barrier.

Patronage is spread among all kinds of stores—specialty, department,
discount, chain. There is little general stigma to shopping in mass
outlets.

Gift purchases are more likely to occur in a department store than
elsewhere.

Specialty stores have a strong reputation for service, quality, and personal touch. For older children, these virtues outweigh economy.

Price

C A S E 4–1

Buffington Wholesale

The Buffington Company was an industrial distributor of builders' hardware. Major items in the line included hinges, bolts, electrical fixtures, locks, and specialty fasteners. Sales and profits at the end of 1978 were reflected in the following profit and loss statement (rounded off):

Sales.	$10,000,000
Cost of goods sold.	8,000,000
Gross margin	2,000,000
Variable costs.	500,000
Fixed costs	1,200,000
Total costs	1,700,000
Profit (before taxes)	$ 300,000

Sales were made to several hundred dealer outlets through an outside sales force of four men and a small sales department (two salesmen), which sold direct to a handful of important builders ($1 million in sales). Competition was severe, since over 20 local competitors and the branch offices of two large national manufacturers serviced essentially the same market. Three "inside salespersons" handled phone and drop-in business. Even though the outside salesmen were responsible for some 250 customers, it was estimated that two thirds of their actual volume was placed by phone or on a pickup basis rather than during a salesman's call.

Although there was some danger in generalizing, the financial manager estimated that costs of goods sold were virtually all variable in character. Thus, the company had a variable cost percentage of 85 percent ($8,000,000 + $500,000 ÷ $10,000,000). The cost relationships were estimated to hold within a volume range of $5 million to $30 million.

As a general rule, Buffington was unwilling to make an investment in either fixed or working capital unless it could anticipate an ROI of 20 percent.[1] The president was concerned about a number of questions:

Questions

1. At what sales level would his firm break even?
2. What sales would a new salesperson have to produce if the annual incremental costs (salary, expenses, other traceable costs) were $30,000 and the firm wanted to realize a 20 percent ROI?
3. Suppose the firm preferred to make a profit of 5 percent on sales rather than 20 percent ROI, what sales would a new person have to produce?
4. What sales would the company have to make in order to produce the same dollar profit (i.e., $300,000) assuming a 10 percent cut in selling prices? What sales would be required to make the same percentage of profit (300,000/10,000,000 or 3 percent)?

---

[1] For our purposes, taxes are eliminated from the case in order to simplify calculations.

C A S E 4–2

Penrod Company

Penrod Company was a U.S. pioneer in the development of solar heating systems. Using the brand name Sun-Save, the firm soon dominated the West Coast market (i.e., California, Arizona, Oregon, Hawaii) for solar swimming pool heaters. By 1978, Penrod had about 55 percent share of a total market that was growing at a yearly compounded rate of over 20 percent. The company's reputation was so strong that the name Sun-Save was more or less synonymous with solar heaters in the Los Angeles and Phoenix markets. The brand franchise was reinforced by an aggressive Penrod advertising campaign. Since its inception, the company had annually invested 10 percent of gross sales in a consumer advertising campaign. Spot TV advertising was backed up with monthly print ads in *Sunset* and in the West Coast editions of *Better Homes and Gardens* and *Reader's Digest*.

Although solar heating systems tended to be similar in both appearance and operation, Penrod's unique characteristics were in the specially designed and patented plastic pipes through which water was passed and heated from a base reflector pad. A typical installation cost the homeowner $3,500 but stretched the swimming season by approximately 50 percent and halved traditional heating costs. Averages varied, of course, due to climatic differences.

Solar heaters were typically sold through specialty distributors and a miscellany of dealers, including swimming pool supply houses, building materials supply outlets, mass merchandisers, and home building centers. In all cases, a special crew was needed to ensure proper installation. Some outlets used house crews, while others subcontracted the work to local contractors. As far as the normal householder was concerned, the "expert" was the local dealer.

Penrod had grown rapidly, as Exhibit 1 indicates.

The company's price index, with 1974 being 100, was an interesting phenomenon. Because of industry growth and inflation, Penrod's

Exhibit 1

	1978 (000)	1977 (000)	1976 (000)	1975 (000)	1974 (000)
Price index	135	140	125	110	100
Sales	$ 6,000	$4,800	$4,000	$3,400	$2,500
West Coast industry sales	11,100	8,000	6,000	4,900	4,000
Profit (AT)	570	550	760	400	250

prices rose steadily. But in 1978, its prices plateaued, due primarily to competition from a growing number of "garage shop" operations.

Competition in 1978 was as shown in Exhibit 2.

Exhibit 2

	Competitor	Market share
1	Penrod	55%
2	Allen Bros. (a company specializing in this line of products)	20
3	Smithson (a division of a large conglomerate)	10
20	Small specialty garage shop type operators	15

The sales of Allen and Smithson had leveled off during the past two years in contrast to the significant growth experience of small competitors who hardly existed before 1976. All competitors sold through standard channels, but only Penrod used its own sales force of four salespeople, in contrast to the others who used specialty reps. In addition, Penrod had two field warehouses, one in San Francisco and the other in Los Angeles.

Price cutting became rampant late in 1978. Small operators typically offered the trade special (extra) discounts of between 10 and 25 percent. Product quality ranged from quite good to poor, although it was virtually impossible for the end users to prejudge actual quality. All suppliers offered some kind of guarantee, from six months to five years (Penrod). Nor was it easy for the customer to know how cost effective the new system was unless he or she kept careful records.

Penrod estimated that every 10 percent cut in selling price cost them $100,000 in profits. Most dealers were willing to carry more than one brand and usually indicated a preference for a high-price and a low-price line.

Question

What price strategy should Penrod follow?

C A S E 4–3

Prentice Machine Tools

Prentice was a moderate-sized, regional producer of consumer hand tools, such as planes, hammers, screwdrivers, saws, chisels, hand drills, and bits. Competition came from a number of large national competitors, such as Rockwell, Sears, Roebuck, and Black and Decker, and many small specialty producers. Low-cost imports were a growing influence in the American market and represented about 10 percent of total sales.

Prentice estimated its regional market share at 5 percent, with the top four competitors accounting for about 60 percent of the total. The largest competitor was substantially bigger than any of the others.

Prentice's strategy had always been to price 10 to 15 percent below the level of the top four. The company spent almost nothing on advertising, relying instead upon price to generate sales in major retail outlets. Point-of-sale material was above average in quantity and quality. Prentice also had an active private label program, which accounted for a growing 30 percent of total sales. It was not unusual in some outlets to find one of the majors, Prentice, and a Prentice-made house label.

Prentice realized a tight 3 percent profit on sales. This margin had been approximately the same over the past four years. Market share in the industry and in the region had not fluctuated much, although there seemed to be increasing price pressure from foreign competitors.

On January 15, 1979, one of the major competitors (the number three brand) announced a new national price program consisting of "permanent" price cuts of 10 to 25 percent at retail, a multimillion-dollar promotion program, and a redesigned product line. The firm's objective seemed to be to buy market share. This company had recently followed a similar strategy in the United Kingdom and had picked up about 10 share points. Whether the gain was profitable or not was not totally clear, though it seemed evident that prices had been lowered permanently.

Prentice's alternatives seemed to be:

1. Do nothing—which might put the firm at a price disadvantage if the other majors moved to match the new schedules.
2. Immediately drop to match the new price, which could cause severe retaliation by some competitors and a major drop in profits.
3. Some combination of marketing effort which would provide the firm with some breathing time.
4. Try to reduce internal costs so as to be better able to handle any required price cuts. There were no obvious alternatives here, although some possibilities were to trim the line, to increase the private label business, to postpone some planned product redesigning, to cut point-of-sale efforts, or to switch from a direct salespeople approach (they had six salespeople who worked with distributors and sold a few large private label accounts directly) to the exclusive use of reps who typically charged 5 percent on sales.

Questions

1. What alternative is best for Prentice?
2. Can Prentice survive in this kind of market? If so, how?

C A S E 4–4

Eindhoven Emballage N.V.

As Hans van der Sanden, sales director for the metals division of Eindhoven Emballage N.V., a large manufacturer of metal and plastic packaging in the Netherlands, left the offices of Windmill Breweries in Kinderdijk, he knew that his plans for the development of the market for the company's new two-piece beverage can had gone badly off the track. It was Wednesday, and Mr. Jan Kalver, managing director of Windmill Breweries, a major Dutch brewery and a major customer of Eindhoven Emballage, had just delivered an ultimatum to Mr. van der Sanden: Either Eindhoven Emballage would agree, in writing, to continue to supply three-piece cans to Windmill Breweries in quantities requested for the next year, or Windmill Breweries was ready to replace its present beer packaging line, which it leased from Eindhoven Emballage, with a line to be installed by American Enclosures. American Enclosures was a strong American competitor in the packaging business that was now trying to find a point of entry into the beverage container market in the Benelux countries. Mr. Kalver had told Mr. van der Sanden that American Enclosures had promised to fly in a complete packaging line within one month and to have it operating within three months. Hans van der Sanden knew that Mr. Kalver was completely serious in his threat. Van der Sanden had been given only until Friday, two days, to decide what to do.

The irony of the situation was that the major issue had little to do with the three-piece can. Rather, the major bone of contention was Eindhoven Emballage's refusal to accept responsibility for a claim that about 8 million cans of Windmill Beer exported to the Middle East had developed leakage problems. Mr. Kalver was insistent that Eindhoven Emballage at least should reimburse Windmill Breweries for the cost of

This case has been prepared by Professor Frederick E. Webster, Jr., Amos Tuck School of Business Administration, Dartmouth College (Hanover, New Hampshire, U.S.) and Visiting Faculty Member, Centre d'Etudes Industrielles (Geneva, Switzerland). All rights are reserved by Amos Tuck School and C.E.I. Revised 12/77.

the 3.5 million cans of beer which had actually been returned to Kinderdijk, a claim amounting to 2 million guilders or about $730,000.[1] Windmill Breweries was unwilling to go ahead with its plans to purchase the new two-piece can from Eindhoven Emballage until this matter was cleared up and until it had conducted further tests to determine that the new can would not develop similar leakage problems, especially when transported long distances into export markets.

With Windmill Breweries' refusal to begin using the new two-piece package, Hans van der Sanden now had two problems—the development of the market for the new package and the fact that the production of three-piece cans currently going to Windmill Breweries had already been committed to other customers, in anticipation of Windmill's change to the two-piece can. It had been expected that Windmill would begin using the two-piece can in February 1973, when the new can production line at Eindhoven Emballage would begin production at the rate of 650 cans per minute or 135 million cans per year. The new line represented an investment of about $3 million (over 8 million guilders). A production line for three-piece cans, by comparison, cost about one third as much and produced at the rate of 400 cans per minute. In addition, plans had already been made and initial work begun for three additional lines to produce the two-piece can. These were scheduled to begin production in January 1974, January 1975, and July 1975, since it took about 18 months to construct each line in order to have necessary capacity as the market developed. A decision to begin a fifth line was only a few weeks away.

Company Background

Eindhoven Emballage was a wholly owned subsidiary of General Container, one of the largest American packaging companies. In addition, General Container had a German subsidiary, Bergdorf Verpackung, which also produced metal containers. The operations of these two subsidiaries were coordinated through a small headquarters staff located in Brussels, although there was no corporate marketing staff. Mr. van der Sanden met regularly with his counterpart, the sales director, in Bergdorf Verpackung to discuss common problems. In addition to these two companies which produced metal containers, General Container also had several subsidiaries in paper, machinery, and plastic operations. Major decisions, such as the introduction of the new two-piece can, were made by the local subsidiaries in close consultation with management from the Brussels and New York offices. Although Eindhoven Emballage and Bergdorf Verpackung were indepen-

---

[1] In mid-1973, the official exchange rate was about U.S. $1 = 2.73 guilders.

dent companies, they were currently considering a joint venture in the production and marketing of aerosol cans, a market where economics suggested one production and marketing operation rather than two in the German and Benelux markets. There was also limited competition between these two companies as, in 1972, Bergdorf Verpackung had sold about 3 million tinplate, three-piece cans in the Benelux market.

At the end of 1972, Eindhoven Emballage was producing three-piece cans on four production lines, each capable of producing 70 million cans per year. The output of the new two-piece can line would be required to meet anticipated 1973 demand for a total of 310 million cans.

The Benelux Market

Metal beverage containers were a relatively new development in the Benelux market, and Eindhoven Emballage's sales volumes had grown rapidly in the past few years. Sales volumes and forecasts are presented in Exhibit 1. Although the Netherlands was a much more important

Exhibit 1
Sales Volume—Tinplated Beverage Cans (millions of units)

| | The Netherlands | | Belgium |
Year	Beer	Soft drinks	beer only
1969	15	1	4
1970	24	18	5
1971	40	38	8
1972	78	92	10
1973 (forecast)	115	180	15
1977 total (forecast)		880	75

Source: Company records.

market for the tinplate three-piece beer can than was Belgium, the average Belgian drank twice as much beer as the average Dutchman, 130 liters per capita per year, compared with 62 liters. The beer market in the Netherlands was increasing 6 to 7 percent per year, however, compared to a growth of only 3 to 4 percent per year in Belgium, about the rate of growth in GNP. There were only three major brewers and two major soft drink producers in the Netherlands. In 1970, the population of the Netherlands had been estimated at 13.2 million compared with 9.6 million for Belgium. In addition to the figures shown in Exhibit 1, which include only cans for domestic beverage consumption, there was an important export market for beer from the Netherlands, most of which came from Windmill Breweries, amounting to about 35

million cans in 1969 and an expected 65 million cans in 1973. This
export market was growing at the rate of 10 to 12 percent per year.

Until 1971, Eindhoven Emballage had had 100 percent of the Benelux market for beverage cans, which was exclusively in three-piece,
tin-plated cans. In 1972, competition had appeared in the form of three
different companies: the German affiliate of an American company
producing a two-piece aluminum can; Bergdorf Verpackung; and American Enclosures, which had begun producing a three-piece tin-plate can
with one production line in Germany, delivering products to customers in the German and Benelux markets. It was estimated, before
the recent problems had developed between Eindhoven Emballage and
Windmill Breweries, that American Enclosures would deliver 3 million cans to Windmill in 1973. Eindhoven's 1973 forecast was that
competition would take a total of 12 million cans out of the 310 million can Benelux market. Eindhoven's 1977 projections were based on
an assumed 75 percent market share.

Pricing Strategy

In order to sell cans, the metals division of Eindhoven Emballage
maintained a large customer service staff which assisted customers,
such as Windmill Breweries, in the design, installation, and service of
package filling and closing lines and in the day-to-day operation of
those lines. It was common for Eindhoven Emballage to arrange with
European Packaging Machinery (EPM), a company also affiliated with
General Container, to actually buy the packaging line for the customer
and install it in his plant on a leased basis. Lease prices were calculated
to allow Eindhoven approximately an 18 percent return on its equipment investment.

Although the packaging business was highly competitive in price
terms, Mr. van der Sanden believed that Eindhoven could command a
slightly higher price for its products because of its better service. The
average price for beer and soft drink cans in 1973 was about 160 guilders per thousand, and it was planned that the new two-piece can
would sell at the same price, although it would cost somewhat less to
make but represented a much larger investment in R&D and in production facilities compared with the three-piece can. Mr. van der Sanden estimated that competitors had to offer a price 4 to 5 percent below
Eindhoven's prices before they became an attractive alternative for a
customer, given the greater value of the technical services offered by
Eindhoven. The cost of these services to Eindhoven was estimated at
between 3 and 4 percent of the cost of the product.

During the negotiations with Windmill Breweries, Mr. Kalver had
taken the position that Eindhoven's price for the two-piece can should
have been less than for the three-piece can because Eindhoven's pro-

duction costs would be lower. Van der Sanden argued that Windmill would achieve a marketing advantage at no additional cost while Eindhoven had a significant increase in investment to recover.

The Product

There are two types of tinplate, three-piece metal cans, a straight-sided version and a so-called necked-in version, as illustrated in Exhibit 2. The three pieces are a top, a bottom, and the body of the can

Exhibit 2
Can Making Processes: Conventional Three-Piece and New Two-Piece Can

A. Conventional soldered-can process

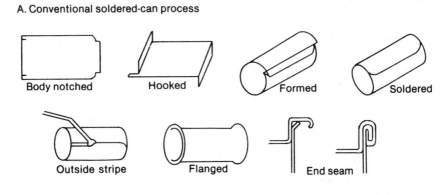

B. Drawn and ironed 2-piece can process

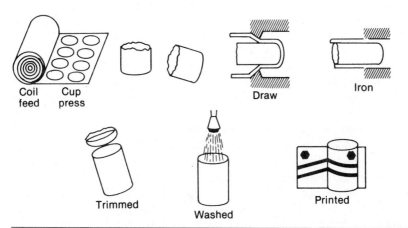

Source: *Modern Packaging Encyclopedia,* 1974 edition.

itself, which is formed from a single sheet of metal wrapped around and welded to form a seam. The presence of the seam makes continuous decoration of the can impossible. All three-piece cans weigh about 65 grams. A variety of new products had been developed by the metal packaging industry in recent years, including a method of electrically soldering the seam which permitted lower priced, uncoated, or "black plate" steel to be used in can construction, the development of plastic materials for less expensive sealing of the ends of the cans, and the use of aluminum rather than tinplate. The American parent company of Eindhoven Emballage had developed an electrical sealing process which offered lower costs to the user and permitted the user to make cans right on his own packaging line. General Container had strongly urged Eindhoven to put this product into its offering. Eindhoven had resisted because the process offered an attractive alternative only to very large brewers and soft drink canners, whereas the typical Benelux producer was much smaller than his American counterpart. Eindhoven Emballage had strongly favored the two-piece can as the direction of new product development.

The beverage producer usually buys a decorated can sealed at one end, and must seal the other end after filling the can. Boxes of cans are delivered to the customer on pallets, and the process by which the cartons are taken from pallets, opened, and the cans put on the line is highly automated. A modern beverage canning line operates at an output rate of up to 1,000 cans per minute, a rate much faster than a glass bottling operation. The flowchart in Exhibit 3 illustrates the principal steps in a canning line.

A two-piece can is produced from a single round piece of metal plate which is drawn to form a cylinder closed at one end. It is sealed on the other end after filling. Before the development of the two-piece tinplate can by Eindhoven Emballage, only aluminum had been used in two-piece cans. A major aluminum company had strongly urged Eindhoven Emballage to build a production line capable of producing both tinplate and aluminum two-piece cans, but this had been decided against for two major reasons. First, aluminum prices in Europe were currently 12 to 15 percent higher than tinplate, although the two metals had about the same cost in the United States. Eindhoven Emballage had estimated that aluminum prices would increase 8 to 9 percent per year in the future, compared to a projected 4 to 5 percent for tinplate. The aluminum company had argued that prices would be equal by the end of 1974. According to Eindhoven Emballage cost estimates, its cost for the two-piece tinplate can would be 119 guilders per thousand compared to 131 guilders for an aluminum two-piece can.

Second, the cost of a dual-purpose, tinplate and aluminum, production line was about $800,000 more than the cost of a line capable of producing only tinplate two-piece cans. After many discussions, Ein-

Exhibit 3
Canning Line Flowchart

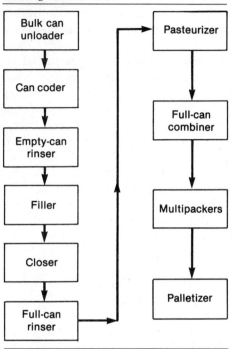

dhoven Emballage had agreed to construct a dual-purpose line *if* the aluminum producer would pay the incremental cost of $800,000 and would guarantee that the costs of producing an aluminum can would be no higher than the cost of producing a tinplate can. In return, Eindhoven Emballage was willing to guarantee to the aluminum producer that 50 percent of its two-piece can production on that line would go to aluminum. The aluminum producer never answered the letter from Eindhoven containing this offer.

Tinplate offered two advantages over aluminum although it weighed more, weight being the big advantage of aluminum. First, tinplate was more rigid than aluminum and therefore offered a better printing surface, a fact which was a marketable advantage for the canner. Second, tinplate was also believed by Eindhoven to offer an ecological advantage because it could be more easily recycled due to the fact that it was magnetic and therefore easier to remove from rubbish for reprocessing. Eindhoven Emballage had plans under way, in cooperation with two Dutch metals producers, to build a total of seven recycling plants, two in Belgium and five in the Netherlands. The recycled beverage cans would most likely be used to produce steel girders for building construction.

The two-piece can offered some important advantages to the canner. Perhaps most important was a marketing advantage from a better-looking package which permitted continuous decoration due to the absence of a seam. Consumer testing also indicated that the absence of a seam made the can somewhat more pleasant to hold and to drink from. With a solid sidewall and only one sealed end, there was also less risk of leakage with a two-piece can, even if damaged by rough handling. Lower weight was another important advantage, especially for export markets, 38 grams for the two-piece tinplate can compared with 65 grams for the three-piece can. The two-piece design used less metal, with a wall thickness of 0.10 millimeters compared to 0.22 for the three-piece can. Because of the lower materials cost which therefore resulted, Eindhoven Emballage had estimated that its total production costs for the new can would be 119 guilders per thousand compared with 138 guilders per thousand for the three-piece can. Although these cost estimates had not been given to Mr. Kalver, Mr. van der Sanden was certain that Windmill's technical people had developed reasonably accurate cost estimates of their own.

Market Development Strategy

The nature of the two-piece can production process was important in determining the market development strategy for the new product. On a three-piece can production line, the metal plate was printed with the decoration required before the can was made. On a two-piece can production line, the can was printed after it was made, and printing became part of the continuous process of production. Machinery for printing the two-piece can had been ordered from an American manufacturer of this highly specialized equipment. The printing machinery would be capable of printing up to 900 cans per minute, printing four colors at once. Although the first two-piece can line would only produce at a rate of 650 cans per minute, it was expected that the third line to come into production would operate at 800 cans per minute. Furthermore, the printing machinery only came in two models, one printing at the rate of 350 cans per minute and the other at 900 cans per minute. It was possible to have two printing machines serving a single can production line so that it was not necessary to shut down the line while changing to a new decoration in the printing machinery, a process which took three to four hours.

The new two-piece can production line would be capable of producing 135 million cans per year, and Mr. van der Sanden believed that this was not enough capacity to satisfy both the beer and soft drink markets. A decision was made to focus market development attention on the beer market for two reasons. First, although there were only two soft drink canners in the Netherlands, using 92 million cans annually, they required about 30 to 35 different decorations for different flavors and brands for an average of about 3 million cans per decoration. By comparison, the three brewers using cans used only six decorations, and of these, three decorations accounted for 85 percent of the total sales in the Netherlands of 138 million cans domestically in 1972 and 55 million export. Furthermore, this export volume was virtually all from Windmill Breweries and required only one decoration.

The second reason related to the ability of the thinner-walled two-piece can to withstand the corrosive effects of the beverage. The inside of a beer can required one coating of varnish to provide the necessary protection, whereas the soft drink can required at least two. Due to the nature of the process, however, there were always a few very small holes in the coating, and this allowed the beverage to react with the metal to some extent, usually not enough to influence the quality of the product or its taste. However, this was a serious problem for certain "aggressive" soft drinks, especially colas and tonics. A conscious strategic choice was made by Eindhoven Emballage, therefore, to avoid trying to sell the new two-piece can to package these more "aggressive" products because they represented the possibility of more serious technical problems. Thus, the decision was made to focus on beer rather than soft drinks and to concentrate effort in the Netherlands, since the Belgian market had not developed as positively as the Dutch market.

Negotiations with Windmill Breweries

In mid-1972, presentations about the new two-piece can were made to Windmill Breweries and to another major Dutch brewery. In his presentation to Windmill Breweries, Mr. van der Sanden had stressed that the two-piece can was "the can of the future" and offered the twin benefits of a marketing advantage and lower handling costs. The marketing advantages were believed to be especially attractive to Mr. Kalver of Windmill Breweries as he placed great importance on the company's worldwide reputation for quality and leadership. There was some discussion of price. Mr. Kalver argued that since the product weighed less it should cost less and therefore the price should be less, whereas Eindhoven had offered it at the same price as the three-piece can, about 160 guilders per thousand. On this question, Mr. van der Sanden had two points to make. First, the greater difference between metal cost and selling price for the two-piece can was made necessary by the much higher product development costs that had been involved. Second, the fact that the two-piece can used less metal meant that prices of the two-piece can could be expected to increase less rapidly in the future than prices of the three-piece can, roughly 2 percent per year compared with 4 percent per year, according to his estimates. Finally, knowing how important the market leadership dimension was to Windmill Breweries, Mr. van der Sanden offered to let them have the two-piece can as an exclusive for three months, giving them time to promote the new can in television advertising before giving it to competitive breweries.

Windmill Breweries was quite interested in the two-piece can, and after Mr. van der Sanden's first presentation, they began a series of tests and studies to consider the new package. They needed to investigate a variety of handling, production, and shipping problems and to assess the promised reductions in cost. Because of the thinner walls of the two-piece can, there was some concern about the ability of the package to withstand rough handling, which was a special problem with the exported product. Particular attention was to be devoted to the lower part of the body where the can production process resulted in a wall thickness somewhat less than for the rest of the can.

Windmill Breweries was, at that time, considering installing a new, high-speed (1,000 cans per minute) canning line. Eindhoven offered to design the new line and to actually purchase it and lease it to them. The presentation was made in June of 1972, and Windmill needed to make a decision on the new production line no later than September of 1972. In August, when Mr. van der Sanden made one of many follow-up calls, Windmill asked if Eindhoven would be willing to design only that part of the line from the depalletizing operation to the filler, but not the filler or the closing operation. Windmill had decided to buy a filling machine from American Enclosures and a closing machine directly from EPM, the company from which Eindhoven often bought machines and leased them back to customers. Van der Sanden stated his opinion that Eindhoven Emballage and EPM could not design a really good system without having responsibility for the entire operation, given the close relationship among the various elements of the total canning operation, especially when high speeds were involved. Mr. van der Sanden finally agreed to design the part of the system up to the filling operation, subject to Windmill's agreement that Eindhoven would not be responsible for the output of the closing operation. In other words, should there be a problem of product quality at the end of the line, it was to be understood that this could not be blamed on Eindhoven. Windmill Breweries agreed to this arrangement and to take the two-piece cans beginning in February of 1973. In his plans for 1973, Mr. van der Sanden expected that Windmill Breweries would take 55 million cans for export sales and between 35 and 40 million cans for its domestic market.

To prepare Windmill Breweries for production of the two-piece can, a change was suggested in their current production operations. Up to this time, Windmill had been purchasing three-piece cans with the "easy-opening" top already sealed by Eindhoven Emballage. The cans were filled through the bottom, and the bottom was sealed by Windmill as this was a somewhat easier operation technically than putting on the easy-opening top. The new two-piece can would, however, require that Windmill install the easy-opening top, so it was suggested that they should begin now to get experience with this part of the operation, and this suggestion was agreed to by Windmill's production management.

Problems in the Middle East

In October of 1972, Windmill Breweries came to Eindhoven Emballage with a complaint that about 8 million cans of beer had developed leaks throughout the market of the Middle East countries, including Lebanon, Kuwait, Bahrain, and so on. About 3.5 million cans had actually been returned to Kinderdijk, and there was no doubt that there was a serious problem of leakage developing around the sealed ends. Eindhoven Emballage agreed to investigate the problem fully but avoided any statement implying that they were ready to assume responsibility for it. After careful study, the customer service and technical personnel of Eindhoven Emballage concluded that the problem resulted from the fact that Windmill Breweries was using the same pasteurization process for both glass and metal containers. After the package was filled, it was passed through a pasteurizer where it was exposed to high temperatures as required to kill bacteria. Because glass was essentially an insulator against heat whereas tinplate was a conductor, the temperature inside the beer can reached much higher levels than inside the glass bottle. This created very high pressures within the beer can, sufficient to destroy the integrity of the seals at the ends of the can and on the seam, creating small holes through which leakage slowly developed. In reporting its conclusions to Windmill Breweries, Eindhoven Emballage pointed out that this problem had been brought to the attention of Windmill's production personnel back in April of 1972. Eindhoven customer service personnel had, at that time, recommended that Windmill Breweries have two pasteurization processes, one for glass and one for metal, but Windmill's technical people had refused to accept these conclusions.

Now, after analyzing the cans that had developed leaks in the Middle East, similar conclusions were arrived at by Eindhoven's technical personnel, and they were once again rejected by Windmill Breweries' personnel. Rather, the brewery came to the conclusion that the problem was with the can itself, because they had never had a problem with cans before and had been using the same production process. They felt that the problem had been caused by the change to closing of the easy-opening end rather than the bottom, plus the fact that they were now using a necked-in can rather than a straight-line can. Furthermore, they argued that even if the problem was caused by the pasteurization process, it was Eindhoven's responsibility to make sure that their cans would actually perform properly in the new application with the sealing of the easy-opening end. Eindhoven's response was that they had faith in their own technical findings, that they had not encountered similar problems with other customers, and that it should be noted that the problem only occurred with product in export countries. Eindhoven Emballage offered to make its own test in the Windmill brewery with 1 million cans at their own expense, but Windmill refused to approve such a test, arguing that "we are in charge of our own business."

At this stage, there was a hardening of positions. Windmill Breweries top management became involved in the discussion, and a decision was made in February of 1973, when delivery of the first two-piece cans was to begin, to postpone the planned introduction of the new can. Mr. Kalver said that they wanted additional time for much deeper study of the entire question of product quality with the new can, including completion of further handling, production, and shipping tests, especially shipments to export countries such as the Middle East. He said he would not move until they were 100 percent certain of the results of their internal studies and that this would take at least six months, postponing introduction of the new can until August or September of 1973.

After this decision, Mr. van der Sanden had no customer for the output of the new production line, which was just about ready to begin production. Furthermore, he was rapidly reaching the point where some of the production of three-piece cans presently going to Windmill Breweries would have to be allotted to other customers. Mr. van der Sanden quickly assembled a team of top management including the president of General Container–Europe, the president of Eindhoven Emballage, the technical director of the two-piece can development project, and others who went to Mr. Kalver to try to get him to change his mind. During this meeting, it was pointed out that not only could Eindhoven no longer agree to hold out the possibility of an exclusive on the two-piece can for Windmill Breweries, but it would also be impossible to promise them delivery of three-piece cans, since planning had gone forward on the basis that Windmill Breweries would begin taking delivery of two-piece cans in February. Mr. Kalver said that he understood their arguments, but he couldn't overrule his production manager. Two days after this meeting, which had occurred on a Monday, Mr. Kalver called Hans van der Sanden to reaffirm his decision and asked to see him. Mr. van der Sanden presented himself in Mr.

Kalver's office that afternoon and was given two days in which to decide either to guarantee delivery of three-piece cans for the remainder of the year or to take back his production line.

As he reviewed the problem with the managing director of the metals division of Eindhoven Emballage, Mr. van der Sanden summarized his impressions as follows:

> Kalver is dead serious. He has offered a take-it-or-leave-it proposition, and he means to follow through. He has got us where he wants us; he knows that we can't go to the soft drink people and that we have a tremendous investment just sitting there. Even if we go to the soft drink people now, he knows it will be late 1974 or early 1975 before they finish testing and we solve the technical problems which are certain to come up. He wants us to lower our prices as he has figured out what our costs and profit margins are. He said we should lower our prices by 15 guilders per thousand to give him a reserve against the risks of being the first to use the new two-piece can. I asked him "What happens to the reserve if there are no problems with the product?" and he answered "We will keep it as a settlement of our Middle East claim." And wouldn't American Enclosures love to steal our major customer from us?

Questions

1.   Evaluate the market development strategy for the two-piece can.

2.   Could the problem with Windmill Breweries have been avoided?

3.   What action should Mr. van der Sanden take now?

C A S E 4–5

Gustav Lübke KG

In the fall of 1974, Carl Löffler, the new managing director of Gustav Lübke KG, was concerned about the future of the "Q Project." Development of machinery for this innovation was on schedule, and Friedrich Pelzer, the innovator, and his technical group were optimistic about the likelihood of its commercial success. Löffler believed that the "Q Project" had created considerable excitement among executives in Lübke, which held a 10 percent market share in the German envelope market, if for no other reasons than that predictions on the future of the envelope industry were gloomy.

As he reviewed the progress of the project, Löffler was concerned with the market's reaction to the "Q" system. Although the system clearly had a large speed advantage over all automatic mailing equipment on the market, he was not yet certain what strategy would be needed to make this innovation a commercial success, nor was he sure of the implications of the system for Lübke.

Company Background

Gustav Lübke KG was founded in 1852 by Gustav Lübke in Erding, a small town in southern Germany. It started with a modest bookbinding operation and later expanded into publishing, book selling, and the manufacture of stationery products. In 1897, the founder's son, Karl, assumed control of the firm and further expanded the business through a series of investments. He stayed as chairman of the board until 1966. In 1974, Lübke was a major stationery manufacturer in southern Germany employing 800 people in its two plants at Grafing and Erding.

274

Sales in 1974 amounted to DM 30 million and were expected to reach DM 33.5 million in 1975.[1] Exhibit 1 contains recent financial statements.

Gustav Lübke KG manufactured several product lines. In Erding, it produced mainly commercial envelopes. Envelopes accounted for 66

Exhibit 1

GUSTAV LÜBKE KG
Profit and Loss Statements
(1972–1975)
(DM in thousands)

	1972	1973	1974	1975 (est.)
Net sales..................	DM 17,224	DM 20,674	DM 30,000	DM 33,049
Cost of goods sold...........	14,980	18,250	24,093	27,828
Gross profit................	2,244	2,424	5,907	5,221
Fixed costs	1,076	1,519	4,283	3,064
Profit before tax.............	DM 1,168	DM 905	DM 1,624	DM 2,157

GUSTAV LÜBKE KG
Balance Sheets
(1973 and 1974)
(DM in thousands)

	1973	1974
Assets		
Current assets:		
Cash..	DM 1,590	DM 1,419
Shares	130	—
Accounts receivable............................	3,140	4,737
Other receivable	437	466
Inventories...................................	1,798	2,862
Total current assets	7,095	9,484
Fixed assets..................................	5,729	6,388
Investment fund with government..................	183	253
Total assets.....................................	DM 13,007	DM 16,125
Liabilities		
Current liabilities:		
Accounts payable..............................	DM 2,730	DM 2,828
Notes payable.................................	1,383	2,293
Deferred taxes................................	29	478
Total current liabilities......................	4,142	5,599
Long-term liabilities	3,218	4,539
Capital.......................................	3,450	3,805
Investment funds and the like....................	2,197	2,183
Total liabilities.................................	DM 13,007	DM 16,125

Source: Company records.

[1] In 1975 U.S. $1 = DM 2.4631 (or about 40 cents for 1 DM).

percent of sales in 1974, with writing and drawing materials (paper for school supplies, note pads, etc.) and private stationery comprising the remainder. More recently, Lübke had been supplying well-known household glassware manufacturers with graphically designed wrapping and packaging materials which served to both protect and merchandise the glassware. Some of Lübke's packaging was designed by free-lance designers and some by Lübke's own graphic artists. The Grafing plant manufactured note paper, duplicating paper, and various special qualities of cut-to-size fine paper.

Lübke's executives thought that their principal marketing asset was a long-standing reputation for quality envelopes. The company considered its envelopes to be of the highest quality available in Germany and prided itself on its wide range of products and superior service. "We are the Rolls Royce in this business," said one Lübke executive, "envelope clients value quality and service of a supplier through consistency of products, ability to rectify any defect, availability of envelopes at short notice, and prompt deliveries. We do these things better than our competitors. Our envelope line is the most complete in the south of Germany and consists of almost 400 types of envelopes for business and private correspondence, bag envelopes for bulky contents, and special envelopes for letter-sealing machines and cardboard-backed bags. We are the only envelope manufacturer in the area who has the equipment to produce this range of products."

The company's prices were generally higher than their direct competitors, except on standard items for which an industrywide maintained price list existed. Higher pricing on nonstandard items was not, according to Lübke executives, a deterrent to sales given the quality and the service customers received. Many bulk mailers were willing to pay a premium for envelopes which would not jam their mailing machines, and for the availability of Lübke service personnel who could quickly solve such problems. The average selling price for conventional envelopes was DM 12 per 1,000. Gross profit on standard items was about 46 percent.

Lübke's had a sales force of 20 men. Two were stationed at the head office in Erding, 7 at various strategic points in southern Germany, and 11 at the three branch offices in Stuttgart, Munich, and Ulm. All salesmen reported to the marketing department, which was run by four section sales managers. Section 1 dealt with direct sales to end users, Section 2 with sales to distributors, Section 3 with export sales, and Section 4 with sales of packaging materials.

Direct sales constituted 54 percent of total sales. These were mainly to large printing companies, advertisers, newspapers, banks, utilities, government agencies, and other bulk mailers. Sales to stationery distributors accounted for 32 percent of the sales in 1974 and were mainly for private stationery which was resold to small retailers. Packaging

Exhibit 2
Company Sales by Major Customer Groups

	Percent of Lübke's sales
Printers	17.0%
Stockers and distributors	16.4
Government institutions	8.8
Other production industry	4.7
Retailers	4.5
Banks	4.2
Other envelope manufacturers	3.5
Insurance	2.9
Mailing houses	2.8
Advertising agencies, copy service	2.9
Newspapers, magazines, publishers	2.5
Photo industry, laboratories	1.9
Municipal institutions	1.3
Others	26.6
Total	100.0%

Source: Company records.

accounted for 6 percent of the sales and export sales for 8 percent. Exhibit 2 gives a detailed breakdown of Lübke's envelope sales by major customer groups.

The Envelope Market in Southern Germany

In 1974, the south of Germany consumed 2 billion envelopes, an annual consumption of 245 envelopes per capita. Lübke maintained a solid position in this market with about a 50 percent market share. Exhibit 3 shows the sales trends for Lübke and its main competitors for 1966–74. They considered two of the competitors, Becker and Eifel (each held a 14 percent market share), as their most important competitors offering a similar product mix. Six other manufacturers accounted for the remainder of industry sales.

Statistics showed a 2 percent annual unit growth rate in the overall consumption of envelopes over the past years. There was a general feeling in the industry that this rate would decrease in the future. The situation was similar in other European countries where quantities of mail were not increasing significantly. Telephone and telex machines were cutting into the use of mail for communication. Postal rates and costs were rising rapidly, and their reliability was decreasing due to labor difficulties and obsolete systems. Exhibit 4 shows the volume of mail telegraph, telex, and telephone consumption in southern Germany for 1964–72. Exhibit 5 presents international comparisons for 1971.

Exhibit 3
Sales Trends for Lübke's and Main Southern German Competitors

	1966	1967	1968	1969	1970	1971	1972	1973	1974
Total envelope consumption in southern Germany (DM 000)	13,746	14,043	14,181	16,967	20,794	20,680	21,891	27,168	38,419
Lübke's sales in envelopes (DM 000)	5,600	6,160	6,398	7,336	8,680	11,095	12,957	13,573	19,417

German market shares (percent)

	1966	1967	1968	1969	1970	1971	1972	1973	1974
Lübke	40.7	43.9	45.1	43.2	41.7	53.7	52.9	50.0	50.5
Becker	11.0	11.5	12.0	12.5	13.0	13.5	14.0	14.0	14.0
Eifel	14.0	14.0	14.0	14.0	14.0	14.0	14.0	14.0	14.0

Source: Company records.

The largest portion of mail was generated by businesses and prepared by mailing machines. Such mailings consisted of personalized items such as billing information sent by large retail companies, advertising mail from advertising agencies and mailing houses, and financial transactions (statements, invoices) from banks, insurance companies, utilities, and government. Any change in the activities of any of these users of bulk mail would strongly affect the envelope industry. It was estimated that almost 70 percent of the southern German mail was sent by business, 5 percent by individuals, and the remaining 25 percent by government. Regarding received mail, the shares were as follows: 50 percent was received by business; 40 percent by individuals; and 10 percent by government.

Direct mail advertising, 36 percent of which consisted of printed matter was growing at 10 percent per year and was generally expanding in Europe. Further expansion was expected due to heavy promotional efforts by the direct mail houses. A 15 percent annual increase was still being recorded, and Lübke's executives were convinced that this expansion would last for several years. This was in contrast to the total envelope industry in which rapid saturation was expected. One of the problems for direct mailing houses was the possibility of government control of the amount of mail which could be directed to private citizens. Mailing equipment was the most important capital expenditure decision for a mailing house and was generally taken by the chief executive.

The second largest users of bulk mail were banks and other financial institutions, insurance companies, and government; i.e., all institutions which had an ongoing need to exchange information with their clients by correspondence. The contents of this mail involved, in most cases, checks, money orders, invoices, and statements. Technological innovations were under way in this segment. One such innovation was the introduction of "electronic funds transfer" whereby financial transactions would be instantly recorded through the use of computers and teleprocessing systems. Another innovation was the "electronic mail system," which would replace some of the post office's labor-oriented material handling services with computer networks and facsimile systems. The introduction of such computerized information exchanges threatened a substantial proportion of envelope production. In these bulk-mailing institutions, mailing machines (inserters) were used in conjunction with computers; and therefore, the person usually responsible for the choice of a mailing machine was the data processing manager. Decisions on the choice of envelopes were usually made by the manager of the mail room where the equipment was operated.

Nevertheless, Lübke's executives were convinced that most of the future transactions would still need some paper systems and that "electronic mail" was not about to take over the industry. They also

Exhibit 4
Mail, Telegraph, Telex, and Telephone Consumption in Southern Germany

Volume of mail (liable to postage; in millions)

	1964	1965	1966	1967	1968	1969	1970	1971	1972	1973
Letters	806	823	876	865	894	903	952	948	959	986
Postcards	46	45	48	43	62	58	56	53	57	54
Printed papers, samples, commercial papers	645	626	651	672	681	674	757	717	732	843
Parcels	33	34	34	34	33	32	33	31	31	31
Money orders	32	32	33	32	31	30	30	31	30	26
Postal cheque form	168	172	179	183	189	191	197	199	205	213
Total	1,730	1,732	1,824	1,829	1,890	1,915	2,026	1,979	2,014	2,153
Of which:										
Registered mail	19	18	18	18	18	18	18	17	17	22
Cash on delivery COD	22	22	21	20	20	20	20	19	19	20
Inland	1,575	1,570	1,653	1,648	1,693	1,708	1,816	1,782	1,844	1,971
To foreign countries	65	70	70	72	81	86	85	82	79	82
Of which by air	41	46	46	47	56	81	60	59	56	59
From foreign countries	30	92	101	109	116	121	125	115	91	100
Number of copies of newspapers	675	662	648	638	645	651	636	614	600	607

Telegraph, Telex

	1963–64	1964–65	1965–66	1966–67	1967–68	1968–69	1969–70	1970–71	1971–72	1972–73	1973–74
Telegraph service:											
Offices Independent	70	62	41	36	33	33	33	30	30	28	25
Small	1,334	1,222	1,444	1,051	997	959	917	891	866	823	785
Circuits 1,000 km	634.7	692.0	721.0	787.0	893.6	1,010.1	1,087.3	1,101.9	1,359.3	1,431.0	1,468.0
Paid telegrams inland (in COD)	3,291	3,240	3,180	2,937	2,735	2,470	2,343	2,134	1,837	1,447	1,187

	1963–64	1964–65	1965–66	1966–67	1967–68	1968–69	1969–70	1970–71	1971–72	1972–73	1973–74
Terminal	2,563	2,579	2,574	2,483	2,318	2,234	2,098	1,848	1,628	1,482	1,424
Transit	556	495	539	515	462	458	422	456	224	—	—
Number of telephones per 1,000 inhabitants	423	440	460	479	499	518	537	557	576	594	612
Telex Service:											
Stations	19	20	20	24	30	31	31	31	31	31	31
Number of subscribers	2,946	3,334	3,791	4,234	4,785	5,418	6,020	6,855	7,575	8,167	8,818
Messages (pulses registered)	13,000	11,821	15,314	17,751	17,923	20,034	20,558	22,485	20,003	22,701	24,383
Minutes of outgoing traffic (in 000)	7,079	8,079	9,241	10,277	12,156	13,154	14,840	16,145	17,494	19,107	20,940
Telephone Service											
Telephone exchanges	6,817	6,796	6,764	6,711	6,685	6,672	6,678	6,687	6,686	6,687	6,687
Telephones (000)	3,223	3,387	3,573	3,757	3,935	4,111	4,307	4,506	4,680	4,829	4,984
1,000-km circuits long distance	7,020	8,348	9,834	10,593	11,067	12,250	13,438	14,429	15,325	16,581	18,109
1,000-km circuits inland	4,385	4,634	4,897	5,181	5,491	5,792	6,112	6,395	6,630	6,837	7,034
Automatic traffic:											
Number of calls	8,120	9,488	10,683	12,067	12,655	13,631	14,489	15,332	15,936	16,233	17,000
Small distance (000,000)	3,264	3,555	3,640	3,848	4,037	4,239	4,436	4,623	4,765	—	—
Long distance, inland (000,000)	372	445	530	609	650	702	749	791	819	—	—
To foreign countries (000)	—	—	371	962	2,050	3,016	5,622	8,264	10,497	12,840	15,750
Manual traffic:											
Number of calls	112,500	86,300	56,264	35,707	22,154	14,363	8,743	4,012	941		
Long distance, inland	72,643	55,303	37,752	21,105	13,170	9,380	7,044	5,068	3,906	3,400	3,446
To foreign countries	3,517	3,904	4,139	4,284	4,352	4,643	4,088	3,800	3,498	3,139	2,862

Source: West German Federal Government.

Exhibit 5
Volume of Mail—Some International Comparisons, 1970–71

	1971							1970	
	Inland letters (000,000)	Letters from and to foreign countries (000,000)	Total letters	Per inhabitant	Cash on delivery (000)	Parcels	Money orders	Total letters	Inland letters (000,000)
Sweden	1,523	192	1,716	211.7	725	30,204	7985	1,764	1,559
Denmark	802	118	920	185.2	152	30,279	7,209	879	757
Finland	618	82	699	149.4	705	16,587	2,011	672	586
Iceland	8	6	14	65.1	7	364	429	14	9
Norway	542	81	623	159.6	586	11,634	3,164	601	520
Belgium	2,391	469	2,860	294.1	391	7,741	3,383	2,754	2,306
France	10,066	721	10,787	210.4	2,489	4,119	317,082	10,436	9,688
Greece	211	61	273	30.5	1	1,419	5,676	270	217
Ireland	294	161	455	153.2	—	9,524	10,278	463	303
Italy	5,786	984	6,770	125.2	21,247	28,853	42,618	6,740	5,924
Yugoslavia	1,095	183	1,278	62.2	1,102	7,485	14,583	1,290	1,115
Netherlands	3,065	426	3,491	264.6	—	12,900	3,086	3,402	2,941
Poland	1,300	125	1,425	43.8	—	—	—	1,361	1,241
Portugal	404	192	596	60.6	282	4,043	9,364	583	397
Rumania	478	56	534	26.4	—	8,300	33,300	488	445
Switzerland	1,682	410	2,092	329.7	190	123,324	9,961	2,042	1,633
USSR	—	—	8,341	31.2	—	—	—	8,220	—
Spain	3,523	666	4,189	122.7	1,218	1,702	30,344	4,067	3,440

Country									
Great Britain	9,958	1,227	11,185	201.3	—	186,151	368,788	11,031	9,985
Hungary	991	136	1,127	188.8	1,192	16,289	45,050	1,064	943
Czechoslovakia	10,330	1196	11,526	188.1	4,724	322,782	30,418	10,680	9,641
Austria	1,277	356	1,634	219.1	358	33,950	11,398	1,596	1,254
Algeria	98	23	121	8.2	81	187	7,599	120	97
Egypt	214	62	276	8.1	13	544	1,736	350	257
Ghana	199	117	316	35.7	—	132	2,186	311	195
Nigeria	252	94	346	6.1	—	366	2,346	271	197
South Africa	1,469	184	1,653	84.3	—	18,067	17,040	1,294	1,076
Canada	4,528	102	4,631	212.5	—	79,215	44,794	4,475	—
Mexico	908	461	1,368	26.9	383	3,449	4,226	1,361	902
United States	86,983	—	—	416.0	—	—	—	85,188	82,824
Argentina	903	164	1,067	45.3	10	5,174	4,000	1,012	833
Brazil	1,084	1,880	2,964	35.3	—	—	—	2,325	1,087
India	6,154	277	6,431	11.7	4,454	64,910	101,479	6,216	5,896
Indonesia	141	26	167	1.3	—	548	2,708	150	130
Irak	63	55	119	13.0	20	100	100	146	87
Iran	858	61	919	30.8	—	400	—	—	—
Israel	258	106	365	121.1	—	2,444	884	319	233
Japan	12,001	244	12,245	117.0	—	154,980	11,734	11,721	11,486
Malaysia	240	99	303	28.4	0	1,667	2,336	291	190
Korea	565	49	614	19.2	—	4,247	4,552	600	550
Ceylon	491	35	527	41.6	—	1,644	3,540	522	490
Turkey	490	126	616	17.0	51	2,424	9,996	610	505
Australia	2,441	289	2,730	214.5	—	24,575	23,176	2,742	2,443
New Zealand	572	104	676	273.1	—	15,759	6,860	677	574

Source: West German Federal Government.

thought that mailers would be interested in any system offering cost savings, and that Lübke should look more closely at the different end uses of their envelopes in order to anticipate the decline of certain types of correspondence.

Inserting Machines

In 1974, there were numerous manufacturers of mailing, or inserting machines, which were competing for the bulk mail market. The principal functions carried out by these inserting machines included folding the letter, inserting it in an envelope, and sealing it. High-speed machines (over 6,000 inserts per hour) were not used for folding since, where needed, the letters ("inserts") were supplied to the mailers in folded form. In virtually all cases where these machines were inserting individually prepared mail items such as invoices or bank statements, the inserts were folded on a separate folding machine. Additional functions included franking and mark sensing. Bulk mailers, who used high-speed inserters, owned separate franking machines which stamped the envelopes with postage due impressions before the envelopes were inserted, although some of the lower speed inserters were also equipped with franking attachments. In cases where a personalized statement was posted, the address was printed on the statement itself and was displayed through a "window envelope." When needed, envelopes would carry addresses; however, owners of high-speed machines used separate machines to do the printing.

High-speed inserters were sometimes equipped with an electronic sensor which was applied to computer generated mail. Those computer printed statements which contained a number of pages marked the final page of each statement to enable the inserting machine to detect when the next statement should be inserted. The sensor was an expensive device which was bought only by those mailers that sent large amounts of varying multipage inserts.

The "cycling speed" of a machine was its highest operating speed. Effective operating speeds were almost always lower than the cycling speed. Since ideal circumstances rarely prevailed, the quality of the insert or envelope could cause jamming when more than one item might be inserted and/or the operator was inexperienced. Three machines which cycled at speeds between 6,000 and 10,000 letters per hour were the Bell & Howell Phillipsburg, the large Pitney-Bowes machines, and the Ertma by Roneo Neopost.

Bell & Howell claimed that its Phillipsburg was the fastest on the market at an effective speed of 7,500 letters per hour. It would insert, staple, nest, spot-glue, print, collate, demand feed, and electronically check or select as required. It required two operators, one for feeding envelopes and one for operating the machine. Its price was DM 35,000, and it was usually depreciated over five years. The user generally paid about DM 12 per thousand envelopes with insurance and maintenance charges of about DM 2,300 annually. Phillipsburg's operating costs (electricity, wages, etc.) were estimated to be DM 15 per hour of operation.

Lübke estimated that the total number of inserting machines sold in southern Germany in 1974 was around 120, of which 35 percent were high-speed inserters (over 6,000 inserts per hour). Phillipsburg had approximately 60 percent of the market, Kern 15 percent, Pitney-Bowes, Ertma, Okafold and others made the remaining 25 percent.

New Management

In the spring of 1973, Hans Lübke, the managing director since 1954, died, and the Lubke family did not have a successor who they felt could head the company effectively. In addition, they did not have enough capital to maintain the rate of growth they considered necessary. The family proceeded to negotiate with Fischer GmbH, a German holding company which had controlling interest in various companies in the building and mechanical industries, for the sale of a part of the equity. On January 1, 1974, Fischer acquired 30 percent of Lübke's voting shares and agreed to help change its managerial structure to one which would allow the company to "go public" in the future. Carl Löffler, who had previously been general manager of Kasel GmbH, a German packaging firm, was appointed managing director in November 1974 as a result of this takeover. Executives at Lübke saw in Löffler's arrival an opportunity to establish a professional management system which would develop business opportunities that had been held back for lack of financial and managerial personnel.

Löffler noticed that 85 percent of Lübke envelopes were sold in the South German market, 5 percent elsewhere in Germany, and 10 percent were exported to about 20 countries. He concluded that possibilities of further expansion in Germany were poor, given the regional nature of the envelope market. He also noted a traditional tendency to try to cover all market requirements even down to small market segments. Possibilities for expansion in the private stationery market were also poor in view of increasing competition. However, Löffler thought that glass packaging presented an opportunity since Erding was surrounded by several leading glassware firms. Moreover, Lübke could not keep up with demand from the glassware companies, as they were expanding the use of graphically designed packaging at a faster pace than originally planned.

A larger commitment to this business had to be made if Lübke were to capture a major market share. Löffler observed, however, that Lübke salesmen were not yet ready for this activity and that orders came in small series. Another disadvantage was that the glassware industry was traditionally very sensitive to general economic conditions. Finally, another alternative was to expand into the mailing equipment market with the "Q Project," which was in progress when Löffler arrived.

The "Q Project"

The "Q Project" began in the late 60s when Friedrich Pelzer, the production manager of Lübke, started questioning the logic behind making an envelope before inserting a letter. He concluded that both operations, making the envelope and inserting, might be performed simultaneously. Pelzer explained his idea to Lübke's management but did not then get the support to develop it. In 1972, Pelzer managed to interest Fleischer, the new marketing manager, in the idea, and the two tried again to convince the management of its merits. In June 1973, they presented an official project proposal which the board of directors approved. "The attitude of the board was a bit reluctant but not negative," recalled Fleischer. "They thought it bordered on science fiction."

In September 1973, the German Board for Technical Development awarded Lübke a loan which was expected to cover 50 percent of the expected project's costs up to prototype stage. The terms of this grant were such that, if the project succeeded, the aid would be repaid within 10 years at a 6.5 percent rate of interest and, if it failed, the loan would be forgiven. Exhibit 6 presents the expected costs up to prototype stage as presented to the Board for Technical Development.

When Löffler arrived, work was under way, and the first prototype was being prepared for tests in actual working situations in July 1976. The "Q Project" consisted of a machine which would construct envelopes around letters and then seal them before they were stamped with the postage due. The Q machine would be faster than any other conventional envelope stuffing machine. It was designed to process between 12,000 and 15,000 letters per hour. Additional attachments might be added, such as address printers, folding machines, franking machines, and multiple insert mechanisms. The Q machine would also have the advantage over conventional equipment of easy paper loading and reduced downtime due to jamming. Production costs for a standard-equipped Q machine were estimated to be DM 49,000.

The paper to be used for envelopes would come in rolls manufactured by another machine Pelzer had developed, the "blank machine." It would produce the envelope blanks according to the size and type of envelope needed (three sizes of envelopes with or without a window) in rolls to be fed to the Q machine. The usage of blank rolls would make

Exhibit 6

September 27, 1973, Application to the Board of Technical Development: R Project Costs (up to prototype stage)

Project budget for the Q machine

1973	
Design work	DM 11,602
Patent applications	1,400
	13,002
1974	
Design work	63,560
Mechanical workshop	
Production of components and mounting	50,400
Purchase of equipment 233,000	
Depreciation	13,048
Interest 8%	5,299
Premises	5,880
Raw material, semiproducts, mechanical and electronic components	72,800
Preparatory marketing costs	68,180
Administration	9,800
Reserve	14,000
	302,967
1975	
Design work (11% of 1974 cost)	69,944
Mechanical workshop ½ year	25,093
Premises ½ year	2,940
Marketing costs ½ year	38,038
Travel expenses	11,200
Advertising	5,600
Other sales costs	28,000
Consultant fees	7,000
Administration	4,200
Reserve	7,000
	199,015
In All 1973–75	
Total project costs 1973–75:	DM 514,984

Project budget for the blank machine

1973	
Design work	DM 3,868
Mechanical workshop hot melt application unit	
Purchase	5,940
Test runs	458
Samples	840
	11,106
1974	
Design work	5,369
Machine FK6 one third of purchase price	46,760
Mechanical workshop modifying jobs	3,360
Travel expenses	2,534
	58,023
1975	
Machine FK6 two thirds of purchase price	93,240
Installation	4,200
Test runs, experiments	8,400
Premises	1,960
Reserve	16,800
	124,600
In All 1973–75	DM 193,729

DM 708,713

the loading of the Q machine easier (a roll would last one hour), and storage of blanks would be simpler and more economical than for envelopes. Boxes of envelopes could not be stored on top of each other to any great height, since the envelopes were packed standing in the boxes and could be distorted by pressure from above, whereas blanks supplied in rolls could be stocked to a greater height.

The Q machine was expected to have a similar economic life as well as insurance and maintenance costs as the Phillipsburg. However, given the easier loading of blanks, the Q machine required only one operator instead of two, which reduced the operating costs to DM 8.5 per hour.

The blank machine was estimated to cost DM 170,000 and to have an economic life of 10 years. Its production speed was 48,000 blanks an hour. Its operating costs would come to DM 43 per hour, and it would consume DM 2 to 4 worth of paper per 1,000 blanks. Other annual expenses associated with the machine were:

Insurance	DM	280
Foreman		6,300
Administration		4,200
	DM	10,780

Pelzer contracted with a North German machine-tool manufacturer for constructing the prototype of the blank machine, while the Q machine was built under his personal supervision at Erding. Although Lübke applied for patents on both machines, there were doubts about whether the process was sufficiently unique to merit patent protection. Those involved in the project felt that Lübke's technological lead time was one to two years before other similar machines would appear on the marketplace.

Market Research

With the machinery development under way, Pelzer and Fleischer realized they had little information on the market for mailing machines. They hoped that a market survey would provide them with useful information as well as give them some technical and commercial specifications needed for the market acceptance of the Q machine. In January 1974, Fleischer hired Industrial Market Research (IMR) of London to conduct a survey of the high-speed mailing machine market. He knew that a large market would be needed in order to make the Q machine a commercial success, but he felt that although he could easily assess the situation in his own region, he needed more information before he could draw any conclusions about the potential of the European market. He therefore asked IMR to carry out the research project in the United Kingdom and the whole German Federal Republic since those countries represented a major part of the EEC market.

a.   The United Kingdom Market

IMR reported that the 1973 annual volume of mail in the United Kingdom was at its 1963 level of 10.7 billion envelopes following a peak of 11.5 billion in 1968. Of this, about 3 billion passed through inserting machines, with accounting-type mail representing 70 percent of this and direct mail the remainder. Direct mail houses achieved an average annual inserting throughput of 3 million pieces with one mailer reaching a 7 million level. United Kingdom banks averaged a 4 million throughput, while post offices and utilities achieved a level of 2.5 million. Finally, about 80 percent of bulk mail in the United Kingdom utilized window envelopes. The major envelope manufacturers were Dickinson, with between 50 and 60 percent of the market, and Spicers, with approximately 25 percent of the market. They estimated that in 1974, there were 3,990 mail inserting machines in use in the United Kingdom, of which 15 percent had a speed range of 6,000 to 10,000 units per hour. The majority of those inserters (68 percent) were in various private industry operations; 22 percent were used by the government, and 10 percent were distributed equally between financial institutions (banks, insurance companies, etc.) and direct mail houses. They also found that 410 inserters were sold in 1973 with the following market shares:

	Market share (percent)	Maximum speed per hour	Average actual speed per hour
Roneo-Neopost's ERTMA	37	6,000	3,000
Pitney-Bowes'	31	7,500	5,000
Bell & Howell's Phillipsburg	13	10,000	6,000
Kern	12	3,500	2,500
Kemp	7	3,600	1,500

Eighty-one of these machines were high-speed, of which 33 were sold to direct mail houses, 24 to the government, 14 to financial institutions, and 10 to industry. Most United Kingdom users expected their machines to last between 7 and 10 years, and up to three quarters of these were expected to be replaced between 1979 and 1982.

b.   The Total German Market

The volume of mail in the German Federal Republic in 1973 was about 10.5 billion letters, of which about 3 billion letters passed through inserting machines. Approximately 87 percent of the inserted letters were bulk direct mail, 11 percent were accounting-type mail, and 2 percent were correspondence-type mail. Many financial institutions sent large quantities of promotional material through direct mail houses. Major manufacturers of envelopes used in inserting machines in West Germany were Ahlers and Lehmann & Hodebrand.

IMR reported that there was a total number of 1,440 high-speed inserters (over 6,000 inserts per hour) in use in West Germany. The user sector with the largest share (35 percent) of the machine population was financial institutions, followed by direct mail (30 percent), the state (30 percent), and industry (5 percent). They also found that 9 percent of all high-speed inserting machines were sold in 1973 with the following market shares:

	Market shares
Roneo-Noepost's ERTMA	52%
Bell & Howell Phillipsburg	44
Pitney-Bowes'	3

Thirty-three of these high-speed inserting machines were sold to direct mail houses, 25 to financial institutions, 23 to state institutions, and 9 to industry. Most German users expected their machines to be replaced after five years.

Pricing of the Q Machine

Unlike regular inserters, which could use envelopes from virtually any supplier, the Q machine could operate only with blank rolls, which were manufactured especially for it by the blank machine. The user of the Q machine was thus restricted in the choice of blank supplier which would naturally make the Q concept less attractive to him. The situation created a variety of alternative pricing schemes, each with different competitive implications.

One extreme alternative would be to place a free Q machine on the users' premises with monthly charges based on the number of blanks used, the blanks being supplied exclusively by Lübke. Another approach would be for Lübke to sell the Q machine to the user on the merits of its advantages over competitive inserters and to liberalize the supply of blanks. A number of other schemes could be envisaged between these two extremes. Lübke executives felt that the problem was to price the Q system in a way which would attract customers and maximize profits.

Customer Reactions

IMR also tested some reactions to the Q concept. It was described to current users of inserting machines, who were then asked whether the principle sounded attractive and whether it could be applied to their own mailing operations.

The initial reaction of most potential users was that increased speed was an obvious advantage. In many cases, however, the respondent was not prepared to believe that a machine could run as fast as was claimed, even when operating at cycling speeds. The highest speed of which users were aware was the 7,500 items per hour claimed by Bell & Howell for their Phillipsburg. This manufacturer had a long-standing reputation for high-speed, reliable machines. Some users believed that if higher speed machines had been practicable, Bell & Howell would have produced them.

Even when the respondents were asked to accept the speeds as given, they could usually foresee drawbacks. One major objection was that by doubling or tripling the speeds at which they were accustomed to running a machine, the number of operators required would be correspondingly multiplied, since the machine would have to be fed and the finished items unloaded and checked. This increase in the mail room staff would, they thought, negate savings obtained by increasing speed. The second category of objections to high speed concerned stoppages due to faults in materials and operations. It was usually assumed that an increase in speed would result in a similar increase in the number of stoppages, and their complexity, and thus in the time taken to free the paper, and in the number of inserts and envelopes destroyed by the failure.

There was a clear division in the reactions to the value of high speeds assuming they could be efficiently achieved. Users of all but current high-speed machines admitted that high speed coupled with reliability obviously made a machine attractive but invariably considered that it would not be appropriate to their mailing operation. In many companies, the mailing schedule and numbers of staff were already geared to the current machine and would need to be revised if a new machine was bought. Users of the fastest inserters usually chose their machines because they were the fastest and most reliable on the market. Most of these users, who included direct-mail houses and banks, would be very willing to purchase higher speed machines, but they would not be prepared to depend on a single Lübke machine, even if its capacity met their requirements, since it was essential for such users to retain a standby machine in the case of a breakdown.

As for reactions to blanks, many firms that had previously relied on one regular supplier of envelopes had spread their accounts to several manufacturers and were adamant in their requirement that the envelope blanks would have to be available from several sources. The only significant objection to using blanks was that if the machine broke down, there would be no other way of sending off the mail using the blanks. Unless two machines were bought, the blanks could not be transferred to another type of machine and therefore could not be mailed until the machine was repaired. With the help of IMR, Fleischer proceeded to estimate the potential for the Q machine in southern Germany, the whole of Germany, and the United Kingdom, by major user types. (Exhibit 7.)

Exhibit 7
Potential Market for Q Machine in West Germany, United Kingdom, and Southern Germany

	1978 Total market			
	West Germany (except south)	United Kingdom	Southern Germany	Total
Direct mail/mail order...............	44	41	3	88
Financial	32	18	4	54
State.............................	30	31	6	67
Total	106	90	13	209

Source: IMR report and company records for southern Germany.

How Should the Q Concept Be Developed

Although long-term prospects for the use of envelopes were threatened by new technologies and various behavioral changes in industrial countries, Löffler, Fleischer, and Pelzer were convinced that envelopes would remain a major element in communication and that the market would not shrink drastically within the 10 to 15 years to follow. They were concerned, however, about the possibility that the Q concept might be introduced by others. They realized that marketing the Q concept represented a number of operations in which they were not experienced and thought that specializing in the supply of blanks to users of the Q machine would not be incompatible with the profile Lübke had maintained. On the other hand, since envelopes were the main business of the company, they realized they had to market the Q machine very carefully not to damage their envelope market.

Löffler hoped that Lübke could utilize its reputation to launch the concept successfully in its own market. In fact, two of Lübke's major clients had already agreed, in principle, to cooperate in the operational testing of the Q machine on their premises. Other markets, however, presented a totally different problem. Lübke was hardly known outside southern Germany and would encounter strong local competition from both envelope manufacturers and the manufacturers of inserting machines. However, Löffler thought that if the Q concept was indeed a viable innovation, Lübke, with its experience in the envelope market, should get "international mileage."

One alternative strategy in Germany and overseas was for Lübke to go direct. Under this alternative, Lübke would both market the Q machine and supply blank rolls. As long as they operated in southern Germany, it was felt that the blank machine could be operated in Erding and that the regular Lübke sales force could be used. However, Lübke could not possibly serve remote markets from Erding, and strat-

---

Exhibit 8

1. Company's Estimate of Average Annual Marketing and Support Cost Selling Direct to End User Market in Southern Germany (DM 000)

	1974
Sales considerations:	
Salesmen's salaries	DM 36
Employees' benefits	11
Overhead	14
Travel and business expenses	25
Recruiting costs	
Training program	
Trade shows	15
Advertising	
Total average sales considerations	101
Support considerations: Maintenance	
Maintenance engineers' salaries	16
Employees' benefits	5
Overhead	9
Travel and business expenses	17
	47
Total average annual marketing and support costs	DM 148

2. Company's Estimate of Average Annual Marketing and Support Cost Selling to OEM'S in Southern Germany (DM 000)

	1974
Sales considerations:	
Salesmen's salaries	DM 21
Employee's benefit	6
Overhead	9
Travel and business expenses	6
Maintenance considerations	
Salaries, benefits, overhead, recruiting costs, training program, travel	14
Total average annual marketing and support costs	DM 56

Source: Company records.

egies of entering those markets and establishing a position there would probably differ.

Alternatively, an office machine equipment manufacturer (OEM) could be used as the distributor of the equipment. Under this approach, the OEM would do the selling and servicing of the equipment, and Lübke would either supply the blanks or be paid royalties of 5 to 6 percent on the blanks used. Exhibit 8 shows the minimum expenses for direct versus indirect distribution as estimated for the southern Germany market.

Löffler was concerned with the future of the Q concept. He felt that it presented an important opportunity. However, based on the studies of the United Kingdom and Germany, there was a need to map out carefully the launching of the Q project in southern Germany and the subsequent expansion elsewhere, and to consider the implications for Lübke's future. As mechanical aspects were well under way, he thought that a timetable should be part of the plan.

The Needlework Company (B)[1]

In early March 1982, Mr. Robert Fisher, vice president of marketing for The Needlework Company, returned from an extensive field trip during which he spent considerable time calling on the trade (independent specialty stores) with several of his sales reps. He was highly concerned with what he had learned about the recent introduction of a new low-cost automated reorder system by a large national distributor located in the New York area.

The Needlework Company, with sales in excess of $28 million in 1981, was a leading supplier of instructional leaflets, floss, fabrics, kits, and tools/accessories to the needlework trade. The company sold its proprietary line of leaflets directly to leading chain organizations and its full line (both proprietary and jobbed) items to over 16,000 independent specialty shops (typically referred to as the regular trade) via some 37 sales reps. Sales to chains accounted for 13.5 percent of total sales. Proprietary items represented 40 percent of total sales to the regular trade. Over the past several years, the company had experienced a rapid growth in both sales and profits. Annual growth in excess of 25 percent was forecast for the next several years.

The reorder system being sold by the large national distributor had been on the market for about three months. While its impact on The Needlework Company's sales to date was hard to measure, it seemed clear to Mr. Fisher that it represented a substantial threat that should be countered as soon as possible. In particular, he thought that the new automated system would be attractive to large stores.

This case was written by Professor Harper Boyd, College of Business Administration, University of Arkansas. Included in *Stanford Business Cases 1984* with permission. © 1984 by the Board of Trustees of the Leland Stanford Junior University.

[1] For more information about the company and its markets, see The Needlework Company (A) Case.

The reorder system currently being marketed consisted of a hand-held, push-button recorder which looked and operated much the same as a hand-held calculator. Indeed, the size was no bigger than the key arrangement and small lighted display space at the top. In the system's simplest form, a person would sight scan the store's various sales racks/displays/bins, determine what needed to be ordered, and manually input the stock-keeping numbers and quantities to be ordered into the machine, which had a memory sufficient to carry over 100 different line items.[2] Once the total order was recorded, the unit was hooked into the phone and the data "dumped" into the supplier's computer via a WATS line. No extra equipment was needed to make the phone connection.

This system required that either the merchandise or the racks/bins in which the items were displayed be identified in terms of the supplier's catalog numbers. This was no small task since the average store carried several thousand stock-keeping units. It was particularly difficult with such products as floss and yarns, which came in a large number of colors and widths. The situation was further complicated by the fact that most stock items did not bear the UPC (Universal Product Code). Also, a good many accounts, even the larger ones, had never developed a consistent set of in-store facilities by which each type of product was properly "housed" and displayed.

The national distributor sold the reorder devise to a store for about $300. In doing so, it was passing along the quantity discount it received for making a purchase of 500 units.[3] The distributor made available (without charge) the required blank rack/bin catalog number identification tags. A store could afix these to the appropriate rack/bin location after imprinting (in ink) the appropriate catalog numbers which were obtained from the distributor's annual catalog. For orders of $100 and over, submitted using this devise, the distributor gave a 5 percent discount.

In further checking into this system, Mr. Fisher found that probably somewhere between 100 and 200 stores had purchased this system from this distributor. He did not, however, know the extent to which the stores were using it. He had heard that once stores had gone on the system, the distributor had stopped paying its sales reps any commissions on these accounts since they were performing the duties of the sales reps. This would explain how the distributor was able to offer a 5 percent discount on all orders over $100. The distributor offering this new system was about the same size as The Needlework Company in

---

[2] A wand or scanner could be attached to the unit which permitted the recording of the desired stock number automatically—i.e., by simply passing the wand over the stock number.

[3] If a scanner was wanted, the price was another $150. For reason indicated earlier, it was thought that few stores had opted for this addition.

terms of the sales of jobbed items. It had no proprietary lines but carried a more extensive line of floss, yarns, and tools/accessories, which it sold nationwide through a commissioned sales force.

Mr. Fisher felt that any new reorder system adopted by the company should be thought of as helping his sales reps do a better job and not as a replacement for them. Even after a store adopted the system, there was, he noted, "a need for our sales force to make sure the system is working, to introduce new items, to make certain the store's catalog is up-to-date, and to provide us with feedback about the market. Also, we'd never be able to convert all the accounts in a given territory to this system. Thus, there will always be a need for a sales force, although I certainly recognize that their duties will change, which may necessitate some changes in their territories and commission structure."

In his attempt to analyze the economics of the new reorder system, Mr. Fisher had a computer run made showing the number of orders placed and the dollars they represented by store category (annual purchases made from the company). For example, stores buying $3,000 and over from the company in 1981 represented 17 percent of all accounts, 43 percent of all orders, and 63 percent of total sales (see Exhibit 1). If all stores buying over $3,000 a year adopted the new system

Exhibit 1
Number of Orders Placed and Dollars Represented by Store Dollar Purchase Category, Regular Trade, 1981

Store category	Percent of total stores	Percent of total orders	Percent of total sales
Under $500	46%	12%	5.25%
$500 to $999	14	11	6.43
$1,000 to $1,999	15	19	13.27
$2,000 to $2,999	8	15	12.25
$3,000 to $4,999	7	17	16.78
$5,000 to $9,999	5	17	22.95
$10,000 and over	5	9	23.07
	100%*	100%*	100.00%

* Based on 15,113 active accounts out of a total of about 16,000 accounts carried on the company rolls. The number of orders placed by regular trade accounts was 229,469 during 1981, of which 18,427 were back orders.

and placed their orders in increments of $100 or more, then over $15.4 million dollars of sales would be affected. If all of this were discounted at 5 percent, company margins would be reduced by $770,000. Perhaps, Mr. Fisher thought, the discount could be applied on only the jobbed items the company sold since the stores would likely continue to buy the company's proprietary products regardless of whether they used an automated reorder system sponsored by a competitor.

The new system would require an investment of about $35,000 in new equipment and software, about half of which could be depreciated over a five-year period. The individual units cost $300 (plus a 4 percent sales tax) when ordered in lots of 500 and more. These could be sold to the stores outright, or the stores could be asked to make a down payment (e.g., $100) with the remainder paid out on a monthly basis. There was also the possibility that the company's sales reps could "contribute" $50 or $75 for each unit installed. The initial per-store cost of the bin or rack catalog number identification tags was estimated at $50 plus $15 per year. Mr. Fisher thought it would be necessary to absorb these costs. If the store was already using the competitor's system, then the tags would be in place but would not use their catalog numbers. Mr. Fisher wasn't sure how he would handle such situations. The hand-held units would also be present but could not be used to place orders with The Needlework Company because they were programmed for the competitors' catalog numbers.

The company would experience several cost savings from orders inputted using the new system. Since such an order would be transmitted in less then a minute versus a much longer period when a regular phone order was placed, a telephone savings (WATS line) of $1.50 per order was estimated. As soon as enough stores adopted the new system to enable the company to reduce its customer service staff (which currently numbered 22 telephone operators), a more substantial savings in personnel costs would occur. On average, a company operator received about $16,000 a year, including fringe benefits. Mr. Fisher decided to use $5 an order for personnel savings. In addition, the new system would impact the company's order-filling costs since it should, over time, increase the average-size order. Further, there was a good probability that sales from the larger stores would increase. Mr. Fisher was not sure how to factor these last two considerations into his analysis.

Sale of the new system would have to be supported by mailings (which would involve a brochure) and at least one home office person who would work directly with the sales reps where necessary. He thought that promotion costs would be about $25,000 the first year and substantially less thereafter. If about 50 percent of the assistant sales manager's time was devoted to this project, then another $25,000 would be involved—of which $10,000 would be for traveling.

It seemed clear, at least to Mr. Fisher, that the new system could not be expected to pay out unless it generated a substantial increase in sales. He wondered to what extent he could get the sales reps to share part of the costs—particularly the 5 percent discount. Sales reps averaged 7 percent commissions and perhaps would accept a reduction of one or two percentage points on the sales to those accounts which adopted the new system.

C A S E 4–7

Global Semiconductors

The marketing vice president of Global, a major producer of semi-conductor devices, was concerned about appropriate pricing strategy. His industry was volatile, to say the least, and profits were highly cyclical.

One of the industry's problems was that it consisted of a large number of sellers and buyers. Technological leads were short lived, and the philosophy of most top management appeared to be summarized in four "management principles":

1. Technological mastery—or understanding the implications of the technology.
2. Alacrity—being able to turn the company rapidly as technology moved.
3. Cost consciousness—particularly in terms of the experience curve and manufacturing yield.
4. Vertical integration—or "don't just make the chip, make the watch!"

The result was severe price pressure and a level of competition that was dynamic and growing. Global made money—as much as anyone could in this industry—because it had a strong manufacturing competence, extensive sales organization, and reputation for service. Its major competitors were Texas Instruments, Intel, Motorola, and Fairchild. In addition, however, there were dozens of other competitors, and more seemed to spring up every day.

The marketing vice president was familiar with the basic theory of economics as it applied to pricing. There was, he remembered:

1. Perfect Competition. Where the demand curve for any competitor was horizontal; the market set the price; the producer could sell

all he wanted at that market price; and there were no "excess" profits.

2. Monopoly.   Where the demand curve was steep, with little or no substitution possibilities, room for monopoly profit, and a tendency for prices to go up (inelastic demand).

3. Monopolistic Competiton.   Where there were a number of both buyers and sellers, product differentiation but buyer willingness to substitute, little long-term opportunity for excess profits, and a tendency for prices to drop (elastic demand).

4. Oligopoly.   Where there were few competitors, with each aware of the other, substitution, and a tendency for a kinked demand curve.

These generalizations were useful as concepts but hardly permitted the determination of a specific pricing strategy. It was too hard to predict what the market and/or competition would permit.

In an effort to gain the experience of other marketing managers, the marketing vice president attended a seminar at a nearby graduate school. During the two weeks of the seminar, he spent considerable time talking with his classmates about their pricing experience. Recognizing that the sample came from a wide range of companies, he was intrigued, nevertheless, with their collective "pricing rules:"

1. Use price as a weapon when there are no other values or benefits of importance to the buyer; you have access capacity and can gain incremental business which will not affect your long-term pricing strategy; and you can discourage competition from entering.

2. The more competent your sales force, the higher the price you can get.

3. Service is worth money to most customers.

4. Maximum pricing occurs only when you can segment your markets and tackle each separately.

5. Price is a function of value or benefits—not of cost.

6. The purpose of marketing strategy is to avoid competing solely on the basis of price.

7. If you compete on the basis of price, be sure you have the most efficient manufacturing facilities.

8. With innovative products, you should be aggressive about pricing, with mature or "me too" products, be prepared for gradual price erosion.

9. It is better to quote a "system price," because you can hide the price of the separate products. System selling is effective when you are the recognized leader in some part of the product line or when you guarantee a "turnkey" operation to the buyer.

10. Demand is much less elastic than you might imagine, due pri-

marily to inertia and to personal relationships (i.e., past service) between buyer and seller.

11. Salespersons should be judged on their ability to match their product and service to the customer's need. This ability avoids most price cutting.

12. In today's world, penetration pricing is better than skimming because:

    a. Market share is ultimately a critical determinant of profits.

    b. Imitators move rapidly.

    c. You can still skim with a "deluxe model" of the product.

13. In a period of inflation, you should raise prices faster than costs— and you can get away with it.

14. Inexperienced managers tend to underprice.

15. Individual product pricing is less important than full-line pricing.

16. In the final analysis, price is a less important buying reason than might be supposed because buyers want quality, dependability, assurance of service, technical advice, and attention before they want minimum price.

17. "Cost plus" pricing is reasonable when your developmental expenses are unpredictable and when there is only one buyer (such as the military).

18. Price setting should be a compromise between marketing and production—with the bias in favor of marketing.

19. Any idiot can cut prices.

20. Producers of components typically have less price freedom than do other industrial goods sellers.

Questions

1. How should the marketing vice president go about determining a pricing strategy?

2. What are his or her alternative pricing strategies?

3. What do you think of the rules? Which ones might he or she consider using? Under what conditions?

Channels of Distribution

C A S E 5–1

The North Face: Distribution Policy for a Market Leader

The North Face was a privately owned company which designed, manufactured, and sold high-quality outdoor equipment and clothing. It began as a specialty mountain shop in San Francisco in 1966, and started manufacturing in Berkeley in 1968. Since that time, the company had emphasized quality backpacking and mountaineering equipment featuring state-of-the-art design and functional detail. The North Face soon dominated this market and became the market leader in three of the four product categories it manufactured—tents, sleeping bags, backpacks, and clothing. Sales in 1980 were in excess of $20 million (see Exhibits 1 and 2 for historical financial statements). All items were produced domestically at the company's manufacturing facility in Berkeley. In the early 1980s, The North Face operated five well-located retail stores and two factory outlets in the San Francisco Bay Area and Seattle. In addition, it employed 14 independent sales representatives who covered 10 sales territories in the United States. Its dealer structure consisted of about 700 specialty shops throughout the United States, as well as representation in 20 foreign countries.

The company's desire for continued growth in the face of a maturing backpacking market prompted Hap Klopp, president of The North Face and the driving force behind its success to date, to investigate expansion into new products related to the current backpacking business. One avenue of growth which appeared to have significant potential

This case was written by Gary Mezzatesta and Valorie Cook, Stanford Graduate School of Business, under the supervision of Professor Robert T. Davis. Financial support for this case was provided in part by the Marketing Management Program, Graduate School of Business, Stanford University. © 1983 by the Board of Trustees of the Leland Stanford Junior University.

Exhibit 1

THE NORTH FACE
Profit and Loss Comparisons
(in thousands)

	1977	1978	1979	1980
Sales:				
Manufacturing......................	$11,437	$13,273	$15,153	$17,827
Retail..............................	2,254	2,570	2,879	3,368
Total.......................	13,691	15,843	18,032	21,195
Cost of sales.........................	9,337	11,188	12,443	13,964
Gross margin	4,354	4,655	5,589	7,231
Selling and operating expense...........	2,186	2,320	2,646	3,306
Contribution to overhead:	2,168	2,335	2,943	3,925
Corporate G&A expense	686	685	777	924
Interest expense.....................	242	268	438	658
Incentive compensation and ESOP......	235	204	253	330
Total........................	1,163	1,157	1,468	1,912
Total pretax profits....................	$ 1,005	$ 1,178	$ 1,475	$ 2,013
Total aftertax profits...................	$ 498	$ 609	$ 776	$ 1,019

Exhibit 2

THE NORTH FACE
Comparative Balance Sheets
Year Ended September 30
(in thousands)

	1977	1978	1979	1980
Assets				
Current:				
Cash	$ 110	$ 149	$ 201	$ 370
Accounts receivable....................	2,765	3,765	3,910	4,573
Inventories	4,496	4,494	4,452	5,947
Other................................	319	329	229	196
Long term............................	803	1,012	1,256	1,437
Other assets..........................	65	68	100	104
Total assets	$8,558	$9,817	$10,148	$12,627
Liabilities				
Current:				
Notes payable to bank..................	$2,624	$3,180	$ 2,563	$ 2,613
Accounts payable......................	2,019	2,186	2,109	2,231
Accrued liabilities	693	589	627	783
Income taxes payable	318	339	360	568
Current portion long-term debt	141	159	222	316
Other:				
Long-term debt.......................	351	302	360	1,103
Deferred income taxes................	33	73	143	230
Stockholders' equity:				
Common stock A	1,687	1,687	1,687	1,687
Common stock B	0	2	2	2
Retained earnings	692	1,300	2,075	3,094
Total liabilities........................	$8,558	$9,817	$10,148	$12,627

was that of Alpine (downhill) ski clothing. This opportunity was pursued, with the result that The North Face Skiwear Line was being readied for formal introduction in fall 1981.

The uppermost question in management minds at this point was, What was the most effective way to distribute the new skiwear line?

Early History

Hap Klopp, 39-year-old president of The North Face and a graduate of the Stanford MBA program, purchased the original company in 1968, following a brief period as manager of another backpacking retail outlet in the San Francisco Bay Area. At that time, the operation consisted of three retail stores and a small mail-order business. The firm sold a line of private-label backpacking and brand-name downhill ski equipment. Klopp closed two stores, brought in equity, and opened a small manufacturing facility for the production of down-filled sleeping bags in the back of the main store in Berkeley, California. Sales in 1969 were just under $500,000.

Prior to 1971, most of the retail sales were in Alpine (downhill) ski equipment, where competition had depressed the margins. To gain relief, management decided to concentrate on the backpacking and ski touring (cross-country) markets, where margins were higher and such adverse influences as seasonality, fashion cycles, and weather conditions were less damaging.

The North Face Products

The North Face manufactured four key lines for the backpacking market: sleeping bags, packs, outdoor clothing, and tents. All products stressed quality, design, and durability and were priced for the high end of the market. All products carried a full lifetime warranty.

Sleeping Bags

North Face sleeping bags ranged from "expeditionary" models (designed to provide protection to −40°F.) to bags offering various combinations of lightness and warmth (aimed at satisfying the needs of the vacationing, leisure-oriented backpacker). The North Face bags were considered superior to competitive products in construction and durability and offered the optimal trade-off between warmth and weight. As the company grew, TNF expanded the variety of sleeping bags offered to meet virtually every environmental condition that a backpacker could expect in the United States. The quality of down used, the nylon fabric thread count, the unique coil zippers, and the stitching were key points of differentiation. Goose down bags retailed from $162 to $400, with the price escalating as the warmth of the bag increased. Initially, the bags were only down filled but in recent years a complete line of synthetic-filled models were introduced. Synthetic fills were preferred by some for damp weather environments and where weight and compressibility were of lesser importance. Synthetic bags ranged in retail price from $75 to $205—also the top end of the competitive market.

From the start, the company had manufactured only two sizes of sleeping bags instead of the usual three found in the industry. This policy not only simplified production but also reduced retailers' stocking needs and retail stock outs. When TNF began, sleeping bags had been the fastest growing segment of the backpacking industry, but this growth had begun to slow during the early 70s.

Parkas and Other Outdoor Clothing

Parkas and functional outerwear were the growth leaders for The North Face in 1981. Their line included a range of parkas designed to appeal to the serious backpacker. Design stressed maximum comfort over a wide temperature range and contained convenient adjustments for ventilation control. Other features such as pocket design, snap-closed flaps over zippers, and large overstuffed collars further enhanced the line. As the industry grew and fashion became more of an element, a much wider range of color surface fabrics were incorporated into the line. Materials such as Gore-Tex (a breathable yet waterproof material) had been introduced which offered a functional advantage over existing products on the market. Two types of parkas were offered: those which afforded primary protection from cold, damp conditions (generally of synthetic material); and those which were intended to withstand cold, dry conditions (primarily of down). As in fabrics, a number of new, strongly promoted synthetics, such as thinsulate, polarguard, and hollofill, had been incorporated into the line to meet expanding consumer base and desires. Parkas varied in price from approximately $50 for a synthetic-filled, multipurpose vest to $265 for a deluxe expeditionary model. The company was in the process of trying to sell a system of clothing called "layering," which utilized multiple layers of clothing confined in a variety of ways to meet climatic conditions.

Tents

In 1981, The North Face had revolutionized the world market for lightweight backpacking tents with its geodesic designs. With assistance from well-known design engineer, R. Buckminster Fuller, the company's employees had created and patented geodesic tents. These tents provided the greatest volume of internal space with the least material and the highest strength to weight ratio of any tent design. They also had more headroom, better use of floor space, and better weather shedding. Because geodesics were free standing, they also required less anchoring to the earth. Competitors throughout the world were beginning to copy the products; but to date, the company had not legally pursued its patent protection. Other special tent features included reinforced seams and polymer-coated waterproof fabric that management believed provided three times the tear strength and superior performance at subfreezing temperatures. The company had helped develop unique tent poles that were available nowhere else in the world. The North Face still carried two A-frame tents for the purpose of price and continuity of line at $200 and $240 price points while the geodesic line had eight tents ranging from $220 to $600. As with the other North Face products, these were at the high end of the price spectrum; but management was convinced that consumers were getting very good value for their money.

The market for tents had accelerated recently with the introduction of the geodesics which met new customers' needs better than did A-frame tents. Management felt that two to four years of rapid growth in geodesic tent sales would continue while A-frames were becoming obsolete, and then the market would return to its former modest levels of growth.

Backpacks

The North Face divided the pack market into three segments:

Soft packs/day packs
Internal frame packs
External frame packs

The North Face introduced the first domestically made internal frame pack which created a market niche and produced extremely good sales for the company. Retail price ranges from $45 to $115 were at the high end of the scale, but management was sure that the quality details (including extra strength nylon, bartack stitching, extra loops and straps, high strength aluminum, etc.) made these good values for the money.

In the soft-pack area, there were fewer features to distinguish the company's products from its competitors'. Price competition—with competitors' prices from $16 to $37—was much more noticeable.

In the external frame market, historically dominated by Kelty, the company had introduced a remarkably different, patented product called the Back Magic. It was an articulated pack with independent shoulder and hip suspension which placed the weight of the pack closer to the backpacker's center of gravity than other packs had done. Although offering an expensive product ($150 to $160) and encountering some bothersome subcontractor delays, the company was significantly increasing its market share in this category.

Additionally, to expand this category of the company's sales and to open up a whole new market for its dealers, The North Face introduced a complete line of soft luggage in 1981. The company was attempting to capitalize upon the peripatetic nature of its customers and its belief that customers wanted the much higher quality traditionally found in luggage shops. Features such as binding on all seams, leather handles on nylon webbing, shoulder straps with leather handles, and numerous zippered internal pockets were incorporated. Prices ranged from $40 to $65.

Marketing Philosophy

The North Face promoted more than just a product; it fostered a way of life. Throughout the ranks of management one found a cadre of outdoor enthusiasts.

It is important to note how Hap Klopp viewed his company's business:

> (The North Face) may be selling bags, tents, packs, boots, or parkas, but I suggest that people are buying better health, social contact, sunshine, adventure, self-confidence, youth, exercise, romance, a change of pace, or a chance to blow off steam and escape from the urban degeneration of pollution, economic collapse, and congestion.

One central theme served as the foundation for The North Face's corporate strategy. It was best summarized by Hap Klopp: "Make the best product possible, price it at the level needed to earn a fair return, and guarantee it forever." Hap contended that profits were not made from the first sale to a customer. After all, it took considerable effort and money to attract that purchase in the first place. Rather, the customer had to be treated well once he had been attracted. Repeat sales were the key to this business' profitability. Hence, there was the need to provide a product that would always satisfy.

A key conceptual tool that North Face used to analyze the backpacking market and similar specialty markets is what Klopp called "the pyramid of influence":

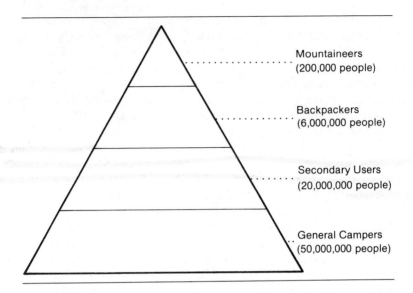

Within this hierarchy, management believed that word-of-mouth communication flowed down a chain of expertise from the mountaineer, to the backpacker, to the secondary user, and finally to the general camping public. Those at the high end of the chain, the "technocrats," tended to influence the buying decisions of the average outdoorsman, who relied upon recommendations and brand image rather than his own research. The North Face characterized the market pyramid as follows:

Segment	Use	Price	Preferred product characteristics
Mountaineer	Frequent, hard	No object	Durable Functional Perfect workmanship
Backpacker	Frequent, careful	Value conscious	Lightweight Repairable Comfortable Brand more important
Secondary user	Inconsistent, careful	Value conscious	Durable Multipurpose Comfortable Brand name
General camper	Inconsistent, careless	Price sensitive	Simple Sturdy Multipurpose Brand name

The Company believed that a number of its competitors had made serious marketing blunders in changing their distribution and products

to meet the needs of the larger, lower strata, thereby ignoring the
pattern of influence of the pyramid and the foundation of the business.
This led to the erosion of their name and franchise in all of the strata.
In contrast, The North Face's long-term strategy was to maintain an
orientation toward the top of the pyramid and quietly broaden the line
so that its existing dealers would be able to meet the needs of both the
peak of the pyramid and the emerging customers.

The North Face adamantly declared that the pattern of influence in
specialty markets only worked one way—downward. By designing and
selling high quality, functional items focused at the top of the pyramid,
a firm could systematically build a strong market image hinging on
credibility. Klopp discounted the integrity and wisdom of the switch
from a "top-down" to a "bottom-up" strategy. Many companies short-
sightedly looked at the financials associated with each segment and
changed their distribution network and products to meet the larger,
lower strata. This process, he claimed, eventually led to failure, since
ignoring the foundations of the business eventually caused a "franchise erosion" at all levels of the pyramid. In short, lowering the quality of product and service to maintain sales growth was a no-win game
which would inevitably lead to erosion of market and image and to the
advancement of someone who was at the top of the cone. If a company
wanted to maintain its commitment to a market and customer group
for the long term, it had to stick to the "top-down" approach.

Because of its strict adherence to this philosophy, The North Face
approached the marketplace with the following strategy: enter specialty markets; nurture them carefully; focus R&D at the top of the
pyramid; use specialty shops to skim the market; target promo efforts
for trendsetters. Once a dominant position in a market was established, growth was sought via two paths:

1. Finding new geographical or new use markets.
2. Introducing new quality products.

The company led the backpacking industry with the following market shares (estimated from available data) in 1980:

	Market share	Industry ranking
Outerwear/clothing	47%	1
Sleeping bags	48	1
Tents	28	1
Packs	20	3

The North Face accounted for 21.9 percent of the sales of backpacking products to specialty stores in 1980, while its closest competitor
achieved a 13.5 percent market share. In summary, the company's
distinctive competence, which distinguished it from its competition,

was the manufacture of high-quality, functional products of classic design, which sold at a premium price and carried a lifetime warranty. The key success factors were thought to be the company's reputation as a specialty supplier of quality products, its strong relationship with its distribution network, and its high-caliber management team. The North Face was generally recognized as having the best management team in the industry, due to its depth of industry knowledge and length of time in the business.

While the backpacking industry had enjoyed substantial growth over the past decade, from total U.S. industry specialty store sales of $15.4 million in 1971 to $81.7 million in 1980, the backpacking market appeared to be maturing, with total sales forecast to grow to $95.1 million by 1985. (See Exhibit 3 for historical and projected market

Exhibit 3
U.S. Industry Specialty Store Sales* of
Backpacking Products (wholesale
prices in thousands)

	Total sales
1971.	$15,400
1972.	21,600
1973.	27,400
1974.	40,700
1975.	44,800
1976.	57,050
1977.	65,850
1978.	70,400
1979.	77,500
1980.	81,700
1981 (est.).	84,300
1982 (est.).	86,900
1983 (est.).	90,100
1984 (est.).	92,400
1985 (est.).	95,100

* Domestic only.

size.) Klopp believed that the industry was out of the high-growth stage of the product life cycle, heading toward the maturity stages; the increasing difficulty the company reported in achieving product differentiation seemed to validate this observation.

Channels of Distribution

The North Face's reliance on the "pyramid of influence" also dictated its handling of distribution channels. Since they were in specialized markets, The North Face preferred to build its brand name carefully by using specialty stores as a foundation. Once this foundation was established, The North Face attempted to nurture it carefully by providing the dealers with new products and techniques (via training classes) to attract new customers. The company only used the more general sporting goods stores (e.g., Herman's, EMS) when it needed geographic coverage in a particular area, and even then tried to limit distribution to certain outlets of the chain. The firm avoided mass merchandising stores as much as possible. TNF felt that specialty shops developed brand awareness and consumer franchise for their products, while the general shops exploited their brand name. Thus, it relied heavily upon the prosperity of these specialty outlets. Careful control of the channels lay at the cornerstone of The North Face's marketing strategy.

Wholesaling.   Backpacking industry sales were distributed among retail stores in the following proportions:

	Dollar value	Number of outlets
Backpacking specialty stores	50%	40%
Sports specialty stores	25	30
General sporting goods stores	10	5
Ski shops, department stores, etc.	15	25

Sales were fairly evenly distributed among the Pacific, North Central, and Northeast regions of the United States, with lesser proportions falling in the Mountain and Southern states.

The North Face sold primarily to approximately 700 retail stores, 75 percent of which specialize in backpacking and mountaineering equipment and the rest in general sporting goods. Wholesale distribution by The North Face was handled by 14 independent sales representatives who carried hiking, mountaineering, and cross-country skiing lines. These representatives covered 10 sales territories in the United States and were paid on commission. The North Face products were their major source of income. Management felt that this network was especially valuable as a conduit for information about market conditions, product knowledge, retail management programs, and competition. It was estimated that 55 to 60 percent of all consumer purchases resulted from word-of-mouth endorsement from a satisfied friend or from a sales presentation in the store. Thus, the primary marketing thrust of The North Face was to (1) sell dealers on the company's products and markets and (2) provide information and point-of-sale aids to help floor salespeople.

The representatives were crucial to this effort and all were carefully chosen by sales and marketing vice president and cofounder Jack Gilbert. As a group, the reps had an average of seven to eight years' experience in the industry, were avid backpackers and lovers of the outdoors, and had been with The North Face since its inception. The reps were highly successful and had been well-treated by the company through the years. Over that time, the nature of their responsibilities had evolved from pioneering or prospecting for new accounts to training existing accounts in industry and management techniques, having established The North Face as the authority in the backpacking field.

The company long pursued a policy of building stable, ongoing relationships with carefully selected dealers. It followed a limited distribution policy, seeking to maintain a balance of dealers and market demand in any geographic area. The company individually reviewed and approved all potential dealer locations, including new locations of existing accounts, and was committed to maintaining and strengthening its dealers. In seeking new product areas in which to expand, it was considered important for The North Face to evaluate the potential of its current dealers to sell the products under consideration.

Retailing.   The North Face's retailing objective was to use its own retail stores to attain its desired market share and profit objectives only where wholesaling was unable to achieve satisfactory market penetration and where the policy had no adverse impact on wholesale distribution. To meet this objective, the strategy was to expand existing outlets and introduce new outlets in an orderly fashion, locating only where conflict with the wholesale division was minimized. This strategy was reinforced in the following policy statement:

> The retail division will continue to examine expansion possibilities on a local basis. The retail division will not expand into any domestic geographic area which will have a significant adverse effect on the wholesale sales of The North Face. The focus of expansion efforts will only be around those areas where The North Face presently has established stores.

The North Face currently owned and operated five well-located retail stores and two factory outlets in the San Francisco Bay Area and Seattle. In 1980, the mail-order operation was closed down due both to its lack of profitability and its perceived conflict with the wholesaling operations. In recent years, the retail division had enjoyed considerable increases in sales and profits, significantly above the industry average:

	Company stores (in thousands)			
	1977	1978	1979	1980
Sales	$2,189	$2,574	$2,884	$3,368
Gross margins	n.a.	974	1,156	1,446
Profits/contribution	n.a.	104	220	364
Inventory turns	1.6X	1.7X	2.1X	2.1X
Transfers to stores	$ 918	$ 908	$ 770	$1,120
(sales from company wholesale to company retail)				

It should be noted that the "transfer" figures represent sales from company wholesale to company retail. Management felt that not all of these sales would have gone to independents if the company stores did not exist. This is important to consider in looking at The North Face's total profitability. The significance of these figures was underscored by the comparison that the average North Face store bought $200,000 from wholesaling while the average wholesale account bought slightly over $30,000 annually. Additionally, the retail division test marketed some promotional programs and products and, through its factory outlets, took nearly $500,000 of seconds—which otherwise would have created image problems if sold through wholesale channels—as well as products which were made out of overstocked materials supplies. While the exact impact on corporate profit of these activities was hard, if not impossible, to calculate, it was thought to be considerable.

Conflict between Retailing and Wholesaling

A continual conflict existed between retail and wholesale because of the feeling that retail might expand into an area which was beyond its domain. In part to alleviate this problem, the retail division closed down its mail-order operation. The retail expansion into Seattle caused the loss of some wholesale business and was used as a lever by some competitive reps; but since The North Face did not terminate any existing dealers, the issue died. Although there were a number of good wholesale accounts left, The North Face did not sell to them because of the geographical protection it had granted its dealers. The company felt it received increased loyalty and purchases because of this protection and would lose them if its accounts were increased randomly.

Differing opinions on the subject of further retail expansion existed even at the highest levels of the company. At one point, at least, Klopp felt that retail expansion was the most effective means of generating market share and promoting brand-name allegiance, while Jack Gilbert, the sales and marketing vice president, had serious reservations in three areas:

1. *The impact on the dealers.* Gilbert felt that retailers in this industry were "very paranoid" that manufacturers would expand their retail operations. Indeed, competitive reps in the industry were known to advise dealers not to "give too much of your business to The North Face because they are out there gathering information about your market area in order to expand their retail operation." He believed that a North Face retail expansion would damage the company's excellent relationship with its dealers.

2. *The profit implications.* While the going margin at retail was 40 percent compared to a target margin at wholesale of 30 percent, entry into expanded retail operations was not a profitable strategy in the short run. The initial investment for a store was $40,000 in fixtures and capital improvements, plus $100,000 of inventory at retail prices. It took three years for an individual store to make the contribution management wanted—12 percent contribution to overhead and 8 percent to pretax profits.

3. *Growth.* Finally, Gilbert was concerned about whether The North Face could meet its growth objectives by going both the wholesale and retail routes, particularly given the company's limited financial resources.

Additional concerns regarding inventory control and the development of capable store managers via a training program were voiced by John McLaughlin, financial vice president for The North Face.

Outlook toward Growth

Maintaining a healthy rate of growth was also a major goal of management. The style of the company was aggressive and entrepreneurial. Hap and his management team did not want to risk frustrating the young, energetic staff they had gathered. As mentioned earlier, the backpacking industry seemed to be entering the maturity phase of the product life cycle. Over the past few years, the total market was growing only at a 5 percent compound annual growth rate. The North Face had grown at a faster rate than the overall market, consistently gaining market share, but it was evident that this situation could not last forever, especially given the company's reliance on the "pyramid of influence" theory.

In evaluating potential new markets, management looked for opportunities that could fulfill the following objectives:

An overlap with current customer base.

A product compatible with current machinery capabilities.

A line that would complement seasonal production peaks.

A market in which "top down" strategy would work.

A line which matched with the interests and expertise of the existing management team.

A line that would maintain and strengthen The North Face's current dealer network.

A line that would not threaten or cannibalize the base business.

TNF's decision-making style added further complexity to the situation. The firm espoused a collaborative style of strategy formation and implementation. Employee input and consensus were essential. Hap fostered this environment by utilizing a paternalistic management style. In fact, each individual felt as if he or she had influence on the direction of TNF. In the context of the approaching decision, this meant that marketing needed to receive a general approval before entering a new business.

The Skiwear Line

The company's desire for continued growth in the face of this maturation of the backpacking market spurred management to investigate expansion into new products. In looking at manufacturing and marketing growth opportunities, the company analyzed its own sales, those of its dealers, and the markets highlighted to see what opportunities were not being completely exploited. Interestingly, the company found that, although it never manufactured or marketed its products specifically for skiing, it held nearly 2 percent of the skiwear market; in some categories such as down vests, it had nearly 5 percent. It was also discovered that over two thirds of all dealers handling The North Face products also sold skiwear. Most appealing was the fact that the market appeared to be highly fragmented. As pointed out in an industry study published in May 1980: "Most skiwear categories have one or two market leaders, but in all areas no one brand dominates the market. In fact, in all categories studied, it required between 9 and 12 brands to make up 70 percent of the market share in dollars."

	Market size—1980 (in thousands)
Adult down parkas/vests	$ 30,000
Adult nondown parkas/vests	54,000
Adult bibs and pants	21,000
Shell pants	1,600
Cross-country ski clothing	2,600
	$109,200

Exhibits 4 and 5 contain details on the skiwear market.

These factors, coupled with an increasing number of requests for uniforms "which work" (i.e., functional, durable, and warm) from ski

Exhibit 4
Skiwear* Market Sales, 1979–80

		Dollars (millions)	Market share
1.	White Stag	$ 27.0	12.5%
2.	Roffee	19.0	8.8
3.	Skyr	13.5	6.3
4.	Head	13.0	6.0
5.	Aspen	12.5	5.8
6.	Gerry	12.0	5.5
7.	Swing West (Raven)	10.0	4.6
8.	Alpine Designs	9.0	4.2
9.	Obermeyer	8.0	3.7
10.	Sportscaster	7.5	3.5
11.	Beconta	7.0	3.3
12.	Bogner America	7.0	3.3
13.	C. B. Sports	6.0	2.8
14.	Serac	5.0	2.3
15.	Profile	5.0	2.3
16.	Demetre	5.0	2.3
17.	Woolrich	4.5	2.0
18.	The North Face	4.0	1.9
19.	Other	41.0	18.9
		$216.0	100.0%

* Excluding underwear.

instructors, ski patrollers, and other professional users thought to influence the market, led The North Face to introduce its skiwear line. The company's strategy in skiwear was predicated on the same strategy as its backpacking business—functionally designed, classically styled clothing. The skiwear was targeted to the "professional skier" (not the racer), since management felt that a trendsetter and uniform program targeted to ski patrollers and lift operators would serve to trigger sales in the same manner that using mountaineers impacted the backpacking pyramid of influence.

Issues with Skiwear

The decision to introduce skiwear was also not without some problems. Although a majority of the dealers carried skiwear, some did not. The latter might oppose "The North Face" trade name going into another local store, even if it was part of a product line they didn't carry. Further, the current dealers were not always the most influential top end shops required to build a market, and their ski departments might not take The North Face's ski-oriented products as seriously as they

Exhibit 5
Estimated Market Share by Segments of Skiwear Market

Down parkas						Nondown	
Men's			**Women's**			**Men's**	
1.	Gerry	21.7%	1.	Gerry	15.0%	1.	Roffee	14.6%
2.	Roffee	8.6	2.	Slalom	9.8	2.	White Stag	8.7
3.	Alpine Designs	7.4	3.	Roffee	8.7	3.	Skyr	8.0
4.	Powderhorn	5.4	4.	Head	7.8	4.	Head	7.7
5.	Head	5.3	5.	Mountain Goat*	6.1	5.	C. B. Sports	7.2
6.	White Stag	4.7	6.	White Stag	4.7	6.	Serac	5.9
7.	Mountain Goat*	3.6	7.	Tempco	4.2	7.	Cevas	4.6
8.	C. B. Sports	3.3	8.	Sportscaster	3.9	8.	Slalom	4.2
9.	Obermeyer	3.1	9.	No. 1 Sun†	3.4	9.	Swing West	4.2
10.	Sportscaster	3.1	10.	C. B. Sports	2.8	10.	No. 1 Sun†	3.8
11.	All other	33.8	11.	All other	33.6	11.	All other	31.1

* Second brand name of White Stag.
† Second brand name of Head.

did the company's backpacking offerings. Similarly, some of the best ski shops which influenced the entire market were not presently The North Face outlets. Out of a total market size of over 3,000 Alpine ski dealers, only about 475 were currently carrying The North Face products. Moreover, the sales reps already had a very extensive line and it was a concern of management that they might have difficulty pushing the ski items during the critical start-up phase. Further, this expansion into a new area in effect required the established sales reps to "start over" again with prospecting for new accounts, a task which might tax their capabilities and desires.

Different complications arose in each of TNF's markets. The following example from a metropolitan center in California highlights some critical issues.

At the time of the skiwear decision, TNF distributed its backpacking products primarily through one, large, specialty backpacking/skiing shop in the city. Suburban, neighborhood stores were utilized for additional coverage. The city store ranked amongst the top 20 percent of TNF dealers. In the past, TNF had rewarded this supplier by witholding merchandise from direct competitors.

TNF serviced this account with regular visits of the local sales representative, frequent visits by sales managers, an annual dealer seminar, and periodic information-gathering visits by top management. The store's annual sales topped $1 million, with 65 to 70 percent of this deriving from backpacking revenue. TNF management felt that this shop, as the largest specialty shop in the area, "made" the area backpacking market. TNF developed consumer awareness via close association with this outlet and by regular co-op advertisements. In short, if a

parkas			Bibs				
	Women's			Men's			Women's
1.	Roffee	12.4%	1.	Skyr	13.7%	1.	Roffee	15.0%
2.	White Stag	12.3	2.	Roffee	12.4	2.	Skyr	14.6
3.	Skyr	10.6	3.	White Stag	11.0	3.	White Stag	9.1
4.	Head	10.2	4.	Head	7.2	4.	Head	6.6
5.	Slalom	6.2	5.	Beconta	5.2	5.	Slalom	6.5
6.	Swing West	5.0	6.	Swing West	4.9	6.	Swing West	4.6
7.	Bogner	4.4	7.	Gerry	4.1	7.	No. 1 Sun†	4.6
8.	Cevas	3.2	8.	Slalom	3.9	8.	Beconta	4.4
9.	No. 1 Sun†	3.0	9.	No. 1 Sun†	3.8	9.	Gerry	3.8
10.	C. B. Sports	2.6	10.	Alpine Designs	3.7	10.	Bogner	3.1
11.	All other	30.1	11.	All other	30.1	11.	All other	27.7

serious local backpacker needed equipment, he would most likely shop at this store.

In backpacking, this shop had little formidable competition. Some second-tier specialty shops existed but they offered less ease of access and a narrower product range. A wide variety of general sporting goods shops also competed in the territory. These stores each had backpacking sections but did not emphasize service. TNF did not associate with these stores.

Unfortunately, the skiing market was much more fragmented in this territory. Although TNF's key backpacking account also sold skiing products, it did not have a dominant position. The store was one of the handful of large dealers that handled skiwear. It did not "make the market." Instead, it often reacted to the environment in setting pricing, merchandising, and product selection policies. In addition, five comparably sized ski specialty shops (no backpacking gear at all) competed in this territory. Each shop carried roughly the same product line frequently featuring loss leadership on hardware (Rossignol, Nordica, Lange, etc.). Soft goods were the primary profit maker. The offerings emphasized aesthetics and functionality.

TNF management obviously faced a serious problem in introducing the skiwear line in this market. On the one hand, they owed special consideration to their key backpacking account. But they also realized that this account alone would not develop sufficient brand awareness as a pioneer for the skiwear line. The key account's owner was concerned about losing backpacking sales if TNF decided to offer its products to other area shops. In this territory, as in others, TNF needed to act quickly and carefully.

Exhibit 6
Partial Organization Chart

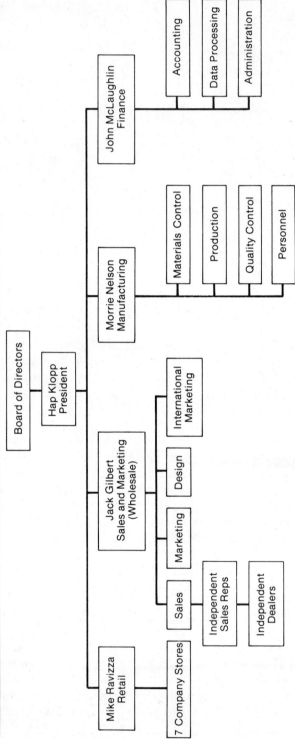

Backgrounds
Mike Ravizza, retail—Joined The North Face in 1969; Stanford undergraduate.
Jack Gilbert, sales & marketing—Co-founder of The North Face in 1968; Stanford undergraduate.
Morrie Nelson, manufacturing—Joined The North Face in 1975; University of Washington undergraduate, Santa Clara MBA.
John McLaughlin, finance—Joined The North Face in 1970; Dartmouth undergraduate, Stanford MBA.

CASE 5–2

Hewlett-Packard
Corporation

Cyril Yansouni sat in bed perusing recent articles about the micro-computer industry. One, "The Coming Shakeout in Personal Computers" (*Business Week*, November 22, 1982), seemed particularly astute; it emphasized distribution and marketing as the crucial determinants of success in the personal computer (PC) industry. As program manager for Hewlett-Packard's personal computers, Yansouni was responsible for the company's marketing strategy. How could HP repeat its successes in other products and become a leader in the microcomputer industry?

The Company

Hewlett-Packard produced a broad array of precision electronic instruments and systems for measurement, analysis, and computation. The company's operations were organized into four business segments: electronic data products, electronic test and measurement, medical electronic equipment, and analytical instrumentation. In the fiscal year ended October 1982, HP earned $383 million on revenues of $4.25 billion. (Sales and earnings distribution by business segment and geography are provided in Exhibit 1.)

HP was founded in 1939 as a partnership between William Hewlett and David Packard, friends from Stanford University's engineering program. The business was formed to manufacture a new type of audio oscillator—an instrument used to test sound equipment—developed

This case was written by Andy Durham under the supervision of Professor Robert T. Davis. Funds for the development of this material were provided in part by the Marketing Management Program of the Graduate School of Business, Stanford University. © 1983 by the Board of Trustees of the Leland Stanford Junior University.

Exhibit 1
(in millions)

	1982	1981	1980
Segment sales:			
Electronic data products	$2,212	$1,816	$1,546
Electronic test and measurement	1,606	1,364	1,215
Medical electronic equipment	325	275	230
Analytical instrumentation	177	185	159
	4,320	3,640	3,150
Intersegment sales:			
Electronic data products	(44)	(45)	(36)
Electronic test and measurement	(21)	(15)	(15)
Medical electronic equipment	(1)	(2)	—
	(66)	(62)	(51)
Net sales	$4,254	$3,578	$3,099
Earnings before taxes:			
Electronic data products	$ 370	$ 314	$ 280
Electronic test and measurement	339	279	267
Medical electronic equipment	60	49	36
Analytical instrumentation	28	31	24
Eliminations and corporate	(121)	(106)	(94)
	$ 676	$ 567	$ 513
Identifiable assets:			
Electronic data products	$1,358	$1,169	$1,000
Electronic test and measurement	903	817	709
Medical electronic equipment	191	175	146
Analytical instrumentation	104	99	94
Eliminations and corporate	914	522	401
	$3,470	$2,782	$2,350

	1982	1981	1980
Net sales:			
United States	$2,304	$1,853	$1,525
Europe	1,334	1,205	1,136
Rest of world	616	520	438
	$4,254	$3,578	$3,099
Exports from:			
United States	$1,083	$ 971	$ 831
Europe	61	50	40
Rest of world	164	206	145
Earnings before taxes:			
United States	$ 554	$ 458	$ 414
Europe	155	155	153
Rest of world	97	80	65
Eliminations and corporate	(130)	(126)	(119)
	$ 676	$ 567	$ 513
Identifiable assets:			
United States	$2,042	$1,817	$1,518
Europe	673	597	565
Rest of world	285	265	192
Eliminations and corporate	470	103	75
	$3,470	$2,782	$2,350

by Hewlett. From its modest beginnings in the one-car garage behind Packard's rented house, the company now manufactures over 5,000 products that are marketed on a worldwide basis.

From its early concentration in electronic instrumentation, the company diversified, in the 1950s, into medical instrumentation and, in the 1960s, into instrumentation for analytical chemistry and also data products—which included calculators, computers, and the associated peripherals. Data products grew so quickly that in 1982 they accounted for more than half of all revenues.

Product Strategy

HP created products that competed by providing new technical contributions; the 8 to 10 percent of sales that was invested in research and development reflected the technical orientation of the founders and provided a constant stream of new products, such that over half of 1982 revenues were derived from products introduced in the past three years (see Exhibit 2). The company avoided both contract business and the design of general-purpose devices suitable for a broad range of customers; rather, HP sought only the most profitable opportunities, leading to an emphasis on many modestly sized market segments. The firm's focus on technical contribution and profit rather than on market

Exhibit 2
HP Product Orders by Year Introduced

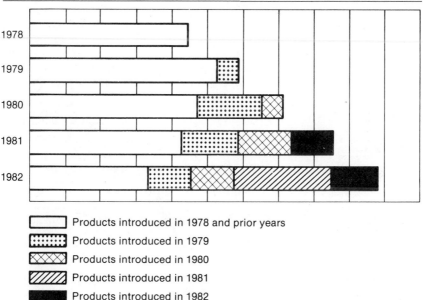

☐ Products introduced in 1978 and prior years

▦ Products introduced in 1979

▨ Products introduced in 1980

▧ Products introduced in 1981

■ Products introduced in 1982

share led to the feeling that introductory price cutting was inappropriate:

> If a new product is really as good as we think it is going to be, we'll be able to sell more than we can make in the initial period anyway, and so you are jeopardizing the whole situation with really nothing to gain. . . . You can reduce the price later on if, in fact, you are able to achieve your lower production costs and keep your costs down. (David Packard)[1]

Financial Strategy

HP had minimal long-term debt, preferring to finance growth almost exclusively through reinvestment of its own funds. As one HP vice president said:

> Our feeling is there is enough risk in the technology—we have all we can handle there. This philosophy provides great discipline all the way down. If you want to innovate, you must bootstrap. It is one of the most powerful, least understood influences that pervades the company.[2]

In order to support growth under the pay-as-you-go rule, asset management was crucial, particularly inventory and receivables.

Organizational Structure (See Exhibits 3A and 3B)

The company was designed to maintain flexibility and responsiveness by decentralizing responsibility and authority to divisions responsible for each market segment:

> The division. . . is an integrated self-sustaining organization with a great deal of independence. The aim is to create a working atmosphere that encourages solving problems as close as possible to the level where the problems occur. To that end, HP has strived to keep (product divisions) relatively small and well defined ("The Hewlett-Packard Organization").

In November 1982, HP had 45 product divisions. Each division had its own R&D, manufacturing, marketing, quality assurance, finance, and personnel departments. New divisions were created by a process similar to cellular division. One of HP's general managers explained:

> New divisions tend to emerge when a particular product line becomes large enough to support its continued growth out of the profit it generates. Also, new divisions tend to emerge when a single division gets so large that the people involved start to lose their identification with the product line.[3]

[1] "Human Resources at Hewlett-Packard," HBS 9–482–125.
[2] Ibid.
[3] Ibid.

Exhibit 3A: Hewlett-Packard Corporate Organization, June 1983

Board of Directors Dave Packard, Chairman Bill Hewlett, Vice Chairman

Chief Executive Officer John Young, President*

Administration
Bob Boniface, Executive Vice President

Corporate Staff

Corporate Controller
Jerry Carlson
Controller

Corporate Services
Bruce Wholey
Vice President

General Counsel and Secretary
Jack Brigham
Vice President

International
Dick Alberding
Senior Vice President

Government Affairs
Bob Kirkwood
Director

Public Relations
Dave Kirby
Director

Patents and Licenses
Jean Chognard
Vice President

Personnel
Bill Craven
Director

Marketing
Al Oliverio
Senior Vice President

Treasurer
Ed van Bronkhorst
Senior Vice President

Operations
Paul Ely, Executive Vice President

Instruments
Bill Terry, Executive Vice President

Electronic Measurements Group
Bill Parzybok, General Manager
- Boblingen Instrument
  - San Diego
  - Colorado Springs
  - Logic Systems
  - Santa Clara
  - YHP Instrument
  - Loveland Instrument
  - Lake Stevens Instrument
  - New Jersey
  - Integrated Circuits
    o Santa Clara
    o Loveland
    o Colorado Springs

Microwave and Communications
Instrument Group
Alan Bickell
Managing Director
- Colorado Telecom
  - Queensferry Telecom
  - Stanford Park
  - Spokane
  - Signal Analysis
  - Network Measurements
  - Santa Rosa Technology Center

Instrument Marketing Group
Bob Brunner, General Manager
Sales: N. America/Europe/Intercontinental
- Instrument Support

Europe
Franco Mariotti
Vice President

Field Sales Regions
France
Germany
Northern Europe
Southeastern Europe
United Kingdom

Manufacturing
France
Germany
United Kingdom

Intercontinental

Field Sales Regions
Australasia
Far East
Japan
Latin America
South Africa

Manufacturing
Brazil
Canada
Japan
Malaysia
Mexico
Puerto Rico
Singapore

U.S./Canada Sales

Field Sales Regions
Eastern
Midwest
Neely (Western)
Southern
Canada

Corporate
Marketing Operations
o Parts Center

Computers

Computer Products Group
Doug Chance, Vice President
- Data Systems
  - Computer Systems
    o CSY/Roseville
  - Ft. Collins Systems
  - Engineering Productivity
  - YHP Computer
  - Computer I.C.
    o Cupertino I.C.
  - Systems Technology
  - Corvallis Components
  - Boblingen Computer Products

Personal Computer Group
Cyril Yansouni, General Manager
- Roseville Terminals
  - Portable Computer
  - Grenoble Personal Computer
  - Personal Office Computer
  - Vancouver
  - Personal Software
  - Puerto Rico
  - Singapore
  - Brazil

Information Products Group
Dick Hackborn, Vice President
- Boise
  - Disc Memory
  - Greeley
  - Computer Peripherals Bristol
  - Roseville Networks
  - Information Networks
  - Colorado Networks
  - Grenoble Networks

Business Development Group
Ed McCracken, General Manager
- Systems Marketing Center
  - Business Development Center
  - Business Development Europe
  - Information Resources
    o Systems Remarketing
    o Guadalajara Computer
    o Manufacturing Productivity
  - Application Marketing
  - Office Productivity

Computer Marketing Group
Jim Arthur, Vice President
Sales: N. America/Europe/Intercontinental
- Computer Support
  - Application Marketing
  - Computer Supplies

Medical
Dean Morton, Executive Vice President**

Medical Group
Ben Holmes, General Manager
- Andover
  - Boblingen Medical
  - McMinnville
  - Waltham
    o Bedside Terminals
    o Medical Systems
  - Medical Supplies

Analytical

Analytical Group
Lew Platt, Vice President
- Avondale
  - Scientific Instruments
  - Waldbronn

Components

Components Group
John Blokker, General Manager
- Microwave Semiconductor
  - Optoelectronics
    o Visible Products
    o Interface Products
  - Singapore
  - Malaysia

Corporate Manufacturing
Hal Edmondson
Vice President

Hewlett-Packard Laboratories
John Doyle
Vice President

Research and Development

Research Centers
Computer Research
Physical Research
Technology Research

Corporate Development
Dave Sanders
Director

Internal Audit
George Abbott
Manager

Hewlett-Packard
Corporate Organization
June, 1983

Corporate and Support Functions

Business Segments

☐ Division
o Operation
* Chairman, Executive Committee
** Chairman, Management Council

Source: Company literature.

Exhibit 3B

HEWLETT/PACKARD
CORPORATE ORGANIZATION
NOVEMBER, 1982

Viewed broadly, Hewlett-Packard Company is a rather complex organization made up of many business units that offer a wide range of advanced electronic products to a variety of markets around the world. Giving it common direction and cohesion are shared philosophies, practices and goals as well as technologies.

Within this broad context, the individual business units—called product divisions—are relatively small and self-sufficient so that decisions can be made at the level of the organization most responsible for putting them into action. Consistent with this approach, it has always been a practice at Hewlett-Packard to give each individual employee considerable freedom to implement methods and ideas that meet specific local organizational goals and broad corporate objectives.

Since its start in 1939, the HP organization has grown to more than 45 product divisions. To provide for effective overall management and coordination, the company has aligned these divisions into product groups characterized by product and/or market focus. Today there are ten such groups or segments. Five sale-and-service forces, organized around broad product categories, represent the product groups in the field.

HP's corporate structure is designed to foster a small-business flexibility within its many individual operating units while supporting them with the strengths of a larger organization. The accompanying chart provides a graphic view of the relationship of the various groups and other organizational elements. The organization has been structured to allow the groups and their divisions to concentrate on their product-development, manufacturing and marketing activities without having to perform all the administrative tasks required of a company doing business worldwide. Normal and functional lines of responsibility and communication are indicated on the chart; however, direct and informal communication across lines and between levels is encouraged.

Here is a closer look at the company's basic organizational units:

PRODUCT DIVISIONS

An HP product division is a vertically integrated organization that conducts itself very much like an independent business. Its fundamental responsibilities are to develop, manufacture and market products that are profitable and which make contributions in the market place by virtue of technological or economic advantage.

Each division has its own distinct family of products, for which it has worldwide marketing responsibility. A division also is responsible for its own accounting, personnel activities, quality assurance, and support of its products in the field. In addition, it has important social and economic responsibilities in its local community.

PRODUCT GROUPS

Product groups, which are composed of divisions having closely related product lines, are responsible for coordinating the activities of their respective divisions. The management of each group has overall responsibility for the operations and financial performance of its members. Further, each group has worldwide responsibility for its manufacturing operations and marketing activities. Management staffs of the four U.S. sales regions and two international headquarters (European and Intercontinental Operations) assist the groups in coordinating the sales/service functions.

CORPORATE OPERATIONS

Corporate Operations management has responsibility for the day-to-day operation of the company. The Executive vice presidents in charge of Corporate Operations are directly responsible to HP's president for the performance of their assigned product groups; they also provide a primary channel of communication between the groups and the president.

CORPORATE ADMINISTRATION

The principal responsibility of Corporate Administration is to insure that the corporate staff offices provide the specialized policies, expertise and resources to adequately support the divisions and groups on a worldwide basis. The executive vice president in charge of Corporate Administration also reports to the president, providing an important upward channel of communication for the corporate staff activities.

CORPORATE RESEARCH AND DEVELOPMENT

HP Laboratories is the corporate research and development organization that provides a central source of technical support for the product-development efforts of HP product divisions. In these efforts, the divisions make important use of the advanced technologies, materials, components, and theoretical analyses researched or developed by HP Labs. Through their endeavors in areas of science and technology, the corporate laboratories also help the company evaluate promising new areas of business.

BOARD OF DIRECTORS

The Board of Directors and its chairman have ultimate responsibility for the legal and ethical conduct of the company and its officers. It is the board's duty to protect and advance the interests of the stockholders, to foster a continuing concern for fairness in the company's relations with employees, and to fulfill all requirements of the law with regard to the board's stewardship. The board counsels management on general business matters and also reviews and evaluates the performance of management. To assist in discharging these responsibilities, the board has formed various committees to oversee the company's activities and programs in such areas as employee benefits, compensation, financial auditing, and investment.

PRESIDENT

The president has operating responsibility for the overall performance and direction of the company, subject to the authority of the Board of Directors. Also, the president is directly responsible for corporate development and planning functions, for HP Labs and for Internal Audit.

EXECUTIVE COMMITTEE

This committee meets weekly for the purpose of setting and reviewing corporate policies, and making coordinated decisions on a wide range of current operations and activities. Members include the Executive Committee chairman, the chairman of the Board, the president and the executive vice presidents for Operations and Administration. All are members of the Board of Directors.

OPERATIONS COUNCIL

Primary responsibilities of this body are to review operating policies on a broad basis and to turn policy decisions into corporate action. Members include the executive vice presidents, group general managers, the senior vice presidents of Marketing and International, the vice president—Europe, and the managing director of Intercontinental.

 HEWLETT PACKARD

Corporate Public Relations
3000 Hanover Street, Palo Alto, Calif. 94304

HP and Personal Computation

HP offered a full range of personal computation devices:

Series 10	Professional calculators
Series 40	Handheld computers
Series 70	Portable computers
Series 80	Personal computers
Series 100	Personal office computers
Series 200	Personal technical computers

This case concerns itself with the 80, 100, and 200 series. The 80 series consisted of three models; the 85 and 87 units were positioned as technical computers, while the 86 was both a technical and a business computer. Models 120 and 125 comprised the 100 series and were marketed to the business market as professional workstations. These two lines competed with the IBM PC, the Apple II and Apple III, DEC's Rainbow and Pro, and Radio Shack's TRS-80. The Series 200 Model 16 was a technical computer that competed with the more expensive business systems made by Fortune, Altos, and Vector Graphics.

While the company's products were judged as competitive in terms of price/performance, HP had not yet been able to duplicate its minicomputer success in the microcomputer market. Hewlett-Packard's share of its traditional minicomputer market grew from 16 percent in 1980 to 19 percent in 1982. Unfortunately, during the same time period, the company's share of the medium-size computer market dropped from 10 percent to 8 percent, and its share of the personal computer market dropped from 20 percent to 17 percent. Some blamed the company's divisional structure:

> The decentralized management style that HP has forged over the years . . . has resulted in overlapping products, lagging development of new technology, and a piecemeal approach to key markets. Indeed, HP often comes across to users as "three or four companies that don't seem to talk to each other," says William Crow, manager of a worldwide association of HP computer users that is based in Los Altos, California.[4]

In fact, different divisions were responsible for the 70, 80, 100, and 200 series of microcomputers.

Another perceived problem was the company's emphasis on profitability at the cost of market share. In the personal computer market, share might be the key to long-term profitability. Consumers wanted machines with the best software library, and software publishers were writing for the best-selling machines to maximize their own sales. Low penetration in this applications-driven market could prove fatal.

[4] *Business Week*, December 6, 1982.

In order to coordinate HP's personal computer activities, Cyril Yansouni was made program manager for personal computers. As chief strategist for this product group, Yansouni was working with the divisions to align product design and software strategies and was coordinating all marketing for personal computers as well.

The Microcomputer Industry

Created by the development of the microprocessor by Intel in 1971, the microcomputer industry had grown at an incredible rate over the next several years; 1980 sales of 425,000 units increased to an estimated 4 million in 1982. Forecasts to 1985 by three leading market research firms (Future Computing, Creative Strategies, IDC) predicted a tripling in market size; this growth would make microcomputers a larger industry than either mainframes or minicomputers by 1988.

Unlike the mainframe market dominated by IBM and the minicomputer market led by Digital Equipment, the microcomputer market was extremely fragmented. There already were over 100 manufacturers competing—with many still expected—and more than 300 competitors in the hardware aftermarket, supplying peripherals such as printers, disk drives, and modems. Peripherals accounted for approximately two thirds of the total hardware market.

As the industry matured, a substantial shakeout was almost certain to occur. Most analysts expected to see no more than a dozen manufacturers of personal computers by 1990. The three key factors for success were:

1. *Low-cost production.* Vertically integrated companies would have an advantage as hardware became standardized and came down in price.
2. *Software availability.* Increasingly sophisticated consumers were applications driven. This would probably cause manufacturers to settle on just a few operating systems, the apparent survivors being CP/M, MS–DOS, Apple DOS, and TRS–DOS.
3. *Distribution.* Industry growth was currently "distribution constrained" as retailers could afford to carry only four or five brands. There was also a shortage of service/support expertise to take care of all potential customers. Direct selling had become almost prohibitively expensive. Competitors were hedging their bets by utilizing as many channels of distribution as they could afford to support and seemed willing to gamble on new formats whether they were invented in-house or not.

With multiple uses and myriad configurations, it was not possible to segment clearly the personal computer (PC) market. Future Computing, of Richardson, Texas, the most widely quoted authority on personal computer market dynamics, segmented the market by price:

Handheld Computers
Portable Computers
$1,000 Home Computer
$3,000 Professional PC
$10,000 Business PC

Exhibit 4 shows the segmentation by major uses and relative prices and lists some of the leading products in each class. This case is confined to the Professional PC ($3K) and Business PC ($10K) markets.

By 1983, the $3K PC segment provided the largest market. Worldwide shipments that year were expected to exceed 1.2 million units, with the United States accounting for three fourths of that total. The Professional PC had the broadest range of applications:

Consumers who purchased these microcomputers used them primarily for personal financial planning, education, and entertainment.

The *institutional education* market consisted of schools using microcomputers to teach computer operating skills as well as traditional subjects.

The *small business* market, which accounted for about one half of Professional PC purchases, was seen as having the greatest potential for growth. The market consisted of more than 4 million businesses with less than 200 employees, along with 6 million offices in the home. Computers were used to automate accounting procedures (general ledgers, accounts receivable, inventory) and upgrade word processing capability; home applications were also considered. Small business users had buying requirements that were different from the consumer, education, and large business markets. Price, service, and basic technical assistance, along with the ability to customize software were the key criteria.

The *large business* market consisted of 15 million managers in large companies. Most of these potential customers wanted a personal computer to automate their daily work; the most desired features were word processing, spreadsheet, graphics, database management, and communications. Many managers bought a computer for their home, then brought it to the office after discovering how it could speed up tasks. Others purchased PCs with company money when they felt that their data processing department was not responsive to their needs.

The $10K PC market was growing at a faster pace than that of the $3K PC segment. Worldwide shipments of 270,000 units in 1983, an

Exhibit 4
Personal Computer Product Classes

	Handheld computers	Portable computers	Desktop computers		
			Consumer personal computers (i.e., $1K computer)	Professional personal computers (i.e., $3K computer)	Business personal computers (i.e., $10K computer)
Main uses	• Problem solving • Learn about computers	• Word processing • Financial planning • Information storage • Data communication	• Entertainment • Education • Personal productivity • Information retrieval	• Financial planning • Word processing • Information storage • Problem solving • Data communication • Entertainment • Accounting	• Accounting • Word processing • Financial planning • Information storage • Data communication
Min price Typical price System price	$200 $400 $800	$2,000 $3,000 $5,000	$400 $700 $1,500	$2,000 $3,500 $5,000	$5,000 $7,000 $10,000
Key products	• TRS-80 pocket computer • Sinclair ZX81	• Osborne 1 • Otrona attache	• TRS-80 color computer • TI-99/4A • VIC-20 • Atari 400	• APPLE II • IBM PC • TRS-80/III • HP-85 • Zenith Z89	• Vector • Cromemco • Altos • TRS-80/II • HP-98XX

The personal computer industry now has five distinct product categories. The professional and business personal computers evolved from the hobby personal computers and are the oldest product classes. The cosumer computer is just now becoming a viable and fast growing business. The portable computer segment was created by the Osborne 1 and is increasing tremendously. The hand-held computer is 1½ years old and already has over 300K units in use.

Source: Author: Egil Juliussen © February 1982, Future Computing, Inc., 634 South Central Expressway, Richardson, Texas 75080.

increase of 50 percent over 1982, were predicted to reach 815,000 units in 1987. As with the smaller systems, the United States now accounted for about three fourths of the total. Substantially all $10K PCs were sold into the small business and large business markets.

Exhibits 5 through 8 provide additional data on the $3K and $10K PC markets, products, and competitors.

Exhibit 5
$3K Personal Computer Customers

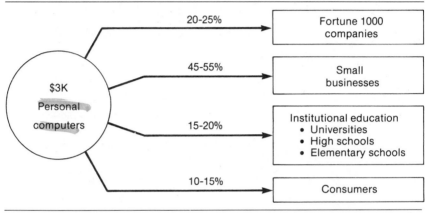

Source: © August 1982, Future Computing, Inc., 900 Canyon Creek Center, Richardson, Texas 75080.

Exhibit 6
The $3K Personal Computer

The best sellers	The also-ran	The newcomers
Apple II	Commodore CBM	DEC Rainbow 100
TRS-80/III	North Star Horizon	DEC PC 325
IBM PC	Zenith Z89	Wang Professional
HP-85	Xerox 820	Sony SMC-70
	NEC PC-8000	Victor 9000
	Exidy Systems	Olivetti M20
	Colombia Data Products	Franklin Ace 1000
	Intertec Superbrain	Sanyo MBC 2000
		Toshiba T200

Source: © August 1982, Future Computing, Inc., 900 Canyon Creek Center, Richardson, Texas 75080.

As the industry matured, larger degrees of freedom could be found in the marketing mix rather than in technical differences.

The technological future seemed clear. The industry would continue to be semiconductor driven; as chip densities increased, products would become smaller or their features would be enhanced. Recent examples of this trend were Sinclair, which marketed a $99, single-

Exhibit 7
$10K Personal Computer Customers

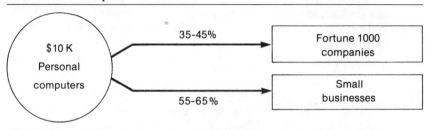

Source: © March 1983, Future Computing, Inc., 900 Canyon Creek Center, Richardson, Texas
75080.

Exhibit 8
$10K Personal Computers

The best sellers	The second tier	The newcomers
Apple III	Vector 3	Fortune 32 : 16
TRS-80 Model II	Cromemco	IBM Personal Computer
Altos 8000	TeleVideo	with Winchester Disk
	Dynabyte 5000	IBM Datamaster
	North Star Advantage	DEC PC 350
	Digital Microsystems	Corvus Concept
	Micromation	Burroughs B20
	Onyx Systems	Sanyo MBC-3000
	Convergent Technologies	
	DG Enterprise	

Source: © August 1982, Future Computing, Inc., 900 Canyon Creek Center,
Richardson, Texas 75080.

board microcomputer, and Hewlett-Packard, which packed the power
of a mainframe into its desktop 9000 model. Operating systems, lan-
guages, and communications protocols were moving toward standardization. Other technical trends included an increase in the number and
usage of data bases and networks and the advancing sophistication of
software.

Trends in the marketing mix were:

Product. There was little room left for another general-purpose
  machine. New entries would be aimed at particular vertical markets or driven by specific applications.

Price. Prices would continue to drop due to lower manufacturing
  costs, more efficient distribution, and more sophisticated customers who required less technical support. (NB, revenues per
  system might rise as the average system included more peripherals.)

Promotions. The increasing emphasis on mass media to generate pull demand would continue. The most popular modes were network television, national magazines, and newspapers. Cooperative advertising programs with retail dealers were also becoming more popular.

Distribution. Not only had the number of distribution channels proliferated, but there was significant variation in the practices utilized by different firms in the same channel. Experimentation was the rule; the markets at stake were too large. While some companies could financially support multiple channels, they also needed to manage the conflict between them. An in-depth description of the current distribution channels follows.

Distribution Channels

Direct Sales

The large dollar amounts and greater technical support involved in selling mainframes and minicomputers made direct sales the appropriate channel. As microcomputers decreased in price and required less support, the direct sale became unattractive except for customers with the potential to make high-volume purchases.

In spite of these economics, an effective direct sales effort was critical to PC manufacturers:

The Fortune 1000 market offered tremendous potential.

Products aimed at vertical markets required specialized, focused sales campaigns.

Increased support necessary to implement networking.

Increased support necessary to establish networking, and other "Office of the Future" applications.

There were four channels for direct selling:

1. Captive sales force.
2. Electronics distributors.
3. Office equipment dealers.
4. Value-added dealers, (also known as systems houses).

The firms with the strongest captive sales forces were those which had them in place from earlier products; i.e., IBM, DEC, Xerox, Hewlett-Packard, and Wang. Their advantages were an installed base of users with whom they already had a relationship and a technically knowledgeable sales staff and service network in place. Firms such as Apple, Fortune, and Radio Shack were expected to have a tougher time selling to large corporations but were attempting to gain ground quickly. Apple, which had tried direct sales through a select few of its retailers, was quickly assembling a 10+ sales force.

Manufacturers' captive sales forces were not the only source of direct sales activity. National *industrial electronics distributors,* such as Hamilton-Avnet and Wyle, and regional firms, such as Algoram, had entered the market but needed to develop technically competent sales forces and service networks in order to become significant channels. It was likely that these companies would utilize third-party service contractors. Industrial distributors were possibly most popular among PC manufacturers pursuing a vertical market strategy since many already served specific industries. Other advantages included an existing customer base and the opportunity for cooperative advertising programs. Disadvantages to the PC manufacturer were that its product would fight with others for sales attention, less control over distribution, and conflict with its own sales force.

Another direct sales channel was provided by office equipment dealers, who already had relationships with customers that needed business computers. The advantages and disadvantages of this channel were similar to those for industrial distributors. Also, major retailers such as Radio Shack and Computerland had developed their own national account programs in an effort to participate in the Fortune 1000 market. Well-known to small businesses and individual consumers, these two companies already had the requisite sales staff and service network in place. They might have difficulty, however, in gaining credibility in this market.

Finally, PC distribution could be done by utilizing value-added dealers, also known as systems houses. These firms bought hardware from manufacturers and integrated it with software packages they had either bought or developed themselves. Many systems houses focused on a particular area and were therefore adept at developing the hardware configuration and the software needed for specialized applications. There were over 1,500 such businesses, most of them small. Customer service played a more important role for systems houses than for other types of distributors.

PC manufacturers could utilize this channel to reach smaller niches more effectively and with more efficiency. Apple had sold on an OEM basis to Bell & Howell in order to penetrate the elementary and secondary education segment. IBM had signed agreements with at least nine value-added dealers; the markets addressed by these firms included insurance, banking, hotels, and agriculture.

The risk to PC manufacturers was that a systems house would go out of business (always a possibility with a small independent operation), leaving the hardware suppliers with some dissatisfied customers through no fault of their own. The other potential conflict arose when the systems house competed for a sale with the PC company's own sales force.

Retailing

Just a few years ago, the concept of selling computers over the counter seemed ridiculous. Now, however, even mass merchandisers such as Sears and Macy's market microcomputers. Driven by decreasing prices and increasing user-friendliness, a wide spectrum of retailing formats has emerged:

Computer specialty stores
   independent
   franchise
   captive
Office products dealers
   independent
   captive
Consumer electronics stores
Mass merchandisers
Mail order/discount houses

In early 1983, there were approximately 2,300 computer specialty stores in the United States. Single-location businesses accounted for 29 percent of all stores but were expected to decline in importance due to undercapitalization, high purchasing prices, low-quality sales and service, and low awareness by the consumer. To remedy these problems, some operators had tried to organize a trade association in order to promulgate standard codes of quality. Another ploy had been to form informal partnerships for volume-buying discounts and to trade sales leads in the others' respective market area.

Independent *multilocation chains* were growing rapidly; this category did not include franchise operators such as ComputerLand, to be described later. Leading examples of the wholly owned specialty chains were Compushop, which had built and operated 18 stores in Dallas, Houston, and Chicago by early 1982; and the Computer Store, a 17-unit, Eastern-based chain. The Computer Store was considering franchise agreements as a way to expand more rapidly.

Chain operations eliminated some of the problems faced by single-unit retailers. They might obtain volume-purchasing discounts and, within reasonable market boundaries, experience advertising economies of scale. The growth of this type of retailer had been constrained by capital, however.

Franchise operations were the fastest growing segment of the specialty retailers. Franchisors offered increased purchasing power, better image and a higher advertising budget, and procedural and training support. The risk of a franchise operation was that sales and service quality could vary widely from site to site, creating a negative impression.

ComputerLand was the dominant participant in this segment. The firm had over 400 stores in operation in early 1983 (with a 98 percent success ratio among its franchisees) with plans for another 200 by year-end. ComputerLand was also the first retailer to go overseas, with over 60 stores spread over the globe. Manufacturers acknowledged the power of ComputerLand's distribution network. Months before they introduced their models, executives from IBM and Xerox met with company officials to discuss their strategies. Edward Faber, who founded ComputerLand in 1976, claimed, "Three years ago, we had to go to the vendors—now, they come to us."

ComputerLand's strategy was to carry a broad range of hardware, price competitively, emphasize software, sell the expertise of their personnel, and offer a series of "Computer-Ease" classes. The firm's centralized inventory carried 20 brands of hardware from which their franchisees could choose according to their local market conditions. In return for a $75,000 franchise fee and 8 percent of revenues, franchisees received substantial price breaks, national and local advertising support, and continuing training programs.

In addition to its retailing activity, ComputerLand developed a network accounts group, which signed contracts with multisite users and coordinated delivery and servicing through the local franchiser. This direct sales force competed with the other sales forces described above.

Other leading franchisors included On-Line Microcenters, which planned to expand from 17 to 100 stores during 1983, and MicroAge, with 40 stores nationwide.

Captive computer specialty stores had been established by Radio Shack and Digital Equipment. Originally known for their consumer electronics products, Radio Shack was the leader in the home office/small business market due to its retailing strength. The company's TRS-80 line was carried in 357 computer centers as well as 480 Radio Shack stores with computer departments. Similar to ComputerLand, Radio Shack had attempted to enter the large corporate market with its own national accounts sales force.

DEC operated 25 retail stores that almost exclusively sold DEC equipment; the three PC products and the video display terminal were carried, along with peripherals, accessories, and supplies. While offering comprehensive expertise and support, these retail outlets suffered from an intimidating image and the parochialism of their inventory. DEC had not announced any plans to open more stores.

Hewlett-Packard and Texas Instruments were considering a move into the retail channel, but appeared to be waiting for signs of success

or failure on the part of others. The captive retail approach offered
these advantages:

Control over retail operations. Quality of service was more easily
assured, price maintenance was facilitated by reducing the number of alternative outlets for the product, and "push" marketing
tactics were guaranteed rather than left to the independent retailer.

Conduit for information gathering. An opportunity to stay close to
the customer.

Facilitation of maintaining a training and service network.

Disadvantages to this format were:

High starting costs. Facilities and inventory, training for sales personnel, and advertising start-up expenses required a substantial
investment. This had been exacerbated by heavy competition for
appropriate locations and sales personnel, both of which were in
short supply.

Entry into a new business. Lack of expertise within the company
made success less assured and demanded a disproportional
amount of management attention that might be better spent on
design and manufacturing of computers.

Office products dealers had gained considerable importance as distributors of PCs. While currently only a small proportion of established
single-location dealers had begun selling microcomputers in significant volume, these outlets were viewed as having tremendous potential. Several major chains had been developed or were in the process.
Sears had mounted the most impressive effort with its Business System Centers. Located primarily in suburbs so as to tap the work-at-
home professional and small business markets, the SBSCs had grown
in number from 5 in 1982 to 43 in 1983; plans were announced for over
200 to be operating by year-end 1984.

California-based Businessland, funded by some of the same venture
capital firms that financed the computer companies themselves, had
positioned itself as a "solver of business problems." The company had
extremely aggressive expansion plans—to grow from four Bay Area
locations to 25 nationwide within 1983 and to add another 75 United
States and 50 foreign outlets in the two years following.

Xerox and IBM had opened their own chains of office products outlets. Exhibiting the same advantages and disadvantages as the captive
computer specialty stores of DEC and Radio Shack, the Xerox and IBM
operations were differentiated by their broader product lines. Xerox
wanted to be known as the "supermarket for the small businessman,"
and so, in addition to computers, they carried copiers, typewriters,

dictation equipment, and calculators from a variety of manufacturers such as Apple, Sharp, Casio, and Sanyo. With 54 stores in place in the spring of 1983, Xerox had plans for 20 more by December.

IBM's stores were similar to those of Xerox, although the outlets did not carry as broad a product line. After a cautious start, IBM doubled its number of stores to 35 within a 12-month period.

Consumer electronics stores were quickly joining in the race to distribute PCs, but with the major exception of Radio Shack, the vast majority of these outlets was selling only home computers.

Mass merchandisers, such as Montgomery Ward, J. C. Penney, and K mart, likewise dealt almost exclusively with home computers. Macy's California, in contrast, was experimenting with the most popular Professional PCs, selling IBM and Apple systems. The mass merchandisers could be expected to increase their participation level as the market matured and the Professional PCs became commodity items.

Mail-order and discount houses, such as Olympic Sales in Los Angeles and New York's 47th Street Photo, accounted for a small share of PC sales yet caused manufacturers a disproportionately large share of anguish. These retailers were able to undercut retail prices by 15 percent or more by virtue of providing less service, particularly with regard to repairs. In an effort to control service quality and maintain prices, manufacturers such as IBM, Apple, and HP had refused to ship any units to the discounters. No matter; inventory was acquired through a "gray market" in which other retail dealers sold off excess inventory in order to raise cash quickly. Some dealers even ordered more than they needed so that they could realize a volume price break, knowing full well that they could immediately convert into any excess cash. Despite the threat of a dealer losing a sales contract if caught transshipping, the "gray market" was estimated at several hundred million dollars. Other moves to discourage mail-order and discount sales included forcing all dealers to make their own repairs, prohibiting them from advertising outside their sales areas, and forbidding them to tout price alone. It was projected that these retailers would become less significant as volume discounts by the manufacturers were reduced or eliminated and as dealers realized that they were cutting their profits by keeping the discounters in business.

Competitors

HP's most significant competitors were Apple, IBM, DEC, and Radio Shack. Some highlights of their respective distribution strategies follow.

Apple had the widest retail distribution; the Apple II was sold in over 2,500 retail outlets. The company provided very heavy support in both "pull" and "push" directions. In addition to spending $12 to $15 million per year on advertising, Apple provided its dealers with sales and product training, toll-free software hot lines manned by specialists, monthly newsletters, an applications-oriented magazine, and even financial support. In 1980, the company introduced the "Apple Means Business" program, designed to teach dealers how to make sales presentations to specific target customers. "Apple saved the dealers," stated an industry analyst. "They helped them make a profit."

Apple sought tight control over its distribution channels. It waged war, with limited success, against the mail-order and discount houses in order to protect its dealers margins. Similarly, the company terminated its central purchasing agreement with ComputerLand. The discounts obtained by ComputerLand franchises were large enough to threaten the livelihood of neighboring independent dealers. ComputerLand outlets still carried Apple products, but now had less incentive, as the margins were less attractive.

The potential of the large corporate market and the entry of IBM created a need to change the retail emphasis. In striving to become a factor in the big business segment, Apple needed to develop a direct sales capability. Its first attempt at this was to designate an elite corps of 100 to 150 dealers as national accounts support dealers. Dealers who applied for the program were selected on their ability to be a full-service support dealer. The dealers chosen earned a 7 percent commission on all sales and an additional 12 percent if they also installed the system. These dealers were also responsible for arranging delivery, installation, and support through separate Apple dealers located near branches of their accounts.

The plan's discount schedule, similar to the one offered by IBM, also called for 5 percent on purchase of 25 to 49 units, 10 percent on 50 to 149 units, 12 percent on 150 to 399, and 15 percent on 400 to 999. Purchases above 1,000 units were negotiated directly with Apple officials.

Dealers were concerned at two levels. While the plan would bring sales to Apple that would otherwise be lost to competitors equipped to sell to corporate accounts through a direct sales team, it would also deprive other dealers of sales. Further, the 12 percent installation commission was far below the 32 to 35 percent that dealers realized on in-store sales. Joe Roebuck, Apple's director of vertical market integration, commented that (the installing dealer) "isn't going to make the sale without the national accounts plan." He added that the dealer was free to "go in on a local basis and sell himself." He said, too, that the 32 to 35 percent margins on dealer sales were misleading in the case of large-volume sales since the dealer would discount those sales and cut into his own margins. In addition, the plan relieved the dealer of inventory expense since product was shipped by Apple to the corporate customer.

During 1982 and 1983, Apple was developing an in-house direct sales force to market its Lisa computer—a more expensive, incredibly user-friendly computer aimed at the large corporate market.

IBM's distribution strategy evolved in the opposite direction. With a formidable direct sales and service network already in place, IBM instantly became a major factor in the large corporate market. The company had extremely limited retail selling experience, having provided typewriters, dictation equipment, and accessories through a small number of "product centers." With the introduction of the IBM PC, the firm, in one year, doubled its number of retail outlets to 35. IBM supported the PC with a heavy advertising budget and an aggressive discount schedule.

To achieve wider distribution, IBM sought out independent retailers. In keeping with their tradition of highest-quality service, the company at first accepted only the strongest of dealers, negotiating agreements with ComputerLand and Sears. IBM later expanded its dealer base, establishing relationships with single-unit retailers. In order to win the loyalty of their independent dealers, the company provided an ample amount of point-of-sale materials, warranty reimbursements, and a hotline to answer questions. All IBM dealers were required to attend a four-day training session in Boca Raton, Florida.

IBM resolved the conflict between its sales force and dealers by requiring that the direct sales force not deal in quantities of less than 20 units. The company faced another potential problem, however; should PC sales outpace production, which channel would they supply with inventory?

A relatively late entry into the PC industry, *DEC*—as did IBM—had a powerful direct sales force. Long criticized because members of his sales force were salaried, Kenneth Olson, DEC founder, claimed that "as far as we can tell, our yield per salesperson is higher than anybody else's. Also, it lets a sales rep stay with a customer even when he's not buying. So our customers are enormously loyal."

DEC had dominated the minicomputer market with this strategy, but the PC business was very different. Unlike the sophisticated minicomputer users, many users of PCs knew almost nothing. They required specific programs and substantial support services when the machines first arrived. And, unlike its head start in minicomputers, DEC entered an already crowded market.

On the positive side, the company had a huge base of potential customers (its minicomputer users) to sell to initially while developing its alternative channels. While DEC was not at all interested in the home market, customers who did buy direct were heavily influenced by the dealer channel. These customers judged a product's success by its acceptance and performance in that channel; they "kicked the tires" in the retail store; and they returned to the stores for add-on sales of peripherals and software.

To complement its sales force, DEC operated 25 retail stores and sold through independent retailers, such as ComputerLand, as well as industrial distributors, such as Hamilton-Avnet.

A leading factor in the home and small business segments due to its retailing strength, *Radio Shack* (a Tandy company) was trying to enter the Fortune 1000 market with its TRS-80 Model 16, the first PC built around a 16-bit microprocessor. A novice at selling to large companies, Radio Shack still suffered from a poor quality image; its earlier models were often referred to as the "Trash-80." The company had succeeded in retailing computers because of its experience in consumer electronics, its willingness to spend advertising dollars, and its aggressive, knowledgeable, and well-rewarded sales staff. Radio Shack had been criticized for not offering any products but its own; the company preferred not to dilute its gross margins, however.

To reach the large corporations, Radio Shack conducted a direct-mail campaign aimed at data processing managers. This was followed by a series of seminars. The company assembled a national accounts sales force, composed primarily of former mainframe sales personnel from other companies. These salespeople offered a 1 percent discount on purchases of at least $75,000 per year. Sales were credited to the location closest to where the machines were to be placed as an incentive for these outlets to provide good service.

Lesser competitors used creative means to obtain shelf space. *Xerox*, as described earlier, diversified into a chain of full-service office products dealers in addition to its direct sales and independent retailing activities. *Zenith* implemented a floor-planning program to finance for dealers one demonstration unit and one inventory system. The company also offered a $5,000 packet of demonstration software for only $500. *Data General* provided video training for both dealers and users, floor-plan assistance, and end-user financing.

Hewlett-Packard's Distribution

The majority of HP's marketing efforts had been through its captive sales force. The commercial sales force (as opposed to the technical force), which was responsible for the model 3000 minicomputer, sold the personal computers. The need to reach their annual quota of $1 million by selling minicomputers at roughly $250,000 apiece and microcomputers at $5,000 to $8,000 apiece did not allow the smaller units to receive sufficient attention. As a result, a new sales force was formed to sell only PCs. Personal Workstation Representatives

(PWSRs) numbered about 150 in early 1983 and called only on potentially large accounts.

In order to reach buyers outside of large corporations, HP attempted to gain distribution in retail outlets. A small group, named "Sales Force 12," was responsible for negotiating agreements with dealers. The group originated with HP's hand-held calculators and had taken on responsibility for the more expensive personal computation products as they were developed.

HP had not been particularly successful in cracking the retail market. In the final quarter of 1982, less than 7 percent of all retail computer outlets carried the 80 and 100 product lines. The majority of their dealers were single-location independent retailers.

The lack of shelf space was a major concern, especially in light of the support that HP provided its dealers. A 3 percent advertising credit, four-color point-of-sale material, free educational seminars, and 33 to 35 percent margins seemed reasonable by industry standards. HP's Personal Computer Centers gave hands-on demonstrations to potential customers but were not allowed to complete a sale. If the customer were a low-volume purchaser, he would be referred to the nearest dealer. High-volume purchasers were contacted by the company's sales force.

His eyelids growing heavy from a long night of reading, Yansouni turned out the light beside his bed. But sleep was a long time coming as his mind continued to churn over HP's distribution tactics. How should the company balance its efforts between channels? And what changes in their retailing practices would gain them entry into more stores?

C A S E 5–3

North Star
Shipping Company

In January 1983, Mr. Peter Kruger, marketing manager of the North
Star Shipping Company's North Continent subsidiary (which serviced
the Benelux countries, Italy, Austria, Switzerland, and West Germany)
was studying the latest company report on shipments from Germany
to North America. Sales and revenue tonnage were again below
budget—sales more so than volume (tonnage). Because of the importance of the German market, both short and long term, Mr. Kruger
knew that he had to take remedial action immediately.

In 1982, German exports provided about 33 percent of the subsidiary's total revenues, but less than 10 percent of those of the parent
company. In tons, the ratios were approximately the same, although
per-ton revenues and contributions were somewhat lower than for
other countries. North Star's share of the total German North Atlantic
tonnage was lower—much lower—than for other countries where a
share of 20 percent was typical. The market share for Germany had
never exceeded much more than 12 percent of total liner traffic in the
North Atlantic and, in recent years, had been declining. The budget for
Germany, set on a port basis and shown in both tons and dollar revenues, had almost never been attained. The German personnel involved
generally explained this "failure" by the longer transit time of North
Star's service versus that of leading competitors, and by the frequent
changes made by the parent company in the type and amount of ship
space allotted to them.

North Star Shipping was formed in the early 1960s, by a merger of
several companies, to serve the highly competitive North Atlantic
trade route via containerization. It was one of the first shipping compa-

---

© by INSEAD, the European Institute of Business Administration, Fontainebleau,
France.

nies to apply the "through" transportation concept; i.e., providing house-to-house service through the use of containers versus the more traditional port-to-port approach. North Star provided a variety of special equipment for both sea and land transportation, ensured the use of the least expensive and fastest land routings, and even provided for fast customs clearance. Its sophisticated communication system, which included computers and private telex wires, made it possible to adopt a high-quality, integrated sales-service approach to the problems posed by shippers, forwarders, and consignees. These services, coupled with convenient and dependable sailing schedules, had made North Star a successful company.

Subsidiary organizations in Canada, the United States, England, France, Scandinavia, and Holland were responsible for marketing the company's services. The central organization was located in New York City and served to control the operation of the vessels, coordinate marketing efforts between subsidiaries, allocate ships and space between ports, undertake general promotional activities, supply marketing information, and prepare budgets. Understandably, the company's North American operation was the largest of any of the country organizations, numbering in excess of 400 individuals.

The German Market for Westbound North Atlantic Liner Trade

In 1982, West Germany was the biggest European exporter to the United States and the second largest importer from there. German exports to the United States included machinery and transport equipment (20 percent) and manufactured goods (46 percent) and chemicals (10 percent). For Canada, Germany was second after Great Britain, and exports to Canada typically represented only 10 percent of total U.S. exports. In 1982, United States imports from West Germany were valued at approximately $13 billion, representing over 4 million tons; about 36 percent of this moved over the North Atlantic.[1] About half of the North Atlantic cargo tonnage was transported by liners, i.e., regularly scheduled ships which were, in 80 percent of the cases, container ships. Exports from Germany fluctuated year to year and were difficult to forecast because they depended on the general economic conditions and particularly on the current exchange rate for the dollar.

Basically, yearly exports from one country were assumed to be connected with its GNP. Any forecast for the lines was made difficult by a lack of current market data; e.g., official statistics in Germany were

---

[1] Compiled from OECD and U.S. Department of Commerce statistics.

restricted to classifications by value, and so were OECD statistics for different commodity groups. The most suitable data were those of the U.S. Department of Commerce (DOC) which classified imports by country, commodity, tons of commodity, percent share of North Atlantic liners, and percent share by shipping company. These data were, however, available with a time lag of at least five months and were, therefore, of only limited relevance to the lines for planning purposes.

Many North Atlantic shippers used liners because they needed a regular service. They often used more than one line in order to balance risks. Typically, less than 50 shippers provided more than half the volume for a particular line. The interest of a shipper in the North Atlantic shipment itself depended largely on the contract by which he sold his goods. If he sold ex works, either the consignee asked for a particular line, or the cargo was simply handed over to a forwarder. In ex work sales the shipper was only slightly interested in the whole transport. This was different when goods were sold on a c.i.f. basis— then the shipper paid greater attention to the transport problem.[2] About 25 percent of the shipments were done on a c.i.f. basis. Consequently, in many cases not the shippers but the forwarders dealt with the lines and thus, constituted a large customer group. Approximately 10 forwarders dominated the German market. Overall, it was estimated that forwarders handled over half of all shipments on a tonnage basis.

It was difficult to separate customer groups by services used, because car shippers, for instance, would also ship automobile spare parts in containers. Statistical groupings were often done by commodities. These groupings, however, gave no indication concerning geographical factors, and little of the profitability per-ton-cargo for the line, because rates could vary within a commodity group and the cost per ton or per TEU[3] was not always the same.

According to Mr. Kruger, a shipper chose a line based on the following:

1. Availability of service.
    House-to-house transit time.
    Availability, regularity, and reliability of shipments.
    Availability of special equipment—special containers or trailers.
    Reliability of the line.
    Availability of special services.
2. Sometimes a shipper had problems in availability on non-North Atlantic shipping routes. Therefore, he had to close a "package deal" with a line serving both the North Atlantic and other routes.

---

[2] c.i.f. = cost, insurance, and freight included, port of destination.

[3] TEU = 20-foot equivalent unit, i.e., unit equivalent to a 20-foot container.

Such a situation worked to the disadvantage of North Star which served only the North Atlantic trade.

3. Price, although conference liners had to maintain price parity. Price sensitivity was greatest with forwarders and could vary with clients.

4. Use of German ports, since German railways offered special rates to these ports.

In most companies, a traffic manager was in charge of shipments. This made personal contact very important and, at the same time, limited a more general approach to transport problems. For instance, it was difficult to convince a traffic manager of the long-term positive effects on investments and costs that could be obtained using a different mode of transportation, such as roll-on, roll-off (RORO) which was especially important for shipping vehicles of almost any size or type. North Star had more RORO capacity than did any of its competition. Sometimes emotional arguments favored a German line.

It was expected that, in the future, transportation would be viewed on a more integrated systems basis—incorporating it into plant location and investment decisions. Moreover, other companies were expected to follow the example of Volkswagen, which operated its own integrated transport system by owning its own trucks and ships.

The Transportation Industry in Germany for the North Atlantic Liner Trade

The "container revolution" had already taken place in Germany. Container shipping required a more careful planning of investments and operations, and therefore, the industry was forced to apply more and more sophisticated technology and management techniques. The old port-to-port approach had given way to an integrated approach. Many difficulties still had to be overcome including the need to close information gaps and update an outmoded and overly complex tariff. Companies had difficulty in determining the profitability by individual units. In general, high-value cargo paid better than did low-value cargo, although there were exceptions to this rule. Conference tariffs in Germany were the lowest in Europe due to the competitive situation. Some shippers from abroad even shipped goods to Germany for transshipment elsewhere in order to obtain tariff advantages (e.g., automobile spare parts from Sweden).

The largest lines were organized in a "conference," which was mainly a tariff agreement. The other lines, the outsiders, were not coordinated as to their prices. Their total capacity was estimated to be about 40 percent of that of the conference lines, but according to the latest statistics, (see Exhibit 1) conference liners transported, in 1982, only about 58 percent of the German North Atlantic tonnage. The

Exhibit 1
Germany to United States North Atlantic Traffic (1980–1982 in thousands of tons)

	1980	1981	1982
Total Germany to United States.	3,108	3,868	4,114
Total North Atlantic	1,373	1,374	1,483
Total Liner N Atlantic	866	860	852
Total Conference Liners	551	558	497
Total North Star	104	112	80

Exhibit 2
Competitive Profile on Major Lines Servicing West Germany—1982

	North Star	Hapag Lloyd	Sealand
Estimated market share of conference liner tons	16%	35–40%	Over 20%
Services.	Container/RoRo	Container	Container
Frequency	Weekly	Weekly	Weekly
Ship speed (knots)	20	21	19
Transit days.	12 days	11 days	9 days
Direct ports in north continent .	Antwerp Rotterdam Hamburg Bremerhaven Halifax	Antwerp Rotterdam Hamburg Bremerhaven Halifax	Rotterdam Bremerhaven
Direct ports in North America.	New York Portsmouth Baltimore	New York Hampton Roads Baltimore Philadelphia	New York Hampton Roads

remaining 42 percent was done by outsiders. The success of the various lines (see Exhibit 2) was based mainly on three factors:

1. Quality of service offered.
2. Representation in Germany.
3. Personal contacts.

Hapag Lloyd, one of the members of the conference, was the most successful line in Germany. It had a 35 to 40 percent market share of the total conference German tonnage. It offered transportation to all parts of the world and was known for reliable and reasonably fast schedules as well as for special services which facilitated customs clearance. Their own suborganization, DCD (Deutscher Container

Dienst), was able to provide containers and special equipment on short notice. Hapag Lloyd used mainly German ports (Hamburg, the largest German port, and Bremen). Approximately half the ocean cargo leaving Germany used these two ports. Hapag had substantially more offices and salesmen than did North Star. Sealand, the next biggest line, had fast ships and could promise an unbeatable transit time to New York, where two thirds of the freight to the United States came in. It served most routes and had substantially more reefer (refrigerated) boxes than any competitor. Sealand had approximately 20 percent of the pool share in Germany.

Traditionally, forwarders had a strong grip on the market. The 10 largest forwarders who dominated the market had their own lorry fleets and booked whole trains for inland moves. They often chartered planes and ship space. Besides their commissions, they earned money by packing goods (an operation typically costing 2 to 5 percent of cargo value and sometimes up to 12 percent). There were indications that in the future forwarders would be "nonvessel operating carriers"; e.g., they would subcontract the sea transportation part of the shipping.

The North Atlantic market was declining, and there was no indication that the market would become less competitive. One threat for the future was the United States-based lines which transported a good deal of cargo back and forth for U.S. military forces in Europe. Since these forces were decreasing yearly, the U.S.-based lines had begun aggressively to seek nonmilitary cargo.

North Star Position in the German Market

North Star's activities consisted of marketing containers and RORO (roll-on, roll-off) space. Compared to other areas in which North Star operated, its market share in Germany was low (see Exhibits 3 and 4). The revenue per ton averaged $175. The contribution from Germany was 25 percent of sales versus 35 percent from other areas. The reasons for this were manifold, according to Mr. Kruger, and included low tariffs and the fact that a small number of competitors dominated the market, thereby picking up the better-paying cargo.

The partial "success" of North Star in Germany was explained largely on the basis of personal contacts, a reliable organization, a relatively good service to Canada, and especially, by the availability of special equipment. Competitors had problems with large equipment, whereas North Star could use RORO. In 1982, 75 percent of North Star's German clients were regular users of their service and some 35 (if forwarders were included) provided 70 percent of the total volume.

Selling in Germany was handled by the Werther Agency which was paid a commission of 2½ percent of sales. This agency, headquartered

Exhibit 3
Exports from West Germany to United States via North Atlantic Route (selected commodities 1980–82 in tons)

Commodity	1980			1981			1982		
	Total liner	North Star	North Star market share	Total liner	North Star	North Star market share	Total liner	North Star	North Star market share
Wine	28,709	1,989	6.9	29,396	2,033	6.9	30,944	3,275	10.6%
Beer	61,506	3,165	5.1	73,666	8,326	11.3	101,088	3,572	3.5
Organic chemistry	55,700	6,266	11.2	59,843	6,622	11.1	57,071	4,043	7.1
Inorganic chemistry	68,725	5,139	7.5	65,586	7,953	12.1	68,290	5,083	7.4
Plastics	35,716	2,887	8.1	28,180	2,865	10.2	30,927	2,012	6.5
Refactory material	34,246	1,384	4.0	32,868	1,714	5.2	40,232	2,425	6.0
Iron and steel wares	64,339	6,137	9.5	50,790	3,639	7.2	65,225	3,139	4.8
Copper	15,649	3,561	22.8	34,789	5,255	15.1	19,064	3,608	18.9
Internal combustion engines	53,967	2,003	3.7	33,040	634	1.9	4,302	120	2.8
Machinery	108,525	14,007	12.9	85,143	12,942	15.2	101,595	12,473	12.3
Motor vehicles and parts	96,342	39,518	41.0	79,442	38,593	48.6	53,820	24,649	45.8
Subtotal for cited commodities	623,424	86,056	13.8	572,743	90,576	15.8	572,558	64,399	11.2
Total for all commodities	866,010	104,270	12.0	859,627	111,869	13.0	851,654	80,380	9.4

Exhibit 4
Revenue Data on a Sample of Selected Commodity Groups Moving out of Bremerhaven between December 1982 and February 1983 on North Star Ships

Denomination	Port of destination	Equipment*	Rate†	Average tons per TEU‡	Average rev per ton (dollars)	Average rev per TCU (dollars)
Cars...........	—	—	—	—	$250	$ 300
Beer...........	NYC	4 × 40' 3 × 20'	$ 71	9	71	640
	BAL	2 × 40' 2 × 20'	71	9	71	640
Wines..........	NYC	6 × 40' 3 × 20'	$160	8.5	160	1,360
	HFX	6 × 40' 3 × 20'	($1,514 @ 20') ($2,456 @ 40')	8.5	152	1,285
Plastics........	PORTS	7 × 20'	$100–135	14	115	1,610
Copper.........	NYC	20 flatbed	$160	14	160	2,240
		50 trailers (40')		8		1,280
Machinery	NYC	2–20' 4–40'	M90–160	9	120	1,080
	HFX	6–40'	$2,000–4,000 per 40'	8	188	1,504
	BAL	9–40' trailers	M100–150	8	130	1,040

* If not otherwise specified, containers (20 feet and 40 feet).
† Per ton, unless an "m" appears, in which case the rate is per cubic meter.
‡ Rounded.

Source: Company records.

in Frankfurt, was formed in 1953 to represent a number of shipping lines. In addition to representing North Star, it served 14 other lines, all of which were conventional, noncontainerized lines; most did not service the North Atlantic route. Mr. Werther, as head of the agency, primarily handled relationships with the various lines his agency represented. His son handled the day-to-day operations which were carried out by some 40 persons of whom 15 were on-the-road salesmen operating mainly out of agency offices located in Frankfurt, Düsseldorf, Berlin, Munich, and Hamburg.

At headquarters, three persons worked full time to coordinate the Werther Agency's North Star marketing effort. Salesmen, of course, sold the services of all lines represented by the agency. They called mainly on traffic managers and occasionally on the large freight forwarders, doing as much of their work as possible by phone. The Werther Agency accounted for approximately 80 percent of North Star's German traffic. The remainder was taken by port agents who handled shipments brought to the port location by the shipper. North Star's business here was but a small percentage of its total sales.

Coping with the Constraints

North Star had developed a budgeting planning system in which profitability per port was carefully watched. Agent commissions were expressed in fixed percentages, but cost performance was reflected in the "revenue guidelines." These guidelines served as a basis for salesmen to determine whether a cargo would be profitable—or profitable enough to accept. The implicit assignment given to the German sales organization was to improve market share and, in the process, to cut costs and increase revenues. This could be done by obtaining better paying cargo and achieving the optimal container balance per area so as to lower "positioning" costs as much as possible. (At the end of 1982, they ranged between $48 and $55 per container.) A typical revenue for a 20-foot container was $1,470.

The quarterly German budget was set in tons and dollar revenue by port and type of equipment. This budget had been developed using estimates from computer forecasts prepared by North Star's central office (essentially an extrapolation of historical data) modified by the German "situation." Forecasts received from each subsidiary were reviewed at the central office and revised only after discussion with the appropriate marketing managers. They were then used to prepare a final budget which was presented to the shareholders for approval. The budget for the following year was processed during the period August/October of the previous year. Additionally, a rolling forecast was made each quarter showing tons and revenues by ports, broken down by equipment. The budget had never been split up by area within Germany, and targets were always in gross terms; i.e., they were not broken down by commodity.

The actual volumes and revenues were compared monthly with the budget, in the "trade report." The RORO traffic was further analyzed monthly in the RORO report. Contribution was watched monthly in the "contribution report" which analyzed volumes, revenues, revenue per TEU, and contributions per TEU. Another monthly report received from each subsidiary dealt (both quantitatively and qualitatively) with past marketing and operational activities.

The Action Plan for 1983

In order to change North Star's approach of soliciting day-to-day cargo as had, more or less, been done in the past, Mr. Kruger had worked out a new approach which was aimed at increasing revenues and market share in the German market. This was termed "the 1983 action plan." This latest planning effort was in line with corporate efforts to take a longer-term view of German problems. The latest step in this effort was the preparation of a five-year tonnage and revenue forecast by port in Germany which was tied to an expected annual growth of some 4 to 5 percent. The goal for Germany was set at a growth in market share during this time period of five share points.

The 1983 budget had already been set by the normal procedure. Tonnage figures were about 5 percent higher than the previous year, but revenue was expected to grow between 10 and 15 percent. For the first time, the budget presented data of a detailed type for Germany, and Werther was asked to split them up by sales area. The new marketing effort provided that the sales force would be helped out by Mr. Kruger and two salesmen from Holland. A list of potential customers was compiled for Germany by area which listed several companies local salesmen had not heard of. This list had been compiled from Germany on port data and was thought to be reasonably good in identifying large, high-value shippers.

A so-called task force was formed; i.e., Mr. Kruger and/or the salesmen from Holland would spend time with local sales people, discussing their future call efforts and visiting difficult and new accounts in their area. This way, North Star's services would be sold to a prospective client more aggressively than before. Werther salesmen were responsible for selling the services of all the lines they represented, but, if a better performance in Germany could be obtained, then Werther received increased commissions. In addition, Mr. Kruger hoped that in the future it could improve his bargaining position (versus the other subsidiaries) in obtaining more space allocation for his operation overall. This, in turn, would have a positive effect on market share in the future.

Mr. Kruger was considering whether the described new efforts could achieve the goals set and to what extent he could undertake further action. He was particularly concerned about the reaction of large forwarders to his plan, since North Star was literally in competition with its own customers. He recognized that other shipping companies competed against the forwarders, but he thought that, because of their size, they might do so more successfully and dominate market share. To what extent forwarders would switch their business from North Star to competitive lines was difficult to estimate. Just what could be done to minimize this possibility was not clear.

Grantree Furniture Rental (B)

In February 1975, the president of Grantree Furniture Rental was considering a major shift in strategy. Because market conditions had changed, there were reasons to suspect a need for a new approach. However, the implications of the change were far-reaching and the consequences difficult to assess.

1972–1973

During the two years between January 1, 1972, and December 31, 1973, sales at Grantree rose somewhat but profits declined seriously. The economy was soft, inflation was causing significant cost problems, real estate financing was getting tight, and the construction industry was in trouble. The analysis of expenses and profits shown in Exhibit 1 indicates that expenses were climbing relatively, while profits were declining. To help reverse the situation, Mr. Bjorklund and the chairman hired a proven professional, Mr. James Jensen, in January 1973 to be vice president of sales and marketing.

During 1973, Mr. Bjorklund also reassessed his own personal goals. Ever since merging with Granning and Treece, he had missed the independence of being an entrepreneur. And he foresaw that as sales grew, organizational complexities would change the nature of his work. The more he thought about the future, the more he realized that he was happiest in a small start-up environment. Therefore, in December 1973, Mr. Bjorklund left Grantree and started another venture in the automobile leasing field, taking the executive vice president with him. On January 1, 1974, Mr. Jensen was appointed president.

Exhibit 1
Relationship between Operating and G&A Expenses to Pretax Profit Contributions, 1967–1973

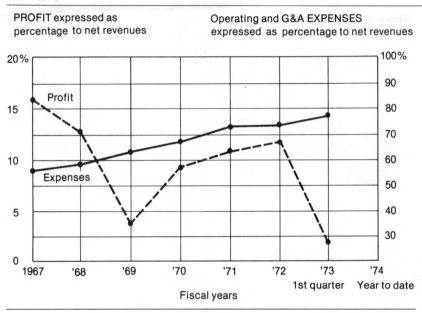

PROFIT expressed as percentage to net revenues

Operating and G&A EXPENSES expressed as percentage to net revenues

Fiscal years

At the age of 32, Jim Jensen was an unusual executive. He had started his career in 1958 selling cookware door to door for four years, while financing his way through the University of Washington. In 1961, he joined Encyclopaedia Britannica, where he achieved an enviable sales record. At the age of 23, he became Britannica's youngest division manager. At 28, he became the youngest corporate officer in Britannica's 200-year history. In 1972, he resigned from his vice president's position with personal earnings well in excess of $100,000 per year.

Jim sought the challenge and opportunity of finding a small conceptual business with unlimited growth potential. In Jim's opinion, Grantree represented such a business. Grantree was a small Oregon concern with presumably large potential and no apparent end to important challenges. Not only were profits falling, but the stresses placed upon operations revealed that the control system was weaker than imagined.

In recalling his first days as president, Jim Jensen described Grantree as poorly organized, not only in terms of lack of organizational structure, but in standardization of procedures and controls. For example, in one profit center, a customer's credit might be checked by the showroom salesperson, whereas in another profit center, that credit check might be made by the operations manager; in still another profit center, there might not be any credit check at all because "the guy looked good." Moreover, there was no clear definition of responsibilities within the home office itself.

As previously stated, there was an alarming trend developing in profits and expenses. According to Mr. Jansen:

> Although sales were increasing at a phenomenal rate, expenses were increasing faster. For example, the Operating and G & A expenses, as a percentage of net revenue, had increased from a low of 57 percent in FY 1967 to 75 percent at the end of the first quarter of FY 1973. At the same time, pretax profits, as a percentage of net revenue, had declined from their high of 16 percent in FY 1967 to a new low of 2 percent at the end of the first quarter in FY 1973.

The business mix was also a problem. As shown in Exhibit 2, the trend was toward de-emphasis of the individual or tenant business and

Exhibit 2
Business Mix: Tenant versus Commercial

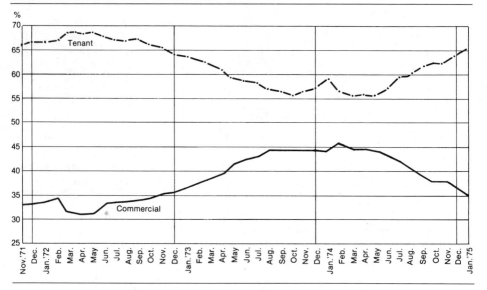

acceleration of commercial business. If one looked at the pretax profit results at the end of March 1973 and matched that graph with the change in business mix, it was easy to see a direct correlation between the increasing less profitable commercial business and the decreasing more profitable tenant business and the overall decrease in pretax profit.

Individual resident business was returning a gross rental revenue of 11 percent per month against the cost of furniture, compared to only a 5 percent gross return on the commercial business. The theory (which proved to be false) that commercial business could be profitable at the lower rate, was that we would get a lot of orders at one time and avoid the cost of generating orders one at a time. In the past, too much attention had been placed on volume for its own sake without regard for the costs of obtaining the extra sales.

Commercial business was, in fact, considerably less profitable. In addition to the lower gross profit margin, it cost just as much to move one unit of furniture on a commercial basis as it does on an individual basis. At least on the individual basis, we were generating a $40 delivery, installation, and pickup fee, plus a waiver fee equivalent to 7 percent of the monthly rental. (Ninety-eight percent of all of our individual business was signed with the waiver fee.) These revenues were in addition to the 11 percent per month return. There was no revenue from delivery and pickup, nor was there any waiver fee with commercial accounts. And the problem of collecting our revenue was monstrous. As you know, the real estate industry was highly leveraged. Consequently, some of the owner-developers were taking the revenues generated from our furniture, and instead of paying us for the rental furniture, they were paying other bills. Consequently, we accrued some revenues into income which, at a later date, we had to charge back to bad debts. Moreover, as the economy turned down, the rate of business failures in the real estate industry was probably as high in 1974 as in any other year since the depression.

Exhibit 3 shows clearly the difference in gross profits on an individual resident account at 11 percent versus a commercial account at 6.5

Exhibit 3
Gross Profit Comparison on a $350 Unit for a Period of Nine Months Rental (created in March 1974)

	Direct to resident 11%	Representative lease 9%	Commercial 8%	Commercial 6½%
Monthly rental...............	$ 38.50	$ 31.50	$ 28.00	$ 22.75
Delivery and pickup.........	35.00	35.00		
Waiver...................	2.90			
Nine months rental..........	$346.50	$283.50	$252.00	$204.75
Plus Waiver.............	26.10			
Delivery and pickup..	35.00 (now 40)	35.00		
Total revenue	407.60	318.50	252.00	204.75
Less: Cost of carrying goods at 3% of $350 per month..	94.50	94.50	94.50	94.50
Gross profit................	$313.10	$224.00	$157.50	$110.25

percent. (The return was raised to 6.5 percent from 5 percent by a change in price during 1974.)

It was also clear that rental rates encouraged the renter to make a decision about buying Grantree furniture after 12 months (in subsequent years the percentage of rent which applied to purchase dropped).

Moreover, the degree of market penetration was disappointingly low. And there were rumors that Mohasco was seriously interested in expanding its role in the rental field via acquisition. (In fact, by 1974, Mohasco had made seven acquisitions.)

Mr. Jensen's Moves

As a first step, Jim Jensen brought in an old colleague from Chicago, Zol Cohen, whose assignment was to take over the administrative and financial details. The firm's name was changed to Grantree and the logo modernized.

In taking stock of his situation, Jim had decided that three things needed to be done:

1. Get the house in order.
2. Prove the concept.
3. Dominate the industry.

Hence, he decided to postpone any major expansion, although he was willing to grow around his present area.

It was obvious that the biggest marketing task was to educate apartment owners that investing in their own furniture was an expensive luxury. (Their skill was property management, not furniture purchasing, rental, and maintenance.) He also knew that he could obtain real selling leverage only if he could get apartment house managers to refer interested tenants to Grantree.

Some Changes

As a prelude to a new approach, Mr. Jensen set some special objectives. He wanted "direct to resident" (he considered "resident" a better term than "tenant") sales to represent 70 to 75 percent of his volume, and he wanted an improvement in returns.

The $35 refundable delivery fee was raised to a $40 charge and was no longer refundable. Charges were increased on rentals of less than six months, so that the firm's return rose from 11 percent to 12 percent on those sales. But most important, and primarily as a sales tool since very few renters exercised the option, the firm adopted a straight purchase option in which 100 percent of all rents could be applied each year to purchase. This meant that in 25 months the tenant had paid enough to own if he decided to exercise his purchase option (not automatic), rather than in 32 months under the sliding scale of earlier years.

Jim also planned for a "representative lease program," which, by January 1975, represented 5 percent of sales. Under this sales approach, the apartment owner was relieved of all responsibility for payment or collection on furniture. The apartment manager was authorized to sign furniture leases on behalf of Grantree. He received, as always, a free "ready to rent" apartment or model and continued to quote a single price to the tenant which included the apartment and the furniture. When the lease was signed, however, the manager presented two leases to the tenant, one for the apartment and the other for the rental furniture. The tenant was told that he would now deal directly with Grantree and was charged a $35 delivery and setup fee. But he was also informed that he had the full purchase option—thus giving the manager or owner a bit of a competitive edge. Grantree thus avoided the large exposure risk of dealing through apartment owner intermediaries. And the strategy anticipated any serious downturn in the fortunes of the owners. At 5 percent return, the loss of two owner units was more than offset by the retention of an 11 percent individual unit. Even at 6.5 percent, when all costs were included, the two were virtually the same.

To facilitate the working of this new strategy, it was necessary to get the active cooperation of the apartment house manager, who might not be the owner. Mr. Jensen introduced an incentive program for these managers in April of 1974. Under the program, managers received prize points for signing up and additional points for each tenant referral. These points were convertible into merchandise selected from a handsomely illustrated catalog.

Used Furniture Program

During this same period, Mr. Jensen made a major change in his used furniture sales strategy. In September 1973, he hired a young aggressive manager from Gold Key, formerly with Levitz, gave him the San Jose used furniture store, and said, "Show me you can run this store profitably, and you can run them all."

In eight months, the young man doubled the volume and converted a $5,000 per month loss into a $5,000 profit. He changed the name of the outlet to "Rental Returns" (who wants to buy used furniture?), hired professional furniture merchandisers and salespeople, increased the new furniture percentage to 40 percent of sales, and increased the average selling price to a 95 percent return on original cost (before sales expense).

The young man's skill was so obvious that in May 1974, Mr. Jensen separated the rental return stores from rental management and centralized their management in Portland under the young executive. The proposed strategy was to increase the number of stores to 12, to increase new furniture sales to 50 percent, and, when there was more capacity, to dispose of used furniture other than the Grantree rental operation provided, by going to apartment owners and buying their furniture. The owner would receive a 30 to 40 percent return over cost (instead of his present 15 percent) in return for signing an agreement for Grantree to supply rental furniture.

In the words of Mr. Jensen, "I want to add used furniture outlets in our present markets until our managers say, 'Jim, we need more used furniture.' That's what I'm waiting for. Then I'll advertise to buy all used furniture from present owners."

As a test of this new concept Mr. Jensen had a special brochure printed which was addressed to apartment owners. He planned to market test the idea in Seattle in April 1975.

Exhibit 4
Rental Return Sales (in thousands)

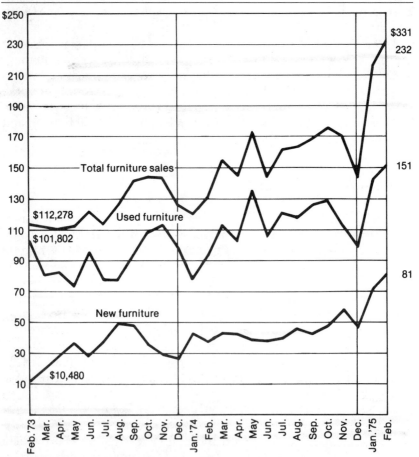

January 1975

The year 1974 was difficult. Although sales continued to climb (see Exhibit 4), losses were incurred (see Exhibit 5). A five-quarter compari-

Exhibit 5
Pretax Profit (percent to revenue)

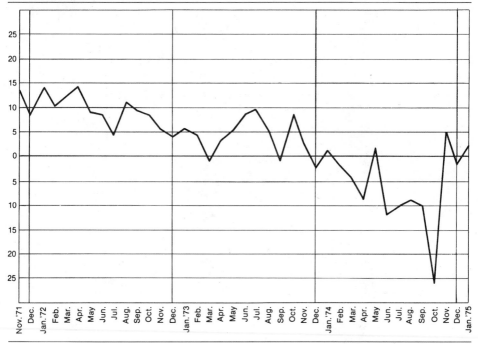

son of sales and profits is included as Exhibit 6. Of interest is the profit in the first quarter of 1975 after the heavy loss in the previous quarter. To quote Mr. Jensen:

> Many people think this is attributed to a reduction in interest expense. However, if you will notice, we have an entry entitled "Operating Earnings before Interest" which shows a $93,000 profit in the fourth quarter and a $215,000 profit in the first quarter of FY 1975. Consequently, we are experiencing increased revenue and decreased expenses, attributable almost entirely to the change in our rental business mix from commercial to direct to resident and our increased rental return sales.

During the year, Grantree also expanded into Sacramento, Riverside, Reno, and Phoenix, but with only modest results. However, on another front, retail operations proved a valuable source of positive

Exhibit 6
Five-Quarter Comparison—Summary of Earnings Furniture Rental (November 1 fiscal)

	1974				1975
	1st Quarter	2d Quarter	3d Quarter	4th Quarter	1st Quarter
Income:					
Furniture rental	$1,602,571	$1,542,399	$1,587,000	$1,603,476	$1,592,986
Furniture sales, net	124,044	109,772	116,534	130,134	154,503
Total income	1,726,615	1,652,171	1,703,534	1,733,610	1,747,489
Expenses:					
General and administrative	1,232,186	1,262,310	1,309,054	1,362,013	1,261,976
Depreciation and amortization	299,847	294,890	280,004	278,443	270,112
Total expenses	1,532,033	1,557,200	1,589,058	1,640,456	1,532,088
Operating earnings before interest	194,582	94,971	114,476	93,154	215,401
Interest expense	194,278	185,757	195,744	214,705	183,267
Earnings before tax	$ 304	$ (90,786)	$ (81,268)	$ (120,551)	$ 32,134

cash flow. In fact, the company borrowed no money for operations after September 1973 and financed internally its newest expansions.

Although Mr. Jensen felt that he was in a strong position after 1974, he was newly concerned about some basic changes that had occurred in his markets during the last few months of 1974. He well knew that his sales success to date rested primarily upon the sales representatives, who softened up managers and owners so they would refer Grantree to prospective tenants. No money, except for telephone book yellow pages, was spent on direct to resident prospects. Owner/managers were good "salespeople" so long as there was a 5 to 10 percent vacancy rate.

But by the end of 1974, new construction had virtually stopped and vacancy rates in some markets were dropping. Owners were getting more choosy about their tenants, preferring those who already owned furniture. (Presumably, they were more reliable.) Thus, apartment owners were potentially less dependent upon Grantree.

Mr. Jensen wondered if he shouldn't switch his entire strategy and go direct to renters. "Why not media advertising instead of (or in addition to) sales representatives?" he asked. Abbey Rents, for example, had been very successful in Los Angeles when it concentrated upon heavy TV advertising. Perhaps it would be wise to switch to a campaign of "Rent to Own."

The implications of such a change were, of course, large. In comparing sales costs and proposed advertising expenses, the following were useful:

Sales and service representatives		
February 1975 salary		$ 11,775
February annualized		141,300
7.5% taxes and benefits		10,600
		$151,900
1974 advertising—rental	$ 97,702	
1974 advertising—used furniture	126,925	
1974 AMIP expense (apartment manager incentive program)	40,272	

As Mr. Jensen put it:

> Since the inception of our business, our primary sales strategy has been to channel all effort through the apartment industry. I am referring here to the owners, property managers, and apartment managers. Consequently, we really have been dependent on a "middle man" over whom we have had no control. If the industry booms, we can boom with it, but if the industry is in a slump, and new construction slows down, it can hurt us. Not hurt us because the demand for our service is decreased (users), but rather the needs for our service from the apartment industry are decreased (i.e., fewer vacant units). We don't believe we are necessar-

ily a cyclical business. Consequently, we are presently developing several marketing plans to test reaching the ultimate user.

We are developing a radio spot which will be tested. We are developing a group discount type of specialized mailing piece for military personnel, teachers, and stewardesses that will be mailed to them from their own associations.

We have also developed a direct mail program to apartment owners offering to buy their used furniture. If we are really going to expand our rental business, we cannot remain dependent upon another industry.

The key is to segment our markets and to move in with the rifle, testing various approaches. Presumably our basic marketing strategy of working primarily through the apartment industry would then be altered. Our intention is not to de-emphasize working with apartment managers, but rather to add additional dimensions to reach our ultimate market.

The proposed strategy and present strategy were compared by Mr. Jensen as shown in Exhibit 7.

Exhibit 7
Present versus Proposed Marketing Strategies

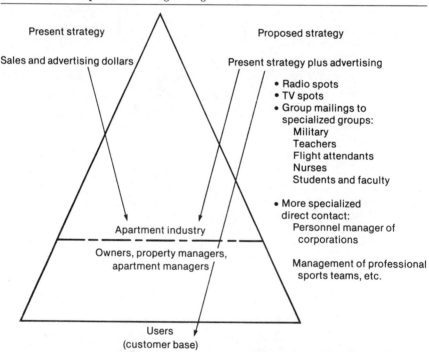

Personal Selling and Advertising

C A S E 6–1

Henderson Service Center

Tom Henderson, president of Henderson Steel Service Center, felt it necessary to review his company's marketing and sales strategies. Early in 1979, it was apparent that old assumptions and approaches had to be carefully examined and updated due to a number of ongoing changes in the environment. To be specific:

1. Specialist service centers were becoming more important and assuming major positions in such lines as tubing, spring steel, aluminum, and tool steel—products characterized as being of relatively high technical content, difficult to comprehend technically, consisting of many small volume grades, with considerable risk of obsolescence, and often with limited sources of supply—but, nonetheless, profitable due to their unique characteristics.

2. A decided upsurge in requests for bids, in which major buyers asked for quotes on a six-month supply contract; contracts which unfortunately might not be honored fully and where shipments might not always be in the specified truckload quantities (in short, a price squeeze).

3. The proliferation of brokers and secondary-line houses, who emphasized distress prices, raised havoc with traditional margins, and were in and out of the markets.

4. An ominous industry drift toward commodity selling, in which old trade names (Shelby Tubing, Jalloy) were being superseded by ASTM numbers, with the resulting willingness of customers to accept "or equivalent" products.

5. The merging of small centers into larger, multilocation houses.

6. And the accelerated trend toward sophisticated management, particularly in regard to asset management in general and inventories in particular.

Henderson was a medium-sized general line steel center in California whose growth made it increasingly difficult for management to stay on top of the details and to maintain its earlier entrepreneurial touch. As Tom Henderson said, "This is a business of inches—of exact control and doing the little things right—where success is closely tied to service and employee attitudes. How do I keep a balanced effort among the salesmen when growth results in a one-inch catalog, specialists eat away at our specialty markets, and the individual salesmen tend to gravitate toward their favorite products?"

Thus, it was timely that he review the company's sales and marketing strategies. Did his sales programs enhance the all-important company-customer relationships? Tom wanted to be sure that there weren't new approaches that warranted implementation. Indeed, he had a number of specific concerns about his sales strategies.

The Steel Service Center Industry

As of 1975, there were estimated to be 1,500 steel service centers (SSC) operated by 700 companies and accounting for 20 percent of the country's steel tonnage. The median firm had annual sales of $3 million. The modern steel service center was a vital link in the chain from basic steel producer (the mill) to user. An SSC was both distributor and processor, who not only handled a great range of mill products, but added considerable value to standard mill output. Steel service center processing included, but was not limited to, cutting, sawing, trimming, slitting, blanking, burning, roll forming, and light fabrication.[1] The mills were only too pleased to see most of this small order, specialty business handled by the centers.

Products handled included pipe, spring steel, sheet, tool steel, bar tubing, and structurals, primarily in steel (or aluminum) and involving a great complexity of specifications and basic processing variations— such as cold rolled carbon. Sales were made by the centers to a wide array of primarily industrial customers, including agriculture and commercial establishments. Needless to say, there were many products that were wholesaled primarily (i.e., no processing) by the steel service centers. And as will be shown, there was a wide difference between different types of centers. Separate from the steel service centers were hundreds of brokers—small independents who bought and sold as the opportunity arose, rarely handled the product, and substituted price for service.

---

[1] Cutting, sawing, and trimming involved reducing mill dimensions to customer requirements. Slitting was represented by the reduction of a wide roll to a narrow one. Blanking was the process of stamping out custom shapes. Burning would involve the "burning out" of a gear design, as an example, from heavy plate. Roll forming would be typified by forming a gutter or down spout. Light fabrication included such activities as punching predetermined holes in structural beams or bending material to a particular shape.

A 1974 study by Republic Steel contained some interesting speculations about the future:

Summary[2]

The service center market will be the largest market for steel by 1980, with shipment of 24.8 million tons in a peak year. This will represent a 25 percent increase over 1974's shipments of 19.9 million tons. Shipments of flat rolled products will increase by 29 percent, and shipments of hot rolled bar products will show a gain of 28 percent. Both tubing and cold finished bar shipments will increase by 22 percent, while the volume of stainless and pipe through service centers should register gains of 16 percent and 15 percent, respectively.

Seven products accounted for almost 75 percent of total service center tonnage in 1974. These products included the following: C HR Sheets, C CR Sheets, C Plates, C Structurals, C Standard Pipe, C HD Galvanized, and C HR Bars.[3] The largest single item was C HR Sheets, accounting for 18.6 percent of total service center tonnage.

Service centers will continue to increase their share of total steel shipments. Although they dropped sharply in 1975, we believe they will recover and take 20 percent in a peak year by 1980.

Our survey revealed four distinct types of service centers: super processors, large general line centers, small general line centers, and specialty houses. We forecast the biggest growth to take place among the large general line centers between 1974 and 1980 because trends to larger minimum order quantities by the mills and the continuation of absorption and consolidation of smaller centers will combine to promote strength in this market segment. The super processor, although showing good growth, will be hampered somewhat by its dependence on the automotive market. The specialty houses will just about hold their own in the marketplace. The small general line center will remain a significant part of the market, although many may be absorbed by large general line centers.

The survey findings indicate that two major changes are likely to take place in the service center market by 1980. If the mills increase and maintain higher minimum quantity extras as our survey indicates, there will probably be fewer service center companies but more locations, as some small centers are likely to be absorbed by larger centers. Those small centers remaining in the business will probably turn to larger centers as a source of supply, creating a two-tier service center market. The average service center of 1980 will be larger than the one of 1975 and will be more professionally managed.

---

[2] "Steel Service Centers in 1980," Republic Steel, pp. 2, 3.

[3] C HR Sheets = carbon hot rolled sheets
C CR Sheets = carbon cold rolled sheets
C Plates = carbon plates
C Structurals = carbon structurals (beams, columns, joists)
C Standard Pipe = carbon standard pipe
C HD Galvanized = carbon hand dipped galvanized
C HR Bars = carbon hot rolled bars

Service centers will not be involved in any different types of processing in 1980 than they are in now but will experience growth in virtually
everything they are doing currently. Slitting and cut-to-length will continue to be bread-and-butter items, but plate burning, blanking, and roll
forming should all show good growth. Pickling and tube manufacturing
could show limited growth at the service center level.

We forecast good growth in hot rolled bar products, particularly carbon hot rolled bars, through service centers based largely on the fact that
the forecasted level of shipments through the rest of this decade will
encourage volume rollings by the mills. Such levels of operations encourage increased minimum order quantity extras at the mill level. This
activity in turn would cause the small purchaser to use service centers as
a source of supply. Good growth in cold finished bars could result from
the same type of circumstances.

Cold finished bars should continue their excellent growth through
service centers, as will tubing products. Stainless and pipe products will
not experience the rapid growth of other products, but will still register
impressive gains.

We estimate that the four major captive service centers handled approximately 20 percent of all steel shipped through service centers in
1974. Captives should grow faster than the average for all service centers
because they fall into the fastest growing category, the large general line
center. However, we do not believe their growth will surpass that of the
independent large general line centers.

Foreign-owned companies have been increasing their holdings in the
domestic service center market. We estimate that 13 percent to 15 percent of the total tonnage handled by domestic service centers goes
through foreign-owned outlets.

In addition to these trends, Mr. Henderson foresaw: (1) continued
emphasis upon sophisticated computer systems to control operations;
(2) increased equipment improvements and costs of investments; (3)
the need to ensure solid supplier relationships, due to limited investment funds for capacity increases among U.S. steel companies; and (4)
continued downward pressures on price unless growing commodity
selling attitudes could be curbed.

The Company

The Henderson company was headquartered in the San Fernando
Valley, north of downtown Los Angeles, having been started by Tom
Henderson in 1958 after his discharge from the army. Over the years,
Tom had developed the company by internal growth and the acquisi-
tion of four smaller firms in San Diego, Bakersfield, Modesto, and San
Jose (all in California). Bank financing had been used recently, but in

his earlier days, Tom relied for financing upon internal funds and the public sale of 60 percent of the ownership.

It is revealing to see how the firm grew with the acquisitions program (see Exhibit 1).

Exhibit 1

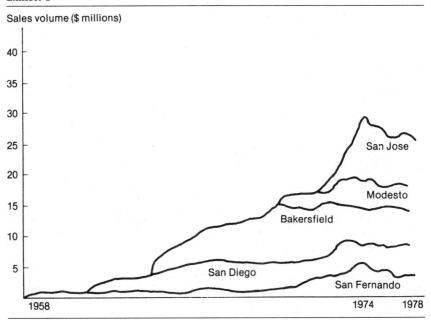

Sales volume ($ millions)

It is reasonably clear that market share was gained fairly early in each market and then maintained or slowly increased over time. Overall growth was primarily a function of acquisition.

As with all steel service centers, profits were sensitive to volume and mix, with different locations having different experiences. Variable costs exceeded 80 percent, which meant that funds available for overhead and profits were narrowly bounded by margins and direct costs. Peak sales for Henderson occurred in 1974, when total volume reached $29 million; 1976 was a poor year for the company and the industry, and by 1978, volume was still below 1974 but recovering.

Tom Henderson was a strong believer in the fact that true profitability was a function of asset turnover and leverage ratio (i.e., relative amount of debt) as opposed to solely conventional profit expressions. To be specific, he had drawn up a simple "strategic profit model" which he also used to compare his results to competition (Exhibit 2).

Exhibit 2
The Strategic Profit Model*

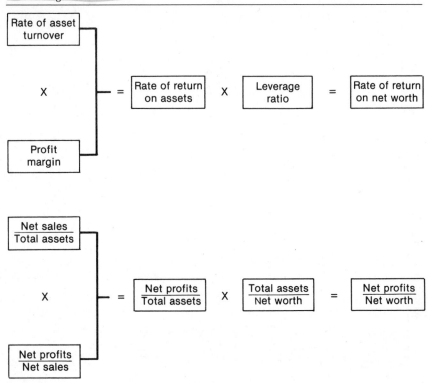

* The strategic profit model excludes leased equipment, fixtures, and facilities. The model also excludes the capital structure of nonconsolidated subsidiaries.

For 1978, to illustrate the model, Tom had drawn the comparisons between his firm and two competitors shown in Exhibit 3.

It was Tom's conviction that strategy should be stated specifically in terms of the model, such as:

Asset Management
Improve asset turnovers to 2.5:
1. Improve inventory turnover to minimum of three times.
2. Eliminate delete when out of items.
3. Maximum use of mother warehouse concept.
4. Maintain accounts receivables at 41 days.
5. Review all fixed assets and remove all nonproductive assets.
6. Study balance of fixed assets to improve their earning power.

Exhibit 3

Competitor	Asset turnover	×	Percent profit margin	=	Percent return on assets	×	Tax return rate	=	Net return on assets	×	Financial LVRG	=	Net return on equity	×	Earn return rate	=	Reinvest rate	Working capital percent sales
No. 1	2.7		1.7		4.4		53.2		2.4		2.2		5.2		32.6		1.7	17.0
No. 2	2.7		4.7		12.6		54.8		6.9		1.7		12.0		76.5		9.2	13.1
Henderson	1.6		4.1		6.6		53.9		3.6		1.7		6.1		100.0		6.1	22.1

Profit Management
1. Tight cost control.
2. Improve plant operating procedure to reduce cost.
3. Better systems to cut out unnecessary work.
4. Improve pricing where possible.
5. Study product lines to emphasize profit opportunities.

Financial Management
1. Find expansion opportunities that meet or equal our asset and profit objectives.
2. Expand debt to 38 percent of total assets.

Competition and Markets

Competition for Henderson was strong—from five majors and 20 times that number of specialists and brokers. It was Henderson's experience that the large, full-line houses were strong but reasonable competitors. Market disruption and cost cutting came from the brokers and a fringe handful of smaller firms whose approach to selling centered around "a good deal." Such tactics were particularly effective with those buyers, who seemed to be increasing in numbers, who preferred to shop around for the lowest offer and who thought that loyalty was for boy scouts.

Henderson's marketing/sales strategy was straightforward. The policy was to carry a good inventory of prime (as opposed to secondary) merchandise, to offer fast response time, and to concentrate on stock parts and cutting at the expense (relatively) of first-stage processing, though 20 percent of sales did come from processing. Whenever the company had to buy out, it examined carefully whether demand for that item would warrant future stocking.

Henderson's markets were diverse, reflecting basic differences among the California territories; 90 percent of the sales, to be specific, were into the farming and farm equipment, railroad, mechanical contractors, industrial equipment, mining, appliance, and furniture segments. Although there were several automobile assembly plants in the state, Henderson had chosen to not go after that very specialized and competitive business. Each market segment represented, obviously, a unique selling problem.

Farm equipment. There were six short-line producers in the Henderson territories, firms which manufactured and sold for their own account or acted as suppliers to full-line houses (such as Deere). By and large, these manufacturers wanted reliability, on-time service, and product quality, as opposed to minimum cost. The service center salesperson was a critical variable in the selling process, though much of his influence was due to the entertainment between supplier and buyer that was common practice. Apparently, the buyers preferred to purchase "from a friend," all other things being equal, and equated supplier reliability with the salesperson's interpersonal skills. This was not meant to imply that product knowledge and service were unimportant; it was rather that the essential catalyst was the salesperson's personal input. Multiple sourcing and bidding, nonetheless, were common, although trusted salespeople typically got "the last look." Buying decisions were made by the purchasing vice president or his buyer (if the firm were big enough).

Railroads were a good market on the West Coast, but in these firms it was difficult to find who buys. The successful salesperson did lots of legwork in engineering, purchasing, and even top management in order to get drawings. As in the case of the farm equipment segment, the role of the salesperson was critical. Cronyism was common, and most sales relationships had been established slowly over the years.

In the case of both segments, Henderson tried to sell the idea of "cost of position," that is, why invest as a buyer in expensive processing equipment when you can share the capital costs with the buyers by dealing with a Service Center?

Mechanical contractors (plumbing and heating, sheet and metal working), on the other hand, were easy to sell in that they bought "off the shelf," but they were price buyers of mixed credit reliability who shopped around. The nature of contractors' businesses caused them to be single job oriented. The salesperson's role was minimal in these instances, and entertainment was of little importance.

Appliance manufacturers (mostly in Los Angeles) were somewhat the same. They were tough buyers who appeared to have little loyalty. They were auction oriented and usually purchased flat rolled products with few components. Salespeople were significant only in respect to maintenance and repair.

Furniture accounts had little need for maintenance and repair. Price, not selling, was the name of the game. Theirs also was a fragmented industry of small, unstable producers.

The **industrial equipment** and **mining** segments were more solid and resembled the farm equipment market—sophisticated, insistent upon reliability and service, and sympathetic to constructive salesperson relationships.

Pricing, Advertising, and Distribution

Henderson was not a price house, although its prices were competitive. In periods of short supply, in fact, the firm had deliberately refrained from gouging its accounts in the hopes that the ensuing goodwill would carry over into buyer markets. Whether this policy was paying off was not at all clear: in 1977 and 1978, there had been a tendency for Henderson margins to slip and for the field salespeople to sacrifice service for discounted prices. Price pressures were growing. In fact, Tom Henderson figured that one of his most pressing needs was to give his salespeople more backbone to withstand such pressures and to sell service instead.

Advertising was a small but useful adjunct to the firm's strategy. Because there were no obvious regional media that matched Henderson's customer base, emphasis was put upon a modest direct mail campaign (which stressed the service dedication of the company, i.e., "Henderson Means Service"), a biannual house publication which went to employees and customers alike, appearance at all relevant conventions, some public relations, and hopefully, positive word of mouth.

The distribution strategy was simple. There were five warehouses in five cities, each stocked to its own market needs. Particular items could be shipped from branch to branch in a matter of hours and were in order to meet special requests. Buyouts were made whenever necessary.

Organization

Henderson's organization was probably representative of the industry (see Exhibit 4).

Exhibit 4

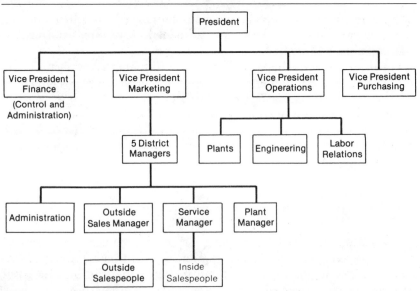

Even though the local plant managers reported to the district managers (for daily administration), they had a dotted-line relationship to the vice president of operations for functional matters. The reporting duality seemed to work.

The sales and service end of the business, because it was of particular concern to Mr. Henderson, deserves more elaboration. Including the San Fernando headquarters, there were five district managers who reported to a marketing vice president. Each manager operated out of a plant and supervised the sales manager, the plant manager, an inside service (sales) manager, and an administrative staff.

Reporting to the outside sales managers were 16 salespeople, for each of whom (with a few exceptions) there was a corresponding inside person. The two worked as a team, although they reported to separate bosses. The team idea was important because most ongoing sales were placed by customers calling in. The role of the outside salespeople was, therefore, to prospect for new accounts, to build established accounts, and to ensure post-purchase service. The inside person's responsibility was to maintain the business.

The district manager was the local authority. He had considerable decision-making leeway, although credit, purchasing, inventory policy, compensation, finance, and labor relations were controlled out of headquarters. The district manager could fire or add to the sales forces (with the concurrence of the marketing vice president), deploy his labor force as he saw fit, and train, supervise, and generally decide sales strategy. He was further responsible for making sure that the plant could meet customer requirements on time.

In a real sense, the district manager was "the leader" and was expected to know intimately the needs of the market. Suffice it to say he reinforced his own observations with data from the field concerning quantity changes, customer new product plans, customer switches in mill purchases, self-fabrication plans, and competitive activity.

The typical district manager earned between $30,000 to $35,000, including a maximum 20 percent of salary bonus based on district profitability. He received a percentage of the profit beyond the plan up to 20 percent of his base pay. Profit was calculated before headquarter's allocations for overhead and support.

The People

The five district managers came from different backgrounds. To single out three as representative:

San Fernando.   Started in accounting and then to inside selling. After two years, became an outside salesman and after three years, fabrication manager. Next, sales manager in a district and finally, at age 40, to district manager. One year of college but . . . "a very strong manager. Pushes hard, sets high standards, lets everyone know where they stand, good on strategy and market penetration."

San Jose.   College graduate, age 45, formerly manager of an advertising agency. Joined Henderson at 34 as outside salesman, then sales manager, manager of corporate development (a staff assignment reporting to the president), and finally district manager. "Sales oriented, well liked, polished, comfortable anywhere, runs tight team, well informed."

Bakersfield.   "Too long in his market. 37 years in the industry, close to retirement, resistant to new techniques but thoroughly conversant with his territory and key accounts. The customers love him, but he is a poor trainer."

The local sales managers had three responsibilities: to supervise and train their salespeople; to handle the key accounts directly; and to establish "executive level" contacts at all accounts. This was a heavy work load, needless to say, and different managers excelled in one or two of the three areas depending upon their strengths and territorial idiosyncracies.

One of them, for example, said that he saw his major job as exciting the salespeople because "attitude is everything in this business." Another felt that sorting out his 900 accounts was a crucial responsibility because "without organization you can't make any territorial headway." A third defined his role as "keeping the men on plan because it's too easy to deviate and do things you own way."

The salespeople were, of course, the prime contact between account and company. They were scheduled to average eight calls each day and to cover their accounts in a three- to four-week cycle. They determined their own callback patterns and varied them by account. Although it is unfair to single out one, the remarks of Harold Murphy (Modesto) are interesting:

> I used to sell insurance. Didn't do well in that environment. All they cared about was the one-time sale. They weren't concerned with building a lasting sales relationship.
>
> I like to think I'm a personal friend of my customers. The two most important things as a salesman are *credibility* and *sincerity*. Customers have got to believe me, or I'm wasting my time. I try to get my inside person out to the customers as much as possible too, so she is more than just a voice on the phone. If they're going to call in an order, then they're more likely to call someone pleasant whom they know.
>
> I've got to have good office support. My job is to introduce customers to Henderson Steel. Then after that, I have to depend on shipping, on production, and especially on my inside person. They make me look good. The first order from a potential new customer is often a token for having visited him three or four times, to "see how the salesman will do." Then I have got to have good support to impress him with my service.

The importance of the inside salespeople isn't recognized adequately at Henderson. Bad inside people slow down a salesman, waste his time and effort doing their jobs for them. The customer may not see any difference and sales may not fall, but the salesman has to cover for his inside person. Inside people were strictly a training grounds for outside salesmen in the past. Now people are beginning to see that some people are best suited there. Some want to stay in the inside.

We're number one in Modesto (the inside person and me), and half the credit goes to her. The inside person doesn't get an incentive bonus, though they should, since they really generate sales. I'm going to share part of my bonus with my inside person. She deserves it.

I run my territory on the basis of customer demand. I go where I can do the most good, be most influential, not based on the size of the account or a certain call frequency. I go to customers with a reason in mind, for a specific purpose. Some of my best customers told me when I first visited them three years ago, "Look, we've been buying from Henderson for years. You can't tell us anything new about Henderson and its service. Don't keep just coming around. We'll call you when we need you!" So I visit them maybe once a month and let my inside person deal with them. If they have a problem, then I am right there. They know whatever the problem is, I take care of it.

At one of my most sophisticated accounts, one of my competitors insists on going out every Tuesday morning to their plant. I don't think it's ever influenced a purchase decision. They joked about his coming every Tuesday.

Henderson Steel gives its sales force too much leeway on how to sell, especially the young ones. But I like it loose. I call my manager daily, and I feel good about calling him in to help if needed.

A rundown of the five districts indicated the situation at the start of 1979 as shown in Exhibit 5.

The salespeople specifics are depicted in Exhibit 6.

Tom Henderson provided a thumbnail sketch on each of the individual salesmen and sales managers:

San Fernando

Smith. An old pro; knows the territory; needs incentives to get full attention; overlooks possibilities in established accounts; about 46 years old; has a "good way" about him; the sales manager, but spends most of his time in his territory; has team which needs little supervision.

Smiley. With us three years; young, comer, eager, wants to advance; liked by customers; only 28; tends to high spot the accounts; somewhat weak on product knowledge; sells service aggressively.

South. Formerly plant superintendent; has done exceptionally well; best suited to country area and will probably have to be transferred; likes farm and mining contacts; thorough but unimaginative; has several key accounts who think the world of him.

Exhibit 5

District and plant	1978 Sales ($000)	1978 Quota	Number of salespeople (including management)	Sales per salesperson ($000)	Gross margin ($000)	Average gross margin per salesperson	Approximate number of accounts	Estimated share of market
San Fernando	$ 7,188	$ 7,000	3	$2,396	$1,798	599	2,500	12 %
San Diego	3,456	3,850	3	1,155	917	306	2,500	7.5
Bakersfield.	4,727	4,650	2 + district manager/ sales manager combined	1,576	1,128	376	1,100	11
Modesto.	2,423	2,600	2 + district manager/ sales manager combined	808	591	197	1,500	10
San Jose/Salinas	5,531	5,100	5	1,106	1,330	265	2,400	8
Total	$23,325*	$23,200						

* In addition there were home office house accounts of $2,550,000 handled by the senior management (but serviced locally).

Exhibit 6

District and territory	Salesperson	1978 Percent of quota	1978 Gross margin	Compensation	As percent of gross margin
San Fernando					
No. 1	Smith	87%	$552,630	$21,166	3.8%
No. 2	Smiley	104	470,912	14,811	3.1
No. 3	South	112	763,215	21,608	2.8
No. 4	Open	—	—	—	—
San Diego					
No. 11	Drudge	61	187,184	—	—
No. 12	Dodge	82	380,747	17,268	4.5
No. 13	Davis	118	320,098	17,963	5.6
Bakersfield					
No. 21	Brown	92	162,165	19,667	12.1
No. 22	Benton	137	468,371	24,055	5.1
No. 23	Bowles*	93	494,120	18,600	—
San Jose					
No. 41	Johnson	86	254,819	22,733	8.9
No. 42	Judas*	65	196,014	16,768	8.6
No. 44	Judd	98	316,592	19,816	6.3
No. 45	James	118	418,211	21,185	5.1
No. 46	Jaedeke	115	143,640	—	—
No. 48	Open	—	—	—	—
Modesto					
No. 51	Murphy	102	301,951	18,355	6.1
No. 52	Minnow*	65	57,853	16,500	28.0
No. 53	Morris*	80	243,582	15,410	6.3

* In territory less than full year. Compensation annualized for comparison.

San Diego

Drudge. The sales manager; well trained but emotional; orthodox in his approach; tends to concentrate on his favorite accounts; 38 years old; has potential; has trouble organizing but does reasonably well as SM.

Dodge. A problem—seems to be drinking too much; recently went through a nasty divorce; was once our best man, now I'm not so sure.

Davis. Shop background; formerly inside salesman; 15 years on the job; seems to be getting bored; OK if closely supervised; no apparent potential; has some well established accounts which he's comfortable with.

Bakersfield

Brown. Combination DM and SM; knows everyone in town; sells entirely on basis of friendship; not running too hard; needs lots of management time; in a tough market; inflexible; close to retirement; good with the petroleum accounts.

Benton. The old pro; a jewel; can always get business; positive; not good on systems or administration; knows markets and products; doesn't want a promotion.

Bowles. Very new in the territory (six months); comes from a competitor where he left under some kind of a cloud; I'm still not comfortable with him—seems slippery, not quite open and honest—though these may be unfair generalizations; I let my DM hire him against my better judgment; has some of our most loyal accounts; shows signs of selling price.

San Jose

Johnson. Lots of experience; was a sales manager but demoted because he couldn't motivate others; needs supervision; knows his product but is easily discouraged; great at knowing the people; spends lots of time on his real estate investments where he has done well; is well-off financially.

Judas. Came from another company where he was a purchasing agent; inside selling for us and has been outside for less than one year; highly religious individual, who occasionally offends others by his inflexible beliefs; not at ease in his territory but seems to be catching on; still a question mark; not fully able to sell on basis of service.

Judd. With us 1½ years from an outside company; good product knowledge but in a tough market; inclined to sell on price; not a strong competitor—wants everyone to like him.

James. An old pro; age 49; lots of experience but needs occasional pumping up; not promotable; the mayor of his town; likes new products and new accounts.

Jaedeke. Recently made SM; too new to judge; has an MBA, which he earned at night; very control oriented; sees the need to concentrate on key accounts and senior managers; well balanced; says he wants to get into marketing management soon; very sharp; should go a long way if handled well.

Modesto

Murphy. 24 years in the industry after a short career in insurance; once a DM but had a nervous breakdown; excellent salesman but very excitable; sees himself as a lady's man; separated from his wife; not fully reliable—some indication that he is slacking off.

Nimow. A new DM; doubles as SM; only three months on the job; has a strong sales background and leads by doing; seems to be a good planner; thorough; tends to be impatient if things don't go his way.

Morris. A new man; just finished his training; college degree; age 24; his father owned and operated a small center but sold out five years ago; seems to be floundering.

Sales Management

The Henderson company's hiring procedures were somewhat a function of local management. Although headquarters set some broad parameters, the district managers were pretty much left to their own. Consider, for example, the remarks of one district manager:

> We hire salesmen primarily through employment agencies. They often have no prior steel experience, though some do. Few even have sales experience; usually they know nothing about sales. We don't require a college degree or screen them with a sales test. What we look for is ambition and good recommendations. Does he want to succeed? The outside salesperson alone is responsible for the territory. Most sales managers, on the other hand, have been with the company many years, since we promote from within.

The training of a new salesperson was supposed to consist of six weeks in the shop learning terminology and the production processes used at Henderson. The content and duration of training varied greatly with the individual managers. Some managers gave trainees two weeks in the plant, some outside selling time, and then four weeks again in the plant. Other managers used six weeks in the plant. One salesman reported that he spent 12 weeks training in the plant, followed by one week each in the credit, billing, and inventory departments. Upon completing the training, the new salesman moved into inside sales. It was not unusual for competition to hire the new employee after his training was completed—at least this was an ongoing threat because a good labor force was at a premium in the industry.

Territorial assignments were largely a function of local needs. A new person might move into an unexpected assignment because of some sudden emergency (i.e., salesperson turnover was 25 percent a year), or territory boundaries might be changed to accommodate a new multilocation account. By and large, however, a salesperson was assigned to a geographic area containing between 500 and 2,500 potential customers and with an industry mix that reflected the local economy.

Sales quotas were established early and were arrived at by adding 10 percent to the person's last year's sales. The marketing vice president recognized that this was a simplistic approach (in fact, the 10 percent figure was only an average; the vice president would vary it by territory depending upon local requirements), but he took comfort in the fact that the resulting target closely reflected what the organization *could* do. Actual results over the years had been remarkably close to the 10 percent average increase, and the firm seemed to be gaining market share (though there were no real data to measure this relative gain).

Sales compensation was tied to the quota. Each person received a salary and a quarterly commission based upon quota. Between 80 and

90 percent of quota, the commission was $10 times the percentage over 80 percent but under 90 percent; $30 between 90 and 100 percent; $35 between 100 percent and 120 percent, and $10 over 120 percent. If a person hit 129 percent of quota during a three-month period, therefore he would receive:

$$\begin{aligned}
\$10 \times 10 &= \$ \quad 100 \\
\$30 \times 10 &= \quad 300 \\
\$35 \times 20 &= \quad 700 \\
\$10 \times 9 &= \quad \underline{90} \\
\text{Total} \quad &= \$1,190
\end{aligned}$$

At 98 percent of quota his commission was:

$$\begin{aligned}
\$10 \times 10 &= \$100 \\
\$30 \times 8 &= \quad \underline{240} \\
\text{Total} \quad &= \$340
\end{aligned}$$

One hundred percent of quota was the expected sales target and represented the "10 percent average over last year" previously described. It was hoped that the typical salesperson would earn about 10 percent of salary in bonus.

Sales supervision, as explained, was centered in the local sales manager, who was both salesperson and supervisor. Normally, however, the sales manager carried a lighter customer load than the full-time salespeople. One manager had this to say about his position:

> I don't think a sales manager can also be his own salesman. Our outside salespeople deserve more attention than I can give them. For example, I don't get out often enough to see other customers. I want to travel more with the sales force, and I plan to. I try to have fewer short sessions with them in favor of longer talks.
>
> Now, Tom Henderson thinks the sales manager can also act as salesman. I'm one reason he thinks so. Sales here have gone up since I took over as sales manager. But I'm the only one who knows I am not doing justice to either job. Our sales are good, but they could be even better. Somewhere between supervising three and seven salespeople, a sales manager becomes necessary. I work hard to do both jobs.

Some Alternatives

As he reviewed his sales strategy, Mr. Henderson singled out a number of issues.

1. Deployment. Was the company's policy of assigning salespeople contiguous geographic areas the best one? After all, the buying habits of the various segments were different, and some salespeople seemed better equipped to sell to sophisticated buyers, while others were at home with more mundane accounts, such as contractors or farmers. Some people were more comfortable in small-town, small-company environments, while others thrived on the big, complex situations. Finally, it was apparent that different salespeople preferred different tasks. For some, prospecting was the challenge. For others, it was developing more business from existing accounts. A few liked to work with development engineers and others with the more commercial side of the customer's operation.

Without even considering the economics of various territory assignment alternatives, Mr. Henderson pondered what were the best overall ways to organize in today's markets? What were the fundamental advantages and disadvantages of each variation?

A part of the development problem was the additional fact that company sales were concentrated. To be exact, volume was distributed as follows:

	Percent of customers	Percent of sales
Largest 20 percent		78.5%
Next 30 percent		12.5
Remaining 50 percent		9.0

This concentration was typical of all of the district offices. In fact, out of ±10,000 customers throughout the company, 250 represented 60 percent of the sales, while the smallest 2,000 averaged only $500 per year. They represented, on the other hand, 18 percent of the calls.

2. Training and Career Development.   A 25 percent turnover of salespeople struck Mr. Henderson as expensively high. He could figure the initial costs of hiring and training a new employee at $18,000. Nor did it make sense that his company should invest heavily in the selection and training of a new salesperson only to have competition raid his ranks with alarming degrees of success. Somehow the company had to convince the new hires that a few more dollars from a competitive firm were a poor trade-off for Henderson's generous retirement and benefit plans. Henderson wondered if more detailed individual career development programs would alleviate the problem and whether ongoing training couldn't be more specifically tied into additional job responsibilities and salary increases. In short, how could Mr. Henderson structure the job, compensation, and career development steps in order to attract and hold superior sales candidates?

One of his friends in the industry sent Tom a summary of a personnel development program that he was using. Excerpts are included below, and Tom wondered whether he should adopt a similar program, one which his friend estimated would add 50 percent to the costs of the normal training program:

Personnel Development Program

The objective of this memorandum is to establish a minimum program to be used in developing new salespeople. The requirements should be expanded to meet the needs of the individual district. For example, those districts with light fab, slitting, etc., should include training in those areas.

The requirements shown should be completed within the time frame of the program, and all portions of one step, including the time involved, must be completed before the change in title is certified.

The district manager will be responsible for arranging outside training, which will have to be adapted to what is available in each area.

Special attention should be directed throughout the program to developing selling skills. Reading material pertaining to products and the industry should be available.

A conference with the district manager is required at the completion of each step of the personnel development program.

Sales trainee—I.	0 to 4 months
Sales trainee—II	5 to 8 months
Sales trainee—III.	9 to 12 months
Salesperson.	Completion

The summary went on to detail each step, listing the specific activities, tasks, and assignments required of the trainees before they could be certified for the next step. Salary adjustments were dependent upon the separate steps. To illustrate, the details under "Sales Trainee I" follow:

STEP 1   0 to 4 Months
A.   Company Orientation
    1.   Salary and review date.
    2.   Insurance programs.
    3.   Savings plan.
    4.   Retirement program.
    5.   Vacations and holidays.
    6.   Safety program.
    7.   Personnel development program written test.
The manager of employee relations will furnish a written test concerning these programs. Completion of this phase will be upon recommendation of the department head and certification by the district manager.

B. Plant Experience
1. People identification.
2. Equipment identification.
3. Equipment capacities.
4. Material identification.
5. Receiving systems.
6. Storage systems.
7. Delivery experience.
8. Order paper flow procedures.

Completion of these requirements will be upon recommendation of the plant superintendent and department head. Certification will be required by the district manager.

3. Future Managers.   Closely related to the problem of salesperson retention was that of preparing a cadre of managers suited to the environment of the 1980s. It was Tom Henderson's conviction that the manager of tomorrow would have to be a true professional—able to think for herself or himself, to strategize, to work with profit models, to analyze, and to lead a group of better trained subordinates.

Would such requirements permit the traditional policy of promotion from within, or should the company begin to go outside for highly talented individuals? It was possible to spot attractive candidates from outside the industry, but whether the risk of force-feeding them upon the existing culture was worthwhile was unclear. To avoid this risk, why wouldn't it be possible for Tom to retrain current managers to fit the new pattern? Such a move would, of course, require a special training effort—one which would be costly and which might or might not work.

4. Quotas and Compensation.   The quota system, as described, concentrated upon experience (10 percent over last year). Why not, wondered Tom, include some measures of potential? After all, the quality of a particular level of performance was a function of both experience *and* potential. It should be possible, he thought, to qualify quotas by such potential measures as industrial activity, level of employment per district, freight car loadings, and changes in employment. If the company were to include such variables, how should they be worked into the present system? How much weight should be placed upon experience? Upon potential?

And even more critical, if there were changes made in the quotas, how should the salespeople be paid? Was straight salary to be preferred, or did there need to be an incentive payment? Similar or different from what now existed?

Another friend of Tom's had suggested a simple diagram for thinking out the problem of compensation (Exhibit 7).

Exhibit 7

Payment alternatives \ Tasks and relative importance	1 To maintain sales* 40%	2 To open new accounts* 30%	3 To sell full line* 20%	4 To supply intelligence* 10%
Salary	$?		$?	
Commission		$?		
Contests				
Bonus		$?		
Expense Accounts				$?
Profit Share				
Other				
			$?	
Dollars for Each Task	$8,000	$6,000	$4,000	$2,000

Note: Total Expected Pay = $20,000.
* Assumed for this example only.

First, you must decide how much the "average salesperson doing an average job" should earn. In this illustration, it was $20,000 as seen at the bottom right. Across the top, the key salesperson jobs and their relative values were listed. Hence, the $20,000 pie was allocated across the tasks. Finally, all of the possible payment techniques were enumerated vertically. The dollars and payment methods were then matched by asking "How do I best pay for this task, and how much?" Obviously a particular task might warrant more than one payment technique.

The resulting matrix would form the base for telescoping the various payment alternatives into a simpler, less complicated compensation plan. But at least the implications of each sales task and the ideal way of paying for it would have been considered.

5. Organization. It was clear, as pointed out earlier, that company growth had come principally from acquisition. Was it possible, considered Tom, to reorganize so as to develop more market share in the existing districts?

For example, would it help to have product managers or even key account managers? After all, business was concentrated both in selected products and customers. Wouldn't specialization in one or both of those dimensions result in better account penetration? But is such a move were to be made, Tom was concerned about how such a modification could be built into the existing structure. Moreover, he estimated that the incremental costs of new managers would be about $60,000 each.

From a field management vantage point, there was the ongoing question of whether the sales managers should supervise and sell, or supervise alone. It was easy to say that supervision was the critical function, but the economics of small districts made it tough to support sales managers who only managed. As the senior salespeople in their territories, their customer know-how was so great that Tom hesitated to set it aside. Could a full-time manager, in other words, pay his own way when he had only two or three salespeople to lead? How best could his job be structured?

6.   Product Lines.   Finally, Tom thought it important to reconsider his product policies. Specialists were growing as were price-oriented brokers and purveyors of secondary lines. Could Henderson hope to survive unless his firm somehow insulated the impact of these competitors from its major markets? Should the company work with one or more of these specialists, become one, or fight them?

Tom knew that he had raised a number of hard questions. It wasn't easy to answer them, but he thought that a good starting point would be to evaluate the effectiveness of his present strategy and to match that strategy against the needs of the marketplace.

C A S E 6–2

Houston Petroleum Company

"Congratulations, Joe," said Phil Keller, a regional credit manager for the Houston Petroleum Company. "Your new assignment to the Watertown sales district is a good promotion." Joe Smith was the district sales manager of Houston's small River Bend sales district and had recently received word of his promotion to Watertown. "Just think" Phil continued, "old Dick Owen has finally reached retirement age. Forty-two years is a lot of service."

The Houston Petroleum Company, a large and well-established oil distributor, operated in Texas, Oklahoma, and Louisiana. The company's Marketing Division was divided into wholesale and retail departments. Both the River Bend and Watertown districts were part of the wholesale marketing department.

Wholesale distribution involved all customers not buying through service stations of the retail marketing department. Customers included farmers, contractors, truckers, and manufacturing and commercial establishments. The three-state marketing area was divided into regions, which in turn were organized into sales districts. As shown in Exhibit 1, a sales district was a purely line organization; staff support was centralized at the regional headquarters.

District organizations varied depending on the business density and volume of the area served. Typically, however, districts consisted of some 10 bulk plants or depots, a majority of which were operated on a commission basis. Facilities included storage tanks for gasoline and diesel products and a warehouse for lubricating oils, greases, and other packaged materials. Tank trucks distributed Houston products from the local bulk plant to the customer, although certain customers with large requirements and adequate storage were served direct from the

Exhibit 1

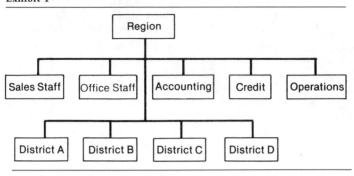

refinery or major distribution terminal. The company owned bulk plant facilities and leased them to commission agents.

A sales manager headed each district, but staffing below that level again depended on the size and nature of the area. Assistant sales managers were assigned to larger districts. An average-sized district employed two to three wholesale salespeople, a fuel and lubricant engineer, and the necessary operating personnel to receive, store, and deliver the products. All operating personnel engaged in some way in direct contact with customers. Office personnel sold to walk-in customers, while truck drivers delivered and sold products from tank trucks. Job titles and brief job descriptions of all district positions follow:

> **District Sales Manager.** Manages the activities of the sales district and administers established policies and procedures relating to sales, delivery, accounting, credit operations, and personnel to secure a representative portion of the available business at maximum realization and minimum operating cost.
>
> **Assistant District Sales Manager.** Assists the district sales manager in managing the activities of the sales district and administering established policies and procedures relating to sales, delivery, accounting, credit, plant operations, and personnel to secure a representative proportion of the available business and maximum realization at minimum operating cost.
>
> **Fuel and Lubricant Engineer.** Provides technical and specialized solicitation and service to accounts which require full engineering help, technical service, and experienced assistance beyond the ability of the general sales organization, through one or a combination of the following activities: (1) solicitation of all product requirements and servicing of accounts requiring constant fuel and lubricant engineering effort beyond the ability of other sales positions; (2) furnishing regularly assigned support to other sales positions on accounts requiring a high degree of fuel and lubricant engineering effort; or (3) providing on-call technical spe-

cialized service to accounts requiring fuel and lubricant engineering effort at intermittant or infrequent intervals.

Wholesale Salesperson. Responsible for sale of the full line of products and related services to an assigned group of accounts (both Houston and competitve) within a designated area. Keeps constantly alert to the entrance of new accounts into the field and programs solicitation efforts to best serve such accounts. As appropriate, and when so directed, performs designated administrative and clerical functions closely related to sales and operations.

Office Salesperson. Directs and performs plant sales and clerical work for the district sales manager. In the absence of the district sales manager, acts as a company representative at the station and coordinates station activities. Responsible for meeting standards in the preparation of reports, records, and correspondence; for accurate advice to customers on products, prices, and sales policies; for securing maximum orders from each customer contacting the plant; and for direction of warehouse and delivery functions as required to coordinate station activities.

Assistant Office Salesperson. As a primary function, i.e., at least 25 percent of the time, performs one or a combination of the following duties: (1) taking orders and soliciting business at the counter and over the phone; advising customers on product characteristics, applications, prices and sales, operating or credit policies; (2) performs negotiation-type credit control duties, such as soliciting payments on accounts from customers on the phone or in person; (3) dispatches delivery trucks. Responsible for giving accurate information to customers and for completing assigned clerical and operating duties accurately and expeditiously.

Head Route Salesperson. Operates a small sales office and bulk plant at a location remote from the district sales office to provide service and facilities for the receipt, storage, sale, and delivery of bulk and packaged petroleum products in the area. Performs all functions involved in the receipt, storage, and delivery of packaged and bulk petroleum products. Responsible for plant and operations, safety practices; solicits business of regular and new accounts; collects and arranges for banking of funds; performs accounting functions; prepares sales, stock, credit, personnel and accounting forms, reports, and necessary correspondence.

Route Salesperson. Delivers company products by tank, combination, or package truck to accounts within an assigned area or an assigned route. Loads or assists in loading trucks, drives truck, delivers product from truck, collects for product at the time of delivery or in accordance with established line of credit. Accounts for all products and funds handled. Reports any pertinent competitive activities observed. Services the truck.

The Job of the District Sales Manager

One of Houston's top wholesale marketing executives explained that: "The job of the district sales manager consisted of three basic functions—to make day-to-day operating decisions to keep the business running smoothly; to plan ahead, setting worthy objectives for each component of the organization, and to follow through to assure that progress actually made was in keeping with goals established; to train, counsel, and motivate the people comprising the organization."

Administering these functions required a number of skills on the part of the district sales manager. He maintained a good deal of the physical plant; he sought out and reported price actions by competitors; he assigned sales territories; he was the company representative in the community; he recommended personnel changes; and so forth. The regional office reserved final approval on price changes, hiring, wage, and salary matters, but the district sales manager initiated such recommendations.

Forms for recording district activity were important to the manager in the effective discharge of basic responsibilities. Several served as the basis for recommendations to regions. For example, Exhibit 2 shows the form used for determining the delivery work load for the route salesperson. The district sales manager used this information periodically to reapportion the work load within the district or to recommend additional personnel to the region.

Sales personnel were expected to record available business information on the customer data sheet, D102 (Exhibit 3). This form provided up-to-date data on the pertinent circumstances surrounding each account, including responsibility for solicitation. Form D105 (Exhibit 4), the account change card, kept the manager informed on sales gains and losses. District managers varied in their insistence on current maintenance of these forms. Some felt that this attention to detail was burdensome and not overly productive, while others insisted that the reported information was their only way of keeping aware of district activity.

The commission agents submitted monthly operating and financial statements which the sales managers were to evaluate and use in consultation with the agents. Agents had no formal business training and relied greatly on the supervision of the district sales manager.

The regional office provided the district with information compiled by three staff services. Form R30, for instance, reported cumulative monthly sales results by product for the district and its components. Form R31 showed the number of accounts to which credit had been extended. Form R35 provided expenses per gallon delivered.

The Watertown District

Following several trips to the Watertown District, Joe wondered just what his course of action would be on assuming his new duties. Dick

Exhibit 2
Tank Truck Performance Analysis

1	2	3	4	5	6	7	8	9	10	11	12
Truck no.	Capacity	Gals. delv'd	No. of loads	No. of del'ys	Miles run	Loads at 25/min.	Deliveries at 20/min.	Drive at 20 mph	Total (7 + 8 + 9)	Office, plant solic. etc.	Total hours required

The following indicates the source of data entered in columns 1, 2, 3, 4, 5, and 6 and the basis as well as method of computation of figures entered in columns 4, 7, 8, 9, 10, and 11:

Column 1   *Truck Number*
From Statement of Miles Run by Motor Equipment—D123.

Column 2   *Capacity*
If the exact truck capacity in gallons is not known, average capacities can be used, i.e., 750 for T1, 950 for T2, 1,250 for T3, and 1,650 for T4.

Column 3   *Gallons Delivered*
From Statement of Miles Run—D123.

Column 4   *Number of Loads*
Divide gallons delivered (col. 3) by truck capacity (col. 2).

Column 5   *Number of Deliveries*
From Statement of Miles Run—D123.

Column 6   *Miles Run*
From Statement of Miles Run—D123.

Column 7   *Loading*
Multiply col. 4 by 0.42 (the fractional hour equivalent of 25 minutes per load). For package trucks, full loads, multiply col. 4 by 1 hour.

Column 8   *Delivering*
Divide col. 5 by 3 (hourly equivalent of 20 minutes per delivery—a liberal average for all types of deliveries).

Column 9   *Driving*
Divide col. 6 by 20 (average truck speed under normal operating conditions).

Column 10 *Total of Loading, Delivery and Driving Time.*

Column 11 *Office, Plant, Solicitation, Collection, and Miscellaneous*
Multiply col. 10 by 0.28, which is the standard percentage of tank truck work load time allowed for these functions. (The office and plant standard allowance to handle daily turn-ins, checking orders, servicing and garaging equipment, etc., is 40 minutes a day. Allowance for solicitation, collection, and miscellaneous is 60 minutes per day. This total, plus 20 minutes for personal time, reduces the average available time for delivery operations to 360 minutes. One hundred minutes is 28 percent of 360 minutes.)

Exhibit 3
Customer Data Sheet—D102

ASSIGNED TO:		CALLS ASSIGNED	NAME				
			LOCATION				
SUPPORTED BY:			HEADQUARTERS				
			TYPE OF BUSINESS				
			EQUIP. OPERATED: PASS. CARS.	TRUCKS	TRACTORS	NO. CREDIT CARDS	
			OTHER EQUIP.:				

KEY PERSONNEL—SPECIAL DATA—CONTRACT INFO.-ETC.		ANNUAL AVAILABLE BUSINESS					
		PRODUCT	STGE. TANKS	TOTAL	HOUSTON	COMPETITIVE	CO.
		GASOLINE (GALS.)					
		DIESEL (GALS.)					
		FURNACE (GALS.)					
		STOVE/KERO. (GALS.)					
		AUTO OILS (GALS.)					
		AUTO LUBS./GRS. (LBS.)					
		INDUSTRIAL OILS (GALS.)					
		INDUSTRIAL GRS. (LBS.)					
		THNRS./SOLVS. (GALS.)					
		WAXES (LBS.)					
		OTHER SPECIAL PRODUCTS (GALS.)					
		TOTAL LIGHT PRODUCTS					

CALLS MADE	JAN.	FEB.	MAR.	APR.	MAY	JUNE	JULY	AUG.	SEPT.	OCT.	NOV.	DEC.

Owen had been at Watertown for 29 years and appeared to be an established part of the community. Joe noted during visits at several service clubs that Dick knew nearly all the town's businesspeople. In fact, at one time or other, Dick had served as president of several of the organizations.

Also going through Joe's mind was the material he had encountered at a recent administrative functions course for district sales managers held at Houston's home office in Dallas. Joe had not been back at River Bend long enough to really apply the material, but he recalled how they had covered the basic management responsibilities of planning, organizing, directing, coordinating, and controlling.

The Watertown district spread over a large area, with a concentration of business activity and population as shown on the map in Exhibit 5. Petroleum and related needs were diversified to the extent that the portion south of the Blue River was highly industrialized, while to the north the mainstay was agriculture. District population figures

Exhibit 4

ACCOUNT CHANGE						CONTRACTS IN EFFECT (IF GAINED, WHAT TYPE SIGNED: IF LOST, WHAT PAPER IN EFFECT):

DISTRICT _____ OFFICE _____ DATE _____

NAME OF ACCOUNT _____

TYPE OF BUSINESS

PRODUCT	ANNUAL REQUIRE-MENTS	VOLUME GAINED LOST	DISTRIBUTION OF REQUIREMENTS AFTER CHANGE		COMPET. GAINED FROM OR LOST TO
			HOUSTON	COMPET.	
Gasoline-gals. Motor Aviation					
Diesel fuel-gals.					
Furnace oil-gals. Stove oil-gals.					
Kerosene-gals.					
Fuel oil-gals.					
Auto oils-gals.					
Auto grease-lbs.					
Ind. oils-gals.					
Ind. greases-lbs.					
Thinners and solvents-gals.					
Liquified pet. gases-gals.					
Other: gals. or lbs.					

REASON FOR GAIN OR LOSS _____

Sales Rep. _____
Office Manager_____
District Manager_____
D105

IF ACCOUNT LOST, WHAT ACTION TAKEN TO REGAIN: _____

SHOULD APPRECIATION LETTER BE SENT TO ACCOUNT?
Yes ☐ No ☐

CHANGES IN KEY PERSONNEL, SUBSIDIARIES, ETC.: _____

recorded at 321,000 in 1974 had reached 400,000 in 1978 and were projected to 675,000 in 1990. This growth was based primarily on expected personnel requirements for new business establishments moving into the area. The following figures show new plant construction since 1974:

Number of New Plants and Expansions (and of capitalization—000,000)

1974.	55 ($10.5)
1975.	82 ($12.0)
1976.	99 ($15.0)
1977.	153 ($24.6)
1978.	176 ($35.1)

Fabricated metal products manufacturers ranked first in number of firms, followed by electrical machinery, chemicals, and food and kindred products. Active promotion of five major industrial parks promised a continuation of this trend. Navigable waters along the Blue River, adequate rail and trucking facilities, and moderate year-round weather were considered basic attractions to new plant growth.

Exhibit 5
Geography of Watertown Sales District

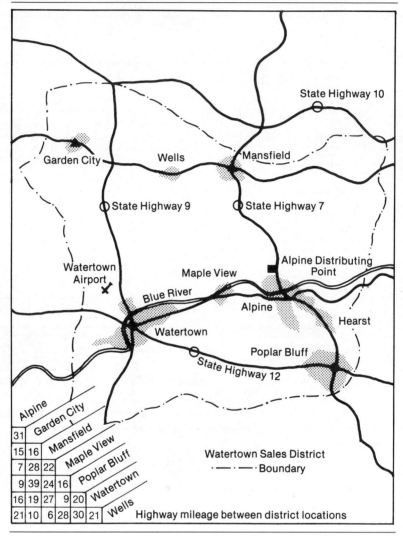

With the increase in population and industrialization, the area within the district devoted to agriculture had been declining over the past five years. However, mechanical efficiencies in farming and an improved price structure in 1978 helped achieve a record value of $16.5 million for agricultural production. Flowers, vegetables, and livestock accounted for the major share of the total.

Watertown, the heart of the area's heavy industrial growth, was the home of the district office and main salaried sales office. Encouraged by liberal zoning laws, "smoke-stack" type operations had increased 40 percent over the last five years. A new 300-acre industrial park was to open soon near the city.

There were four rather sizable airports in the sales district—located at Watertown, Alpine, Poplar Bluff, and Garden City. The Watertown Airport, five miles outside city limits, was the largest, providing facilities for commercial and private aircraft. The district had been successful in establishing dealerships at each of these airports. Bulk storage facilities at the Watertown Airport were under supervision of the district sales manager and required the services of four warehouse-workers.

A smaller salaried sales office was located 20 miles from Watertown, in the city of *Poplar Bluff*. This was primarily a residential center, but a recently developed light industrial tract had brought 20 new manufacturing firms to the city within the past two years. Commercial establishments, warehousing facilities, and some farming rounded out the activities of the area. Several large accounts were important in maintaining the gallonage position at this station. The light industrial plants, in general, were not large users of petroleum products.

The city of *Alpine*, served by a commission agent, was involved in an overnight transition from an agricultural-commercial economy to one centered around light industry. Electronics and precision-type manufacturing firms were predominant in the area. At the time, industrial sites covering 250 acres were being sold along the Blue River, with reports that actual sales and inquiries had already exceeded expectations. Keeping pace with industrial growth, the city's population, now at 50,000, had doubled in the past five years. Joe was visiting the Watertown office when it was learned that Mac McMurtry, a commissioned distributor for Houston's largest Alpine competitor, was going to retire in several months. McMurtry had always been a leader in Alpine (mayor, city council, etc.) and was held in high esteem by many accounts in the area. A salaried plant was scheduled to replace the old operation.

Garden City and *Mansfield* were both unincorporated farming centers served by commission agents. The total number of agricultural accounts had been declining over the last three years due to the failure of the marginal operators to keep up with new farm innovations. However, those still in business were producing larger quantities through use of more and more mechanized equipment. The Garden City area showed the most promise in terms of agricultural growth, while the future of Mansfield was uncertain. Recent plans for improving Highway 7 and the low cost of land had attracted the interest of several real estate promoters to the Mansfield area. One manufacturing firm had already constructed plant facilities near Mansfield, and from all reports, its management was quite happy with the results.

An organization chart for the Watertown Sales District is shown in Exhibit 6.

Exhibit 6
Watertown Sales District Organization Chart

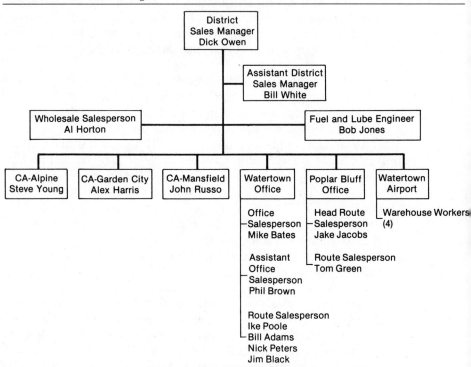

Exhibit 7 shows the district's 1978 market position in terms of number of accounts and percent of gallonage for both motor gasoline and diesel sales. These figures were developed from existing customer data sheets, Form D102, which admittedly had received very little attention from the district sales manager. Comparable figures for prior years had never been developed. Some picture of district growth, however, can be gained from a composite of the $31 credit statements. Quarterly and yearly averages of accounts to which credit had been extended are shown in Exhibit 8 for the last four years.

Sales results for the district and its components are shown in Exhibit 9 for the period covering 1976–78. Dick set the district goals for

Exhibit 7
Houston Petroleum Company Market Position, 1978 (by number of accounts and percent of gallonage)

Watertown district (5,000 gal. per year and over)

Company	Motor gasoline CA & I No. of accounts	Motor gasoline CA & I Percent of gallonage	Motor gasoline Other No. of accounts	Motor gasoline Other Percent of gallonage	Diesel fuels CA & I No. of accounts	Diesel fuels CA & I Percent of gallonage	Diesel fuels Other No. of accounts	Diesel fuels Other Percent of gallonage
Houston	244	38.3	8	34.1	69	30.6	2	12.3
Company A	61	14.7	2	11.7	18	15.3	1	5.5
Company B	95	25.7	—	—	20	19.8	—	—
Company C	86	11.3	6	19.0	16	5.6	—	—
Company D	6	1.1	11	25.5	5	20.1	1	54.3
Company E	10	2.4	2	2.3	1	.5	1	27.9
Other	55	6.5	2	7.4	11	8.1	—	—
Accounts available	557		31		140		5	
Total gallonage	8,918,800		1,118,400		2,776,700		107,200	

Watertown office (5,000 gal per year and over)

Company	Motor gasoline CA & I No. of accounts	Motor gasoline CA & I Percent of gallonage	Motor gasoline Other No. of accounts	Motor gasoline Other Percent of gallonage	Diesel fuels CA & I No. of accounts	Diesel fuels CA & I Percent of gallonage	Diesel fuels Other No. of accounts	Diesel fuels Other Percent of gallonage
Houston	81	46.1	3	24.3	27	25.7	—	—
Company A	14	15.8	1	16.0	7	7.9	—	—
Company B	56	25.3	—	—	7	20.9	—	—
Company E	5	2.5	—	—	1	1.0	1	34.1
Company C	19	6.4	3	26.4	3	4.1	—	—
Company D	1	.9	6	22.6	3	36.4	1	65.9
Other	16	3.0	1	10.7	2	4.0	—	—
Accounts available	192		14		44		2	
Total gallonage	5,009,000		409,000		1,515,000		88,000	

Exhibit 7 (concluded)

| | Motor gasoline | | | | Diesel fuels | | | |
| | CA & I | | Other | | CA & I | | Other | |
Company	No. of accounts	Percent of gallonage	No. of accounts	Percent of gallonage	No. of accounts	Percent of gallonage	No. of accounts	Percent of gallonage
Poplar Bluff Office (5,000 gal. per year and over)								
Houston	27	25.6	1	70.8	3	17.0	1	100
Company A	13	14.1	1	26.4	5	49.3	—	—
Company B	3	8.2	—	—	—	—	—	—
Company F	4	5.4	—	—	1	19.7	—	—
Company G	3	10.8	—	—	1	9.8	—	—
Company C	23	28.5	—	—	3	4.2	—	—
Other	2	7.4	1	2.8	—	—	1	—
Accounts available	75		3		13		1	
Total gallonage	1,980,000		212,000		507,000		12,000	
Alpine (1,200 gal. per year and over)								
Houston	34	23.0	2	24.0	6	48.5	1	100
Company A	16	13.9	—	—	3	5.3	—	—
Company B	35	38.9	—	—	13	41.3	—	—
Company C	31	12.9	2	20.4	2	3.2	—	—
Company D	5	2.3	5	48.5	2	1.7	—	—
Other	18	9.0	2	92.9	—	—	1	—
Accounts available	139		11		26		1	
Total gallonage	2,391,000		416,000		562,000		13,000	

Mansfield (1,200 gal. per year and over)

Company	Gasoline CA & I No. of accounts	Gasoline CA & I Percent of gallonage	Gasoline Other No. of accounts	Gasoline Other Percent of gallonage	Diesel fuels CA & I No. of accounts	Diesel fuels CA & I Percent of gallonage	Diesel fuels Other No. of accounts	Diesel fuels Other Percent of gallonage
Houston	49	52.8	—	—	10	62.1	—	—
Company A	5	7.5	—	—	5	12.2	—	—
Company F	6	10.1	—	—	3	6.2	—	—
Company C	10	29.6	1	100	7	19.5	—	—
Accounts available	70		1		25		—	
Total gallonage	199,000		4,000		98,000		—	100

Garden City (1,200 gal. per year and over)

Company	Gasoline CA & I No. of accounts	Gasoline CA & I Percent of gallonage	Gasoline Other No. of accounts	Gasoline Other Percent of gallonage	Diesel fuels CA & I No. of accounts	Diesel fuels CA & I Percent of gallonage	Diesel fuels Other No. of accounts	Diesel fuels Other Percent of gallonage
Houston	53	76.6	2	100	23	43.3	1	
Company A	13	8.1			4	12.8		
Company F	11	8.3			4	6.9		
Company C	3	7.0			1	37.0		
Accounts available	81		2		32		1	
Total gallonage	239,800		17,400		94,700		1,200	100

Source: D-102. Excludes some company activities where minor sales involved.

Exhibit 8
Number of Accounts to Which Credit Has Been Extended

	1978	1977	1976	1975
District				
1st qtr.	701	648	730	677
2d qtr.	706	651	705	685
3d qtr.	721	659	680	685
4th qtr.	713	676	689	650
Year avg.	710	659	701	674
Watertown				
1st qtr.	223	177	188	167
2d qtr.	224	172	184	183
3d qtr.	238	173	174	177
4th qtr.	234	220	184	163
Year	230	186	182	172
Poplar Bluff				
1st qtr.	91	78	88	85
2d qtr.	88	83	81	86
3d qtr.	96	93	89	85
4th qtr.	93	81	87	79
Year	92	84	86	84
Alpine				
1st qtr.	123	119	148	121
2d qtr.	131	118	142	129
3d qtr.	132	130	135	129
4th qtr.	133	121	123	129
Year	130	122	137	127
Mansfield				
1st qtr.	93	84	112	104
2d qtr.	96	95	109	104
3d qtr.	94	96	111	104
4th qtr.	86	89	108	102
Year	92	91	110	103
Garden City				
1st qtr.	171	190	194	200
2d qtr.	167	182	189	183
3d qtr.	161	167	171	190
4th qtr.	167	165	187	178
Year	166	176	185	188

Source: R 31 (compiled through averaging obtain data by quarters).

1978 at a general increase over the 1977 results. Several large losses, as noted in the exhibit, resulted from situations over which the district had no control. Expenses, as listed in Exhibit 10, showed some improvement for the year. The large decrease per gallon at the Poplar Bluff plant related to the elimination of a route salesperson following a regular workload study.

Exhibit 9
Sales Results by Product, 1976–1978 (gallon)

District	1978	1977	1976
Motor gasoline:			
Agriculture..........................	413,211	410,733	423,592
Construction and contractor	675,031	518,116	634,570
Commercial and industrial	2,316,641	2,187,287	1,973,751
Jobbers	30,264	137,998	25,861
Government	429,345	146,052	179,462
Total	3,864,492	3,400,186	3,237,236
Auto diesel	126,705	114,517	114,100
Truck diesel........................	695,846*	1,083,705	877,275
Aviation gasoline.....................	18,699,930	18,961,370	16,483,800
Auto oils............................	113,000	118,899	112,000
Thinners and solvents.................	2,350,074	2,334,249	2,561,540
Refined wax........................	476,344	660,778	191,297
Total light products..................	26,326,937	26,673,704	23,577,248

Watertown Plant

	1978	1977	1976
Motor gasoline:			
Agriculture..........................	141,119	137,365	144,307
Construction and contractor	304,499	287,146	292,250
Commission and industrial	1,876,132	1,832,996	1,559,580
Jobbers	11,014†	125,015†	12,500
Government........................	209,300	100,105	50,674
Total	2,543,084	2,482,627	2,059,143
Auto diesel	76,443	78,388	82,647
Truck diesel........................	346,360	454,469	406,284
Auto oils............................	52,543	54,997	50,674
Thinners and solvents.................	2,046,644	2,149,941	2,180,938
Refined wax........................	367,334	264,037	287,653
Total light products..................	5,314,195	5,386,709	5,071,204

Poplar Bluff Plant

	1978	1977	1976
Motor gasoline:			
Agriculture..........................	8,934	12,699	8,710
Construction and contractor	136,126	94,674	96,852
Commission and industrial	173,003	168,020	164,412
Government	115,884	34,169	36,358
Total	433,547	309,562	306,332
Truck diesel........................	77,975‡	182,892	92,783
Aviation gasoline.....................	137,859	117,468	100,848
Auto oils............................	9,245	10,327	9,503
Thinners...........................	48,493	62,564	81,098
Total light products..................	743,474	694,813	602,564

Exhibit 9 *(concluded)*

Alpine

	1978	1977	1976
Motor gasoline:			
Agriculture	29,842	25,315	22,358
Construction and contractor	232,033	121,384	218,095
Commission and industrial	202,618	258,345	282,590
Jobbers	19,250	–0–	–0–
Total	483,743	405,044	523,043
Auto diesel	5,740	7,644	7,534
Truck diesel	191,378	351,600	269,199
Aviation gasoline	136,937	127,613	105,006
Auto oils	20,856	22,447	18,142
Thinners and solvents	253,776	145,277	230,305
Refined wax	10,010	49,737	20,013
Total light products	1,227,232	1,149,630	1,201,038

Mansfield

	1978	1977	1976
Motor gasoline:			
Agriculture	82,455	77,448	87,824
Construction and contractor	311	5,432	15,131
Commission and industrial	28,507	29,228	32,977
Total	111,273	112,108	135,931
Auto diesel	14,961	16,450	10,741
Truck diesel	40,879	49,092	81,668
Auto oils	3,122	3,220	4,720
Bottled gas	58,968	61,969	64,831
Total light products	203,082	211,544	270,628

Garden City

	1978	1977	1976
Motor gasoline:			
Agriculture	150,861	142,304	148,142
Construction and contractor	1,062	–0–	–0–
Commission and industrial	33,650	37,673	44,042
Government	13,800	2,400	2,111
Total	199,373	182,277	194,285
Auto diesel	21,766	3,871	3,377
Truck diesel	39,245	45,644	51,080
Aviation gasoline	28,640	25,844	25,413
Auto oils	4,043	4,274	4,067
Refined wax	99,000	61,600	64,000
Total light products	472,064	447,046	390,532

Watertown Airport

	1978	1977	1976
Aviation gasoline	18,396,500	18,690,445	16,252,433

* Lost (completed) highway contract—nonrecurring business.
† Gained and lost jobber—not under district or region control.
‡ Loss of large account—moved to other district.

Source: R 30, based on 10-month period.

Exhibit 10
Expenses per Gallon Delivered, 1977–1978*

	1977 (cents)	1978 (cents)
Total sales district:		
1st qtr.	3.34	3.06
2d qtr.	3.00	2.93
3d qtr.	3.20	2.75
4th qtr.	3.30	2.94
Year	3.21	2.92
Supervision/solicitation:		
1st qtr.	0.64	0.69
2d qtr.	0.57	0.58
3d qtr.	0.49	0.48
4th qtr.	0.56	0.57
Year	0.56	0.57
Plant cost—Watertown sales office:		
1st qtr.	1.05	0.71
2d qtr.	0.50	0.75
3d qtr.	0.82	0.86
4th qtr.	0.80	0.83
Year	0.79	0.79
Marketing delivery cost—Watertown sales office:		
1st qtr.	2.07	1.90
2d qtr.	1.78	1.72
3d qtr.	2.04	1.47
4th qtr.	1.95	1.70
Year	1.96	1.70
Total cost—Watertown sales office:		
1st qtr.	3.12	2.61
2d qtr.	2.28	2.47
3d qtr.	2.86	2.33
4th qtr.	2.75	2.53
Year	2.75	2.49
Plant cost—Poplar Bluff sales office:		
1st qtr.	0.78	0.51
2d qtr.	0.76	0.27
3d qtr.	0.72	0.42
4th qtr.	0.77	0.40
Year	0.76	0.40
Marketing delivery costs—Poplar Bluff sales office:		
1st qtr.	2.12	2.24
2d qtr.	2.15	2.04
3d qtr.	2.27	1.75
4th qtr.	2.17	2.01
Year	2.18	2.00
Total cost—Poplar Bluff sales office		
1st qtr.	2.90	2.75
2d qtr.	2.91	2.31
3d qtr.	2.99	2.17
4th qtr.	2.94	2.41
Year	2.94	2.40

Exhibit 10 *(concluded)*

	1977 (cents)	1978 (cents)
Total cost—commission agents:		
1st qtr.	1.99	1.89
2d qtr.	2.35	2.02
3d qtr.	2.35	1.89
4th qtr.	2.36	1.91
Year	2.26	1.93

* Excludes airport gallonage.

Source: R-35.

Credit collections for the district ran below company objectives of 75 percent current. Figures (dollars and accounts current) for September 1977 and September 1978 are indicative of the yearly results:

	September 1977		September 1978	
	Dollars	**Accounts current**	**Dollars**	**Accounts current**
District	$71	62	66	63
Watertown	77	68	71	70
Poplar Bluff	78	63	68	60
Alpine	75	54	63	60
Mansfield	52	48	53	50
Garden City	54	61	71	59

Source: CD-35.

Commission agent operations are outlined in Exhibit 11, which shows the number of employees, major expense items, gross commissions, total expenses, net commissions, commission rates, and equipment. Several monthly statements (Exhibit 12) are included for the operation at Mansfield. Realizing that such earnings would not support the distributorship, John Russo was paid, as a common carrier, for picking up and transporting the product needs for both his own and the Garden City operation. As part of the trucking business, Russo often hauled farm products for other members of the community. Such trips might cover a distance of 200 miles, with fertilizers often making up the load for the return haul. Russo's 22-year-old son tended the CA operations during these absences.

Dick Owen, the retiring district sales manager, had, during his tenure, advanced with the organizational changes of the company. His duties over the past 29 years had changed from agency manager to

Exhibit 11
Commission Agent Operations

	1976	Alpine 1977	1978
Gross commissions	$24,240	$23,395	$25,193
Expenses			
Salaries	$7,621	$7,986	$8,274
Gas and oil	1,225	1,091	1,294
Tires and batteries	195	178	329
Repairs	923	711	383
Rental	—	—	—
Deposits	2,136	637	323
License and tax	191	145	195
Insurance	723	769	774
Business license	56	130	126
Workman's compensation	103	190	138
Unemployment compensation tax	—	—	—
F.O.A.B.	201	147	173
Utilities	137	111	137
Postage	268	301	307
Telephone and teletype	572	390	409
Tool and supply	243	164	228
Dues and donations	212	231	194
Advertising	196	—	—
Dep. P & T	—	—	—
Storage deductions	—	—	—
W/D Allowance	739	13	—
Special allowance	—	—	—
Entertainment	381	548	680
Other	64	161	110
Total expenses	$16,186	$13,903	$14,074
Net commissions	$ 8,054	$ 9,492	$11,119

Commission rates	Cents	Equipment	Full-time employees
Airport and airline	1.10	1972 Dodge—710 gal.	1 at $500 per month
All other resale	1.10	1971 Ford—12 bbl.	
Government	.80	1976 Dodge—Pickup	
Other consumer—gasoline and kerosene	1.70		
Diesel/furnace and auto	1.35 + 0.2 = 1.55 cents gas oil		
Stove oil	1.45 + 0.2 = 1.65		

resident manager and finally district sales manager. He was alert, enthusiastic, and a good personal salesman. As a result of his long association in Watertown, he knew most of the accounts in the immediate area and often supplemented the solicitation efforts of other district employees. To make sure operations continued smoothly, Dick was quite active in checking on clerical details, handling many himself. He insisted on opening all the company mail as a precaution against missing any important correspondence.

Exhibit 11 *(continued)*

	1976	Garden City 1977	1978
Gross commissions.	$15,457	$14,464	$18,222
Expenses			
Salaries.	$3,900	$3,900	$5,608
Gas and oil.	650	574	721
Tires and batteries.	394	465	356
Repairs.	1,009	720	550
Rental	—	—	—
Deposits.	1,320	1,320	1,416
License and tax	217	175	342
Insurance	712	1,011	759
Business license	—	—	—
Workman's compensation	—	—	—
Unemployment compensation tax.	—	—	—
F.O.A.B.	—	—	—
Utilities.	144	144	145
Postage.	122	121	144
Telephone and teletype.	562	561	516
Tool and supply.	—	—	—
Dues and donations.	300	275	300
Advertising.	—	—	—
Dep. P & T	—	—	12
Storage deductions	87	115	54
W/D Allowance	—	—	—
Special allowance	—	—	47
Entertainment	—	—	—
Other.	—	—	—
Total expenses.	$ 9,417	$ 9,381	$10,970
Net commissions.	$ 6,040	$ 5,083	$ 7,252

Commission rates	Cents	Equipment	Full-time employees
Airport and airline*.	1.60	1977 Chev—970 gal.	1 at $457 per month
Government—all bulk products.	1.60	1966 Chev—930 gal.	
All other resale*	1.60	1969 Ford—Pickup	
Other consumer—gasoline and kerosene*.	2.10		
Diesel/furnace and auto*	1.95		
Stove oil*.	2.05		

The following people were relied upon to carry out district operations:

White-Collar Personnel

Bill White—Assistant District Sales Manager. Age 36, had been with the company 11 years and in his present position 3 years. Held a B.S. degree in engineering and started with Houston as a route salesperson. His ability was obvious, as he moved rapidly through the positions of head route salesperson, fuel and lubricant engineer, and regional specialist. As assistant district sales manager, he handled a number of accounts, which greatly relieved the load on the wholesale salesperson. He

Exhibit 11 *(concluded)*

	1976	Mansfield 1977	1978
Gross commissions............	$7,971	$6,812	$6,986
Expenses			
Salaries.....................	$1,597	$1,812	$1,956
Gas and oil..................	690	724	678
Tires and batteries...........	506	161	408
Repairs.....................	1,830	280	270
Rental......................	—	—	—
Deposits....................	564	564	654
Licenses and tax.............	132	150	138
Insurance...................	337	458	162
Business license.............	10	—	—
Workman's compensation.......	—	—	—
Unemployment compensation tax .	—	—	—
F.O.A.B.....................	—	—	—
Utilities....................	54	54	52
Postage....................	50	38	43
Telephone and teletype........	118	108	131
Tool and supply..............	73	53	29
Dues and donations...........	47	42	36
Advertising..................	27	—	—
Dep. P & T..................	—	—	—
Storage deductions...........	22	12	19
W/D Allowance...............	—	—	—
Special allowance............	—	—	—
Entertainment................	343	327	387
Other......................	114	178	9
Total expenses...............	$6,514	$4,961	$4,972
Net commissions.............	$1,457	$1,851	$2,014

Commission rates*	Cents	Equipment	Full-time employees†
All other resale...................	1.40	1969 Chev.—760 gal.	1 at $163 per month
Consumer—all gasoline		1968 Ford—Stake	
and kerosene...................	2.10	1972 De Soto—Sedan	
Diesel/furnace and auto............	1.95		
Stove oil.......................	2.05		

* Plus 50 cents TSC (temporary supplemental commission).
† Work load shows that TSCs not warranted.
‡ Paid to Pete Russo, John's son.

also took the responsibility for planning the activities of the fuel and lubricant engineer. Joe had formed the impression that Bill was not being used to his full capabilities and was not functioning within the proposed scope of the ADSM position.

Bob Walters—Fuel and Lubricant Engineer. Age 62, had been with the company 35 years and in his present position 16 years. A graduate engineer, he had held a previous position as a home office specialist. He was very conscientious but needed to be told exactly what to do, where

Exhibit 12
Monthly Statement for Mansfield, 1978

	June	July	August	September
Gross commissions	$607.35	$591.49	$608.06	$533.65
Expenses:				
Wages	163.13	163.13	163.13	163.13
General:				
Gas and oil	57.03	45.47	75.71	61.76
Tire and battery	53.48	156.06	—	—
Repairs	11.53	7.94	52.95	34.06
Depreciation	57.00	57.00	57.00	57.00
Licenses	2.40	2.36	2.61	2.22
Insurance	15.64	15.64	15.64	15.64
Utilities	13.85	24.98	18.82	25.27
Miscellaneous	7.89	—	—	—
Club dues	2.50	2.50	2.50	2.50
Advertising and entertainment	22.20	19.90	32.70	20.95
	$243.52	$331.85	$257.93	$219.40
Total expenses	$406.65	$494.98	$421.06	$382.53
Total net commissions	$200.70	$ 96.51	$187.00	$151.12

to be at a given time. The ADSM had set up certain days when the engineer was to be at stations in the district. He reported to the district office twice a week for instructions.

Al Horton—Wholesale Salesman. Age 60, with the company 35 years and in his present position 12 years. A high school graduate, previously a bottled gas salesman, he was considered to be a good salesperson and was energetic and enthusiastic. While not particularly effective in organizing his own time, once told to do something, he required little follow-up. He reported each day to the district office, left (about 9.30 A.M.) to make his calls, returned in the afternoon to set up appointments on the telephone, and then left again about 3.00 P.M. Al seemed to be left pretty much on his own in terms of planning his sales approach and setting up his calls for the day. Very little of his time was actually spent in the area north of the Blue River. Occasionally, when a problem was heard of through one of the commission agents, Dick would instruct him to take a run out and see what was taking place. According to both Dick and Al, the nature of these accounts did not warrant a more intensive solicitation effort.

Operating Personnel—Watertown Sales Office

Mike Bates—Office Salesperson. Age 32, with the company 10 years and in present assignment for the last 4 years. Had completed two years of college and seemed to possess the necessary qualifications for the job, although it was noted that he was not particularly exacting in his work. There was evidence that he needed training in the clerical aspects of his job, but this seemed to stem from the fact that he had not been delegated the full responsibility called for in this position. Normally Mike should have been the spokesperson for the rest of the operating personnel, but very seldom was he included in problem-solving or planning conferences held by Dick Owen.

Phil Brown—Assistant Office Salesperson. Fifty-nine years old, had been with the company 35 years and in his present assignment for the past six months. Previous positions included time as a field salesperson and head field salesperson. There were indications that he didn't work well under pressure and lacked knowledge of many company policies.

Ike Poole—Route Salesperson. 57 years old and had been with the company for 30 years in his present position. Performed his work well.

Bill Adams—Route Salesperson. 59 years old and had been with the company for 40 years as a field salesperson. Performed work well and required a minimum of supervision.

Nick Peters—Route Salesperson. Age 45, with the company as a field salesperson for 20 years. An energetic and enthusiastic worker with real concern for company welfare. Well acquainted with company policy and required little supervision.

Jim Black—Route Salesperson. Age 38, had been a field salesperson for 11 years. Had potential for position of head field salesperson or head office salesperson. Followed directions well.

It was noted that the work done by the above men consisted principally of delivering to accounts, taking orders, truck maintenance, etc. However, in terms of solicitation of new and existing small accounts, all needed development of sales desire and techniques. Few tangible results were being recognized from their efforts to gain new accounts or increase sales from present customers.

Personnel—Poplar Bluff Sales Office

Jake Jacobs—Head Route Salesperson. Age 58, had been with the company 38 years. Very energetic and conscientious. Required a minimum of supervision but did require occasional counseling from the district management. Noted as a good salesperson.

Tom Green—Route Salesperson. Fifty-eight years old and with the company 35 of these. Had no formal sales training, but was very alert to duties involving filling orders, maintenance, etc.

Commission Agents

Steve Young—Alpine. Fifty years old with eight years as agent. Was at one time a bottled gas salesperson for the company. Steve was sized up as a rather retiring individual and, while effective in selling agricultural accounts, he was not particularly suited to the growing industrial trend of his area. It was felt that he was making little effort to keep the district office posted on potential business that entered the area.

John Russo—Mansfield. Age 59, had been an agent for 15 years. Previously worked 15 years for the company. In addition to the low area potential, his operation was somewhat sloppily run. John did not seem to be particularly concerned with company welfare. Much of the area was of the same nationality and was extremely clannish. Consequently, there was danger that business could well follow the distributor rather than the company, should he become alienated. The present CA agreement was soon due to expire, and regional reports that always preceeded renewal of such contracts showed considerable weakness, particularly in the areas of plant maintenance and credit collections.

Alex Harris—Garden City. Fifty-eight years old, with 16 years as agent. Was head field salesperson at the same station before it was converted to an agency. Similar to John Russo, he had greatly tied up the area business in an extremely clannish community. Although he needed considerable supervision, the operation had always been independently profitable. Alex had always been very cooperative and receptive to suggestions.

As implied earlier, supervision of district functions was closely held by Dick Owens. Having grown with most of the local accounts, he seemed to feel that he owed personal attention to them. During one of the visits, Dick said to Joe, "I know everything that happens in this district. If I walk into the front office of any of our accounts here in Watertown, they know who I am. Knowing as much as I do about the accounts saves a lot of time in working with my sales personnel. Unless a special problem arises, it's very seldom that we have to sit down and plan an approach to a particular customer."

"One thing I've really limited," continued Dick, "is the use of sales meetings for district personnel. If you ask me, they are a pure waste of time; most people form a negative attitude when they are asked to attend these meetings. I see all of my white-collar people every day, and, believe me, the grapevine takes care of passing on information of interest to the operating personnel."

Apparently Dick was satisfied with the job being done by his sales force, as he spent relatively little time with them observing sales techniques. "If I play nursemaid to these people," he said, "they would never learn to go out on their own. Hell, I'll know anyway when one of them goofs up."

District sales coverage logically broke down into geographical areas, with the wholesale salesperson and fuel and lubricant engineer providing white-collar support to the entire district. Alpine, Poplar Bluff, Garden City, and Mansfield, with their relatively limited number of accounts, posed no real problem of area breakdown. Within the Watertown area, the responsibility of the four route salespersons was originally organized by geographical boundries. However, local revisions over a period of time had finally resulted in each route salesperson serving a certain list of accounts. This occurred as account status changed and Dick found it necessary to add or subtract gallonage as a

Exhibit 13
Route Salesperson Performance, 1977–1978

Route salesman	Miles run		Light products delivered (gallon)		Number of deliveries		Average gal./del.	
	1977	1978	1977	1978	1977	1978	1977	1978
Jim Black—T2—Capacity 850								
1st quarter	3,146	2,547	78,697	99,554	217	318	312	313
2d quarter	3,473	5,044	89,256	124,525	258	440	344	287
3d quarter	2,899	3,404	58,282	119,132	167	330	304	358
4th quarter	3,133	3,191	62,878	118,005	209	410	292	282
Year	12,651	14,186	289,113	461,216	851	1,498	313	310
Bill Adams—T2—Capacity 977								
1st quarter	2,719	1,963	114,693	141,621	406	431	281	328
2d quarter	2,664	2,113	127,813	157,392	457	484	280	325
3d quarter	2,687	2,182	127,633	176,900	451	629	283	283
4th quarter	2,369	2,023	120,889	177,000	452	590	252	300
Year	10,439	8,281	491,028	652,913	1,766	2,134	274	309
Ike Poole—T2—Capacity 814								
1st quarter	3,225	3,293	168,433	128,564	487	435	342	296
2d quarter	2,813	3,585	162,500	157,624	503	509	329	310
3d quarter	3,317	3,490	156,824	178,958	487	522	322	348
4th quarter	3,050	3,030	133,122	134,368	383	442	366	299
Year	12,405	13,398	620,879	599,514	1,860	1,908	340	313
Nick Peters—T3—Capacity 1,130								
1st quarter	2,360	3,457	157,020	126,627	449	408	351	288
2d quarter	1,970	3,938	166,070	158,651	435	430	375	369
3d quarter	2,178	3,688	162,693	170,154	452	520	339	329
4th quarter	3,033	4,462	152,109	157,885	474	468	299	358
Year	9,541	15,545	637,892	613,317	1,810	1,826	341	336
Composite	45,036	51,410	2,038,912	2,326,960	6,287	7,366	317	317

Source: D-123.

means of maintaining an equal work load for each salesperson. Finally, Jim Black was pulled off regular business and given the responsibility to service contractor accounts only. The net results of the shifting had been a composite of accounts for each salesperson which no longer followed the original geographical breakdown. A two-year record by route salespeople of miles run, gallons delivered, number of deliveries, and average gallons delivered is offered in Exhibit 13.

C A S E 6–3

Sierra Chemical Company

Jay Rossi, recently appointed as marketing vice president for the Sierra Chemical Company, was troubled about his firm's ability to execute an effective sales program. As he summarized, "Good sales management requires sales forecasts and reasonable cost estimates. Otherwise you can't price to value or control your profits. To do this you've got to get hold of your sales force." His reservations were based on the fact that even though sales growth seemed reasonable in dollars, unit volumes almost always fell short of forecasts. Moreover there was a primitive, at best, sales information system and almost no formal control mechanism. Hence, Jay really didn't know what sales to anticipate, what level of effort to require, what standards and evaluation criteria to apply. He was literally starting from ground zero. His task was complicated further by the fact that he was new to the industry and had no related market experience.

Sierra Products and Markets

Sierra produced and sold slow-release fertilizers, Osmocote and Agriform by name.[1] Pellet-like in form, similar to B-Bs, the products were coated with a patented rosin material. This coating had tiny pores which allowed small amounts of water to seep into the fertilizer ingredients, which then seeped out at a predictable rate (i.e., over two months, four months, six months, etc.). Product uniqueness was in the

---

This case was written by Professor Robert T. Davis, Graduate School of Business, Stanford University. It is based in part on his 1977 case of the same title. © 1983 by the Board of Trustees of the Leland Stanford Junior University.

[1] Agriform represented 10 percent of Sierra sales and was sold only as a landscape product; that is, it was bought by commercial landscapers. The same distributors handled this product as Osmocote, and it was sold by the same Sierra representatives. Hence, for the rest of this case, Agriform remains unmentioned but can be assumed to run parallel to Osmocote.

coating (the manufacturing process) and product form, not in the fertilizer. Fertilizer is primarily a standard commodity, consisting of varying proportions of nitrates, phosphates, and potassium. Growers buy different combinations, depending upon individual needs.

Growers could apply fertilizer three ways: by liquid feeding, dry application to the soil, or by slow release. The greatest tonnage of fertilizer was sold in dry form to agricultural markets and consisted of the three essential ingredients named above. Prices per ton were in the $100–$150 range.

Slow-release products were designed for specialty markets, not the huge field crops such as corn and wheat. There were four specialty markets: (1) nursery, (2) landscape, (3) row crops or agricultural (such as strawberries and tomatoes), and (4) retail. It was estimated that slow-release fertilizers were distributed in these four markets in the proportions 60 percent, 10 percent, 30 percent and negligible.

Slow-release fertilizers, needless to say, were not without competition in these markets. Growers often used dry and liquid alternatives, sometimes in combination. Most growers were convinced that they were experts at growing their particular product(s). Whether they used dry, liquid, or slow-release fertilizers was a function of their particular plants, prejudices, soil and weather conditions, and timing problems (i.e., did they want to "force bloom" roses for Mother's Day). It was not unusual, therefore, to find use of all three application techniques within a single establishment.

Liquid systems normally made use of local fertilizer ingredients. The problem with liquid systems was that they were continuous and many of the nutrients were washed or leached away. Dry fertilizers were limited by the fact that release was not controlled and application might be required several times during the season.

There were quite a few large companies in the dry, liquid, and slow-release fertilizer business. For example, firms like International Chemical, Scott, Swift, DuPont, and Hercules were important Sierra competitors. Urea Formaldehyde was a controlled-release product, as were some of Scott's items. Osmocote was the only product, however, which controlled the release of all three fertilizer ingredients.

It was estimated by Sierra management that slow-release products were gaining share in the total specialty markets and accounted for almost 30 percent of the nursery market in 1976. One out of four nursery plants was grown on Osmocote, and it was the only national label in its segment.

There were many reasons why growers accepted or rejected Osmocote. On the positive side:

1. It produced better plants—greener, healthier, faster, more consistently.

2. It was safer—reduced the chance of error (human or environmental).
3. It saved money—primarily in labor savings (compared to dry types) and in less raw material waste (compared to liquid feeds).

And on the negative side:

1. Its initial price was high—four times normal fertilizers and two times most slow-release types.
2. It was inflexible—once applied, it went! There was no way to slow it down, speed it up, or stop it.

Growers tended to be concentrated in southern California, northern California, and the Seattle-Portland belt; Florida, North Carolina, and Connecticut; and Texas, Wisconsin, and Ohio. Growers were reached through approximately 200 distributors, who carried thousands of items and regularly serviced their accounts. Manufacturers' salespeople, such as Sierra's, were supposed to establish and maintain distribution and do missionary selling among nurseries. For instance, in creating a new grower-user, it was essential that the grower be induced to set up some test plantings, measure the results, and compare these results with alternative fertilizing techniques. Distributor salespeople rarely were effective in this kind of selling; they were, essentially, sources of supply for already established users. Moreover, test plantings took time and effort.

The nursery business was heavily populated with "cottage type" operators. Large, 100-plus acre nurseries were important, but Sierra's real expansion has been among "start-ups" with one to five acres under shade but planning to add more each year. As a rule of thumb, each new acre was a potential one-ton sale for Sierra. There were several thousand such small operators.

Osmocote, by 1976, was the single most important specialty fertilizer on the market and was well known and well regarded among commercial growers and state extension agents. The agents were important product endorsers, since they were the acknowledged experts. Their "stamp of approval" was virtually mandatory, though approval by no means guaranteed purchase. A summary of the product lines and markets is contained in Exhibit 1 (company brochure).

Sales, by 1976, had reached 247,494 units or $4 million for the domestic market. The table below summarizes the Company's unit sales for 1976 and the previous five years, with 1977 forecasted:

Sales in Units (50-pound bags)*

	1971	1972	1973	1974	1975	1976	1977 (est.)
Domestic......	111,290	147,639	214,043	233,666	211,315	247,494	305,956
Foreign	6,932	6,659	22,900	47,834	36,028	82,600	104,000

* Included were sales of about $300,000 in small bags through professional nurseries to homeowners.

Exhibit 1

Osmocote® is the most economical, efficient controlled release fertilizer available.

Osmocote® provides a steady, continuous metering of N-P-K nutrients corresponding closely to the requirements of all nursery stock. This prolonged, constant feeding helps ensure an ideal level of nutrients for optimum plant growth.

One application of Osmocote® lasts for an entire crop cycle.

Osmocote® is available in a variety of formulations: 3 to 4 months, 8 to 9 months and 12 to 14 months. This offers the grower a nutrient release rate based on individual crop cycles.

Osmocote® is safe and efficient.

There is virtually no risk of burning plants with Osmocote® when used at recommended rates. Nutrients are released approximately 1% per day with the 3 to 4 month formulations, 0.4% per day with the 8 to 9 month formulations, and 0.25% per day with the 12 to 14 month formulation.

Osmocote® is economical.

There is less labor cost and management concerns involved with the use of Osmocote® because one application is sufficient for an entire crop cycle. And, since Osmocote® is resistant to leaching loss, the grower also saves on materials.

Osmocote® releases nutrients as plants need them.

The rate of nutrient release from Osmocote® is *not* significantly affected by:
•Soil moisture levels
•Total volume of water applied
•External salt concentration of the soil
•Soil pH
•Soil bacteria
   Nutrient release from Osmocote® is *only* affected by changes in soil temperature. The release rate increases as the soil warms, and decreases as the soil cools, therefore corresponding to plant needs.

Osmocote®

Product	Longevity	General Use	Specific Use
Osmocote 14-14-14	3-4 mo.	Greenhouse Nursery	Pot plants, bedding plants, foliage plants, nursery stock. For use in growing media containing no soil.
Osmocote 19-6-12	3-4 mo.	Greenhouse Nursery	For plants requiring high nitrogen. For use in growing media containing 25% soil or more.
Osmocote 18-6-12 Regular	8-9 mo.	Nursery	For all nursery stock. For propagation and establishment of young transplants. Spring, summer, or fall application.
Osmocote 18-6-12 Fast Start	8-9 mo.	Nursery	For use only with established, rapidly growing plants that require nutrients immediately. Spring, summer, or fall application.
Osmocote 18-5-11	12-14 mo.	Greenhouse Nursery	For mild climate, long season areas, spring and summer use on long term crops. Not generally used for fall feeding. For long term greenhouse crops (roses, carnations).
Osmocote 14-14-14 Retail Pack	3-4 mo.	Home & Garden	House plants, flowers, and vegetables.
Osmocote 18-6-12 Retail Pack	8-9 mo.	Home & Garden	House plants, flowers, and vegetables.

Agriform^T

Product	Longevity	General Use	Specific Use
Agriform 16-7-12-1 Iron	5-6 mo.	Landscaping	Turf, hydroseeding, flowers and ground covers, trees and shrubs.
Agriform 21-8-8	3-6 mo.	Landscaping	Maintenance of turf, ground cover and landscape plants.
Agriform 18-18-6	3-6 mo.	Landscaping	Establishment of turf, ground cover and landscape plants.
Agriform Planting Tablets			
Planting Tablets 20-10-5	24 mo.	Landscaping	New tree and shrub plantings, established trees and shrubs, liners, ground covers, and perennials.
Agriform retail pack 20-10-5	24 mo.	Home Landscaping	New tree and shrub plantings, established trees and shrubs, ground covers, perennials.
Container Tablets 14-4-6	3-4 mo.	Nursery Greenhouse	Pot plants, retail nursery stock.
Orchard Starter Tablets 28-8-4	24 mo.	Orchards	New plantings or young established trees.
Grape Starter Tablet 28-8-4	24 mo.	Vineyard	New plantings or young established vines.
Forest Starter Tablet 22-8-2	24 mo.	Tree farms	Xmas trees, reforestation, land reclamation.
Forest Starter Tablet 18-8-3	24 mo.	Tree farms	Xmas trees, reforestation, land reclamation. This formulation used in magnesium deficient areas as in S.E. U.S.

The Company

   The Company traced its history to Agriform of Woodland, which was later acquired by Leslie Salt. In 1967, a new venture capital team purchased the company from Leslie and established it as the Sierra Chemical Company in Newark, California, after combining its Agriform technology with a fertilizer rosin coating process developed by Archer Daniel Midland (Osmocote). A final series of transactions resulted in a new management takeover in 1971 under Robert Severns as president.

By the middle of 1976, Sierra was beginning to generate a healthier cash position, although funds were not plentiful by any means. Jay Rossi estimated that the company could probably borrow $500,000 from banks if it had to. Current assets exceeded current liabilities in the ratio of 1.3 to 1.0. The company had moved to a new plant in Milpitas, California, during 1973, and in 1976, the plant was operating at 50 percent of capacity.

Rossi Hired

By 1975, Sierra had experienced a slow but acceptable growth. Dollar sales were steadily rising, and business was beginning to develop in Europe. In the United States, penetration of particular markets was encouraging, such as tomatoes and strawberries, but the overall situation was deceptive. Between 1973 and 1975, the potential market grew an estimated 30 percent, but Sierra's unit sales were fairly flat. Inflation and European dollar sales had disguised the domestic unit sales problem.

Then suddenly, in October of 1974, Sierra sales growth ground to a halt for six to eight months. The economy was bad, but that didn't seem to be the entire explanation. Growers were still in business; they just appeared to be turning away from Osmocote and its higher prices, and substituting alternative fertilizer. In an attempt to better understand the real problem, the company president made a number of field visits. He was appalled at the level of sales performance. The salespeople were not aggressive, appeared to consider themselves as advisors and horticultural experts to the growers, and blamed the distributors for all their selling problems. While it had been true that this type of advisory selling was desirable in the early introduction of the controlled-release fertilizer, this innovation stage of the selling cycle had been over by 1970.

Some indication of the firm's lack of sales aggressiveness could be inferred from the existing job description of regional managers, i.e., salespeople (Exhibit 2), and one typical sales call report (Exhibit 3). The decision was made to bring in an experienced and professional marketing executive. Continued success, it seemed, would require a new look in both sales and marketing.

Jay Rossi was offered the job. Not only had he enjoyed a successful career in marketing, but he had been a consultant to Sierra. Bob Severns and his management team knew and respected Jay. And Jay knew enough about the Sierra products and markets to be optimistic about the future. There were some short-term problems of immediate concern. For half of the previous six quarters, for example, Sierra had experienced losses in operations. Cash itself was tight. Not only were

Exhibit 2
Job Description—Regional Manager (i.e., salesman)

The regional manager is responsible for the representation of the company, its products, and policies to customers, distributors, dealers, and the general public within his area. The manager is responsible for maintaining contact with universities, experiment stations, corporate research facilities, and other areas where technical interest may be expressed in controlled-release fertilizers. He strives to maintain a favorable public relations image for the company in his territory and works in conjunction with the advertising and sales promotion manager as required.

He is responsible for the securing, training, and supervision of distributors for Sierra products within his territory. The following specific responsibilities apply:

1. Selection and evaluation of candidate distributors.
2. Recommendation of distributor appointments to home office.
3. Training of distributor salesmen to acceptable levels of product knowledge and proficiency.
4. Establishment of goals and programs with the distributor to provide acceptable sales levels for our products.
5. Maintain overview of distributor's operations to be certain that they are conducted on a businesslike and creditworthy basis.
6. Maintain distributor interest in our programs, products, and activities so that vigorous representation of our products to the trade is maintained.

The manager will be responsible for a knowledge of the market within his territory. This knowledge shall include:

1. The major users and customers within the area.
2. The size, location, and trends of the various markets within the region.
3. Advice to the home office on business opportunities requiring development of new products or adaptation of existing products to new opportunities.
4. Investigation of new crops or uses or industries as may be requested and directed by the main office.

The manager is responsible for securing and maintaining an acceptable sales level within his region:

1. An annual sales plan will be prepared and presented to management for acceptance.
2. Quotas for distributors will be assigned and discussed with the responsible distributor personnel.
3. Adequate representation of our products to meet sales plan throughout the region by dealers or distributors is required.
4. Performance of distributors and dealers in compliance with the distributor agreements is the responsibility of the regional manager.
5. Development of sales programs specifically tailored to an area or region as may be required to develop and maintain sales.
6. Giving advice to dealers and distributors on the most profitable ways for them to handle Sierra Chemical Company's product line is also within the regional manager's area.

The regional manager is responsible for the investigation and evaluation of complaints registered by customers:

1. A report of the situation as determined by personal investigation will be made to the home office, attention technical director.
2. A recommendation on the disposition of the complaint will be made by the regional manager to the operating vice president.
3. A complaint settlement up to $200 invoiced cost may be made by the regional manager at his own discretion.

The regional manager is further responsible for the following activities:

1. Preparation of an expense budget for the operation of the region each year and operation within the accepted budget level.
2. Recommendations for attendance at regional trade shows.
3. Maintaining office complete with necessary records for distributor follow-up, correspondence with customers, and activity reports to sales management.

Exhibit 3

To: David Martin
From: George Parker
Subject: Call Report for the Week of May 25

Harvey Blake Poinsettia Ranch, Sonoma, California

We were able to confirm this morning that the problem in the stock bench area at the ranch was twofold, as George and I suspected, but previously were unable to confirm:

1. The rooted cuttings were slightly infected with Pythium when they were set out in the stock benches. Mr. Metkin at Soil & Plant Laboratory had earlier confirmed this point and further indicated that poinsettia plants could, in fact, recover from a slight infection of Pythium.
2. The workers assigned to apply Osmocote to the surface of the test benches were using a drop-type spreader, the result being that several of the particles of the Osmocote were crushed. Sally Jones, their in-house technical advisor, further stated that when the Osmocote granules would clog up the applicator, the workers merely lifted the spreader and forced the wheels around until they again moved freely. The Osmocote was substantially worked in the top six inches of planting bed with a rototiller, which would tend to erase any severely turned areas across the bench.

Dave, we understand that all of the principals of the Blake organization are away on their annual selling trip, but when they return, I will make sure that they are aware of the cause of the earlier damage.

B&D Wholesale Nursery

I left a sample of our Osmocote 18-5-11 with Mr. Bill Ramsey, who is the head grower for their container division. We outlined a trial for Bill similar to the one we have set out earlier at Valborg's Nursery, and I'll be checking back with Bill in three to four weeks to make sure that the trial was set out in a proper manner.

Mr. John Liddicoat, who is in charge of their rose breeding program, is also the man we'll have to talk to about setting up Osmocote trials in their field-grown roses. John is already aware, as previously reported, of the benefits derived from using Osmocote, and there is a good chance we can get him to begin using the product in certain sandy fields this next February.

Our first meeting with John was rather brief, due to a previous commitment on his part, and John is now away on a six-week business trip through Europe. I plan to see him as soon as he returns from his trip and will keep you posted as to the progress we make.

Willamette Chemical, Eugene

The recent 10-ton (approximately) order from this company should have been a full truckload and reflects a continuing desire on the part of our major distributor to carry a reduced inventory in the hope that prices on all fertilizer products will eventually come down.

I'm having a meeting the week of June 16th with Steve Lookabill, who is in charge of specialty sales programs through the various branch offices. I told Steve that we would shortly be selling some of the major accounts on a direct basis in the Salem basin, but there was still a huge potential in that area that was not being tapped by any of our present distributors.

I feel this company has a place in our chain of distributors, even though they did not sell their initial truckload as quickly as we would have liked. I feel that Steve in his new position will certainly enhance our total sales program.

Eureka Plant Growers

I reported earlier that Eureka had placed a small initial order for Osmocote through Willamette Chemical, and I was supposed to meet him at the Summit growing grounds this morning to instruct the workers on the proper amount of Osmocote to apply to each

Exhibit 3 *(concluded)*

can. Little did we know that the Immigration Department was going to raid their field yesterday, so they are without help for two or three weeks until workers can get back up and begin working again.

I reported earlier that George is having middle management problems and has a new grower in charge of the Summit growing grounds, so it may be a while until we really get the program started here, even though we have sold the merchandise and made the initial delivery.

Butler's Mill, Crescent City

Open house was a tremendous success, both in terms of general interest in our product line and the number of people who attended. Between 200 and 300 people came to the exhibit area (outside) between 10 A.M. and 2 P.M., and it seemed that most of them either knew about Osmocote or were using one of our products, and I was extremely grateful for Dick Spray's assistance during this time.

We picked up several good leads of people who deserve a follow-up call, and we'll certainly sell a lot more merchandise as a result of being at this meeting.

The dealers only portion of the open house was held in the evening between 5 and 7 P.M. Approximately 36 dealers showed up, and although many of them were from the various chain store garden departments, we did sell three new Green Green accounts. In addition, there was a great deal of interest in Green Green on the part of both Sears Roebuck and Handyman, so we should begin to see real movement of this product in the Del Norte County area. Dick Spray was going to spend all day Friday, the 30th, detailing some of the region accounts in the Crescent City area and will be anxious to hear how well he is able to do.

---

all sales factored, but projections for 1975 indicated that cash flow would barely be enough to cover a bank repayment due in January.

Jay Rossi had graduated from one of the top universities on the West Coast and earned an MBA at its business school. He spent four years at Maxwell House in product management; seven years at Basic Vegetable Products Company (San Francisco) as marketing manager; 18 months as an independent consultant; and 6 months as vice president of Marketing for Saga Corporation. He left Saga with no ill feelings, since Saga management recognized that the Sierra offer was "one in a lifetime."

Jay arrived at Sierra in May 1975 and took immediate stock of his situation. In terms of people, he inherited the following:

1. *David Martin—Sales Manager.* Age 62, highly competent and experienced—a slow-release fertilizer salesman since 1957 (in the predecessor company) and sales manager since 1973. Dave had earlier owned a small chain of greenhouses and three retail outlets in Wisconsin and was a well-known and respected member of the industry. He was an active participant on many industry committees.

2. *William K. McFarland—Marketing Manager.* Age 53, very strong in advertising and publicity. A frequent writer for trade magazines and the "book editor" of *Nursery Business* magazine. He admittedly had no interest in profit and loss statements, nor did he enjoy his management responsibilities.

3. *Beverly James—Regional Manager or Saleswoman.* Age 32, a horti-cultural graduate from Ohio. Work experience with Procter & Gamble, Horticultural Division. She was an excellent saleswoman but weak on administration; i.e., paper work, reports.

4. *George Parker—Salesman.* Age 45, one of Martin's first hires in the predecessor company (early 1960s). He had an excellent understanding of horticulture matters.

5. *Dick Smith—Salesman.* Age 45, with Sierra since 1972. Smith previously sold insurance and fertilizer on the East Coast. An "old time, stand up and tell you what you have to do" salesman.

6. *James Van Horn—Salesman.* Age 26, a former plant superintendent, who asked for a field-selling assignment and seemed to be floundering.

7. *George Schwartz—Technical Director.* Age 52, the "dean" of slow-release fertilizer technology and the company's best asset "as a spokesman." Schwartz was a sought-after speaker, respected scientist, and friend of many major growers. He had a master's degree in horticulture.

For complete organization chart, see Exhibit 4.

What Rossi Found

It didn't take Jay Rossi long to discover that his sales manager, David Martin, was right in his diagnosis of the problem. Here was a selling group with little marketing direction, strategy, controls, or leadership. Forecasts were useless (as much as 50 percent off), and there were no records that indicated how the company was doing with its various lines in the separate markets. Field reports were filled in sporadically, and weekly reports were sometimes backed up in the system for two weeks by the two typists. Phone calls were used to get things accomplished, since reports were useless. Penetration rates were rarely known, and most sales efforts seemed to be reactive. There was no professional selling. Servicing old accounts and distributors was the focus—prospecting was given little attention. In short, management was entirely reactive. All information was after the fact. "We were always putting out fires," was a common complaint. Quotas were ignored, and compensation was by straight salary.

An extended field trip confirmed Jay Rossi's fears about the sales force. The first person he contacted criticized his "dumb distributors," complained about the tough market conditions, and never even talked about Osmocote's advantages to a new customer because "he didn't ask." The second salesman evidenced reasonable activity but had neither a sense of urgency nor any apparent professional selling skills. The third was a great saleswoman but terrible at managing her time. She

Exhibit 4: Table of Organization as of July 1976

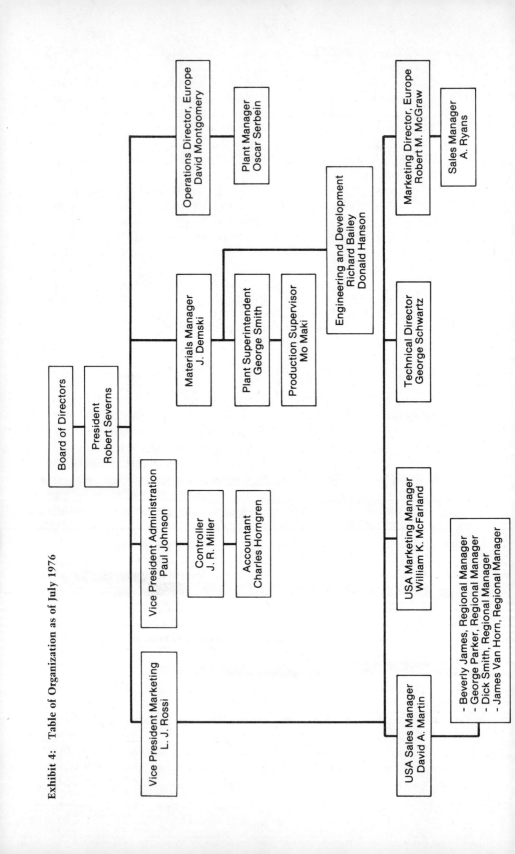

would spend hours driving between calls and averaged only two calls per day (which was below the company average of 2.9).

Each seemed to blame problems on the distributors, and their visits to users were courtesy calls. They didn't feel they were supposed to "sell." It was apparent, furthermore, that the group believed strongly in a number of "principles":

1. You can't do much about sales in the short run. After all, growers are reluctant to try a new technique until they have been conditioned, educated, and made confident that the new supplier is reliable. And this takes time.
2. Salespeople have to be horticulturists first. Because controlled-release fertilizers are a technical innovation and commercial growing a scientific endeavor, it is obvious that horticultural skill is the most important prerequisite for selling. Advice and counsel are crucial if the salesperson is to successfully convert growers into Osmocote users.
3. The product is expensive and therefore hard to sell (a typical price is $650 per ton to the user).
4. Quality is irregular and a complication for the sales personnel.
5. Comparison between salespeople and regions is not possible because of the great differences between various parts of the market.
6. Distributors are not on "our team" but rather are "our customers." And you can't ask your customers to do things for you!

New Product Possibilities

There was a second pressure on Jay to bring the sales force under rapid control; namely, the firm's plans for new product and market opportunities. He had first read some information from one of Sierra's new product groups:

> OSMOCOTE 14^3 and urea-only products have been undergoing recent trial work in mushroom cultivation. At this time, it seems that our products may be able to prove their value and gain acceptance in this high-value market.
>
> During trial . . . it has been found that one-quarter pound of OSMOCOTE increases mushroom yields from 4.15 to 4.69 pounds per square foot, an obvious economic advantage.
>
> Another potential market where extensive work with our products is being done is in British Columbia stream fertilization. It has been found that nitrogen and potassium increase algae populations in streams and this, via several food steps, increases the size of the salmon that travel these streams to the ocean. Hence, more salmon survive this trip. Since salmon always return to the same stream where they were spawned,

there is then not only more but larger salmon available for the commercial fisheries.

Fish sizes and populations have increased so much that return on fertilizer investment can be anywhere from 3–6 to 1. Trial measurements—fish weights and lengths—will be conducted throughout the summer, and economic measurements—the number of fish leaving the stream—will be available by early fall. Initial studies have shown fish size doubling with frequent applications of soluble N&P fertilizer.

OSMOCOTE economics seem very favorable assuming fish sizes double with only one fertilizer application. The potential market for Sierra's products could be between 100 to 300 tons per year.

Deciduous fruit and nut trees will also be an area of trial study for Sierra next year. Some are currently under evaluation, while others are scheduled to begin earlier this year. Since the fertilization of mature, bearing trees is currently not economical when compared to standard practice, Sierra is interested in entering the area of establishment fertilization of young deciduous fruit and nut trees. Favorable trial work in Washington has shown that trees which are expected to mature in five years have begun bearing fruit one year earlier, thus giving the grower an extra year of production. Trials are also being set on citrus trees in Florida, where we believe that the sandy soils, high rainfall, and crop value will be responsive to our product.

Another market where Sierra products can prove their value is in sugar cane fertilization. Trials are currently in place at Maunakae Sugar Plantation in Hawaii, where our custom-blend OSMOCOTE 17-0-23 product is being used on restricted areas.

It is believed that our technology will allow the sugar plantation to provide nutrients for the second half of the crop cycle. Normally, nutrition cannot be applied in these restricted areas as they are underneath power lines. Planes cannot fly over them to supply nutrients, and the thick growth of the sugar cane prohibits ground application.

The near-term market potential is felt to be between 15,000 to 20,000 units if these trials prove successful. We currently believe we have a 50 percent chance of obtaining this business.

Rossi's Challenge

As Jay Rossi and sales manager David Martin saw their problem, it was to:

1. Change the attitude of the sales force from horticultural specialists to aggressive salespeople.
2. Introduce controls that would direct the sales force toward a more productive use of its time.
3. Establish new incentive systems that would redirect the selling effort.
4. Give the organization a sense of mission and direction.

5. Be sure that the sales force was positioned to take advantage of the growth opportunities.

Questions

1. What specific action do you suggest that Rossi take?
2. What specific controls, reports, incentive systems, etc., would you adopt?
3. What would you do with the data?
4. How would you organize for growth?

C A S E 6–4

Golden Bear Distributors

John Gray, president and owner of Golden Bear Distributors (GBD), had been pleased by his firm's progress and by the growth in sales and profits. Only 10 years old, GBD had grown to be generally regarded as number three in its area and was definitely a marketing force to be reckoned with. But there were some storm clouds on the horizon:

1. The rate of growth for GBD (in sales and profits) had decreased in the past two years—in fact, Gray suspected his firm may have lost market share (there were no hard data by which to accurately measure this surmise).
2. Mass merchandisers and other volume retailers were beginning to dominate the markets, and GBD's traditional independent dealers were hard pressed to survive.
3. For the first time, Gray was experiencing a worrisome increase in salesman turnover.
4. The dealers were increasingly vocal in asking that GBD provide ever greater sales and promotional help.
5. The largest competitor, a national distributor, had recently installed an expensive and extensive sales training program.

Gray decided therefore to launch a study intended to reassess the firm's selling strategy. His first step was to engage a local consulting firm with the charge of "evaluating GBD's sales strategy and, in particular, the training needs of the sales force."

The Company and Its Lines

GBD carried a wide line of consumer products including refrigerators and kitchen ranges, TVs and radios, home video players, and a

---

limited line of medium- to low-priced computers. All told, there were over 2,000 different items in inventory. Sales in 1983 exceeded $55 million with the bulk of the dollar volume centered in home appliances. Computer volume, although small, was expanding at a 45 percent annual rate.

Sales were made to 500 independent retailers as well as to a growing number of small chain operators and about 35 industrial accounts (i.e., contractors and local manufacturers primarily). The large chains, as implied earlier, preferred to purchase direct from the manufacturers and from the distributors for small, fill-in orders. Increasingly, these direct buyers purchased their product requirements on a bid basis. Not all dealers carried all the GBD lines.

GBD had a number of distribution arrangements with its suppliers. The great bulk of the products represented merchandise in open distribution. However, one third of GBD's business represented products that were either exclusively handled or distributed on a selective basis. GBD made considerably more profits in these specialty items.

The firm's sales organization included six product sales managers who reported to the president. (See Exhibit 1.) Each product sales man-

Exhibit 1
Organizational Chart

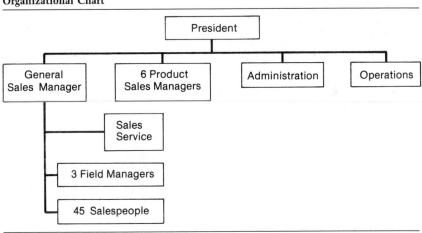

ager was assigned a number of the company's lines and was held responsible for sales and profits.

The sales force consisted of 45 individuals supervised directly by three field managers and indirectly by the product sales managers. Each salesperson was assigned a specific geographic territory made up of approximately 1/45 of the total Retail Distribution Index of GBD's trading area (calculated from the Survey of Buying Power). Each time a new person was hired, he or she was assigned a territory equal in potential to the others.

There was little formal sales training. The field managers and product sales managers took turns "going the rounds" with the new hire to acquaint him or her with the territory and to introduce the customers. Each salesperson sold all of the products in the company's line; if sales fell off in one product area, that product sales manager usually discussed at regular bi-weekly meetings any problems the sales rep had encountered.

Each sales individual received a draw of $300 a week against commissions. Since the average commission rate was 3 percent, each salesperson had to sell slightly over $500,000 per year in order to cover the draw. Net annual commissions for the different members of the sales force varied between $15,000 and $65,000. All selling expenses were paid by the company.

The sales force filled out individual detailed weekly route sheets describing all planned activities for the following week. In addition, they made out a daily call report which was mailed to the home office at the end of each workday as well as a "special attention" memorandum for unusual situations.

Selling to independents was quite different than selling to chains and large operators. The latter, as stated, preferred to buy direct and expected a considerable amount of promotional and advertising support. They were, by and large, reasonably able merchandisers and put a great deal of pressure on their suppliers for deals, special prices, and point-of-sale assistance. There wasn't much demand by these big operators for selling assistance, though they did welcome abundant product information and unique product features.

The independents were much more dependent upon their suppliers for credit terms, selling assistance, product availability, and service. Although they talked price, they were equally concerned with ongoing support and service. In recent months, however, there was a noticeable increase in retail price cutting.

The Consultant's Interviews

The consulting firm assigned the GBD account to one of its top young men, Kevin Murphy. Murphy had received an MBA from a leading western business school in 1975 and, upon graduation, had taken a job with the General Electric Company. He left his sales management job there four years later to join the consulting group.

Shortly after John Gray's initial discussion with the consultants, Murphy contacted GBD's general sales manager, Harry Overstreet, at the home office in Oakland. After getting some background data on the sales organization, Murphy asked Overstreet for his views on sales training at GBD. He responded:

> As far as I'm concerned, the training job has to be twofold; retail salesclerks need training just as much as our field salespeople. Right now we have a policy whereby we invite dealer personnel to our home office in small groups for meetings to demonstrate and discuss all of the products that we carry. On the other hand, as I mentioned earlier, our salesmen's only on-the-job training is the initial joint calling by the product sales managers and the field sales managers. Such limited training probably isn't sufficient, but I'm not sure what kind of training they do need. That's what I expect you to tell me after you spend some time with them.

Overstreet then arranged for Murphy to "make the rounds" with several of the GBD salesmen. Murphy first met Bob Benton, who serviced part of Monterey County south of San Francisco. Bob was 34 years old and had been with GBD over 7 years. His initial reaction to Murphy was one of suspicion. "I never hear from the office unless my sales are down." But when Murphy explained that he was merely interested in learning how he sold as part of a general study on sales training, Bob talked more freely:

> You have to learn to sell like a retailer sells. New salesmen should be given all kinds of product information, and the company should demonstrate the operation of our products to them.
>
> Next, you need to follow up on the new people so they tell their story to the retailer every time they go into a store. The idea is to get them to give the story to the retailer and his floor people so many times that when a customer walks in the store and asks about a recorder or TV, the retailer goes into "the pitch" on our equipment automatically.
>
> According to management, we're supposed to be "sales consultants" to the dealers, but I think that's a lot of baloney. I tried to help out a couple of small retailers once by showing them how I'd sell our product line, but they both thought I was trying to run their business. I think the best training is to bring the retail salesmen into the home office every once in awhile and show them how to operate our equipment and explain it thoroughly—just like we do now. That's how to train.

Bob's first stop was at the Mission Home Center, a successful San Francisco retailer. Before he and Murphy went in, Bob explained his sales approach:

> I go in and say hello to the salespeople first because, if there's any service problem with our products, they're sure to know about it. That way, the boss won't surprise me if something's gone wrong. Next, if I have a chance, I slip back into the stockroom to see how many of our items they have in stock. Mission is a good operator and sells a pretty good mix of our products. Incidentally, most of my sales are TV and appliances—I can't sell many computers down in this part of town.

Well, after that, I check with the service manager to make certain that anything I've promised him in the last week or so has been taken care of. Then, of course, I tip my hat to the secretary and ask to see the boss.

When Bob entered the store, he greeted the two retail clerks, walked over to a quiet corner and conversed with one of them in low tones. Shortly thereafter, he and the consultant went downstairs to the storeroom for about 40 minutes. When they came back, Benton headed for a desk at the back and motioned for Murphy to follow. He greeted the service manager and introduced Murphy as his helper. The service manager was apparently mad at GBD and Bob in particular because Bob had promised him some special software for the computers which had not yet been delivered. After Bob stated that he had relayed the information to GBD's service department a week or so ago, he phoned the GBD service manager and a short, heated argument ensued. When Bob finished the call, he informed Mission's service manager that he would have to "check further." Although the service manager was not satisfied, Bob explained that he wanted to see the boss first and that he would talk later.

Bob then knocked on a door marked "Private" and waved Murphy to follow. As they entered, a man on the telephone looked up and motioned them to a seat. After he hung up, Bob introduced Murphy to the owner and proceeded to ask if there was anything he needed. The owner answered by questioning Bob about the missing software. When Bob assured him that he was following it up, the owner stated: "That's OK for me, Bob."

The salesman then began to explain a new TV floor display GBD had designed for its dealers for the Christmas holidays. The owner turned down the offer because "Panasonic pays me $250 bucks a year to put their line on special display during the first three weeks of December, so you can forget about it."

Bob glanced at his note pad and informed the owner that he was running low on a couple of popular models. The owner replied, "I'm OK for now, but I'll give you an order next week." After leaving the office, Bob stopped by the service manager's desk and reviewed the software situation. He concluded by stating that he would check on the material the following morning when he reported to the home office. He promised to call the service manager with a report.

As they left the store, the salesman remarked. "The owner evidently wasn't in a buying mood today, but I'll definitely get an order from him next week." Since it was then nearly 4:30 P.M., Bob wanted to call it a day, but he offered to take Murphy to visit other stores on Monday if he wished.

The following week, Murphy spent most of one day with Grace Adams. She was a divorcee, about 35 years old, who had been selling for GBD for almost three years. She had left a sales job with the J. C. Penney organization because she preferred the relative freedom of an outside position. Grace had a large territory north of San Francisco which covered a number of small towns. Murphy met her about 9 A.M., and they chatted over a cup of coffee before beginning their calls.

When Murphy explained that he was helping to do a study for GBD on methods of training salesmen, Grace evidently interpreted this to mean that she should talk about her job, for she started explaining her daily call routine. Her suggested approach to the retailer was much the same as that of Bob Benton.

Grace and Murphy first visited the Petaluma TV and Radio store, which sold additionally a broad line of home appliances. Adams quickly introduced Murphy to Mrs. Smith (the owner's wife), listened to a complaint about a scratched cabinet on a television set, and checked the company's inventory. After discussing with Mrs. Smith the aggressive price cutting initiated by a local discounter, Grace took an order for two home video units. The call lasted about 20 minutes.

As they walked toward the second stop several blocks away, Grace confided:

> I always try to get on a first-name basis with my retailers as soon as I can because it helps me establish rapport. We all like to do business with our friends. Another secret to calling in a territory that you haven't visited for a week or so is to walk along the main street and window shop and see who's got what bargains displayed. I also buy a local paper most every time I come into these little towns to see who's advertising what. I think that helps me to get a feel for my competition too.

The second call, which lasted about 45 minutes, was at a large home service center. As soon as they entered the store, Grace introduced Murphy to Joe, the owner. The following conversation took place:

Adams: I see you're featuring a couple of our home computer systems, Joe. Great—that should help to boost your sales.

Joe: Yeah, that's true. But the reason I'm promoting them is that I can't sell them at full retail. As long as I make some profit, though, I should care.

Adams: Joe, that business should be picking up pretty soon now—Christmas, you know. Over half of these sales should come in November and December.

Joe: What's good in the rest of your lines?

Adams: Everything, Joe.

Joe: *[Looking at some promotional material]* I've got some Sonys here, got them at a special price. But the last I sold was about three months ago.

Adams began to talk about a new warranty program on the food mixer. Joe explained he was aware of it.

Adams: Well, we do have a nice gift promotion on the mixers.

Joe: I don't need all that stuff. I've got plenty now.

Adams: We can send it to you prepaid you know, Joe, plus a 10 percent dating. These mixers will really go well . . .

Joe: I just don't need any.

Adams: Well, anything else? How about taking an ad in your local paper on the video player? I've never seen your newspaper feature any of our products. What's the cost over there anyway?

Joe: $2.60 a line.

Adams: Well, of course, we'd split the cost 50-50 with you, Joe, on any ads you'd like to run.

Joe: 50-50?

Adams: Yes, on all the lines you run with our mats.

Joe: On everything?

Adams: That's right. Just send us the tear sheets.

Joe: Why don't you mail me some mats then? I can use them.

Adams: OK. Now, how about the TVs, Joe?

Joe: Send me a couple of those new Sony portables—you know the ones I mean?

Adams: The FM-36B? A good choice. That's the popular one, Joe.

Joe: OK. I'll see you next week.

Adams: Fine, Joe, see you.

As they left the store, Grace remarked, "Gee, sure looks like a good day. You know, the personal approach means everything in this business. I'm trying to build goodwill so that when I leave a store, those retailers will want to sell GBD because of me. Now Joe there thinks that I'm a pleasant person, so he tries to sell my line. Incidentally, the reason I pushed some advertising is that he's got to advertise if he wants to sell. These dealers often look upon advertising as a cost instead of an investment. Or they think the manufacturer should do it all."

The next stop was a new TV dealer. Grace had taken an order from the dealer for a new combination stereo TV and home recording system on the promise that it would be delivered in two days. Three days after taking the order, she had received a phone call from the dealer who stated that unless the set was delivered that very day, Grace was to cancel the order. She commented to Murphy, "I checked with our delivery people yesterday after I got the call, and they weren't sure the set would go out. If it isn't there now, I'll be in trouble with him. Seeing as how he's a new dealer, I don't want to rock the boat."

In the TV dealer's window was the system distributed by GBD. "Well," remarked Grace, "I guess it's safe to go in." As soon as they entered the store, a thin man greeted her with, "The set arrived just as I was closing last night." Grace explained some of the features of the set to the dealer and gave him some literature on several other models. Then she inquired about what other sets the dealer was planning to install. The dealer replied that he wouldn't carry any others until he had sold this one. After a few more words, Grace and Murphy left the store. Several minutes later she remarked, "You know, bringing people around with you hurts your sales . . . but he's a tough dealer to sell, anyway."

Murphy and Adams then drove 20 miles to another town further north. During the trip, Grace talked about why she had left the retail business and why she liked selling. When they arrived at the next stop, Grace explained, "I have to try to collect a check from the dealer and report my results back to the home office by telephone." Since the man she wished to see was not in, she made arrangements to call back later that afternoon.

During lunch at a small diner, Grace talked more about the retail business. She also expressed a desire to obtain a territory closer to the city. After lunch, as they began walking toward the next call, they passed a newly renovated electronics store. Grace paused, "This is a new store. I haven't gotten them for an account. It's just possible they don't have a computer line. I think I'll go in cold and see what I can do." They entered the store and looked around for a clerk. A woman came out, and Grace explained the purpose of her call, stating that her company had just started up with a new line of complete computer systems. When she mentioned the brand names, the woman remarked that the store carried one well-known brand and added that she could show it to them. In a corner of the store, a special display was devoted to the computer and peripherals. The shopkeeper explained that she and her husband had recently purchased the store, didn't know much about personal computers, and were in the process of rethinking the business. Grace noted the inventory that she had and explained that, on her next call, she would supply some promotional materials. She also added that the distributor who formerly handled the line had gone out of business and that GBD would gladly provide the components from now on. The woman thanked her, and they left the store.

After similar experiences traveling with three other salespeople, Kevin Murphy felt that he had a good feeling for the GBD selling job and its requirements. Since two men were retiring soon from GBD's sales force, John Gray was very anxious that Murphy complete his recommendations for a sales training program before new recruits had to be hired to take over the territories. Thus, Murphy began outlining a training program for GBD which would include recommendations for training dealer sales personnel as well as the firm's own sales force.

Questions

1. What is the basic role of the distributors' salesmen in this situation?
2. What skills do these salesmen need?
3. What specific training program (coverage, subjects) do you recommend?
4. Elaborate upon one particular training subject in your program that you consider important—points to be covered, specific training technique to be used, measurement objectives, etc.

C A S E 6–5

Western Industrial Supply Company

Western Industrial Supply Company, located in Los Angeles, distributed janitorial supplies—waxes, cleaners, paper toweling, and the like—to industrial and institutional users in California from San Diego to Fresno and east as far as Needles. Salesmen called mainly on custodians who, if sold on the product(s), requisitioned the purchase through the firm's purchasing department. Western was one of the larger companies of its type in the state and, within its sales area, competed with some 30 to 40 other companies—many of which were small, local distributors. In both the Los Angeles and San Diego metropolitan areas, competition came mainly from distributors of a size similar to Western.

Population and industrial growth had increased the demand for janitorial supplies substantially during the early and mid-1970s. In more recent years, market growth had slowed, and competition had become more intense with the result that profits had declined when measured in real dollar terms. Mr. Randy Cross, the company's president and chief executive officer, felt that a new sales strategy was needed which included a different way of compensating the sales force.

In the past, Western had tried to minimize competition by emphasizing proprietary products through aggressive selling. Over the years, the company had increased the number of its proprietary products which yielded a gross margin considerably higher than did jobbed items. Such products were manufactured under contract by a variety of

This case was written by Professor Harper Boyd, College of Business Administration, University of Arkansas. Included in Stanford Business Cases 1983 with permission. © 1983 by the Board of Trustees of the Leland Stanford Junior University.

small manufacturers located in southern California. The company had a laboratory which developed the product's specifications, tested it against competitive products under a variety of use conditions, and made certain that it was produced to specification. Proprietary products represented about 18 percent of total sales but nearly 35 percent of total gross margin.

Western Industrial salesmen were expected to call regularly on their accounts, although their call frequency by account type and size was not known since salesmen did not make out call reports. Once on the premises, they were expected to demonstrate items—especially proprietary ones—whenever possible in an effort to call attention to those features which made the product unique. This required them to have a good technical knowledge of the product and a willingness to "get their hands dirty." Salesmen were trained to work with custodians to show them how to make their jobs easier and at the same time to improve the hygiene and cleanliness of the facilities they maintained.

The company employed 14 salespersons working under a vice president in charge of sales. Each salesperson had an assigned territory the size of which depended upon the number, size, and density of accounts. Outside salespersons were paid on a commission basis backed by a monthly guarantee based on the individual's earning record. In addition, each member of the sales force received either a $250 or $150 monthly car allowance (depending upon the size of the territory) plus fringe benefits. Three members of the sales force were "insiders" in that they handled phone orders and service requests. These persons were paid on a salary basis. Of the 11 outside salespersons, 4 were still on monthly guarantee, having been with the company less than one year. An average salesperson earned $1,500 per month while the better ones exceeded $2,000. Most of the better salespersons had been with the company a long time.

A number of trends had conspired to make the industry increasingly competitive. One was the growing consolidation of supply distributors. The small local distributor was fast becoming extinct. Cost of capital associated with inventories and accounts receivable coupled with high inflation had forced many small firms to exit the industry. A second trend was that an impressive number of medium to large customers had contracted out their cleaning activities, thereby reducing their direct purchases of janitorial supplies substantially. The larger contract cleaning firms either bought direct from manufacturers or acquired their supplies from distributors on a bid basis. A third trend was the increased importance of the purchasing department in the purchase of janitorial supplies. This tended to downplay the role of the custodian in the purchasing decision. Yet another trend was that more and more of the larger accounts were requesting bids on major supply items.

In view of the above, Mr. Cross thought that Western had to make some important decisions near term if the company was to survive and prosper. In commenting on the situation he said:

> The basic trends have dried up a number of our larger accounts since our company has never learned how to bid successfully. We really do very little bidding, but we've got to start learning how soon. Also, we're stuck with an increasing number of small accounts which means lots of small orders. These have increased our sales, order processing and fulfillment, delivery, and bad debt costs to a point where something significant has to be done. And we're having trouble holding our better salesmen. Our turnover here is not good.

Mr. Cross outlined his tentative corrective plan as follows:

1. Price the company's proprietary products more competitively. This meant that prices on present proprietary products would be reduced by as much as 10 to 20 percent through the use of quantity discounts.
2. Increase the number of new products. To accomplish this, two new technicians would be added to the company laboratory.
3. Divest in the very small accounts by using a minimum order size requirement in an effort to lower costs and allocate more resources to the larger accounts. These actions would likely result in a substantial shift in the composition and size of the sales territories.
4. Undertake aggressive bidding which would be accomplished by establishing a special inside unit to work with the sales force in the preparation of bids.
5. Better service to a point "where it is at least as good as any competitor and better than most." The plan called for all orders to be shipped within 72 hours after receipt. This was to be made possible mainly by a computerized order processing system which prepared all necessary documents and identified the exact warehouse location (bin number) of each invoice line item. In addition, a computerized inventory model would be installed which would hopefully reduce out-of-stocks to less than 2 percent of all items stocked.
6. Professionalization of the sales force. Given the actions cited above, it seemed clear that a different kind of salesperson would be needed. Some of the present sales force could be retrained, but it was anticipated that probably half would need to be replaced. It was likely that a new sales manager would have to be hired; further, that the infrastructure within the sales department would have to be improved (e.g., addition of the estimating unit and an increase in the number of inside salesmen).

Mr. Cross recognized that considerable fact-finding had to take place before he could make his plan operational. He also recognized that he should move slowly in this regard, perhaps taking several years to implement it. He thought the place to start was with the sales force. In this regard, he reasoned that since several salespersons needed replacing in the near future, the first step would be to draw up a new compensation plan which would retain the loyalty of those asked to stay while attracting the caliber of person desired. If a satisfactory plan could be developed which could accommodate both the present and the future, Mr. Cross was willing to install it for the next fiscal year, which started some five months hence.

The present outside sales force was paid a 10 percent commission on the sales of all proprietary items and a 5 percent commission on all jobbed items. In addition, each had a car allowance and received fringe benefits mostly in the form of health and life insurance and social security. Each had a monthly guarantee which was expected to be equaled or bettered by commissions. The company paid no bonus to the sales force, although all other workers received one in those years when before-tax profits exceeded a certain percent of sales. This was distributed on the basis of an employee's annual wages. Typically, this amounted to a week's salary.

The new compensation plan called for the setting of a dollar quota for each outside salesperson in three product categories—proprietary, high-margin jobbed products, and low-margin jobbed products. The quotas would be based on an extrapolation of sales from the three previous years with the last year carrying a double weight. This result would then be subject to adjustment based on the forecast for the coming year. The forecast would take into account new products, price changes, general economic conditions in the territory, and any change in competition. Adjustments would also need to be made to accommodate territorial shifts or realignments.

All salespersons would be paid a monthly salary in the future. This would be calculated by applying the present commission system to the quota for proprietary products and a total of the high- and low-margin jobbed items. Every effort would be made to approximate the present remuneration of a salesperson, although it was recognized that this could prove difficult when substantial territorial adjustments had to be made. In addition to salaries, salespersons would receive car mileage and the company's fringe benefit package and participate in the annual bonus plan. Quotas were to be set for each month of the year.

In addition to the base compensation plan, salespersons had the opportunity of earning an "improvement over standard bonus" each quarter for the three product categories as follows:

Percent improvement over standard (quota)	Commission rate to be paid
Category A—proprietary (18 percent of sales):	
0 and under 5.	8%
5 and under 10.	9
10 and under 15.	10
15 and under 20.	11
20 and over	12
Category B—high-margin jobbed items (26 percent of sales):	
0 and under 5.	4.0
5 and under 10.	4.5
10 and under 15.	5.0
15 and under 20.	5.5
20 and over	6.0
Category C—low-margin jobbed items (56 percent of sales):	
0 and under 5.	2.0
5 and under 10.	2.5
10 and under 15.	3.0
15 and under 20.	3.5
20 and over	4.0

To ensure that the sales force did not neglect the high-volume but low-margin items completely, the plan provided that *no* improvement over standard bonus would be paid unless the quotas were met in each of the three product categories. This seemed critical, given the relatively high fixed costs associated with the company's warehouse and delivery operations.

A possible alternative to the above was to set up a point system whereby an underage in one category could be offset by an overage elsewhere. Points would be assigned to each category based on its percent of the total quota which equaled 100 points. In the case of Category A, any deficit would be translated into a gross margin dollar figure which would have to be equaled by some combination of gross margin overages from the other two categories. A deficit in Category B could only be made up from a gross margin overage in Category C, while a deficit in the latter could only be accommodated by an overage in Category B. Average margins would be used to calculate overages and underages and were expected to be approximately 54 percent for Category A, 26 percent for Category B, and 16 percent for Category C.

While quota by product category was to be set monthly, commissions would be based on a quarterly basis, thereby enabling the salesperson to make up for a bad month; i.e., there would be four chances during the year for a salesperson to earn extra compensation in the form of a commission bonus since a failure to meet or exceed quota for any one quarter would not be cumulative.

Bidding posed a special problem. Since the company had little experience here, there was some question as to how best to handle it in terms of the new compensation plan. Sales from successful bidding activities could be large, but margins would be reduced. Thus, if successful, the sales force could meet the sales quotas but at a considerably lower average gross margin. One possibility was to credit sales on the basis of gross margin; e.g., if the company made a successful bid by cutting its margins by half, then the salesperson would receive credit for 50 percent of the dollar sales involved. The objection here was that, under such conditions, salesmen would shy away from bidding situations. Much the same would happen if quotas were established on the basis of gross margin dollars and not sales dollars. Once the company had developed a history of bidding, then the problem would be less acute.

Another problem was whether the new compensation plan would in any way inhibit the motivation of the inside sales force. A smart outside salesperson would likely use the insiders to do as much of his/her follow-up work as possible and would set high service standards. This could generate the feeling by the inside sales personnel that they were making a significant contribution to company sales and profits and yet did not participate in the rewards.

C A S E 6–6

The Webb Office
Products Company

The Webb Office Products Company manufactured a wide line of office productions including adhesives, sealers, glue sticks, cleaners and solvents, markers, laundry pens, a variety of inks, stamp pads, and erasers (a relatively new addition). Webb had originally specialized in adhesives and was an old and well-established company. Over the years, it had added office-product lines partly by acquisition and partly by internal development. For the most part, the new products were produced under contract by a number of small manufacturing firms.

Company sales over the past five years (1976–80) had increased substantially despite the business recession. In late 1980, the company's sales manager resigned because of poor health. The new sales manager, Robert Fischer, joined the company early in 1981. He had formerly been employed as a regional sales manager for a large office-products manufacturer specializing in writing instruments. After familiarizing himself with the company's product line and its sales policies, he spend considerable time in the field visiting the trade with the company's sales representatives. While he was generally pleased with what he found, he was concerned that he had no way of evaluating their individual performances. This was made difficult by not only a lack of industry sales data at the national level but by the substantial differences in the individual company sales territories based on number of accounts and geography covered.

The company's regular sales force consisted of 27 manufacturer representatives who, in 1980, generated sales of $14.4 million. Sales were made directly to large retail office-product stores (often called statio-

This case was written by Professor Harper Boyd, College of Business Administration, University of Arkansas. Included in *Stanford Business Cases 1983* with permission. © 1983 by the Board of Trustees of the Leland Stanford Junior University.

ners by the trade) and the wholesale office-product companies. Many customers were both wholesalers and retailers. The company did not sell to industrial, institutional, or government agencies since these organizations typically bought from local sources—usually large stationers.

Four company salespeople sold all major chains (regardless of buying office location) and large office supply distributors. The former often required private-label merchandise specially packaged to meet their requirements. The latter were often referred to as brokers, although this was a misnomer, given that they stocked a full line of products which they typically sold over a several-state area to local retailers and wholesalers. More often than not, such distributors served an area which could be reached overnight by truck. For the most part, they were large, highly automated units of a large national organization (e.g., Boise Cascade). Because of their volume and overall efficiency, they were able to operate on low margins; indeed, it was often less expensive for retailers to buy from them than direct from manufacturers—especially when relatively small quantities were involved. Such distributors did not sell to industrial, institutional, and government accounts. Sales reps were not allowed to solicit these accounts.

Company sales reps sold not only the company's products but other noncompetitive lines. It was estimated that on average company products accounted for about 60 percent of their sales, although there was considerable variation between individual reps. An exclusive sales territory was assigned each rep who received credit for all sales from that territory regardless of order mode—i.e., orders could be phoned or mailed in by either the customer or the sales rep. Sales reps received no credit for sales made to chains and the large distributors which, as noted earlier, were sold direct.

Sales reps worked on a commission basis out of which they paid all of their own expenses. Commissions ranged between 5 and 10 percent depending on the product line's margins. Because of their independent middlemen status, it had proved difficult to get them to render call reports. It was also a question of whether it would be wise to do so since the Internal Revenue Service might then classify them as employees and force the company to pay fringe benefits, including contributions to the Social Security system. In any event, call frequency by type and size of account was not known.

The duties of the sales reps included line placement, the introduction of new items, setting up in-store merchandise displays, and handling any complaints. Only a few of the orders placed were written by the reps—over 90 percent of all orders were received by phone over the company's toll-free service. The company had 12 incoming WATS lines staffed by 14 experienced order takers. The order processing system was computerized to a point where, within but a few minutes after receipt, the order was delivered to the warehouse for picking, packing, and shipment. The company prided itself on shipping a high percentage of all orders within 48 hours—two working days.

In the past, the company had not used any criteria to evaluate the performance of individual sales reps other than a percentage increase in sales over the prior year. For example, if company rep sales were forecast to grow by 20 percent, then each rep's sales were expected to increase by this amount. Over the past several years, the company's sales force had remained relatively stable; only four reps had been turned over during the previous three years including one who had been killed in an automobile accident.

One reason why no performance criteria has been set up was, according to the sales manager, a lack of industry sales data. In particular, there were no national sales data by product lines. Thus, the company had no reliable base from which to compute its market share at either the national or individual sales territory levels for each of its product lines.

After considerable discussions with a variety of individuals including the company's senior chain salesman, the sales manager came up with six different evaluation ratios as follows (see Exhibit 1).

1. Percent dollar increase 1980 against 1976, company versus territory.
2. Company 1980 average dollar sale per outlet versus territory average dollar.
3. Percent of territory sales 1980 to total sales versus percent territory's population to total U.S. population.
4. Company average sales of adhesives per outlet 1980 versus that of the territory.
5. Percent erasers 1980 to total company sales versus percent to total territory sales. Erasers were a relatively new addition to the company's product line.
6. Percent cleaners and solvent sales 1980 to total company sales versus percent to total territory sales. Cleaners and solvents were long established items.

If the ratios generated in 4 through 6 proved meaningful, it was planned to calculate similar ratios for the company's other product lines.

In commenting on his sales analysis to the company executive vice president, Mr. Fischer noted that the evaluations used were "purely objective with no weights added." He went on to say that "after digesting this information, we should determine if these are the areas we want to use to measure our reps. Perhaps we should be using additional

Exhibit 1: Sales Territories Evaluation Ratios Based on Sales Credited to Sales Reps

Sales territory	Sales increase over 1976 (company average = 98.6%)	Average $ sales per outlet (company average = $1,318)	Percent of total sales made by reps	Percent of total population	Average adhesive sales per outlet	Percent erasers to total territory sales (company = 1.1%)	Percent cleaners/ solvents to total territory (company = 19%)
1	34.0%	$ 688	3.74%	8.38%	$239	.50%	10.95%
2	67.2	804	3.30	4.88	326	.83	7.89
3	210.1	728	1.72	4.54	264	.53	5.75
4	202.8	1,365	2.83	2.36	240	1.25	18.21
5	118.5	1,267	4.11	3.55	267	1.14	18.91
6	189.8	2,041	3.85	2.02	381	3.21	8.50
7	103.6	1,276	2.22	3.40	443	1.46	5.19
8*	5.7	916	6.50	5.51	217	.27	29.16
9	72.6	498	1.28	4.88	168	.41	10.38
10	75.5	1,274	2.88	5.33	268	.84	12.72
11	176.3	1,887	4.05	2.30	384	1.75	21.23
12	113.6	1,415	1.56	.94	281	2.01	9.28
13	168.0	1,248	3.48	3.97	298	1.38	14.44
14	155.1	1,701	3.19	1.90	315	2.26	21.15
15	151.0	1,868	5.93	3.41	225	1.07	27.50
16	114.6	1,707	5.85	5.78	321	.89	21.84
17	117.9	1,385	1.62	1.46	398	1.84	1.78
18	81.7	1,456	.85	.74	259	1.16	15.63
19	350.4	1,522	4.93	5.24	317	.84	24.76
20	93.9	1,199	2.10	2.65	288	1.18	5.82
21	134.8	1,465	6.48	5.36	232	.92	24.84
22	94.8	2,216	9.46	4.52	224	.46	35.99
23	78.9	1,526	7.69	6.56	292	1.03	28.66
24	88.3	871	2.91	4.28	270	1.16	7.29
25	121.9	1,604	4.65	4.06	312	.91	14.84
26	149.6	1,622	2.53	1.44	307	2.99	16.35
27	49.8	1,239	.18	.41	305	.48	18.70

* Territory 8 represents a special case. It matched total company percentage increases in 1977 and 1978. In 1979, the sales rep responsible for the territory was killed in an automobile accident, and his successor was let go after some six months. Also in 1979, a super distributor was established in the approximate center of this territory, causing a sharp drop in rep sales.

measures, and perhaps we should weight some heavier than others. In any case, what I'm looking for is a way of identifying our weaker reps. Thus, those who exceed the evaluation criteria in four categories are not where we should focus our time and attention. If you agree with what we have done, I plan to use it as a way of taking corrective action with problem reps. I'd appreciate your candid comments as soon as possible."

CASE 6–7

Gerrish Motors

As he reviewed the monthly profit and loss statement for November 1983, Mr. Kurt Gerrish, president of Gerrish Motors, was generally pleased with the results for the first 11 months of the year. Nineteen eighty-three had been a year of recovery for the American economy and for the automobile industry, and Gerrish Motors was also seeing a marked increase in consumer interest in buying automobiles. Gerrish and his vice president for administration, Mr. John Sloan, were estimating sales of 390 units for the full year, compared with 310 units in 1982. Looking out the showroom window at the snow-dusted hills of Woodstock, Vermont, Kurt Gerrish saw a car lot that was virtually empty, a frustrating sight. One salesman had just complained that he had lost at least five deals that week because he couldn't get cars for people who wanted them. "Sales have become a function of supply, not demand, for every make we sell," Gerrish reflected out loud. As he scanned the income and expense statement searching for areas for improved productivity, he looked at the $56,400 spent for advertising so far in 1983 and wondered whether he was wasting his money when he couldn't meet current customer demand. At least, he thought, it was time to reconsider the role played by advertising and sales promotion for Gerrish Motors.

Gerrish Motors was an authorized dealer for Mercedes-Benz, Honda, and Porsche and Audi automobiles. Located in the beautiful resort town of Woodstock, Vermont, Gerrish served a market area, roughly estimated to contain a population of 250,000, that stretched from the New York State line on its western edge, to Randolph and Barre, Vermont, on the north, Springfield, Vermont, to the south, and the White River Junction, Vermont/Hanover-Lebanon, New Hampshire, area to the East. A significant portion of Gerrish Motors' sales came from the

White River Junction/Hanover-Lebanon area, where there was a population estimated at close to 100,000 people (including all of Grafton
County and the northern portion of Sullivan County, New Hampshire)
and a concentration of medical, educational, and manufacturing activity with resulting favorable impact on disposable personal income.

Each agreement between Gerrish Motors and the respective automobile companies specified the geographic area that was to be served
by the dealership, held the dealer responsible for sales results in this
"area of primary marketing responsibility," and stated that the manufacturer would not appoint another dealer in that area. These area

Exhibit 1
Map of Area Served by Gerrish Motors

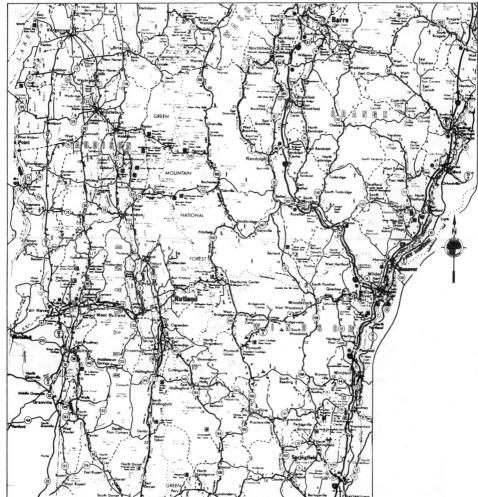

Source: *1982–83 Official State Map of Vermont.*

definitions varied from one company to another. For example, the
Mercedes-Benz area assigned to Gerrish was larger than the Honda
area, reflecting Honda's more extensive distribution on a national basis. In addition, it was not uncommon for customers to come from as
far away as Burlington, Vermont, where there was a well-established
dealer for Mercedes-Benz and Honda, or from other market areas that
were not within Gerrish's assigned areas of marketing responsibility.
As Kurt Gerrish put it, there was "more pump-in than pump-out" of
customers from other market areas for Gerrish Motors. Exhibit 1
shows a map of Gerrish Motors' market area.

Product Line

Gerrish Motors had started as a Chevrolet dealer in 1957, a line that
was dropped in 1982 based on Mr. Gerrish's judgment that it was no
longer compatible with the other automobile lines being sold. He referred to this decision as the decision to "focus on the carriage trade in
the market, the sophisticated driver." The Mercedes-Benz line had
been taken on in 1968 and was expected to account for about 65 units
at an average retail value of $35,000 in 1983. Mercedes-Benz automo-
biles sold at prices ranging from $23,000 for the newly introduced
Model 190 sedan to over $56,000 for the 500 SEC two-door coupe. The
Honda line was added in 1973 and would account for about 255 units,
at an average price of $8,800 in 1983. Honda prices ranged from $6,800
for the small Civic sedan to almost $13,500 for a Prelude "loaded" with
air conditioning and other accessories. BMW automobiles had been
added in 1980 but had not been particularly well received in the market. The BMW line had been dropped in 1982 in favor of the Porsche-
Audi line. Gerrish expected to sell 20 Porsches in 1983, at an average
price of about $26,000, along with 50 Audis averaging $18,000. Porsche
models, all sports coupes, sold at prices from $22,000 to $50,000,
whereas Audi's two-door and four-door sedans sold in the $14,000 to
$23,000 range. Gerrish would also sell about 200 used cars in 1983, but
only half of these would be sold at retail, the others being sold to other
dealers. Kurt Gerrish wished to have only a few high-quality used cars
on his lot, which Gerrish Motors could stand behind and which could
be sold at a reasonable profit.

Gerrish Motors had also been a dealer for the short-lived DeLorean
automobile for a brief period in 1981–82. The Toyota line had been
handled from 1964 to 1968, when it was transferred at Gerrish's request to a White River Junction dealership. Gerrish had also been the
dealer for the Mercedes-Benz bus for several years, with an assigned
market area that included all of northern New England plus parts of
Massachusetts and New York State. However, Mercedes-Benz had
withdrawn this bus from the United States market when it determined
that it would be economically impossible to meet new federal regula-

tions requiring a wheelchair ramp on every vehicle along with other demands relating to emissions and safety.

The front-wheel drive Hondas and Audis were popular because of their traction on the area's hilly, snowy roads. Audi's new 4000S Quattro four-door sedan had all-wheel drive and was expected to have strong demand in this market. Honda, Audi, and Mercedes-Benz had all introduced new models in late 1983 and were generating a great deal of excitement in the automotive press. Gerrish Motors had hosted over 300 of its customers at a black-tie cocktail buffet "Salon Show" to introduce the Mercedes-Benz 190 in mid-November. At this affair, several other new and established models of Mercedes-Benz, Honda, Porsche, and Audi were also displayed, along with a selection of vintage Mercedes-Benz automobiles owned by customers. Several customers had already ordered cars as a direct result of this show. The Salon Show represented an expenditure of almost $16,000, of which approximately $4,000 was for renovation and redecoration of a second showroom. The remaining $12,000 was allocated to advertising expense at the rate of $3,000 for November and December and $2,000 per month for the next four months, with some offsetting reductions in media expenditures.

A series of follow-up letters was planned for mailing to all who had attended the Salon Show. Gerrish had recently purchased a word processor that was being used to create as many as 250 letters per week to be sent to customers. The main point of these letters was to ask for referrals, as well as to promote the customer's own interest in purchasing additional automobiles and service. All sales personnel were encouraged to take advantage of this capability, and letters could be tailored and personalized easily with the new machine. (See Exhibit 2.) Kurt Gerrish strongly believed that referrals were the key element in his business.

Gerrish Motors' showrooms were quite sumptuous, with carpeted floors, antique furnishings, original artwork on the walls, and stained glass decoration. Each of the five salesmen's offices was furnished with an antique, oak roll-top desk. Mr. Gerrish worked hard to project an image of quality and service that he believed fit the product line and the clientele he served. The sale of service and parts was an important source of revenue and profit for Gerrish Motors. A major objective of all of the company's marketing activities was to sell automobiles to people who would return for service and would become regular customers of the dealership. John Sloan estimated that over half of all new car sales were to people who had previously purchased automobiles from Gerrish or who had been referred by satisfied customers. It was not uncommon for a customer to own two or more Mercedes-Benz automobiles at the same time, or a Mercedes-Benz and Honda or Audi. These customers also tended to be very important purchasers of service.

Exhibit 2
An Example of a Letter Encouraging Referrals

GERRISH MERCEDES-BENZ • HONDA • PORSCHE • AUDI • MERHOW HORSE VANS

&DATE&

&NAME&
&ADDRESS&
&ADDRESS1/o&
&C-S-Z&

Dear &SALUTATION&:

We are writing this letter to update our close friends and associates with the progress of The Gerrish Difference which includes:

    1. lifetime transferable rustproofing guarantee
    2. guaranteed extended warranties up to 50,000 miles
        or five years
    3. very flexible lease and finance arrangements
    4. a service shuttle to the central Upper Valley
        area
    5. a 12 month/12,000 mile used car guarantee for
        qualified orders.

With our hard work, and the cooperation and assistance of friends,
we are motivated to set very high goals for the future. To achieve
these goals, we will be relying on two major factors:

    1. our experience in the automotive field

                 AND...

    2. your referral of me to anyone who is thinking of buying or
        selling a car.

Please mention my name to your contacts, but also I ask that you
CALL ME PERSONALLY SO THAT I CAN CONTACT THEM DIRECTLY.

If I'm away from the dealership, please leave your name. I will
return your call promptly.

Let me extend my thanks for your help.

Sincerely,

Kurt D. Gerrish
President

KDG/jlb

WOODSTOCK EAST • WOODSTOCK, VERMONT 05091—802/457-2222

Source: Company files.

Promotional Activities

Automobile companies were among the largest national advertisers in the United States. It was estimated that the General Motors Corporation, for example, had spent $549 million for advertising in 1982, making it the third largest advertiser in the United States. Ford Motor Company was estimated to be number 12, with $313.5 million. The leading Japanese importer, Nissan Motors Corporation USA, ranked 55th with spending of $117.6 million, and Toyota Motor Sales, another leading Japanese importer, ranked 58th with $111.3 million. American Honda Motor Corporation had spent $94.9 million and ranked 64th, with an estimated $42.1 million of this amount spent for its automobile lines. Volkswagen of America, whose products included Porsche and Audi automobiles, was 61st with total expenditures of $98 million, of which an estimated $11.4 million was spent on Audi and $8 million on Porsche. In every case, network television received most of the spending, followed by magazines, spot television, radio, and newspapers.[1]

Published estimates of advertising spending by Mercedes-Benz were not available, but Kurt Gerrish estimated these to be in excess of $50 million. It appeared that Mercedes-Benz had been spending conservatively for much of 1983 until the introduction of the Model 190, at which time major increases in print and television advertising were observed.

Kurt Gerrish, John Sloan, and Jim Bailey, vice president and sales manager, all agreed that the automobile companies were responsible for promoting the individual car makes, whereas Gerrish Motors' advertising and promotional activities were intended to identify Gerrish Motors with the car names and to attract prospective customers to the dealership. Customers for each of the three product lines were described by John Sloan as "people who buy the car because they want it, not because they need it." Mercedes-Benz, Honda, and Porsche-Audi were cars held in high regard by the "auto buff," the person with above-average interest in automobiles, who read such publications as *Auto Week*, *Road & Track*, *Motor Trend*, and *Car & Driver*. These magazines regularly featured articles about performance tests and new models from these manufacturers, a very important source of promotion for these makes. Each of the manufacturers supplied the dealer with a description of customer demographics and other characteristics of their target customer, to help the dealer identify and sell to the right prospects.

In recent months, Gerrish advertising had been modified away from "Gerrish Motors" in favor of identifying Gerrish with the specific

---

[1] All of these expenditure estimates are taken from *Advertising Age*, September 8, 1983.

makes—Gerrish Honda, Gerrish Mercedes-Benz, Gerrish Porsche, and Gerrish Audi. There was some concern that mentioning all lines at the same time created confusion or the impression that Gerrish was a huge, impersonal organization. Following each mention of the Gerrish name with a single automobile name was believed to be a way of creating stronger identification for each make with the Gerrish operation. Jim Bailey said, "We believe the manufacturers are doing a very

Exhibit 3
Recent Print Advertising

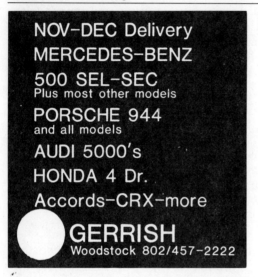

Source: *The Valley News*, White River Junction, Vermont.

Exhibit 3 *(concluded)*

Source: *TRAVELHOST* Magazine 17, no. 11 (December 11, 1983).

good job of selling the specific car. Our objective is to let the prospect know that we sell that product. We do not have a highly competitive market area where we have to steal the sale from another dealer with the same lines."

Kurt Gerrish always served as the spokesman for his company in its television and radio advertising. The current campaign used the theme "The Gerrish Difference," and stressed the quality of Gerrish Motors' service, including such specific things as "the Tri-Town Shuttle," a Mercedes-Benz 300TD station wagon that transported customers between Woodstock and the White River Junction/Hanover-Lebanon area while their cars were in Woodstock for service. Other ads featured the distinctive lineup of automobiles, the elegance of the showroom, the fact that Gerrish sold only official factory parts, and the training of the service technicians. Exhibit 3 shows some of Gerrish Motors' recent print advertising. Exhibit 4 is a script for one of the radio commercials.

Sales personnel were instructed to ask every prospect with whom they had contact in the showroom or on the telephone where they had learned about Gerrish Motors. A recent tabulation produced the following results:

Source	Number	Percentage
Yellow Pages	25	17.9
The Valley News*	1	0.7
WNNE-TV (White River Junction)	1	0.7
Other TV	1	0.7
Road sign	2	1.4
Radio	1	0.7
Referral (word of mouth)	60	42.9
Just walked into showroom	21	15.0
Telephoned (no source given)	23	16.4
Came to car lot outside	5	3.6
Totals	140	100.0

* *The Valley News* was the local newspaper, published in Lebanon, New Hampshire.

Exhibit 4
Examples of Radio Commercials, 1983

Remember 1973, the Honda Civic?
The right time, the right place
with exactly the right car.
Then 1976, Honda Accord—sporty and quick
dazzling the market place
with super value.
Last year, Honda Prelude, acknowledged
as best by far in its class.
Now Honda Civic for 84—bold space,
efficient design—CRX sporty performance.
Wait until you see the new Civic wagon.
Honda—light years ahead. Test drive and
buy a Gerrish Honda
where the Gerrish Difference continues.

*   *   *   *   *

Have you ever been fooled by auto parts
that might cost a bit less, but appear as
the genuine article? These "gypsy parts"
are often quality control rejects
from the original equipment manufacturers.
At Gerrish Mercedes-Benz, Honda, Porsche, Audi,
Rick and Stewart rely on genuine parts.
Parts guaranteed by the manufacturer and Gerrish.
We don't cut corners.
You pay a fair price for the genuine article.
When you drive the best, maintain it with the best.
Gerrish Mercedes-Benz, Honda, Porsche, Audi.
In Woodstock, where the Gerrish Difference continues.

Source: Company files.

Since 1977, American Honda Motor Company had provided to each of its dealers the results of its biannual Honda Dealer Image Study conducted by J. D. Power & Associates. This survey involved national samples of over 50,000 Honda customers and evaluated every dealer on a variety of dimensions relating to sales information, service, parts, warranty, etc. It also reported detailed information about customers' shopping habits, what other makes they considered, and where they first learned about their Honda dealer. Selected results from the previous four surveys are presented in Exhibit 5.

Expenditures

Gerrish Motors tried to take maximum advantage of the multiple media available in its market area. Expenditures for advertising by media type are shown in Exhibit 6. Drive-time radio was favored for reaching people in their automobiles traveling to and from work. The

Exhibit 5
Results of Honda Customer Survey, 1977–1983

Survey year	1977	1979	1981	1983	1983
Number of Gerrish customers	88	69	64	71	
Total U.S. sample					57,168

How did you first learn about the dealer from which you purchased your Honda?

	Percent Gerrish customers				Percent total U.S.
	1977	1979	1981	1983	1983
Friend/relative/Honda owner............	30.7	53.6	29.7	43.7	37.4
Drove by/saw sign...................	27.3	13.0	21.9	7.0	18.7
Yellow Pages.......................	9.1	11.6	6.3	5.6	9.2
Newspaper ad......................	5.7	1.4	6.3	1.4	9.3
Television ad......................	—	—	—	5.6	2.5
Radio ad	3.4	1.4	9.4	7.0	1.6
Magazine ad	—	—	—	—	0.5
Only one local Honda dealer	—	—	—	29.6	20.6
Auto Show	3.4	—	—	—	—
Other	20.5	18.8	26.4	7.0	8.3*

Why did you decide to buy your Honda from the dealer you did?

From the 1983 survey	Percent Gerrish customers	Percent total U.S.
Car available/delivery sooner	32.4	30.5
Lower cost than other dealers	12.7	36.0
Closer than other dealers.........................	15.5	21.5
Salesman's attitude/knowledge	23.9	27.8
Reputation for good service........................	22.5	16.1
Only one local Honda dealer.......................	23.9	16.8
Recommended by friend/relative....................	9.9	13.1
Bought previous car here..........................	18.3	12.4
Showroom looked better...........................	8.5	1.8
Service facility looked better	7.0	3.2

* Only this last column sums to more than 100 percent, reflecting a few multiple answers; no Gerrish customer gave more than one answer.

Source: Company files.

rather large variety of local newspapers were also used extensively. With the range of automobiles from the small Honda Civic and CRX to the large Audi and Mercedes-Benz automobiles, Gerrish Motors believed that virtually the entire adult population of the area were potentially customers for Gerrish Motors. However, the stress was always on the sophisticated customer, even for the small Hondas, the driver who appreciated quality and performance in an automobile.

Expenditures for advertising had been relatively consistent over the years, reflecting Gerrish's commitment to continually developing the market and to projecting a quality image. Exhibit 7 summarizes advertising expenditures and sales over the previous five years. It was common to cut back on media expenditures during the month of Decem-

Exhibit 6
Advertising Expenditures, January 1 to November 30, 1983

Radio:
WNHV–White River Junction	$ 4,861
WTSL–Hanover/Lebanon	1,607
WECM–Claremont.	2,090
WDCR–Dartmouth College (Hanover)	726
WRUT–Rutland (Swap for car)	10,800
Total radio	20,084

Television:
WNNE–Hanover	5,300
Total television	5,300

Print:
The Wall Street Journal.	1,400
New York Times	60
Rutland Herald	900
Valley News (Lebanon).	1,200
Vermont Standard (Woodstock)	6,000
Quechee Times.	250
White River Valley Herald (Randolph)	100
Wagon-Wheels	500
TRAVELHOST (distributed to hotels & motels)	3,600
Total print media	14,010

Other:
Yellow Pages.	1,750
Vermont Institute of Natural Science (Use of car for year)	2,500
Salon Show	3,000
Manufacturers' brochures	2,500
Business cards, printing, etc.	400
Miscellaneous promotional activities.	3,256
Administrative expense.	3,600
Total other	17,006
Total.	$56,400

Source: Company files.

ber, and to spend more on alternative forms of promotion, in order to avoid the advertising clutter of the Christmas season. Many dealers used a rough rule of thumb of approximately $100 per car sold to determine their annual advertising expenditures. Gerrish avoided reliance on such rules, preferring instead to look at overall economic conditions and business requirements.

As he reflected on what to do for the remainder of 1983 and for 1984, Kurt Gerrish thought he was faced with a real dilemma. On the one hand, it didn't seem to make much sense to spend advertising dollars to create demand that he couldn't satisfy. On the other hand, continued sales performance was vitally important to the morale and profitability of his organization and to his success in obtaining allocations of additional automobiles from the manufacturers. He described the allo-

Exhibit 7
Advertising Expenditures and Sales Volume, 1979–1983

Year	Automobile sales	Advertising
1979	$5,391,926	$24,019
1980	5,617,258	31,896
1981	6,845,314	48,341
1982	6,325,010	47,109
1983 (est.).	8,000,000	60,000

Source: Company records.

cation process as "very political." Dealers actively competed for the allocation of additional cars from the manufacturers. To receive higher allocations, it was necessary to demonstrate real need and success in moving the cars at a high gross profit after they had been obtained. The higher allocations then provided the basis for future allocations. Not only the number of cars allocated but the quality, in terms of model mix, color, special features, etc., was influenced by this process. At the current time, the new Mercedes-Benz 190E and 500 SEL models, as well as the established 380SL, the new Audi 5000S and Quattro, and the new Honda CRX and the Prelude models were all described by Gerrish as "very hot." Gerrish believed he was one of only a few dealers on the East Coast selling Hondas at sticker price; most dealers were believed to be "packing" their cars with "additional dealer profit," and so noting it on the window price stickers. Commenting on his decision to not ask for additional profit, even when customers apparently were willing to pay it for cars in short supply, Gerrish commented, "We like to sell each car as if it is the first of many we are going to sell to that customer, not the last."

Returning to the monthly financial statement for November, Kurt Gerrish continued to worry about what changes he should make in the allocation of his promotional and other expenditures. Among his options, he thought, was to shift some of his advertising dollars into additional charitable contributions and into travel and entertainment. He had actively encouraged his salespeople to spend money on customer entertainment. Total expenditures for travel and entertainment to date had been $14,197, a figure which he believed might be too low. He stated bluntly, "You can buy customers. If you treat them well on a personal basis, they have confidence they will be treated well on a business basis." While he knew that specific sales results could not be traced to his advertising activities, he realized that ongoing awareness of Gerrish Motors was an important factor. At the same time, he thought current market conditions might permit an experiment in which he would cut off all media advertising for a period of time, spend an equal amount on direct mail, customer entertainment, and other forms of nonmedia promotion. If he did so, he would want to be sure that he could measure the results of the experiment and come to a better determination of how to allocate his promotional resources in the future.

Questions

1. What is the role of advertising in Gerrish's promotional strategy?
2. Who is Gerrish's target customer? How can they reach that customer?
3. How can Gerrish measure the effectiveness of its advertising expenditures?
4. What would happen if Gerrish eliminated all advertising?
5. How should the level of advertising expenditures be determined?
6. What action would you recommend?

C A S E 6–8

Perdue Foods, Inc.

"It Takes a Tough Man to Make a Tender Chicken" had become the theme of the advertising campaign developed for Perdue Foods, Inc., of Salisbury, Maryland, by its New York-based agency, Scali, McCabe, Sloves, Inc. The campaign often featured Mr. Frank Perdue, president of Perdue Foods who had become something of a celebrity as a result in the New York market and elsewhere where the print and radio and TV ad campaign had been run. From an obscure position as one of several hundred companies raising broilers in 1968, Perdue Foods had become, by the end of 1972, the largest producer of branded broilers in the United States, killing about 1.5 million birds each week, almost twice as many as when the new agency had acquired the account in 1971.

Such visibility attracted competitors as well as customers and in February of 1973 a major competitor, Maryland Chicken Processors, Inc., had launched a direct frontal attack on Perdue Chickens with ads in the New England trade press carrying the headline

> Read how Otis Esham's Buddy Boy chicken is going to beat the pants off the other guy's chicken.

The "other guy," of course, was Frank Perdue, and the Buddy Boy trade ad even featured a back-of-the-head picture of Frank Perdue with the caption "the other guy." It was a no-holds barred approach which made direct and frequent reference to Perdue Chickens. For example, the trade ad began:

> The other guy has been a friend and neighbor of ours for years, as well as a competitor.
> To be truthful about it, our hat's off to him. In the past year or so, he's probably done more for the chicken business than any other guy we know.
> With his help and the help of his fine New York advertising agency, the consumer is now beginning to realize that it's worth paying a few

more pennies a pound to get the kind of fine, plump, tender, golden-yellow chicken we produce down here on the Eastern Shore of Maryland.

What this means is that the days of footballing the price of chicken all over the lot are probably numbered.

The new name of the game is Profits, and that's not just profits for the chicken business but profits for you, too.

So, as far as we are concerned, that other guy is doing a real good job. But he's vulnerable.

The other guy is a spunky little guy (no offense intended, Frank) who loves to go on television and the radio and tell folks about the fine kind of chicken we produce down home.

You think those commercials are going to hurt us?

Uh-uh. They can't do anything but *help* us.

What those commercials are doing is making the consumer aware that a chicken that's good enough to carry the brand name of a proud producer is going to be a *better* chicken than the one that is only good enough to be acceptable to the U.S. government.

Well, the actual truth is, those commercials could just as well be talking about Otis Esham's fresh Buddy Boy chicken. Because Otis's methods of raising and processing chicken are just about identical to the other guy's.

Except for one very important thing and here's where we get to the part about how the other guy is vulnerable.

That was only the first of four columns in a double-page spread. The ad went on to say that "the other guy's" chickens are packed and shipped in ice and that, as the ice melts, "your chicken is going to begin to get all waterlogged," whereas Buddy Boy chickens are quick-chilled to 30°F and shipped in refrigerated trucks. The ad reported that Purity Supreme, a major New England chain, had taken on the Buddy Boy product and that a "hot" Boston-based ad agency, Pearson and Mac-Donald, had been given the Buddy Boy account. The ad also featured pictures of Otis Esham (whose position was not disclosed[1]), Jack Ackerman, head meat buyer for Purity Supreme (with the caption "Jack Ackerman of Purity Supreme, a 'tough bird' "), Pearson and Mac-Donald, and a crate of dressed broilers showing the "old-fashioned 'ice-packed' method." The ad went on to explain that "By the time you're reading this, Otis Esham will be on the major Boston radio stations telling your customers about how his fresh Buddy Boy chicken is a better chicken because it's a chilled chicken." More information about media plans was given, and readers were given a telephone number to call collect in Parsonsburg, Maryland, to talk with "Bubba Shelton, Otis Esham's right-hand man for sales."

---

[1] In point of fact, Esham was president of Maryland Chicken Processors, a family-owned business. Esham and Perdue had known each other all their lives; at one time they had owned abutting properties.

An executive at Scali, McCabe, Sloves called this "one of the most blatant frontal assaults I have ever seen in advertising" as the account executive and top agency personnel began to talk about their response. Three classes of action were being considered. Some favored simply ignoring the Buddy Boy campaign because "it can't hurt us, it can only help us." Others wanted to respond directly, with trade and consumer ads, to the charge that ice-packing was an inferior method and that chickens became "waterlogged" because this was not true. A third group suggested that now was the time for an entirely new Perdue campaign to take the initiative away from Buddy Boy and go after entirely new segments.

Growth of Perdue Foods, Inc.

An article in *Esquire* magazine in April 1973, described chicken farming as "about the last free enterprise industry in America. Chicken is produced in a no-holds barred, rags-to-riches, no-control system, at the fascinating confluence of all the commercial strains in the land: the chicken is where the most volatile elements of the assembly line, of the farm and the field, and bid-and-ask all come together." Until 1968, Perdue was raising chickens for resale to other processors. In 1967, sales had been about $35 million, mainly from selling live birds, but the business also included one of the East Coast's largest grain storage and poultry feed milling operations, soybean processing mulch plants, a hatchery, and 600 farmers raising broilers under contract to Perdue.

A buyer's market existed in 1967 which had squeezed chicken profits. More and more processors were lining up their own contract growers and cutting out Perdue and other middlemen. As Frank Perdue noted, "The situation was good for processors. As in all commodities, profit depends on high volume and small margins. A processor's normal profit on chickens runs 1/4 cent to 1/2 cent per pound. But in 1967's market, processors were paying us 10 cents a pound for what cost us 14 cents to produce, and their profits were as much as 7 cents per pound."

As a result of these conditions, Frank Perdue decided to redesign his business to coordinate egg hatching, chick delivery and feeding, broiler processing, and overnight delivery to market, and to develop his own brand. The aim was to develop a quality chicken that could demand premium prices. Special attention was devoted to development of exact feeding formulas which would optimize the chickens' growth rate and give the chicken a golden-colored skin preferred by consumers.

Over the next three years, Perdue began consumer advertising on a limited basis. Distribution was concentrated in New York, with a small percentage in other East Coast cities and as far west as Cleveland. The Perdue brand was identified by a tag on the wing of the processed chicken. Distribution was concentrated in butcher shops and smaller chain food outlets.

Perdue Advertising

As the new strategy of integrated production and product differentiation began to prove itself in the form of increased sales and profit margins, Frank Perdue became increasingly concerned with the quality of his advertising. After a period of intensive reading on the subject and interviews with almost 50 agencies, Perdue selected Scali, McCabe, Sloves, Inc. in April of 1971. The agency immediately began to prepare for a major campaign to be launched in New York City in July. Over Frank Perdue's initial objections, the agency developed a campaign featuring him as the spokesman for the product.

The campaign focused on the quality of Perdue's product, often using subtle humor to make the point. The direction of the campaign is indicated in Exhibits 1–4, photo-boards of four TV commercials. Radio and newspaper advertising was also planned. A new wing tag was designed featuring the company name and a money-back guarantee of quality. In an early 60-second TV commercial, Frank Perdue made the following comments:

> When people ask me about my chickens, two questions invariably come up. The first is "Perdue, your chickens have such a great golden-yellow color it's almost unnatural. Do you dye them?" Honestly, there's absolutely nothing artificial about the color of my chickens. If you had a chicken and fed it good yellow corn, alfalfa, corn gluten, and marigold petals, it would just naturally be yellow. You can't go around dyeing chickens. They wouldn't stand for it.
>
> The other question is "Perdue, your chickens are so plump and juicy, do you give them hormone injections?" This one really gets my hackles up. I do nothing of the kind. When chickens eat and live as well as mine do, you don't have to resort to artificial techniques.

In the first year with the new agency, all advertising expenditures were aimed at the consumer. Only after consumer awareness and preference had been created was trade advertising begun. By the end of the first year, Perdue had achieved distribution in more than half of all New York butcher shops and small retail food outlets. Consumer surveys showed well over 50 percent awareness of the Perdue brand. While financial information was not publicly available, Perdue said "you have to assume it paid off." Competitors estimated that Perdue's costs increased between 2 cents and 4 cents per pound due to promotional expenses. At the retail level, Perdue chickens were able to command a premium of 5 cents to 10 cents per pound. One out of every six

Exhibit 1

1. FRANK PERDUE: A chicken is what it eats. And my chickens eat better than . . .

2. people do. I store my own grain and mix my own feed.

3. And give my Perdue chickens nothing but pure well water to drink.

4. That's why my chickens always have that healthy golden-yellow color.

5. If you want to eat as good as my chickens, you'll just have to eat my chickens.

IT TAKES A TOUGH MAN TO MAKE A TENDER CHICKEN.

PERDUE

6. That's really good.

Exhibit 2

2. That's why you can only buy Perdue chickens . . . .

3. in butcher shops and better markets.

1. FRANK PERDUE: I don't . allow my superior chickens in just any store.

4. (VOICE OVER): I don't want to give my name a bad name.

Exhibit 3

1. FRANK PERDUE: Nobody gets near my chickens unless they wear this fancy get-up.

2. This is not to protect people from my chickens.

3. It's to protect my chickens from people.

4. My competitors think I'm nuts to go through all this.

5. But why do you suppose my chickens always have that healthy golden-yellow color . . .

6. instead of a pale one. I'll tell you why. Clean livin'.

7. (SILENT)

Exhibit 4

1. FRANK PERDUE: Knowing how good my chickens are isn't good enough for me.

2. So every week I have my people go out and buy cases of my competitors' birds.

3. We put them through the same rigid inspection that our own Perdue chickens have to . . .

4. go through. It costs me a lot of money. But it's worth it.

5. It's the only way I have of knowing that I'm ahead of these guys.

6. How're we doing? Did we win yet?

chickens sold in the New York market carried the Perdue brand. Similar campaigns were launched in Hartford, Connecticut (March 1972), and Baltimore (April 1972). Sales in 1972 exceeded $80 million.

Perdue advertising attracted a good deal of public attention, partly due to the distinctiveness of Frank Perdue's presentation which was described by one commentator as having the sincerity and fervor of a southern preacher. Stories about the company and its advertising appeared in *Business Week* (September 16, 1972), *Newsweek* (October 16, 1972), and *Esquire* (April 1973), among other places.

The Boston Campaign

Perdue's Boston campaign was launched in December of 1972, following the basic pattern now established. The Boston market was somewhat different from New York in that a high percentage of chicken sales occurred through chain store supermarkets, whereas in New York, the majority was sold through butcher shops and independent food outlets.

Shortly thereafter, Otis Esham publicized his plans to advertise in Boston and even gave the exact dates on which consumer advertising would break. Perdue's immediate response had been to triple GRP TV and radio coverage and to contract for additional newspaper coverage on heavy food-buying days in anticipation of Buddy Boy's campaign. Perdue's first radio ads ran on December 18, and TV ads began on January 15.

Now that Buddy Boy's first trade advertising had appeared early in February, executives at Scali, McCabe, Sloves were wondering what steps to take next. Esham was planning radio for the second week of February, and TV was scheduled for the beginning of April. It would be possible for Scali, McCabe, Sloves to prepare television ads within 72 hours to refute the points about "waterlogged" chickens in the Buddy Boy advertising.

A principal of Buddy Boy's agency, Terry MacDonald, was quoted as saying "We're going to kill them. They have brilliant advertising. But we have the product advantage."

Question

What action should Scali, McCabe, Sloves recommend to Frank Perdue?

C A S E 6–9

Pennwalt Corporation

Corporate Advertising Campaign

As the year 1977 came to a close, executives of Pennwalt Corporation were evaluating the company's corporate advertising program. Media commitments on the campaign extended through the third quarter of 1978, but strategic planning and copy development for a new campaign would have to begin very soon if any significant changes in the campaign were to occur at that time. The current corporate campaign had been closely identified with the personal business philosophy of Mr. William P. Drake, chairman of the board and chief executive officer of Pennwalt, who was reaching mandatory retirement age in April 1978. Thus, the end of 1977 was a particularly opportune time to evaluate the company's corporate advertising program.

Mr. Drake's Management Philosophy

In the early 1960s, Mr. Drake had begun to discuss matters of business philosophy and economic principles in his annual reports to his shareholders. He stressed his faith in the free enterprise system, the importance of reasonable profits, and the fact that the firm's growth in sales revenues and earnings reflected the dedicated efforts of thousands of hardworking employees, who Mr. Drake referred to as "our fundamental resource." Over the years, this thinking had evolved into a statement of corporate purpose, stated in the company's 1976 annual report as follows:

> Pennwalt's Purpose is to provide, profitably, socially useful products and services through the efficient use of the resources available to us for the benefit of our five major publics: our customers, our employees, our shareholders, our suppliers, and the general public. This last public in-

---

cludes, of course, federal, state, and local governments and the commu-
nities in which we operate. In fulfilling this purpose, we shall continue
to rely on the integrity and good judgment of all our employees—as we
have for the past 126 years.

The rank ordering of publics in terms of importance, putting customers first, was quite intentional. In the 1976 annual report, Mr.
Drake also made a point of noting that the basic viability of the competitive enterprise system had been maintained by "the competitive
enterprise of free people," despite increased government regulation
which made the system no longer "free enterprise."

Company Background

Pennwalt Corporation had net sales of $777,315,000 in 1976 and
earned $34,910,000 after taxes, equal to 12.2 percent on shareholders'
investment. This represented the sixth consecutive year of growth in
earnings per share, from $1.16 in 1971 to $3.56 in 1976, an average
annual growth rate of over 20 percent. Over a 19-year period, earnings
had increased every year except two, 1969 and 1970, which reflected,
in Mr. Drake's words, "acquisition indigestion." He believed that the
risks involved in this acquisition strategy had been worthwhile, however as illustrated by the company's continued growth in earnings
through the 1974–75 recession. At the end of 1976, the company had
17,450 persons or institutions as shareholders of common stock, and
an additional 6,900 holders of preferred stock.

In 1977, Pennwalt was a highly diversified firm, manufacturing
products aimed at five carefully chosen major markets: health care, the
chemical process industry, agriculture and good processing, plastics,
and environmental cleanup. These five markets constituted over 80
percent of company sales. (See Exhibit 1.) Virtually all of the company's products were related to the chemicals industry, including
chemically oriented precision equipment. Consumers undoubtedly

Exhibit 1
Pennwalt's Five Major Markets as of 1976

Major market	Sales volume (000)	Share of sales
Health	$218,000	28%
Chemical process industry	171,000	22
Agriculture and food processing	78,000	10
Plastics	78,000	10
Environmental cleanup	85,000	11
	630,000	81
Other	147,315	19
Total	$777,315	100%

Source: *Annual Report*, 1976.

knew Pennwalt best through its over-the-counter health care products including Allerest® and Sinarest® brands of decongestant, Fresh® deodorant, Cruex® skin powders, the Desenex® line of antifungal agents, Caldesene® medicated powder, and Bare Face® acne skin medicine, as well as the ethical (i.e., prescription) products of its pharmaceutical division and its dental products, but this represented only $218 million or 28 percent of Pennwalt's total sales. Other product groups included inorganic chemicals, organic chemicals, chemical specialties, fluorochemicals, plastics, food processing and agricultural chemicals, water treatment equipment (including chlorinators, flow meters, a fluoride saturator, and other control units), centrifuges of several different types, plastic molding equipment, navigational aids, dental chairs and related equipment, dental burrs, etc. All in all, there were over 1,200 primary products in the Pennwalt product line. About 10 percent of Pennwalt's sales came from products that were new in the past five years. Pennwalt spent $18.7 million on R&D in 1976, an increase of 10 percent over the prior year. Pennwalt Corporation purchases from outside vendors in 1976 equaled $472 million.

"The Little Red Hen"

At the conclusion of required business at the 1975 annual shareholders' meeting, Mr. Drake had read his own adaptation of the classic children's fable of "The Little Red Hen." The adaptation reflected Mr. Drake's deep concern that the American business system was poorly understood. Many shareholders who had attended the meeting subsequently wrote to Mr. Drake and Pennwalt's corporate headquarters requesting a copy of his remarks. In the fall of 1975, in response to the large amount of interest shown, executives responsible for corporate advertising decided to publish the full text of Mr. Drake's remarks as a corporate advertisement in several national publications such as *Business Week, Forbes, Newsweek, The Economist,* and *The Wall Street Journal,* and similar journals. The advertisement that resulted is shown in Exhibit 2.

The 1976 Corporate Campaign

In 1976, these officials decided to launch a more significant corporate campaign, based on the tremendous response to "The Little Red Hen" advertisement. A basic reason for the campaign was the belief that Pennwalt, as distinct from its subsidiaries and divisions, was not well known. One objective, therefore, was to make Pennwalt better known among the various publics important to it. Management felt that a well-known corporate identity could help Pennwalt sell its products, especially undifferentiated commodities such as chlorine, caustic

Exhibit 2
"The Little Red Hen" Advertisement Run in 1975

The <u>Modern</u> Little Red Hen.

Once upon a time, there was a little red hen who scratched about the barnyard until she uncovered some grains of wheat. She called her neighbors and said, "If we plant this wheat, we shall have bread to eat. Who will help me plant it?"

"Not I," said the cow.

"Not I," said the duck.

"Not I," said the pig.

"Not I," said the goose.

"Then I will," said the little red hen. And she did. The wheat grew tall and ripened into golden grain. "Who will help me reap my wheat?" asked the little red hen.

"Not I," said the duck.

"Out of my classification," said the pig.

"I'd lose my seniority," said the cow.

"I'd lose my unemployment compensation," said the goose.

"Then I will," said the little red hen, and she did.

At last it came time to bake the bread. "Who will help me bake the bread?" asked the little red hen.

"That would be overtime for me," said the cow.

"I'd lose my welfare benefits," said the duck.

"I'm a dropout and never learned how," said the pig.

"If I'm to be the only helper, that's discrimination," said the goose.

"Then I will," said the little red hen.

She baked five loaves and held them up for her neighbors to see.

They all wanted some and, in fact, demanded a share. But the little red hen said, "No, I can eat the five loaves myself."

"Excess profits!" cried the cow.

"Capitalist leech!" screamed the duck.

"I demand equal rights!" yelled the goose.

And the pig just grunted. And they painted "unfair" picket signs and marched round and round the little red hen, shouting obscenities.

When the government agent came, he said to the little red hen, "You must not be greedy."

"But I earned the bread," said the little red hen.

"Exactly," said the agent. "That is the wonderful free enterprise system. Anyone in the barnyard can earn as much as he wants. But under our modern government regulations, the productive workers must divide their product with the idle."

And they lived happily ever after, including the little red hen, who smiled and clucked, "I am grateful. I am grateful."

But her neighbors wondered why she never again baked any more bread.

At the conclusion of the required business of the 1975 Pennwalt Annual Meeting, Chairman and President William P. Drake, commenting on the state of the company in today's economy, read this, his own adaptation of a modern version of the well-known fable of The Little Red Hen.

For 125 years we've been making things people need – including profits.

PENNWALT

C O R P O R A T I O N
Three Parkway. Philadelphia. Pa. 19102
Chemicals • Health Products • Specialized Equipment

soda, and caustic potash. Another objective, albeit secondary, was to enhance the view which financial analysts had of the firm and thereby to influence the price/earnings ratio of Pennwalt stock. For this reason, it was deemed appropriate to include a brief review of the firm's recent financial performance in the advertising. Another set of objectives for the corporate advertising campaign were reflected in Mr. Drake's comments to shareholders in the 1975 annual report, in a section labeled "Challenges." After commenting on some specific operating problems, Mr. Drake continued:

> As I see it, all of us as business people, as shareholders, as employees, and yes, as parents too, have failed miserably in extolling the virtues of our competitive enterprise system and how it works. Unfortunately, part of this is due to the fact that many of us don't understand the competitive enterprise system and how it works. This is particularly true among some of our elected or appointed representatives in government, in some of the news media and among other thought leaders such as may be found on college campuses and even in pulpits.
>
> This country, now in its 200th year, was built by producers—physical producers and mental producers. It hasn't been simply by chance that such producers created and built a country in which today's citizen enjoys more benefits and greater freedom than may be found in any other country in the world. I can think of no better way for each of us to commemorate this, our Bicentennial year, than to go back to basics and really learn what the competitive enterprise system has done and can continue to do if we will just understand it and let it work unshackled by the myriad of governmental regulations that are being imposed these days.
>
> Unfortunately, many of these regulations have come about as a result of the misconception that every economic ill, real or imaginary, that might befall us can be corrected by new regulations or laws.
>
> This, to me, is the biggest challenge confronting all of us who would like to create more and better jobs for self-respecting producers who are able and willing to work. And, I might add, for people who seek an opportunity to create their own security through their own efforts rather than being satisfied with having their security provided by someone else. Success in meeting this challenge will, in turn, enable those of us who are so fortunate as to be able to work to provide also for those who are legitimately unable to work.

The specific advertisements constituting the 1976 campaign are reproduced as Exhibits 3–6. The above philosophy was reflected in the "tag line" on each ad—"For 126 years we've been making things people need—including profits." This tag line had been chosen against the recommendation of the advertising agency, The Aitken-Kynett Company, which had advocated "these ads ask only that you stop and think."

Exhibit 3
An Advertisement in the 1976 Campaign

THE COMPETITIVE
We believe in it...

The <u>Modern</u> Little Red Hen.

Once upon a time, there was a little red hen who scratched about the barnyard until she uncovered some grains of wheat. She called her neighbors and said, "If we plant this wheat, we shall have bread to eat. Who will help me plant it?"

"Not I," said the cow.

"Not I," said the duck.

"Not I," said the pig.

"Not I," said the goose.

"Then I will," said the little red hen. And she did. The wheat grew tall and ripened into golden grain. "Who will help me reap my wheat?" asked the little red hen.

"Not I," said the duck.

"Out of my classification," said the pig.

"I'd lose my seniority," said the cow.

"I'd lose my unemployment compensation," said the goose.

"Then I will," said the little red hen, and she did.

At last it came time to bake the bread. "Who will help me bake the bread?" asked the little red hen.

"That would be overtime for me," said the cow.

"I'd lose my welfare benefits," said the duck.

"I'm a dropout and never learned how," said the pig.

"If I'm to be the only helper, that's discrimination," said the goose.

"Then I will," said the little red hen.

She baked five loaves and held them up for her neighbors to see.

They all wanted some and, in fact, demanded a share. But the little red hen said, "No, I can eat the five loaves myself."

"Excess profits!" cried the cow.

"Capitalist leech!" screamed the duck.

"I demand equal rights!" yelled the goose.

And the pig just grunted. And they painted "unfair" picket signs and marched round and round the little red hen, shouting obscenities.

When the government agent came, he said to the little red hen, "You must not be greedy."

"But I earned the bread," said the little red hen.

"Exactly," said the agent. "That is the wonderful free enterprise system. Anyone in the barnyard can earn as much as he wants. But under our modern government regulations, the productive workers must divide their product with the idle."

And they lived happily ever after, including the little red hen, who smiled and clucked, "I am grateful. I am grateful."

But her neighbors wondered why she never again baked any more bread.

At the conclusion of the required business of the 1975 Pennwalt Annual Meeting, Chairman and President William P. Drake, commenting on the state of the company in today's economy, read this, his own adaptation of a modern version of the well-known fable of The Little Red Hen.

For 125 years we've been making things people need–including profits.

PENNWALT
CORPORATION

Exhibit 3 *(concluded)*

Exhibit 4
An Advertisement in the 1976 Campaign

"Let's commemorate the Bicentennial by understanding fully the benefits of competitive enterprise."

This country was built by *producers*—both mental and physical.

It wasn't by chance that such producers created and built a nation in which today's citizen enjoys more benefits and greater freedom than in any other nation on earth. The bedrock of our system is competitive enterprise, from which come the profits that permit people in business to help meet society's needs—both as individuals and as part of an organization.

Only from profits come scholarships, aid to charities and hospitals, and taxes that support all government activities—unemployment compensation and social security, for example.

Sound and consistent profitable growth enables our own company to do the things we feel a good corporate citizen should do. I can think of no better way to honor our Bicentennial than to really learn what our competitive enterprise system is capable of if we will just understand it and allow it to work.

Adapted from remarks made by the chairman in Pennwalt's 1975 Annual Report.

Operating Record (000):	1971	1972	1973	1974	1975	First Quarter 1975	First Quarter 1976
Net Sales	$405,507	$441,010	$504,034	$641,002	$713,736	$169,521	$190,137
Net Earnings	$ 13,050	$ 16,072	$ 20,113	$ 26,983	$ 31,633*	$ 5,407*	$ 8,455
Per Share of Common Stock	$ 1.22	$ 1.58	$ 2.13	$ 2.81	$ 3.25*	$ .56*	$ .86

114 consecutive years of regular dividend payment on our common stock.

*Before special credit of $1,813,000 or $.19 per share.

For 126 years we've been making things people need—including profits.

Our Modern Little Red Hen speaks out for competitive enterprise. For her most recent message, write Director, Corporate Communications.

≥ PENNWALT
CORPORATION
Three Parkway. Philadelphia. Pa. 19102
Chemicals · Dental Products · Pharmaceuticals · Specialized Equipment

Exhibit 5
An Advertisement in the 1976 Campaign

Does business today need comprehensivists?

Is there a place for Renaissance man in today's computerized, automated, specialized world?

For men and women who scorn "group-think" for individual creativeness?

Who are as much at ease with the great masters as with computers, slide rules and test tubes?

For people who can master a field of specialization without becoming intellectually imprisoned by it?

For those who enjoy the excitement of a challenge more than the security of playing it safe? In short, for those who can operate in the many gray areas where things are neither black nor white?

We think so.

For these are the kinds of men and women who nurture our growth. Dreamers and thinkers. Risk-takers. Individuals who combine technological skills with a solid grounding in the humanities.

It's because of comprehensivists that Pennwalt today is stronger in products, in markets, in financial structure—yes, and more profitable —than at any time in our history.

Operating Record (000):	1971	1972	1973	1974	**1975**	First Quarter 1975	**First Quarter 1976**
Net Sales	$405,507	$441,010	$504,034	$641,002	**$713,736**	$169,521	**$190,137**
Net Earnings	$ 13,050	$ 16,072	$ 20,113	$ 26,983	**$ 31,633***	$ 5,407*	**$ 8,455**
Per Share of Common Stock	$ 1.22	$ 1.58	$ 2.13	$ 2.81	**$ 3.25***	$ .56*	**$ .86**

114 consecutive years of regular dividend payment on our common stock.

*Before special credit of $1,813,000 or $.19 per share.

For 126 years we've been making things people need—including profits.

Our Modern Little Red Hen thinks comprehensively. Write for her latest message to our Director of Corporate Communications.

PENNWALT
CORPORATION
Three Parkway, Philadelphia, Pa. 19102
Chemicals · Dental Products · Pharmaceuticals · Specialized Equipment

Exhibit 6
An Advertisement in the 1976 Campaign

To avoid risk, do nothing.
(But even then, you can't be sure.)

Risk is what life is all about. And business, too.

A risk is an opportunity. Even failure is an opportunity to risk again, but with more experience.

We risk our reputation on every new product; and our progress with every expansion. Our shareholders, too, accept a risk every time they invest in our future.

You might say that Pennwalt's successful growth has come from a *series* of carefully calculated risks in every aspect of our operations.

You see, we learned long ago that doing nothing can be the greatest risk of all. And that's a risk we shall never take.

Operating Record (000):	1971	1972	1973	1974	1975	First Quarter 1975	First Quarter 1976
Net Sales	$405,507	$441,010	$504,034	$641,002	**$713,736**	$169,521	**$190,137**
Net Earnings	$ 13,050	$ 16,072	$ 20,113	$ 26,983	**$ 31,633***	$ 5,407*	**$ 8,455**
Per Share of Common Stock...............	$ 1.22	$ 1.58	$ 2.13	$ 2.81	**$ 3.25***	$ .56*	**$ .86**

114 consecutive years of regular dividend payment on our common stock.

*Before special credit of $1,813,000 or $.19 per share.

For 126 years we've been making things people need—including profits.

Our Modern Little
Red Hen isn't afraid to
stick her neck out. For
her most recent message,
write Director, Corporate
Communications.

⊠ PENNWALT
C O R P O R A T I O N
Three Parkway. Philadelphia. Pa. 19102
Chemicals · Dental Products · Pharmaceuticals · Specialized Equipment

The 1976 campaign was deemed to be highly successful based on several hundred letters received at corporate headquarters, feedback from the field sales force of 1,300 persons, and from several conversations Mr. Drake and his colleagues had had with executives and directors of other corporations.

Organization of Marketing Communications

Throughout this period, Pennwalt's operating divisions had continued their own programs of product advertising and sales promotion. There was no assessment levied on the divisions for corporate advertising, the cost of which approached $1 million in 1976. In contrast, product advertising for the consumer products of Pennwalt was substantially greater than advertising and sales promotion budgets for industrial products, and both exceeded the amounts spent for the corporate campaign.

Until mid-1977, both corporate advertising and public relations had been the responsibility of the director of corporate communications. In June 1977, these responsibilities were divided between a director of advertising, Mr. Peter McCarthy, who supervised a staff of 10, and a director of public relations, Mrs. Kathleen Putnam, with a staff of 3. Both directors reported directly to the chairman of the board.

In 1977, the company was involved in a major corporate identity campaign which would more strongly emphasize the name Pennwalt. Division names such as S. S. White, Jelenko, Pharmacraft, Stokes, and Sharples would not be replaced but would supplement the corporate name. This program was the responsibility of the director of advertising. The director of public relations was responsible for the company's quarterly and annual reports to shareholders, for all press contacts, financial and editorial contacts, as well as the publication, six times each year, of the company's newspaper, *Profile*. The company's corporate advertising budget was about twice as large as the public relations budget.

The 1977 Campaign

Management was highly satisfied with the results of the 1976 campaign and hoped to build on that success. Mr. Drake continued to feel that there was a need to acquaint the public at large, and especially opinion leaders and "thought leaders," with basic economic concepts, as well as to continue to increase awareness of the Pennwalt name. At the same time, he was of the opinion that a large portion of corporate advertising by other companies lacked credibility because of the one-sidedness and self-interest often characterizing these campaigns.

"The Little Red Hen" had been Pennwalt's first attempt at corporate advocacy advertising. Before that, Pennwalt's corporate advertising had been of the type categorized by Pete McCarthy as "catalog" advertising, stressing the diversity of the company's product capability and intended to generate company and product awareness, with a resulting favorable impact on sales volume. The company's 1975 "capabilities" campaign, prior to "The Little Red Hen," and following such an approach, is illustrated in Exhibits 7 and 8, which show two of the six ads that appeared in the series.

Exhibit 7
Pennwalt's 1975 "Capabilities" Campaign

From a few grains of salt in 1850 has grown a worldwide corporation--a growing company with over $600 million in sales--whose efforts are creating sophisticated products from some of nature's most basic substances. We are that company. All 14,600 of us.

We make things people need.

1850-1975

C O R P O R A T I O N
Three Parkway, Philadelphia, Pa. 19102
Chemicals • Health Products • Specialized Equipment

Exhibit 8
Pennwalt's 1975 "Capabilities" Campaign

Man's best friend may be the chicken. Poultry, you see, is possibly our most efficient source of dinner table protein. Pennwalt's role: world leadership in organic sulfur chemicals, one of which is the essential ingredient in a remarkable feed supplement that brings chickens to market faster, healthier, and at lower cost.

We make things people need.

PENNWALT
CORPORATION
Three Parkway, Philadelphia. Pa. 19102
Chemicals • Health Products • Specialized Equipment

The impact of "The Little Red Hen" advertisement was indicated by the fact that by August 1977, the company had received requests for over 60,000 reprints of this specific ad. In contrast, Pete McCarthy, the director of advertising, questioned whether the "capabilities" campaign had been of much interest to anyone except those customers who purchased the products mentioned in a specific advertisement.

The 1977 campaign was developed with the objective of "declaring a leadership position for Pennwalt," in the words of Pete McCarthy. The audience was defined as "activists and skeptics." An activist was defined, for the purposes of the campaign, as any person who had, in the past 12 months:

1. Written to a magazine/newspaper editor.
2. Written to an elected official.
3. Addressed a public meeting.
4. Taken part in a civic issue.
5. Worked for a political party.
6. Engaged in fund raising.
7. Belonged to a board/civic club, etc.

This definition had been developed by the Target Group Index (TGI), a media research and consulting organization. Their research indicated that activists were generally better educated, had higher incomes, and had professional/managerial occupations. For example, TGI stated that:

1. College-educated adults are 27.2 percent of the total population but account for 55.1 percent of all adults who wrote to an editor.
2. 15.8 percent of all adults have professional/managerial occupations but account for 44.9 percent of all adults who have addressed a public meeting.
3. Only 19.7 percent of all adults have household incomes over $20,000, but these persons equal 33.1 percent of all adults who reported working for a political party.

The advertising agency used these data in its selection of the media for the campaign.

Conversations with media representatives indicated that each ad in the campaign should be run four times in order to have maximum impact. The program that evolved included six specific advertisements to appear in print media, such as The New Yorker and The Atlantic, over a two-year period. The media schedule that was developed for 1977 included 15 publications such as The Wall Street Journal (national edition), New York Times (Sunday edition), Change magazine, Newsweek, Saturday Review and smaller and more local publications such as Stockbroker's Observer and Wharton magazine. It was expected that repetition in individual media could achieve penetration and "top-of-mind" awareness among a larger portion of the target audience. The specific ads used for the 1977 campaign are shown in Exhibits 9 through 14.

While Mr. Drake, Pete McCarthy, and other executives recognized that the 1977 campaign could not go on forever, they were very pleased with the results apparently achieved. Mr. Drake had received many

Exhibit 9
An Advertisement from the 1977 Campaign

It may not be the best system the world will ever see. But it's the best one we've seen yet.

We Invite Comparison

And it's up to us to keep it working.

The rest of the world acknowledges the American economy as the most productive in history.

Other governments envy the system that has made such giant contributions to the human condition.

As men and women in business, we know our system affords more opportunity for fulfillment than any other yet devised.

We know that only when business is permitted to operate profitably can we discharge the many obligations to society of responsible corporate citizens.

And that taxes on corporate profits enable society to share, with those who cannot work, the benefits of productive effort.

We also know the system will only work as well as we do.

Some people argue that competitive enterprise has outlived its usefulness. That the time has come to replace it with something else.

But nobody quite knows what to replace it with, and still preserve our freedom.

Faith in the system gave Pennwalt its start a good many years ago. Faith in the system guides our successful growth today.

But it's not a blind faith. We know there are problems. We also know from experience that every problem carries with it the chance of a workable solution.

So while competitive enterprise may not be the best system the world will ever see, it *is* the best one we've seen yet.

(If this ad makes sense to you, why not share it with someone of a more skeptical bent.)

Pennwalt Corporation, Three Parkway, Philadelphia, Pa. 19102.

For 126 years we've been making things people need – including profits.

CHEMICALS ■ EQUIPMENT
HEALTH PRODUCTS

Too many people believe business doesn't give a damn about the public.

Minds are tough to change.

Times *do* change, though. And business is changing. Faster than a lot of people's attitudes toward business.

American business invests more money every year in strenuous efforts to communicate the benefits of competitive enterprise. (Including ads like this one.)

Yet survey after survey shows that public sentiment is against big business.

This suggests to us a communications problem. And a credibility problem.

It also suggests some possible corrective steps toward more effective communications with the public.

First, let's stop talking mostly to ourselves.

Let's stop resorting to one-sided arguments that thoughtful adults are no longer willing to accept on faith.

Let's stop pretending that there aren't any flaws at all in our system, and the way it works.

Instead, let's face up to our mistakes, and correct them. Admit that we're not perfect. And engage in open discourse instead of arm-twisting diatribes.

Since public opinion is ultimately the controlling force in our democracy, an informed public is really one of the costs of staying in business.

Thus there may be only one way for business to restore its credibility. And that's to level with the public.

It's definitely worth a try.

(Why not try these thoughts out on somebody who's turned off by business?)

Pennwalt Corporation, Three Parkway, Philadelphia, Pa. 19102.

For 126 years we've been making things people need—including profits.

CHEMICALS ■ EQUIPMENT
HEALTH PRODUCTS

Exhibit 11
An Advertisement from the 1977 Campaign

We need to have faith in the system, but not <u>blind</u> faith.

No one has to sell American business on competitive enterprise.

We know how good the system is.

But when it comes to communicating its merits to a skeptical public, the business community isn't getting through.

It's not that we don't have a story to tell. Our system affords greater opportunity for the realization of human potential than any other yet devised.

But in our eagerness to point with pride, we often convey the false impression that there's nothing at all wrong with the way the system works.

We know better, of course. So does the public.

Since society cannot function very long without public confidence in business, we think it's time to shelve the one-sided arguments that turn people off.

When we run ads to explain competitive enterprise, let's be candid. Let's demonstrate that our concern with meeting broad social needs is just as real as the public's.

When we appeal for understanding, let's do so not in the language of the boardroom but in terms of better jobs and productive, useful lives.

The point is simply this. Survival of our system requires that profitability and public accountability go hand in hand.

Because what happens to business happens eventually to all of society.

So faith in the system is fine, but it needn't be blind faith.

(Why not use this message to open someone else's eyes?)

Pennwalt Corporation, Three Parkway, Philadelphia, Pa. 19102.

For 126 years we've been making things people need–including profits.

CHEMICALS ■ EQUIPMENT
HEALTH PRODUCTS

Exhibit 12
An Advertisement from the 1977 Campaign

No one ever had to sell American business on free enterprise.

As men and women in business, we *know* how well the system works.

We know it affords greater opportunity for fulfillment than any other yet devised.

We know the importance to this country of an economy regulated more by free markets than by the federal government.

We know that only when business is permitted to operate profitably can we meet broader social needs.

We're sold on the system, but we haven't yet sold the public on it.

Most Americans, we suspect, have no quarrel with the profit motive. At the same time, every new poll shows that public sentiment is against big business.

This can only mean the business community has been less than adept at putting across the essential role of competitive enterprise in our society.

We complain that people won't listen, but we've been talking to ourselves.

Since society can't function effectively without public confidence in its institutions (including business), we'd like to propose a change of tactics.

Let's substitute the shock value of absolute truth for one-sided arguments that turn people off.

Let's own up to some shortcomings in the way our system operates, and take steps to correct them.

Let's stop communicating with the public and start talking to people. Not in the language of balance sheets and the "bottom line," but in terms of our mutual stake in a better America.

Since we're already sold on this imperfect system, we hope these thoughts will help sell you.

Pennwalt Corporation, Three Parkway, Philadelphia, Pa. 19102.

For 126 years we've been making things people need – including profits.

CHEMICALS ■ EQUIPMENT
HEALTH PRODUCTS

Exhibit 13
An Advertisement from the 1977 Campaign

A code of ethics isn't something you post on the bulletin board. It's something you live every day.

Suddenly everybody seems to be rediscovering ethics.

In the business community, in Congress, on the campus and in the pulpit.

We think the trend is healthy. And needed. So we'd like to disclose a discovery of our own on this subject.

We found a long time ago that when it comes to any sort of corporate decree, the more you reduce it to writing the more you reduce participation.

It's much better, we learned, to create a working environment in which communication is a two-way process. And corporate goals are shared.

So that your code of ethics is expressed not in a news release, but in the release of appropriate thought and action.

Nobody's perfect, but it seems to work.

As our chairman put it: "The character of this company is simply a reflection of how Pennwalt people think and act. *That's* our code of ethics."

And so it is.

Admittedly, it's an approach that places more stress on the integrity and good judgment of our people than on manuals from Personnel. (A *lot* more stress.)

But it pays off. In pride. In performance. In a belief that the work we do is important. And in the enhancement of our worldwide reputation.

You might say it's the difference between a bulletin that goes up on the board, and the life that goes on every day.

(We have a brief booklet on corporate citizenship which we believe covers this subject. If you'd like one, just write our Director of Corporate Communications.)

Pennwalt Corporation, Three Parkway, Philadelphia, Pa. 19102.

For 126 years we've been making things people need—including profits.

CHEMICALS ■ EQUIPMENT
HEALTH PRODUCTS

Exhibit 14
An Advertisement from the 1977 Campaign

Jack Block's class of business majors politely suggested what we could do with this ad.

Mr. Block teaches Business Communications at Mesa College in San Diego.

When our ad ran, he asked his students to make suggestions.

They did. All eighty-five of them. Thoughtfully and pointedly.

"Don't tell us people distrust big business," they suggested. "Tell us what you intend to *do* about it."

If only it were that simple.

As we've said before in this space, loss of credibility is just one reason why business is in trouble with the public. But loss of credibility leads to erosion of confidence in the whole system.

This alarms us. Because we believe in competitive enterprise, despite its defects.

We hate to see the whole system condemned for the questionable or unethical practices of a relatively few people in business who ought to know better.

Too many people believe business doesn't give a damn about the public.

But *we* know better than to try to defend the system with one-sided sermonettes that insult your intelligence.

Instead, we hope you'll stop and think. We hope the skeptics among you will question certain attitudes of your own.

Maybe nothing business says will ever change the mind of anyone not already sold on the system.

We certainly don't expect an ad to do it. That's not the point at all.

The point is to make you think. To replace a monologue with a dialogue. Judging from our mail, it's working.

Thus the ads themselves are an example of what we "intend to *do* about it."

The dialogue is healthy. We hope it continues.

We also hope we've shown Jack Block's students that we're open to suggestion.

Pennwalt Corporation, Three Parkway, Philadelphia, Pa. 19102.

For 126 years we've been making things people need–including profits.

PENNWALT
CHEMICALS ■ EQUIPMENT
HEALTH PRODUCTS

letters from directors and officers of other corporations and from a number of Pennwalt's shareholders. In an issue of *The New Yorker* that had been evaluated by *Starch Reports*, the Pennwalt ad had received 17 percent readership ("read most"), the highest of any ad in the issue. Pennwalt's 1,300 salespeople had responded very favorably, reporting back specific instances where they felt that sales had resulted from the ads and many more instances where the ads had been commented on favorably.

Management had been especially pleased with the amount of public reaction (most, but by no means all, of it favorable) that had been generated by the ads. (See Exhibit 15 for examples of responses.) As he

Exhibit 15
Selected Comments from Letters Received about Pennwalt's Corporate
Advertising Campaign

This is a cute statement, and makes an interesting point . . . But . . . when you use an expression like "free enterprise system" . . . you dilute some of the effect. There is not—now, or ever before—anywhere—a "free enterprise" system. It's not only a misnomer, it has become a propaganda expression.

As a college student about to enter the "real world," I was interested in this topic and posted it for others to read. The commentary and response has been so great (and the original so well worn) that I'm writing to obtain several additional copies. Is that possible?

Your ad reeks of guilt. Should a Communist read your ad, it ought to provoke a complacent smile and sense of satisfaction: "We've got them on the run! Because the best way to beat an enemy is to get him to doubt his own worth to start with."

America, and Americans, and American enterprise are hated all over the world, not by everyone, but by those who hate success, who hate ability, who hate human life; and the people who hate these things, really hate themselves more than anything else, but they turn their hatred on everything that accuses them of their own evil, their own failure, their own worthlessness.

Don't accept the allegations made by the people who hate you not for your mistakes, but for your success—something they will never, ever tell you. Don't continue falling into the trap of unearned guilt.

I have just read your ad on page 3 of the February 19, 1977, issue of *Saturday Review*. If big business had any creditability with me before reading this ad, it certainly has none now. I do give you credit for publishing your address so that you could be written to! Most corporations on TV won't even do that.

Why should we have any creditability in Big Business? The oil corporations have not only had a 26 percent depletion allowance for decades but they have used their profits to corner all of the other energy sources, coal and uranium. They own the entire distribution chain, and only federal government keeps their greed in check.

If you and the rest of big business told it like it really is, there would be a legitimate clamor in Congress to put restraints upon you! All I hear from my stockholder friends is that their dividends have not gone up even though the

Exhibit 15 *(concluded)*

corporations they have invested in are now becoming diversified corporation giants.

Mr. President of Pennwalt Corporation, why should we trust "Big Business?"

In a recent issue of *Newsweek* I noticed your advertisement entitled, "A code of ethics isn't something you post on the bulletin board. It's something you live every day." I wanted to write to you to congratulate you on the excellent reasoning expressed in that advertisement. It is the most mature advertisement about ethics and their place in everyday life that I have yet seen.

I find it interesting, but not surprising, that it is a business corporation (or an advertising agency) that shows more acumen about the nature of ethics and their practice than many of the things currently written by professional ethicists and moral philosophers. I would be interested to see your brief booklet on corporate citizenship, and I encourage you to produce other advertisements in the spirit of this one.

I am sending copies of your advertisement to colleagues who, I think, will agree with my assessment of the cogency of your presentation. Someone was right on target. Thank you.

reflected upon the results that had been achieved, Mr. Drake, in June of 1977, had put forth the following statement about the campaign:

> The overall purpose of this campaign is to encourage a friendly dialogue with a skeptical public. We want simply to stimulate thought on the part of the reader and, hopefully, to encourage some people to question cherished misconceptions of their own and thereby trigger reader reaction.

In establishing this campaign we recognize:

1. That public opinion ultimately is the controlling force in a free society.
2. That the pursuit of profit and public accountability go hand in hand.
3. That public confidence in big business is dangerously low.
4. That business must come clean with the public and admit its mistakes if it wants to repair its damaged credibility.

Mr. Drake had no doubt that the campaign had established the company as one having corporate integrity, that it had helped to sell products, and that it had attracted shareholders, although he did not feel that the effect on sales should be a major objective. The 1977 campaign, in the opinion of Pete McCarthy, had gone considerably beyond the relatively unsophisticated approach of "The Little Red Hen" ad and had clearly established Pennwalt as a major corporation in the minds of opinion leaders in education, government, industry, the arts, and the public at large.

Now, however, there was growing uncertainty about the direction future corporate advertising should take. Many corporate advertising campaigns of the advocacy variety were clamoring for the public's attention. Among the decisions called for at Pennwalt was whether to continue the campaign in its present format or to go to a fundamentally different approach such as once again emphasizing specific products. Some managers favored keeping the present format but focusing more specifically on the financial community through media such as *Barron's* and *The Wall Street Journal*. Others felt the 1977 campaign had been excessively noncommittal and advocated taking a definite stance, as a matter of corporate policy, on such specific issues as environmental quality, development of alternative energy sources, excessive government regulation, and so on, and publicizing these policies through a corporate advertising campaign, now that Pennwalt had emerged from its prior "low profile" status. Regardless of format, there was the question whether Pennwalt should increase, maintain, or decrease its level of spending for corporate advertising.

Mr. Drake felt that he should remain somewhat aloof from these discussions, given his pending retirement, but he did hope that some effort would continue to be devoted to explaining the "competitive enterprise of free people" and to explicating the "five publics" philosophy of corporate purpose.

C A S E $6-10$

Castle Coffee Company

In May of 1972, Mr. Adrian Van Tassle, advertising manager for the Castle Coffee Company, tugged at his red mustache and contemplated the latest market share report. This was not one of his happier moments as he exclaimed, "I've got to do something to turn this market around before it's too late for Castle—and me. But I can't afford another mistake like last year."

Indeed, Mr. William Castle (the president and a major stockholder of the Castle Company) had exhibited a similar reaction when told that Castle Coffee's share of the market was dropping back toward 5.4 percent—where it had been one year previously. He had remarked rather pointedly to Mr. Van Tassle that if market share and profitability were not improved during the next fiscal year "some rather drastic actions" might need to be taken.

Adrian Van Tassle had been hired by Mr. James Anthoney, vice president of marketing for Castle, in the summer of 1970. Prior to that time, he had worked for companies in the Netherlands and Singapore and had gained a reputation as a highly effective advertising executive. Now, in the spring of 1972, he was engaged in trying to reverse a long-term downward trend in the market position of Castle Coffee.

Castle's Market Position

Castle Coffee was an old, established company in the coffee business, with headquarters in Squirrel Hill, Pennsylvania. Its market area included the East Coast and southern regions of the United States and a fairly large portion of the Midwest. The company had at one time

Reprinted from *Stanford Business Cases* with the permission of the publisher, Graduate School of Business, Stanford University. Copyright © by the Board of Trustees of the Leland Stanford Junior University. This case was developed by Professors William F. Massy, David B. Montgomery, and Charles B. Weinberg of the Graduate School of Business, Stanford University.

enjoyed as much as 15 percent of the market in these areas. These were often referred to as the "good old days," when the brand was strong and growing and the company was able to sponsor such popular radio programs as "The Castle Comedy Hour" and "Castle Capers."

The company's troubles began in the 1950s, when television replaced radio as the primary broadcast medium. Castle experienced increasing competitive difficulty as TV production and time costs increased. Further problems presented themselves as several other old-line companies were absorbed by major marketers. For example, Folger's Coffee was bought by Procter and Gamble and ButterNut by Coca-Cola. These giants joined General Foods Corporation (Maxwell House Coffee) among the ranks of Castle's most formidable competitors. Finally, the advent of freeze-dry and the increasing popularity of instant coffee put additional pressure on Castle, which had no entry in these product classes.

The downward trend in share was most pronounced during the 1960s: The company had held 12 percent of the market at the beginning of the decade but only about 5½ percent at the end. Share had held fairly stable for the past few years. This was attributed to a "hardcore" group of buyers plus an active (and expensive) program of consumer promotions and price-off deals to the trade. Mr. Anthoney, the vice president of marketing, believed that the erosion of share had been halted just in time. A little more slippage, he said, and Castle would begin to lose its distribution. This would have been the beginning of the end for this venerable company.

Operation Breakout

When William Castle was elevated to the presidency in 1968, his main objective was to halt the decline in market position and, if possible, to effect a turnaround. His success in achieving the first objective has already been noted. However, both he and Anthoney agreed that the same strategy, i.e., intensive consumer and trade promotion, would not succeed in winning back any appreciable proportion of the lost market share.

Both men believed that it would be necessary to increase consumer awareness of the Castle brand and develop more favorable attitudes about it if market position were to be improved. This could only be done through advertising. Since the company produced a quality product (it was noticeably richer and more aromatic than many competing coffees), it appeared that a strategy of increasing advertising weight might stand some chance of success. A search for an advertising manager was initiated, which culminated in the hiring of Adrian Van Tassle.

After a period of familiarizing himself with the Castle Company and the American coffee market and advertising scene, Van Tassle began developing a plan to revitalize Castle's advertising program. First, he "released" the company's current advertising agency and requested proposals from a number of others interested in obtaining the account. While it was generally understood that the amount of advertising would increase somewhat, the heaviest emphasis was on the kind of appeal and copy execution to be used. Both the company and the various agencies agreed that nearly all the advertising weight should go into spot television. Network sponsorship was difficult because of the regional character of Castle's markets, and no other medium could match TV's impact for a product like coffee. (There is a great deal of newspaper advertising for coffee, but this is usually placed by retailers under an advertising allowance arrangement with the manufacturer. Castle included such expenditures in its promotional budget rather than as an advertising expense.)

The agency which won the competition did so with an advertising program built around the theme, "Only a Castle is fit for a king or a queen." The new agency recommended that a 30 percent increase in the quarterly advertising budget be approved in order to give the new program a fair trial. After considerable negotiation with Messrs. Castle and Anthoney and further discussion with the agency, Van Tassle decided to compromise on a 20 percent increase. The new campaign was to start in the autumn of 1971, which was the second quarter of the company's 1972 fiscal year (the fiscal year started July 1, 1971, and would end June 30, 1972). It was dubbed "operation breakout."

Performance during Fiscal 1972

Castle had been advertising at an average rate of $1 million per quarter for the last several years. Given current levels of promotional expenditures, this was regarded as sufficient to maintain market share at about its current level of 5.4 percent. Castle's annual expenditure of $4 million represented somewhat more than 5.4 percent of industry advertising, though exact figures about competitors' expenditures on ground coffee were difficult to obtain. This relation was regarded as normal, since private brands accounted for a significant fraction of the market and these received little or no advertising. Neither Mr. Van Tassle nor Mr. Anthoney anticipated that competitive expenditures would change much during the next few years regardless of any increase in Castle's advertising.

Advertising of ground coffee followed a regular seasonal pattern, which approximated the seasonal variation of industry sales. The relevant figures are presented in Table 1. Total ground coffee sales in

Table 1
Industry Sales and Castle's Advertising Budget

Quarter	Industry sales		Maintenance advertising		Planned advertising for FY 1972	
	Cases (000,000)	Index	Dollars (000,000)	Index	Dollars (000,000)	Percent increase
1. Summer........	18.7	0.85	0.8	0.80	.8	0%
2. Autumn........	22.0	1.00	1.0	1.00	1.2	20
3. Winter.........	25.3	1.15	1.2	1.20	1.44	20
4. Spring.........	22.0	1.00	1.0	1.00	1.2	20
Average......	22.0	1.00	1.0	1.00	1.16	16

Castle's market area averaged 22 million cases per quarter and were expected to remain at that level for several years. Each case contained 12 pounds of coffee in one-, two-, or three-pound containers. Consumption in winter was about 15 percent above the yearly average, while in summer, the volume was down by 15 percent.

Advertising expenditures by both Castle and the industry in general followed the same basic pattern, except that the seasonal variation was between 80 percent and 120 percent—somewhat greater than the variation in sales. The "maintenance" expenditures on advertising, shown in Table 1, were what the company believed it had to spend to maintain its "normal" 5.4 percent of the market in each quarter. Van Tassle had wondered whether this was the right seasonal advertising pattern for Castle, given its small percentage of the market, but decided to stay with it during fiscal 1972. Therefore, the 20 percent planned increase in quarterly advertising rates was simply added to the "sustaining" amount for each quarter, beginning in the second quarter of the year. The planned expenditures for fiscal 1972 are also shown in Table 1.

In speaking with Mr. Castle and Jim Anthoney about the proposed changes in the advertising program, Mr. Van Tassle had indicated that he expected to increase market share to 6 percent or perhaps a little more. This sounded pretty good to Mr. Castle, especially after he had consulted with the company's controller. Exhibit 1 presents the controller's memorandum on the advertising budget increase.

Mr. Van Tassle had, of course, indicated that the hoped-for 6 percent share was not a "sure thing" and, in any case, that it might take more than one quarter before the full effects of the new advertising program would be felt.

The new advertising campaign broke as scheduled on October 1, 1971, the first day of the second quarter of the fiscal year. Adrian Van Tassle was somewhat disappointed in the commercials prepared by the agency and a little apprehensive about the early reports from the field. The bimonthly store audit report of market share for September–Octo-

Exhibit 1

August 1, 1971

Confidential

Memo to: W. Castle, President
    From: The Controller (I. F.)
 Subject: Proposed 20 percent increase in adversiting

I think that Adrian's proposal to increase advertising by 20 percent (from a quarterly rate of $1 million to one of $1.2 million) is a good idea. He predicts that a market share of 6 percent will be achieved, compared to our current 5.4 percent. I can't comment about the feasibility of this assumption. That's Adrian's business and I presume he knows what he's doing. I can tell you, however, that such a result would be highly profitable.

As you know, the wholesale price of coffee has been running about $8.60 per 12-pound case. Deducting our average retail advertising and promotional allowance of $0.80 per case, and our variable costs of production and distribution of $5.55 per case, leaves an average gross contribution to fixed costs and profit of $2.25 per case. Figuring a total market of about 22 million cases per quarter and a share change of from 0.054 to 0.060 (a 0.006 increase), we would have the following increase in gross contribution:

$$\text{Change in gross contribution} = \$2.25 \times 22 \text{ million} \times 0.006$$
$$= \$0.30 \text{ million}$$

Subtracting the change in advertising expense due to the new program and then dividing by this same quantity gives what can be called the advertising payout rate:

$$\text{Advertising payout rate} = \frac{\text{Change in gross contribution—change in advertising expense}}{\text{Change in advertising expense}}$$

$$= \frac{\$0.10 \text{ million}}{\$0.20 \text{ million}} = 0.50$$

That is, we can expect to make $0.50 in net contribution for each extra dollar spent on advertising. You can see that as long as this quantity is greater than zero (at which point the extra gross contribution just pays for the extra advertising), increasing our advertising is a good deal.

I think Adrian has a good thing going here, and my recommendation is to go ahead. Incidentally, the extra funds we should generate in net contribution (after advertising expense is deducted) should help to relieve the cash flow bind which I mentioned last week. Perhaps we will be able to maintain the quarterly dividend after all.

I. F.

---

ber showed only a fractional increase in share over the 5.4 percent of the previous period. Nevertheless, Van Tassle thought that, given a little time, things would work out and that the campaign would eventually reach its objective.

The November–December market share report was received in mid-January. It showed Castle's share of the market to be 5.6 percent. On January 21, 1972, Mr. Van Tassle received a carbon copy of the memorandum in Exhibit 2.

Exhibit 2

January 20, 1972

Memo to: W. Castle, President
   From: The Controller (I. F.)
Subject: Failure of advertising program

I am most alarmed at our failure to achieve the market share target projected by Mr. A. Van Tassle. The 0.2 percent increase in market share achieved in November–December is not sufficient to return the cost of increased advertising. Ignoring the month of October, which obviously represents a start-up period, a 0.2 increase in share generates only $100,000 in extra gross contribution on a quarterly basis. This must be compared to the $200,000 we have expended in extra advertising. The advertising payout rate is thus only −0.50: much less than the break-even point.

I know Mr. Van Tassle expects shares to increase again next quarter, but he has not been able to say by how much. The new program projects an advertising expenditure increase of a quarter of a million dollars over last year's winter quarter level. I don't see how we can continue to make these expenditures without a better prospect of return on our investment.

cc: Mr. J. Anthoney
    Mr. Van Tassle

Private postscript to Mr. Castle: In view of our autumn 1971 performance, we must discuss the question of the quarterly dividend at an early date.

I. F.

On Monday, January 24, Jim Anthoney telephoned Van Tassle to say that Mr. Castle wanted an immediate review of the new advertising program. Later that week, after several rounds of discussion in which Mr. Van Tassle was unable to convince Castle and Anthoney that the program would be successful, it was decided to return to fiscal 1971 advertising levels. The TV spot contracts were renegotiated, and by the middle of February, advertising had been cut back substantially toward the $1.2 million per quarter rate that had previously been normal for the winter season. The agency complained that the efficiency of their media "buy" suffered significantly during February and March due to the abrupt reduction in advertising expenditure. However, they were unable to say by how much. The spring 1972 rate was set at the normal level of $1 million. Market share for January–February turned out to be slightly under 5.7 percent, while that for March–April was about 5.5 percent.

Planning for Fiscal 1973

So in mid-May of 1972, Adrian Van Tassle was faced with the problem of what to recommend as the advertising budget for the four quarters of fiscal 1973. He was already very late in dealing with this assignment, since media buys would have to be upped soon if any substantial increase in weight were to be effected during the summer quarter of 1972. Alternately, fast action would be needed to reduce advertising expenditures below their tentatively budgeted "normal" level of $0.8 million.

During the past month, Van Tassle had spent considerable time reviewing the difficulties of fiscal 1972. He had remained convinced that a 20 percent increase in advertising should produce somewhat around a 6 percent market share level. He based this partly on "hunch" and partly on a number of studies that had been performed by academic and business market researchers with whom he was acquainted.

One such study which he believed was particularly applicable to Castle's situation indicated that the "advertising elasticity of demand" was equal to about ½. He recalled that the definition of this quantity when applied to market share is:

$$\text{Advertising elasticity of demand} = \frac{\text{Percent change in market share}}{\text{Percent change in advertising}}$$

The researcher assured him that it was valid to think of "percent changes" as being deviations from "normal levels" (also called maintenance levels) of advertising and share. However, he was worried that any given value of advertising elasticity would be valid only for moderate deviations about the norm. That is, the value of ½ he had noted earlier would not necessarily apply to (say) plus or minus 50 percent changes in advertising.

Van Tassle noted that his estimate of share change (6.0 − 5.4 = 0.6 percentage points) represented about an 11 percent increase over the normal share level of 5.4 points. Since this was to be achieved with a 20 percent increase in advertising, it represented an advertising elasticity of 11 percent/20 percent = 0.55. While this was higher than the 0.5 found in the study, he had believed that his advertising appeals and copy would be a bit better than average. He recognized that his ads may not actually have been as great as expected but noted that, "even an elasticity of 0.5 would produce 5.94 percent of the market—within striking distance of 6 percent." Of course, the study itself might be applicable to Castle's market situation to a greater or lesser degree.

One lesson which he had learned from his unfortunate experience the last year was the danger inherent in presenting too optimistic a picture to top management. On the other hand, a "conservative" estimate might not have been sufficient to obtain approval for the program in the first place. Besides, he really did believe that the effect of advertising on share was greater than implied by performance in the autumn of 1971. This judgment should be a part of management's information

Exhibit 3
Theater Tests

In theater testing, an audience is recruited either by mail or by phone to attend a showing of test television programs. When the members of the audience arrive, they are given a set of questionnaires, through which an emcee guides them as the session progresses. Usually, data on the audience's opinions and preferences regarding the various brands in the product categories being tested are gathered before the show begins. The show consists of a standard television program episode (or two or more such episodes) in which several television commercials have been inserted. At the close of the showing, audience members are asked to fill out questionnaires, reporting on the commercials they remember, and are again asked to give their opinions and preferences concerning the various brands of the advertised products. In many cases, the members of the audience (or some proportion of them) also record their interest in the show as it progresses by turning a dial as their interest level rises and falls, which permits the analyst to trace "interest curves" for the program. One service, Audience Studies, Inc., of Los Angeles, also measures basal skin resistance continuously for some members of the audience, for recent studies have suggested that there is a connection between this measure and the audience's degree of involvement with the material on the screen.

The theater test is one of the most versatile of the available test methods. It can be used to test television commercials in many different stages of development, and it has sometimes been used to test radio commercials and print ads (presented in the form of slides). To offset the high cost of this method, several advertisements for noncompeting products are normally tested in a single session, thus splitting expenses among several advertisers. The method yields fair measures of attention-getting power. credibility, and motivating power. However, it is not very valuable in diagnosing specific problems in the commercials. To some extent, interest curves and measures of skin resistance can help to pinpoint weak spots, but the best way to obtain information that will point the way to improvement is to hold a group interview session immediately after the showing, using a few people selected from the audience.

Source: From Kenneth A. Longman, *Advertising*. (New York: Harcourt Brace Jovanovich, Inc., 1971), pp. 326–27. Reprinted with their permission.

set when they evaluated his proposal. Alternatively, if they had good reason for doubting his judgment, he wanted to know about it—after all, William Castle and Jim Anthoney had been in the coffee business a lot longer than he had and were pretty savvy guys.

Perhaps the problem lay in his assessment of the speed with which the new program would take hold. He had felt it "would take a little time" but had not tried to pin it down further. ("That's pretty hard, after all.") Nothing very precise about this had been communicated to management. Could he blame the controller for adopting the time horizon he did?

As a final complicating factor, Van Tassle had just received a report from the agency about the "quality" of the advertising copy and appeals used the previous autumn and winter. Contrary to expectations these ads rated only about 0.9 on a scale which rated an "average ad" at 1. These tests were based on the so-called theater technique, in which various spots were inserted into a filmed "entertainment" program, and their effects on choices in a lottery designed to simulate purchasing behavior were determined (see Exhibit 3 on theater tests). Fortunately, the ads currently being shown rated about 1 on the same scale. A new series of ads scheduled for showing during the autumn, winter, and spring of 1973 appeared to be much better. Theater testing could not be undertaken until production was completed during the summer, but "experts" in the agency were convinced that they would rate at least as high as 1.15. Mr. Van Tassle was impressed with these ads himself but recalled that such predictions tended to be far from perfect. In the meantime, a budget request for all four quarters of fiscal 1973 had to be submitted to management within the next week.

Questions

1. State precisely what you think the objectives of Castle's 1972 advertising plan should have been. Were these the objectives of Van Tassle? William Castle? I.F. (the controller)?

2. Evaluate the results obtained from the 1972 advertising campaign prior to and after the cut in advertising funds. What do you think the results would have been if the 20 percent increase had been continued for the entire year?

3. What should Van Tassle propose as an advertising budget for 1973; how should he justify this budget to top management?

4. How should Van Tassle deal with the issues of seasonality and copy quality?

SECTION SEVEN

Organization

C A S E 7–1

Nike, Inc.

During the fall of 1982, the Nike company was recognized generally as one of the phenomenal success stories of the recent decade. From its small base in 1972, the firm had blossomed into a $450 million giant in 1981 and expected sales to reach $650 million in 1982. It had passed Adidas in the United States and held an estimated 30 percent of the American market. Most Nike executives were confident that a $1 billion sales year was imminent. Although the company owed much of its success to a vibrant management team, it was also very much the brainchild of a remarkable entrepreneur, Phil Knight, who still served as president, CEO, and major stockholder.

The company's incredible growth rate was not without its problems. As Phil Knight reflected:

> There has been a severe overload on marketing exacerbated by our need to organize for new opportunities as our old products and markets mature. We are geared to handle existing lines where we have 30 or 40 percent of the market. But how about new areas which must be developed, like leisure products, international, the children's line, clothing, and cleated shoes?

The Industry

Nike competed in an industry that could be variously described as shoes—running, sports, leisure, participation—and sportswear, both of which were estimated to exceed $10 billion in sales in 1982. In a way, the company was all of these descriptors, and there seemed to be a gradual evolution, certainly for Nike, from left to right. Running, the

This case was written by Robert T. Davis, Professor of Marketing. Financial support for this case was provided in part by the Marketing Management Program of the Graduate School of Business, Stanford University. © 1982 by the Board of Trustees of the Leland Stanford Junior University.

company's foundation, was primarily an American phenomenon, though it had been copied in varying degrees elsewhere. By 1980, however, the running boom was leveling off and, as Phil Knight stated, "We see only a couple more years of strong growth in shoes in the United States, though we are sure that fitness is here to stay."

Because of the industry's evolution, there was a wide range of competitors and strategies. In running, for example, there were Adidas (the largest firm in total, worldwide sales), Puma, Converse Rubber, Pony International, Asics (Tiger brand), New Balance, and Brooks (acquired by Wolverine in 1982), to mention the most obvious. Reliable data about these competitors were sketchy because many were privately owned or divisions of larger operations. Market share estimates, for example, were based largely on one commercial service which regularly surveyed 200 retailers for competitive comparisons.

The market segments were diverse. In addition to the serious runners, the observer might distinguish the faddist, the casual exerciser, the trend follower, the price buyer, the leisure-time devotee, the amateur sportsman, the high-fashion, status-conscious user, and any other number of variants. In recent months, some observers felt that color coordination (between shoes and clothing) was a coming consumer consideration. Indeed, one competitor (New Balance) had succeeded in drawing favorable comments about its grey, light brown, burgundy, and navy colors early in 1982. This same firm had recently increased its margins to the trade (to 55 percent), upped its innovation rate, and put heavy emphasis on the specialty retailers. These actions appeared to have increased that firm's penetration of the innovator segment.

The clothing business was even more fragmented, consisting of thousands of designers, cutters, finishers, stylists, knitters, weavers, etc. Raw materials ranged from cotton and wool to a great variety of synthetics and blends. In the relevant world of Nike, the key actors were such competitors as Levi Strauss, Head, Adidas, and hundreds of prestige designers (e.g., Pierre Cardin, Bill Blass). There were, in addition, many retailer brands such as Brooks Brothers, Saks, and I. Magnin.

During the 60s and 70s, Levi's grew spectacularly on the basis of its "Western-cowboy" look, and thanks partly to James Dean and Marlon Brando, jeans became the uniform for every self-respecting teenager or young adult. By 1980, however, there was some speculation that "the look" was about to shift to a new life style—the fit, the jock, the athlete-winner. If this materialized, the implications were great for the trade.

It was also reasonably obvious that traditional manufacturer labels in fashion merchandise were under seige by the aforementioned designer labels. Large numbers of department stores and mass merchandisers were trying to gain distinction through the handling of such "prestige" labels and the use of the "boutique look" within their stores. It almost seemed that there were two fundamental strategies at work—the price-oriented mass market appeal and the high-income, status appeal. The distinction between these two was somewhat clouded by the adoption of "prestige labels" by the more aggressive mass merchandisers. Even Sears Roebuck had relaxed its policy of carrying only house labels.

Adidas, Head, and Nike represented firms that expanded into clothing from "hardware lines," whereas Levi Strauss experimented, not too successfully, with shoes. All of these firms, of course, vied for the same basic distribution system. At the retail level, the outlets could be classified as: mass merchandisers (Sears), discounters (Marshalls and Mervyn's), department and specialty stores (R. H. Macy and I. Magnin), and a wide variety of small independents (sporting goods, shoe stores, running stores). These outlets could be reached through company salesmen, manufacturers' representatives, distributors, or even direct mail. Adidas, for example, covered the United States with four independent distributors; Levi Strauss used company salesmen; Nike, manufacturers' representatives; and Sears Roebuck sold direct through mail order and/or retail stores.

Nike's niche in the industry was solid. It appealed to the market on the basis of quality, technical innovation, and high performance, all of which attracted the serious runner. This position among the experts was the lever to open up the mass markets. The firm had also been aggressive in product line and brand name extensions (such as leisure shoes and clothing).

Nike Organization

One of the intriguing characteristics of the company was its informal organization. From its beginning, Nike had been run as a small operation by a close-knit group of top managers. Most of them were sports enthusiasts and athletes and thus understood and appreciated the Nike line. A surprisingly large percentage also had legal or accounting backgrounds. But, as Phil Knight explained, "We mostly want people who are company experts, not functional experts."

The organization chart (next page) is therefore deceptive. It portrays the formal pieces of the organization, but not the way it works.

Management assignments across these functions were frequent. One senior manager moved from legal to R&D, to lobbying, to marketing, and there were other equally dramatic assignment changes. Territorial imperatives were held to a minimum, and such words as budgeting, planning, and control were dirty ones—even though the company did have effective systems. The emphasis was upon informality, will-

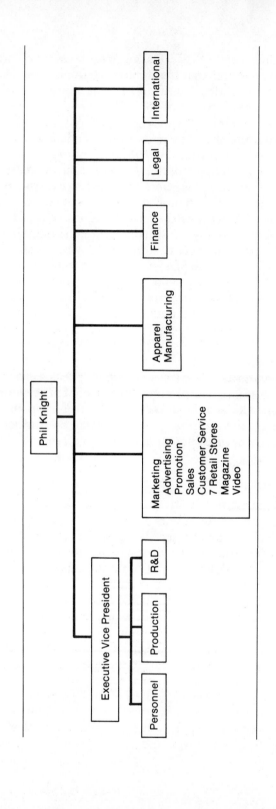

ingness to change, experimentation, and mutual decision making. The Friday Club was the chief management tool of the company. This group of 11 top managers[1] was called together regularly, as Phil Knight laughingly described, "to shout at each other." The meetings were open and informal, and everyone contributed, with enthusiasm, his ideas and solutions to the topics. Phil Knight played the catalyst role in eliciting ideas and in meshing the various personalities. There were no functional restrictions. The informality of these sessions was evident on one occasion when a visitor commented that Nike management "was a shambles." The next day, at a follow-up meeting, each executive wore a T-shirt which said, "It's a shambles."

Even though the Friday Club was a key decision-making group, it wasn't as omnipotent as it might appear. In the first place, it was, in practice, a floating group with varying degrees of autonomy. There were five so-called old-timers who were really "the chairman's office" and who were considered the ultimate decision-making unit. The Friday Club itself could expand or shrink in size depending on the issue. There had been some meetings, to illustrate, at which over 30 managers participated. Perhaps more important was the fact that reporting to these senior executives was a "conventional" organizational hierarchy. Marketing, to select one example, included research and advertising components, while manufacturing had plant and quality assurance managers. The unique aspects of the Nike organization were the degree of mobility, the generalist perspective of the senior group, and the participative decision-making style.

History

Knight's enthusiasm for sports started early, and by his senior year in high school, he was already an accomplished runner who had caught the eye of Bill Bowerman, the track and field coach at the University of Oregon. Knight attended that school and then received his MBA from Stanford in 1962. For one of his term papers, the budding entrepreneur developed an idea for a new business. He knew that running shoes were dominated by two German firms, Adidas and Puma, and he wondered why the Japanese couldn't do in shoes what they had already done in TV and cameras. After graduation from Stanford, Knight joined a CPA firm in Portland, Oregon, but as a sideline, decided to import and sell Japanese running shoes. He traveled to Japan and contracted

---

[1] These included, in 1982: chairman, executive vice president, vice presidents of apparel, finance, production, chief counsel, manager MIS, vice president international, director of marketing, treasurer, and manager Far East operation.

with Onitsuka to supply him, as their exclusive agent for the 13 western states, with their Tiger line. He also persuaded his former track coach to join in the venture. Between them, they invested $1,000 in inventory for shoes that cost $3.50 a pair but which they sold for $9.95. By 1966, the fledgling company had branched out to the East Coast, and by 1971, sales reached just over $1 million. At this point, Knight broadened his product line to include soccer, basketball, and tennis shoes.

In 1972, Onitsuka sought more control of marketing operations, and Knight decided to strike out on his own. Furthermore, even though his growth had been rapid, virtually doubling every year, it was still a small company, and Knight was hard pressed to obtain adequate financing. For each purchase, he had to put up a letter of credit which, for approximately 90 days, tied up his credit. As luck would have it, he had recently read a *Fortune* article which suggested that Japanese trading companies could, among other things, extend credit on flexible terms, though at a slight premium. A few inquiries soon unearthed Nissho-Iwai, the sixth-largest trading company in Japan. Knight and Nissho-Iwai soon agreed to a deal. Through Nisso-Iwai, Knight also acquired some manufacturing contacts which agreed to produce shoes to Nike's specifications.

The Nissho-Iwai deal gave Nike an important financial and business ally which made subsequent rapid growth possible. By putting up the necessary letters of credit every month, Nissho-Iwai freed Nike to concentrate on operating matters. In fact, the trading company went well beyond the strict limits of the agreement and gave Nike much needed flexibility. Nissho-Iwai served, furthermore, as the financial and administrative intermediary between Nike and the contract manufacturers. During these same early days, Phil established a strong accounts receivable group which managed to keep receivables in line despite the explosive growth in sales.

The development of these contract manufacturers was an early preoccupation of top management. A traditional problem in the leisure shoe industry had been the lack of dependable supply and delivery, particularly for the retailers. Knight saw this as an opportunity. He first tied up a considerable percentage of the available shoe capacity in Japan and later in Taiwan and Korea. These vendors were delighted to supply such a fast-growing, profitable customer. By 1982, 100 percent of the company's production was centered in 28 plants of which 84 percent was in Taiwan and Korea. There were also three plants in the United States. Knight also introduced a futures program for retailers whereby the company guaranteed the price and delivery terms for any retailer who ordered six months in advance. The system worked as follows:

Illustrative data	Event	Elapsed time
March 30	Retailer places order with Nike (order is noncancellable by the retailer and guaranteed by Nike)	0
April 15	Nike places order with NIAC	15 days
April 25	NIAC orders from the plant	25 days
July 30	Plant completes manufacturing and ships order	120 days
September 1	Shoes come to warehouse in Seattle, Boston, or Memphis	150 days
September 15	Shoes shipped to retailer	165 days

Since 65 percent of the orders followed this sequence, the futures program, in effect, served as a planning device by giving Nike reasonably accurate sales forecasts and shipment schedules. By 1982, monthly shipments were averaging 4.5 million pairs. The other 35 percent of the orders were placed by the dealers on a "when needed" basis. Delivery, in this second case, was not guaranteed.

Production costs were low, but quality was high because all output was made to Nike specifications and the firm maintained its own quality control staff at each plant. In fact, the first expatriot employee was assigned to Taiwan in 1976. The table below summarizes the cost buildup from a hypothetical $1 manufacturing base:

Cost buildup

Cost to manufacturer (for a Korean plant)	$1.00
Price from Nissho-Iwai Corp. (Japan)	1.04
Price from Nissho-Iwai, U.S. (this is Nike cost)	1.08 + interest (near prime)
Price to the retail store	1.60
Price to the customer	2.80–3.00

As one of the early employees of the firm said, "Product control is our forte." Indeed, the plants had considerable product flexibility and could easily handle volume swings of 25 to 35 percent. The three U.S. plants were useful as a backup to the overseas contractors.

Another early focus of Nike management was product innovation. Bowerman, for example, was a particularly creative individual who contributed the famous "waffle sole" (though at the expense of his wife's waffle iron). In fact, when Nike split originally from the Onitsuka group, the founders took with them two important product innovations which they had developed on their own time. Management's interest in innovation was so high that in 1974, while still small, the firm bought a factory in Exeter, New Hampshire, and dedicated it to R&D. This group subsequently developed a number of major innovations, including the airsole, the nylon top, and the full-cushioned midsole.

Innovation, in practice, was a constant give-and-take between marketing, production, and Exeter. For example, as marketing identified new product needs, it asked Exeter to conduct extensive research and testing in design and biomechanics.

Phil Knight was an important innovator in an even broader sense— not only in product but in several aspects of the operations. He was described by one colleague as "farsighted and alert to new opportunities." To be specific, Knight foresaw the desirability of expanding production out of Japan, the opportunity in a guaranteed retailer delivery system, the potential of manufacturing in China, and the advantages of working with a trading company instead of a bank. Moreover, he anticipated a number of market changes and moved his company into other sports shoes (basketball, court, cleated, etc.), a children's line, nonathletic leisure and work shoes, and clothing. The firm's early concentration on running represented superb timing (either by luck or brilliant deduction) and positioned Nike in the consumer's mind as "a running company."

The marketing program, in turn, was developed over several years. To start, the company hired sales representatives who, of necessity, were new, enthusiastic, hardworking shoe amateurs. They were supervised by an East Coast and West Coast field manager. The number of representatives was gradually increased, and their territories decreased until, in 1982, there were 28 representative organizations employing 180 salespeople. Some carried other lines, some did not. But all had thrived under Nike and depended upon the firm for their well-being. Sales were so large that representative commissions averaged 2½ percent instead of the more traditional 6 percent.

The representatives sold to 8,000 retailers who operated 13,000 outlets. Almost 2,500 of these outlets were classified as mass merchandisers, 2,500 specialty (i.e., running) stores, 1,500 sporting goods, and the rest shoe stores and miscellaneous. The premier mass merchandiser for Nike was J. C. Penney, which was added in 1977 before Nike was particularly well known. (Adidas elected to go through J. C. Penney in 1981). Quite obviously, the distribution system was effective and covered a wide range of clientele—from low-end to high-end specialty. Furthermore, the Nike line, priced between $19.95 and $70, was broad enough to accommodate each segment. Those relatively few dealers who sold primarily the top of the line to the serious, innovative runners were handled through a "torch program" and received special attention. For all dealers, Nike offered a number of special inducements: a generous 46 percent margin; guaranteed prices and delivery; and a coordinated program of promotions, advertising, training, and sponsorships.

Nike also owned and operated seven retail stores. Their volume of $4 million was minor, but they were regarded as valuable training centers. There were no expansion plans.

The distribution story was different overseas where Nike was just beginning to expand. In Europe, the jogging boom had not yet taken off, though Nike expected that it would. Adidas and Puma dominated the European distribution system and concentrated on the huge soccer market. These German competitors would not be easy to replace, particularly since their loss of market in the United States. As one industry executive stated, "Adidas and Puma will let the other American companies do whatever they want in Europe because they're not much of a threat. But after what Nike did to them in the United States, they simply will not let themselves be embarrassed in their own backyards." It would not be easy for Nike to gain dealers whose livelihood depended on Adidas and Puma.

Japan was an easier target. Not only did the Japanese perceive American products as high quality, but Nike had had years of contact with that market. England was another attractive market, and Nike not only acquired its distributorships but opened a manufacturing plant to permit inexpensive access to the European markets.

Nike's promotion and advertising strategy was another ingredient of its success. The company, to start, employed a pull, not a push, approach built around its distinctive "swoosh" trademark. Its recent $18 million budget was spent as follows:

25 percent product advertising in such vertical publications as *Running, The Runner*—and stressing general concepts like cushioning and shoe weight.

Point-of-sale devices such as a retailer poster program, the use of technical tags and brochures, and dealer clinics.

25 percent dealer co-op advertising, where Nike would match the dealers' advertising outlays up to a specified limit.

50 percent promotions, which included free goods and/or cash payment to about 2,500 athletes as well as the sponsorship of selected athletic events (including a women's pro-tennis circuit).

The critical part of Nike's selling approach was the endorsement by these athletic "heroes." From the firm's first endorsers—Steve Prefontaine and Geoff Petrie—the list grew to include 40 pecent of the players in the NBA, a large percentage of the top runners, and such individual stars as John McEnroe, Sebastian Coe, and Dan Fouts. As one of the Nike managers said, "These athletes are our promotional team."

Exhibit 1

NIKE, INC.
Profit and Loss Summaries

	1981	1980	1979
Revenues	457,742	269,775	149,830
Cost of sales	328,133	196,683	103,466
Selling and administrative	60,953	39,810	22,815
Interest	17,859	9,144	4,569
Other	92	107	(443)
Income before taxes	50,705	24,031	19,423
Taxes	24,750	11,526	9,700
Net income	25,955	12,505	9,723
Earnings per share	1.52	.77	.58

Breakdown of Sales

	1981	1980	1979
Domestic footwear	398,852	245,100	143,400
Domestic apparel	33,108	8,100	2,200
Foreign sales	25,782	16,575	4,230
Total	457,742	269,775	149,830

Exhibit 2

NIKE, INC.
Balance Sheet

	May 31, 1981	May 31, 1980
Assets		
Cash	$ 1,792	$ 1,827
Accounts receivable	87,236	63,861
Inventories	120,229	55,941
Deferred taxes	1,300	135
Prepaid expenses	2,487	2,151
Current assets	213,044	123,915
Property, plant, equipment	23,845	14,193
Accumulated depreciation	(7,673)	(4,027)
Other assets	1,073	534
Total assets	$230,289	$134,615
Liabilities		
Current portion of debt	$ 6,620	$ 3,867
Notes payable	61,190	36,500
Accounts payable	42,492	36,932
Accrued liabilities	15,401	10,299
Income taxes payable	12,654	6,693
Current liabilities	138,357	94,291
Long-term debt	8,611	11,268
Common stock	28,600*	71
Retained earnings	54,721	28,985
Total liabilities	$230,289	$134,615

* In 1981, Nike went public with the sale of 1,360,000 shares of common stock, with Knight retaining 51 percent of the outstanding shares.

The effectiveness of Nike's strategies is reflected in their financial statements. (See Exhibits 1 and 2.)

Current Concerns

Obviously, Nike had been a tremendous success. Nonetheless, size created its own problems and caused Phil Knight to review, more specifically, some of the important marketing issues.

The channels, as a case in point, represented one such area of concern. To quote from a company document:

> Given the present management's obsession with increased "numbers," it is not surprising that we are witnessing an increased emphasis on self-service in branded footwear retail sales. You need only look as far as the local G. I. Joe's, J. C. Penney, Meir & Frank, or Athletic Shoe Factory Outlet to see why the technical portion of our line is so badly misunderstood. In self-service retail outlets, you are hard pressed to find any sales help, let alone well-informed assistance from users of athletic footwear. Perhaps it is a function of our stagnant economy, but every retailer is talking about how to reduce his "selling costs" by employing mass merchant mentality, i.e., read *Proportionally Fewer Customer Service-Oriented Retail Outlets* to intelligently sell our technical line.
>
> With a significantly smaller and diminishing percentage of our products being sold in specialty or Torch accounts, it is no wonder that our reputation is being redefined in the consumer's mind with descriptive phrases such as, "low-end, nontechnical, pricepoint, and promotional." The bulk of our sales volume is now attributable to dealers who are providing less and less point-of-purchase information about how our shoes perform to customers as retailers strive for more volume and fine tune their selling efficiency. The result of this shift in selling technique and brand identity puts increased pressure on Nike to presell our products while making the shoes easily visible and recognizable as high-quality, innovative products.
>
> In the midst of the recent frenzied growth of mass consumption of branded athletic footwear, there has developed a reaction among both the more technically aware and prestige-seeking, affluent consumers to distinguish themselves from the pack. With increased discretionary buying power, these consumers are demanding high-tech products and are willing to "pay a little more to get just what I wanted." This *is* the segment of the market we have ignored and, as a result, have been losing to New Balance, Tiger, and Saucony. If Nike is going to continue to have mass volume sales and retain a strong share of the high-end sales, it is obvious we need to segment the product line and distinguish the product in this market so that it appeals to the high-tech, affluent consumers.
>
> The high-tech segment of the branded market is becoming substantially more crowded with new products and new brands. This is particularly true of running flats. Avia, for example, is gearing its entire en-

trance into the technical branded segments of the athletic footwear market with advertising and packaging that connotes high technology and new design innovations. Advanced technologies (materials, construction techniques) are creating a more confusing product environment for consumers to make buying decisions in. The expanded array of products and advertised product features, each (Puma, New Balance, Tiger) claiming to perform breakthroughs in sports research, is making our brand prey to slick (well-segmented) marketing strategies.

Of particular note was the recent incursion by some mass merchandisers into the high end of the shoe market. Mervyn's, to be specific, in early 1982, sold 300 pairs of Nike's newest technical product at very low prices. Nike received the income, to be sure, but was unable to capitalize in the consumer's mind on the technical advantage of the new product. To the consumer, it was only a price deal.

Another matter of worry had to do with individual responsibilities as opposed to company-wide responsibilities. Size had increased the breadth and depth of the various lines. For example, there were over 200 shoe types alone. But as no one was responsible for any one line, this led to a lack of focus and attention to details in several lines. Moreover, as implied earlier, there were few formal lines of communication and very little hierarchy between managers and locations. And finally, in Phil's opinion, the company was relying on too few key people who were close friends and saw the company as fun more than as a business.

It was within this special environment that Phil was considering his possible moves. It was not easy to trade off more control and formality against the current organizational culture. And yet he was very much aware that the market's and his own company's evolution required a new look at how to organize for growth.

Although he was well aware that there were other choices, he thought he might ask the Friday Club to consider the implications of the following alternatives:

1. Do nothing.
2. Divisionalize (and decentralize) by product category.
3. Organize by channel.
4. Organize by markets or segments.
5. Fragment the marketing function.
6. Adopt a product management system, such as for running, court, cleated, etc.
7. Split the marketing group into "established businesses" and "new opportunities."
8. Establish and use "task forces" to handle critical problem areas as they arose.

CASE 7–2

Traditional Building Systems, Inc.

"I'm not going to ignore any suggestion that might prevent fiscal 1982 turning into the financial disaster it appears to be headed for. I'll try to keep an open mind on this, but you are going to have to convince me that changing the organization is going to improve anything." Walter Dwyer, president of Traditional Building Systems, Inc. (TBS), had reacted to a suggestion by his director of marketing, Scott Hamlin, that the company should reorganize its marketing and sales organization so that marketing managers no longer reported to the eight subsidiary company general managers but to the director of marketing. Each of the company's eight manufacturing facilities, located across the United States, was organized as a separate subsidiary under the direction of a general manager who had clear profit-and-loss responsibility. At every plant, a marketing manager and a production manager reported to the general manager. In most cases, an assistant marketing manager reported to the marketing manager. At each plant location, a sales staff of two or three people handled the clerical and administrative aspects of order processing, customer service, and delivery and reported to the marketing manager. Exhibit 1 depicts the current corporate organization, and Exhibit 2 shows the marketing organization.

Company Background

Traditional Building Systems, Inc., was one of the oldest companies in the United States manufacturing complete precut log building

This case was prepared by Frederick E. Webster, Jr., E. B. Osborn Professor of Marketing, Amos Tuck School of Business Administration, Dartmouth College, as the basis for classroom discussion. It is not intended to illustrate either correct or incorrect handling of a management situation. All rights reserved by the author. © 1984 by the Trustees of Dartmouth College.

Exhibit 1
Corporate Organization Structure

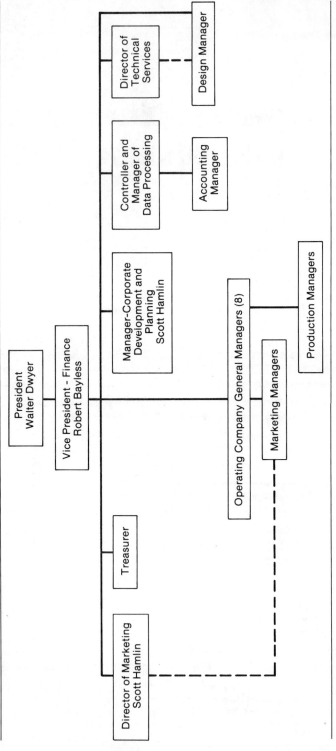

Exhibit 2
Marketing Organization

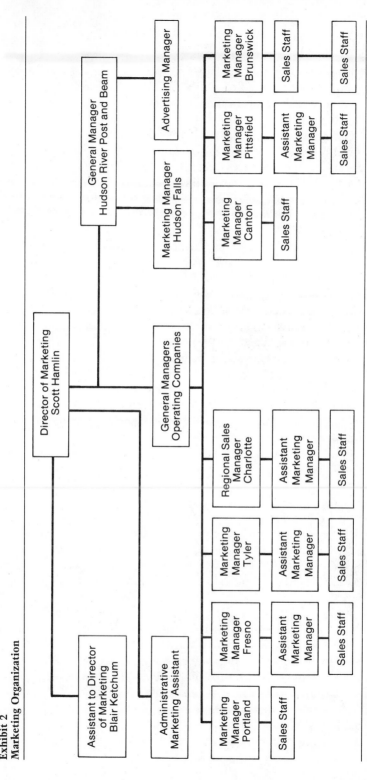

Source: Company records.

packages for private residential and light commercial construction. A complete set of building materials (except for electrical and plumbing components) was delivered to a building site on flatbed tractor trailers (usually two) where it was typically erected by a local contractor. A significant number of customers, however, elected to build their own houses, contributing what was called by company management "sweat equity" to the project. Building models and packages were designed to make the construction process as easy as possible, although some basic carpentry skills were required. Building packages sold to the customer for prices ranging from $15,000 to over $30,000 and represented about 40 percent of the total cost of the completed structure if built by a general contractor.

Manufacturing facilities were located in Portland, Oregon; Fresno, California; Tyler, Texas; Charlotte, North Carolina; Canton, Ohio; Pittsfield, Massachusetts; Hudson Falls, New York; and Brunswick, Maine. In addition to manufacturing regular log home models, the Maine plant also specialized in the manufacture of windows and doors for shipment to other plants where they were incorporated in the building packages shipped to local customers. (Some millwork was also purchased by the general managers from other sources.) Corporate management was located in Pittsfield, Massachusetts, a few miles away from the Pittsfield plant, the company's first manufacturing facility. There had been no acquisitions in the 30-year history of the company; all plants had been built for the specific purpose of making log building packages.

The plant in Hudson Falls, New York, had a distinct line of home designs, marketed under the brand name Hudson River Post and Beam. The Hudson River product was sold through a separate dealer organization. Packages were either standard or custom designs, with the latter running as high as $70,000, whereas standard packages averaged about $35,000. The post and beam product line featured a much more contemporary design and appealed to a higher income market than log buildings. Additional Hudson River Post and Beam operations were in the process of being established at the California and Carolina plant locations.

The product (both TBS log homes and Hudson River Post and Beam homes) was sold through 210 dealers, also called independent sales representatives (ISRs), each functioning as a separate and independent business. The dealers were organized on a regional basis defined by the market served by a given subsidiary. That is, each dealer sold the product of a single plant and was serviced by the marketing manager at that plant. Some were simple proprietorships, others were partnerships, and a few were incorporated. Although there were some professional people such as lawyers and real estate agents who represented

TBS as one part of their business dealings, the typical ISR was an individual with experience in the building trades, perhaps as a carpenter or independent building contractor. Very few of the ISRs had construction capability, however. Typically, the ISR worked with the customer to make the necessary arrangements with a local contractor.

Each ISR had an assigned geographic area of responsibility as part of his formal agreement with the subsidiary but could not be prevented legally from selling outside that assigned area. Every ISR was the responsibility of a single TBS marketing manager and was supplied by a single plant. Thus, each subsidiary general manager had a set of roughly 20 to 30 independent sales representatives who were responsible for selling the product of his plant. Seventy percent of the dealers produced 10 or fewer orders in the typical year; 30 percent of the dealers produced 70 percent of annual sales. A study at one plant recently showed that 9 of 28 dealers had sold no units in the previous year.

Industry and Market Conditions

Market conditions in recent years had been the worst in the history of the homebuilding industry in the United States since World War II. Housing starts in 1982 were running at an annual rate of slightly under 1 million units, less than half that experienced through most of the decade of the 70s. TBS unit sales in the past year were only about 50 percent of what they had been a few years before, the best years in the company's history of, to that point, uninterrupted growth. Hudson River Post and Beam sales had actually continued to increase while the rest of TBS plants suffered major declines in orders.

Industry conditions in 1982 reflected a period of general economic recession in the United States and, more specifically, interest rates that had moved in a range from 15 to 20 percent for the better part of the past two years. It was not clear whether potential home buyers were becoming used to such high interest rates or whether they expected rates to decline in the future. In the most recently completed fiscal year, TBS reported a before-tax loss, although a modestly positive cash flow had been preserved and the company had been able to service all its debt obligations.

TBS sales volume for the first quarter of 1982 was off approximately 40 percent from the same period in 1981. The best performing company, in terms of both volume and profit, during this time period was the Tyler, Texas, subsidiary, one of the newer companies. The three oldest subsidiaries—Pittsfield, Brunswick, and Canton—were mediocre performers in the first quarter of 1982. The two plants with the worst performance in this period were the two newest subsidiaries, in California and Carolina, both located in favorable climates and housing markets.

TBS sales forecasts were not optimistic for the coming months. A price increase had been announced effective May 1. Most of the plants were virtually booked full for the month of April, but orders for March had been very light, and May and June orders were almost nonexistent. The exception was the Hudson Falls plant, which had a strong order picture right into the summer months. The spring months were always the strongest months for orders, given the effects of weather on plans for building construction. Seasonality even existed to some degree in the order patterns in the milder climates of the markets served by the California, Texas, and Carolina plants. Forecasts and budgets for the previous fiscal year had been revised downward three times. Most of the general managers and marketing managers had earned little or no bonus.

The Marketing Organization

The TBS marketing organization (see Exhibit 2) was headed by Scott Hamlin, a 35-year old graduate of Williams College with a background in corporate planning and small business management. Mr. Hamlin was originally hired by Walter Dwyer and Robert Bayless, the vice president of finance, to help study acquisition opportunities and to manage other aspects of corporate development and planning. A few months after Hamlin joined TBS, the vice president of marketing resigned after two years with the company.

The vice president of marketing position was created in 1976 as the company began to expand nationally, beyond its traditional northeastern U.S. market. Prior to that time, marketing functions were performed at the plant level and focused on the dealer organization. The position was created during a major upswing in the housing market, with interest in log homes at a historic high and many new firms entering the industry. TBS management believed that company growth and expansion to cover the total U.S. market, combined with increased competition, created a need for a professional approach to its marketing and more careful coordination across subsidiaries. A young man with a background in consumer marketing was hired and immediately turned to the task of upgrading the catalog, creating a company-wide brand name, Traditional Building Systems, and developing a national advertising campaign. Prior to this time, each subsidiary had its own brand name (e.g., Maine Log Buildings), but each plant offered the same selection of models, common prices, etc. Responsibility for the dealer organization remained with the local subsidiary, but the vice president of marketing was directed to develop an approach for assisting in recruiting, developing, and supporting a strong dealer network.

When market conditions began to soften while competition continued to increase, according to Dwyer and Bayless, the vice president of marketing seemed unable to develop programs to effectively counter the downturn. He was criticized for lack of planning and spending too much time on details, such as catalogs and brochure design, and finally resigned. Top management remained uncertain as to whether a corporate marketing slot was necessary, believing that effectiveness depended very much on the quality of the person filling the post.

The top marketing slot was vacant for several months as Dwyer and Bayless interviewed several candidates identified through their own efforts and with the assistance of a Boston placement organization. When none of these candidates was judged satisfactory, it was decided to ask Hamlin to fill the top marketing post on a temporary basis as director of marketing. Hamlin was not unhappy in this post; neither did he consider himself to be a real marketing professional. Weak market conditions gave this temporary assignment more permanence than originally intended. Top management thought Hamlin had performed well, and the company was no longer thinking about acquisitions. On the other hand, Hamlin did not intend to stay in his present assignment much longer and was eager to return to issues of corporate development, strategic planning, and related long-range matters.

One of Hamlin's accomplishments during the three and a half years he had been serving as director of marketing (as well as continuing as manager-corporate development and planning) was to develop job descriptions for the marketing department, including his own position (see Exhibit 3).

An administrative marketing assistant reported directly to the director of marketing and was responsible for handling many details relating to advertising, sales promotion, and marketing administration. The company's annual advertising budget in national media exceeded $250,000. About half of the advertising budget was spent for national media, principally "shelter" magazines (like *Better Homes and Gardens*) and "lifestyle" magazines (like *Sunset* and *Country Journal*), and this advertising was placed from corporate headquarters in Pittsfield. The other half was placed in regional media following directions set by the local subsidiary management and included local home show promotions, regional co-operative advertising programs with the dealers, local media targeted at specific markets, etc. Regional media often featured the names of local dealers. The principal objective of virtually all national advertising was to generate inquiries and sales leads for the dealer organization.

The TBS National Information Center (NIC) was an 800 number that could be dialed toll free from anywhere in the continental United

Exhibit 3

Traditional Building Systems, Inc.

Job Description

Position: Director of Marketing

Basic function: Responsible for planning, directing, controlling, and coordinating the marketing functions of the company, including pricing, distribution, forecasting, customer service, market research and marketing studies, advertising, and public relations. This responsibility should be conducted in such a way to meet or exceed established volume and profit goals within approved budgets.

Reports to: President—Traditional Building Systems, Inc.

Supervises: Administrative marketing assistant

Specific duties:

1. Develop for approval by the president long- and short-term marketing objectives and strategy concerning:
   a. Overall sales, advertising, promotion, public relations, and planning and research activities.
   b. Recruiting, training, and development programs for marketing personnel.
   c. Operating budgets to control expenses and allocate efforts for all marketing activities.
   d. Pricing policies to market the company's products profitably and competitively.

2. Direct the development of strategic and tactical marketing plans and programs. Part of this effort should be to develop input for long-range company plans in the marketing area.

3. Maintain close liaison with Traditional Building Systems, Inc., management, operating management, and other company groups to assist in the sharing of both company and marketing policies.

4. Recommend marketing department organization, personnel assignments, and wage and salary programs in accordance with established policies.

5. Review and control the performance of the marketing department by:
   a. Reviewing actual expenses against budgets and established standards.
   b. Appraising the company's market position relative to that of competitors.
   c. Appraising the results of special project assignments.

6. Develop marketing strategy for operating companies in keeping with established marketing objectives.

7. Review license agreements for president's approval and establish dealer quotas for TBS dealer network. Approve policies to be followed by dealers for proper territory coverage.

8. Submit annual dealer network review to president together with recommended changes.

9. Approve all operating systems and procedures for the collection, analysis, and dissemination of market information.

10. Keep fully abreast of market developments through analysis and review of sales, research, and trade reports.

Exhibit 3 *(concluded)*

11.   Direct the planning for new products to serve market needs and direct the development of new markets for the profitable sales of new and future products.
12.   Coordinate overall marketing strategy with the general manager in each plant to promote a good working relationship between the general manager and the marketing manager.
13.   Work with the president and the Hudson River Post and Beam general manager to develop a marketing program for the post and beam product. Projects in this area will be specifically defined and assigned.
14.   Work with counsel on legal questions that involve the marketing function after each instance is cleared with president.

States. Every national advertisement carried the NIC telephone number as well as a coupon which could be completed by an interested consumer and mailed to the NIC, which was physically located at the Pittsfield plant. The woman who answered NIC calls worked an eight-hour day five days per week and used a computer terminal to enter information about each inquirer into a data base. (Calls after business hours were answered with a recorded message, and the caller was asked to leave a name, address, and telephone number.) The callers were asked whether they wished to receive a brochure or the TBS full-color catalog, which showed all building models and included detailed floor plans and drawings and sold for $6. A set of full-sized blueprints for each of the models could also be purchased for $25 per model. Any person ordering a catalogue or requesting a brochure was considered a prospect, and information about each was sent to the appropriate dealer within a few days after the call.

The NIC operator was managed by the general manager of the Pittsfield plant, and the position therefore does not appear on the marketing organization chart. The NIC activity, however, was planned and monitored by the director of marketing, and the expenses of the NIC were part of the corporate marketing budget. In the last year, the NIC received more than 5,000 telephone calls. A good deal of lead generation also occurred at the local level, in response to regional media usage, and did not pass through the NIC. Calls and mailed coupons as well as dealer requirements yielded sales of more than 30,000 catalogs in that year. Dealers purchased the catalogs at $2 and either gave them to prospects or sold them for $6.

The national marketing organization developed and distributed a large variety of public relations, publicity, and promotional materials, especially brochures, slide shows, ad mats, catalog sheets, product specification sheets, and the like to and for the dealer organization. For example, over 200 publicity kits describing a new joining system to be incorporated in TBS buildings had recently been distributed to media serving the building industry and consumer markets. For 1982, a cooperative advertising program was underway in which TBS would pay half of any dealer's advertising expenses up to a maximum determined by the dealer's annual quota.

Company management believed that the dealer organization was not as strong as it could be although it was believed to be the strongest in the industry. Scott Hamlin saw a serious problem in the dealers' failure to follow up on leads. One study indicated that fewer than 15 percent of the leads sent to dealers by the NIC were followed up by the dealer within 30 days. Among the possible explanations considered by Hamlin were a fear of cold calling by the dealers, a dealer's belief that these leads were not as good as those he could generate locally, poor dealer planning and time management, and a basic lack of selling skills. To address this issue, Hamlin had arranged a series of dealer training sessions, conducted by a professional training organization, on lead follow-up and telephone selling. Several had been conducted at local plant sites and had been well received by the dealers and marketing managers who attended. Typically, the stronger dealers showed the most interest in such training opportunities.

The marketing managers reported directly to the general managers. The reporting relationship (illustrated in Exhibit 2) of the marketing managers to the director of marketing was a "dotted line" or advisory relationship. (See Exhibit 4 for the marketing manager job description.) The marketing manager's major responsibility was to develop and support the dealer organization for that plant. Marketing managers could also become deeply involved in the dealer-customer relationship, especially when problems developed at the construction site. Needless to say, a log building package was a complex product, and problems such as improper dimensions on a building component, improper construction, faulty materials, or a builder's confusion about instructions, while not an everyday occurrence, were inevitable and needed to be dealt with in a timely and courteous manner.

Each sale required careful administration in terms of order processing, documentation, production scheduling, package assembly, and delivery. Follow-up with each project at the building site was also necessary, as just noted. Many initial customer inquiries were made directly to the local TBS company rather than to the National Information Center. At many plants, these day-to-day details were handled by an assistant marketing manager, freeing the marketing manager to spend more time in the field with the dealers. In actual practice, the functioning of the assistant marketing manager varied significantly from plant to plant, reflecting both the person in the job and his supervisor. There was no formal job description for this position. Where there was no assistant marketing manager, the marketing manager spent a good portion of his time responding to inquiries and complaints, solving problems, and "putting out fires."

Exhibit 4

Traditional Building Systems, Inc.

Job Description

Position: Marketing manager

Basic function: Responsible for implementing marketing objectives and maintaining a good business relationship with the dealer network.

Reports to: General manager

Specific duties:

1. Dealer support—the marketing manager must dedicate the majority of his time to working in support of our dealers. Each dealer should be met at his location twice a year for a formal evaluation period. Thorough records of dealer performance, license agreements, quotas, adherence to administrative and sales guidelines, and customer complaints should be maintained on a current basis. The marketing manager is also responsible for the adding on of new dealers and their development.

2. Customer relations—since our customers are usually working through our dealers, the marketing manager's efforts should be aimed at harmonizing that relationship. Courtesy, speed, and accuracy of response are essential to a continued positive company image. The marketing manager is initially responsible for handling all claims, short shipments, and other customer complaints. Recommendations for a financial or material settlement are to continue to be submitted to the general manager for a final decision.

3. Scheduling product and shipping—the marketing manager is to be in charge of scheduling product based on the general manager's stated level of production. This product schedule is then to be arranged in concert with trucking companies to assure the smooth flow of product from the plants.

4. Contract processing—the contract processing function lies primarily in the hands of the clerical force, but the marketing manager must be able to determine the acceptability of buildings vis-a-vis the codes, available options, production limitations, pricing, etc. It is his sole responsibility to provide for the accuracy of the contracts in regards to pricing and the calculation of commissions. This requires an up-to-date knowledge of the buildings, options, and sales policies.

5. Corporate marketing input and projects—the marketing manager is expected to provide corporate marketing input in terms of creating better marketing systems for an improved marketing administration program, producing ideas for the improvement of the product's marketability, and relating individual company experiences for the education of the total marketing department. In addition, the marketing manager will be asked to complete several corporate marketing projects under the supervision of the director of marketing.

6. Financial planning—the marketing manager is to be responsible for formulation of a yearly budget for marketing activities. His ability to meet this budget will be a measured criterion for successful job performance. The budgets will be reviewed quarterly with the new year's budget due in November.

7. Assistant to general manager—the marketing manager is an assistant to the general manager and should be capable of acting on the behalf of an absent general manager. This necessitates a strong communications link between the general manager and the marketing manager so that each is aware of the other's duties and objectives.

8. Dealer development—responsibilities include soliciting, interviewing, assessing, and selecting new independent sales representatives in areas needing representation.

9. Dealer training—a constant effort is needed here to train the ISR in all aspects related to lead generation, lead follow-up, contract initiation, product knowledge, company administration and billing policies, marketing and sales policies, and such other areas as may be required to facilitate the ISR's sales performance.

Exhibit 5

Traditional Building Systems, Inc.

Job Description

Position: Regional sales manager—Texas, Arkansas, Oklahoma

Basic function: Responsible for implementing marketing and sales objectives and maintaining a good business relationship with dealer network.

Reports to: General manager—Tyler

Specific duties:

1.   Independent sales representative development—responsibilities include screening, interviewing, testing, and developing ISR applicants pursuant to developing an efficient ISR network within the region. The time and effort expended in this area should be significant.

2.   Direct selling—the sales manager will be expected to have sufficient product and market knowledge to effect sales of the product in both the residential and commercial areas throughout the region where there are no ISRs.

3.   Customer relations—the responsibilities here will be a result of direct sales which require technical building assistance and direct customer support throughout the building process. Courtesy, efficiency, and accuracy are essential to maintaining a strong public image. Recommendations related to financing, building customization, material shipping, and supply will also be required.

4.   Dealer support—existing dealers will require consultation and advice in selling, customer service, and solving of problems related to scheduling of the shipping of the product.

     Other responsibilities:

     a.   Hold periodic sales meetings with the dealers to convey policy, strategy, and techniques related to marketing and to convey other pertinent information.

     b.   Assess the market potential for the ISR's service area, arrive at an annual unit sales expectation(s), and help the ISR reach that goal.

     c.   Assist ISR where necessary with customer relations.

5.   Marketing strategy—in concert with the director of marketing (TBS), marketing strategies will be set out on an annual basis for the region. Sales expectations will be detailed, as well as strategy(s) as to how those sales will be realized. One semiannual ISR review will be due simultaneously detailing which ISRs will be dropped and how many will be added. New service areas not occupied will be identified and prioritized in groups.

6.   Intercompany communications—the sales manager will be responsible for maintaining a high level of communications with his immediate supervisor, as well as with TBS. Well-developed writing and verbal skills are required. Good reporting skills are also necessary.

7.   Other general requirements—as this is a field position with no day-to-day support of supervision, the individual must be highly motivated, capable, self-starting, conscientious, and honest. A significant amount of travel is required.

Scott Hamlin believed that the effectiveness and productivity of the marketing organization would be improved if the director of marketing had direct control over the marketing managers. He described himself as "a general without troops" and felt that many marketing plans and programs failed to achieve their goals because he lacked authority over the marketing managers. He perceived the general managers as product, production, and cost oriented, more concerned with the control of short-term operations than with long-term market development. The general managers were evaluated and rewarded based primarily on annual profit performance. Hamlin believed that the typical general manager was much more likely to cut personnel and programs rather than commit resources to developing orders when he saw a developing short-fall in profit. In addition, he felt that control over marketing and sales plan implementation was lost when the general managers felt pressure to meet short-term performance goals in weak market conditions.

One approach to improving marketing activity by the operating companies had been tried as an experiment in part of the market served by the Tyler, Texas, plant. A sales manager position was created (see Exhibit 5), and a person was hired and located in the Dallas/Fort Worth area, by far the strongest market area served by the Tyler plant. The idea was to have a person who could be free of the need to respond to day-to-day problems and complaints and who could concentrate on developing sales and improving the dealer organization. The new man was responsible for generating business in Texas, Oklahoma, and Arkansas and reported to the general manager at Tyler. After about eight months, no positive results were observed, and the man was terminated. In the meantime, the marketing manager at Tyler had resigned, and the general manager had been fired because of a number of problems related to inventory and production control. A new general manager had been hired, but the marketing manager position was still vacant. Given the importance of the Texas market, Hamlin preferred hiring only a new sales manager rather than a new marketing manager. Neither post was currently filled, and budget constraints would prohibit filling both positions at this time. Hamlin was thinking that the newly hired sales manager could focus on the Texas market, with the general manager serving as his own marketing manager and overseeing the other markets until market conditions improved. A position for a sales manager to be responsible for Louisiana, Mississippi, and Alabama had been discussed but never filled.

The General Manager

The general manager of an operating company was viewed by TBS top management as responsible for running his own business with

Exhibit 6

Traditional Building Systems, Inc.

Job Description

Position: General manager

Basic function: To control the manufacture and distribution of our product through management of facilities, inventories, and personnel with profit responsibility for financial objectives. This position is responsible for promoting our corporate image and maintaining good community relations.

Reports to: President—Traditional Building Systems, Inc.

Specific duties:

1. Prepare annual budget for operating company for review and approval by TBS. Perform periodic review of performance using company's financial budgets with operating authority over income and expense functions at the operation level.

2. Capital budgets should be prepared annually. Fixed asset proposals should be reviewed by the general manager and submitted to TBS in writing for approval.

3. Interpret and implement company policies and procedures as well as maintain the safety and health of assigned personnel.

4. Maintain accurate records at the operating company level and transmit timely required information to the parent company.

5. Supervise the installation and maintenance of plant equipment.

6. Direct the marketing manager and production manager to carry out the objectives of the company.

7. Insure stable and adequate supply of raw material.

8. Maintain good business relationships with vendors, customers, and dealers.

9. Institute a systematic basis for appraising personnel performance.

10. Review and make recommendations for corporate objectives and policies.

---

clear profit and loss responsibility. (Exhibit 6 is a position description for the general manager.) The principal element of corporate control over the operating companies was the annual budget, developed by the subsidiary general managers under the coordination of Robert Bayless, the vice president-finance. Sales and profit projections were originated by the general manager and his staff and reviewed by Dwyer, Bayless, and Hamlin. Sales figures were rarely subject to challenge, although TBS management often asked the general managers to revise specific expense items and profit estimates.

In a good year, the general manager could receive a bonus, based on profitability, equal to up to 40 percent of his annual salary. The typical general manager was between 35 and 45 years old and had extensive previous experience in the homebuilding industry. Some general managers had been with the company for over a decade, rising through the ranks. Others had been hired very recently.

Walter Dwyer and Robert Bayless were both philosophically committed to the concept of a decentralized, profit-center organization. Dwyer, in particular, was adamant in his belief that recent problems were primarily a reflection of bad hiring decisions rather than flaws in the organization itself. A local manager with direct knowledge of local conditions, full responsibility and authority for all aspects of the operation, and the incentive of a reward system based on profit performance seemed to Dwyer to be the best guarantee for corporate profitability. He believed this system was most responsive to changes in market conditions and best able to solve problems as they appeared. Bayless agreed and added, "You can look at the bottom line and know whether the general manager has done the job or not. If he hasn't and doesn't seem to know how to correct the problem, you replace him."

Both Dwyer and Bayless understood Scott Hamlin's desire to have responsibility for the marketing managers but believed that they couldn't take marketing responsibility away from the general managers without fundamentally undercutting the profit-center concept.

Hamlin was convinced, after almost four years of trying to improve marketing effectiveness, that the general managers were, with only a few exceptions, unable to execute their marketing responsibilities adequately. He commented:

> In the good old days when we had a seller's market, the dealers were order takers who needed no selling skills, and the general managers had to allocate buildings to dealers. Sales and marketing are no problem when you have the plant full and three- to six-month order backlogs. The GM's problems are all production problems, which he typically knows how to handle.
> Today's markets are another matter. Our dealer organization is weak. Most of the dealers don't know how to sell. Our marketing managers are go-fers for the general manager. They don't spend enough time working with the dealers in the field. When the general manager sees that he can't make budget, he is reluctant to put more effort into marketing to generate more orders. He tries to cut back on marketing and plant expenses to improve his bottom line. As far as I'm concerned, that's suicidal from a business development viewpoint.

Bayless had a different viewpoint. He pointed to a record of increases in spending for promotion, significant increases in commission amounts, and increased marketing personnel expense to support his view that the general managers did not shortchange marketing when business was off. Dwyer agreed but felt that there was little planning for these adjustments in spending.

As a first step toward the revised organization he had in mind, Scott Hamlin was considering proposing that three regional sales managers be hired and that they should report to him directly, coordinating marketing effort across subsidiary boundaries. The eastern regional sales manager would be responsible for the marketing managers at

Exhibit 7

Traditional Building Systems, Inc.
_____
Job Description
_____
Position: Regional sales manager (preliminary draft)
_____

     Basic function: Responsible for implementing marketing objectives on a re-
gional basis, and for stimulating sales in the multiresidential
and nonresidential markets, along with assisting plant personnel, directly and indirectly, in maintaining good dealer relations.

     Reports to: Director of marketing

     Specific duties:

1. Dealer support—the regional sales manager must dedicate a portion of his
   time to supporting all dealers within his region, although his responsibility
   and support will be in coordination with, and secondary to, the local plant
   marketing manager's. Additional responsibilities will include dealer training
   in the areas of lead generation, lead administration and management, sales,
   promotions, and seminars.

2. Advertising and public relations—responsibilities will include recommending regional publications for advertising to the director of marketing, recommending projects for cooperative funds and budget funds by quarter
   throughout his region, developing local photographs and stories for regional
   and local media editorial placement, and establishing relationships with
   free-lance writers and editors of publications so as to maximize placement
   opportunities.

3. Sales management—the regional sales manager will be responsible for the
   following sales management areas:
   a. Train plant marketing managers on an ongoing basis.
   b. Train dealers in concert with plant marketing managers in the areas of
      sales, lead generation, etc.
   c. Assist marketing managers with developing an effective dealer network.
   d. Direct dealer support in support of the local marketing managers for
      home shows.
   e. Assist in development and maintenance of a sales manual.
   f. Assist and aid all dealers in advertising and lead generation.
   g. Assist in overall consultation with dealers on general business manage-
      ment.

4. Direct sales—the regional sales manager will be responsible for penetrating
   the multiresidential and nonresidential marketplaces. Specifically, generation of leads through advertising and sales calls; administration and management of lead follow-up; pursuing large, single-family developments with
   local dealers; and generating interest in chain stores, restaurants, churches,
   retail stores, and other nonresidential applications of TBS products will be
   part of this effort. In addition, he will aid and assist with the syndication of
   office buildings and other light commercial uses.

5. Marketing support—the regional sales manager will be responsible for developing market information for his region in coordination with the director of
   marketing. Any demographic surveys, secondary sources of information not
   currently held by TBS, and local knowledge will be gathered in support of
   more comprehensive knowledge of market conditions.

6. Evaluation—performance evaluation will be made on an annual basis.
   Quantitative sales expectations will be established within the sales region
   for two areas: (1) multi and nonresidential sales and (2) overall dealer sales.

Exhibit 7 *(concluded)*

> Compensation will, in part, be based on realization of sales expectations. Other qualitative review criteria include:
>
> a. Dealer training in the areas of lead generation and sales.
> b. Management effectiveness in advertising and public relations.
> c. Marketing manager training and development.
> d. Marketing support.
>
> 7. Corporate planning—input and direction will be expected during corporate planning sessions. Responsibilities will include preparation of marketing strategy options, marketing project identification and prioritization, identification of market segments, alternatives to increase market penetration, and sales projections.

Pittsfield, Hudson Falls, and Brunswick. A central regional sales manager would serve Canton, Charlotte, and Tyler. The western regional manager's responsibility would include the dealers and markets served by Portland and Fresno. A new job description for the regional sales manager had been developed by Hamlin (see Exhibit 7). Because this arrangement would leave the marketing managers reporting to the general managers and because it proposed that the regional sales manager have a direct selling responsibility as well as a management responsibility, Hamlin hoped it might be more acceptable to Dwyer and Bayless. But he wasn't sure it would really solve the problem. He was undecided whether to put forward this compromise or to argue forcefully for what he believed was the better idea—to take line responsibility for marketing away from the general managers and reassign it to the corporate director of marketing.

Questions

1. How has Scott Hamlin defined the problem?

2. Is it possible for an operating company general manager to execute his marketing responsibilities? Under what conditions?

3. Evaluate the various marketing job descriptions, especially the marketing manager's (Exhibit 4).

4. Was the regional sales manager—Texas, Arkansas, and Oklahoma—a good idea? Should the position be filled again?

5. Evaluate Hamlin's suggestion for three regional sales managers to report to him and evaluate the job description in Exhibit 7.

  a. Is it possible for one person to be responsible for both direct selling/commercial market development *and* management of the regional dealer organization?

  b. Would it be wise to have marketing managers report to both the regional sales manager *and* the general manager in a "matrix organization?" What does that do for the director of marketing?

C A S E 7–3

Barney Corporation

Barney Corporation was founded in 1958 to develop an entirely new field of technology based on the control of the crystalline structure of metals and alloys to a degree not thought possible prior to this development. A whole new product line had been developed from this technology.

Between 1956 and 1967, company sales had grown to about $42 million, and the average growth rate during the past five years had been in excess of 20 percent. In 1958, Barney stock was offered to the public at a price of $12.50 per share. In 1960, Barney obtained listing on the American Stock Exchange, and in 1967, the stock was trading in the range of $98 to $142 after splitting two for one in 1966. The management of Barney felt that this impressive growth rate was due to two factors. First, the vigorous research and development program undertaken by the company and, second, a dynamic and aggressive organization which prided itself on modeling its unique technical capabilities to the needs of the market place.

However, conflicts had started to develop within Barney's marketing organization as a result of the rapid expansion experienced by the company. To illustrate some of the problems, the following are excerpts taken from a recent meeting of product managers:

> So for the second time in a month, I had to ring St. Francis[1] to ask for more time on their order because you guys in manufacturing don't know the meaning of the word "priority." You also remember the trouble I had persuading R&D to work on this problem in the first place. Now we get a $150,000 order just as a starter, and we can't deliver on time!"
>
> Why do you ask me to spend my time trying to sell tubing when the

---

[1] St. Francis Roller Bearing Company was a major customer of Barney.

time given up could be spent on chain, for which I have profit responsibility?

All I do all day is put out fires. I have no time left to perform my other functions, especially long-range planning.

I wish you guys would wake up and see that we must move away from product management. Market orientation, that's what we need.

Look, we sell metal products; sure it's high-grade stuff, but it's all based on our product technology. A specialized, single-line sales force under these circumstances doesn't make sense to me.

Comments such as these worried the management of Barney, and they wondered what changes, if any, should be made in Barney's marketing organization, to maintain the expected rapid growth rate in the future.

Company History

In 1955, while working for the Great Western Steel Company's R&D division as metallurgists, Ken Barrington and George Whitney made an important discovery. Using various metals or alloys and subjecting them to a variety of physical and chemical treatments, they were able to produce compounds with extraordinary properties. These included an extreme degree of hardness, light weight, elasticity, and an ability to change the electrical conductivity of the metal.

Toward the end of 1955, Barrington and Whitney resigned from their positions with Great Western Steel and started their own company, which they called the Barney Corporation. After a great deal of discussing, it was decided that Barney Corporation would manufacture the finished products resulting from the new technological development rather than license other companies to use the technology or to manufacture the metal raw materials only. The company became a supplier to the electronics, aircraft, and aerospace industries almost immediately, although some time had to be spent with the engineers of each customer to acquaint them with the attributes and performance of these new materials.

The company grew rapidly between 1956 and 1960. Barney continued to concentrate on furthering research and development in the whole field of metal technology. Many patents were applied for, and new product development was taking place at an extremely rapid rate. Whitney commented that "hardly a day went by without someone calling us up with the 'greatest' new idea ever! We received a lot of good ideas in this way."

Marketing of the product line also received a good deal of attention. In order to build for long-range growth, management decided upon the following strategies:

1. Manufacturing representatives were to be used initially, in order to
    gain national distribution and rapid customer acceptance, until a
    competent internal marketing organization consisting of metallur-
    gical engineers could be developed.
2. Commercialization of new products would initially be restricted
    to those with only limited sales potential.

These strategies proved successful, and by the early 1960s, Barney
had developed to the point where it was able to launch a major expansion program. Existing product lines were greatly expanded, and several new high-volume product groups were introduced. The Cincinnati
Chain and Cable Company, located in Cincinnati, Ohio, was acquired,
which opened up markets not served by Barney prior to the acquisition. Barney also purchased the Curtis-Conway Manufacturing Company located in Chicago. Although under the financial direction and
control of Barney, this wholly owned subsidiary continued to operate
as a separate and autonomous company under the direction of Mr. John
Curtis.

At the same time, Barney began the transition to an in-house technically trained marketing team through the establishment of the product
management group and a direct sales force. The marketing group increased from only 10 people in 1960 to 104 in early 1968; in addition,
22 field sales offices were opened. Barney also began a major domestic
plant expansion to supplement its leased facilities in an industrial park
south of Cleveland. The company purchased 100 acres of land in an
industrial park nearby, on which some 420,000 square feet of manufacturing, research, and office facilities were constructed. Present facilities had the capacity to handle up to $80 million of business a year.
Much of this expansion and construction was financed from the sale of
some $7 million of convertible debentures.

Barney also began to expand internationally. In conjunction with
Uni-Metals Ltd., Barney set up a subsidiary in England, which had
research, manufacturing, and marketing facilities, to exploit potential
markets in the United Kingdom. Complete control of this British affiliate was acquired in 1966. As overseas marketing efforts were extended
to Western Europe, a second manufacturing facility was established in
West Germany. Most of the requirements of the European market
could be produced by the English and West German facilities.

Although Barney's record had been highly successful to date, management was anxious to maintain the company's impressive growth
rate. As such, management's stated financial objectives were to obtain
at least a 20 percent increase in sales per year, a 40 percent annual
return on invested capital, and an after-tax profit on sales of 7 to 9
percent. Management considered three courses of action prerequisite
to fulfilling these objectives: continued technological innovation, adequate patent coverage, and vertical integration.

Product Line

Technology

Nearly all of Barney's products were based on the science of metal crystallography. The company had developed over 100 different metals and alloys, which, when changed by several chemical and physical processes, had desired chemical, physical, and electrical properties. Barney utilized these properties to develop novel products and applications ranging from ball bearings to top secret materials for defense contracts, and had over 8,000 different types and sizes of products.

Research and Development

In early 1968, Barney's R&D staff totaled 170, nearly double that of the previous year. Approximately half of the staff were degreed personnel, including 31 with doctorates in metallurgy, engineering, and chemistry. Research was carried out in new facilities which included a materials processing area, product development laboratories, and technical service laboratories. England and West Germany had a separate development and technical service group which supplemented the U.S. activity for service to these Western European subsidiaries.

Many of the research projects were initiated by the product management group based on market research or on information from the field sales force. In order to supplement the market research and product development efforts of the product managers, a venture analysis group, which consisted of three men, was set up in early 1967 to explore whole new areas within the technical competence of the company. This group originally reported directly to the president, but was later transferred to the R&D area under vice president Greenhalgh.

All Barney products were developed through its own research efforts. Over 60 percent of 1967 company sales were comprised of products introduced in the preceding three years. In addition to patent protection on substantially all of its significant patentable developments, the company had many trade secrets and a large body of confidential technical information and skill. Barney also adopted and used many trademarks. A description of the major product lines follows.

Electrical Wiring

Prior to the development of special alloys for high-performance electrical wiring by Barney, electrical wiring could be made to withstand only quite narrow extremes of physical conditions. For example, there was high-temperature wire and low-temperature wire, each being suitable for applications only in a fairly narrow temperature range. The alloys developed by Barney allowed one wire to be used under all tem-

Ball and Roller Bearings[2]

Barney had made a major breakthrough with this product line recently. For a number of years, Barney had been working in close cooperation with the St. Francis Roller Bearing Company, one of the major producers of ball and roller bearings in the United States. In the past, St. Francis had manufactured over 300 different types of bearings in many different sizes and shapes depending upon the application, required life, load carrying capacity, and many other factors. Many different alloys were used to produce this large product range. After several years of testing, St. Francis had recently decided to standardize on ball and roller bearings manufactured by Barney. As a result of this change, St. Francis was able to reduce its line of bearings to about 35 basic types with great savings in manufacturing and inventory costs.

The first commercial order had been received about six months ago, and it would appear that potential business for this application would reach at least $10 million within a very short space of time.

Barney was now actively soliciting business with other bearing manufacturers and had initiated a study project to determine whether it should begin to manufacture finished bearings. Barney had been approached recently by one of the major motor car manufacturers, regarding the supply of finished bearings manufactured from Barney alloys.

Chain and Cable

These products were sold to a wide variety of industrial users. The major product advantages over competing lines were a high degree of hardness and high tensile strength. Chain was sold to automobile companies and other engine manufacturers for timing chain, to bicycle and motor bicycle manufacturers as driving chain, and to other industrial users for a variety of applications. Another line of chain was manufactured for cutting purposes and found a major outlet in power saw manufacturers either as chain or band saws.

Mechanical cable was also manufactured in a wide variety of alloys depending upon the required application. Some cable went into aircraft and to automobile manufacturers. Other high-tension cable was sold to contractors involved in the construction of bridges and commercial office buildings. One major customer was the Langsford Elevator Corporation, one of the major manufacturers of elevators in the United States. Both the main cable and the safety cable of lifts manufactured by Langsford were made from Barney cable.

---

[2] The company did not produce finished bearings. It produced only spherical or cylindrical-shaped alloy ball and roller bearings, ground and polished to the required tolerances. These "ball bearings" were then sold to bearing manufacturers who made a final polish and then manufactured the bearings.

Castings

Barney had developed many alloys for use in a wide variety of castings. In addition to a wide variety of castings manufactured in its own foundries, Barney sold metal to other foundries for casting purposes. This was the only purpose for which Barney sold raw metal or alloy.

Barney owned several foundries in different parts of the United States located close to major customers. Major use for casting was in a wide variety of precision items. Automobile manufacturers were major customers, and others included manufacturers of earthmoving and agricultural equipment. The leading edges of bulldozer blades, power shovels, plows, and harrows were major outlets for Barney castings.

Another group of important, potential customers for castings was the nation's railways. Rails are laid in 100-foot lengths but cannot be welded together since expansion during hot weather would lead to buckling. A gap of about one to one and one half inches has to be left between these lengths to allow for expansion. This means that the wear at the end of the rail is about three times as great as that on the rest of the rail, leading to costly maintenance problems. Barney had conducted tests for some years with a variety of alloys, whose special attribute was extreme hardness, to combat this problem. It currently had a cast sleeve in the final stages of testing which looked very promising. It appeared that it would need replacement only once during the life of a rail rather than three or four times. If this product proved acceptable to the railways, a market of some $20 to $25 million annually was projected by the product manager responsible for casting products.

Welding and Soldering Devices

Because of the special nature of Barney alloys, they could not be welded or soldered with ordinary equipment. Barney, therefore, produced a line of welding equipment and soldering guns, as well as special welding and soldering rods for use with its product line. These devices accounted for less than 3 percent of Barney sales.

Manufacturing

Manufacturing at Barney took place in two distinct phases:

1.   A smelting and treatment plant, where metals and alloys were melted, mixed, and treated in batch quantities, depending upon the use to which the metal was to be put.

2.   Product lines for wire, bearings, cable, tubing, etc., where the products in question were manufactured from the alloys produced in the smelting and treatment plant.

Conflicts between product groups could, therefore, take place at both of these phases of the manufacturing process. About 80 to 85 percent of the time, the conflict occurred in the smelting and treatment plant. Two or more product managers might, for example, ask the plant, at the same time, to produce alloy on an urgent basis for orders which they had obtained and for which manufacture had not been planned.

The remaining 15 to 20 percent of conflicts occurred on the product lines, where, for example, two urgent orders for cable might arrive at the same time, and some means of setting priorities had to be arrived at.

Marketing

Barney attributed much of its success to its desire and ability to respond quickly and effectively to the needs of the marketplace. If a customer wanted an item at a given time, which manufacturing could not fit into the production schedule, then manufacturing would be asked to work overtime to complete the order. Likewise, if a product manager wanted R&D to design a new application for a customer with a significant potential, then R&D would set aside less pressing projects in order to satisfy the customer's requirements.

Markets and Customers

Barney's sales were concentrated in a relatively small number of accounts and industries. In 1967, the three largest customers accounted for approximately 21 percent of sales, and the 10 largest customers accounted for 41 percent. The industry breakdown for 1967 sales was approximately as follows: aircraft (principally military), 29 percent; missiles and space, 14 percent; electronics, telecommunications, and computers, 26 percent; automobiles, 18 percent; other, 15 percent. The profitability of sales to all the industries was roughly comparable.

Sales for U.S. government end use (estimated at approximately 48 percent of sales during fiscal 1967 including approximately 3 percent direct sales to the U.S. government) were dependent upon continuance of appropriations and requirements for national defense and aerospace programs and were subject to renegotiation. Most of Barney's sales for governmental end use were to customers operating under government prime contracts and subcontracts which contained standard provisions for termination or curtailment at the convenience of the government. Sales for commercial use had expanded to approximately 60 percent in the first six months of fiscal 1968, primarily due to increased commercial aircraft business and to the addition of the ball bearing business plus much higher sales to the automotive market.

Competition

Although Barney's products were sold in highly competitive markets, there were few directly comparable products. Barney competed with many companies and divisions of companies both larger and smaller than Barney, but only a few of these companies supplied competitive products that provided similar technical solutions to the functional problems of customers. Barney competed primarily on the basis of its unique technical capabilities and the advantages thereof—high reliability, labor cost savings, less repair work.

Sales Organization

Barney sales were originally handled primarily through manufacturer's representatives who sold both Barney's entire product line and other related products. These representatives were used to set up a national sales network at a low cost (average 4.5 percent commission). Barney utilized some distributors for casting products and a small direct sales force which handled sales in some eastern states, missionary sales, and contacts with the manufacturer's representatives.

When Barney's rapid expansion made a direct sales force expedient, the manufacturer's representatives were phased out. Barney found it advantageous, however, to retain its distributors for casting sales even though it built up its own direct sales force. The nature of the casting market lent itself to mass distribution because approximately 80 percent was sold in small quantities. Furthermore, only the distributors could effectively provide the necessary local service to this diverse market. Because Barney was able to offer its distributors a high markup (45 to 55 percent), the distributors pushed Barney casting products so that Barney became a major line with most of them. And even though castings became more price competitive, the distributor rather than Barney absorbed the price erosion; yet the line's volume still commanded a great deal of his time and effort. Moreover, the distributor presently had an added incentive to find new applications for Barney products, in that he was in direct competition with Barney; only if the distributor found a new market or application was he allowed to sell it; otherwise, Barney handled the new accounts directly.

As Barney expanded its direct sales force and district offices were opened throughout the United States, the current sales organization took shape (see Exhibit 1).

Exhibit 1

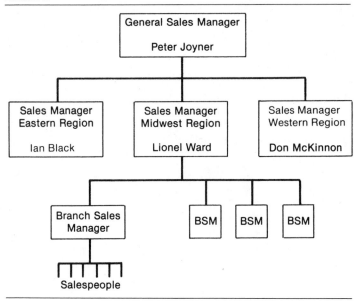

The general sales manager's position was established, in December 1966, to coordinate the activities of the three regional managers who had previously reported directly to vice president Ron McOnie. Peter Joyner, the current field sales manager, defined his job as mostly administrative at the outset; however, in the long run, he expected to spend about half of his time selling and half on administrative detail.

The regional sales managers were responsible for all accounts within their respective regions. They worked with the salesmen and branch managers to set priorities and to sell to major or difficult accounts. According to Joyner, "the regional manager should spend at least 80 percent of his time actually selling."

The Barney sales force in the United States consisted of 58 men, of whom 24 were managers of branch sales offices. The branch managers had anywhere from one to seven salesmen working out of their individual offices. Much of the sales effort was directed toward project selling. Of the 24 branch sales offices in the United States, most were established in response to the needs of specific projects or accounts. For example, an office was set up in St. Louis, Missouri, to gain and service the St. Francis account.

The Barney sales force ranged in age from 23 to 52 and averaged eight years of sales experience. Sales compensation consisted of a salary (ranging from $12,000 to $18,000 per year) plus a bonus based on

each salesman's performance. The basis for evaluating performance
was the quarterly sales forecast, which was a combination of:

1. The forecast made by the salesmen in conjunction with their
    branch and regional managers, based on key accounts, distributor
    sales, and new projects.
2. The forecast made by the product managers based on their work in
    the field and new product developments.

Sales performance was reviewed monthly by the sales managers. Of
the 58 sophisticated and technically trained salesmen in the United
States, three quarters had scientific or engineering backgrounds, and 12
held M.B.A. degrees. They attempted to create the image of being "consultants" to their accounts based on their high technical competence.
Primary emphasis was placed upon working with the engineering and
manufacturing departments of customers and potential customers.

Barney had another 31 salesmen working out of its 11 sales offices in
Europe and Canada. These offices, staffed with engineering personnel,
provided a full range of marketing services and maintained inventories
to meet customer requirements. Foreign sales accounted for about 14
percent of the company total in 1967.

All of the salesmen went through a rigorous three-month training
program which emphasized company philosophy, product knowledge,
and company capabilities. Nearly two thirds of the program was devoted to detailed technical information and applications of the company's products and processes. The other third of the time was spent on
sales training including role playing, information on customers and
markets, and field experience. Upon completion of the training course,
a salesman was assigned to the field either as a multiline salesman
covering a given geographical area or as a specialized salesman selling a
given line of products to specific markets. Although each salesman had
originally handled all products, the demands of the marketplace had
recently made expedient the use of a specialized sales force oriented to
specific products and markets.

Product Management

According to one of Barney's six product managers, "The product
manager has the best job in the company. The whole structure here is
such that things get funnelled to the product manager, and then he
crosses whatever lines he needs to get things done. It's where the
action is." Each of Barney's major product lines was under the direct
control and responsibility of a product manager who coordinated and
directed the entire marketing program for his particular product line.

Barney's product managers ranged in age from 29 to 38. All but one
had both sales experience and a scientific or engineering background;

in addition, all of them held M.B.A. degrees. Their compensation consisted of a salary (ranging from $14,000 to $22,000) plus a bonus (based on management's estimates of each man's relative contribution to profitability and sales growth). The organization of the product management group, under the direction of Terry Westwood, is shown in Exhibit 2.

According to Westwood, "The product manager should operate much as a general manager of his own business with P&L responsibility but without his own sales force or manufacturing facilities." One of the product managers described the role in more detail:

> The product manager is responsible for the profitability and growth of his product line, and a major part of that responsibility should be the long-range planning for that line. He is essentially a coordinating function between sales, manufacturing, and R&D. He is responsible for training and equipping the sales force to sell the existing product line, which boils down to training new men, retraining existing people, promotional material, literature, and sales aids. He's also in charge of advertising—where, what media, how much. He is responsible for guiding R&D in the design of new products to meet whatever requirements he finds. The product manager is also directly involved with field sales problems. Often, he will go to specific areas where there are major problems or major sales efforts or programs and will assist the local guy in whatever way he can.

The product manager also had pricing responsibility. Since Barney had little direct competition because of the unique properties and applications of its products, customers were often willing to pay a premium for Barney products which offered such advantages as high reliability or savings in labor and repair costs. Prices were usually based on value to the customer, rather than cost plus a fixed percentage. As such, most of Barney's products were very profitable.

Although the product manager was responsible for the profitability of his product line, he was technically in a staff position with no direct authority. He had to deal directly with the people in manufacturing, R&D, and sales and "sell" them on his projects and ideas. According to another of the product managers, "The basic philosophy at Barney essentially promotes a nonorganizational type of function. In other words, each guy is pretty much on his own to accomplish what has to be done to fulfill his job function without a lot of mickey mouse organization stuff. If I want R&D to work on something, I talk to the guy who knows the most about what I want done, and I get it done."

Occasionally, however, conflicts would arise between product areas, and these conflicts were becoming increasingly difficult to resolve within the growing company framework. The unique characteristics of each product line presented different requirements and marketing problems for each product manager as the following examples show.

Exhibit 2

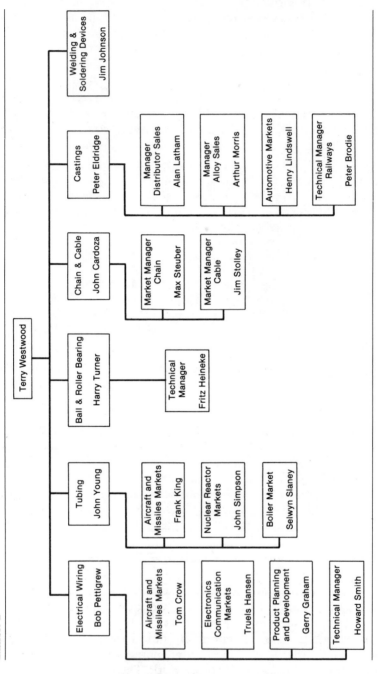

Welding and Soldering Devices.   This product line, under the direction of Jim Johnson, crossed all other product lines except ball bearings because of its essentially supportive nature. Johnson did not look to the marketplace itself to ascertain the need for his type of product as the other product managers did. He had to deal with the needs of the other product managers and field salespeople since his devices provided them with a great deal of leverage to generate sales in other product lines.

Although Johnson theoretically had the same profit and loss responsibility as the other product managers, he did not have the same pricing authority that they did—they could "give away" one of his devices in order to close a sale. Furthermore, his line was characterized by low-volume and high unit cost, and thus, he could not be evaluated on the same basis as the other product managers.

Castings.   This line also differed from the other product lines in several respects. First, most of the casting products were marketed through a series of distributors who took title to the products. Second, castings were subject to more direct competition than the other product lines.

Eldridge had three staff marketing assistants to cover the four major markets for his products, and the fourth of Eldridge's assistants was in charge of distributor sales.

Electrical Wiring.   Bob Pettigrew, who was responsible for the large electrical wiring line, had four men working with him. Howard Smith was primarily involved in the technical aspects of the line including technical problems both in the plant and in the field, writing product specifications, and preparing sales literature. Because of the nature of the product line, electrical wiring experienced far more technical problems than the other lines.

Pettigrew also had one man aiding him with product planning and development. Gerry Graham had recently been transferred to the product management group from his position as midwestern regional sales manager. Pettigrew himself was very involved with the selling function, and he estimated that 75 percent of his time was spent dealing directly with the sales force.

Barney's electrical wiring line had significant competition from the many other producers of coated wire products. Since Barney's products were often quite different, the salesmen sometimes had difficulty getting their products specified by the customers because Barney would then become their sole source of supply.

Tubing.   John Young was responsible for the tubing product line. Since this product line differed from the others somewhat in that a larger portion of his orders were manufactured on a custom basis, he spent a good deal of his time on new product strategy—determining which had the greatest potential, establishing prices, etc. Recently, two men had been hired to work with him on the nuclear reactor and boiler markets.

John Simpson was in charge of tubing for the nuclear reactor market and had responsibility for sales development to contractors and industries where the major potential for high-pressure tubing was. These included the electric utilities companies, shipyards involved in the nuclear submarine program, and companies working on a variety of other projects utilizing nuclear reactors such as desalination. It was anticipated that once all these markets became fully developed, the regular sales force would have to be supplemented with a group of six to seven specialists. The reasons for this expansion were that the potential was expected to be very large and that the construction work would be carried out by a large number of subcontractors, all of whom would have to be familiarized with the special properties of Barney tubing.

Selwyn Slaney was responsible for the development of sales to the boiler and steam generator markets. Included in his list of potential customers were public and private electric utilities and equipment manufacturers. It was Slaney's job, also, to identify other possible major markets for high-pressure tubing and to ensure that such products were developed to add to the present line.

There was some duplication in terms of product responsibility between Simpson and Slaney. Often contractors were quoting on both nuclear and conventional power generators so that two sales engineers might be working with the same contractor at the same time. The characteristics of the tubing used in nuclear and conventional power generators were quite different, but Young wondered whether the present system was the best way to utilize very high cost sales resources.

In addition, this line of tubing shared production facilities with tubing required for use in aircraft and missiles. Occasionally a conflict would arise in manufacturing. For example, Simpson recently ordered a considerable quantity of specialized tubing for extensive testing purposes by one of his potential customers at the same time as Frank King received a large tubing order for an aircraft application. Terry Westwood had to resolve the conflict by authorizing the use of both overtime and subcontracting to complete the two projects in time.

Product Manager's Meeting

The following dialogue concerning Barney's marketing operations took place at a recent meeting of the product management group:

Cardoza: One of the basic defects in our present product management setup is that we're too concerned with day-to-day problems and we're unable to spend as much time as we should looking ahead and planning what direction the product line should be taking. Basically, there's just too much to do, and we've really got to skim the top.

Turner: Yeah! Day-to-day ticky-tack gobbles up a fierce amount of time. It's easy to put off formal, long-range planning and sales forecasting in favor of more pressing immediate needs.

Johnson: True. With so many men in the field now, I sometimes never get the phone off my shoulder all day long. But, after all, the open phone-open door policy is our real strength. We've maintained our growth record by being able to react quickly to the customer's needs rather than by sitting down and figuring out by market research what area we really want to shoot at, then designing a product to meet that need, and then going out and promoting it.

Young: But one of the biggest problems ahead is going to be to keep developing new products and new potentials so that we can sustain that growth rate.

King: John's right. And the product management concept was set up at Barney to create new products and new markets.

Young: Long-range planning may not be the panacea, but I think you'll agree with me, John, that as the field sales organization grows, product management has got to grow to support the activities of the product in the field.

Pettigrew: I have to disagree with you, John. This may be a sacrilegious statement in this group, but I think we're going to have to get away from the product management concept toward that of market management, which I've already done to a certain extent in my line. I have two staff marketing assistants in charge of the big potential wiring markets. I've come to the conclusion that if we intend to turn an almost job shop kind of business into a high-volume operation, we need market development and emphasis.

Simpson: I agree, Bob. After all, I'm basically a market manager myself. I think it's inevitable that we ultimately organize on a market basis because our products and markets are not clearly and exclusively defined. I say that we should be oriented on a market basis—including the sales force. We've got to fit our company capabilities to the needs of an industry.

Johnson: Your product areas may need market specialists but that doesn't hold for me. We all need more time for planning, etc., but what I need is an applications engineer to do some of my legwork. I suspect that more technical support might be valid for electrical wiring, too.

Smith: Well, that's pretty much how Bob and I have things divided now anyway. I'm taking care of most of the technical problems, but we need a larger technical backup staff to keep up with them.

Turner: As I see it, we have a couple of alternatives for evolution. First, if the company organized itself into product divisions—when we're big enough to afford the luxury of it—the product management concept would make some sense because one guy would have real control and responsibility for manufacturing, marketing, sales, and new product development for his line. Then Terry's definition of a product manager as a minigeneral manager with his own business would be realistic. Right now we don't really have that flexibility because we're single-sourced by manufacturing and R&D, and we always have to work within the framework of the whole company.

An alternative to the division manager would be to have market managers, which probably makes more sense from a growth and marketing standpoint. We already have some market specialists under the product managers, but since they sometimes have to cross product lines, we find ourselves in competition with each other, or the wrong guy gets the credit for making things happen, and so on.

King: I can vouch for that. The markets I deal with buy tubing, but I'm sure they could use some electrical wire, too. But there's no incentive for me to spend my time trying to sell them wire if it takes time away from the products where I have authority and profit responsibility.

Turner: Yeah, we keep saying we're marketing oriented, but boy, the whole concept of product management is a very unmarketing oriented way to do things. It's a manufacturing approach. I mean, I will sell bearings to anyone who wants to buy them. But what if my customer needs some castings or cable? I'm not really going to get credit for it on a formal basis unless we install a halfway decent profit-compensation plan which gives credit where it's due.

Hansen: Isn't that what you guys from biz school would label the authority/ responsibility syndrome? It's inevitable that a conflict will come up now and then where there's an authority/responsibility gap, but if you can persuade people, it really isn't that much of a problem.

Cardoza: Right. We're recognized as the guiding group, and our requests are respected by the various functions. It may take a certain amount of salesmanship to sell a point, but if the project's any good . . .

In spite of some problems inherent in the product management system, Terry Westwood felt that it had operated effectively at Barney. He was, however, concerned that additional problems might arise as the company continued its rapid expansion. One of his current concerns was how to allocate R&D time among the various projects recommended by the product managers. The relative importance of each project was not always clearcut since the product managers frequently did not have enough time to devote to market research.

Current crises generally commanded most of the product manager's time, and the results of the time so expended were often more measurable than that spent on long-range plans or new product development. As a result, Westwood felt that the company might unintentionally exclude itself from new markets or applications. Active evaluation and pursuit of new markets and applications were essential if Barney expected to maintain its ambitious growth rate.

Development of Marketing Plans

C A S E 8–1

Thousand Trails

It had been only three months since Jim Jensen, the new CEO, had taken over the reigns from Milt Kuolt, entrepreneur and founder of Thousand Trails, Inc. Since 1972, when the company recorded its first sale, volume had grown to over $40 million by year end 1981. Nineteen eighty-one had been a year of upheaval for the sales and marketing department. In late December, the Seattle-based organization was about to welcome its fourth "new" VP of sales and marketing, Bob Mayes.

The arrival of Jensen in September and Mayes in late December came none too soon. Many of the old sales methods were no longer working, and several new ideas had recently been introduced. It was getting to the point where it was hard for the average employee to keep track of all the programs.

Jensen came to Thousand Trails with a solid background in operations, sales, and marketing. From 1974 to 1979, Jensen served as chief operating officer of Grantree Furniture Rental of Portland. In that six-year period, Grantree's revenues soared from $6 million to $70 million. Prior to Grantree, Jim Jensen worked for Encyclopaedia Britannica where, in a period of 11 years, he advanced from sales training positions to vice president of sales and marketing and chief operating officer for the Great Books division.

History

Thousand Trails had its foundation in a true entrepreneurial effort. In 1969, Milt Kuolt, a business manager for the Boeing Company in

Financial support for this case was provided in part by the Strategic Management Program of the Graduate School of Business, Stanford University. This case was revised by Gary Mezzatesta under the supervision of Robert T. Davis, Professor of Marketing, Stanford Graduate School of Business. © 1982 by the Board of Trustees of the Leland Stanford Junior University.

Seattle, Washington, took his family on a camping trip. What was to have been a pleasant five-day vacation turned out to be a three-day disaster. His wife complained of the unsanitary restrooms and lack of security. Their children, after setting up camp, complained of boredom. Moreover, as a result of trying to make life bearable for his family, Kuolt had no time to relax.

The camping disaster, however, highlighted for Kuolt the need for good, clean, outdoor recreational facilities. In the ensuing year, Kuolt set out to further define what he saw as a void in the outdoor recreational industry. He passed out questionnaires to and talked with recreational vehicle (RV) owners and campers. He found that many of them were also dissatisfied with outdoor recreational facilities. Kuolt determined that an outdoor enthusiast generally camped at several different areas, desired clean and safe camping facilities, and often felt burdened with having to provide activities for the family when they became bored.

In 1970, Kuolt purchased 640 acres in Chehalis, Washington. With its accessible location, less than two hours from either Seattle or Portland, the spot was perfect for the concept. Milt left his job and began to construct roads and campsites in the woods. Kuolt and his three sons spent two years developing their dream. Most of his personal assets, including his wife's jewelry, were risked on the project. Kuolt put in roughly $40,000 of his savings and was able to raise $90,000 from the Canadian Imperial Bank of Commerce by using some real estate as collateral.

By July of 1972, the pioneers were ready to unveil their product to the public. Kuolt sent letters to all those who had answered his marketing questionnaire, offering them a lifetime membership for a $295 contribution fee and dues of $60 a year.

The first memberships were sold in 1972, and Thousand Trails was born. It was a division of the Pacific Rim Group, a land management company started by Koult in 1969. The ensuing two years were devoted to the development of the Chehalis preserve. A 4,000-square-foot clubhouse, a swimming pool, tennis courts, all-purpose sports courts, and campsites with power and water were built. From 1972 to 1974, the number of active memberships grew slowly. In 1974, active memberships numbered 384; sales amounted to $113,000, and 18 people were employed during peak months.

In 1975, Thousand Trails acquired a second preserve near Leavenworth, Washington. The Leavenworth preserve, formerly a private camping club, was perfect for Thousand Trails because it bordered on the Wenatchee National Forest and provided year-round recreational opportunities for members. The acquisition increased Thousand Trails' credibility. It signified to the members and the public Thousand Trails' commitment to multiple locations.

In 1976, two more preserves were added, one near Hood Canal, Washington, and another near Mount Vernon, Washington. Due to legal proceedings, the development of the Hood Canal preserve did not start until 1980.

Rather than acquiring new preserves in 1977, Thousand Trails devoted its capital to the development of its existing properties. During the years 1975 through 1977, the company's sales grew from $113,000 to $7,713,000, memberships rose from 384 to 3,575, and the number of employees during peak seasons increased from 18 to 175.

Thousand Trails experienced phenomenal growth in the years 1977 to 1980. The company acquired 10 preserves (bringing its total to 14), 6 of which were located in California. During these three years, the number of existing memberships rose from 3,575 to 27,620 (see Table 1), sales increased from $7,713,000 to $33,950,000, and the number of

Table 1
Membership History

	1976	1977	1978	1979	1980
Outstanding memberships	1,117	3,575	7,664	12,926	27,620
Average price per membership	$1,900	$2,725	$3,375	$3,825	$4,400
Memberships sold	614	2,826	4,263	5,581	7,704
		Percentage change			
Outstanding memberships	—	220.1%	114.4%	68.7%	59.9%
Average price per membership	—	43.4	23.9	13.3	15.0
Memberships sold	—	360.3	50.2	30.9	38.0

people employed during peak months increased from 175 to 960. (See Exhibit 1.)

By 1981, Milt Koult felt that he had made his greatest contribution to the company and began to look for a replacement. Forty-year-old Jim Jensen was chosen to take over the management of Thousand Trails in September of that year.

The Company

Thousand Trails owned and operated outdoor recreational campground resorts commonly referred to as "preserves." The company's marketing staff, operating at these preserves, sold family memberships which entitled purchasers to use any existing or future locations for visits extending up to two weeks at a time. In contrast to most parks which were part of the National Park System or operated or franchised by Kampgrounds of America, the Thousand Trails preserve was de-

Exhibit 1

THOUSAND TRAILS
Financial Statement
Year Ended December 31

	1981	1980	1979
Sale of memberships	$40,006,000	$33,950,000	$21,396,000
Costs attributable to membership sales:			
Marketing expenses	19,831,000	15,323,000	8,159,000
Preserve land and improvement costs	5,753,000	4,825,000	2,832,000
General and administrative expenses	7,141,000	5,760,000	3,980,000
Provision for doubtful accounts	1,866,000	824,000	886,000
	34,591,000	26,732,000	15,857,000
Income from membership sales	5,415,000	7,218,000	5,539,000
Preserve operations:			
Membership dues	3,304,000	2,048,000	1,170,000
Trading post and other sales	1,482,000	868,000	389,000
	4,786,000	2,916,000	1,559,000
Less:			
Cost of trading post sales	1,346,000	675,000	148,000
Maintenance and operations expenses	2,470,000	1,858,000	1,045,000
General and administrative expenses	801,000	524,000	498,000
	4,617,000	3,057,000	1,691,000
Income (loss) from preserve operations	169,000	(141,000)	(132,000)
Other income (expense):			
Interest income	4,153,000	2,530,000	1,267,000
Interest expense	(3,213,000)	(1,332,000)	(1,470,000)
Gain on sale of property held for investment		437,000	122,000
Other	(147,000)	24,000	50,000
	793,000	1,659,000	(31,000)
Earnings before taxes	6,377,000	8,736,000	5,376,000
Deferred income taxes	3,050,000	4,200,000	2,586,000
Net earnings	$ 3,327,000	$ 4,536,000	$ 2,790,000
Net earnings per share:			
Primary	$1.06	$1.69	$1.17
Fully diluted	$1.02	$1.42	$1.17

Source: Company annual report.

signed to serve as a destination campground. That is, members would typically spend two or more consecutive nights at the site, most often on weekends and during vacations.

In consideration of this, as well as of the fact that memberships were sold primarily to middle-income families with children and to retired individuals, each preserve employed a staff of recreational supervisors who organized activities such as swimming and tennis lessons, dances, parties, tournaments of various types, and a large assortment of games. Amenities included swimming pools, indoor recreational centers, tennis courts, basketball and athletic courts, other outdoor game areas and fields, hiking trails, restrooms and showers, chapels, and other resort facilities. A year-round trained recreation, maintenance, and security staff was employed at each preserve.

Product

The appeal of a Thousand Trails membership consisted of several key elements. These included:

Effective use of an existing recreational investment. Most Thousand Trails members had already made a major investment in their choice of outdoor recreation. Eighty-nine percent of the members were committed to utilizing their recreational vehicles. The Thousand Trails concept was designed to effectively meet that desire. By providing security, cleanliness and maintenance, supervised recreation, quality amenities, and aesthetically pleasing locations, TT attempted to meet the expressed needs of the RV owner.

Cost of alternatives. Vacation homes, cabins on the lake, vacation travel, etc., had become increasingly expensive. Most consumers were not in a position financially to afford such a purchase. While a Thousand Trails preserve did not offer the same degree of privacy as an individual second home, by placing four to five campsites per acre and leaving 30 to 40 percent of each property in an undeveloped state, a certain ability to "get away from it all" was offered to the members. In addition, because of the availability of multiple locations offered by a Thousand Trails membership, the members could "pick and choose" between a mountain, desert, ocean, or lakefront environment.

Deterioration of public/government provided alternatives. Due to continuing budgetary restrictions by state and federal governmental agencies, the alternatives available to the consuming public were diminishing. Most of the facilities offered by these agencies had a lower quality of amenities, minimal security, and a lack of maintenance. Additionally, budgetary cuts had resulted in the closure of many campgrounds across the country, further increasing occupancy pressure on a system already overcrowded with campers.

Security. Perhaps the most desirable feature of a Thousand Trails membership was that of security. Controlled entry to the preserves, combined with 24-hour uniformed security personnel, provided the member with a high degree of assurance that their personal possessions would not be subject to theft or vandalism. Coincidental with funding reductions of state and national park systems had been a decrease in security provided by those organizations. Accordingly, the benefits provided a member in this area became even more apparent.

Supervised recreation. The "fun" aspect of a membership in Thousand Trails was also an extremely important component of the product. Movies, dances, athletic events, instruction in sports activities, hayrides, etc., were all key elements to a happy member. Most members stated that the social experience was what they enjoyed most about Thousand Trails.

By the end of 1981, Thousand Trails was operating 15 preserves with an agreement in principle to acquire five more units. These ranged in size from 11 to 754 acres, with the average running 175 acres. A map showing the locations of these preserves is included as Exhibit 2. From its roots in Washington state, the company began its expansion south into Oregon in 1978 and California in 1979. A preserve in British Columbia opened in 1978. In selecting its preserve sites, TT considered a variety of criteria, including:

Proximity to a market area—Preserves should be located within approximately 60 miles of a population center of at least 500,000.

Proximity to a natural amenity—Preserves should be located on or close to a lake, river, ocean, or national forest.

Popularity of a general area for outdoor recreational use.

Topography—Preserves should have ample tree cover and terrain suitable to the company's typical recreational facilities. (See Exhibit 3.)

Availability of domestic water supply and suitable soil conditions.

Accessibility from primary roads—Preserves should be located in close proximity to a major highway.

Suitability of any existing improvements for the company's operations.

Exhibit 4 summarizes the acquisitions through 1981.

Membership

A membership in Thousand Trails was similar to memberships in golf and country clubs or tennis clubs. The membership provided an unlimited right to use the company's facilities subject only to published company rules and guidelines. The membership was nonproprietary, and the company reserves the right to remove any property from the system subject to a "best effort" replacement in a similar geographic area.

Exhibit 2
Preserve Locations

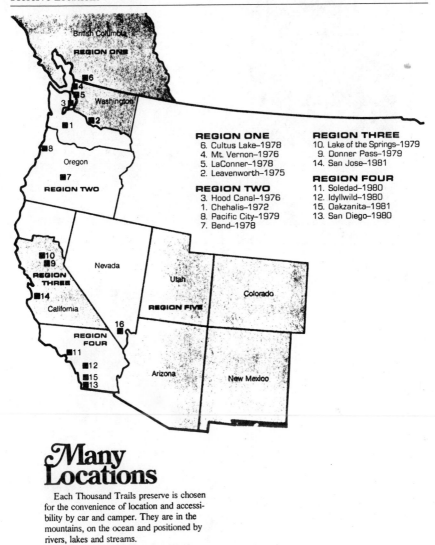

REGION ONE
6. Cultus Lake–1978
4. Mt. Vernon–1976
5. LaConner–1978
2. Leavenworth–1975

REGION TWO
3. Hood Canal–1976
1. Chehalis–1972
8. Pacific City–1979
7. Bend–1978

REGION THREE
10. Lake of the Springs–1979
9. Donner Pass–1979
14. San Jose–1981

REGION FOUR
11. Soledad–1980
12. Idyllwild–1980
15. Oakzanita–1981
13. San Diego–1980

Many Locations

Each Thousand Trails preserve is chosen for the convenience of location and accessibility by car and camper. They are in the mountains, on the ocean and positioned by rivers, lakes and streams.

Prior to October 1980, company memberships permitted unlimited usage of all preserves regardless of location. After that time, the company offered two types of memberships: an unlimited membership entitling the member and his family to use all existing and future preserves operated by the company and regional membership which restricted usage to existing and future propeties located within one of four geographic regions. Unlimited memberships were sold at $5,795

Exhibit 3

Staff member preparing Sunday brunch

Typical preserve campsite

Exhibit 4
Preserve System

Location	Year acquired	Acreage	Total planned	Existing campsites	Approved campsites	Cost of existing property and investments (in thousands)	Estimated cost of planned improvements (in thousands)
Chehalis, Wash.	1973	218	600	425	600	$2,318	$ 775
Leavenworth, Wash.	1975	135	400	275	275	1,666	536
Hood Canal, Wash.	1976	199	252	80	252	1,487	1,428
Mt. Vernon, Wash.	1976	260	500	275	275	2,869	1,054
La Conner, Wash.	1978	108	500	288	500	3,042	869
Cultus Lake, B.C.	1978	84	530	400	530	1,546	562
Bend, Oreg.	1978	156	520	330	530	2,438	839
Pacific City, Oreg.	1978	108	651	251	251	1,971	2,607
Donner Pass, Calif.	1979	238	406	310	310	3,879	680
Lake of the Springs, Calif.	1979	754	960	387	560	4,446	2,746
Soledad, Calif.	1980	230	1,100	—	1,100	3,662	6,228
Idyllwild, Calif.	1980	120	360	105	286	2,446	1,185
San Diego, Calif.	1980	88	600	234	234	2,152	1,899
San Jose, Calif.	1980	62	320	140	170	3,631	1,847
Oakzanita, Calif.	1981	75	350	100	142	1,220	2,370

and regional membership at $4,795. A regional member could convert to an unlimited membership within one year by paying an additional $1,500. Since October 1980, approximately 90 percent of all new members had purchased unlimited memberships. Although memberships were sold on the basis of the existing preserve network, families could use facilities developed in the future subject only to the restrictions of their particular type of membership.

Members, regardless of type of membership, could use the preserves on a first-come, first-served basis except when reservations were requested on busy holiday weekends such as Memorial Day, Fourth of July, and Labor Day.

Memberships could not be transferred during the initial two years of ownership except to family members or by operation of law. Otherwise, memberships being sold could be transferred twice and would then expire upon the death of the second transferee. By policy, the company had restricted memberships at each preserve to 10 times the number of constructed campsites, which prevented overcrowding of the preserves and promoted good member relations. Detailed statistical records were maintained to monitor this policy. As a preserve approached capacity, additional campsites were added. All existing properties had planned and regulatorially approved, but undeveloped sites available for future expansion.

The Customer

As mentioned earlier, 89 percent of Thousand Trails members were RV owners. The RV market was segmented as follows:

Motorized motor homes and vans	31%
Truck campers	20
Travel trailers	35
Folding camping trailers	14

RV owners represented roughly 8.3 percent of vehicle-owning families in the United States. Regionally, the western states had the highest preponderance of RVs:

	Percent of RV market	Percent of U.S. population
West	34%	21%
South	29	32
North central	26	28
North east	11	19

Forty-eight percent of all RV owners were from households without children, 20 percent of RV owners had one child, 18 percent had two children, and 14 percent had three or more children.

Age of household head	Percent owning RVs
25	3.1%
25–35	7.4
35–44	11.7
45–54	10.1
55–64	10.1
65	4.9

Family income bracket (1980)	Share of RV market
$15,000	22%
$15,000–25,000	40
$25,000	33

Even with the amazing growth of the past five years, Thousand Trails had yet to saturate the market. With its almost 28,000 members at the end of 1981, Thousand Trails had achieved the highest penetration of RV owners in the state of Washington (5.1 percent). Only 1.3 percent of all California RV owners were members of TT. (Additional data about members are in Exhibit 5.)

Exhibit 5
Member Survey

A. Age of head of household: 52.3   Retired: 36% Yes   64% No

B. Occupation of head of household: *See attached page.

C. Length of time with present employer: 14.3 years.

D. Occupation of spouse: *See attached page.

E. Length of time with present employer: 10.3 years.

F. Number of dependent children: 0.9   Ages: 11.2

G. Do you own your place of residence?   91.9% Yes   8.1% No

H. Length of time at present residence: 11.7 years.

I. Length of paid vacation of head of household (if not retired):   3.7 weeks

J. Family income range for 1980:   (percent in each income bracket)

5.7	under $10,000
12.6	10,000–15,000
12.4	15,000–20,000
18.3	20,000–25,000
17.9	25,000–30,000
12.0	30,000–35,000
6.7	35,000–40,000
5.1	40,000–45,000
2.5	45,000–50,000
6.9	Over 50,000

Exhibit 5 *(concluded)*
1981 Member Survey, Head of Household by Age Bracket

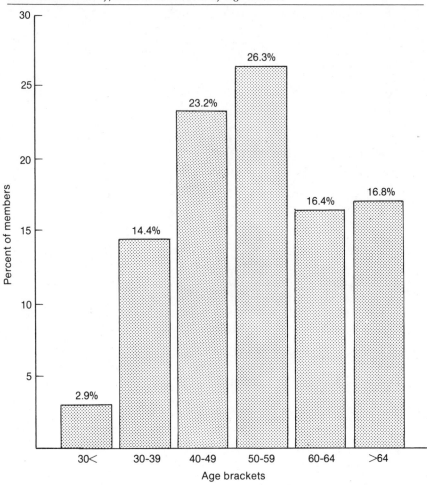

Competition

Management believed that the company was in an excellent position vis-a-vis the competition. Thousand Trails did not compete directly with transient campgrounds such as Kampgrounds of America (KOA), which were generally located on or near major highways and used by recreational vehicle travelers principally on an overnight basis. Rather, the company's preserves were developed and marketed as family "distinction" recreational resorts catering to member families for weekend and vacation use. Numerous private campgrounds existed throughout the western United States which competed directly with TT through marketing nonexclusive memberships usable at multiple destination campground locations. The two largest of these were American Campgrounds, Inc., with 30 locations and 1980 sales of $21 million and the Great Outdoor American Adventure with 11 sites and 1980 sales of $11.1 million. In addition, there were approximately 400 "ma and pa" single-site establishments. Of these, 180 joined a network called Camp Coast to Coast.

In general, it was management's opinion that Thousand Trails was the industry leader by a wide margin. The vast majority of competitive personnel were former TT employees. Almost all of the pricing structures and marketing concepts were directly copied from TT. One marketing manager asserted, "We have not had the time to go out and learn about the competition; quite frankly, I just don't think they are all that important."

Organization

The company was really four different businesses: a financial company that provided funds for expansion and managed the substantial receivables; a resort service company with a large staff dedicated to creating preserve services for members to enjoy; a construction and engineering concern that concentrated on locating and developing new properties in addition to improving existing properties; and a sales and marketing organization that focused on selling memberships to the preserves. See Exhibit 6.

Each of the four subdivisions ran fairly autonomous operations. There was substantial managerial communication at the top level. The CEO played a very pivotal coordinating role in facilitating the efforts of each group.

Marketing and Sales

The company marketed memberships in Thousand Trails through its own sales organization. Because the product that this firm offered was not readily available for evaluation, the marketing effort became very crucial. In fact, back in the early years of the company, Milt Kuolt saw the marketing efforts as the key constraint on growth.

Although marketing and sales were both under one vice president, they were seen as distinctly different functions. (See Exhibit 7.) Marketing attempted to build awareness of the product and entice people to visit the preserves for a tour. A sales force was located at each preserve and guided tours around the local facility, making a sales

Exhibit 6
Table of Organization

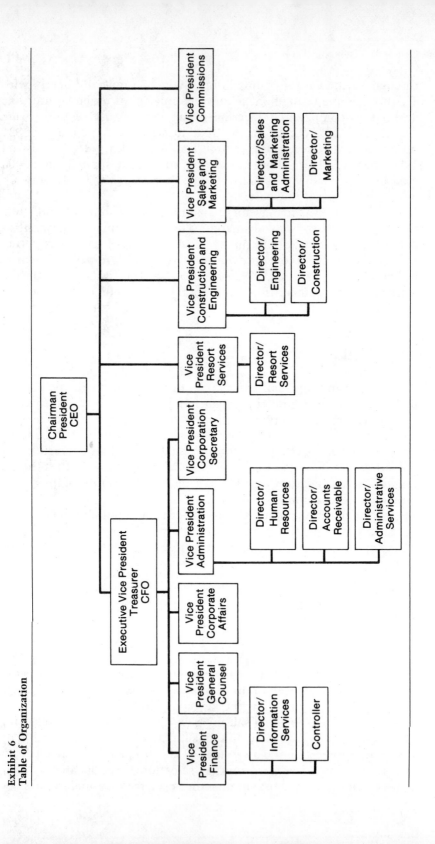

Exhibit 7
Marketing Organization Chart

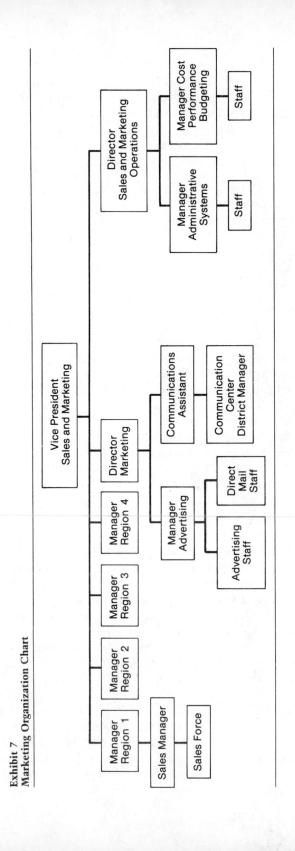

presentation throughout the tour. Since a sale could not be closed
without inspection of the actual site, the marketing effort was concentrated on areas surrounding existing Thousand Trails preserves. The
prime target base was the RV owner.

The marketing effort consisted of a number of programs whose goal
was to attract members to visit a TT site. The primary methods were:

1. Member personal referral program.
2. Direct mail promotion.
3. Professional referral program.
4. Two-step program.
5. Phone sales effort.
6. Attendance at fairs and shows.
7. Advertising.

> *The member personal referral program*—The basic concept be'iind
> the program was the use of the existing membership base to locate
> prospective new sales. Members received compensation for each
> completed tour they generated as well as for each membership
> purchased as a result of referral. In more recent years, Thousand
> Trails changed the compensation formula frequently. Prior to
> April 1981, members received $50 per tour generated and $200 for
> each generated prospect that purchased a membership. Since sales
> were strongest on weekends, they received an extra $50 for sales
> developed between Monday and Friday.
>
> In April 1981, TT changed compensation with the initiation of
> The Friends of Thousand Trails Program. Under this new system,
> member compensation was determined by a very complicated
> award points system. Cash and/or merchandise awards were of-
> fered.
>
> *Direct Mail*—Thousand Trails generated a significant proportion of
> total prospects by mailing information about the company to peo-
> ple with an interest in the outdoors. Large quantities of mail
> (150,000 pieces per week) were sent out to residents in areas con-
> venient to the 15 preserves. Mailing lists utilized included the
> California RV ownership list, the Oregon RV ownership list (the
> Washington RV list was not public information), and West Coast
> subscribers to *Field and Stream, Campers World, Camping Jour-
> nal,* and *Hunting and Fishing Review.* The company used outside
> agencies to design, develop, and mail the items.
>
> The mailers tried to sell Thousand Trails by offering free gifts
> in return for a visit to a preserve. The standard gifts were items
> like Coleman sleeping bags, barbecue grills, and cameras. Mailers
> offered a wide range of information on the actual product. Some
> pieces mentioned the product concept with little elaboration,

whereas others devoted considerable space to a description of the product. Many gimmicks, such as enclosing credit cards or running sweepstakes, were used to get people to open the mail. The average rate (i.e., actual tours generated) was .53 percent. See Exhibit 8 for sample mail pieces. Exhibit 8A is an example of an unsuccessful ad, while 8B presents a more successful one.

The large volume and diversity of mailings made the mail department a sizeable operation. Prior to the end of 1981, very few systems were in place to monitor mailing results. For example, a person who had already purchased a membership or had gone on a tour without purchasing could receive numerous additional mailings. In general, the approach was a shotgun attempt which tended to be biased towards quantity rather than quality. Very little systematic pretesting of mailers were done. (See Exhibit 9.)

Professional referral program—The professional PR program was similar to the member PR program except for the fact that non-members were used to identify and send prospects to the preserve sales office for tours. Pro PR workers were paid $50 for each tour generated. They were chosen and managed by the preserve sales manager. The number of pro PR workers used was at the discretion of the individual manager. Company management was known to change its mind frequently with regard to the value of the program and the level of support lent to it.

Two-step program—In 1981, management decided that a major disincentive for prospective customers was the distance to a Thousand Trails preserve. To deal with this issue, the company initiated a series of presentations on the Thousand Trails concept in large population centers. These presentations generally occurred on a monthly basis. Attendees were offered free dinner and cocktails at a local hotel plus a small gift. The main sources of recruiting people for these meetings were "cold" phone calls and the membership base who were encouraged to attend with some friends.

These presentations were run by the sales manager of the local preserve. No attempt was made to close a sale. Instead, these meetings were seen as a prescreening. Interested attendees were encouraged to set up a visit to the local preserve at their earliest convenience (the second step).

Phone sales effort—Thousand Trails had over 10 communications centers in the western states. Each center had six phones and a supervisor. Most calls were cold calls made between 3 and 9 P.M. The calls followed a standard format (see Exhibit 10) and attempted to solicit either tours at the local preserve or attendance at a two-step presentation. Gifts were offered as enticement.

Exhibit 8A
Direct Mail Ads

THIS IS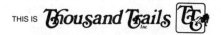

Dear friend:

We _really_ want you to see Thousand Trails, so we're offering you your choice
of _3 valuable free gifts_ and _take a free tour_ of the finest outdoor recreation preserves in the west. It's our way of saying "thank you" for driving
out to hear our story and see our preserve.

When you leave for home, take with you any one of these _valuable free gifts_!

      * _ELECTRIC CHAR-B-QUE_. A real energy-saver that ends
          forever the charcoal mess.
      * _REMINGTON CHAIN SAW_. Here's a trusted name and a
          handy tool to have around -- at home or in your RV.
      * _2 COLEMAN SLEEPING BAGS_. A name synonymous with
          outdoor recreation for years.

Thousand Trails is _more than a dozen private preserves_ from Southern California
to Canada -- yours whenever you plan your family's outdoor recreation.

Imagine these _exclusive resort-preserves_ complete with clubhouses, swimming pools,
clean and fully equipped campsites with recreational areas for young and old alike.
PLUS acres and acres of NATURAL WILDERNESS where you can _walk and talk with your
kids_ and share the great outdoors -- maybe just like it was when you were younger.

THOUSAND TRAILS: _A WAY OF LIFE_. _AN ATTITUDE_.

Honestly, one of the biggest decisions a member-family has to make is _which
preserve to visit_!

The _friendly_, _comfortable_ and _safe_ environment of each Thousand Trails campground poses the dilemma to _rekindling last visit's relationships_ or to head
out for a _brand-new experience_. In any case, you'll be assured that your
Thousand Trails neighbors will be the kind of people that you'd choose for _your
own friends_, and _those of your family_.

Thousand Trails _has it all_ in outdoor recreation and entertainment -- we're the
original and _the standard_ for the industry to match. We're still way out front
and intend to stay that way!

Come visit Thousand Trails. You deserve it.

Stu Harelik
Stu Harelik
for Thousand Trails

    P.S. Your _gift_ is waiting. _Plan now_ to drive out and see us. You'll like what
          you see and hear!

© 1981 TT Printed in the USA

Exhibit 8B
Direct Mail Ads

$250,000

...Like a dream come true!

CONGRATULATIONS   THE SAVAGE FAMILY HAS DEFINITELY
WON AT LEAST TWO PRIZES IN THE THOUSAND TRAILS $250,000 LUXURY
SWEEPSTAKES. AS A SWEEPSTAKES WINNER, YOU MAY HAVE WON $250,000
IN CASH. AT LEAST TWO OF THE FOLLOWING LUXURY GIFTS, WITH A
COMBINED MINIMUM SUGGESTED RETAIL VALUE OF $174.95, WILL
DEFINITELY BE YOURS:

SUGGESTED RETAIL VALUE

1.	$250,000 CASH	$250,000.00*
2.	1982 CADILLAC COUPE DEVILLE	$ 16,009.50
3.	RANCH MINK COAT	$ 6,110.00
4.	TRIP FOR 2 TO LONDON, PARIS & ROME -- 7 NIGHTS, 8 DAYS, AIRFARE & ACCOMMODATIONS	$ 4,050.00
5.	MAGNAVOX COLOR 25" TV WITH VIDEO CASSETTE RECORDER	$ 1,814.25
6.	$500 CASH	$ 500.00
7.	DELUXE GAS-FIRED, FAMILY-SIZED BARBEQUE	$ 119.95
8.	$100 CASH	$ 100.00
9.	AM/FM MULTIPLEX STEREO WITH HEADSET	$ 99.95
10.	$75 CASH	$ 75.00

THERE'S NO OBLIGATION TO PURCHASE ANYTHING. TO RECEIVE YOUR
PRIZES, SIMPLY PRESENT THIS MAILER AT THE THOUSAND TRAILS
INFORMATION OFFICE. YOUR PRIZE CLAIM NUMBERS WILL BE MATCHED
TO THE NOTARIZED MASTER PRIZE LIST POSTED IN THE OFFICE IN
ORDER TO DETERMINE WHICH SPECIFIC PRIZES ARE YOURS.

IMPORTANT...YOU MUST CLAIM YOUR PRIZES BY NOVEMBER 14, 1982, OR
YOUR SELECTION AS A WINNER IN THE $250,000 LUXURY SWEEPSTAKES
WILL BE VOIDED. THE THOUSAND TRAILS OFFICE IS OPEN FOR PRIZE
CLAIMS FROM 9:00 A.M. TO DUSK, MONDAY THROUGH SUNDAY. SEE THE
BACK OF THIS LETTER FOR MAP AND ELIGIBILITY CONDITIONS.

SINCERELY,

Julie Cooper
JULIE COOPER

P.S. VISIT THOUSAND TRAILS MONDAY THROUGH FRIDAY AND RECEIVE A
MYSTERY GIFT VALUED AT $39.95.

* PRIZE WILL BE PAID AT $12,500 PER YEAR FOR TWENTY YEARS.

The number of centers and the organizational structure varied substantially over the years. In 1981, the number of centers ranged from 7 to 14. Centers were known to open and close within three months.

Attendance at fairs and shows—Thousand Trails participated in roughly 30 West Coast outdoor recreational fairs and shows. These activities were conducted by the regional sales manager. The booths were set up and moved by a special fairs and shows staff. Company representatives informed people about the Thousand Trails concept and tried to convince them to take a sales

Exhibit 9
Direct Mail Results 1981 Year End*

	Total pieces mailed	Number of tours resulted	Percentage return	Actual sales	Sales closing percentage
Chehalis.........	237,979	870	.356%	61	7.00%
Leavenworth......	19,401	176	.907	11	6.25
Hood Canal	11,449	91	.795	9	9.89
Mt. Vernon	35,009	119	.339	9	7.56
La Conner........	197,003	790	.401	79	10.0
Bend............	376,143	1,786	.475	102	5.7
Pacific City.......	695,775	3,220	.463	204	6.3
Donner Pass......	333,669	1,705	.511	96	5.6
LOTS............	615,384	1,969	.32	251	12.7
Soledad	940,773	5,118	.544	594	11.6
Idyllwild	682,085	3,197	.469	342	10.7
San Diego........	830,658	5,331	.642	708	13.3
San Jose.........	851,669	6,187	.726	723	11.7
Oakzanita........	31,834	199	.625	10	5.0
Santa Ana........	22,598	270	1.19	10	3.7
Total as of December......	5,881,429	31,028	.528%	3,209	10.30%

* This includes mailings made between January 1 and December 4, 1981.

Exhibit 10
Two-Step Phone Presentation

Taken directly from company literature

Hello Mr. or Mrs. _____ this is _____ calling for "Thousand Trails," and the purpose of my call this evening is to invite you and your _____ to see a film presentation of our Thousand Trails camping areas. We have 12 different locations from Canada to California, and we have a lot to offer in the way of camping and family recreation. And just for taking your time to see our film we'd like to give you a 3 lb. sleeping bag.

"How does that sound?"

We will send you a reservation in the mail with complete directions. Also, we'll be giving you a call back just to see if everything is OK.

Name _____ Mr. and Mrs.
Age _____
Correct addresses _____
Camping equipment _____
Employment _____ Works where _____

tour. The shows were also used to generate additional leads for future mailings.

Advertisings—The advertising program consisted of placing ads in media that reached areas close to the various preserves. Placement decisions were made by the director of marketing, who received input from the regional sales managers, who in turn received requests from preserve sales managers.

Sales

As mentioned earlier, the sales force sold memberships at the preserve sites. Each preserve sales force had a manager, and depending on the size of the preserve, the manager might also have an associate. Most of the sales manager's time was spent recruiting and training staffs, developing the "team," achieving monthly and annual sales projections, scheduling the sales crew, handling sales premiums, coordinating member PR and pro PR programs, coordinating two-step programs, and interfacing with the preserve operations manager to ensure the quality of the TT product. The 15 sales managers reported to 4 region managers, and these managers reported to the director of sales and marketing.

In 1981, the average number of salespeople was 145. The total ranged between 112 and 220. Total hires for the year numbered 440. The top-paid salesperson earned $78,500, while the average salary was a little over $40,000 on an annualized basis. The company experienced large turnovers in the sales force, especially in the Pacific Northwest. Salespeople in Washington and Oregon eyed the greater opportunity in the newer preserves in California. Many of the salespeople from the North quit and applied for jobs when a new preserve opened.

Selling Methods

When selling a membership, Thousand Trails salespeople followed a prescribed sales presentation which included the following 10 steps:

The greeting. A friendly greeting was given to a prospect and the prospect's family by a salesperson, welcoming them to the preserve.

Registration. The greeter introduced the prospect to the receptionist who took down pertinent information such as the address and phone number, the marketing effort which influenced the prospect to visit Thousand Trails, and the gifts he or she was to receive. The receptionist then assigned the prospect to a salesperson for a sales presentation. If the prospect was generated by the efforts of a specific salesman, the prospect was assigned to that salesman for the presentation.

Introduction to the salesperson. The receptionist introduced the prospect and the prospect's family to the assigned salesperson who then gave them the appropriate gift. Then they went to a private room where the salesperson became further acquainted with the prospect. After preliminary introductions, the prospect was asked to fill out a consumer survey. The consumer survey provided answers about outdoor recreational preferences and interest which alerted the salesman or saleswoman as to what Thousand Trails should emphasize during the presentation. The survey also provided the company with information concerning consumer attitudes and demand.

The fact sheet. After the prospect completed the "consumer survey," the salesperson used a "fact sheet" to acquaint the prospect with and establish the credibility of the company. Although some salespeople presented the "fact sheet" differently, many used the format suggested in the sales manual.

Alternatives to Thousand Trails. Once the prospect was given an introduction to the company and the product, the salesperson illustrated the value of a Thousand Trails membership by presenting and comparing the alternatives—camping at state and national parks (which tended to be overcrowded, dirty, and unsafe), purchasing a private campsite (which, in 1980, on the average cost over $10,000), and buying a membership to a camping club (most of which provided only one camping location).

Description of Thousand Trails preserves and regional memberships. After comparing the alternatives, the salesperson showed the prospect pictures and maps of the company's 14 preserves, described the attributes of each preserve, and then explained details of the company's regional membership. At this point, mention was made of a special membership offer available for those who took advantage of their initial purchase opportunity. The special offer referred to was the chance to buy an unlimited membership. No details concerning the "special offer" were given at this time.

The video presentation. Following the description of the preserves and the regional membership, the prospect and the prospect's family were shown a 15-minute videotape which highlighted the many merits of the Thousand Trails concept.

The tour. Immediately following the videotape, the prospect and the prospect's family were given an automobile tour of the grounds. The salesperson stopped and got out of the car with the prospect and the prospect's family to view various points of interest.

The map presentation. While heading back to the sales office, mention was made of additional maps of each campground which the prospect should see. While the maps were being displayed, all the benefits of membership were reviewed.

The close. Finally, it was up to the salesperson to complete the sale. As an added incentive to the prospect to purchase a membership, he/she extended the "one time special offer" mentioned earlier in the presentation. The offer was the opportunity to purchase an unlimited membership if the prospect acted immediately. Salespeople often used the crew manager, the associate manager, or the preserve sales manager to help close a sale.

Immediately after a membership was sold to a prospect, the new member was told about the details and monetary benefits of the PR program and given a schedule of preserve events. Then a picture of the new member and his family was taken and placed on display with pictures of other families who had purchased a membership at that preserve. They were now part of what the company referred to as the "Thousand Trails family." They were welcomed to the "Thousand Trails family" by everyone in the sales office. That night, the salesperson called the new member, congratulating and again welcoming him/ her to Thousand Trails and asking if there were any questions. The following day a thank-you letter was mailed to the new member. All post-sales efforts were a means of allaying buyers' possible doubts and ensuring the satisfaction of new members with their purchases. Member satisfaction was not only essential to the image of the company and the effectiveness of the PR program, but was important to company personnel because they took pride in their product.

Compensation

In 1981, the company varied its compensation plan at least three times. This caused uneasiness at the sales force level since a salesperson often did not understand how gross pay was decided. Throughout the year, this issue caused the development of a hostile attitude toward the home office in Seattle. Home office personnel were referred to as "corporate pukes" in the field.

Their typical sales manager's compensation package included these features: a base pay, a standard per sale ($25) rate, plus a bonus based on a monthly closing rate and percent of target reached. Exhibit 11 presents a version of the compensation program.

The salesperson compensation plan included: a base pay of $200 per week, commission rate per sale based on the type of membership sold and the cash down payment and length of payment term (see Exhibits 11 and 12), volume commission incentive which paid an additional set fee for each sale over a certain number of sales, and a monthly bonus stock plan.

Exhibit 11
Sales Managers Compensation, United States, February 1 to April 30, 1981

Effective February 1, 1981
1. Expense allowance = $2,600 per month—($1,300 paid twice monthly)
2. Base compensation = $25 per sale—override paid weekly
3. Performance compensation
    (To qualify for the performance compensation, the preserve unit sales for the month have to be 100 percent of the monthly quota).
    a. Closing sales percentage

Direct		**Two-step**	
16%–	$30 per sale	28%–	$30 per sale
17–	35 per sale	30–	35 per sale
18–	45 per sale	32–	45 per sale
19–	55 per sale	34–	55 per sale
20 and over	75.00 per sale	36 and over	75.00 per sale

    b. 100 percent of volume target—$60 per sale—paid monthly (on all sales over monthly targets).
    c. Quarterly closing percent bonus—a stock bonus plan to be used on quarterly closing rates is currently being finalized.

Exhibit 12
Compensation Schedule (On-Site), United States, Effective June 13, 1981

	Length of Contract				
Down payment	24 months	36 months	48 months	60 months	72 months
Cash day of sale	Unlimited regional membership–$5,795 650				
$1,995	525	500	475	425	375
1,595	500	475	450	400	350
1,295	475	450	425	375	325
1,095	455	430	405	355	305
995	425	400	375	325	275
795	375	350	325	275	225
All	Regional membership with option–$4,795 200				

Preparing for 1982

The new management team had many issues to deal with as it entered 1982. The fourth quarter of 81 was the firm's first losing quarter in years. Net earnings for the year 1981 were below the 1980 level, although sales were higher. The stock price had fallen from a peak of near 14 in 1980 to the current 5 to 7 range.

Clearly, many of the major problems could be found in sales and marketing. (See Exhibit 13.) Marketing costs as a percentage of membership sales had risen:

Table 2
Marketing Costs as a Percentage of Sales

1976	1977	1978	1979	1980	1981
51.9%	46.9%	41.5%	38.1%	45.1%	49.6%

From top down, the entire marketing and sales department had been in a state of upheaval throughout 1981. Four different individuals occupied the position of VP of sales and marketing; compensation programs changed every few months until it got to the point where staff members could barely understand their checks; rapport between the home office and the field personnel increasingly weakened; and many new programs had been initiated.

Two major mistakes epitomized the misguided strategy out of Seattle:

The April mailing—in early 1981, management decided to get away from the junk mail "gimmicky" image of its mail program. An elaborate product mailing that focused on the beauty and quality of the preserves was developed in house instead of by one of the regular agencies. Over 1 million pieces were printed. After mailing out 400,000 units it became apparent that the response was not as high as anticipated—the return rate was only .3 percent. The estimated cost of this blunder was $750,000.

The Friends of the Thousand Trails program—around mid-1981, the VP of sales and marketing decided that the cash incentive for the member PR program was losing its effectiveness. He introduced an extremely complicated program which assigned bonus points to members for their referral assistance. These points translated into cash or merchandise from an extremely elaborate hardbound color catalogue. Implementing the new format cost $1.75 million and did not substantially increase member PR efforts.

As Bob Mayes accepted his position of sales and marketing vice president in late December 1981, he was excited about the firm's tre-

Exhibit 13
Marketing Statistics

	1978			1979			1980			1981		
	Tours	Sales	Cost per sale	Tours	Sales	Cost per sale	Tours	Sales	Cost per sale	Tours	Sales	Cost per sale
Member PR	14,502	1,828		13,692	2,531		12,195	2,399	457	10,308	2,493	765
Pro PR	—	—		—	—		4,883	670	606	1,773	250	766
Advertising	—	—		216	21		1,607	175	1,258	548	46	1,331
Fairs and shows/phone	3,582	974		8,560	1,137		6,841	875	1,723	9,840	1,271	1,419
Direct mail	1,593	302		5,683	822		17,371	1,999	600	30,721	3,221	783
Self-generated	2,511	346		1,411	282		1,644	440	n.a.	1,609	364	159
Other	3,924	831		2,220	394		5,189	767	n.a.	621	87	58
Total	26,112	4,281	n.a.	31,782	5,187	n.a.	49,730	7,325	627	55,420	7,732	847

mendous potential but a bit confused about where to focus his attention. Fortunately, the firm had recently installed a sophisticated MIS system which provided good up-to-date information of sales activities. After spending some time selling in the field, he drew the following conclusion: "The product is a definite 10, but our sales effort is a 2 or a 3. We really need to get things in shape quickly or the company will lose the momentum it has built up over the years."

C A S E 8–2

![header bar]

The Needlework
Company (C)

The Needlework Company's sales and profits had increased dramatically over the past several years. The company sold not only a proprietary line of instructional skill leaflets (e.g., knit/crochet and surface stitchery) and kits but a line of approximately 5,000 jobbed items. Sales were made both to leading chain store organizations (e.g., K mart and Wal-Mart) and to over 14,000 independent specialty stores referred to as the regular trade. The latter were serviced by a sales territory.[1] As a preliminary to developing the company's strategic plan for the period 1982–86 and the annual business (action) plan which would follow, the company president asked each department manager to prepare a report outlining the opportunities and problems facing the company. It was within this framework that Mr. Robert Fisher, vice president of marketing, began his assignment.

One of the primary areas of concern to Mr. Fisher was the mix between the sales of proprietary and jobbed items. Since proprietary items had substantially higher margins (71 percent versus 28 percent in 1981), it was critical that their sales be emphasized. In recent years, they had dropped below 50 percent of total sales, although they had improved slightly during the last year (from 48 percent in 1980 to 48 percent in 1981). One reason for the declining relative importance of proprietary items was that the company had added a substantial number of jobbed items. It had done so at the outset primarily as a convenience to the regular trade. The response was so enthusiastic that the

This case was written by Harper Boyd, Professor of Business Administration, University of Arkansas. Included in *Stanford Business Cases 1983* with permission. © 1983 by the Board of Trustees of the Leland Stanford Junior University.

[1] For information pertaining to sales and profits as well as the market place and the industry (including competition), see The Needlework Company (A).

company rapidly expanded its line of jobbed items. The company still, however, considered itself as being essentially a leaflet publisher.

Mr. Fisher was not certain that the margins of proprietary versus jobbed items was an adequate reflection of the profitability of these two types of business. More specifically, he thought that when the cost of buying, receiving, selling, order processing and fulfillment, and collections with reference to the approximately 5,000 jobbed items (stock-keeping units) were taken into account, the company's jobbing business might, at best, show a small profit. Since it was not likely that the company would divest itself of this business, the problem was one of how best to improve its profitability.

Another problem with jobbed items was that competition came primarily from local jobbers. These middlemen carried many of the same brands as did the Needlework Company. This was particularly true in three major categories—floss, fabric, and needles—where one brand in each was dominant. Local jobbers provided overnight delivery (versus 7 to 10 days on average for the Needlework Company) and, in some cases, lower prices. Further, local jobbers provided free transportation while the company's terms were FOB warehouse except for West Coast shipments where it paid 50 percent of the freight. The reason why the company's jobbing business had been at all successful was because of its in-depth inventories and prompt order handling. Less than 3 percent of its invoice line items were back ordered. When this happened, the company paid the cost of shipping.

Jobbers were particularly strong in the Northeast, including the large metropolitan areas of Boston, New York, Philadelphia, Washington, and Baltimore. In recent months, many such jobbers had offered discounts on the leading floss brand (the one also carried by the company) of up to 10 percent for quantity purchase. In some cases, the order was of sufficient size to warrant being drop-shipped by the floss manufacturer. In other cases, a quantity discount would be given on a cumulative basis. Since the floss manufacturer typically gave jobbers a 33 percent margin, these quantity discounts lowered the jobbers' margins to 23 to 25 percent. Company sales of floss had been strongly impacted by such discounting, and Mr. Fisher was fearful that it might spread to other national brands—particularly in needles and fabrics.

Another area of growing company concern was selling costs. The interaction of the regular trade's retail structure (which was dominated by small stores) with those costs relating to commissions paid to the sales reps (at an average of 7 percent), order size, trade mailings, and order mode (phone versus mail) was thought to be substantial. Over the years, the company had paid little attention to this interaction with the result that some costs had perhaps gotten out of hand. This was particularly the case with respect to handling small accounts which tended to generate small orders (see Exhibit 1 for an analysis of

Exhibit 1
Distribution of Orders and Sales by Order Size, First
Quarter 1981

Order size	Percent of total orders	Percent of total sales
Under $10.00	17.85	.92
10–19.99	17.58	2.80
20–29.99	6.15	1.47
30–39.99	6.04	2.05
40–49.99	3.85	1.67
50–74.99	16.02	8.70
75–99.99	5.45	4.58
100–149.99	9.63	11.54
150–249.99	8.03	15.90
250–499.99	6.56	21.73
500–999.99	2.03	15.71
1,000 and over	.81	12.93
Total	100.00	100.00

company sales by order size). Since sales reps did not typically make calls on such accounts, they were serviced largely by phone and mail. Thus, they received by mail at regular intervals—as did all other regular trade accounts—product literature describing all company products along with price information about each. They typically availed themselves of the company's WATS line service in placing their orders.

There was a strong difference of opinion within the company as to what to do about the "small store problem."[2] The president, for example, felt that the small stores should be taken away from the sales reps (who presently received a commission on such sales even though they rarely called on them) and handled directly out of company headquarters. In commenting on this subject, he said, "I'd suggest we hire an assistant sales manager to deal with these accounts. If he or she really showed some imagination in dealing with this problem, I'm sure we'd increase our sales to them." He mentioned that the customer service department, which received and processed all orders (both phone and mail), could be programmed to call these stores at regular intervals to solicit their business. This suggestion was based, in part, on a recent study which showed the department as having about 12 percent "free time" due to being staffed to handle the peak loads (both time of day and day of week) of incoming WATS order calls.

Another executive thought the company should make no effort to solicit business from small accounts on the basis that the company would be more profitable without them. Yet another person suggested

---

[2] Some 40 percent of the regular trade accounts purchased $1,000 and more from the company in a year, 20 percent buy between $500 and $1,000, and the remainder buy less than $500 yearly.

that the company find some way of selling only its proprietary products to such accounts.

Small orders were of increasing concern to the company. A recent study showed that orders of $30 and under represented 41.5 percent of all orders received. Another study showed that the variable costs associated with the receipt, processing, order picking, packaging, and shipping totaled $12.53 per order. One explanation for the volume of small orders was that the regular trade was minimizing its inventory and relying more and more on the company to provide backup inventories. The sales manager thought that as the company added more products to its line, the average order size would increase. While he recognized the costs involved in processing small orders, he felt that the company had generated a lot of goodwill in the market place because of its willingness to accept them without requiring a minimum order size or levying a special handling charge.

The performance of the sales reps was another problem which bothered Mr. Fisher. He was particularly concerned that the reps were not checking store inventories of the company's proprietary products. Because of the length of the jobbed line, he was reasonably certain that they did little to sell such items. He had recently asked the sales manager to study these and related problems and suggest ways of improving the situation. The sales manager's response is shown in Exhibit 2.

Uncertainty about the future demand for surface stitchery products and the fad nature of the company's kit business emphasized the need for some kind of market information system. This need was particularly acute during the time when the company updated its strategic plan and prepared its business plan for the next year. In an effort to obtain market trend data on surface stitchery, locate possible new items for the company to carry, and obtain an appraisal of the company's sales and service activities, a store audit among 50 regular trade stores had been attempted. The results had been most disappointing.

The sample of 50 stores was selected on the basis of size (sales by the company), geographical location, and friendships. Thus, the sample consisted of 50 stores which annually purchased more than $3,000 in company products, were distributed across the United States, and the management of which was known by one or more company executives. The sample was activated by a personal phone call made by the appropriate company executive to each store asking for cooperation and offering $25 for completing a three-page questionnaire. All sample stores agreed to cooperate, and shortly thereafter, the questionnaire and instructions were mailed. Respondents were asked to complete the study within two weeks. Two months after the mailing, only 30 completed questionnaires had been received despite numerous follow-up phone calls. Further, of the 30 received, only 23 were usable.

Exhibit 2
Suggestions from the Sales Manager as to How to Improve the Sales Force Coverage/Home Office Support System

Based on a recent study, over 40 percent of regular trade accounts buy over $1,000 worth of goods from us in a given year. About 20 percent do between $500 and $1,000, and the remainder do less than $500 annually. The sales force concentrates on about the upper 30 percent by calling on them three to four times a year. In addition, some calls are made on new accounts as well as potentially large accounts; i.e., those doing over $500. These calls are made on an "as needed" or convenience basis (sales reps happen to be in same town, etc.). The balance of the company's accounts are handled by:

1. Trade shows.
2. Automatics (sending all new leaflets to stores who request such service).
3. Periodic general mailings.
4. Telephone calls to and from the customer.

For the most part, our sales reps are strong professionals who are well entrenched in their respective territories. They pay their own travel expenses and, thus, will not go where there is neither easy profit nor strong potential. With the encouragement of the company, some of our reps have begun to build organizations to accommodate the growth of the company and to better service their growing customer needs. At this point, one third of our territories have more than one sales or sales/service person in the field. Thus, many of our reps are making a real investment in the future of our business. Since the company is a large part of the total business of our reps, those making such an investment, and those that haven't but intend to, deserve our support.

The support I suggest consists of several steps, each of which will strengthen the total sales and service effort. The first is to assign proven, reliable customer service personnel to specific sales reps. Doing this will accomplish several good things and will lay the groundwork for other moves later. By taking this step, we establish accountability on the part of each and every customer service person. The rep will know with whom he/she is dealing because that person always remains the same. Every day I hear from reps and customers referring to the fact that they spoke to someone in the customer service department but forgot who it was. The individual customer service person will also get familiar with the rep, his or her customers, and their particular problems. They'll have to because they will be their responsibility. A bonus to all this will be the spreading of the call load among customer service personnel. Most reps have a few favorites in the department, and they end up being the same.

Finally, all customer service personnel will not be assigned to individual territories. Several will be available to handle orders and other overflow when the phones are particularly heavy. Understand that this first part of the program is only for the reps and not *their* customers.

The second step is a natural outgrowth of the first. As the sales rep refers his customers to his service rep, they will become familiar with a specific individual. This is when things really begin to get good. All of a sudden we have two people working an account, one who comes through the door and one who is at the other end of a phone. The customer is not calling just a company but rather a known and proven person who will look after the order or handle any problems. This teamwork between outside and inside—working a territory together—will inevitably help the customer, which has to benefit us.

The third step should occur when the rep is convinced that the new relationship between the sales force and customer service is viable. We next need to address the problem of the small account (which may be under $500 or even $250). As the company's sales manager, I need to go over all customer service on a regular basis via our outgoing WATS lines.

In order for us to assume the costs of a call-out program of this nature, we will pay only half commission on these small accounts. If a time comes when an account reaches $500, it will be turned back to the rep on a full commission basis. In this manner, we save our reps the costs associated with travel to small accounts, we help small accounts to grow, and finally, turn over a stronger, more important customer to the rep for further growth.

Mr. Fisher was surprised at the failure of the company's marketing research effort, especially since "we didn't ask them for any confidential information and the questionnaire could be completed in less than an hour. In any event, there is nothing we can do about our need for market information this year. But we're going to have to try again as soon as possible. At this point, I think we should go back to basics and decide what information we want, how often, and how we can best obtain it."

Throughout its history, the company had indicated that its primary concern was the regular trade. The president often stated that sales to chains should not exceed 33 percent of total company sales. At the present time these sales were only about 15 percent of total company sales. But since the company sold only proprietary products to the chains, the percentage of leaflet sales going to chains was considerably higher as a percentage of total leaflet sales than the overall percentage. Since chains were becoming increasingly aggressive in seeking out the better selling leaflets regardless of skill area, there was every reason to believe that the company would become increasingly dependent upon chains. Several years earlier, when the company had started to sell chains, only knit and crochet leaflets had been involved. As chains became more and more successful in the sale of knit and crochet leaflets, sales of these products to the regular trade declined substantially.

That the company had experienced few complaints from the regular trade about its sales to chains was explained by Mr. Fisher by the fact that the regular trade had benefited enormously from the growing demand for surface stitchery leaflets, which to date had not been stocked by the chains. But there was ample evidence that chains would soon start stocking such leaflets. "Even though they sell for about the same price, this will certainly hurt the regular trade," said Mr. Fisher. He went on to say that this time the regular trade might well protest any action taken by the company to sell chains since there was nothing on the horizon to take the place of surface stitchery. Mr. Fisher summarized his concern here by emphasizing that, to the company's knowledge, "there's no new skill waiting in the wings to take over after the popularity of surface stitchery starts to fade. If there is, we certainly don't know about it. Besides, I don't like to be all that dependent on a few large accounts."

The marketing department had three product managers—one each for kits, knit and crochet leaflets, and surface stitchery leaflets. The latter two were responsible not only for the company's proprietary products but for the jobbed leaflets as well. This involved primarily the selection of what leaflets to stock as well as the size of the initial order. The other jobbed items were handled by the purchasing unit which reported to the vice president in charge of finance. Mr. Fisher felt that this meant that such items—particularly tools and accessories—were not being properly managed, especially with respect to the selection of which items to carry, what suppliers to choose, packaging, pricing, and merchandising. The president was opposed to the idea of an additional product manager because of not only the cost but the possible organizational problems that might arise.

C A S E 8–3

Jennings National Bank

In early December 1981, Mr. Earl McWilliams, vice president of marketing at the Jennings National Bank, was going over his recommendations for the marketing of the bank's new individual retirement account (IRA) product. Over the past several months, Mr. McWilliams and several other members of the marketing department had been studying the market potential for IRAs. It was now time to finalize a marketing plan which would be submitted to the bank's executive committee in about two weeks. The main reason for the delay in developing such a plan was the difficulty in obtaining information from a variety of sources about the market potential for IRAs.

The Jennings National Bank was located in a metropolitan area of about 400,000 population. With total deposits of $324 million, it was the third largest bank in the city. The leading bank had total deposits in excess of $600 million, while the number two bank had $373 million. Two large savings and loans with deposits of $600 million and $400 million, plus a number of smaller financial institutions, comprised the remainder of the city's banking industry.

The Economic Recovery Tax Act of 1981 increased tax-deferable IRA contributions from $1,500 or 15 percent of earned income to $2,000 or 100 percent of earned income (whichever was less) for individuals; for spousal IRAs, the increase went from $1,750 to $2,250. IRAs were permitted for individuals already covered by pension plans. The law also increased Keogh plan tax-deferable contributions for the self-employed from $7,500 to $15,000, or 15 percent of earnings (whichever was less). Moreover, the Depository Institutions Deregulation Committee (DIDC) was established under the Depository Institutions Deregulation and Monetary Control Act of 1980 (DIDMCA) to

---

This case was written by Professor Harper Boyd, College of Business Administration, University of Arkansas. Included in Stanford Business Cases 1983 with permission. © 1983 by the Board of Trustees of the Leland Stanford Junior University.

deregulate interest rate ceilings. It thus created a new IRA/Keogh investment instrument with no interest rate ceiling which could carry a fixed or a floating rate provided it had a minimum 18-month term. This new feature of deregulation was an extremely important one since it permitted institutions to pay tax-deferable money market rates for certificates of deposit (CDs) *without* requiring minimum deposits. This made the IRA a more attractive alternative for the typical investor, while significantly increasing competition among financial institutions for retirement dollars.

In the view of Mr. McWilliams, IRAs would be important sources of bank funds and especially so longer term since they encouraged stable savings. While it would be expensive to get deposit money at market interest rates, the trend towards deregulation was such as to suggest that banks and others would have to pay market rates for whatever savings instruments would henceforth be offered. Moreover, the deferred tax advantages and severe penalties for each early withdrawal made IRA monies a source of stable, long-term deposits.

Mr. McWilliams expected the competition for IRAs to be strong from the outset because individuals who opened their accounts in one institution could not switch them to another without substantial penalties. Also, individuals who established an IRA at a given institution were thought likely to establish other accounts at the same institution. Further, there was really no alternative but for a bank to offer an IRA product since not to do so ran the risk of losing existing deposits to competing institutions. He recognized that, in the short run, any IRA accounts would be expensive to obtain because investors could be expected to switch money out of low-interest-paying checking and savings accounts within the same financial institution, not to mention the promotional and administrative expenses involved. Strong competition could be expected from other banks, savings and loans, insurance brokers, and security brokers.

It was difficult to estimate the longer-term market potential for IRA. By December 1981, there were about $18 billion invested in these funds for the total United States, and some estimates for 1982 suggested that another $25 billion might be generated. The size of this potential would likely cause all major financial institutions to push heavily for a large share from the very beginning. In prior years, only savings and loans had shown any real interest in IRAs. There share was 35 percent followed by 18 percent each for life insurance companies and commercial banks, 15 percent for mutual funds, and 13 percent for mutual savings banks.

The initial advantage held by the savings and loans was not expected to endure, although both of the two largest local S&L organizations gave every evidence of competing strongly for IRA funds. The performance of the largest of the two S&Ls had been particularly impressive. Mr. McWilliams thought that while some of its IRA funds had originated from liquidated savings balances, most had come from competitors or the income of regular customers. This also appeared to be the case with the other S&L, although to a lesser extent. The success of both organizations was attributed to in-house retirement expertise and an integration of IRAs with retirement planning in general. Both appeared willing to pay a high price for new IRA deposits.

Major brokerages firms were also expected to move strongly in seeking to attract IRA funds. For example, Merrill Lynch, Pierce, Fenner, & Smith had recently announced the creation of a "mini-trading account" which allowed investors to trade $2,000 on the stock market. Merrill Lynch planned to charge $30 to set up a self-directed IRA account which would allow the customer to invest in stock, stock funds, bonds, bond funds, and money market funds. In addition, regular commissions and an annual fee of $50 would be charged.

Life insurance companies were also thought to represent potential competition, but since most life insurance products were sold by commissioned salespersons, it was thought that the would have some difficulty in attracting new customers. It was recognized, however, that some companies might reduce the large first-year commission fees or try other innovative arrangements in an effort to attract a larger share of the market. Allstate Life Insurance Company (a part of Sears Roebuck & Company) offered standard annuities with guaranteed payouts but flexible minimum payments.

Mr. McWilliams thought that the new 18-month variable rate certificate of deposit had given commercial banks the best opportunity of any of the competing financial institutions to attract IRA money. His reasoning was that since there was no interest rate ceiling and banks had a more profitable short-term asset base than S&Ls—as well as stronger ties to business—they should have an excellent opportunity to obtain IRA payroll deductions.

IRA profitability would depend primarily on the amount of new deposits generated, the rates offered by competing institutions, fees charged, and the timing of deposits. The interest rates offered on IRAs would increasingly be determined by the marketplace. The key problem was to match sources of funds (e.g., IRAs) with the uses of funds (e.g., loans). The difference is the "spread" which, in effect, was a gross margin. Mr. McWilliams targeted the spread for IRAs at 1.5 to 2 percentage points. The overall spread for the bank was nearly 2.

Institutional profitability would be affected strongly by the source of the IRA funds. If, for example, the only new IRA funds obtained by a particular bank came from existing customers who simply switched money without replacement into their IRA accounts from checking accounts, then the opportunity cost of IRAs would be substantial. On the other hand, if new deposits were to come directly from customer income, they would add to the total deposit base and provide a new customer relationship. The cost of the new money would simply be a function of the interest rate offered. It would be still better if the money going into bank A came from bank B because this would increase the former's relative market share. It would likely also result in bank A "selling" this customer other services.

The first three months of 1982 were expected to generate some $8 to $9 billion in IRAs at the national level, of which banks would account for 50 percent. The local scene was apt to be somewhat different, given the unusual strength of the savings and loans. Mr. McWilliams thought banks would do well to take 35 to 40 percent. Further, it was not at all certain that individuals would invest in IRAs to the extent they indicated they would. One reason for some caution in accepting the forecast given above was that consumers appeared to have relatively little knowledge about IRAs. Apparently whether, where, and when to open an IRA account was not a clear cut question for most people.

Studies showed that many people thought they could not invest less than $2,000 per year in an IRA and assumed, therefore, that they could not afford one. The message that the IRA was a retirement account and not simply a tax shelter for the rich had not come across clearly to the average potential customer. People seemed unaware that the deposits would be fully taxable when taken out at retirement. Most banks and S&Ls had sold IRAs like a retailer sells his wares and thus had not been overly concerned with developing the market by providing information which would create more favorable attitudes towards IRAs. Few had tried to think of themselves as retirement specialists.

Market segments for IRAs could be classified in a number of ways. Demographically, one would guess that IRAs would appeal strongly to middle-age persons; white-collar and professional workers; and those with higher incomes, better educational attainment, and more substantial savings balances. Younger, less affluent, and less well-educated individuals were thought, however, to be important potential customers if only because of their numbers. Studies had shown that, in general, the younger the individual the more likely he/she would be to open an account with a bank versus a savings and loan.

Segments could also be thought of in terms of those corporations offering payroll deduction IRAs and simplified employee pension plans and those businesses with no pension plans.[1] Publishing studies had shown that many major corporations were studying how IRAs could be adapted to their organizations. About 30 percent were considering im-

---

[1] Simplified employee pension plans were employer-sponsored IRAs in which the employer made a contribution to the employee's IRA. The employee could, of course, contribute to the full standard IRA limit. It should also be noted that monies derived from terminated pension plans could be rolled over into IRAs without paying taxes.

plementing payroll deductions, while another 30 to 40 percent were thinking about amending their qualified pension plans to allow for these deductible contributions. It is important to note that legally an employer cannot endorse a particular financial institution as being the recipient of IRA depositors from employers.

In the late fall of 1981, the bank's marketing department had made a study to determine total IRA deposits accumulated to date for local banks and S&Ls. These were as follows:

	Bank/savings and loan	Total deposits (in thousands)	Estimated number of IRA accounts	Total (in thousands)
1.	Dixon Commercial	$600,000	Refused	Refused
2.	The First State Bank.	373,000	543	$ 3,425
3.	Jennings National	324,000	500	3,000
4.	Atlantic	298,000	480	2,700
5.	Seaboard Federal S&L.	625,000	3,405	11,200
6.	Main S&L	412,000	2,603	5,400

None of the other banks had aggressively promoted the purchase of IRAs. To Mr. McWilliams' knowledge, about all that had been done was some mailings to trust accounts. Thus, most of the purchases from banks had been largely customer initiated. Savings and loans, on the other hand, had been more forceful and especially so through their payroll deduction plans. Both Main and Seaboard Federal had spent considerable effort to attract payroll deductions for savings and IRAs from the business community during the past few years. While some of the IRA funds undoubtedly originated from liquidated savings balances, it was thought that most had come from outside institutions or from regular income. In its presentation to the business community, Seaboard Federal emphasized their in-house retirement expertise and that any IRA account could avail itself of such expertise which included a full-time retirement specialist who would develop, with the aid of a computer, alternative retirement plans.

It was expected that all of the above six institutions plus a number of smaller ones would compete aggressively for new IRA accounts. In addition, there were several insurance companies, a number of national brokerage firms with local offices (e.g., Merrill Lynch and Dean Witter), and a few large local independent broker firms who could be expected to enter the market although their efforts would be more limited. Banks and S&Ls were expected to spend heavily on TV, direct mail, and radio advertising. All could be expected to offer similar payroll-deduction plans which did not include employer participation.

While some banks in other cities had announced their intentions of using a fee schedule which decreased as deposits increased, Mr.

McWilliams did not feel that such would apply to the local market. In the case of Jennings, there would not even be a minimum deposit requirement. Most local financial institutions were expected to offer both the fixed and floating rate 18-month CD, probably tying the rate to Treasury auction rates. In the past, most of these rates had been above the inflation rate, thereby allowing institutions to point out that people could keep ahead of inflation with an IRA. Jennings planned to emphasize this fact in their advertising. Jennings also planned to tie its minimum rate on the 18-month variable CD to the actual 6-month Treasury bill auction rate. The maximum rate would be set by senior management in an effort to enhance the bank's flexibility and make their IRA more appealing.

Dixon Commercial's IRA offering rate was expected to equal that of Jennings with respect to the minimum rate, but the maximum rate would probably be tied to the 6-month Treasury bill auction *plus* 50 basis points (one half of 1 percent). The two savings and loans were expected to price their IRAs in a similar fashion but with a 75 point "bonus."

The Jennings' IRA plan relied heavily on a strong sales effort starting in January to explain the bank's IRA product to key potential customers. A team of trained salespersons would be recruited from existing bank personnel to contact those bank customers with savings or checking balances of over $5,000 (about 3,500 out of some 17,000). Only about 5 percent of these were thought to already own an IRA. A sales commission of one half of 1 percent would be paid on sales; in addition, each buyer would receive a $10 bonus. It was not planned to try to sell the self-directed IRA which was available through the trust department for a $75 annual fee. Only six such accounts were in existence.

The bank also planned to offer a payroll deduction plan which did not include employer participation. The monies would be deducted directly from the employee's paycheck through a corporate clearinghouse account. The individual employees would, however, have to open an account themselves at a bank of their choice. It was recognized that companies would be reluctant to spare company time to permit a bank presentation. Nevertheless, it was thought that the bank had enough corporate clients who were sufficiently "friendly" to put on at least 100 presentations during the first six months of 1982 with a total of 3,500 in attendance.

The bank's advertising strategy consisted of three phases. The first would attempt to attract large depositors—those with sufficient discretionary income to invest immediately in an IRA account. Phase two would start just before personal income tax time and stress the tax-deductible nature of the IRA. Starting in May 1982, phase three would be launched. It would seek to appeal to a broader base, including those who considered themselves ineligible for an IRA. The advertising copy to be used would stress that IRA deposits were "secure, pay high interest, and do not require a minimum deposit."

Mr. McWilliams had not yet decided how many TV commercials he would use in each phase since he wanted to see what results were obtained on a month-to-month basis. The bank annually spent about $625,000 in radio and TV advertising, with the latter accounting for nearly 75 percent—including production costs. It was planned to divert part of these monies to support the IRA marketing program— perhaps as much as $100,000 to $150,000. Phase one advertising was budgeted to spend $5,000. This would include some 160 30-second TV spots and 600 radio spots during the months of January, February, and March. About 20 percent of the TV commercials would be during prime time (7 to 9 A.M. and 4:30 to 7 P.M.). The bank typically bought special packages from the local TV and radio stations. Production costs were expected to total about $10,000 for this advertising phase. No newspaper or billboard advertising was planned.

In addition to the above, a direct mail campaign was planned (occupant-addressed, 3rd class) which would cover most of the city and proximate suburbs. This would be undertaken during phase three and was expected to cost about $30,000. During the first three months of 1982, well-designed, four-color inserts promoting IRAs would be placed in all bank mailings at a cost of about $7,500.

The bank planned to feature in their advertising the availability of investment counselors who, in fact, would be branch managers trained to answer basic questions about IRA accounts—such as which investment instruments were offered, current interest rates paid, and customer eligibility. These investment counselors could be contacted in person or by phone. All inquiries would be channeled to such "experts."

It was expected that the IRA product would lose money the first year and very likely the second and third. How much of a loss would be experienced was hard to estimate. Much depended upon the length of payback period used and the extent to which IRA accounts represented a transfer of funds from other accounts within the bank.

C A S E 8–4

Concorn Kitchens

Mr. Conrad, marketing director of the packaged foods division of the Concorn Kitchens, expressed reservations about the planning process used in his division. Previously, brand managers had prepared a document containing a review of the performance of each product and a pro forma profit and loss statement which implicitly contained a recommended price, promotion, and advertising strategy for the following year. It was viewed by most brand managers as a "commitment" for sales and profits that would be forthcoming from the product.

Mr. Conrad felt that these documents were "ploys" used by his subordinates to obtain as many marketing resources as possible. He felt that the plans often had little relation to historical performance and that generally no clear meaning could be assigned to the sales and profit numbers included in the plan. He was frequently not sure if these numbers represented goals or predictions. It was never clear how the sales figures were related to the marketing inputs or what would be the consequences of certain resource allocations.

As an example, he cited the lack of relationship between the 1969 plan and actual performance, particularly for one of the company's products—instant puddings. He noted that because sales did not develop as anticipated during the first part of the year he had been forced to cut advertising budgets for subsequent quarters. He stated, "If the original projections had been better this would not have happened and we would not be in the profit squeeze we now face."

The operations research manager, Mr. Kendall, suggested that the preparation of the marketing plan could be expedited by the development of some computer models. He recommended that he be autho-

---

This case is based on one prepared by Gerald J. Eskin. Reprinted from *Stanford Business Cases* with the permission of the publisher, Graduate School of Business, Stanford University. Copyright © by the Board of Trustees of the Leland Stanford Junior University.

rized to develop such models. An operations research project was approved and undertaken, the results of which were summarized in a report to Mr. Conrad from Mr. Kendall (see Appendix A). Based on this report, Mr. Conrad decided to try the system out on two products—instant puddings and instant breakfasts. The marketing research staff was requested to get together the necessary information to use the models. The result of this effort is reported in Appendix B. Mr. Conrad issued orders to the applicable product managers to, first, develop a planning base which would typically require modifying the straight-line projections made by the computer. He requested that all changes be supported with a "logical explanation." Once a base plan had been accomplished, his instructions were to get quantified goals for the period 1970–74 with respect to the company's case sales, dollar sales, total dollar gross margin contribution, and profits before taxes.

He reminded all concerned that these goals should be consistent one with another. Once the goals were set then the individual managers were to determine how they should be obtained. This required set annual expenditures with respect to advertising and promotion and possible changes in the list price of a case. All strategy decisions were to be supported logically.

In setting forth the new strategic planning method, Mr. Conrad noted that it might be that the goals which were set were unobtainable, in which case the manager would explain "why" and then proceed to set up new goals. If the goals, were attainable, then the manager would be asked to determine whether higher goals were possible. "In this way," stated Mr. Conrad, "we hope to come reasonably close to an optimization scheme through interactions which match inputs with outputs. While I'm very interested in the numbers which emerge from this planning exercise, I am more interested in how they were derived. In this connection, a man's thinking will be on display—starting with the magnitude of the planning gap; i.e., the difference between his goals and the planning base. To repeat, each product manager should do the following:

1. Analyze the past data on his brand and evaluate the complete projected data for 1970–74. (See Appendix B for data on instant puddings and instant breakfasts.)
2. Make any changes in the projected data thought necessary based only, however, on historical trends.
3. Set goals for this brand; i.e., sales in cases, market share, and profit goals for the period 1970–74.
4. Determine the "gap" between goals and the corrected projections.
5. Strategize expenditures to accomplish these goals.
6. Change goals up or down to optimize expenditures (as best possible).

Appendix A

To: Mr. Conrad
From: Mr. Kendall
Subject: Computer planning model (PLAN)

We believe that a planning process should include the following steps:

1. Data on past performance should be stored in an easily accessible way, and these data should form the basis of a first projection of future outcomes.
2. Projections of key components of the plan should be made assuming continuation of past trends and strategies. These component projections should then be combined into a pro forma profit and loss statement for each product. (We call this a *Planning Base.*)
3. Alternate plans should then be developed which explicitly take into account the relationships between changes in spending, prices, and resulting levels of sales and profits. These alternate plans *should be* evaluated by comparison to the Planning Base.

These ideas have been incorporated into a model called PLAN. It should be possible for your staff to use the model simply by making either manual or machine changes in the sample output.

The model has made linear extrapolations of key planning components. These extrapolations are purely mechanical in nature and will not always be appropriate. Provisions for overriding the projections have been made so that when you feel market share or costs can be better projected subjectively this can be done—again manually or by the computer. In the case of costs, we have projected totals, but as you can see from the printout, you can consider cost of function of sales rather than fixed in total.

Given that these first projections are intended to show the results of *continuing historical strategies,* any changes or overrides should not be used to indicate new trends that might develop *from a shift in strategy.* Such effects are considered in the next stage of analysis.

The remainder of the effort is designed to allow experimentation with alternate marketing plans in order to improve on the base projection—i.e., obtain any goals which have been set. To use this section, the individual involved must know something about the responsiveness of sales to various marketing tools. This knowledge is summarized in the form of response coefficients to be supplied by the user. These are defined as:

$$\frac{\text{Percent change in sales}}{\text{Percent change in inputs (e.g., price, advertising, etc.)}}$$

The way in which these coefficients affect sales is illustrated in the following tables:

Change in advertising (percent change from planning base)	Percent change in sales for an advertising response coefficient of:	
	.2	.4
+20%	+4%	+8%
+10	+2	+4
Same Advertising as in Planning Base	Same Sales as PB	Same Sales as PB
−10	−2	−4
−20	−4	−8

Change in price (as percent of price planning base)	Percent change in sales for a price response coefficient of:	
	−1	−2
+10%	−10%	−20%
No change	No change	No change
−10	+10	+20

We realize that complete knowledge is not always available on response coefficients but believe that your years of marketing experience and past research efforts should allow reasonable estimates to be made. When are unsure of the exact value, you may wish to use sensitivity testing through trying the same plan with different response coefficients.

When attempting to test the sensitivity of response coefficients remember that the coefficients are defined in terms of *changes* from the planning base; hence, a sensitivity test can only be performed on a plan that is *different* from the base plan.

The following technical notes are provided on the program:

A. Units of measure.
   1. Market and sales are measured in thousands of cases (12 units to the case).
   2. All dollar values are in thousands.
   3. Price is the case price charged by Concorn. Retail prices are roughly 30 percent higher.
B. Accounting conventions.
   1. Gross contribution margin = Price − Variable production cost.
   2. Overhead includes only manufacturing expense. General and administrative expenses are not included in product level

profit and loss statements at Concorn (sales force expense is considered G&A).

3. Promotional includes expenditures on:
    a. Trade allowances (temporary price reductions).
    b. Cents-off packs and coupons.
    c. Point-of-sale material.

C. A sample output follows.

Which product do you want to consider?
$ *"test product"*

	Historical file				
	1965	**1966**	**1967**	**1968**	**1969**
Market—total cases	1,000	2,000	3,000	4,000	5,000
Share	0.20	0.20	0.20	0.20	0.20
Price per case..............	$ 2.50	$ 2.50	$ 2.25	$ 2.25	$ 2.25
Gross C margin..............	1.00	1.00	0.80	0.80	0.80
Sales volume in cases	200	400	600	800	1,000
Sales	500	1,000	1,350	1,800	2,250
Gross C margin..............	200	400	480	640	800
Overhead...................	100	100	100	150	150
Gross margin...............	100	300	380	490	650
Advertising	20	20	20	20	20
Promotion..................	30	30	30	30	30
Net operating profit..........	$ 50	$ 250	$ 330	$ 440	$ 600

	1970	**1971**	**1972**	**1973**	**1974**
Market—total cases	6,000	7,000	8,000	9,000	10,000
Share	0.20	0.20	0.20	0.20	0.20
Price per case...........	$ 2.125	$ 2.05	$ 1.98	$ 1.90	$ 1.825
Gross C margin...........	0.70	0.64	0.58	0.52	0.46
Overhead...............	165	180	195	210	225
Advertising..............	20	20	20	20	20
Promotion...............	30	30	30	30	30

Do you wish to override any projections? "Yes."
Which line? 3.
Input new values for line. 2.25, 2.25, 2.25, 2.25, and 2.25.
Any others? "Yes."
Which line? 4.
Input new values for line. 0.8, 0.8, 0.8, 0.8, and 0.8.
Any others? "Yes."
Illegal use of tabs, please retype.
Any others? "Yes."
Which line? 6.
Input new values for line, 150, 200, 200, 200, 250.
Any others? "No."

Planning base P/L

	1970	1971	1972	1973	1974
Sales volume—cases	1,200	1400	1,600	1,800	2,000
Sales	$2,700	$3,150	$3,600	$4,050	$4,500
Gross C margin	960	1,120	1,280	1,440	1,600
Overhead	150	200	200	200	250
Gross margin	810	920	1,080	.1,240	1,350
Advertising	20	20	20	20	20
Promotion	30	30	30	30	30
Net operating profit	$ 760	$ 870	$1,030	$1,190	$1,300

Specify response coefficient to be used for each of five years.
Price . . . . −2,−2,−2,−2,−2
Advertising . . . . .2, .2, .2, .2, .2
Promotion . . . . .4, .4, .4, .4, .4
Time dependency
0,0,0,0,0
Which marketing variable do you wish to change "advertisng?"
Specify new levels by year. 30, 40, 50, 60, 70
Any others? "No."

	1970	1971	1972	1973	1974
Sales volume	1,301	1,608	1,922	2,242	2,569
Sales	$2,928	$3,618	$4,324	$5,045	$5,781
Gross C margin	1,041	1,287	1,537	1,794	2,056
Overhead	150	200	200	200	250
Gross margin	891	1,087	1,337	1,594	1,806
Advertising	30	40	50	60	70
Promotion	30	30	30	30	30
Net operating profit	$ 831	$1,017	$1,257	$1,504	$1,706

Do you wish to try another plan? "Yes."
Which marketing variable do you wish to change? "Price."
Specify new levels by year. 2,2,2,2,2
Any others? "No."

	1970	1971	1972	1973	1974
Sales volume	1,647	2,035	2,432	2,838	3,252
Sales	$3,294	$4,071	$4,865	$5,676	$6,504
Gross C margin	906	1,119	1,338	1,561	1,789
Overhead	150	200	200	200	250
Gross margin	756	919	1,138	1,361	1,539
Advertising	30	40	50	60	70
Promotion	30	30	30	30	30
Net operating profit	$ 696	$ 849	$1,058	$1,271	$1,439

Do you wish to try another plan? "No."
Do you wish to change a response coefficient? "Yes."
Which one? "Price."
New values. −2.5, −2.5, −2.5, −2.5, −2.5
Any others? "No."

	1970	1971	1972	1973	1974
Sales volume	1,747	2,159	2,580	3,010	3,449
Sales	$3,494	$4,318	$5,160	$6,020	$6,898
Gross C margin	961	1,187	1,419	1,656	1,897
Overhead	150	200	200	200	250
Gross margin	811	987	1,219	1,456	1,647
Advertising	30	40	50	60	70
Promotion	30	30	30	30	30
Net operating profit	$ 751	$ 917	$1,139	$1,366	$1,547

Do you wish to try another plan? "No."
Do you wish to change a response coefficient? "No."

Appendix B

To: Mr. Conrad
From: Marketing research staff
Subject: Data for PLAN computer model

Per Mr. Kendall's request, we have provided historical data on instant breakfasts and instant puddings for inclusion in the computer
data base.[1] This information will be updated as it becomes available.

The request for response coefficient information is more difficult to
satisfy. A controlled experiment was conducted on these products two
years ago which provides some information on this product. The
results of that test were:

Price coefficient	−1.6
Advertising coefficient	0.1

We suspect that, over time, the price elasticity coefficient is rising
(larger negative values) while the advertising coefficient is falling, although we cannot prove this assertion.

---

[1] No effort was made in the initial plan to detail the sales of the product in question
by subproducts. Thus, with regard to puddings, no plans were to be formulated by type or
flavor of mix. Such detailing would be accomplished later.

There are no data available on instant breakfasts, but we do have some estimates on some other products which may have similar values to those of instant breakfasts in that they are also *new* package foods in our line.

They are:

	Price coefficient	Advertising coefficient
Corn muffin mix	−1.2	0.3
Soy Snacks.	−1.4	0.4

There does not exist any hard data on the promotions question, although our sales manager feels that the response to cents-off promotions is rather large for all our products. He feels that doubling promotional allowance might increase sales by 50 to 70 percent (he is unable to say which of our products are most responsive to promotion). We feel that his estimates represent a short-run view and that such promotion may not be nearly as effective in the long run.

Instant Puddings

Product History.   The instant pudding market started in the early 1950s as a commercialization of some processing methods that were developed as part of World War II technology. Concorn was one of the first national brands in the market and, for a number of years, was the leading brand.

As the market grew, several other major companies entered the market. These companies had the advantage of having major sources of revenue in other higher margin industries plus experience in technologies important to the instant pudding market.

By 1965, the market had slowed, and Concorn was tied for second with Julia Childs at about 20 percent of the market. Gambles Deluxe had become the leading brand with 27 percent of the market following many years during which they dominated the market in terms of spending, primarily on advertising.

During the past five years, sales promotion has become an increasingly important marketing tool. In 1969, 90 percent of Concorn's volume moved at a dealing rate of 50 cents per case. There are no clear data about whether as high a percentage of competitor tonnage moves under a deal. About 40 cents per case is spent on cents-off promotions which are not typically supported by media advertising.

There is some indication that Concorn technology has not kept pace with the industry and that Concorn may have a marginal product disadvantage.

Ingredient costs have been rising causing a deterioration in our margin. In the past, Concorn has felt that these rising costs could not be passed on to the consumer given the highly competitive nature of the market.

While ad tests show Concorn advertising to be of equal quality to competition and perhaps marginally superior, awareness studies show the leading brand to be getting credit with consumers for the principal product benefits claimed by Concorn.

The following are the 1969 share of market and media expenditure data:

	Share (percent)	Media ($ million)
Concorn.	16	1.5
Gambles Deluxe.	30	3.5
Julia Child.	20	2.5
Private label	25	—
All others.	9	—

Plan versus actual	Plan	Actual
Market (000)	41,000	40,800
Share.	0.17	0.157
Sales volume (000)	6,970	6,406
Sales (price $5.25 case $0.55 per package retail. $000)	$36,592	$33,629
Gross contribution margin.	12,615	11,466
Unit.	(1.81)	(1.79)
Overhead ($000)	$ 2,000	$ 2,000
Gross margin ($000)	10,615	9,466
Advertising ($000)	2,000	1,500
Promotion ($000)	5,500	5,783
Net operating profit ($000)	$ 3,115	$ 2,183

Which product do you want to consider?
$ Instant Puddings

Historical file

	1965	1966	1967	1968	1969
Market (000 cases)	39,000	40,000	40,600	40,800	40,800
Share	0.192	0.1849999	0.16	0.165	0.1569999
Price	$ 5.25	$ 5.25	$ 5.25	$ 5.25	$ 5.25
Gross C margin	$ 1.9	$ 1.87	$ 1.839999	$ 1.809999	$ 1.79
Sales volume (000)	7,488	7,400	6,496	6,732	6,406
Sales	$39,312	$38,850	$34,104	$35,343	$33,629
Gross C margin	14,227	13,838	11,953	12,185	11,466
Overhead	2,160	2,160	2,100	2,100	2,000
Gross margin	12,067	11,678	9,853	10,085	9,466
Advertising	2,114	2,105	1,561	1,610	1,500
Promotion	5,028	5,032	5,101	5,500	5,783
Net operating profit	$ 4,925	$ 4,541	$ 3,191	$ 2,975	$ 2,183

	1970	1971	1972	1973	1974
Market (000)	41,559.98	41,999.98	42,439.98	42,879.98	43,319.98
Share	$ 0.145	$ 0.136	$ 0.127	$ 0.118	$ 0.109
Price	5.25	5.25	5.25	5.25	5.25
Gross C margin	1.757999	1.73	1.702	1.674	1.646
Overhead constant	1,990	1,952	1,914	1,876	1,838
Advertising constant	1,261.1	1,088.8	916.5	744.2	571.8999
Promotion constant	5,882.191	6,079.992	6,277.789	6,475.59	6,673.391

	Planning base P/L				
	1970	1971	1972	1973	1974
Sales volume (000)	6,018	5,704	5,381	5,051	4,713
Sales	$31,594	$29,944	$28,252	$26,519	$ 24,744
Gross C margin.............	10,579	9,867	9,159	8,456	7,758
Overhead.................	1,990	1,952	1,914	1,876	1,838
Gross margin..............	8,589	7,915	7,245	6,580	5,920
Advertising................	1,261	1,089	917	744	572
Promotion.................	5,882	6,080	6,278	6,476	6,673
Net operating profit..........	$ 1,446	$ 746	$ 51	$ −640	$−1,325

Instant Breakfasts

Product History.   Concorn entered the instant breakfast market in
1964, correctly anticipating the growth trend in that segment of the
food market. At that time, the major competitors in the market were
the first national brands—Paulicci's Best with 40 percent, O'Brien
with 20 percent, and a number of local or regional brands concentrated
in major metropolitan areas—New York, Miami Beach, Los Angeles,
Chicago, and Philadelphia.

By 1967, the growth trend in the market and the attractive margins
had led the major chains to introduce private labels (store brand) with
strong local advertising and shelf space support. Paulicci's Best initiated a price cut—which the other brands followed—in an effort to
reduce the price spread between the advertised and private label
brands.

In addition, each brand reacted to the 1967 market situation in
different ways. Paulicci's Best de-emphasized sales promotion, and increased its advertising. O'Brien held to its historical pattern of promotion and advertising spending.

Concorn's response to the situation is reflected in the historical
file—a strong emphasis on sales promotion and sales execution efforts
to get in-store trade support.

The following are the 1969 share of market and media expenditure
data:

	Share (percent)	Media ($ million)
Concorn....................	10.0	2.0
Paulicci's..................	42.5	7.5
O'Brien....................	18.0	4.0
Private label	21.0	
All others..................	8.5	

Product quality and advertising claims are effectively equal for all
brands.

Historical file

	1965	1966	1967	1968	1969
Market	21,000	24,500	28,900	32,700	36,500
Share	8.999997E–02	.105	.105	9.999996E–02	9.999996E–02
Price	$ 4.599999	$ 4.599999	$ 4.099999	$ 4.099999	$ 4.099999
Gross C margin	2.599999	2.599999	2.2	2.2	2.2
Sales volume	1,890	2,572	3,034	3,270	3,650
Sales	8,694	11,833	12,441	13,407	14,965
Gross C margin	4,914	6,688	6,676	7,194	8,030
Overhead	1,500	1,500	1,500	1,500	1,500
Gross margin	3,414	5,188	5,176	5,694	6,530
Advertising	2,000	2,000	2,000	2,000	2,000
Promotion	1,420	1,700	3,030	3,200	3,600
Net operating profit	$ –5	$ 1,488	$ 146	$ 494	$ 930

Input projections for use in base plan

	Line number	1970	1971	1972	1973	1974
Market	1	40,479.93	44,399.98	48,319.98	52,239.98	56,159.98
Share	2	0.10399997	0.1059999	0.107	0.109	0.11
Price	3	$ 3.849999	$ 3.7	$ 3.549999	$ 3.4	$ 3.25
Gross C margin	4	$ 2	$ 1.879999	$ 1.759999	$ 1.639999	$ 1.52
Overhead per unit	5	0	0	0	0	0
Overhead per constant	6	1,500	1,500	1,500	1,500	1,500
Advertising per unit	7	0	0	0	0	0
Advertising constant	8	2,000	2,000	2,000	2,000	2,000
Promotion per unit	9	0	0	0	0	0
Promotion constant	10	4,347.992	4,933.992	5,519.992	6,105.992	6,691.988

	1969	
Plan versus actual	**Plan**	**Actual**
Market	36,500	36,500
Share	0.105	0.10
Sales volume	3,832	3,650
Sales (price contribution $4.59 case, 0.49 retail)	$15,711	$14,945
Gross contribution margin	8,430	8,030
Unit	(2.20)	(2.20)
Overhead	$ 1,500	$ 1,500
Gross margin	6,930	6,530
Advertising	2,000	2,000
Promotion	3,400	3,600
Net operating profit	$ 1,530	$ 930

Which product do you want to consider?

$ Instant Puddings

Do you wish to override any projections? "No."

Planning base P/L	**1970**	**1971**	**1972**	**1973**	**1974**
Sales volume	4,230	4,706	5,194	5,694	6,206
Sales	16,286	17,414	18,440	19,360	20,168
Gross C margin	$ 8,460	$ 8,848	$ 9,142	$ 9,338	$ 9,433
Overhead	1,500	1,500	1,500	1,500	1,500
Gross margin	6,960	7,348	7,642	7,838	7,933
Advertising	2,000	2,000	2,000	2,000	2,000
Promotion	4,348	4,934	5,520	6,106	6,692
Net operating profit	$ 612	$ 414	$ 122	$ −268	$ −759

Specify response coefficient to be used for each of 5 years.

Index of Cases